FUNDAMENTALS OF SPORT MARKETING

Other Titles in the Sport Management Library

Professor Packets are now available at no charge for many of our best-selling textbooks. Visit www.fitinfotech.com for details.

FUNDAMENTALS OF SPORT MARKETING

THIRD EDITION

Brenda G. Pitts

GEORGIA STATE UNIVERSITY

David K. Stotlar

UNIVERSITY OF NORTHERN COLORADO

Fitness Information Technology
a Division of the International Center
for Performance Excellence
262 Coliseum, WVU-PE, PO Box 6116
Morgantown, WV 26506-6116

Library of Congress Card Catalog Number: 2007928453

ISBN 13: 978-1-885693-78-5

Production Editor: Matt Brann
Cover Design: Bellerophon Productions
Typesetter: Bellerophon Productions
Copyeditor: Anita Stanley
Proofreader: Maria E. denBoer
Indexer: Maria E. denBoer
Printed by: Sheridan Books
Cover Photo: The cover photo is of the opening event ceremony of the Amp'd Mobile World Supercross GP competition in February 2007 at the Georgia Dome in Atlanta, Georgia. Courtesy of The Georgia World Congress Center Authority.

10 9 8 7 6 5 4 3 2 1

Fitness Information Technology
A Division of the International Center for Performance Excellence
West Virginia University
262 Coliseum, WVU-PE
PO Box 6116
Morgantown, WV 26506-6116
800.477.4348 (toll free)
304.293.6888 (phone)
304.293.6658 (fax)
Email: icpe@mail.wvu.edu
Website: www.fitinfotech.com

Contents

Detailed Contents

Foreword

Subsequent editions of textbooks usually do not surpass their predecessors; however, the third edition of *Fundamentals of Sport Marketing* has far exceeded all expectations. This latest version provides future sport management professionals as well as practitioners with substantial knowledge and skills required for all aspects of the sport business industry.

Dr. Pitts and Dr. Stotlar are proven sport marketing innovators and not only do they recognize the necessity for staying abreast of current trends, but they also keep readers up to date on what is *new* and *cutting edge* in sport industry marketing. This is evident in their unique method of imparting information on basic sport marketing concepts, market conditions within the sport industry, how these conditions are changing, the demands and requirements of key industry players, and the global impact of sport marketing over the past few years, ranging from economic and social concerns to an increase in participation in sport business by foreign countries.

Further, *Fundamentals of Sport Marketing, Third Edition,* places a strong emphasis on research and how it is conducted. I personally gained invaluable, professional experience in sport marketing research under the tutelage of these renowned authors. You can expect to enhance your research skills dramatically from what is taught in this portion of the textbook.

Fundamentals of Sport Marketing covers every facet of the sport business industry—from sport history to sport marketing theory, from marketing information systems to elements of sport marketing (the marketing mix), from promotion of the sport industry to how to market a sport business through endorsements and sponsorships. It is far and away the most comprehensive textbook ever written on this subject.

In addition to being an excellent current resource, *Fundamentals of Sport Marketing* provides extensive practical instruction and real-world case studies covering an array of issues in the sport marketing field. It is designed to help students and practitioners develop a thorough understanding of sport marketing from both a theoretical and applied perspective.

If you want to gain expertise and considerable experience in sport marketing as well as explore groundbreaking research in this industry, this textbook is for you. Congratulations to Dr. Pitts and Dr. Stotlar for another stellar job in providing the most authoritative source for the study of sport marketing.

Carol Lucas
Market Research Manager
Georgia World Congress Center Authority

Preface

Welcome to the leading sport marketing textbook—and it is now in several languages and sold around the world! We are very excited about this third edition of *Fundamentals of Sport Marketing*. When we started our careers as professors in sport management and developed our first courses in sport marketing, there were no journals or textbooks in the field. Although this might sound as though it was a very long time ago, it was only about 20 years ago. As we developed our course lectures and materials, we used the theories and fundamentals of marketing from general business literature as the primary foundation because sport marketing is marketing applied to one industry—the sport industry. We created sport marketing language, developed terminology and definitions, and developed theories, models, and fundamentals. This is what differentiates sport marketing courses from general marketing courses. It is what distinguishes the study of sport marketing. And this, we believe, is what gives this book a sound basis and distinguishes it from other marketing textbooks. Everything we have developed is based on sport marketing's foundation studies, such as, marketing, communication, athletics administration, the media, consumer behavior, sport history, internet marketing, sport sociology, sales, advertising, sport psychology, sponsorship, brand architecture, and marketing management.

In this third edition, there are numerous updates and new material. The updates and developments in this edition are based on research and developments that have taken place in sport marketing, sport management, and the sport industry since the publication of the second edition. We believe the new material provides the best and most current information and tools that students need as they prepare to begin their careers in the sport industry.

In addition, we, as authors, have unparalleled years of experience consulting and working in the industry, and of applying the theories and fundamentals of the first two editions in theoretical and applied research. The result is a third edition that is the most current, contemporary, and indispensable book on sport marketing on the market.

Further, we are excited about the companion workbooks that complement the main text. These include *Case Studies in Sport Marketing, Developing Successful Sport Sponsorship Plans, Second Edition*, and *Developing Successful Sport Marketing Plans, Second Edition*. Never before has there been such a complete and comprehensive set of materials to prepare students for their careers in sport business. We know that students in sport management today will end up in a wide variety of jobs and careers in sport business, so they will need sport marketing fundamentals that can be used in those jobs in any area of the sport industry.

Since the publication of the first edition of this textbook more than a decade ago, there have been many changes in the sport business industry. Today, for example, the Web is a critical marketing tool for companies, NASCAR has become the most popular spectator sport, and women's sports, such as basketball and soccer, have exploded in popularity and commercial value. The evolution of "media content" as opposed to TV and broadcast rights has changed the way marketers distribute their products through video streaming via Wi-Fi and increased consumer interfaces through these technologies.

In addition, there have been changes in the world that will most assuredly impact sport business. We have always stressed the study of the interrelatedness between sport and society, culture, business, and the world. We can forget talking about the impending globalization of sport; it's here. Multinational mergers of companies like adidas and Reebok, the expansion of professional schedules into international markets, and the ongoing trade developments in developing countries are but a few of the examples.

As this book went to print, we are in wonder of what the future holds for sport business. Students in sport management will be faced with new problems to manage. This will certainly affect sport marketing efforts for a period of time. As in the first and second editions, this new edition stresses the importance of analyzing socio-cultural issues and events and predicting how they influence sport business.

Acknowledgments

We first want to recognize and thank all the students who helped us gather material. Dr. Pitts specifically thanks Ken Goglas, a dedicated graduate assistant. We both want to thank all the students and faculty over the years who have been willing to tell us exactly what they think about the book. Students working in industry who call to tell us how they are using everything they learned and have kept the book as a guide have provided helpful suggestions for updating material. Faculty and instructors who use the book for their classes have also offered valuable feedback and suggestions.

We want to thank the publisher, Fitness Information Technology, and its editors for their patience and persistence in the development and publication of this third edition and we look forward to many future editions.

Finally, Dr. Pitts thanks her family and partner, Melita, for her patience during those long hours at the laptop; and her Corgi, Jazz, for his complete commitment to fun—and the knowledge that deadlines are not what's important in life. Rather, the purpose of life is to get outside and play, chase a squirrel up a tree, and have fun!

Introduction

Fundamentals of Sport Marketing, Third Edition is a textbook on the theories, fundamentals, and practical application of marketing to sport business. Our approach has been to apply sound principles of marketing to the sport industry, modify and refine, define and develop, and eventually present theories and fundamentals of sport marketing that we know work in the sport business industry.

In this book, we use the definition of sport management and sport industry as it has been defined in the field of sport management by leading scholars who have extensive experience working in both academia and industry. According to these definitions, the sport industry is broad and varied, includes the many segments of businesses that toil behind the scenes, and is not limited to the selling of sports events. Two schools of thought regarding sport management and sport industry have emerged through the development of sport management as a field of study over the last three decades. One supports the notion that sport management is limited to the study of mainstream sports events and how to market and sell those to spectators. The other supports the position that sport management is the study of all businesses that exist in the sport industry, and the sport industry is defined as all businesses and enterprises whose products are sport or recreation-business related.

Like no other book in the field, *Fundamentals of Sport Marketing, Third Edition* covers the diversity of sport business, not merely professional and collegiate sport. This would include, for example, sport marketing research companies, sport sponsorship management companies, sporting goods manufacturers and retailers, sports broadcast companies, web sport enterprise, and sport tourism companies. All of these different types of companies are places where sport management and sport marketing students will be working. It is therefore incumbent upon sport management educators to prepare students with foundational knowledge that can be carried into any one of these types of companies. Therefore, our third edition is once again designed to meet these needs: sound foundational sport marketing knowledge that students can apply in any sport business.

This book is designed to introduce students to the business and practice of sport marketing. It provides an overview of the sport business industry, sport management, and sport marketing. It further provides detailed theories, fundamentals, and practical applications about how to conduct sport marketing. In conjunction with the companion books, these books offer the most comprehensive set of sport marketing materials to date. Moreover, sport marketing professionals working in the industry could easily use these books as handbooks for sport marketing, kept on-hand for constant reference.

This book is based on the belief that current and future sport industry professionals should be able to apply the fundamentals of sport marketing to any sport business. Therefore, different types of sport businesses are included as examples throughout the book.

Chapter 1 presents an updated overview of contemporary sport management definitions and concepts for sport, sport industry, sport business, sport management, and sport marketing.

Chapter 2 introduces the student to the global characteristics of sport business and how sport and global markets merge.

Chapter 3 orients the student to the foundations of sport marketing and introduces the Sport Marketing Management Model, which provides an illustration of the elements and tasks of the practice of sport marketing.

Chapter 4 introduces sport marketing research and its importance, as well as new examples of actual survey instruments that can be used for sport marketing research.

Chapter 5 presents the important sport marketing element of segmentation. Used to categorize and focus marketing efforts for consumer and business-to-business marketing, the importance of both consumer and industry segmentation are presented and thoroughly explained.

Chapter 6 provides the necessary tools for information management.

Chapter 7 lays the groundwork for the four Ps of marketing, each of which is the foci of chapters 8, 9, 10, and 11. Each chapter has been updated with new information from the sport business industry that arms the student with contemporary knowledge in relation to product, price, place, and promotion.

Regardless of which area of the sport industry or what type of sport business an individual is working in, at some point they will work with the media, sponsorship, and/or licensing and endorsements. Therefore, chapters 12, 13, and 14 cover these important sport marketing elements.

The Appendices—completely updated—are very important and are continued in this edition. Appendix A provides a brief directory to sport businesses. Appendix B contains a directory of sport business trade organizations. Appendix C provides a directory of sport business trade publications. For nearly every specific area of sport business, there is a trade publication to which you may subscribe. Appendix D provides a directory of sport management, sport marketing, and sport law journals and their information; it also contains directories of related sport business journals, sport management associations, sport management conferences, and information about the sport management curriculum standards. Appendix E contains several examples of sport marketing academic research. These will be helpful in finding research and locating where it is published. Finally, Appendix F contains seven different examples of research instruments commonly used in sport marketing that can be modified and used for actual research. This book is the only textbook that offers sport marketing instructors, students, and practitioners actual research instruments at their fingertips. Further, each instrument is provided with a description of the topic of study, its purpose, type of instrument, methodology, and some practical uses of the data gathered by this instrument. Actual studies may be conducted using these instruments with appropriate guidance from the sport marketing course instructor.

Underlying Philosophies of this Book

Readers will welcome that fact that this book, like no other, is inclusive of diverse populations, such as people of various ages, genders, races, abilities, classes, sexual orientations, and cultures. The sport business industry contains these diverse populations, therefore, our philosophy of sport marketing reflects this position. For example, there are examples and information offered throughout the text concerning the many different populations and sport businesses. Further, the unbiased language used throughout the text is reflective of our recognition and embraces the diversity in sport business.

The sport business industry is vast and varied. We believe that today's sport business management and sport marketing students will attain jobs and careers in any one of the many different types of sport businesses in the industry. Therefore, we believe the student should be educated about fundamental sport marketing theories and practices that can be used and applied in any sport business. As such, we present a variety of sport businesses in discussions and as examples throughout the text.

Further, although this book is grounded in marketing theory as its conceptual framework and "parent discipline," we have intentionally presented the material in such a way that it can be used as a practical guide to sport marketing. In addition, the sport marketing theories and models developed and presented in this book may serve researchers in sport marketing well as their conceptual frameworks for important academic sport marketing scholarship.

Special Package: The Companion Books and Language Editions

This book is part of a package of sport marketing books by the authors which, when used in concert and with other sport marketing literature, offers the most comprehensive set of materials in sport marketing education available today. The main textbook provides the foundation of sport marketing theory and fundamentals. It also provides directories for networking and professional growth and instruments for practical application. *Case Studies in Sport Marketing* offers situations in which students can use their new sport marketing knowledge and analyze sport businesses and their possible marketing problems. Finally, *Developing Successful Sport Sponsorship Plans, Second Edition* and *Developing Successful Sport Marketing Plans, Second Edition* offers the student the opportunity to develop contracts and business plans involving sponsorship management and marketing planning.

In addition, this textbook is available in the following languages: Chinese, Polish, and Spanish, with plans for it to be translated into more languages.

Benefits to the Reader

Fundamentals of Sport Marketing, Third Edition is a book written by authors with unparalleled academic and sport business industry experiences, knowledge, consulting, research, and practical experience in sport marketing, both in the US and in countries around the world. Some of their international experiences include speaking, working, teaching, or consulting in South Africa, The Netherlands, Spain, England, France, Singapore, Malaysia, Hong Kong, Mauritius, Australia, Zimbabwe, Japan, Cyprus, Scotland, China, Saudi Arabia, Hungary, Greece, Italy, Germany, Korea, and Taiwan. Both authors have received the top awards in the field: the North American Society for Sport Management Research Fellow Award and the Dr. Earle F. Zeigler Scholar Award—both of which recognize top scholars each year in sport management. Therefore, readers can be assured that the book is developed by years of scholarship and practical experience in sport marketing.

It is a book that can be used on the job as a handbook, guide, and reference. Since the first edition was published, students working in the industry report that they continue to use it and follow it as a handbook. The third edition builds on the foundation laid in the first and second editions.

It is a book that we believe can be used in practically any country. Even though the examples and businesses cited are primarily North American, the theories, fundamentals, and the Pitts & Stotlar Sport Marketing Management Model (found in Chapter 3) can be applied in any sport business in any country.

Chapter One

THE SPORT BUSINESS INDUSTRY

"Know what you sell, and sell what you know."

—The Bottom Line to the Sport Business Industry

Sport business is one of the largest industries in the United States and in many regions of the world. Estimates vary on just how large it is because it is too large and varied for any one study to provide a single number. However, when one begins to consider all of the parts of the whole, one can easily recognize that this industry is massive—placing it among the top few largest industries in the world. The sport business industry consists of numerous segments, some of which include sports tourism, sporting goods (manufacturing and retail), sports apparel, amateur participant sports, professional sports, semi-professional sports, recreation, high school and college sports, outdoor sports, sports service businesses such as sport marketing firms, sport sponsorship management companies, and sport governing bodies.

Segments of the Sport Business Industry:
- Sports tourism
- Sporting goods
- Sports apparel
- Amateur participant sports
- Professional sports
- Recreation
- High school and college athletics
- Outdoor sports
- Sport marketing firms
- Sports sponsorship industry
- Sports-governing bodies

In addition, each of the segments is comprised of a plethora of sub-segments. Examine, for instance, outdoor sports. How many outdoor sports can you name? How many involve mountains? How many involve water? How many involve vehicles? How many involve animals—horse racing, bull riding? How many involve competition? Additionally, how many outdoor sports events are held each year? How many of these are held weekly, monthly, or annually? If you really thought hard, you could potentially list thousands.

Take another segment—professional sports. How many sports have a professional league, event, or circuit? How many cities host professional sports teams or sports? How many facilities are built just for professional sports? How many individuals are involved in building professional sports facilities? How many individuals work for professional sports—either for the actual team, league, or circuit; and how many work either full time or part time?

Jobs and careers in the industry are seemingly endless and are as varied as the segments and businesses. It is an industry in which a person can often find success by linking an interest in sports with an interest in something else. For example, a person interested in shoe engineering and sports can design sports shoes as a career. A person who writes computer programs and likes sports can design programs for exercise equipment, for use in athletic training, or for gauging the air drag of race cars, speed-skating suits, or bobsleds.

With its size, variety, and flexibility, it is no wonder that sport management is one of the fastest growing, most popular college degree programs today. Because so many students want a career in the sport business industry, many colleges and universities are adding degree programs in sport management, also called sport administration and sport business. Despite recent sport program additions, there are still too few programs and students in sport management to support the constantly growing industry. It will be several years before there are enough students trained in sport management programs to fill all of the available jobs. Until employers in the industry begin to demand employees with the appropriate sport management education, people without a sport management background or a college education will fill the positions in the sport industry. Therefore, it is important that colleges and universities continue to promote sport business management education.

It is important for all students in sport business management to know and understand as much as possible about their chosen career and industry. For example, it is vital that every sport management student have an understanding of sport marketing. The student must understand sport marketing fundamentals and how they can be used in every segment of the sport industry. This knowledge will positively affect the student's success in a chosen career in any segment of the sport industry.

The application of sport marketing fundamentals to the sport business industry is best accomplished when the student has full knowledge and understanding of the sport business industry and its segments. It is important to understand what this industry is, how it develops, how it grows, what feeds its growth, who its consumers are, and the nature of its linkages with society and culture.

In this first chapter, the student will learn about the sport business industry. Toward this goal, it is first essential to understand the "sport business industry" as it is being defined in sport business management today. To do this, it is important to understand the terms *sport* and *industry* individually and also as they are defined in sport management today.

Industry

An "industry" is "a market in which similar or closely related products are sold to buyers." Some industries may contain only one product. It is more typical that an industry comprises a variety of product items sold to many existing or potential consumers who vary demographically and psychographically, and who may change in need, want, desire, or demand. The tennis racket industry is an example of a single-product industry. Within this industry, there are different variations of tennis rackets ranging in size, color, material, and price to meet the demands of the many different consumer markets. Additionally, the tennis racket industry is part of a multi-product industry, the sporting goods industry. The sporting goods industry is an example of an industry comprising many different but related products. It comprises all products sold as goods, equipment and apparel for use in sports, recreation, and fitness activities. This industry can be subdivided into several segments using different ways to define those segments. To see the many segments of the sporting goods industry, look inside a sporting goods store. There are departments, representative segments of the industry, for a variety of sports and activities, categorized according to their similarities such as water sports, camping activities, and soccer apparel. Keep in mind, however, that your local sporting goods store doesn't carry goods for every sport that exists. For example, to find equestrian or rodeo equipment, you would have to go to a specialty store.

Within a department, the products can be further subdivided into groups of individual sports or closely related sports. In the water sports department, for example, you will find equipment, goods, accessories, and apparel for several different sports such as scuba diving, fishing, water skiing, snorkeling, and swimming. In the tennis department, you will find tennis rackets, from the single-product industry, but you will also find many other tennis products—tennis balls, shoes, socks, bags, towels, tennis ball holders, water bottles, caps, shirts, and many more. You will also find products not needed to play tennis. These are products that promote the sport of tennis such as tennis bumper stickers, key rings, jewelry, posters, and T-shirts. As you can see in the examples, an industry can be composed of one product or many products. Those products can be very closely related and similar in nature or very loosely related and dissimilar. Moreover, it is important to recognize that products can be goods, services, people, places, or ideas. An industry can be composed of one of these or a combination of them. Either way, the products are usually related in some way as defined by those involved in the industry.

Sport and Sport Business Management

"Sport" is defined in many different ways depending on the context in which it is used. In many fields such as sport sociology, physical education, and recreation, sport is used to denote sporting activities such as basketball, hiking, snowboarding, and boating. Sport sociology is the study of people and sport and society. Physical education involves teaching sports to people. The term *sport*, as used in the field of sport business management and in relation to the sport business industry, is a broad concept term used to denote all people, activities, businesses, and organizations involved in producing, facilitating, promoting, or organizing any activity, experience, or business enterprise focused on fitness, recreation, sports, sports tourism, or leisure. At some institutions, sport management is also often called sport administration, sport business, and sport business management. To classify an enterprise as a sport business, then, doesn't necessarily mean it is a business that sells sports. It might be a company in the business of sport marketing research, a sports tourism business that sells snow ski packages, a Web sport company that sells Women's World Cup souvenirs via the Internet, a sponsorship management business specializing in handling sports sponsorship packages, or a sporting goods company that manufactures mountain-climbing gear.

Notice that the title of this book is *Fundamentals of Sport Marketing* and not *Fundamentals of Sports Marketing*. Also note the use of the term *sport management* instead of *sports management*. The term *sport* has a very different meaning than *sports*. According to the North American Society for Sport Management (Parks and Zanger, 1990), "sports implies a collection of separate activities such as golf, soccer, hockey, volleyball, softball, and gymnastics—items in a series that can be counted" (6). This is the way most people define sports—as sports activities. This reflects primarily two things: first, exposure to sports in our schools and colleges; second, exposure to sports every day through the media. That is, what the average person sees and hears through television coverage of sports events, the sports section in the newspaper, and the sports report on TV news broadcasts covers sports activities as they take place or a report of the outcome—the final score and who won. Therefore, *sports* management implies only managing sports activities. Sport, however, is a collective noun and a more all-encompassing concept. Therefore, the North American Society for Sport Management (NASSM), the professional association comprised of university academicians, students, and scholars in sport business management, chose the word *sport* as a term that more correctly identifies and defines the sport management field of study.

Sport business management implies a much broader concept. Therefore, the contemporary definition of sport business management is as follows: *Sport business management* is the study and practice involved in relation to all people, activities, businesses, and organizations involved in producing, facilitating, promoting, or organizing any product that is sport, fitness, and recreation related. Sport products can be goods, services, people, places, or ideas. This includes, for example, a company that manufactures sports equipment, clothing, or shoes; a person or company who offers promotion services for a sports organization; an organization charged with governing a sport; a person who represents a professional athlete as an agent; people who own and manage a sports facility; people who design and construct those sports facilities; a person who teaches golf; a company that manages the promotional merchandise and licenses for a sports event; and television companies that are involved in broadcasting sports events.

> **Sport Management Defined:**
>
> Sport Management is the study and practice of all people, activities, businesses, or organizations involved in producing, facilitating, promoting, or organizing any sport-related business or product.

This is what *sport* means when used in the context of sport management, sport marketing, and the sport industry. It is an all-inclusive term representing every person and business involved in producing, facilitating, promoting, or organizing sports, fitness, play, leisure, or recreation activity and all related products.

The Sport Business Industry

We may now define the term *sport business industry*. A variety of research provides descriptions of the many different products and businesses that comprise the sport industry. The products and businesses focus on sports, fitness, recreation, or leisure products. There are many different groups of consumers for these products, and they can be broadly categorized as either end consumers or business consumers.

Based on this research and the definitions of *sport* and *industry* presented earlier, the definition of *sport business industry* follows:

> The *sport business industry* is the market in which the products offered to its buyers are sport, fitness, recreation, or leisure related and may be activities, goods, services, people, places, or ideas.

Here are some examples of the types of products offered in the sport industry:

• Sports are products and can be offered as a participation product such as participation in a women's recreational basketball league;

- Sports can be offered as an entertainment product, primarily for spectating, such as the offer to watch a field hockey game, a snow-boarding competition, or the X-Games;

- Equipment and apparel are sport products needed or desired to participate in sports and fitness activities such as softball uniforms, ice-hockey pads, body-building apparel, in-line skates, and bicycle helmets;

- Promotional merchandise is a sport product used to promote a sport business, a sports league, a sports event, or fitness activity such as logo caps and shirts, fitness club shirts or towels, stadium cushions and blankets with the company logo;

- Sports facilities are sport products needed or desired for producing sport such as the construction of a new sport stadium or the remodeling of racquetball courts to accommodate wallyball; the design and the construction company for the facility are also products;

- Service businesses offer such sport products as sport marketing research, tennis racket stringing, or golf course care;

- Recreational activities are sport products sold as participation products such as mountain bicycling, hiking, camping, horseback riding, boating, cross-country skiing, sailing, and mountain climbing;

> **Sport Industry Defined:**
>
> The sport industry is the market in which the businesses and products offered to its buyers are sport related and may be goods, services, people, places, or ideas.

- Complete management and marketing professional services are sport products offered for a variety of markets such as the management of a large marathon, the promotion and management of a sports tourism package, or the management and marketing for an athlete; and

- Sport media businesses offer such products as magazines about specific sports such as *Runner's World* magazine and trade magazines targeted to industry business such as *The Boat Dealer*. There also are these products and companies: sports television companies, sports radio shows, and Internet sports companies.

The Size of the Sport Business Industry

The sport business industry has experienced phenomenal growth in a relatively short period of time. Although sports and recreational activities, events, and businesses have been around for a very long time, there has never been a period of explosive growth like that of the last 30 years. There are many reasons for this growth. Those are presented in the next section in this chapter. These changes represent both horizontal and vertical expansion. Horizontal growth involves the addition of new markets and new products such as new sport businesses like sport marketing research firms. Vertical growth involves the growth of existing markets and products such as the explosion of girls and women in traditional sports like basketball and volleyball.

A few studies have attempted to place a dollar value or economic impact number on the sport business industry. Although the studies were not conducted the same way and did not look at the same factors, they at least provide an estimate of the size of the industry and the various segments that have composed the industry since

1986. You may be surprised to learn that men's professional sports are not the largest segment of the industry even though there is a lot of money in some men's professional sports and some of them are the primary, and prime-time, focus of most media. However, as you will see in the tables, the largest segments of the industry are sports for the masses and sporting goods. When you give thought to what comprises these segments, then you see that it makes sense. Five studies on the size of the sport business industry offer an illustration of its size, segments and its growth over two decades. The first was a series of three studies about the industry in 1986, 1987, and 1988 (Comte and Stogel, 1990). A summary of the studies is presented in Table 1.1. In this sum-

Table 1.1
Two Decades of Growth in the Sport Industry.

Study	Year	Size of Industry	%Growth Annual/Between		Rank
1st study	1986	$47.3 billion	—		
2nd study	1987	$50.2 billion	+6.1		23rd
3rd study	1988	$63.1 billion	+7.5		22nd
4th study	1995	$152 billion	+13.0	+141.0	11th
5th study	1999	$213 billion	+10.5	+40.1	6th

Note: The results of these five studies cannot be compared. Although each study included similar segments of the industry, they included different segments. Moreover, methodologies were not similar. However, some general conclusions can be made.
* between 1986 and 1988, the annual increase averaged +6.8%
* from 1988 to 1995, the average increase was +13%
* from 1995 to 1999, the average increase was +10.5%

Note: Research in the first three studies was conduced by Sport Inc. and Sporting News with WEFA (Wharton Econometric Forecasting Association); the fourth study is from Meek, A. (1997). An estimate of the size and supported economic activity of the sports industry in the United States. *Sport Marketing Quarterly, 6* (4), 15–21; the fifth study was conducted by *SportsBusiness Journal* and published in the December 20–26, 1999 issue (1999, volume 2, issue 35, pages 23–30).

Table 1.2
The Top Fifty Sport Industries in 1987 (in billions).

1. Real estate $519.3	26. Paper and allied products 39.5
2. Manufacturing 479.9	27. Auto repair garages 38.9
3. Retail trade 427.4	28. Security/commodity brokers 36.7
4. Regulated Industry 408.2	29. Primary metals 36.4
5. Manufacturing (non-durable goods) 373.6	30. Lodging 35.7
6. Wholesale trade 313.0	31. Personal services 34.4
7. Health services 223.7	32. Air transportation 34.2
8. Business services 179.3	33. Petroleum and related products 33.6
9. Communications 120.9	34. Rubber and plastics 29.9
10. Radio and television 108.3	35. Educational services 29.6
11. Insurance 101.3	36. Insurance agents and brokers 28.6
12. Miscellaneous professional organizations 86.4	37. Lumber 27.7
13. Electrical machinery 85.0	38. Stone, clay, and glass 27.5
14. Banking 84.8	39. Instrument manufacturing 26.9
15. Chemicals and allied products 77.1	40. Amusement and recreation services 24.0
16. Food and kindred products 74.0	41. Apparel 22.5
17. Insurance carriers 72.7	42. Textile mills 19.9
18. Trucking and warehousing 64.2	43. Credit agencies 17.0
19. Legal services 62.3	44. Holdings and other investment firms 16.2
20. Fabricated metals 60.3	45. Tobacco 15.5
21. Printing and publishing 58.2	46. Furniture and fixtures 14.9
22. Non-auto transportation equipment 56.0	47. Miscellaneous repairs 13.9
23. SPORTS 50.2	48. Miscellaneous manufacturing 13.9
24. Motor vehicles and parts 49.9	49. Telephone and telegraph 12.7
25. Social and membership organizations 45.3	50. Transportation services 12.0

Source: (Comte & Stogel, 1990).

Table 1.3
Rank of the sport industry in 1995 compared to other industries according to the Meek study (Meek, 1997).

Industry	Value in billions
1. Real estate	$850.0
2. Retail trade	$639.9
3. Wholesale trade	$491.0
4. Health services	$443.4
5. Construction	$277.6
6. Business services	$275.3
7. Depository institutions	$225.9
8. Utilities	$205.3
9. Other services	$195.0
10. Telecommunications	$156.0
11. Sports	$152.0
12. Chemicals and allied products	$141.0
13. Electronics and electrical equipment	$138.5
14. Industrial machinery and equipment	$123.3
15. Insurance carriers	$115.4
16. Food and kindred products	$113.3
17. Trucking and warehousing	$100.6
18. Legal services	$100.5
19. Printing and publishing	$89.7
20. Motor vehicles and equipment	$88.7
21. Fabricated metal products	$86.0
22. Farms	$85.0
23. Security and commodity brokers	$75.6
24. Oil and gas extraction	$62.7
25. Auto repair, services, and parking	$60.5

mary, we see that from 1986 to 1988 the sport industry grew an average of 6.8% yearly. This is an important figure to note when comparing the sport industry to other industries that usually average a yearly growth of one to three percent. In the first edition of this textbook, we predicted that if the sport industry grew at the annual average rate of 6.8%, it would grow to $139 billion by 2000 and would more than double in size. We admit we were wrong. The industry is much larger than the prediction! In 1995, a study showed the sport business industry to be a $152-billion dollar industry and the 11th largest industry in the United States. That represents a 242% increase, indicating that the industry has grown almost $2^{1}/2$ times larger in a 10-year period. Tables 1.1, 1.2, 1.3, 1.4, and 1.5 show the information from those studies.

In 1999, a fifth study was conducted and reported by the *SportsBusiness Journal*. This study estimated the industry to be $213 billion ("The Answer," 1999). Table 1.6 illustrates the size of the industry segments as reported in the *SportsBusiness Journal*. Table 1.7 shows the segments of the industry that were included in the *SportsBusiness Journal* study.

Table 1.4
Sport Industry Segments, 1987–88.

Segment	1987 (in millions)	1988	Percent change
Leisure and participant sports	$21,599.5	$22,789.3	+5.5
Sporting goods	18,069.3	19,012.8	+5.2
Advertising	4,058.6	4,388.5	+8.1
Net take from legal gambling	3,504.8	3,618.3	+3.2
Spectator sports receipts	3,050.0	3,240.0	+6.2
Concessions, souvenirs, novelties	2,100.0	2,348.1	+11.8
TV and radio rights fees	1,209.2	1,415.8	+17.1
Corporate sponsorships	1,012.0	1,140.0	+12.6
Golf course, ski area construction	542.3	946.9	+74.6
Sports insurance	722.0	830.0	+15.0
Magazine circulation revenues	658.6	773.0	+17.4
Royalties from licensed properties	584.0	735.0	+25.9
Athlete endorsements	520.0	585.8	+12.7
Trading cards and accessories	350.0	408.3	+16.7
Sports book purchases	241.0	330.7	+37.2
Stadium and arena construction	250.0	319.3	+27.7
U.S. Olympic Committee, NGB budgets	98.2	114.2	+16.3
Youth team fees	95.3	97.0	+1.8
Halls of fame	5.4	6.0	+11.1
Total	$58,670.2	$63,099.0	+7.5

Note: Several categories have been statistically adjusted with updated 1987 figures, which may vary from previous publication; sports insurance premiums include professional and amateur teams, and individual players, but not multi-purpose facilities.

Source: (Comte & Stogel, 1990).

Table 1.5

Sport Industry segment sizes in 1995 according to the Meek study (Meek, A. 1997).

Segments	Estimated Value
1. Sporting goods, footwear, apparel	$71 billion
2. Participant sports	$32 billion
3. Sports medicine	$18.5 billion
4. Construction	$11.8 billion
5. Sponsorship, endorsements, radio, TV, newspapers	$7.5 billion
6. Admissions (spectators)	$5.3 billion
7. Trading cards, video games, tapes, books, magazines	$3.5 billion
8. Concessions and souvenirs	$3.4 billion
9. Betting	$3.3 billion

When you compare these studies, you can see that the *SportsBusiness Journal* study included the fewest segments of the industry. Their study was limited to organized sports that they defined as "spectator sports" and their related industries.

In the most recent study of the sport business industry, PricewaterhouseCoopers looked at a portion of the industry globally. In their study, labeled "Global Entertainment and Media Outlook: 2005–2009," they found that the global sports market will reach sales of $111.1 billion in 2009 at a 6.1% compound annual growth rate (CAGR) (Zimmerman, 2005).

PricewaterhouseCoopers is a company that serves as "accountant and business advisor to many of the world's leading entertainment and media companies" (http://www.pwc.com). Through this work, the company develops its analyses of several industries. Some segments of the sports industry are included in their work. Their definition of the "sports market" as

Table 1.6

Where the sport industry ranks compared to other industries in the *SportsBusiness Journal* study.

1. Real estate	$935 billion
2. Retail trade	$713 billion
3. Health care	$460 billion
4. Banking	$266 billion
5. Transportation	$256 billion
6. Sports business	$213 billion
7. Communications	$212 billion
8. Public utilities	$210 billion
9. Agriculture	$132 billion
10. Mining	$121 billion
11. Motor vehicles and equipment	$85 billion
12. Motion pictures	$31 billion

Source: *SportsBusiness Journal*, December 20–26, 1999.

". . . consisting of gate revenues for live sporting events; rights fees paid by broadcast and cable television networks and television stations to cover those events; merchandising, which includes the selling of products with team or player logos; sponsorships, which include naming rights and payments to have a product associated with a team or league, as well as, in Asia/Pacific, actual team ownership; and other packages with rights to sports events or programming. Concession revenues are not included, consistent with the definition of box office spending in the Filmed Entertainment chapter" (http://www.pwc.com). Therefore, they do not include all of the segments of the industry. However, it is beneficial to look at their numbers. Table 1.8 presents some of the information from their study.

Integral to determining the size of the sport industry is the study of individual industry segments. Although there may be some overlap, this can be used as an esti-

Table 1.7
Estimated Value of Various Spectator Sports Segments.

Spectator Sports Segment	Estimated Value	% of Total
1. Travel transportation, accommodations, meals of spectators, colleges, the 'big four' leagues, other	$44.47 billion	20.92
2. Advertising telecasts, cable, regional, print, signage, radio	$28.25 billion	13.29
3. Equipment, apparel, footwear. sportswear in competition	$24.94 billion	11.73
4. Gate receipts admission, concessions, merchandise, parking	$22.56 billion	10.61
5. Team operating expenses 'big four' player salaries and operating expenses; colleges; others	$19.23 billion	9.05
6. Legal gambling wagers, horses, dogs, jai alai, internet	$18.55 billion	8.73
7. Licensed goods apparel, footwear, housewares, media, miscellaneous	$15.1 billion	7.10
8. Professional services agents, sport marketing firms, facility management, financial, legal, and insurance services	$14.03 billion	6.60
9. Media broadcast rights 'big four,' college, other, radio telecasts	$10.57 billion	5.0
10. Sponsorships events, teams, leagues, broadcasts	$5.09 billion	2.40
11. Medical treatment baseball, football, basketball, soccer, softball, other	$4.1 billion	1.93
12. Facility construction stadium, track, arena construction	$2.49 billion	1.17
13. Publications/videos. magazines, videos, video games, books	$2.12 billion	1.0
14. Endorsements value of top 80 athletes and coaches	$730 million	.34
15. Internet revenue from advertising and access fees	$300 million	.14

Note: The study by the *SportsBusiness Journal* included only these few segments of the industry. The methodology included selected organized sports: those that are defined as 'spectator sports' and their related industries, as listed above. Further, the study does not reveal which sports organizations are included and which are left out. Note that this study does not include such segments as participant sports, recreational sports, or others that are listed in other tables here in Chapter one (*SportsBusiness Journal*, December 20–26, 1999).

Table 1.8
Estimated growth of entertainment sports gate revenues, rights fees, merchandising, sponsorships as defined by PricewaterhouseCoopers (www.pwc.com).

Country	2004	2009 projected
United States	$42.1 Billion	$57.4 billion
Europe, Middle East, & Africa	$24.9 billion	$32.9 billion
Asia/Pacific	$12.7 billion	$17 billion
Latin America	$2.82 billion	$3 billion
Canada	$440 million	$878 million

mate of the size, as well as the variety, of the sport industry. Tables 1.9 and 1.10 present lists of some of the many different sport business segments and sports events in the United States and their estimated economic value. You can easily see that the sum of just a few of these segments of the sport industry exceeds the reported 1999 $324-billion-dollar size of the industry in the *SportsBusiness Journal*. (Note: No studies are available since 1999.)

Using studies and reports about numerous different industry segments might be a better way to study the sport industry. Each sport management student will work in an industry segment and must continuously monitor the research about that segment as well as the entire sport industry.

This information can be found in a variety of such resources as the following:

- Industry publications: These include, for example, trade or business magazines, journals, newsletters, and Internet sites.

- Sport business conventions and exhibitions: These include such annual convention and trade shows as the Snow Sports Industries of America and the National Sporting Goods Association's Super Show.

- Sport management or marketing research businesses: There are numerous companies that specialize in conducting research. Some of these include Joyce Julius and Associates and Simmons Market Research Bureau.

- Local or national news publications: Much can be learned about sport industries from published articles in newspapers and magazines. Local papers carry information about local sports businesses, and national papers provide articles with a more national focus about individual sport-related businesses and whole industries.

Another way to help us determine the size and especially the depth and breadth of the sport industry is to look at the factors that have affected growth and development of the industry and at what exists in the industry.

Table 1.9
Examples of Sports Business Industry Segments and Their Values.

Sport Business Segment	Value
The New York Yankees	$1.026 Billion
The Boston Red Sox	$617 Million
Golf Equipment, Apparel, & Footwear	$5.8 billion
Indianapolis, Indiana Sports Industry Impact	$3 Billion
Atlanta, Georgia Sports Industry Impact	$4.5 Billion
Global—Sporting Goods Industry	$150 billion
USA—Sporting Goods Industry	$25.6 billion
Segments: Equipment	$10 billion
Sportswear	$8 billion
Footwear	$7.8 billion
Global—Tourism 2004	$4.5 Trillion
Segment—USA—Tourism from abroad	$93.5 billion
USA—General Tourism	$462.2 billion
USA—Sports Tourism 2005	$69.33 billion
Canada—Sports Tourism 2005	$2.4 billion
Sports Sponsorship	$24.8 Billion
Sports Licensed Products 2005	$13.23 billion
NASCAR Licensed Products	$2 billion
Canada—Sport Travel	$1.17 billion
Online Sports Advertising	$4 billion
U.S. Winter Sports 2005 season	$2.25 billion
Golf Charitable Giving Impact Estimate	$3.25 billion
Golf Industry	$62.1 billion
Golf Facilities	$20.5 billion
Angling (fishing)	$35.6 billion
Corps of Engineer Lakes & Surrounding Area	$5.6 billion
Spectator Sports Expenditures (pro & amateur; racetradks)	$8.1 billion
Outdoor Recreation	$350 billion
Winter Sports (2004–05 season)	$2.25 billion

Sources: http://www.sportbusiness.com; http://www.marketresearch.com.

You can keep up with the latest in your industry by
- Reading trade or business magazines, journals, newsletters, and Internet sites
- Attending sport business conventions or exhibitions
- Obtaining research from sport marketing firms
- Reading local or national news publications

Table 1.10
Examples of Sports Events and Facilities and Their Values (Usually in Economic Impact).

Sports Event	Value (Economic Impact)
Men's World Cup Championship (2002)	$260 Million
Arizona Cardinals New Stadium	$455 Million
Triple Crown Brighton Baseball Bash (a high school baseball tournament)	$1 Million
AAU Junior Olympic Games	$60 Million
Tour de Georgia—impact on one town	$2 Million
Nextel All-Star Challenge, a NASCAR race	$94 Million
CIAA Basketball Tournament (Central Intercollegiate Athletic Assoc.)	$15 Million\
Florida State High School Association Boys & Girls State Basketball Tournament	$7 Million
NASCAR NEXTEL Cup event—2004	$146 Million
NCAA Division I-AA Football Championship 2003	$1.1 Million
Super Bowl XXXVII, Houston 2005	$367 Million
Nokia Sugar Bowl 2005	$210 million
Capital One Bowl	$42.3 million
Mississippi State Games	$5.5 million
Bank of America PGA Classic 2005	$25 million
Alamo Bowl 2004	$35 million
Opening Day Baltimore Orioles	$4 million
World Golf Championship 2004	$24 million
USA Volleyball Junior Olympics 2005	$27 million
Atlanta Football Classic 2005	$28 million
NCAA Women's Final Four 2003	$34 million
Chick-Fil-A Peach Bowl 2004	$35 million
National Field Hockey Festival 2004	$3 million
WIBC (bowling) Championship	$40 million
Honolulu Marathon 2005	$90 million
New York City Marathon 2005	$130 million
2010 Winter Olympic & Paralympic Games: Vancouver, British Columbia, Canada	$8.4 billion (est.)
2006 NFL Super Bowl Championship Game	$300 Million
2006 IIHF World Junior Hockey Championship	$36.7 Million
Gay Games VI, 2002, Sydney, Australia	$116.8 million
Super Cross event Atlanta	$12 million
Men's NCAA Div. I Regional Basketball Tournament—Atlanta	$23.4 million
Professional Bull Riders—2005 single event	$5.9 million

Sources: http://www.sportbusiness.com; http://www.azcentral.com; http://www.SGMA.com.

Studying the factors that influence the sport industry can reveal what types of jobs are available and help you decide on a future career.

FACTORS INFLUENCING THE GROWTH AND DEVELOPMENT OF THE SPORT BUSINESS INDUSTRY

The sport business industry is large and diverse. There are numerous kinds and types of businesses and organizations. Your career in the sport industry will be greatly enhanced if you understand why the industry is so large and diverse and what drives its growth. To gain this understanding, it is important to understand the factors that have influenced the growth and development of the industry in the past, those that affect it currently, and those that will have an influence in the future (see Table 1.11).

The sport business professional must constantly analyze what is affecting the industry because such influences may affect the success or failure of a product or business. If the sport businessperson studies and understands how the factors affect the product or business, he or she can develop decisions and strategies that will lead to success.

The factors that influence the industry are grouped into the following categories: people; sports activities and events; sporting goods; facilities, sports medicine, and fitness training; commercialization and marketing; service businesses; education; and media. Factors within these categories have been among the many causes for the growth of the industry in the past and will continue to affect growth in the future.

Additionally, studying these factors can help us identify the number and types of jobs and careers in the industry. As you read about the factors listed and explained in this section, think about the number and types of jobs necessary in that area. You just might discover your future career.

Table 1.11

Factors That Influence the Sport Business Industry—Why the Sport Business Industry Is So Large and Diverse.

I. People

1. Constant Human Interest in Sport and Recreation
2. Increase in Sport Business Among Diverse Market Segments

II. Sports Activities and Events: Sports, Recreation, Fitness, Leisure, Sports Tourism

1. Constant Increase in the Number of New and Different Sport, Recreational and Fitness Activities, and Events
2. Constant Growth in the Offering of Traditional Sports
3. Constant Increase in the Number and Type of Professional Level Sport, Fitness, and Recreational Activities
4. Increase in Sports Tourism and Adventure Travel Products

III. Sporting Goods

1. Increase in Sporting Goods and Apparel Designed for the Diversity of Markets and Their Demands
2. Influence of Technology on Sport-Related Goods, Services, and Training

IV. Facilities, Sports Medicine, and Fitness Training

1. Increase in Number and Type of Sports Facilities and Events
2. Movement of Facilities From Single-Purpose to Multi-Sport and Full-Service Facilities
3. Constant Increase in the Amount and Type of Sports Medicine and Fitness Training Services

V. Commercialization and Marketing of Sport

1. Packaging of Sport as an Entertaining Product
2. Increased Marketing and Marketing Orientation of the Sport Industry
3. Increased Understanding and Knowledge of Customers of the Sport Business Industry
4. Promotion Perfection as the Goal of Sport Marketing Professionals
5. Growth of Corporate Sponsorship
6. Increased Endorsements
7. Growth in Importance of Licensing and Merchandising

VI. Sport Industry Professional Service Businesses

1. Extraordinary Growth in Service Businesses for the Sport industry

VII. The Sport Industry, Media, and Sport Media

1. Sport Industry Benefits Greatly From Mass Media Exposure
2. Sports Activities and Events as a Popular Entertainment Product
3. Constant Increase of Television and Radio Coverage
4. Increase in the Number and Variety of Magazines, Trade Magazines, and Academic Journals Devoted to Sport
5. The World Wide Web

VIII. Sport Industry Education

1. Increase in Sports and Sport Business Education for Executives, Administrators, Athletes, and Other Personnel
2. Increase in Competency of Sport Management Professionals
3. Increased Prevalence of Sport Management as an Academic Discipline and as a Career

I. People

People are the reason sports and the sport business industry exists. If it were not for people's interest in and demand for sports, recreation, fitness, adventure travel, and sports tourism, the industry would not survive. Sports activities, for example, do not exist until individuals play them. That is, a basketball game does not occur

until individuals get together and play the sport. Further, a lot of people are fascinated with sports and recreational activities of all kinds. Additionally, when people become bored with one sport they change to a new one. Here are some factors relating to people and the sport business industry.

1. Constant Human Interest in Sports and Recreation

A look at the studies presented earlier in this chapter on the size of the sport business industry shows that participant sports constitute the largest segment of the industry. People participating in sports, recreation, and fitness activities are the primary reason the sport industry exists. It is people who drive the growth of the sport industry because they are the consumers of sports, recreation, fitness, tourism, and leisure products.

Millions of individuals participate in such activities. They play, run, climb, scoot, ride, and perform numerous other skills for a variety of reasons, including, to have fun, to compete, to improve, to lose weight, to socialize, to have a good workout, and to learn a new sport. Moreover, they invent new activities. As you will learn, new and different sports and activities are invented almost daily. These millions of people spend billions of dollars to participate in sports, recreation, fitness, travel, and leisure activities annually. The majority of this money includes the cost of admission to the activity, which carries such labels as entrance fee, registration fee, membership fee, greens fee, and league fee. To get an idea about how much money can be spent on sports activities, try to find out how much money people in your city spend on entering and participating in some of the sports activities such as softball, basketball, and golf offered by the city parks and recreation department.

Another large portion of the dollars spent on sports is the millions spent for items needed or desired in order to participate such as equipment and apparel. For example, to play softball, the player needs a softball glove and a bat. This player might also want to use other products that are produced for a variety of reasons. These might be batting gloves, cap, helmet, special softball shoes, specialized socks, sunglasses, customized uniform shirts, undershirts, pants or shorts, and a customized softball bag to carry it all in. Finally, many players will want merchandise that speaks to their identity as a softball player such as funny softball T-shirts, a softball-glove key ring, and a tiny softball glove and bat to hang on their car's rearview mirror.

Moreover, this continuous interest in sports and recreation activities influences many other segments of the sport industry. Consider this: For every coed basketball league, there must be many people and products in order for that league to exist—a basketball facility, basketball officials, scorekeepers, score sheets, facility managers, facility maintenance people, facility groundskeepers, a league director, a league on-site supervisor, staff people for such jobs as paperwork, record keeping, registration and other forms, a certain number of teams registered, coaches, team managers, uniforms, shoes, socks, water bottles, towels, a coach's note pad, officials' evaluation forms, rulebooks, pens and pencils, and basketballs.

There are many different companies needed to supply all of these people and to create and produce all the necessary products. Further, if the basketball league is the WNBA or the NBA, many more businesses are needed to provide additional items or services needed or desired to produce just one game. Some of those are special officials, statisticians and other specialized people, reporters, radio, television, facility security, concessions and concession stand staff, office staff, hospitality staff, promotions and promotions people, parking facilities and parking lot staff, and trophies and awards.

It is easy to see that because so many people participate in sports, fitness, and recreation activities, the sport industry is especially affected. People who participate are the primary reason the industry exists and is so large and diverse. Additionally, they are the reason that the industry has so many other segments.

2. Increase in Sport Business Among the Range of Diverse Market Segments

The sport business industry is a vast multi-business and multicultural industry. It always has been and always will be. What is perhaps different is that there has been significant growth, development, and commercialization of the multitudes of sports activities and organizations that are created for and managed by the many different populations of people who live in the United States. Table 1.12 illustrates some of the categories of different sports events. As diverse market segments such as people who are African-American, Asian-American, Jewish, Hispanic, lesbian and gay, young and old, and disabled grow and emerge as viable markets, two things are happening. First, existing sports companies are targeting them and courting them as potential consumers either for existing products or potential products.

Table 1.12
Examples of Diverse Market Sports Events and Organizations.

Geographical Regions:	African Games
	Asian Games
	Pan American Games
	National Games of India
States:	Alabama State Sports Festival
	Southeastern Sports Festival
	Rocky Mountain State Games (Colorado)
	Empire State Games (New York)
Disabilities:	Special Olympics
	Paralympics
	World Games for the Deaf
	Disabled Swimming
	O & P Extremity Games
Religious Affiliation:	Maccabi Games (Jewish Olympics)
	Athletes in Action (Christian sports)
Career/Profession:	Police Games
	World Student Games
	U. S. Corporate Games
	Australian Corporate Games
Sexual Orientation:	Federation of Gay Games:
	Gay Games VII, Chicago, USA, July, 2006;
	Gay Games VIII, Cologne, Germany, 2010.
	The European Gay & Lesbian Sports
	Championships: EuroGames
	International Gay and Lesbian Aquatics
	Gay and Lesbian Rowing Federation
	ForeUS Lesbian Golf Tour
	International German Gay and Lesbian Golf
	Championships
	International Gay and Lesbian Ice Hockey
	Association (IGLIHA)
Political Affiliation:	Commonwealth Games
	International Sports Initiatives, U.S. Department
	of State
	Men's & Women's World Cup (soccer)
	The Olympic Games
Race/National Origin:	North American Indigenous Games
	World Games for Indigenous Peoples
	Cherokee Nation Youth Fitness Camp
	Colorado Indigenous Games
	NDN Sports: First Nation Golf Association
	National Brotherhood of Skiers (African American)
	National Association of Black Scuba Divers (NABS)
	Northwest Hispanic Soccer League
	Sacramento Asian Sports Foundation
	Seattle Asian Sports Club
Age:	National Senior Games Association
	National Youth Soccer Championships
	National Youth Bowling Championships
	U.S. Masters Swimming
	World Masters Weightlifting
	Pan Pacific Masters Games
	World Youth Athletics Championships

Second, many of these groups are creating their own sports companies and industries. Here are some examples:

- The National Brotherhood of Skiers Association (NBSA) for African American snow skiers has over 14,000 members. The NBSA hosts over 800 events each year. One annual event can reach an estimated economic impact of $10 million. Go to www.nbs.org for more information.

- The Women's World Cup was created by FIFA to meet the demands of women's soccer worldwide. After the first tournament, in 1991, tournaments have been held every four years. The media and fan attention has grown at an extraordinary rate since 1991; and at the World Cup of 1999 and 2003, there was a record breaking number of spectators at the games and a record breaking number of people watching on television. Go to www.fifa.com for more information.

- There is a gay and lesbian sports organization, business, league, or team in almost every city in the United States. These organizations offer tens of thousands of sports and recreation events each year for the lesbian and gay sports market. The events range from archery to equestrian to rodeo to snow sports to volleyball. The top event, the Gay Games, held every four years, is a major sports event and festival. Go to www.GayGames.com for more information.

- Master's swimming organizations offer swimming opportunities, events, and competitions for a variety of age-groups from 20 to 90 years of age. People of different ages compete in groups of their ages only. Go to www.usms.org for more information.

- The ESPN X Games were invented specifically for an age-group—18 to 34—labeled the Generation X. There are now Summer and Winter X Games; and sports include skateboarding, downhill and aggressive in-line skating, bicycle stunt racing, street luge, snowboarding, snow mountain biking, and skysurfing. Started in 1995, the 1998 X Games boasted over 400 athletes, $450,000

Table 1.13
Some Events Offered by Disabled Sports USA During 2005–2006.

BlazeSports Ability Games	BlazeSports Quad Rugby
First Swing Golf clinic	STRIDE Swimming
Desert Challenge Games	National Sports Center for the Disabled Rock Climbing
Michigan Association of Blind Athletes Sports Education Camp	Adaptive Adventures' Adaptive Cycling
2006 Women's Wheelchair Basketball National Championship Tournament	Adaptive Adventures Rafting Experience
	DS/USA Far West Water-Skiing
STRIDED Wounded Warriors Weekend	Disabled Sports Eastern Sierra Adventure Cycling/ Mountain Biking
Maine Handicapped Skiing's 21st Anniversary Ski-A-Thon	
25th Anniversary Windsor Classic Indoor Games	National Sports Center for the Disabled Therapeutic Horseback Riding
Ladies with Abilities Winter Adventure & Ski Camp	Source: http://www.dsusa.org.

in prize money, 225,000 spectators, and a proclaimed economic impact of $20 million. Having grown in popularity, today the X Games boasts EXPN.com, EXPN radio, official X Games sporting goods and X Games merchandise, EXPN Podcasts and more. Go to http://expn.go.com for more information.

NASCAR-licensed products generates $2 billion in annual sales.

• The Paralympic Games are Olympic-style Games designed for people with physical disabilities. Disabled Sports USA, established in 1967, offers nationwide sports programs, activities, and events to anyone with a permanent disability. Table 1.13 shows a few of the many events offered during the year 2005. Go to www.dsusa.org to find out more about this organization.

One of the reasons so many groups of people create their own sports businesses and organizations is to socialize and participate in sports with individuals with similar backgrounds and interests.

A second reason is that as populations fight for and gain civil rights, new legislation brings about increased opportunities in sport, fitness, or recreational activity. For some populations, the increase in sports opportunities has almost paralleled the fight for civil rights. The involvement of the African-American population in sport, fitness, and recreation activity increased as their struggle for civil and equal rights progressed. Women and girls gained more opportunities in organized high school and collegiate athletics because of legislation aimed at stopping discrimination based on gender in educational institutions. The number of women and girls participating in sports and athletics has increased significantly since the early 1970s.

A third reason is that people like to enjoy sports activities with their friends. Typically, a person wants to be around and do activities with people they like, who have similar characteristics, who enjoy the same things, who share the same culture, and

Table 1.14
Facts about the Gay Games.

Gay Games Event	Participants	Countries	Sports	Economic Impact
Gay Games I San Francisco, 1982	1,300	12	16	not known
Gay Games II San Francisco, 1986	3,482	22	17	not known
Gay Games III Vancouver, Canada, 1990	7,300	28	31	$30 million
Gay Games IV New York City, 1994	10,864	40	31	$112 million
Gay Games V Amsterdam, 1998	14,864	78	31	$300 million
Gay Games VI Sydney, Australia, 2002	15,000	70	31	$116 million
Gay Games VII Chicago, USA, 2006	12, 000	50	30	not known

with whom they are most comfortable. It is no surprise that most groups of people with common interests organize their own sports activities and businesses. For example, the number of sport businesses, organizations, and events for the lesbian and gay population has grown at a very fast rate (Pitts, 1997, 1999). The event that exemplifies the growth of sport in the lesbian and gay population is their Olympic sporting event, the Gay Games. The Games are held every four years; and the number of events, participants, sponsors, and spectators has grown at an extraordinary rate. The number of participants increased 1200% from the first Gay Games in 1982 to the fifth Gay Games in 1998. Over 14,000 athletes from over 70 countries competed in 1998. Table 1.14 shows the growth and size of the Gay Games since 1982.

Laws and other legislation have been passed to stop discrimination against the handicapped population. The passage of the Americans with Disabilities Act of 1990 has helped in the increased opportunities in sports and fitness activity for the handicapped and has had a significant impact on forcing the accessibility of sports facilities for the disabled. The Paralympics receives major sponsorship today. In addition, there are now numerous sports organizations and equipment designers for people with disabilities.

II. Sports Activities and Events: Sports, Recreation, Fitness, Leisure, Sports Tourism

The creation, management, marketing, and production of sports, recreation, fitness, leisure, and sports-tourism activities and events offer a world of opportunities to people. Many sports activities are created specifically for a particular group. For example, the popularity of the sports has led to the creation of state games such as the Bluegrass Games (Kentucky), the Sunshine State Games (Florida), and the Big Apple Games (New York). These events are multisport festivals designed for recreational athletes who live in a particular region.

Table 1.15 shows some of the many different sports and recreational activities today and the changes in participation rates over a period of time as compiled by the Sporting Goods Manufacturers Association (SGMA). Indeed, the SGMA believes that participation figures are the most important information in defining the size of a market. According to the SGMA, "sports participation defines the size, composition, and ultimately the trend of the product market and is, in effect, the 'gold standard' to which all markets eventually return" ("Sports Participation Trends," 1999, p. 4).

1. Constant Increase in the Number of New and Different Sports, Recreational, and Fitness Activities and Events

Since the middle 1970s, the United States has experienced a consistent and fast growth in the number and type of new sport—fitness, or recreation-related activities and events—offered to a variety of sport market consumers. Consider the following examples. In the late 1970s, a seemingly new way to get fit was offered. This was called aerobics—exercising to music. Today, there are hundreds of different kinds of aerobics offered to a wide variety of consumers. Some of these programs are soft aerobics, hard aerobics, jazzerobics, elderobics, and baby-robics.

Table 1.15
SGMA Sports Participation Trends. U.S. Population, 6 years or older, at least once per year (thousands). Released April 2005.

[1] Fourteen-year change   [2] Eleven-year change   [3] Seven-year change   [4] Five-year change   [5] Four-year change   [6] Two-year change

[7] 2003 figure is elevated due to change in category definition from "Pistol" to "Handgun."

Bold type face indicates statistically significant change at 95% confidence level

	1987 Benchmark	1990	1993	1998	2000	2002	2003	2004	1 Year % Change (2003-2004)	6 Year % Change (1998-2004)	17 Year % Change (1987-2004)
Fitness Activities											
Aerobics (High Impact)	13,961	12,359	10,356	7,460	5,581	5,423	5,875	5,521	-6.0%	**-26.0%**	**-60.0%**
Aerobics (Low Impact)	11,888	15,950	13,418	12,774	9,752	9,286	8,813	8,493	-3.6%	**-33.5%**	**-28.6%**
Aerobics (Step)	n.a.	n.a.	11,502	10,784	8,963	8,336	8,457	8,257	-2.4%	**-23.4%**	**-28.2%** [2]
Aerobics (Net)	21,225	23,015	24,839	21,017	17,326	16,046	16,451	15,767	-4.2%	**-25.0%**	**-25.7%**
Other Exercise to Music	n.a.	n.a.	n.a.	13,846	12,337	13,540	14,159	16,365	**+15.8%**	**+18.2%**	n.a.
Aquatic Exercise	n.a.	n.a.	n.a.	6,685	6,367	6,995	7,141	5,812	**-18.6%**	**-13.1%**	n.a.
Calisthenics	n.a.	n.a.	n.a.	30,982	27,790	26,862	28,007	25,562	**-8.7%**	**-17.5%**	n.a.
Cardio Kickboxing	n.a.	n.a.	n.a.	n.a.	7,163	5,940	5,489	4,773	**-14%**	n.a.	**-33.4%** [5]
Fitness Bicycling	n.a.	n.a.	n.a.	13,556	11,435	11,153	12,048	10,210	**-15.3%**	**-24.7%**	n.a. [1]
Fitness Walking	27,164	37,384	36,325	36,395	36,207	37,981	37,945	40,299	**+6.2%**	**+10.7%**	**+48.4%**
Running/Jogging	37,136	35,722	34,057	34,962	33,680	35,866	36,152	37,310	+3.2%	**+6.7%**	0.0%
Fitness Swimming	16,912	18,045	17,485	15,258	14,060	14,542	15,899	15,636	-1.6%	+2.5%	**-7.5%**
Pilates Training	n.a.	n.a.	n.a.	n.a.	1,739	4,671	9,469	10,541	**+11.3%**	n.a.	**+506.2%** [5]
Stretching	n.a.	n.a.	n.a.	35,114	36,408	38,367	42,096	40,799	-3.1%	**+16.2%**	n.a.
Yoga/Tai Chi	n.a.	n.a.	n.a.	5,708	7,400	11,106	13,371	12,414	**-7.1%**	**+117.5%**	n.a.
Equipment Exercise											
Barbells	n.a.	n.a.	n.a.	21,263	21,972	24,812	25,645	24,103	**-6.0%**	**+13.4%**	n.a.
Dumbells	n.a.	n.a.	n.a.	23,414	25,241	28,933	30,549	31,415	+2.8%	**+34.2%**	n.a.
Hand Weights	n.a.	n.a.	n.a.	23,325	27,086	28,453	29,720	30,143	+1.4%	**+29.3%**	n.a.
Free Weights (Net)	22,553	26,728	28,564	41,266	44,499	48,261	51,567	52,056	+1.0%	**+26.2%**	**+130.8%**
Weight/Resistance Machines	15,261	16,776	19,446	22,519	25,182	27,848	29,996	30,903	+3.0%	**+37.2%**	**+102.5%**
Home Gym Exercise	3,905	4,748	6,258	7,577	8,103	8,924	9,260	9,347	+1.0%	**+23.4%**	**+139.4%**
Abdominal Machine/Device	n.a.	n.a.	n.a.	16,534	18,119	17,370	17,364	17,440	0.0%	+5.5%	n.a.
Rowing Machine Exercise	14,481	14,639	11,263	7,485	6,229	7,092	6,484	7,303	**+12.6%**	-2.4%	**-49.6%**
Stationary Cycling (Upright Bike)	n.a.	n.a.	n.a.	20,744	17,894	17,403	17,488	17,889	+2.3%	**-13.8%**	n.a.
Stationary Cycling (Spinning)	n.a.	n.a.	n.a.	6,776	5,431	6,135	6,462	6,777	+4.9%	0.0%	n.a.
Stationary Cycling (Recumbent Bike)	n.a.	n.a.	n.a.	6,773	8,947	10,217	10,683	11,227	+5.1%	**+65.8%**	n.a.
Stationary Cycling (Net)	30,765	39,823	35,975	30,791	28,795	29,083	30,952	31,431	+1.6%	+2.1%	+2.2%
Treadmill Exercise	4,396	11,484	19,685	37,073	40,816	43,431	45,572	47,463	**+4.2%**	**+28.0%**	**+979.7%**
Stair-Climbing Machine Exercise	2,121	13,498	22,494	18,609	15,828	14,251	14,321	13,300	-7.1%	**-28.5%**	**+527.1%**
Aerobic Rider	n.a.	n.a.	n.a.	5,868	3,817	3,654	2,955	2,468	-16.5%	**-58.0%**	n.a.
Elliptical Motion Trainer	n.a.	n.a.	n.a.	3,863	6,176	10,695	13,415	15,678	**+16.9%**	**+305.9%**	n.a.
Cross-Country Ski Machine Exercise	n.a.	n.a.	9,792	6,870	5,444	5,074	4,744	4,155	-12.4%	**-39.5%**	-35.0% [1]
Team Sports											
Baseball	15,098	15,454	15,586	12,318	10,881	10,402	10,885	9,694	**-10.9%**	**-21.3%**	**-35.8%**
Basketball	35,737	39,808	42,138	42,417	37,552	36,584	35,439	34,223	-3.4%	**-19.3%**	-4.2%
Cheerleading	n.a.	n.a.	3,257	3,266	3,377	3,596	3,574	4,131	**+15.6%**	**+26.5%**	**+35.9%** [1]
Ice Hockey	2,393	2,762	3,204	2,915	2,761	2,612	2,789	1,998	**-28.4%**	**-31.5%**	-16.5%
Field Hockey	n.a.	n.a.	n.a.	1,375	1,349	1,096	n.a.	n.a.	n.a.	n.a.	n.a.
Football (Touch)	20,292	20,894	21,241	17,382	15,456	14,903	14,119	12,993	-8.0%	**-25.2%**	-35.9%
Football (Tackle)	n.a.	n.a.	n.a.	n.a.	5,673	5,783	5,751	5,440	-5.4%	n.a.	-4.1% [5]
Football (Net)	n.a.	n.a.	n.a.	n.a.	18,285	18,703	17,958	16,436	**-8.5%**	n.a.	-10.1% [5]
Lacrosse	n.a.	n.a.	n.a.	926	751	921	1,132	914	-19.3%	-1.3%	n.a.
Rugby	n.a.	n.a.	n.a.	546	n.a.	n.a.	n.a.	n.a.	n.a.	n.a.	n.a. [4]
Soccer (Indoor)	n.a.	n.a.	n.a.	n.a.	n.a.	n.a.	4,563	4,349	-4.7%	n.a.	n.a. [4]
Soccer (Outdoor)	n.a.	n.a.	n.a.	n.a.	n.a.	n.a.	16,133	14,608	-9.5%	n.a.	n.a.
Soccer (Net)	15,388	15,945	16,365	18,176	17,734	17,641	17,679	15,900	**-10.0%**	-12.5%	+3.3%
Softball (Regular)	n.a.	n.a.	n.a.	19,407	17,585	14,372	14,410	14,267	-1.0%	**-26.5%**	n.a.
Softball (Fast-Pitch)	n.a.	n.a.	n.a.	3,702	3,795	3,658	3,487	4,042	**+15.9%**	+9.2%	n.a.
Softball (Net)	n.a.	n.a.	n.a.	21,352	19,668	16,587	16,020	16,324	+1.9%	**-23.5%**	n.a.
Volleyball (Hard Surface)	n.a.	n.a.	n.a.	n.a.	n.a.	11,748	11,008	11,762	+6.9%	n.a.	+0.1% [6]
Volleyball (Grass)	n.a.	n.a.	n.a.	n.a.	n.a.	8,621	7,953	9,163	**+15.2%**	n.a.	+6.3% [6]
Volleyball (Beach)	n.a.	n.a.	13,509	10,572	8,763	7,516	7,454	7,741	+3.9%	**-26.8%**	-33.0% [1]
Volleyball (Net)	35,984	39,633	37,757	26,637	22,876	21,488	20,286	22,216	**+9.5%**	**-16.6%**	**-38.2%** [4]
Racquet Sports											
Badminton	14,793	13,559	11,908	9,936	8,490	6,765	5,937	6,432	**+8.3%**	**-35.3%**	**-56.5%**
Racquetball	10,395	9,213	7,412	5,853	5,155	4,840	4,875	5,533	**+13.5%**	-5.5%	**-46.8%**
Squash	n.a.	n.a.	n.a.	289	364	302	473	290	-38.7%	0.0%	n.a.
Tennis	21,147	21,742	19,346	16,937	16,598	16,353	17,325	18,346	+5.9%	**+8.3%**	**-13.2%**

Continued on next page

Table 1.15 (continued)
SGMA Sports Participation Trends. U.S. Population, 6 years or older, at least once per year (thousands). Released April 2005.

[1] Fourteen-year change   [2] Eleven-year change   [3] Seven-year change   [4] Five-year change   [5] Four-year change   [6] Two-year change   [7]

2003 figure is elevated due to change in category definition from "Pistol" to "Handgun."

Bold type face indicates statistically significant change at 95% confidence level

	1987 Benchmark	1990	1993	1998	2000	2002	2003	2004	1 Year % Change (2003-2004)	6 Year % Change (1998-2004)	17 Year % Change (1987-2004)
Personal Contact Sports											
Boxing	n.a.	n.a.	n.a.	n.a.	1,085	908	945	1,140	+20.6%	n.a.	+5.1% [5]
Martial Arts	n.a.	n.a.	n.a.	5,368	5,722	5,996	6,883	6,898	0.0%	**+28.5%**	n.a.
Wrestling	n.a.	n.a.	n.a.	n.a.	2,405	2,026	1,820	2,303	**+26.5%**	n.a.	-4.2% [5]
Indoor Sports											
Billiards / Pool	35,297	537	40,254	39,654	37,483	39,527	40,726	36,356	**-10.7%**	**-8.3%**	+3.0%
Bowling	47,823	53,537	49,022	50,593	53,844	53,160	55,035	53,603	-2.6%	**+6.0%**	+12.1%
Darts	n.a.	n.a.	n.a.	21,792	18,484	19,703	19,486	n.a.	n.a.	n.a.	n.a.
Table Tennis	n.a.	20,089	17,689	14,999	13,797	12,796	13,511	14,286	+5.7%	-4.7%	**-28.9%** [1]
Wheel Sports											
Roller Hockey	n.a.	n.a.	2,323	3,876	3,287	2,875	2,718	1,788	**-34.2%**	**-53.9%**	**-23.0%** [2]
Roller Skating (2x2 Wheels)	n.a.	27,101	24,223	14,752	10,834	10,968	11,746	11,103	-5.5%	**-24.7%**	**-59.0%** [1]
Roller Skating (Inline Wheels)	n.a.	4,695	13,689	32,010	29,024	21,572	19,233	17,348	**-9.8%**	**-45.8%**	**+269.5%** [1]
Scooter Riding (Non-motorized)	n.a.	n.a.	n.a.	n.a.	13,881	13,858	11,493	10,196	**-11.3%**	n.a.	**-25.5%** [5]
Skateboarding	10,888	9,267	5,388	7,190	11,649	12,997	11,090	10,592	-4.5%	**+47.3%**	-2.7%
Other Sports/Activities											
Bicycling (BMX)	n.a.	n.a.	n.a.	n.a.	3,977	3,885	3,365	2,642	**-21.5%**	n.a.	**-33.6%** [5]
Bicycling (Recreational)	n.a.	n.a.	n.a.	54,575	53,006	53,524	53,710	52,021	-3.1%	-4.7%	n.a.
Golf	26,261	28,945	28,610	29,961	30,365	27,812	27,314	25,723	**-5.8%**	**-14.1%**	-2.0%
Gymnastics	n.a.	n.a.	n.a.	6,224	95,268	5,149	5,189	5,273	+1.6%	**-15.3%**	n.a.
Swimming (Recreational)	n.a.	n.a.	n.a.	94,371	93,976	92,667	96,429	95,268	-1.2%	+1.0%	n.a.
Walking (Recreational)	n.a.	n.a.	n.a.	80,864	82,561	84,986	88,799	92,677	**+4.4%**	**+14.6%**	n.a.
Outdoors Activities											
Camping (Tent)	35,232	36,915	34,772	42,677	42,241	40,316	41,891	41,561	-0.8%	-2.6%	**+18.0%**
Camping (Recreational Vehicle)	22,655	20,764	22,187	18,188	19,035	18,747	19,022	17,424	**-8.6%**	-4.2%	**-23.1%**
Camping (Net)	50,386	50,537	49,858	50,650	51,606	49,808	51,007	49,412	-3.1%	-2.4%	-1.9%
Hiking (Day)	n.a.	n.a.	n.a.	38,629	39,015	36,778	39,096	39,334	+0.6%	+1.8%	n.a.
Hiking (Overnight)	n.a.	n.a.	n.a.	6,821	6,750	5,839	6,213	6,396	+3.0%	-6.2%	n.a.
Hiking (Net)	n.a.	n.a.	n.a.	40,117	40,133	37,888	40,409	40,713	+0.8%	+1.5%	n.a.
Horseback Riding	n.a.	n.a.	n.a.	16,522	16,988	14,641	16,009	14,695	**-8.2%**	**-11.1%**	n.a.
Mountain Biking	1,512	4,146	7,408	8,611	7,854	6,719	6,940	5,334	**-23.1%**	**-38.1%**	**+252.8%**
Mountain/Rock Climbing	n.a.	n.a.	n.a.	2,004	1,947	2,089	2,169	2,161	-0.4%	+7.8%	n.a.
Artificial Wall Climbing	n.a.	n.a.	n.a.	4,696	6,117	7,185	8,634	7,659	**-11.3%**	**+63.1%**	n.a.
Trail Running	n.a.	n.a.	n.a.	5,249	5,232	5,625	6,109	6,486	+6.2%	**+23.6%**	n.a.
Shooting Sports											
Archery	8,558	9,252	8,648	7,109	6,047	6,650	7,111	6,756	-5.0%	-5.0%	**-21.0%**
Hunting (Shotgun/Rifle)	25,241	23,220	23,189	16,684	16,481	16,471	15,232	15,196	-0.2%	**-8.9%**	**-39.8%**
Hunting (Bow)	n.a.	n.a.	n.a.	4,719	4,120	4,752	4,155	3,661	-11.9%	**-22.4%**	n.a.
Paintball	n.a.	n.a.	n.a.	5,923	7,121	8,659	9,835	9,640	-2.0%	**+62.8%**	n.a.
Shooting (Sport Clays)	n.a.	n.a.	3,100	2,734	2,843	3,017	3,867	3,222	-16.7%	**+17.8%**	+9.9% [1]
Shooting (Trap/Skeet)	5,073	n.a.	n.a.	3,800	3,827	3,696	4,496	4,059	-9.7%	+6.8%	**-20.0%**
Target Shooting (Rifle)	n.a.	n.a.	n.a.	14,042	12,984	14,336	15,176	14,057	-7.4%	+0.1%	n.a.
Target Shooting (Handgun)[7]	n.a.	n.a.	n.a.	12,110	10,443	11,064	13,836	11,932	-13.8%	-1.5%	n.a.
Target Shooting (Net)[7]	18,947	21,840	23,498	18,330	16,293	17,558	19,788	18,037	-8.9%	-1.6%	-4.8%
Fishing											
Fishing (Fly)	11,359	8,039	6,598	7,269	6,581	6,034	6,033	4,623	**-23.4%**	**-36.4%**	**-59.3%**
Fishing (Freshwater-Other)	50,500	53,207	50,198	45,807	44,050	42,605	43,819	39,433	**-10.0%**	**-13.9%**	**-21.9%**
Fishing (Saltwater)	19,646	19,087	18,490	15,671	14,710	14,874	15,221	13,453	**-11.6%**	**-14.2%**	**-31.5%**
Fishing (Net)	58,402	58,816	55,442	55,488	53,846	51,426	52,970	47,906	**-9.6%**	**-13.7%**	**-18.0%**
Winter Sports											
Ice Skating	n.a.	n.a.	n.a.	18,710	17,496	14,530	17,049	14,692	**-13.8%**	**-21.5%**	n.a.
Skiing (Cross-Country)	8,344	7,292	6,489	4,728	4,613	4,080	4,171	4,007	-4.0%	**-15.2%**	**-52.0%**
Skiing (Downhill)	17,676	18,209	17,567	14,836	14,749	14,249	13,633	11,971	**-12.2%**	**-19.3%**	**-32.3%**
Snowboarding	n.a.	n.a.	2,567	5,461	7,151	7,691	7,818	7,110	-9.1%	**+30.2%**	+41.0%
Snowmobiling	n.a.	n.a.	n.a.	6,492	7,032	4,515	5,509	4,688	**-14.9%**	**-27.8%**	n.a.
Snowshoeing	n.a.	n.a.	n.a.	1,721	1,970	2,006	2,479	2,302	-7.1%	**+33.8%**	n.a.

Continued on next page

Table 1.15 *(continued)*

SGMA Sports Participation Trends. U.S. Population, 6 years or older, at least once per year (thousands). Released April 2005.

[1] Fourteen-year change   [2] Eleven-year change   [3] Seven-year change   [4] Five-year change   [5] Four-year change   [6] Two-year change   [7] 2003

figure is elevated due to change in category definition from "Pistol" to "Handgun."

Bold type face indicates statistically significant change at 95% confidence level

Water Sports	1987 Benchmark	1990	1993	1998	2000	2002	2003	2004	1 Year % Change (2003-2004)	6 Year % Change (1998-2004)	17 Year % Change (1987-2004)
Boardsailing/Windsurfing	1,145	1,025	835	1,075	655	496	779	418	-46.4%	**-61.1%**	**-63.5%**
Canoeing	n.a.	n.a.	n.a.	13,615	13,134	10,933	11,632	11,449	-1.6%	**-16.0%**	n.a.
Kayaking	n.a.	n.a.	n.a.	3,501	5,562	5,562	6,324	6,147	-2.8%	**+75.6%**	n.a.
Rafting	n.a.	n.a.	n.a.	5,570	4,431	4,431	4,553	4,209	-7.6%	**-24.4%**	n.a.
Jet Skiing	n.a.	n.a.	n.a.	11,203	10,835	9,806	10,648	7,972	**-25.1%**	**-28.9%**	n.a.
Sailing	6,368	5,981	3,918	5,902	5,271	5,161	5,232	4,307	**-17.7%**	**-27.0%**	**-32.4%**
Scuba Diving	2,433	2,615	2,306	3,448	2,901	3,328	3,215	3,430	+6.7%	-0.5%	**+41.0%**
Snorkeling	n.a.	n.a.	n.a.	10,575	10,526	9,865	10,179	11,112	+9.2%	+5.1%	n.a.
Surfing	1,459	1,224	n.a.	1,395	2,180	1,879	2,087	1,936	-7.2%	**+38.8%**	**+32.7%**
Wakeboarding	n.a.	n.a.	n.a.	2,253	3,581	3,142	3,356	2,843	-15.3%	**+26.2%**	n.a.
Water Skiing	19,902	19,314	16,626	10,161	10,335	8,204	8,425	6,835	**-18.9%**	**-32.7%**	**-65.7%**

During the past two decades, in-line skating made its way across the continent. Boogie-boarding and snow-boarding were invented. Here are some others that have been created in the last 10 to 15 years: snow kayaking, parasailing, ice surfing, mountain boarding, two-person and three-person beach volleyball, skydive dancing, street luge, indoor soccer, snow biking, ice climbing, and the X-Games. With this fast and diverse innovation in sport and fitness activities comes increased participation by a wider spectrum of consumers. Whereas the traditional sport of outdoor 11-on-11 soccer played for two 45-minute halves might not interest someone, that person might be interested in trying a modified game of indoor soccer, 5-on-5, and consisting of four 12-minute quarters. These innovations have increased the number and types of sport-activity products offered to the consumer and have reached an increased number and type of consumer market segments. This kind of new product development is one key to success in competitive strategy.

2. Consistent Growth in the Offering of Traditional Sports

Even though there are a multitude of new sports activities, traditional sports haven't been set aside. Instead, there has been growth in the offerings of traditional sports and activities. In other words, if you wanted to play volleyball a few decades ago, you most likely would have had to join a YWCA, YMCA, or a local city parks and recreation league. Today, volleyball is offered by many different businesses and organizations such as multisport centers, clubs, independent organizations, individual tournaments, and even by local pubs or bars. Along the same line, soccer was a sport almost unknown in the United States just a few decades ago. Today, soccer may be found at many parks and recreation facilities, privately owned facilities, state facilities, and on the campuses of schools and colleges. It is offered to consumers of all ages. There are leagues for children who are 4 years old as well as the fast-growing leagues for the 30-something, 40-something, and 50-something year-old player.

In addition, fueling this growth are the increasing numbers of sports and recreation organizations among the many diverse populations. For example, the number and variety of sports and recreational activities and events for people with disabilities have exploded. Limited only by imagination, people with a vision or hearing impairment, for example, can participate in a multitude of sports, recreation, and fitness activities.

3. Constant Increase in the Number and Type of Professional Level Sport, Fitness, and Recreational Activities

When a new sport activity is invented, sometimes that sport will become a professional sport activity. A professional sport is one in which the participant is paid to perform or in which the participant is making a career of the activity. Consider the number and range of sport and fitness activities that are professional today: racing cars, trucks, boats, horses, dogs, and other items; Frisbee throwing; water sports such as water skiing, knee boarding, trick skiing, jet skiing, surfing, boogie-boarding, windsurfing, sailing, yachting, fishing, and other water activities; snow sports such as downhill and cross-country racing, trick skiing, ice sailing, the Iditarod, ice fishing, and others; bowling; billiards; hang gliding; aerobics competition; and body building. These have increased the number of professional sports participants as well as the number of opportunities available for the sport management and sport marketing professional in producing, facilitating, promoting, or organizing the events. In addition, such a growth in activity increases the need for sports equipment and apparel designed for the sport and participant.

4. Increase in Sports-Tourism and Adventure-Travel Products

Combining travel and sports is not new. Every time a person travels to another city to participate in a marathon or to go hiking in the Himalayas, this is sports tourism. Every time a group of baseball fans travels to another city to watch the World Series, this is sports tourism. When people travel to Fort Lauderdale to see the Swimming Hall of Fame or travel to tour a sports facility to pay homage to it, this too is sports tourism.

During the past decade, sports-tourism, sports-travel, and adventure-travel products have increased. Additionally, the number and diversity of businesses offering these products have increased. Sports tourism is a combination of sports activities and travel, either for participatory, spectatorial, or homage purposes (Gibson, Attle, and Yiannakis,1998; Pitts, 1999; Standeven and DeKnop, 1999). The World Travel & Tourism shows that tourism in the United States has an economic impact of $462.2 billion. If sports tourism is an approximate fifteen percent of that, then sports tourism is $69.33-billion-dollar industry in the United States (refer to Table 1.9).

Some sports businesses such as snow ski resorts rely heavily on people's willingness to travel to their place of business in order to participate in a sports activity. Others such as golf promote their resort as a golf-vacation destination even though local consumers support the resort. Some businesses are in the business of developing sports travel packages by developing a trip specifically for the purpose of participating in an activity. For example, numerous companies now specialize in organizing trips for hiking, camping, climbing, running, kayaking, scuba diving, and many other activities.

There are now many companies that specialize in putting together travel packages for the purpose of attending sports events. A few of the many sports events designed for spectatorial and entertainment purposes include the Super Bowl (a national football championship game), the Women's or Men's World Cup (the international soccer championship held every four years and requiring more than a month of time, several matches), or a local college women's or men's basketball play-off games. In addition, people do sports-related travel not to participate in a sports activity or to watch a sports event, but to see sports-related places such as sports museums, halls of fame, arenas, stadiums, facilities, memorabilia, or monuments. In one example, companies were selling tours to Atlanta prior to the 1996 Olympic Games for people who just wanted to see the sports facilities that would be used for the Olympics. Additionally, there are people who want to visit and tour sports areas such as halls of fame to study history and see the memorabilia of big-name sports people from over the years. Sports tourism is also an emerging field of study. There are a few textbooks such as *Sport Tourism* (1999) by Standeven and De-Knop and a journal, the *Journal of Sport & Tourism*.

> What is new about sports tourism is the increasing number of businesses, types of products offered, and focus on sports tourism as a developing identifiable industry.

III. Sporting Goods

Sporting goods and equipment can fuel people's interest in sports and recreational activities. That is, when you browse through a sporting goods store, you may see equipment for sports that are new to you. This can sometimes catch your interest and you'll purchase that equipment and learn how to play that sport. Refer to Tables 1.9 and 1.10 as you read this section.

1. Increase in Sporting Goods and Apparel Designed for the Diversity of Markets and Their Demands

It wasn't so long ago that all sporting goods, equipment, and services were designed and made only for the male participant. Today, sporting goods manufacturers are designing goods and equipment for a variety of market segments. Further, the number of companies, retail or manufacturer, owned and managed by people who are not white males is increasing. These companies are set up to specifically design sports equipment, apparel, and services for other markets. A woman, for example, may look for running shoes made for a woman's foot instead of having to purchase a shoe made for a male. A child who wants to play soccer can buy soccer shoes made specifically for children. A person with only one leg can purchase specially designed snow-ski equipment. A Jewish person can participate in an Olympic-style event created just for Jewish people. At the same time, technology and design have influenced sports equipment and apparel. Tennis rackets are available in a variety of sizes: The grip is offered in several sizes, shapes, and materials; the racket head is offered in several sizes and materials; the string is offered in a variety of type; and the

Sporting goods and equipment can peak people's interest in sports.

weight of the racket varies. Uniforms also come in a variety of styles, sizes, and materials. Most sports have clothing or equipment custom designed for enhancing performance. Consider the one-piece vinyl-looking suits worn in the sport of luge. The style and material are aerodynamically designed for speed.

Today, sporting goods, as well as sport activity, are much more available, more affordable, and more accessible to more consumer segments. Historically, tennis was enjoyed exclusively by the wealthy. Today, tennis is affordable to and enjoyed by people of many income levels.

Services surrounding sport and fitness activities have expanded. Services offered in some fitness clubs include laundry service, racket stringing, golf-club cleaning, child-care, concessions, restaurants, lounges, tanning beds, valet parking, and massage.

> The sporting goods industry is one of the largest segments of the sport business industry because people must have equipment and apparel in order to participate in most sports activities.

The variety of goods and services is expanding to accommodate the many diverse populations participating in sport. The demographics and psychographics of the people in the United States change almost constantly. At one time a marketer could safely assume that the greatest majority of people living in the United States were white, Christian, and heterosexual, and that a household consisted of a traditional family consisting of a woman, man, and children. The general make-up of the current "household" is very different today. Knowledge of and sensitivity to current household structure is important in decisions concerning all marketing strategies.

Sports equipment designed for the disabled is being developed more frequently today. There are softballs that emit a beeping sound. These are used in softball games for people with vision impairments. There are wheelchairs designed for speed. Materials are very lightweight, and the chairs are aerodynamically designed and constructed. This type of wheelchair is used in basketball, running, and tennis participation, for example.

2. Influence of Technology on Sport-Related Goods, Services and Training

The sport industry has benefited from advances in technology. Technology has influenced sports equipment, facilities, clothing, and shoes and has affected performance through sophisticated training programs. Some specific examples include computer assisted programs in nutrition, training, skill analysis, and equipment design; and materials used in equipment, uniforms, shoes, and other gear.

IV. Facilities, Sports Medicine, and Fitness Training

Is it the facilities or an athlete's natural skill that enhances performance? If an athlete believes that a facility makes him or her perform better, is it true? Perhaps we will never know the answer to such questions. We do, however, know that what people believe can be a powerful influence on their mental or physical state. Sports facilities today are state-of-the-art and place the athlete in an ultimate surrounding for enhanced performance. In addition, many modern sports facilities are designed with the spectator in mind. At no other time in history have so many multimillion-dollar facilities been built than in the 1990s. Many are taking into consideration the many needs of and the diversity of the people who will watch the spectacle. Facilities influence and are a major segment of the sport industry.

1. Increase in the Number and Type of Sports Facilities and Events

The increased interest in sport, fitness, and recreation activity over the last few decades has influenced the number and type of facilities and events offered. Sports and fitness facilities are constantly being built to meet the demand for sports, fitness, and recreation activities, new sports, and for sports entertainment purposes. For example, a record number of football stadiums for professional teams were built in the late 1990s. These facilities incorporate full-service communities including restaurants, shopping malls, hotels, and fitness centers.

Another factor influencing this growth in building sport facilities and offering events is money. Call any city's visitors and convention office, and they can tell you how many sports events were hosted in the city during the prior year. They can also give you an estimate of the economic impact of each of those events. Economic impact includes the money brought in to the city because of the event—money spent by the event attendees on lodging, eating, shopping, and transportation. Realizing the money involved, many cities build sports facilities and have committees whose primary responsibility is to attract sporting events. The sporting events might include small events such as a 10k run, a car race, a three-on-three basketball tournament, a beach volleyball tournament, or a rodeo. It can also include trying to attract events as large as the Olympics.

> The sporting goods industry is increasingly focused on developing products for non-traditional markets such as women, disabled athletes, and children.

2. Movement of Facilities From Single-purpose to Multi-Sport and Full-Service

Facilities

Early sport, fitness, and recreation facilities were typically single sport or single purpose. Today, sport facilities are built with the capability to serve many purposes and to accommodate many sport events as well as nonsports events. Consider today's fitness centers. Most will have the usual weight-lifting room, sauna, and tanning beds. Further inspection will reveal large multipurpose rooms for aerobics and other activities, an indoor and outdoor pool, steam rooms, whirlpool baths, plush locker rooms and full-service dressing rooms, childcare services, restaurants, lounges, volleyball courts, racquetball courts, basketball courts, tennis courts, massage services, a pro shop, and many auxiliary services such as racket stringing, laundry services, hair dryers, shampoo, and even toothbrushes and toothpaste.

The multipurpose, multisport facility serves the modern fitness and health-minded consumer as a home away from home. Such facilities are more accessible, more convenient, and more efficient; they can accommodate the consumer's desires for something different when he or she becomes bored with one sport.

There are still some single-sport facilities built today whose primary purpose is to accommodate one sport. As examples, look at the Toronto Sky Dome, the Joe Robbie Stadium in Miami, and the Super Dome in New Orleans. However, even though they were built to primarily service one or two sports, other events are staged in the facilities.

3. Constant Increase in the Amount and Types of Sports Medicine and Fitness Training Services

Regardless of status, skill, or fitness level, if an individual wants or needs medical treatment for a sports injury or professional training, it is available today like in no other period of time in history. During the late 1970s and throughout the 1990s, the importance of keeping college, professional, and Olympic athletes healthy, in top physical condition, and in the game produced a need for professionals who specialized in taking care of sports injuries with an emphasis on speedy and accurate recovery and professionals who specialized in perfecting the physical. Hence, the athletic training, sports medicine, and fitness training fields of study proliferated. Today, every city has sports medicine, sports-injury rehabilitation, and fitness training clinics. It is a growing industry segment of the sport business industry. For the professional, there are degrees, certification clinics, workshops, seminars, exhibitions, conferences, magazines, newsletters, professional journals, web sites, and even consultants, all designed to support, and make money from, this growing industry.

Its effects on the sport business have been many, but the individuals reaping the benefits are people who participate in sports. Getting professional attention to injuries and professional training enhances an athlete's performance.

> Taking care of the athlete, regardless of level, has become big business.

Therefore, fewer sports participants have to give up participating due to an injury. Furthermore, the growth of such services is one reason for the growing numbers of people participating throughout their lifetimes, regardless of age. It is no secret that one of the fastest growing age segments in the sport industry are people 45-plus. The industry is scrambling to meet the demand, offering increasing numbers of age-group categories in most sports for those who are 50, 60, 70, 80, and even 90-plus. Those of you reading this textbook who want to play sports forever should know that this is increasingly becoming possible.

V. Commercialization and Marketing of Sport

The word *commercialization* is derived from the word *commercial*. A check of any thesaurus will give you these words: business, mercantile, trade, trading, marketable, salable, vendible, wanted, advertisement, ad, plug, promo, promotion, sponsorship, and sport. Most sports and recreational activities are all these things today. The increasing commercialization and marketing of more and different sports, recreation, fitness, tourism, and leisure activities and events as well as sport-related products such as sports magazines are having a tremendous impact on the growth and development of the sport industry.

1. Packaging of Sport as an Entertainment Product

Companies with sports events for sale have done a much better job of packaging sports to attract a wide variety of consumers. Fitness centers and sports clubs have enhanced their offerings to attract and keep consumers. As you learned earlier, fitness centers have become almost a 'home-away-from-home.' Every convenience and service are offered to catch and to keep the consumer's attention.

Sports for sale as a spectatorial or entertainment product are being packaged to attract more and a greater variety of consumers. For example, consider a minor league men's professional baseball game. The consumer is lured to the park with accommodations for tailgating (partying in the parking lot before and after a game) and offered a chance to be one of the first 2,000 people through the gate to receive a huggie (a plastic can cooler); he or she might win a brand-new truck during the seventh-inning stretch (as the result of a ticket-stub number drawing); and, for one hour after the game, a local country music band will play their hearts out while consumers two-step on the infield. What a bargain!

In another example, the Kentucky Derby offers over 70 events leading up to and surrounding the Kentucky Derby horse race. The actual race lasts only about two minutes, but the events surrounding the race now last about four weeks! The primary reason for offering the consumer more than just the sports event is to make the sports event the centerpiece of a larger event. Of course, another reason is money. Many people and businesses profit from the Kentucky Derby. Therefore, everyone cooperates in order to bring in more consumers. Table 1.16 illustrates a sample of the events. Notice how many are sports events!

The fans' interest in sports is what keeps sport businesses surviving and thriving.

Table 1.16
Sample of Kentucky Derby Events.

26th Annual Poster Premiere	Don Fightmaster Golf Outing for Exceptional Children
50th Annual They're Off! Luncheon	Festival Appearance in Gator Bowl Parade
adidas Derby Festival Basketball Classic	Festival Exhibit at Annual Home and Garden Show
adidas Derby Festival Night of Future Stars	Festival Merchandise at Stewart's Flea Market
Aquafina Derby Festival Student Art Desplay	Fifth Third Bank Derby Festival $1 Million Hole-in-One Ladies Day
Aquafina Student Art Contest Awards Ceremony	Fifth Third Bank Derby Festival $1 Million Hole-in-One Contest
BellSouth Derby Festival Morning Line	
BellSouth Derby Festival Pro Beach Volleyball Exhibition	FOX 41 Thunder Harley Raffle
BellSouth Derby Festival Volleyball Classic	King Southern Bank Derby Festival Foundation Pro-Am Golf Tournament
Bluegrass Family Health Running Wild Expo	
Boys' Haven Corn Toss Competition	Meijer Derby Festival Marathon/miniMarathon
Derby Eve at the Chow Wagon	Thunder Over Louisville
Derby Festival Battle of the Bounce	U.S. Bank Derby Festival Great Balloon Race
Derby Festival Foundation Academic Challenge	

2. Increased Marketing and Marketing Orientation in the Sport Business Industry

As more sport management professionals learn and then apply the fundamentals of sport marketing to the sport industry, the sport industry is treated more as a business than as a recreational interest and sport products are designed with consumer needs in mind. Maybe you have heard the expression, Give consumers what they want! This certainly applies to the sport industry. Take, for example, basketball rules changes specifically for entertainment value: The dunk was legalized because the fans loved it; there are TV time-outs because television's advertisers need the time for their commercials. Why isn't soccer televised in the United States on a regular basis? Because there are no time-outs in order to assure advertiser's commercials? Television officials are pressuring soccer officials to change the rules in order to make it 'TV-friendly." In other words, rules in sports are changed to make it more marketable.

3. Increased Understanding and Knowledge of Consumers of the Sport Business Industry

As you will learn in this book, there are a multitude of different products in the sport business industry and, therefore, a multitude of different consumer groups. Gone are the days when a sport business such as college men's basketball could simply offer the game and expect large crowds. Gone, too, are the days when an athlete-management consulting company was the only one in existence. Because of the increased competitive structure of the industry, there are many more products from which to choose. For a sport company to thrive, therefore, it must constantly analyze its consumers. Sport management professionals are increasingly doing a better job of studying consumer groups and meeting their demands for products. Additionally, literature in sport management and sport marketing has begun to recognize that there is much more to the industry and many more types of consumers than sports participants and spectators. Therefore, sport management education materials are better preparing students for careers throughout the industry.

4. Promotion Perfection as the Goal for Sport Marketing Professionals

Many in the sport business industry have perfected the art of promotion, partially out of a desire to truly promote a product and partially out of the increasingly competitive nature of the industry. For example, there are more home fitness-equipment products on the market than ever before. In order to entice the consumer to purchase one company's product instead of the other company's product, sport marketing professionals go to great lengths to create the optimal promotional plan.

In another example, it might seem that sport marketing professionals have taken the art of promotion perhaps too far. Modern spectators of sporting events expect more than just the event. They expect to be entertained before, during, and after an event. They expect to be bombarded by advertising messages, and they expect promotional activities such as giveaway merchandise, souvenir stands, food and drink, instant replay on gigantic screens, and much, much more. At any rate, the sport marketing professional has perfected this craft.

5. Growth of Corporate Sponsorship

Sport sponsorship is estimated to be a $24.8-billion-dollar industry (refer to Table 1.9). Sponsorship is the exchange of something for something. In its simplest form, sponsorship occurs when a company or person gives money to financially support an event, organization, or person. The return is an advertising benefit. Some exchanges can be quite complex and involve goods and services as well as funds. In exchange, the company might receive such benefits as advertising, having the event or facility named for the company, product tie-ins, on-site sales or giveaways, goods, and tickets. Companies are heavily involved in sponsorship in the sport industry today. Because it is such a large and popular industry, companies use sponsorship primarily as an advertising tactic. Other reasons are to reach specific market segments, to increase grassroots marketing, to be associated with sports, and to do "cause" marketing. Watch any racecar driver step out of her or his car. Look at the uniform, and what do you see? The uniform is covered with patches of the many companies that provided money to the racing team organization. Look at the car. It's almost impossible to see the car because it is covered with sponsor's logos. Why do companies get involved in sponsorship? The most common reasons include the company's desires to have the public think of it as a caring company, to have the public see and remember its name, and, to use its resources wisely (in many cases, sponsorship is less expensive than other forms of advertising).

> Decisions in the sport industry are increasingly based on consumers' desires.

Sponsorship is a multibillion-dollar industry and growing. There are a multitude of opportunities for companies for sponsorship because there are hundreds of thousands of sports events, organizations, governing bodies, and athletes, many of which are looking for sponsorship. Sponsorship is such a large industry segment that there are conferences, trade shows, magazines, companies, and directories serving the industry.

6. Increased Endorsements

Over the last couple of decades, the use of endorsement as an advertising and promotional tool has increased. The product may or may not be a sport product. The agreement may involve a fee or goods and/or services traded for the individual's or company's time. Use of the endorser brings attention to the product by capitalizing on the popularity of the endorser. There are different categories of endorsement. The following are some examples:

* Individual endorsement: use of an athlete, coach, owner, or other individual person

* Team endorsement: use of a full team

* Full organization: use of an entire organization such as the use of the NCAA (National Collegiate Athletic Association), the NFL (National Football Association), the IOC (International Olympic Committee) or USOC (United States Olympic Committee) to endorse a product.

7. Growth in Importance of Licensing and Merchandising

Licensed merchandise in the United States and Canada is estimated to be worth $71.21 billion, of which sports licensed products in 2005 were $13.23 billion (refer to Table 1.8) (SGMA). NASCAR, for example, reports an estimated $2 billion in licensed merchandise sales. A way to promote and to add extra income for many sports companies is to use licensing and merchandising. In the last decade, licensing and merchandising have become big business. It involves copyright protection for a company's name, logo, mark, or events and using those to create lines of souvenir merchandise. This has become so much a part of sports events that spectators expect to be able to purchase souvenir merchandise. Licensing and merchandising have had a tremendous impact on the sport business industry, primarily as income boosters, but also as ways to develop brand-loyal consumers.

> **Company sponsorship:**
> * promotes a caring image
> * familiarizes the public with the company name
> * provides relatively inexpensive advertising

VI. Sport Industry Professional Service Businesses

There are a number and variety of businesses that offer such professional services as legal, sport marketing, sport finance, sport management, and consulting to the sport business industry. These have become an integral part of the industry. Some specific examples, shown in Table 1.9, are sports medicine at $64.6 billion; Agents Interpublic Groups of Companies (agents) at $4 billion; Huber, Hunt, and Nichols (sports facility construction) at $1.01 billion; and Ticketmaster at $341 million. Most of these are business-to-business companies: Their products are sold primarily to sport businesses. You will learn more about business-to-business markets in later chapters.

1. *Extraordinary Growth in Service Businesses for the Sport Industry*

Those service businesses provide legal representation, consulting, and research, marketing, and financial services. For almost every area of the industry, there are now businesses that want to provide services to help—and profit from—that part of the industry. For example, for professional athletes, there are several service businesses and consultants to help them with their legal, financial, licensing, sports equipment, clothing, and endorsement possibilities.

These offers of help now start when athletes are very young, even sometimes when they are still preteens. For other areas of the industry, there are service businesses. For example, if your company is a laundry detergent company and you want to know exactly how effective your $15-million racing boat sponsorship is, you can hire a sport marketing company to do the research for you. Moreover, although these service businesses have sprung up to offer help in the sport industry, and, of course, to profit from it as well, they have created new professions, which translates into new jobs and careers for people.

VII. The Sport Industry, Media, and Sports Media

The sport industry and the media have a relatively long history. Sports have been broadcast or reported through such media forms as television, radio, newspaper, and magazines. There are more forms of media today, and the sport business industry has benefited greatly from most of them. Additionally, a new sport business industry segment, sports media, has emerged as a result of the popularity and growth of both media and sports as well as media technology. For instance, sports events were first televised by existing broadcasting companies. During the 1960s, a couple of hours per week might be programmed for broadcasting sports coverage. The growth in popularity of sports, fitness, and recreation gave rise to new sport media businesses such as ESPN and FOX Sports, whose exclusive programming focus was sports events and news. The continued popularity of such businesses has spawned specialization. Today, for example, there is a sports television company, the Golf Channel, that focuses only on one sport; and there are companies that focus on a region of the country such as the Sunshine Sports Network, which focuses on sports in the southeastern region of the United States. In 2000, it was reported that there were 48 sports channels in the United States that were producing 235 hours of sports programming each day ("ABC Evening News," 2000). Today, that number has increased almost exponentially. For example, that number of programming hours was carried by 48 sports channels; whereas today, each sports channel carries 24-hour programming. See Table 1.17 for a sample list of sports television channels.

Other forms of sport media include print media, the World Wide Web, film, and radio.

As with television, coverage of sports started with existing companies. Later, companies whose exclusive product was sports proliferated. Today, sports print media, sport web companies, sports films, and sports radio are growing segments of the industry. More recently, combinations of media forms have begun to redefine the sports media industry. For instance, a sports television broadcasting company that

Table 1.17
Sample List of Sports Television Channels.

ESPN	Empire Sports Network	Sportsnet World
The Golf Channel	Surf TV	Sportsnet America
FOX Sports Network	GolTV	EXPN
Resort Sports Network	Football Network	ESPN2
Extreme Sports Channel	NFL Sunday Ticket	ESPN News
College Sports Television	Black Belt TV	SUN Sports
Golden Sports	MLB Extra Innings	Fuel TV—Action Sports Television
The Tennis Channel	The Ice Channel	Cox Sports TV
Showtime Boxing	Outdoor Life Network	Speed Channel
Madison Square Garden Network	TSN—The Sports Network	Guangdong Sports Channel
New England Sports Network	Sky Sports	Shanghai Sports Channel
NFL Network	Rogers Sportsnet (Canadian)	

also produces sports events, sports magazines, a sports website company and sponsors a variety of sports events becomes a sports media conglomerate and can cross-market its many products. For example, the TV channel will advertise its event on TV, in its magazine, and on its website. The company can link promotional activities and fan participation activities, thus enticing the fan (consumer) to use products all produced by the same company.

1. Sport Industry Benefits of Mass Media Exposure

The advent of television and certainly the broadcasting of sports on television have had a tremendous impact on the growth of the sport industry. Through television, people are exposed to a variety of sports and sport events. The demand for sport on television gave way to advertising dollars for the networks and for the sport enterprise as well. The exposure has influenced the awareness of sport, the popularity of sport, and the participation in sport. Television has also created new sport business opportunities and a new sport industry segment has taken off—TV sports. Gone are the days when people were limited to watching a few select sports events on national broadcasting channels sandwiched between other programming. Today, numerous sports channels offer the consumer the chance to watch sports and recreational events 24 hours a day, 7 days a week—as shown in Table 1.17. Fueling this increase is target marketing.

Sports channels are being created to meet the desires of target markets. Some of those targeted channels include the Golf channel, the Tennis channel, the Speed channel, NBA channels, soccer channels, and the outdoor life channel.

These sports channels are having profound effects on the sport business industry. Not only are they an enormous industry segment creating millions of jobs, but they also introduce, educate, and entertain millions of consumers each day. They have launched two more industry segments: non-sports companies that use televised sports events for advertising their products and sports created for TV. In the first instance, which is sometimes called "marketing through sports," many companies pay millions of dollars to advertise during televised sports events, or to sponsor the event, to reach certain markets. In the second instance, sports, fitness, and other recreational activities and events are invented specifically for television. For example, ESPN2 created the X-Games as a television sports event commodity.

> Exposure to TV, the radio, and the Internet has increased popular interest in sports and the sport industry.

Another mass media outlet includes print media such as newspapers. No other industry enjoys its own separate section in nearly every newspaper worldwide. Reading about sports and recreation increases the awareness of sport and the desire to participate in sports and recreation.

The Internet, which continues to revolutionize business and the way people shop, interact, and communicate, has also had an enormous impact in the sport industry. There are already numerous sport businesses and other opportunities on the web. To find some of them, simply go to any search engine and type in "sports" or "sport business" as the subject. In one example, www.CBSsportsline.com is a company created specifically to be a web company. It offers information and is a sports shopping mall.

2. Sports Activities and Events as a Popular Entertainment Product

As presented earlier, many sports and recreation activities and events have become very popular events. This makes them great products for media. Some of the American culture is built around using sports activities and events as entertainment. For example, a family can use the fact that one of their children participates in mountain biking as an excuse to get a long weekend vacation and family outing to attend the event. In another example, tailgating has become an American phenomenon, and some have turned it into an art form. The SBJ study, shown in Tables 1.6 and 1.7, focused on spectator sports and estimated the value of that industry and its segments.

This entertainment value of a sports activity or event makes the event a great media event. For example, live television coverage of the Kentucky Derby begins at 6:00 a.m. on the day of the race, a 2-minute sports event usually run at around 4:30 p.m. However, television crews and reporters are at every possible spot on the track and talk with many different people: inside and outside the track, at the stables, at the corporate tent areas, up in Millionaires Row, on the infield, in the trailers with the jockeys, and at the gates to interview people as they arrive. The media know this event has become a major entertainment event, and they are there to cover all aspects of it.

3. Constant Increase in Television and Radio Coverage

Coverage of sport activities and events on television and radio is big business. Most major and minor broadcasting companies compete for the rights to broadcast events, large and small, traditional and contemporary. In addition, there are several sports broadcasting companies whose full-time coverage is sports activities and events. It has been estimated that there is 235 hours of sports programming in a 24-hour period on 48 sports channels ("ABC Evening News," 2000). This constant and growing coverage of sports, recreation, and fitness events has helped increase the popularity of sports.

4. Increase in the Number and Variety of Magazines, Trade Magazines, and Academic Journals Devoted to Sport

Walk into any local bookstore and go to the magazine section. How many magazines can you count that are sports, fitness, health, leisure, travel, and recreation magazines? If the activity exists, there is or soon will be a magazine for it. The variety includes boating, sailing, in-line skating, fishing, flying, running, walking, adventure travel, camping, hiking, mountain biking, four-wheeling, canoeing, water sports, and snow sports.

What are the purposes of these magazines? What do they offer the consumer? They expose the consumer to a sport. They educate, encourage, and support participating in the sport or becoming a spectator of the sport. They serve as a source of

Table 1.18
Examples of Sports Magazines.

Aikido Today	Hoop	Southern Sports Journal
Auto Racing Digest	Horse Illustrated	Sporting News
Backpacker	Inside Kung Fu	Stock Car Racing
Baseball Digest	Inside Pool Magazine	Surfer's Journal
Basketball Times	Inside Wrestling	Swimming World
Billiard Times	International Figure Skating	Tae Kwon Do Journal
Black Belt	Junior Baseball	Tennis
Blue Water Sailing	Kite Boarding	Thoroughbred Times
Bowling Digest	Motorcycle World	Track & Field News
Buffalo Sports Report	National Masters News	Transworld Skateboarding
Camping Life	Personal Watercraft Illustrated	USA Gymnastics
Canoe & Kayak	Pro Bull Rider	VeloNews
Climbing	Racer	Volleyball
Dick Berggren's Speedway Illustrated	Road & Track	Volleyball Canada
Diehard	Rugby	Wahine
Dirt Rag (bicycle racing)	Runner's World	Wake Boarding
ESPN Deportes	Scuba Diving	Wind Surfing
Fantasy Sports	Senior Golfer	Women's Basketball
Footbag World	Ski	Women's Soccer World
Golf	Skydiving	Yachting
Golf for Women	Snowboarder	
Hockey Business News	Soccer Digest	

Table 1.19 Sample of Trade Magazines. See also Appendix C.
Boat & Motor Dealer
Boating Industry International
Bicycle Retailer and Industry News
Golf Product News
Tennis Industry
Fly Fishing Retailer
NCAA News
Ski Area Management
Sporting Goods Business

Table 1.20 Example of Sport Business Academic Journals. See also Appendix D.	
European Sport Management Quarterly	Journal of Sport and Tourism
International Journal of Sport Finance	Journal of Sport Management
International Journal of Sport Management and Marketing	Sport Management and Other Related Topics Journal (SMART)
International Journal of Sport Management	Sport Marketing Quarterly

information and as a resource for networking. They serve as a catalog of sport equipment and apparel and therefore offer manufacturers a source of advertising directly to a target market.

Consumer magazines serve to address a sport consumer's interest in a sports activity. Trade magazines serve industry individuals who want industry news, ideas on marketing, and business information. Academic journals serve teachers, professors, and students studying sport business. Tables 1.18, 1.19, and 1.20 present examples of these magazines and journals and Appendix C and D offer extended directories.

Trade magazines are primarily for people in the various careers and trades in the sport business industry. For example, there are magazines that provide boating industry information, market data, and business strategies for the owners and managers of boat dealerships. For the sports tourism company, there are sports travel magazines and, for snow sports businesses, there are snow sports business magazines such as *WinterSport Business* and *Snowboarding Business*.

Additionally, there are annual convention and trade shows for many businesses such as the annual sporting goods manufacturers' trade show held annually in Atlanta and the snow sports industries trade show held annually in Las Vegas.

This proliferation of information has influenced both the popularity and growth of participation in sport-, fitness-, and recreation-oriented activity and the effectiveness of the sport business. As people read about, hear about, or see sports, they are more inclined to become involved. As sport businesses study and learn more about their business and industry segment, they more effectively manage and market their business. Both groups reap great benefits.

5. The Internet and Other New Media

As yet another media outlet, the Internet has had an impact on the sport industry in an instantaneous way. The Internet is now a major business force, creating a way for communication and conducting sports businesses in an instant. It joins the sport business industry, what we call e-sport business, as another new product and part of the burgeoning sport business industry. For existing companies, the Internet serves as a new way to distribute the sport product to the consumer. Further, the Internet is now a place of business for new sports businesses that exist only as on-line companies.

VIII. Sport Industry Education

Where there is an industry, there is a need for appropriately educated individuals. The vastness and diversity of segments, jobs, and careers in the sport business industry have led to a constant increase in the number and type of educational opportunities. From certifications to doctoral degrees, education for the sport industry professionals can't grow fast enough.

> The plethora of magazines devoted to particular sports not only promotes awareness of specific sports, but also provides education, encouragement, and support for the sport's participants.

1. Increase in Sports and Sport Business Education for Executives, Administrators, Athletes, and Other Personnel

There are several categories of sport education. There are people who want to learn how to play sports, games, and other activities. Some want to learn how to officiate, coach, or train athletes. Some want to learn how to organize and manage sporting enterprises. Others want to learn how to produce or promote sports events. When people desire something, it is usually (eventually) offered for sale. Today's consumer is offered an abundance of sports and/or sport business educational opportunities that range from rock-climbing lessons and biking instruction to sport business CEO workshops and coaching clinics. In addition, there are meetings and clinics to educate officials.

A vast array of books, videos, and magazines offers lessons, suggestions, hints, and tips for improving performance. All of these products have positively affected the sport industry. The opportunities help educate people who are already working in the industry and people who want to work in the industry.

2. Increase in Competency of Sport Business Management Professionals

Although sport business management is still a new field of study when compared to most other disciplines, it is having a positive influence on the competency level of those working in the sport business industry. The number of undergraduate, graduate, and doctoral programs of study in sport management continues to increase in the United States, Canada, and around the world. In 1993, the members of the North American Society approved curriculum standards for Sport Management, and in 1994, an approval process began, headed by a joint committee called the Sport Management Program Review Council of NASPE-NASSM (Fielding, Pitts, and Miller, 1991; Parks and Zanger, 1990). As students complete degrees in sport management, they will fill the jobs in the sport industry. Eventually, there will be more employees and executives in the sport industry who have a sport management degree than those who do not. As appropriately educated sport administrators begin to manage in the sport industry, they will have a positive effect on the industry.

3. Increased Prevalence of Sport Management as an Academic Discipline and a Career

Sport management is growing as an academic discipline. In the United States alone, there are approximately 280 undergraduate programs, 130 master's degree programs, and seven doctoral programs. The growth of sport management academic programs is creating jobs for those interested in education and research and the sport business industry. Today, there are more sport management faculty than ever before. With the growth in the number of programs comes growth in sport management as an academic discipline, and an academic discipline must have a scholarly body of knowledge. Today, the body of knowledge in sport management is larger than ever before. For example, there are now over a dozen sport management academic journals; some of these journals are the *Journal of Sport Management*, the *International Journal of Sport Management*, the *European Sport Management Quarterly*, the *Sport Management Review* (Australia), the *Sport Marketing Quarterly*, the *International Journal of Sports Marketing and Sponsorship*, the *International Journal of Sport Management and Marketing*, the *International Journal of Sport Finance*, *Sport and Other Related Topics Journal*, and the *Journal of Sports Economics*. Additionally, there are closely related journals such as the *Journal of Vacation Marketing*, the *Journal of Sport and Social Issues*, and the *Journal of Sports Tourism*. For a more complete list, see the appendix.

There is a scholarly society in North America, the North American Society for Sport Management, and some in other countries such as the Sport Management Association of Australia and New Zealand, the European Association for Sport Management, and the Taiwan Association for Sport Management. Each of these groups holds annual conferences during which numerous academic papers are presented.

You should have a good start on understanding the depth and breadth of the sport industry. As you have read in the preceding sections, the industry is quite large and varied. It is so large and diverse that it is necessary to organize what exists in the industry to make it easier to study and easier to understand everything that might be included in the industry.

Think about conducting an experiment in determining exactly everything—sport activity, sport business, and all related products—that is included in this super-large industry. Do this by developing a list. You could get organized by creating categories. The categories could contain products in the industry that have commonalities such as categories of sporting goods and equipment, clothing, shoes, sport activities, sport marketing companies, and fitness centers. Of course, trying to list everything in the United States would be practically impossible. You would end up with an enormous list. So let's start with your hometown. Consider some resources that will help you such as the yellow pages and copies of your local newspaper. List all the YMCAs and YWCAs and what each one offers. Write down every activity, service, good, league, tournament, and other products offered at the Ys. Now list city recreation offices and everything offered. List the fitness centers and health clubs and everything offered. Develop a list of youth sport organizations and everything offered. Add to your list sporting goods outlets (hunting, fishing, general), golf courses and driving ranges, sports clubs, recreation centers, company recreation and fitness centers, sports magazines, newspapers, books, videos, television shows, local college athletics departments, professional sports teams, church-affiliated sports or fitness centers, water-sport outlets and marinas, sailing clubs, snow-ski outlets and clubs, bowling centers, tennis centers, running clubs and events, and everything related to sport. How many pages do you have so far? You should have several even if you live in a very small town. You may not have realized just how much you are surrounded by sport and sport-related products. Now multiply the number of items on your list by the number of towns and cities in your state. Remember, the lists will grow longer as population and city size increase.

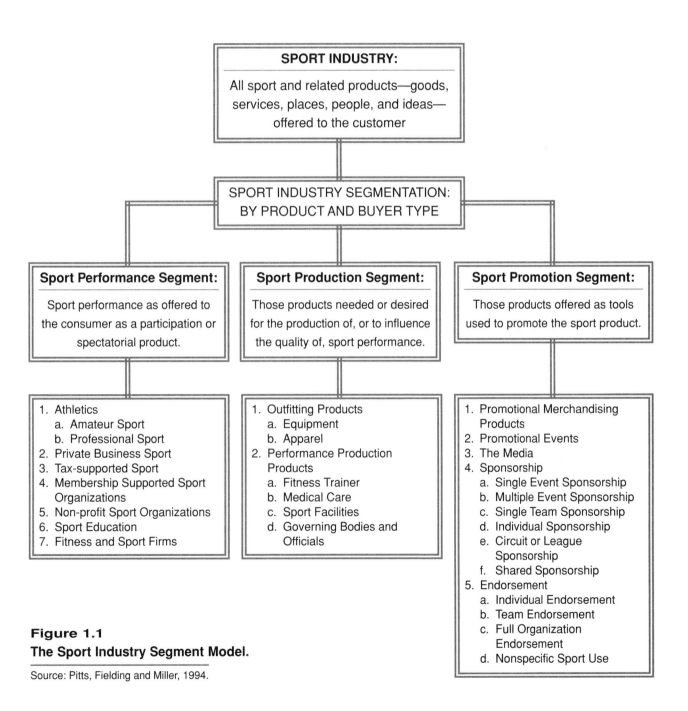

Figure 1.1
The Sport Industry Segment Model.

Source: Pitts, Fielding and Miller, 1994.

Now you have an idea of the size of the sport business industry in your town and in your state and of the many different companies in that industry. All of these businesses can be categorized to help you make sense of such a large and diverse industry. One method is *industry segmentation*. In a study by Pitts et al. (1994), a model for categorizing and segmenting the industry into product function was developed. Figure 1.1 illustrates that model.

It shows that the industry can be categorized into three industry segments: sport performance, sport production, and sport promotion. Their theory is that every product and business in the sport business industry falls into one of these three segments. This kind of research can help the sport management and sport marketing professional better understand their products and their consumers, and therefore enhance their decisions regarding their particular sport business. For example, if your business manufactures tennis rackets, this product falls into the sport production segment in the Pitts, Fielding, and Miller model. That is, a tennis racket is a product needed or desired for the production of or to influence the quality of sport performance. To play tennis, one must have a tennis racket. There are, however, a great variety of tennis rackets, and they vary by color, material, grip size, weight, head size and configuration, and string. As a player increases in skill level, the player might desire a custom-made racket in order to try to enhance performance. Your tennis racket company, then, might consider manufacturing a line of rackets that range from the inexpensive one-size-for-all racket to an expensive custom racket. Your knowledge of this product segment, sport industry segment, purposes of the racket, and your consumer greatly enhances your decision making. You will learn more about segmentation in later chapters..

Chapter Summary

The student in sport business management and in sport marketing must develop an understanding of the sport business industry, sport management, and sport marketing. An industry is a market containing similar products. Some industries contain only one product. The sport industry contains many. The sport industry is a market in which the products offered to its buyers are sport, fitness, recreation or leisure related; these products may be activities, goods, services, people, places, or ideas. The sport industry is a large, broad, and very diverse industry. Its products serve a large and diverse base of consumers. Studies have created categories or industry segments as a way of organizing the sport industry in order to better define and understand it.

Many factors have affected and will continue to affect the sport industry. Some impact the growth and development of the industry. Some will continue to have an effect on the industry. The sport management and sport marketing person should constantly monitor these factors and others in order to develop educated decisions and strategies.

Women's Basketball Online: Where Women's Basketball Meets the Internet

In the world of sports, women's basketball at all levels has been experiencing unprecedented growth in participation numbers and in spectator popularity. As a spectator sport, the numbers are increasing annually. For example, the annual NCAA Women's Final Four championship tournament rapidly sells out of tickets as soon as they go on sale. The NCAA has staged the Women's Final Four Basketball Championship since 1982. Prior to the NCAA control, the championships were managed by the Association for Intercollegiate Athletics for Women (AIAW). In the first decade, cities didn't want to bother hosting an event that drew relatively small numbers of spectators. But the passage of 20 years has brought more fans, prestige, media exposure, and money to this annual event. In addition, the Women's Final Four has been sold out each year since 1993.

The WNBA was created in 1996 and has enjoyed a decade of popularity. It is not the first women's professional basketball league. That honor goes to the Women's Professional Basketball League (WBL), which started in 1978 and lasted for a decade despite temporarily shutting down during its tenure. It features eight teams: Chicago Hustle, Dayton Rockettes, Houston Angels, Iowa Cornets, Milwaukee Does, Minnesota Fillies, New Jersey Gems, and New York Stars. They play a 34-game schedule the first year, and 6,000 fans in Houston watched the Angels defeat the Cornets 111-104 for the first WBL Championship. In its second year, the WBL expanded to 14 teams, adding the Dallas Diamonds, San Francisco Pioneers, California Dream, New Orleans Pride, Philadelphia Fox, and Washington DC Metros. In that year, New York won the WBL championship.

The WBL and two research studies are credited as the beginning of the new sized women's basketball—the current women's basketball is about one inch smaller in circumference and a few ounces lighter than the men's basketball. Wilson Sporting Goods developed this ball specifically for the first WBL. Although perceived mostly as a publicity stunt, the ball had a sound argument for its size. Karen Logan, a pioneer in women's basketball, made the argument that women should have a ball that better fits their hand size, which is on average smaller than male basketball players. Karen argued that many sports have equipment that is custom fitted for its players, or for categories of players. The WBL liked the idea and used it.

After that, two research studies are credited with being the foundation for the adoption of the basketball for girls and women's basketball at the high school and college level. The researchers found that in studies in which female players were skills tested using the "regular" size ball and the "women's" size ball, all players tested significantly better when using the smaller ball. One of those studies was conducted by the author of this textbook, Dr. Brenda G. Pitts, who also played in the first league. For more on the study, refer to Brenda G. Pitts, 1984, dissertation, University of Alabama, "Effects of a Smaller, Lighter Basketball on Skill Performance of Female Basketball Players."

Studying *why* spectators like and dislike certain sports, sporting events, sports on TV, or specific characteristics about sports is important for sport marketing professionals. This information helps with making decisions about the company and its products. There is quite a bit of research about women's sports and why spectators like to watch women's sports. This is an area of market research called consumer behavior. In sport marketing, it is also called *factors that affect attendance*.

The popularity of girls' and women's basketball is partially evident in the number and variety of internet resources and businesses related to women's basketball. On any day, one can do a subject web search using the words *women's basketball* and typically hit millions of sites.

In one example, http://www.wbmagazine.com is a website extension of its print magazine. The website offers instant news and stories about women's basketball that supplement the print version.

In another example, the website Women's Basketball Online (http://www.womensbasketballonline.com) provides historical information about women's basketball as well as current information and topics. The hardcore basketball fan will find plenty of information here to feed their need for stats and data.

Case Activity

How many websites can you find and summarize; and can you create categories for them? Conduct a study of the websites and write a report of your findings.

QUESTIONS FOR STUDY

1. What is the sport business industry? Give some examples.
2. Describe the size of the sport industry in dollars.
3. What is sport business management?
4. What is the North American Society for Sport Management?
5. What are the many factors that influence the growth and development of the sport industry? Give examples and explain how each factor influences the industry. Why is it important to know this?

LEARNING ACTIVITIES

1. Create a list of sport industry businesses, organizations, clubs, and other enterprises in your city or community. Categorize everything according to the three sport industry segments created by the Pitts, Fielding and Miller (1994) model: sport performance, sport production, and sport promotion.
2. For each item on your list, list the jobs within each.
3. For each item on your list, list the sport products offered to the consumer.
4. Write to the North American Society for Sport Management and ask for information about the organization.
5. Subscribe to sport management-related journals such as the *Journal of Sport Management*, *Sport Marketing Quarterly*, and the *Seton Hall Journal of Sport Law*. Read and summarize the studies you find in the journals. Describe how sport management and sport marketing professionals can use the information.
6. With a group, create a list of 10 very different products offered in the industry. Determine which industry segment of the Pitts, Fielding and Miller model each product falls into and why.

Chapter Two

THE GLOBAL MARKET FOR THE SPORT INDUSTRY

Globalization is not coming—it is here. "Many people believe that nowhere is the triumph of globalization more clear than in the world of sport" (Bairner, 2003, p. 34). The NBA, NFL, Nike, and nearly every major sport enterprise in the United States are doing business in a global environment. Yeh and Li (1998) noted that "the globalized economy has imposed a great challenge on sport management professionals to develop an understanding of issues associated with the globalization of sport, and accordingly come up with appropriate coping strategies" (p. 32). The value of the global sports equipment market is a staggering $85.66 billion and is expected to grow through 2010 at 5% per year (SMGA, 2005, Global Sport Equipment, 2004). Currently, Europe represents the largest segment of the sports equipment market at 44.4% followed by the United States at 25.4% and Asia-Pacific with 21.8% (Global Sports Equipment, 2004).

As a multinational corporation, Nike cornered 32% of the worldwide market in athletic footwear, bringing in over $13.7 billion in annual sales. Reebok was second in the market and adidas was third, but with the 2005 merger of those two companies, they could give Nike stiff competition (Laessing, 2005). In total, the United States exported more than $2 billion in sporting goods in 2004 and imported over $10 billion (SGMA, 2004). It's not just sports products companies that are going global; sport services are involved as well. The world renowned sports agency, International Management Group (IMG) has 70 offices in 30 different countries (http://www.imgworld.com, 2005). As you can see, the sport industry is a global marketplace.

> The globalized econommy has imposed a great challenge on sport management professionals to develop an understanding of issues associated with the globalization of sport.

The purpose of this chapter is to enable sport marketers to think in international and global terms. It is not intended to provide the forum for billion-dollar multinational corporations. Although many lessons and examples can be learned from such companies, you do not have to play in their league to learn from their experiences. To illustrate the complexities of international sport marketing, IMG founder Mark McCormack once commented that "I worry that the people in our Stockholm office don't talk to the people in our Sydney office. I worry that they don't know our people in the Sydney office. Worse yet, I worry that they don't know we have a Sydney office!" (McCormack, 2000, p. 248). This chapter has been written with the following objectives in mind: (a) to provide information about the global marketplace for the sport marketer, (b) to identify information and knowledge necessary for entry into a global market, and (c) to present a context for thinking about marketing internationally.

According to Pride and Ferrell (2003), fewer than 15% of small-to-midsize companies participate in global marketing and trade, but 70% express an interest in international sales. Thus, it seems only natural that many businesses have limited knowledge of international trade. This information void may contribute to a reluctance to begin examining global aspects of the sport industry.

Traditional concepts of import and export arise when international markets are mentioned, yet these are not the only factors in a global approach. It will become increasingly necessary to view all corporate resources, finances, manufacturing, distribution, retailing, and human resource management, from a global perspective. As Americans have experienced, much of our sport equipment is manufactured abroad, but have we truly examined foreign markets for the sale of our products and services? Are there markets where our products or services could dominate? Could mergers and cooperative agreements provide increased revenue and markets for US and foreign companies?

With these questions in mind, it becomes necessary to investigate the global market in more detail. Although the global marketplace is ever changing, the areas presented below may provide some knowledge and insight for international market exploration.

The Global Business Structure

The structure of the international business environment is complex. Business schools offer complete courses in international business, and some graduate programs are designed with international commerce as their focus of study. Following is an overview for the sport marketing professional of the key topics in the area.

Several avenues are available for entering international markets. The Internet and the World Wide Web certainly provide opportunities for engaging in international commerce. However, because individual consumers are burdened with clearing items through customs and paying duty on goods (over $400 for goods imported into the United States), this option is not prevalent in the sport industry.

> Exporting provides the easiest avenue for international marketing.

The easiest and least complicated avenue available for entering international markets is exporting. This practice depends on either corporate or agency interest in domestic products. For example, a sporting goods company in Argentina may contact your firm about the possibility of purchasing in-line skates from your company for export. You would simply supply them with the product, and they would deal with the issues of duties and tariffs to import the items into Argentina. The benefits are easy to see.

The Four Steps in the US Customs Process:
1. Filing of the appropriate entry documents
2. Inspection and classification of the goods
3. Preliminary declaration of value
4. Final determination of duty and payment

Source: Tuller, 1991, p. 332.

Your outlay of capital is negligible, and you are not overburdened with customs procedures. Perhaps the only modifications that you would need to make would be in package labeling or modifications in color to satisfy local appeal. On the other hand, exporting in this manner depends on the emergence of demand, as opposed to activating demand (Pride and Ferrell, 2003).

In some instances, trading companies can more actively identify markets and move your products more effectively into international channels. Trading companies typically purchase goods in one country and then resell them in various international markets. Again, the advantage for you is that the risks and capital outlay are minimal. If the products don't sell, the trading company absorbs the loss.

The formation of *joint ventures* and *strategic alliances* are two additional forms of penetrating international markets prevalent in the sport industry. These marketing techniques involve a greater level of risk and the commitment of more corporate resources.

Joint ventures are characterized by partnering with a corporation residing in the target nation. This practice has been successfully implemented in the athletic footwear industry. Major US shoe companies have formed partnerships with Asian factories to dedicate portions of their factory space or a percentage of their production-line time to produce shoes. Pride and Ferrell (2003) noted significant growth in the implementation of strategic alliances in the late 1990s.

What differentiates strategic alliances from joint ventures is that in the formation of a strategic alliance, partners "often retain their distinct identities, and each brings a distinctive competence to the union" (Pride and Ferrell, 2003, p. 128). Thus, a Korean golf-equipment manufacturing group could receive much needed capital for expansion and engineering innovation from a US sporting goods company. The US firm would obtain high-quality products manufactured at labor and material costs far lower than it could have secured domestically.

Direct ownership is the final alternative to entering a foreign market. In this instance, the domestic company commits significant resources to build a factory and corporate office and hire a local work force to manufacture goods and distribute them within the market. Because of the level of capital required and the tremendous risk involved, few sport firms are willing to select this strategy. Regardless of the structure selected for international marketing, a thorough understanding of the business environment is required. Additional topics presented below provide information that should prove useful.

International Economics and Finance

Gaining a working understanding of world banking and finance is essential for sport marketers. Most Americans are accustomed to dealing with commercial banks through such services as deposits, loans, and checking accounts. In the United States, commercial banks are widespread and need only a license to operate. However, most industrialized nations have a system controlled by a central national bank. For the sport entrepreneur, two choices exist: You can deal with the central bank of the host country, or you can deal with a foreign branch of an American bank.

American banks may have familiar-sounding names and executives who understand the American way, but overall, foreign banks have fewer restrictions and less regulation than do American banks. For that reason, "foreign banks are generally easier to deal with, cheaper, and less inclined to hassle the customer, than their American counterparts" (Tuller, 1991, p. 214).

In selecting a bank for foreign business activities, the size of the bank is not as important as are the services it can provide. Managers should look specifically for banking institutions that can:

1. Move money from banks in one country to banks in another through wire transfer.

2. Handle export financing through personnel in their internal department.

3. Arrange for collections and payments in various currencies.

4. Process foreign currency through exchange conversion at the lowest possible rate.

5. Issue and process letters of credit to guarantee payments and collections from clients.

A common nightmare for sport marketers is foreign currency. If the only experience you have in dealing with foreign currency is exchanging your dollars for pesos on your Mexican vacation, you are in for an education. Not all international monetary units are the same with regard to exchange and convertibility. The term *hard currency* has generally been defined as a unit of monetary value readily convertible to other units. In international business transactions, the US dollar, Euro, the Japanese yen, and the British pound are all convertible with one another at established rates of exchange. However, because of fluctuating exchange rates, variance in financial backing, and government stability, not all world currencies are equally acceptable.

Problems can easily result in situations where the standard payment method has not been well conceived. Suppose you close a deal to provide 100,000 baseball bats at 264 Chinese Yuan each ($1.00 US = 8.104 Chinese Yuan). Once the shipment arrives, payment is required within 30 days. However, because of currency fluctuations within the international monetary system, the value of the payment may be less than expected at the time of delivery to your account in Shanghai. Until 2005, the Yuan was pegged to the US dollar, but with the strength of the Chinese economy, it was allowed to float freely in the international system (How China runs the world, 2005). The international monetary system may have devalued the dollar against the Yuan. The result could be that you would actually lose money on your deal.

With the 2008 Olympics on the horizon, this change in monetary policy meant that the Beijing Olympic Organizing Committee would receive less money from the IOC's television contract, but would have to pay a lower amount in rights fees to the IOC. In another example, the Golf Channel began negotiating with Taiwanese television officials to supply 24-hour programming. However, when "the Taiwanese dollar plunged, the deal fell apart" (Mullen, E. 1998, p. 46).

This same situation can also wreak havoc with international employees. If agreements for salary were negotiated in local currency, employees might find that their

Did you know . . . ?

You can become a millionaire playing billiards? In May 2006, the Cujoroho Challenge Series™ at the Alan Hopkins Super Billiards Expo in Valley Forge, Pennsylvania is the first amateur only pool/billiards match play system in the USA to offer a $1,000,000 prize to a single winning player.

http://www.insidepoolmag.com /content/blogsection/7/76/9/18/

standard of living deteriorates considerably with inflation or devaluation. On the other hand, if they contracted to be paid in US dollars and the local currency decreased in its value against the dollar, they could have expanded their buying power immensely. Precisely this situation occurred with the Asian Games in Bangkok. In an 8-month period, the Thai *baht* dropped in value against the US dollar by more than 54%. However, because most of the expenses incurred by the organizers were in *baht* and their income from sponsors was in US dollars, the event and revenues were protected. Most international corporations have contractual language that addresses this issue. When possible, avoid taking foreign currency in payment for an account.

> To avoid a common sport marketer's nightmare, don't take foreign currency in payment for an account and consider using countertrade agreements.

In dealing with the problems of international currency, many companies use countertrade agreements.

These agreements are similar to barter in which products and services are exchanged for other products or services that can be resold to another party for hard currency. According to Tuller (1991), "countertrade is probably the best guarded secret in international trade" (p. 263).

One multinational sport corporation, ProServ, encountered a situation such as this in negotiating with Eastern European backers for a professional tennis tournament. Although the promoters wanted television production and coverage of the event, they did not have any hard currency with which to pay. However, a German firm was located that needed to make a series of payments for their employees in the local currency, and ProServ agreed to make the payment for the German firm, which would in turn pay ProServ in deutsche Marks (Briner, 1992).

Finally, Tuller (1991) recommends the following guidelines for using the global banking system:

1. The education process—Get up to speed in international finance as soon as possible. Take a college course in international finance. Spend some time with the head of the international department of a regional bank.

2. Read, read, read—The fastest way to learn about global banking and develop a global financial mentality is to read everything available on the subject.

3. Choosing a commercial bank—Determine which local bank has an international department. Interview the department manager.

4. Experiment—Open a foreign bank account. Transfer small amounts back and forth. Incorporate exchange rate variances in forecasts—even if you have to use fictitious entries.

5. Conquer the "big boy" syndrome—The more a person investigates global banking the more one realizes it is not just for the "big boys." (p. 221)

Trade Regulations

Since the industrialization after World War II, the General Agreement on Tariffs and Trade (GATT) has governed much of international trade. Through this accord, member nations agree to certain practices involving international commerce.

Although it may be beneficial for sport marketers to review this agreement, relatively few of the member countries meticulously follow its bylaws. Many countries in the world continue to establish and enforce trade agreements and tariffs that protect their products and restrict competition. However, the success of GATT agreements between the 124 participating nations has reduced the average tariff on manufactured items from 45% to 5% (Pride and Ferrell, 2003). In 2004, the US congress passed legislation (Foreign Sales Corporation/Extraterritorial Income bill) that lowered tariffs for 1,600 products including many US manufactured sporting goods.

Before sport marketers want to become involved in global efforts, it is important to gain an understanding of world finance.

Examples of trade regulation affecting sports organizations are numerous. In 1994, the United States, Mexico, and Canada entered into the North American Free Trade Agreement (NAFTA) and, in 2005, the Central American Free Trade Agreement (CAFTA), which reduced and eliminated many previously imposed tariffs across North and Central America. By 2009, almost all tariffs between these nations will disappear. If you had been contemplating creating a product to compete with a Canadian firm, the price differentials pre- and post legislation could have been substantially affected. However, lifting trade regulations has provided greater access to Canada's more affluent population and has increased trade from the United States by 50% since NAFTA's inception. Although many consumers in Mexico and Central America are less affluent than those in either the United States or Canada, trade between the United States and Mexico was enhanced because of a strong desire for US-made products. US firms were also able to redirect manufacturing to Mexico and Central America, where the costs of labor have traditionally been much lower. In the manufacture of sporting goods, this labor market may prove attractive in business relocation and product sourcing. As will be discussed later, the practice of using cheap labor to produce US consumer goods has created considerable controversy in some segments of the sport industry. NAFTA and CAFTA could also have an impact on the export of products where previous tariffs may have priced US goods too high for some consumers; thus, additional markets for US sporting goods and equipment companies could be more accessible (A weighty matter, 2004; Pride and Ferrell, 2003).

Free-trade agreements could also affect sport-related corporations in terms of liability costs. In the last 20 years, many sporting goods corporations relocated to foreign countries because of the growing cost of equipment-related liability in the United States. If import tariffs were eliminated between the United States and the manufacturer's host country, some corporations might be able to realize greater profit margins by relocating to a foreign manufacturing site.

Specifically in Europe, the formation and liberalization that took place with the European Union (EU) in 1992 also brought many challenges and opportunities in sport. This event had dramatic effects on the sport industry. One example surfaced in Formula One (auto racing), where officials in charge of regulating antitrust situations across the European Union have challenged F1 authorities' restrictive television contracts. One of the main issues pertains to whether or not sport is a business and subject to regulation (Stewart, 1999).

Prior to the unification of the EU, sport marketers who desired to do business in Europe had a multitude of rules and regulations specific to each country. However, with consolidation in many key business areas, the bureaucracy of transacting business in Europe has been standardized, if not reduced. The 1999 introduction of a standard currency, the Euro, also helped with international transactions. Although not all member countries adopted the Euro as domestic currency, inter-European and international trade was calculated in Euros.

In sport marketing, we must be careful not to become too restricted in our perceptions. Although EU regulations may allow for more standardized products to be sold, the sport marketer should not automatically conclude that European consumers have similarly homogeneous needs and desires. Specific demographic and psychographic research will continue to be required. As an example, the spread of income across the richest EU member nations to the poorest has been as high as 138%. EU markets have become more accessible, but not significantly more similar (Quelch, Buzzell, and Salama, 1990).

Another area of concern has been in sports equipment. Manufacturers in England had previously been required to follow one set of product safety codes whereas those in France had another. These and other issues related to sport and commerce are continually being clarified.

The general strategy predicted for companies in the EU will be that as new markets open, price-cutting is likely to be a popular move to increase initial market share. New products will also be used as development will have been made less costly through standardization. New products will also help attract consumers who may have been previously unfamiliar with a company's product line. Experts have also postulated that distribution of goods will also be facilitated because regulations covering truck transport (accounting for 80% of EU goods) will be reduced and border clearances will be considerably faster (Quelch, Buzzell, and Salama, 1990). The EU unification therefore brought serious issues to light for sports professionals and sporting goods companies.

Other areas of the world also offer opportunities for sport-related businesses. In Saudi Arabia, the United States Sports Academy, an American college located in Alabama, has conducted business affairs since the mid 1970s, at one point having over 500 employees in the region. However, by modifying regulations in the 1980s, the Saudi government changed the rules for calculating taxes and income for foreign corporations. Excellent planning by the CEO provided for the formation of a locally held corporation to take over the sport and recreation services once provided by the United States Sports Academy. By seeking local executives and changing the business structure of the venture, the United States Sports Academy was able to continue to effectively do business with the country.

Free-trade zones also provide interesting opportunities for sport marketers. These zones are regulated by government agencies in host countries. In the United States, such zones allow for the manufacture and/or assembly for goods that are not intended for national consumption. Thus, you could import parts for gymnastics equipment from Asia, assemble them in a Colorado free-trade zone, and ship them to Europe without paying customs duties. Similar situations have also been developed in foreign nations. On a recent trip to Taiwan, a sport executive planned to purchase a high-quality set of golf clubs that he had discovered were manufactured in Taiwan. Figuring that he could find a great bargain, he began to search for his prized clubs. Much to his surprise, he learned that they were manufactured in Taiwan, but they were produced for "export only." Yes, they could be purchased in Taiwan, but only when reimported from the United States. With twice the shipping expense, the clubs were cheaper in the United States.

International Marketing Structure

The structure of international marketing in contrast to that of domestic sport enterprises contains more similarities than differences. Tuller (1991) reports that the main concepts of selling directly to consumers or selling through agents are indeed the same. Other traditional marketing activities contained in this book are also required in global marketing efforts. The process is similar, but the information and sources will be significantly different.

Differences come in the format that facilitates transactions. Terms such as *foreign trading corporations* and *export management companies* are unique to international business. Sport marketers who choose to compete in the global market will invariably learn to deal with these terms and to work effectively with foreign distributors.

Probably the most difficult aspect of foreign trade is customs. If you are dealing in sports goods and products, successfully negotiating the customs system is key to your success. If you are importing goods into the United States that have been manufactured overseas, you will be required to clear the goods through customs at their port of entry.

> The formation of the EU is expected to have significant effects on the sport industry such as a decrease in prices and increased ease of distribution as restrictions are lifted and a potential for either the elevation or equalization of player salaries.

Kapoor and McKay (1971) also cite factors that differentiate international marketing from domestic. There appears to be greater government regulation in foreign markets and consequently a greater need for feedback and control. In addition, more data are needed for marketing decisions because of the cultural differences that exist. Many marketing decisions are made in US sport organization because of a high level of sports knowledge in our societal context. This knowledge simply does not exist for US sport managers making decisions in foreign countries. To offset this problem, most organizations will enlist the assistance of national experts from the target nation.

These experts can also be helpful in communicating value differences between cultures. For example, US and German executives typically value punctuality and promptness, whereas in other cultures a 10:00 a.m. meeting simply means sometime in the morning. It is not that executives in other cultures are being rude; punctuality is just not important in their value system. International managers must learn to respect the value systems of others, not merely tolerate them.

Another difference in international marketing is that in many countries, government-owned business can compete with privately held companies. For instance, you may own a sport concession management business similar to ARA-MARK Corporation in the United States. ARAMARK Corporation has a variety of contracts with professional and collegiate stadiums around the country to supply concession and facility management services. However, in some foreign countries, government-owned corporations may be granted exclusive rights to public stadiums. Another complication could be government subsidies to local corporations. Either of these practices would severely restrict the ability of a successful US company to compete in that market.

The Global Sports Structure

A precursor to involvement in international sport management is a thorough understanding of the global sport environment.

The framework for comprehension begins in the United States with the recognition that the United States Olympic Committee (USOC) is chartered by Congress to oversee amateur sport in the country. This encompasses all sports that are in the Olympic and Pan-American Games. Sports that fall outside those parameters may hold membership with the USOC, but are not governed by them. Professional and collegiate sports in the United States are self-governing through private voluntary associations such as the major league offices and the National Collegiate Athletic Association.

> The best source for a study of the global sport environment is Chalip and Thoma's book entitled *Sport Governance in the Global Community* (1993).

In the international sports environment, the International Olympic Committee (IOC) maintains authority over the Olympic Games and regional Olympic-style competitions (Pan-American Games, Asian Games, etc.). It is only these multi-sport competitions where the IOC retains control. The IOC manages and markets these events internationally. The Olympic Partners (TOP) sponsorship program includes multinational corporations such as Coca-Cola (US), Panasonic (Japan), and Samsung (Korea).

Each specific sport is governed by an international federation for that sport. Track-and-field is a member of the International Amateur Athletic Federation; basketball has its International Amateur Basketball Federation; and each sport maintains an affiliation with its International Federation (IF). These federations work very closely with the IOC in staging the Olympics, but have their main purpose is to set rules and regulations for their sports; they also conduct the world championships in their sport on a yearly basis.

The organizations are also linked through national governing bodies (NGB). Each IF designates an NGB in each country to organize and govern a specific sport within national borders. This NGB must be recognized by its national Olympic committee (i.e., USOC). As such, the NGBs work with the IFs for rules and regulations dealing within a one-sport setting, yet for Olympic competition, the NGBs work with their national Olympic committee to ensure participation in the Olympic Games. Several corporations have secured official supplier contracts through positive relationships developed with Olympic-governing bodies. This status was effective in invigorating product sales. As a sport marketer, it is imperative that you become well versed in the relationships between each of these groups and tune into the political dynamics of the world sport community.

Global Market Selection and Identification

Global markets can seem overwhelming if viewed as a whole. Only when they are dissected and analyzed individually can the sport marketer make wise marketing decisions. Market conditions vary considerably in different countries, and thus, the sport industry exhibits varying growth rates. For instance, the global growth rate for the industry was projected to be 12% for the athletic footwear market, yet the US rate was 5% whereas the projected growth of the Asian market was 36%. These data indicated that average yearly per capita spending on athletic footwear in the United States was $30.88 at wholesale; Japanese consumers spent $10.36, whereas the Chinese market figures indicated spending of only $0.02 (but remember, the Chinese market is 1.2 billion people). Overall, 65% of the global sporting goods market is comprised of products made in China (Yang, 2005). China dominates among exporters of athletic footwear to the United States with a market share of 76% of the total import dollar value in 2004. Indonesia's share declined from 11.3% in 2003 to 8.6% in 2004. Vietnam's share increased from 5.9% in 2003 to 7.6% in 2004. Vietnam, as you may know has been a significant producer of sporting goods for many years, with company-owned and licensed factories around the country. In 2005, a Taiwanese sportswear producer (Pou Yuen) under contract with Nike, adidas, Reebok, Puma, and Lacoste invested $480 million to build a new plant in Vietnam. Thailand's share was unchanged from 2003 (SGMA, 2005). For any single company like Nike, the percentage of company profit derived from international sales can run as high as 37% (Himelstein, 1997). Fortunately for the sport marketer, there are a variety of ways to investigate foreign markets.

Contrary to what you may think, your tax dollars really do provide services for you and other American citizens. The US government is one of the best sources of information on foreign markets.

As an example, the US Information Agency(USIA) (http://www.usia.gov) manages US Pavilions at the World trade expos around the globe. They create excellent opportunities for American firms to demonstrate their products and services to worldwide consumers. One example was the 2005 Volvo Sports Design Forum in Munich where snowboard manufacturer Burton utilized the opportunity to discuss and showcase

> For information on foreign markets, consult the US Information Agency, the US Agency for International Development, or other agencies in the Department of State.

their new snowboard products designed specifically for women (Walzer, 2005). Information and contacts obtained through the USIA offices and their numerous publications can be invaluable in developing a network of sport professionals.

Other government offices in the Department of State also have reams of information about foreign economies, information that is available at little or no cost. Consideration also should be given to contacting the US Agency for International

It is important for sport marketing professional to acknowledge that sport leagues continue to expand internationally.

Development, which has as its main purpose improving trade with developing countries.

Interestingly, most foreign governments are also attempting to attract US business and have personnel at their embassy to accommodate your needs. Brief meetings or telephone conversations with their staff are often beneficial during the early stages of project development. Other sources for international marketing contacts can be made through international trade associations, economic development councils at the state or local level, and international trade shows. With a little digging, even small sport companies can obtain quality information for entering the global marketplace.

According to Tuller (1991), key issues include whether a market economy exists or one that is government controlled, the existing market demand, growth, and competitive forces, US government trade policies, and the local government policies toward trade with the United States. Each factor should be evaluated, and as Pride and Ferrell (2003, p. 113) noted, before a company enters a foreign market, it must "thoroughly analyze the environment." Similar to marketing to domestic customers, marketers must evaluate cultural, social, technological, political, and economic forces in target regions. Considerable attention over the past 15 years has been focused in varying degrees on Japan, the Pacific Rim, Europe, South America, and developing nations throughout the world. In no particular order, a discussion of several of these markets follows.

JAPAN, CHINA AND ASIA

Why, you might ask, has this section been called Japan, China and Asia? Aren't Japan and China part of Asia? Yes, from a geographical perspective, but not from a marketing point of view. For many years Japan and China have presented obstacles to American sport marketers. With the endless debate over Japan's high tariffs, complex system of distribution and sales, and governmental reluctance to encourage foreign business activity, sport marketers have not generally been successful. The climate has appeared positive for them with a stable hard currency and an attractive market size. Regardless, many sports companies have taken the approach of trying to sell the Japanese on American products.

China, with a population in excess of 1.26 billion people (22% of the world population), has commanded considerable attention from sport marketers. Trade with China has been hobbled by bureaucracy and political interference with business for many years. Yet the prospects for the future of the sport industry in China are based on a new policy of decreased government intervention and increases in private ownership (Yang, 2005). The increasing international focus on trade with China (2008 Olympics) and its participation in the World Trade Organization (WTO) has improved the situation (Yang, 2005). The official policy for the development of the sport industry in China is to create and market their own brands. The government believes that too much of the productivity of China has gone to furthering international brands such as Nike and adidas and the shift must now be to home-grown Chinese brands. Estimates reveal that in 2005, China will import $1.2 trillion in products from the international market, making it the world's largest consumer market. With the 2008 Olympic Games in Beijing, the pace of growth is sure to accelerate.

Asia, as a geographic and social region, is extremely diverse. Social and political conditions affecting sport vary considerably from predominantly Muslim nations such as Malaysia to the socialist ideology in the People's Republic of China.

Some regions and other industrialized nations (Singapore, South Korea, Taiwan) and can provide active, growing markets for both consumption and production of sports products, whereas other nations are still in the stages of economic development. As noted previously for other regions, the US government has also worked to make entry into Asian markets easier. The Asia-Pacific Economic Cooperation alliance in place since 1989 has enabled its 21 member nations to work through many trade barriers to enhance both import and export business (Pride & Ferrell, 2003). Entry into the sports markets of Japan, China and Asia will demand considerable study and analysis, but the rewards can be immense.

EASTERN AND WESTERN EUROPE

Considerable attention has already been given to Western Europe. The dynamic changes with the formation of the European Union have in some ways helped sport marketers and in other ways hindered their success. A unified Western European market has allowed for much freer access to markets than was previously available, yet the enhanced competitiveness of EU companies has also increased competition. The generally held view is that in most sport industry segments, the opportunities are still limited and extremely competitive.

Eastern Europe, on the other hand, may provide more opportunities. With pent-up consumer demand and a reduction of government controls, sport purchasing and sponsorship avenues may proliferate. However, some of the problems that sport marketers will encounter include the lack of hard currency and unstable governments. It is also important to realize that sport expenditures are often considered luxuries and are made with discretionary funds. These funds may be limited in the Eastern European communities well into the next decade.

Specifically, the situation in Hungary was reported by Dénes and Misovicz (1993). Their research indicated several phenomena that may be similar in other parts of

Did you know . . . ?

The Health Club Trend Report included the following facts:

- Another 25.5 million non-members used health clubs in 2004. They either paid a daily fee or gained access to a club via a hotel, hospital, on-site work facility, etc.;

- 25% of all health club members are aged 55+;

- 51% of all health club members are women;

- 60% of all health club members have earned four-year degrees from college

Eastern Europe. In Hungary, the demise of socialist rule in the early 1990s meant that the sport economy changed as well. Previously, the government had subsidized, yet with the political changes, governmental resources were allocated to other parts of the economy. Ticket prices for sports events rose with inflation that impacted the economy, yet few citizens could afford to attend, instead diverting their income to cover the costs of food and shelter. In addition, many workers took on second jobs to generate funds necessary for maintaining an acceptable lifestyle. The market for leisure sports products, once supplied by the government, had all but disappeared (Denes and Misovicz,1993).

THE CARIBBEAN AND CENTRAL AND SOUTH AMERICA

In 1983, the US government passed a law that made trade with the Caribbean nations both more accessible and more lucrative. The Caribbean Basin Initiative (CBI) was designed to increase trade and assist in the economic development of this region. The 1989 report indicated that recreational items and sporting goods were some of the products that had benefited the most from this legislation (Tuller, 1991).

> Sport marketers can take advantage of special conditions in the Caribbean, including tax breaks and the reduction of import duties.

The business climate in the area has been enhanced through this Act. Sport marketers should examine the possibility of taking advantage of the benefits extended through the CBI Act. These include tax breaks and the elimination or reduction of import duties. In addition, special financing programs are available for start-up companies. Of special note is the fact that many of these nations also have special agreements with European nations for importing and exporting goods and services. Therefore, it may behoove the sport marketer to investigate the range of possibilities of operating out of the Caribbean.

Central America presents several points of interest. With the previously discussed free trade possibilities, manufacturing potential exists in the sports goods industry. Depending on the economic and political fortunes of the area, additional consumer demand for both goods and services may also exist.

South America has been under the shadow of its severe debt crisis for the past two decades. As mentioned in the section on international economics and finance, triple-digit inflation and hard-currency issues will hamper sports entrepreneurs in South America. The sport marketer should realize that the public interest in sport is especially high in much of the region and that considerable potential exists in numerous market segments.

Conducting business in the Caribbean and Central and South America has positive attributes, but only if the sport marketer is able to cope effectively with the business and political idiosyncrasies of the region. The 2005 CAFTA agreement should accelerate business in the region.

AFRICA

As diverse as Central and South America are, the African market is understood by even fewer American companies (Tuller, 1991). Generally, the continent consists of

Muslim North Africa, Central, East and West Africa, with South Africa presenting a special case of its own. Sports activities in North Africa are, in line with traditional Muslim view, predominantly male and rooted in tradition. For American sport managers to conduct business here demands an understanding of the culture and the emphasis on sport. Within that context, the markets are available to US representatives.

West Africa has, for the most part, resolved its political upheaval and is entering an era in which sport market development is possible. Of specific importance will be sport equipment and supplies as well as sport services in coaching and sport management. However, many of these markets offer limited growth potential. As recently as 1990, the product advertised in the window of a sporting goods store was a pair of adidas Rome running shoes, popular in the United States in the early 1970s. Central Africa has yet to achieve the stability conducive to market entry. This will of course be an area to watch for future growth and development in sport.

In South Africa, enough wealth exists for any multinational corporation to flourish. However, because of past economic and political practices, a two-tiered economic market exists. For the sport marketer, both segments offer possibilities. With the political changes in the country in the early 1990s, the lower class was provided greater access to sport and recreational facilities. This created immense demand for sports equipment. Corporate sponsorship and financing for sport activities also created an atmosphere conducive to a growth market. Another factor in favor of expansion into South Africa is the abundance of well-educated and effective sport management personnel. These have been most apparent in South Africa's hosting major international sports events such as the FIFA 2010 World Cup.

As with other regions in the world, the problems of soft currency and political instability will restrict many African sport-marketing opportunities. Yet, with attention to these factors and a careful study of the market, sports marketers can successfully meet the demands of these consumers.

International Sport Marketing Personnel

The selection of well-trained and experienced personnel is essential. Tuller (1991) indicated that trying to enter global markets without the expertise of someone experienced in international trade is a common error made by American executives: "To try and arrange financing, market products, or negotiate contracts with foreign customers without assistance from internationally experienced management personnel will always lead to disaster" (p. 12).

In a 2004 study by *Sports Edge* magazine, they found that European companies prefer to have US personnel manage US offices and European executives staff their European operations. The issue seems to be that the US market is relatively homogeneous whereas success in the European market demands a multitude of language skills and cultural sensitivity lacking in many US executives (Going Global, 2004). The selection of personnel for managing foreign markets or for heading up foreign units is affected by several criteria. Among those found to be most important were proven domestic marketing ability, foreign national status, prior international training, and a strong desire for global involvement. Personnel training can be performed through a variety of different methods. Some corporations conduct in-house training sessions using the expertise and experience of their existing staff. Some corporations handle the training through their foreign offices. Both of these methods have proven to be successful in the sports environment. Outside resources have also been retained for the training process. This method is often expensive, but without internal expertise, it is essential.

> It is imperative that personnel be educated for cultural sensitivity prior to their involvement in international affairs.

Speer (1999) indicated that the main difficulty experienced by foreign market managers was adapting to cultural diversity.

Research has indicated that adaptability to foreign cultures is equal in importance to marketing skills developed in a domestic position.

ADAPTATION TO CULTURAL DIVERSITY

Sport business personnel have a common bond with sport executives in other nations through their athletic experiences; however, culture variations on appropriate business and sport etiquette can sabotage chances for success. The successful sport marketer needs to have a clear understanding of the dos and don'ts of foreign culture. What follows are some national and international customs in business relations.

> Review and understand the following issues about your host nation before traveling and dealing with international executives.
> * Touching
> * Relationships between males and females
> * Drinking
> * Gifts
> * Time and schedules
> * Business etiquette

Before traveling and dealing with international executives, be sure to review the special characteristics of your host nation.

Touching. In much of North America, touching is acceptable between friends, but overt touching of casual acquaintances in a business setting is not tolerated. The local custom in many Latin countries allows for hugs following an introduction. In the Middle East, on the other hand, you may find two men walking down the street holding hands to signify their friendship (Axtell, 1991).

Relationships between males and females. Women have for many years played increasing roles in the conduct of sport business in the United States. Many women serve as CEOs of major sport corporations, sport marketing firms, and professional team franchises. Yet, in other parts of the world, women may not be accepted in business meetings. Because we believe in equality of the sexes does not mean that everyone in the world does. Your firm must make a decision whether to do business with countries that have different beliefs about the role of women in business relations and follow a strategy that will produce the best business results.

Drinking. The easiest rule for drinking is to follow the lead of the host. If the host orders a drink, you are welcome to imbibe. Be cautious about bringing alcoholic gifts for your host. Even though you are from the South, possession of a fifth of Southern Comfort will land you in prison in almost any Islamic nation. On the opposite end of the spectrum, refusing a glass of wine in France or a cup of sake in Japan will be considered rude. One experience at the International Olympic Academy in Greece found that the Russian delegation's vodka was one of the most cherished barter items between participants—worth at least five Olympic pins.

Gifts. Exchanging gifts is a custom that is more prevalent in other countries than it is in the United States. In fact, in the 1970s the US government passed the Foreign Corrupt Practices Act to curtail bribes and kickbacks (Tuller, 1991). The line is very vague as to what constitutes a payoff and what is a generous gift (Speer, 1999). Most sport marketers will face difficulty in this area. Try to learn ahead of time from a confidante or fellow sportsperson the tradition and local custom. A good practice is to carry small company pins or souvenirs and to graciously accept similar extensions from your host.

Time and schedules. In many parts of the world, time is a relative concept. This is especially true in many Latin countries and in the Middle East. Both of the authors of this text have conducted sport-marketing seminars around the globe and can attest to this phenomenon. In Malaysia, an 8:00 a.m. meeting means sometime in the morning, yet just across the bridge in Singapore, you had better be there at 7:30 a.m. to get a seat. One style is not right or wrong; it is just different. It is also important that everyone be clear on how dates are written. The US military writes dates with the day first, then the month and year (i.e., 7 June 1999). This does not create confusion until it appears as 7/6/99. Much of the world uses the same style as does the US military, so when placing the order for the delivery of your tennis rackets, be specific.

Business etiquette. Every country will have its unique protocol for conducting business. In England, you had better wear a jacket and tie for your initial business meeting; however, try that in Manila, and you will not only roast but will also look like a fool in the process. The mix of business attire and casual sports clothing is something that should be explored carefully; it never hurts to ask. Careful determination should also be made in deciding when and where to talk business. In England, work is work and play is play. Don't confuse the two. However, in many other countries, the best deals are put together on the golf course. You should also be perceptive about special interrelationships. In England, you seat the most important person to your right, British military custom. In South Africa, you rise to greet your Afrikaner guest, but don't when meeting a Zulu guest; according to tribal custom, such a movement is confrontational. In South Africa and other parts of southern Africa, sports marketers and event organizers have experienced problems from a simple question, "Do you understand this proposal?" When the answer was "yes," all matters seemed settled. Only later was it determined that all was not well. The polite answer to the question was "yes." To answer "no" would imply that you had not explained it well and be considered insulting. Better initial questions would have been "What is your understanding?" or "Do we have an agreement on these points?" Similarly, in negotiating with Asian executives, "We'll consider it" means "no" (Morrison, Conaway, and Borden, 1994).

The integration of international marketing into the domestic corporate culture is also of great importance. Depending on the size and nature of the international versus the domestic market, jealousies and conflicts can arise if executives are not adamant in clarifying the priority of both global and national marketing activities (Tuller, 1991). The selection and training of international sport executives encompass many different considerations. They often involve difficult and awkward adaptations to normal business practices. However, if you invest the time, the results can be rewarding.

Specifics of International Sport Marketing

The expansion of professional and amateur sports internationally has been well recognized in the sport-marketing arena. "Faced with a maturing US sports market, the [professional] leagues have looked overseas" (Ozanian and Taub, 1992, p. 49). One of the first professional sport organizations to recognize the global demand for its product was the National Basketball Association. From a historical standpoint, professional boxing has had worldwide events for many years, but these have been primarily single events. Professional baseball had early opportunities to restructure and include demand in Asia and Latin America, but decided that such a move was not in its best interests. The NBA, on the other hand, has viewed international markets from an entirely different perspective.

In recognition of the 200 million people around the world who participate in basketball, the NBA embarked on a global marketing campaign in 1989. Sixty-nine percent of international youth (age 12–17) play basketball. In 2005, the NBA had 81 international players from 35 different countries. Games played in Europe and Asia spawned a growth in NBA television rights of 30% per year with the sales of licensed goods growing at twice that rate. The NBA also held development clinics in Africa in 2003 and its first games in China (Shanghai) in 2004. During the summer of 2004, the NBA hosted 36 international events and continued its very successful Basketball Without Borders program for international youth development.

The NBA sells licensed products in more than 200 countries with international sales accounting for 25% of product sold (Sports licensed products, 2005). Since the success of the 1992 US Olympic (a.k.a. NBA "Dream Team") basketball team, the NBA commissioner recognized the global nature of basketball and positioned the league to capitalize on the phenomenon (Ober, 1992). For the 2005–2006 season, the NBA scheduled over 20,000 hours of international television programming in 43 languages to over 214 countries (NBA and Russell, 2005). International broadcasting produces 15% of the TV revenues and 20% of the merchandising dollars. In addition, 40% of the NBA's web traffic originated from outside the US. MLB has also pushed the international spectrum signing a $46 million per year television deal with Japanese agency Dentsu who resold rights to the major broadcaster in Japan. The estimated per game audience was pegged at 12.5 million with a total of 630 games aired in 2004. Still moving into international markets is the NFL, where the popularity and understanding of the game lags. Still, the NFL is considering hosting the American Bowl (2004 in Japan) in Shanghai for 2006. NFL Games are currently available to 500 million homes outside of the US (Kaplan, 2004). NASCAR has moved more slowly into international markets and has run Busch series races in Mexico and non-points races in Japan.

As the NBA has stressed global marketing, basketball equipment manufactures have followed suit. Nike, Reebok, adidas, and Spalding all saw tremendous growth in global sales of basketballs and basketball shoes in conjunction with NBA positioning. Spaulding sells their NBA licensed basketballs through 18,000 retail outlets in 74 countries, which together with their backboards (Huffy division) totaled $3 billion in sales (NBA and Russell, 2005).

World tournaments and international events are at the center of many international marketing activities. Because the recognition and value of international events grew considerably in the 1980s and 1990s, most television agreements, sponsorship contracts, and licensing programs have necessarily become international. Without attention to these details, sport marketers could find themselves in the same situation as Nike during the 1992 Olympic Games when another company in Spain had registered the word *Nike*, thereby complicating the US firm's marketing efforts.

"The international reach of the fitness business is also noteworthy. Overseas clubs call on US fitness experts to fashion American-style clubs that meet the demands of style-conscious clientele" (Holland, 1992, p. 40). The depth of the market is such that International Fitness Association (IFA) has representatives in more than 80 foreign countries.

The sport of soccer (football, in the international community) is the most popular sport on television across the globe. The projected worldwide cumulative audience for the 2006 World Cup was over 40 billion. This popularity has affected the sport industry in many ways. Many of the world's top teams have been able to secure sponsorship from multinational corporations. Nike has sponsored the perennial power, Brazil, whereas adidas sponsored Germany. Within the European league, teams like Manchester United attract a global audience and annually earn several million dollars from licensing rights fees and has proven a model of licensing business through its joint dealings with Nike.

It should also be noted that global demographics are significantly different from those in the United States. An amazing 70% of the world's consumers reside in developing countries. The United States has an aging population, yet in much of the developing world, the population is considerably younger and becoming even younger. Children tend to buy shoes more frequently than adults do, which contributes many of the marketing decisions for sporting goods manufacturers.

Trends for the Future

As the United States and many leading economic powers evolve as information societies and reduce their strength in manufacturing, the licensing of sport manufacturing technology and professional services will be a major growth area in the sport industry. Sporting goods companies and sport consultants will protect products through extensive licensing and manufacturing agreements and will issue "covenants not to compete" to ensure the protection of their intellectual properties. The result will be a greater emphasis on strategic alliances, mergers, and joint ventures than in the past.

Sport marketers will begin to think more of international demographics in the development of products and services in the sport industry. Pan-European consumers will begin to develop more similarities than differences as EU markets mature. Around the world, the newly industrialized nations will begin to demand more sport-related products and services, and new markets will emerge. However, friction between the countries that supply the cheap labor for sporting goods production and those that consume the goods will continue.

> Companies that can communicate their concern for global problems through the delivery of the sport products and services will be more highly valued than will those who ignore this social component.

Cause-related sport marketing will also make favorable impressions on consumers. These humanistic trends must be incorporated in the operation of all sport organizations in the global environment.

With the developments outlined in this chapter and evidence in the professional literature, there will undoubtedly be a greater need for internationally trained and educated sport managers. Professionals in the area and aspiring sport managers should become well versed in international sports affairs. This training will open a vast new job market and should provide an array of exciting experiences.

Chapter Summary

The purpose of this chapter was to provide information about the global marketplace for the sport marketer. It is clear that sport is a major component in the global economy and that sport marketers must be prepared to work in this environment. Specific skills and knowledge regarding the international banking system, world sport structure, and the application of marketing principles in specific cultural contexts are necessary to succeed in international markets, and sport marketers must obtain the requisite training. Furthermore, Pride and Ferrell (2003) noted that marketers must "customize marketing mixes according to cultural, regional and national differences"(p. 115). The global sport marketplace provides a wealth of opportunities for corporations and organizations that commit to spending the time for market research and flexibility in market perception.

CASE STUDY CHAPTER 2

Read the information provided on the adidas and Reebok companies and the 2006 merger and answer the case study questions at the end of the section. (including excerpts from http://www.adidas-group.com/ and http://www.reebok.com/

adidas Profile

adidas executives cited financial growth and global market position as primary reasons driving the 2006 merger of adidas and Reebok. adidas-salomon and TaylorMade-adidas Golf (adidas Group) achieved excellent finanacial growth in recent years, and are committed to bringing the Reebok brand in line with the adidas Group's profitability standards. The combination of adidas and Reebok accelerates the adidas Group's strategic intent in the global athletic footwear, apparel and hardware markets. The new Group will benefit from a more competitive platform

continued on next page

worldwide, well-defined and complementary brand identities, a wider range of products, and an even stronger presence across teams, athletes, events and leagues. (http://www.reebok.com/useng/ir/press/2005/adidas.htm)

2005 adidas Corporate Mission Statement

http://www.adidas-group.com/en/investor/
reports/annually/ar2005.asp

The adidas Group strives to be the global leader in the sporting goods industry with sports brands built on a passion for sports and a sporting lifestyle.

We are "consumer focused" that means we continuously improve the quality, look, feel and image of our products and our organizational structures to match and exceed consumer expectations and to provide them with the highest value.

We are innovation and design leaders who seek to help athletes of all skill levels achieve peak performance with every product we bring to market.

We are a global organization that is socially and environmentally responsible, creative and financially rewarding for our employees and shareholders.

We are committed to continuously strengthening our brands and products to improve our competitive position and financial performance.

In the medium term we will extend our leading market positions in Europe and Asia, expand our share of the US footwear market and be the fastest growing major sporting goods supplier in Latin America. The resulting top-line growth, together with strict cost control and working capital improvements, will drive over-proportionate earnings growth.

2005 adidas Brand Strategies

adidas has a clear mission—"to be the leading sports brand in the world". To accomplish this mission, the organization at adidas is matched to the needs of three groups of sport-oriented consumers: Our Sport Perfor-

mance division is aimed at meeting the sport-specific needs of athletes at all performance levels. Sport Heritage targets trendsetters who seek sport-inspired streetwear with an authentic origin, and Sport Style focuses on young cosmopolitan consumers who look for exclusive, fashion-oriented sportswear products. This three-divisional approach helps us to develop and market innovative products to best meet the needs of today's diverse consumers.

adidas Sport Performance: Focusing on Functionality and Innovation

adidas Sport Performance focuses on offering functional and innovative products in all our sports categories. Our top five priorities are football, running, basketball, tennis and training. We currently hold the number one or number two position globally in each of these categories. Exciting new products are introduced within these categories every season. In 2006, our major initiatives will include the extension of our global "Impossible Is Nothing" communications campaign, special attention to the football, running and basketball categories as well as continued efforts to commercialize our major promotion partnerships.

Impossible Is Nothing: adidas' Attitude Drives Brand Campaign

A key factor to securing the brand's long-term success is to continuously expand a strong global brand positioning. To achieve this, we believe a global brand campaign is critical. adidas launched the "Impossible Is Nothing" brand campaign in 2004 with tremendous success and we will continue to strengthen this message in 2006. Our goal is to present "Impossible Is Nothing" in innovative and challenging ways and to use it to further inspire and involve consumers. As in 2004 and 2005, we will celebrate the power of sport and demonstrate our confidence that "Impossible Is Nothing". The fully integrated communication campaign will feature numerous adidas athletes from various sports who share our desire to surpass limits and to challenge the impossible.

Leveraging adidas Strength in Football and Using FIFA World Cup™ as Brand Platform in 2006

At adidas, football is the heart and soul of our brand. The history of the sport has always been closely connected with adidas. For example, our founder Adi Dassler supported the German national team on their way to the "Miracle of Bern" surprise World Cup victory in 1954 by providing the players with revolutionary boots for the first time featuring screw-in studs. Ever since then, adidas has led all major developments in football boot technology and balls. And the name adidas has become synonymous with the passion of how football is played, shared, enjoyed and celebrated. This is why adidas is the world's leading football brand, both in terms of market share as well as in overall net sales. An important component of our future growth strategy is to further strengthen and extend our leadership in this category. The 2006 FIFA World Cup™ will be the most viewed sports event of all time and adidas intends to be the most visible brand on and off the pitch. Six of the qualified federations will be wearing adidas apparel: Argentina, France, Germany, Japan, Spain and Trinidad & Tobago. Hundreds of players will be wearing adidas footwear during their 2006 FIFA World Cup™ games. adidas will deliver hundreds of thousands of products to fully equip federations, players, referees, ball boys, stewards and volunteers. And our exciting "+10" advertising campaign will communicate our unique commitment to football (see Innovation and Marketing).

New Technologies and Products Support Running's Race for the Number One Position

Running is the world's largest footwear category and an area where adidas has always been strong. We strive to be the leader in performance, innovation, design, and ultimately in volume. We will create excitement amongst runners of all skill levels by providing the most innovative products and addressing specific performance needs.

With the adidas_1, intelligence level 1.1, we have launched an updated and improved version of the adidas_1 running shoe. It features a built-in microprocessor for intelligent cushioning that automatically and continuously adjusts to the unique needs of individual athletes and changing surface conditions. In addition, we will expand our successful Ground Control System™, ClimaCool® and a3® technologies. Furthermore, we will continue to attack and grow in the technical running market by further developing our three, strongly established running families. The adiStar® family consists of premium performance products, built with our newest technologies. The Supernova™ line includes highperformance products constructed using our most viable technologies. Finally, our Response™ family features performance products with our most commercial technologies. We will support these innovations and the rest of our strong offering in running with high-impact marketing and communication around the world.

Sponsorship with Key Players and Innovation to be Drivers of Basketball Business

The basketball category plays a key role in our initiatives to drive sales growth and to position the adidas brand as young and creative, particularly in North America. As a result, we will continue to intensify our basketball efforts and grow our basketball business around the world, especially in the USA and in Asia. Three of the best and most inspirational NBA players spearhead adidas basketball: Tracy McGrady, Kevin Garnett and Tim Duncan. In addition, with athletes such as the most dominant young player in Dwight Howard, the game's fastest player in Gilbert Arenas, the most clutch players in Chauncey Billups, Grant Hill, Jerry Stackhouse, Slam Dunk Champion Josh Smith and the first guard drafted out of high school Sebastian Telfair we have an exciting stable of established and young NBA stars that will showcase the entire range of adidas basketball products. Since we are committed to constant innovation for our superstars in 2006, we will

(continued)

launch new signature products for Kevin Garnett and Tracy McGrady. Two-time MVP and three-time Champion Tim Duncan will help us launch the world's first intelligent basketball shoe: the adidas_1 Basketball. This product concept ushers in a new generation of innovative footwear design that could revolutionize the industry. At adidas in 2006, will move closer to our goal of having the most innovative and most complete basketball product offering ever.

Strategic Partnerships Help Propel adidas Forward

To further extend our position as a global performance brand, adidas has recently entered into strategic partnerships with Stella McCartney, Polar and Porsche Design. Each is a unique arrangement that allows us to partner with leaders in design and innovation to extend the reach of the adidas brand. The "adidas by Stella McCartney" collection introduced in 2005 was the first ever functional performance range for women created by a high-end fashion designer. The collaboration with Stella McCartney is intended to combine Stella's unique design and her instinctive insight into women with adidas' knowledge in creating breakthrough functional sports products. In 2006, this collection will be expanded and extended into new sports categories. adidas has also formed a partnership with Polar, the innovative market leader in heart rate monitoring technology. In 2006, we plan to introduce the world's first completely integrated training system which seamlessly integrates Polar monitoring equipment into adidas apparel and footwear. Additionally, adidas and the Porsche Design Group have entered into a long-term strategic partnership and licensing agreement, to jointly establish an exclusive, high-tech premium brand in the sports sector. Footwear, apparel and hardware for golf, tennis, running and possibly other sports will all be designed and developed under the name "Porsche Design" and co-branded with adidas and TaylorMade.

adidas Sport Heritage: Continued Growth Worldwide

Over the past five years, sports lifestyle has been the fastest growing segment in the sporting goods industry. And our goal is to be the brand of choice in the global sports lifestyle market. This division, started in 2000, has become a more than € 1 billion segment for adidas, which is now one of the key trendsetting brands in the market for the sports lifestyle consumer. Selective distribution to prevent dilution of the brand plays a major role in the development of this division. Our ambitious own-retail strategy will also help us to further commercialize this success. In 2006, we will further sharpen our market segmentation with exciting new concepts to directly address today's lifestyle consumer. Additionally, we will expand our apparel offering and our distribution to directional accounts.

adidas Sport Style: Expanding the Power of the Brand

The adidas Sport Style division is entering its fourth year in 2006. At adidas, we know that niche marketing is increasingly important and that successful brands are those which can reach not only larger audiences but also small and influential ones. Our Y-3 collection, developed with designer Yohji Yamamoto, is helping us extend our product appeal to cosmopolitan consumers who are looking for exclusive, style-leading active sportswear products. The collection is limited to fashion-oriented accounts in Europe, North America and Asia. Influential designs combined with the highest quality standards clearly distinguish Y-3 from any other product in the market. With Y-3, the adidas brand has distinctly established itself as a design leader in the industry. Yamamoto's strong presence in this area allows us to expand the power of the adidas brand to help reach out to style setters and fashion industry visionaries.

adidas Lines

adidas Sport Performance

The largest adidas division (78% of adidas sales) features highly innovative products for athletes around the world. Technological innovation and a commitment to performance are the cornerstones of this division.

adidas Sport Heritage

Once innovative, now classic, always authentic. The Sport Heritage division (22% of adidas sales) extends the unique and authentic heritage of adidas to the sports lifestyle market.

adidas Sport Style

The Y-3 collection, designed in collaboration with Yohji Yamamoto, represents the future of sportswear: an original blend of sport, fashion and fine craftsmanship. With adidas Sport Style, we address the cosmopolitan, fashion-conscious consumer.

http://www.adidas-group.com/en/investor/reports/
annually/ar2005.asp

Reebok Profile

The Reebok Brand's stated 2004 mission was "to enroll global youth through sports, music and technology." From http://www.reebok.com/NR/rdonlyres/eoikict34q5sjstvaq 7hp2rmpb7dwxomgotgnmzjztk3mgnywdim2bgnyoie47h wvgo3uik5zd4zc/FinalShareholdersReport.pdf

Reebok Product Lines

During 2004 the Reebok Brand was organized around integrated product development and marketing teams focused on each of three main product lines: Rbk; Performance; and Classic. Each of these product lines featured product offerings for men, women and children that were designed for specific consumer groups, and each line was supported by targeted marketing and advertising initiatives. In February 2005 the Reebok Brand introduced its comprehensive new advertising campaign, "I Am What I Am." This campaign, which celebrated authenticity and individuality in sports and life, was the cornerstone of Reebok's Brand positioning and flowed through the marketing of Rbk, Performance and Classic lines. One of the Reebok Brand's product initiatives during 2005 was incorporating their inflatable shoe technology, The Pump, into a new selection of products.

Rbk

Reebok's Rbk product collection features footwear, apparel and accessories designed to appeal to young, fashion-oriented consumers. Rbk represents the fusion of sports, music and fashion, and incorporates cutting-edge fashion and technology into performance products that are relevant to today's youth culture. During 2004 we began to expand our Rbk platform into a broader initiative that includes performance products that incorporate our leading technologies, as well as classic and lifestyle products for both men and women. We introduced Rbk products in multiple categories including basketball, running, training, tennis and boots designed for both the suburban and urban consumer. Throughout 2005 we plan to continue to broaden our Rbk product collection by introducing additional performance categories and product offerings to our Rbk collection, including products featuring our Pump inflation technology. During 2005 we also plan to introduce a line of Rbk-branded basketballs, footballs, soccer balls and volleyballs, which will be available at sporting goods retailers. The Hockey Company will also introduce Rbk-branded hockey skates, sticks, helmets, equipment and hockey-related apparel at retail during 2005.

During 2004 we utilized the "Sounds and Rhythm of Sport" marketing platform for Rbk, which emphasizes the connection between sport, music, fashion and entertainment in youth culture. Our Rbk footwear products include the "S. Carter Collection by Rbk," the signature footwear collection of hip-hop star Jay-Z, and the "G-Unit Collection by Rbk," the signature footwear collection of hip-hop artist 50 Cent. Both of these collections experienced strong sales growth during 2004 and successful new product launches. During 2004 we expanded the S. Carter Collection to include the S. Carter Tennis shoe as well as basketball and casual footwear, and we added cross-training product to our G-Unit collection, introducing the G-Unit XT cross trainer. In addition, for the 2004 holiday season we expanded our G-Unit collection by introducing the G-Unit Boot. We plan to evolve this platform in 2005 to address a broader base of consumers with our "I Am What I Am" marketing campaign.

Our Rbk line also includes products designed and marketed under our relationship with National Basketball Association (NBA) star Allen Iverson of the Denver Nuggets. We market a signature line of footwear and apparel bearing Iverson's endorsement, and we have the right to use his name and image throughout his playing career and beyond. Our Iverson products include the I3 basketball footwear and apparel collection, as well as our Off the Clock Signature Collection, which features footwear that reflects Iverson's off-court lifestyle. We believe Iverson's performance on court as well as his compelling lifestyle and attitude resonate with Rbk consumers. In November 2004 we launched the Answer 8, Iverson's newest game shoe, to coincide with the start of the 2004–05 NBA season. At the 2005 NBA All-Star game Iverson showcased our The Pump inflation technology, setting the stage for the introduction of a new Iverson shoe in the second half of 2005 that will feature our latest The Pump technology, The Pump 2.0.

Our Rbk product line also includes our Above the Rim (ATR) basketball collection of footwear, apparel and accessories. In 2004 we promoted our ATR products with endorsements from NBA stars Baron Davis of the Golden State Warriors and Steve Francis of the New York Knicks. During 2004 we updated the styling of our ATR footwear, featuring more aggressive upper patterns, new materials and cutting-edge midsoles. In February 2005 we introduced our new ATR The Pump basketball footwear, which features our The Pump inflatable custom fit technology, at the 2005 NBA All Star Game. Our ATR The Pump shoe is now being worn on court by a number of NBA players, including Yao Ming of the Houston Rockets, Peja Stojakovic of the New Orleans Hornets, Baron Davis and Steve Francis. In February 2005 we also introduced at retail the ATR Clear Out and ATR 5 Star, which feature our new DMX Micro cushioning technology.

We continued to emphasize grassroots marketing in 2004 to promote our Rbk products and enhance Rbk brand awareness, particularly among young consumers. During 2004 we placed marketing teams in 18 cities throughout the United States that are focused on enhancing our street awareness and targeting our marketing message to the places where our consumers live and play. As part of our effort to connect with young consumers, our Rbk-branded products are featured in the latest releases of basketball and football video games released by EA Sports. In 2004 we also sponsored the Entertainers Basketball Classic (EBC) tournament at Rucker Park, the premier street basketball competition in the U.S., in connection with which we seeded certain of our ATR basketball products. We have agreed to continue this sponsorship through 2007. We sponsor several high-profile amateur basketball tournaments in the United States, including the elite Reebok ABCD Basketball Camp. We believe these camps significantly enhance our Brand's visibility with elite high school basketball players who are trend-setters among American youth. In Summer 2004 we marketed our ATR collection in conjunction with the 2004 Reebok ABCD Camp, which features approximately 400 of the most elite high school basketball players in the U.S. During 2004 we ran a national print advertising campaign featuring the Reebok ABCD Camp. Also during 2004 we sponsored the two leading high school basketball all-star games in the U.S., the EA Sports Roundball Classic and the McDonald's High School All-America game. Internationally, we sponsored the Reebok Eurocamp and the Reebok Big Men Camp, which featured the top basketball players in Europe, as well as two NBA-run camps in Africa and Asia called Basketball without Borders. We plan to continue our emphasis on innovative grassroots marketing for Rbk in 2005.

We distribute our Rbk products through a limited number of authorized Rbk retailers, including athletic specialty retailers, independent retailers located primarily in urban areas and select sporting goods retailers. During 2005 we plan to expand the number of retailers within these channels that carry our Rbk products. Our distribution strategy is focused on those retailers at which younger, fashion-oriented consumers tend to shop, and which we believe will enhance the retail presence of our Rbk products. We operate a company-owned Rbk concept store in Philadelphia that features our Iverson and other Rbk products in an atmosphere that combines music, sports and entertainment with fashion. In addition, during 2004 we opened our Rbk store in West Hollywood, California, which features a 3,300-square foot retail store, a VIP lounge and a product showroom that converts to a screening room, and which is designed to showcase Rbk's dynamic fusion of sports, music, entertainment and technology.

Performance

The products in Reebok's Performance line are designed for, and marketed to, athletic consumers who seek performance from their footwear, apparel and accessories. The Performance line includes products designed for basketball, running, fitness, football, baseball, soccer, tennis and other sports. Our Performance products incorporate technological features such as our The Pump inflation technology, our DMX footwear cushioning technology, our 3D Ultralite footwear material and our Play Dry moisture management systems. Performance products are also designed to reflect a sense of fashion and style.

Included in the Performance line are apparel and footwear products designed and marketed under the licensing agreements we entered into during 2001 with the National Football League (NFL) and the NBA. Our Performance line also includes footwear designed and marketed under the license agreement we entered into in February 2004 with Major League Baseball (MLB) and apparel designed and marketed under The Hockey Company's license agreement with the National Hockey League (NHL). These agreements and our NFL, NBA, MLB and NHL products are described below under the heading "Sports Licensing."

The cornerstone of our Performance category is our Premier Series of performance-oriented products designed for serious runners. We introduced the Premier Series in 2003 with the goal of re-establishing Reebok with our heritage as an authentic running shoe brand. Premier Series running shoes are designed for technical performance and incorporate features such as our DMX Foam and DMX Shear cushioning technology and our Play Dry moisture management system. The Premier Series was launched in the running specialty channel, which we believe is critical to re-building the authenticity of our Brand with runners. During 2004 our marketing for the Premier Series of running products focused primarily on print advertising in running periodicals and grassroots marketing at running events, including our Reebok Running Mobile Running Tour that brought the mobile Reebok Running Zone vehicles to major running events and select athletic retailers nationwide. Also during 2004, Reebok's grassroots Local Heroes program sponsored top race participants in communities throughout the U.S. In 2005 we plan to continue our emphasis on building our running business in the United States and internationally. In early 2005 we sponsored the Rbk Boston Indoor Games, one of the leading indoor track meets in the U.S., and in April 2005 we will sponsor the Paris Marathon. Also during 2005 we plan to launch a fully integrated new grassroots marketing initiative for our Performance running products that will be focused on the key running specialty channel of distribution. During 2005 we plan to build on the success of the Premier Series by introducing three new running product collections related to the Premier Series called the Vision, Aztec and Versatec collections, which we plan to segment by distribution channel in the athletic specialty, sporting goods and department store channels, respectively, in order to meet consumer needs in each channel.

During 2004 we entered into a new license agreement with the NBA covering the Asia Pacific market. In October 2003 Reebok entered into a multi-year endorsement agreement with Houston Rockets star Yao Ming, a native of Shanghai, China. Our relationship with Yao is at the center of our efforts to develop the basketball apparel and footwear market in Asia. In 2004 we began working with the NBA to leverage our relationships with both Yao and the NBA as we develop an integrated marketing plan for China. In October 2004 Reebok sponsored the first NBA China Games, featuring pre-season games played in Beijing and Shanghai between Yao's Houston Rockets and the Sacramento Kings. Leading up to the NBA China Games we featured Yao in television, print and billboard advertising in China, as well as in an extensive public relations campaign. Also at the China Games, we debuted Yao's signature NBA High Post shoe. In addition, in June 2004 Reebok and Yao Ming worked together to build "Yao's House," a renovated outdoor basketball park in downtown Shanghai that is free to the public. During the Summer of 2004, Yao's House hosted a series of Reebok-supported basketball programs. We also sponsored a high school basketball league in China.

Classic

Reebok's Classic lifestyle product line includes Classic originals—long-time consumer favorite Reebok footwear and apparel products—as well as more fashion forward, lifestyle collections that incorporate new technologies, fabrics and materials. Many of our Classic products feature "retro" styling that reflects distinctive design elements from past Reebok products. During 2004 we continued to focus on print advertising for our Classic products. In addition, we worked with a number of our customers on cooperative television advertising. We also promoted our Classic products in connection with the release of a new album by popular rap artist Twista.

Our product and distribution strategy for our Classic line focuses on segmenting our products in those distribution channels that reflect the different types of consumers for whom our Classic product collections are intended, and on merchandising and assortment planning to ensure that our products are effectively presented at retail. For example, during 2004 we introduced high-end, fashion-forward Classic footwear products with targeted trend-setting retailers in New York and Los Angeles.

Reebok Kids

During 2004 Reebok renewed its focus on kids footwear. We believe that the Reebok Kids footwear business is important to establishing a relationship between our Brand and young consumers who we can cultivate as Reebok customers as they grow into adulthood. Our kids business includes both take-downs of Reebok's key adult initiatives as well as several kids-only concepts.

During 2004, we introduced kids versions of S. Carter Collection and G-Unit Collection products such as the S. Carter Tennis shoe and the G-Unit Boot. Our 2004 Kids collection also included versions of our Iverson shoes, including the Answer 8, as well as take-downs of other popular adult shoes. During 2004 we also introduced three new footwear collections created specifically for kids: Sweets, Hard Wear and Classic Lights. Launched in Fall 2004, the Reebok Sweets collection, which we market as "eye-candy for your feet," is designed to appeal to fashion-forward "tween" girls between the ages of six and twelve, and features glitter, sparkles and rhinestone detailing in fun, feminine colors. The Hard Wear collection for boys, which we launched in Europe in 2003 and in the U.S. for back-to-school in 2004, features high abrasion resistant uppers and soles and double stitching for extra durability. Hard Wear shoes also feature a "Grow Through Guarantee," which assures parents that their kids will outgrow the shoes before the shoes are worn out. Finally, our Classic Lights collection offers classic-styled footwear that lights up. During 2004 we supported the launch of our Sweets collection with a print advertising campaign, and we supported the launch of both our Sweets and Classic Lights collections with online advertising campaigns as well as television advertising campaigns that we ran on Nickelodeon.

Case Questions

1. Should adidas integrate the corporate structure of Reebok into the existing structure or allow Reebok to retain its separate structure under adidas Board of Directors review?

2. Having reviewed the adidas and Reebok position in the market relating to performance and fashion, should adidas force Reebok to move more in line with the performance image of adidas or should adidas allow Reebok to explore a higher profile and fashion image?

3. How could adidas leverage Reebok's licensing agreements with the NBA, NFL, NHL and MLB?

QUESTIONS FOR STUDY

1. Diagram the relationship of the International Olympic Committee to a specific International Federation. Include a discussion of how each functions with the United States Olympic Committee and a national governing body in the United States.
2. What are the keys to successful banking in international sport marketing?
3. How does marketing a sport product internationally differ from marketing the same product in the United States?

LEARNING ACTIVITIES

1. Investigate opening a Swiss bank account. It could be a lot of fun and a great conversation topic among friends.
2. How would you handle the following situation? You just completed a consulting project negotiating sponsorship deals for the Lithuanian National Basketball team and were due to be paid $10,000 in US dollars. At the last minute, you were informed that they could pay you only in the local currency. What is that currency? How much of it would you get? Would you accept payment in that form, and if not, what would be an alternative?

PROFESSIONAL ASSOCIATIONS AND ORGANIZATIONS

World Federation of the Sporting Goods Industry
La Maison du Sport
CH-1936 Verbier Switzerland
http://www.wfsgi.org

United States Information Agency
301 4th Street SW
Washington, DC 20547
http://www.usia.gov

International Events Group
640 N. LaSalle, Suite 6000
Chicago, IL 60610-37777
http://www.sponsorship.com
1-800-834-4850

SUGGESTED READINGS

Axtell, R. E. (1991). *Gestures: The do's and taboos of body language around the world.* New York: John Wiley and Sons.

Chalip, L., and Thoma, J. (1993). *Sport governance in the global community.* Morgantown, WV: Fitness Information Technology, Inc.

Morrison, T., Conaway, W., and Borden, G. (1994). *Kiss, bow, or shake hands.* Holbrook, MA: Bob Adams, Inc.

Tuller, L. W. (1991). *Going global.* Homewood, IL: Business One Irwin.

Chapter Three

SPORT MARKETING THEORY

Sport marketing defined:

The process of designing and implementing activities for the production, pricing, promotion, and distribution of a sport or sport business product to satisfy the needs or desires of consumers and to achieve the company's objectives.

Sport marketing is the process of designing and implementing activities for the production, pricing, promotion, and distribution of a sport product to satisfy the needs or desires of consumers and to achieve the company's objectives. It is a complex and dynamic part of every sport business. In fact, most business decisions are based on the activities of marketing. All sport marketing activities are developed with specific and strategic decisions based on research and information. These activities are typically based on a strategic process, or model, such as will be presented in this chapter (see Figure 3.3).

To understand sport marketing, it is first important to understand the components of its definition and how the definition was developed. This definition is derived primarily from sport marketing theory, which is built on fundamentals of marketing, marketing theory, sport business industry knowledge, and the sport marketing and sport management bodies of knowledge. Although sport marketing textbooks and courses are relatively new when compared to other fields of study, such as law, sport marketing is as old as ancient sports and sports events. Sport businesses have been practicing sport marketing for as long as they have been selling sport products.

What is new about sport marketing is the development of sport marketing as an academic field of study. Sport marketing involves marketing fundamentals applied in one industry, the sport business industry. The development of sport marketing fundamentals is therefore based on basic marketing principles. The practice and activities of sport marketing are also based on basic marketing activities, but are modified and adapted to one industry—the sport business industry. Therefore, sport marketing is based on its primary and parent discipline—marketing. However, it is not enough that students who will work in the sport business industry take only marketing classes in a business school. Those students will learn basic marketing principles, but will not learn sport marketing, that is, the principles and fundamentals of marketing as they have been modified and adapted to the sport business industry. Hence, it is imperative that a sport management student's college education be primarily comprised of sport management courses.

Sport marketing is one of the most important functions of a sport business. This is because the sport marketing activities will define the business. The growth of the sport industry is phenomenal and shows no signs of slowing. It has grown from the 23rd largest industry in the United States to the 6th largest industry in a short period of 10 years. Growth means there are increasing numbers of sport companies and products. Each sport product or company is competition. The concept of competition in business is the idea that a sport business is competing against another business to win the consumer's dollar. Winning in business means staying in business at a successful level. Success is defined by the sport company and is usually measured by achieving the company's objectives.

Companies in the sport industry have plenty of competitors. A sport company today must employ sport marketing as a significant business function to the extent that every facet of the company is guided by sport marketing concepts. It is the function that guides the sport business toward identifying the products that consumers need or desire, that identifies and analyzes competitors, that develops pricing strategies, that develops the promotional strategies to be used for the company's products in order to get the consumer to the product, and that identifies how to get the product to the consumer.

To more completely understand sport marketing, let's look at its base—marketing. After that, we'll study the theory and fundamentals of sport marketing.

Marketing Defined

Marketing is a business process that developed along with the development and growth of business. Bartels (1988) wrote that marketing is the element that "revolutionized the economy of the country and gradually affected the whole world" (p. 1). The word *marketing* comes from the word *market,* which means a group of buyers and sellers (consumers and producers) negotiating the terms of exchange for something. Buyers are consumers, and there are many different categories of consumers as you will learn later in this book. Sellers can be manufacturers, producers, retailers, promoters, and wholesalers. Negotiation takes many forms such as deciding to buy or not to buy simply based on a nonnegotiable price, making offers and counteroffers until agreement is reached, and determining a fair or satisfactory exchange. Terms can involve negotiating over delivery and acceptance, warranty, after sales service, payment methods, and promises of quality. The exchange can involve many such factors as delivery, terms of payment or trade, and transaction. Finally, the word *something* in the definition usually involves the trade of something for something else; "something" could be goods, services, ideas, benefits, perks, deeds, and, of course, money. One example of the market at work is a flea market. It is an area, or a marketplace, where sellers bring their wares and buyers come to shop. At a flea market, it is expected that buyers and sellers will haggle in the exchange process to trade something for something else.

Usually, in this setting, the buyer and seller negotiate over the worth, or value, of a good. The seller has established a price, but the buyer will offer a different price based on the buyer's belief of the good's value—or to try to get the good at below a fair market price. Buyer and seller negotiate until some exchange agreement is reached.

> Marketing is the study of people and what they buy, how much they will pay, where they want to purchase a product, and how they are affected by promotional tactics and messages.

In another example, the value of goods in a sporting goods store is set using pricing strategies. The buyer typically enters the store and decides whether or not to purchase the good at its "sticker" price (the price placed on the good by a little sticker). Usually there is no negotiating between buyer and seller like the kind of bargaining we find in a flea market. However, the buyer can send a message to the seller about price by making the decision to buy or not to buy. If a product is not selling, the company must determine why. If the company discovers the product does not sell because too many consumers think the price is too high, the company can relay this important information to the producer. The producer now has to analyze the situation and make a decision about what to do about the price. It's not a simple decision of lowering the price because perhaps the price is high because of the high cost to manufacture the item.

Marketing as a business activity developed and evolved primarily from the study of

> The sport marketer must be able to recognize and analyze business environments, determine their effects, and make strategic decisions that will enhance the success of the sport business.

people and what they buy, how much they will pay, where they want to purchase a product, and how they are affected by promotional tactics and messages. Additionally, the elements, functions, principles, and theories of marketing were also developed through the study of many other factors such as industrial production expansion, the invention of new products, the study of human behavior (sociology and psychology), population studies, education and income studies, and studies of new and diverse markets. As a response to these and other factors, a market-driven economy developed. This meant that businesses paid increasing amounts of attention to consumers and studied what the consumer needed or wanted (Bartels, 1988).

Today's marketing concepts evolved from a simple to a complex and broad concept of marketing. The concepts are drawn from the social sciences and are more than merely a business activity. Businesses exist in a variety of environments such as political, social, and economic environments that constantly provide opportunities and threats for a business.

Although marketing is a business function that should be a significant part of every business, the functions of marketing should be a critical part of every department within the business. Companies faced with the challenge of achieving profitable growth in an environment of intense competition, product proliferation, and escalating costs must make marketing a priority function throughout the company. Marketing must be a total company effort, and the company therefore should develop a marketing orientation—that is, every task and decision of the company should be made based on its marketing plan.

The marketing orientation, or concept, is a philosophy concerning the way a company should be managed. It consists of three requirements (Cravens and Woodruff, 1983):

1. Examine people's needs and wants as the basis of deciding what the business (or economy) will do.

2. Select the best way to meet the consumer's needs that are targeted by the firm.

3. Achieve the organization's performance objectives by meeting the consumers' needs satisfactorily.

In short, the company must study what the consumer wants and provide it. Although this seems like an easy rule to follow, there are many functions that must be performed and receive critical analysis and proper management in order for successful marketing decisions to be developed. It is not an easy task to identify what someone wants or needs and then to provide it. The human being is a complex organism affected by a remarkable variety of influencing factors. Although the marketer might discover what the consumer wants today, that desire may be different tomorrow.

> The company's every task and decision should be a reflection of its marketing plan.

Complicating the task of producing what the consumer wants is the company's capacity to manufacture it, distribute it, and offer it. In addition, the company must consider its values and objectives and decide if it can ethically offer the products. Therefore, careful management of the marketing functions and critical analysis before decision making can increase the company's chances for success. The incorporation of a marketing management strategy is critical.

Sport Marketing Fundamentals and Theory

Theory can be defined as "a system of assumptions, accepted principles, and rules of procedure devised to analyze, predict, or explain a set of phenomena" (*Webster's*, 1978). Theory is built from a foundation of research and knowledge and may be tested through research and application. Research can be defined as a systematic and organized investigation. When the research is complete, the results may be used in a variety of ways, some of which are to add to one's knowledge or a body of knowledge solutions for problems and to discover answers to specific questions.

Sport marketing is a relatively new academic field of study. It does not yet contain a substantial body of knowledge when compared to many other fields of study. However, the body of knowledge is growing. Sport marketing is very new when compared to fields of study like law, education, management, medicine, or marketing. For example, this textbook is one of only five textbooks about the fundamentals of sport marketing. In addition, there are three academic journals for sport marketing, the *Sport Marketing Quarterly, International Journal of Sport Management and Marketing,* and the *International Journal of Sports Marketing and Sponsorship.*

Finally, sport marketing is just beginning to be considered a singular academic discipline. As a course of study, it has typically been offered as one individual course among several other sport management courses. Today, a few institutions offer two or more sport marketing courses. Additionally, a smaller number of institutions offer sport marketing as a concentration.

Although sport marketing is becoming an academic discipline, academicians have created two different sport marketing areas of focus (see Figure 3.1). First, one group of academicians teach that sport marketing involves just the selling of sports events to two groups of consumers: sports participants and sports spectators. This group uses the terminology of "sports" marketing, or, the marketing of sports.

Second, other academicians believe that sport marketing is closely related to the contemporary definition of sport management and the sport industry. That is, sport management is the study and practice of management and business princi-

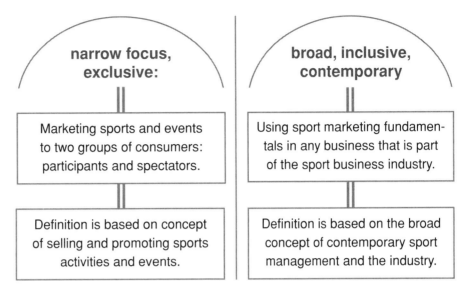

narrow focus, exclusive:	broad, inclusive, contemporary
Marketing sports and events to two groups of consumers: participants and spectators.	Using sport marketing fundamentals in any business that is part of the sport business industry.
Definition is based on concept of selling and promoting sports activities and events.	Definition is based on the broad concept of contemporary sport management and the industry.

Figure 3.1
The two different concepts of sport marketing being used today.

Table 3.1
Some segments of the sport business industry.

Paricipation Sports

Spectatorial Sports Events

Sporting Goods

Sports Media—Print

Sports Media—Broadcast

Sports Media—Electronic

Sponsorship

Athlete Management

Sports Tourism and Travel: for participation or spectatorial

Facility and Venue Design and Construction

Licensing and Merchandising

Sport Marketing Research

Web Sport Business

Sport Law Firms

Sport Event Management

Sports Medicine

Sports Governing Organizations

Advertising

Endorsement Management

ples in the sport industry. The *sport industry* includes all businesses offering any sport, recreation, fitness, tourism, and leisure-related product (See Table 3.1). As you learned in chapter one, there are many different types of sport businesses that offer many different types of products to many different consumers. Therefore, sport marketing should be broad enough so that students will learn how to apply the fundamentals of sport marketing to any sport business, in any industry segment, and to all of its consumers.

It is the contemporary definitions of sport marketing and the sport business industry that are used in this text to define sport marketing and the sport marketing management model.

Although sport marketing is a developing field of study, this does not mean that marketing has never been used in the sport industry. As pointed out earlier, marketing practices and principles have been used in the sport industry throughout history and are still being used today. Sport marketers have drawn from and continue to draw from marketing and other fields of study. In addition, academicians and practitioners are hard at work conducting research in sport marketing as is evidenced by the studies published in a variety of research journals and trade magazines. Further, this book adds to the young but growing body of knowledge in sport marketing. As marketing principles are applied to the sport industry, they are modified as necessary. As marketing strategies and models in the sport industry are studied and research is published, the body of knowledge will be developed. As higher education responds to the needs of the sport industry, textbooks, courses, and curriculum in sport marketing will be developed. Each will add to the development of the body of knowledge and to sport marketing as a field of study and will serve as the foundation of a theory of sport marketing.

The theory of sport marketing is still developmental and constantly evolving. These theories and fundamentals should be used as conceptual frameworks for research. To study the developing theory of sport marketing, we must study the foundation from which it is being built. Foundation refers to the basis on which something stands or is supported. Foundation is research, fundamentals, principles, and theories. The foundation of sport marketing knowledge is being built primarily from five broad fields of study: sport studies, business administration studies, social science studies, technology, and communications (see Figure 3.2).

Within each broad field of study are specific or specialized areas of study from which sport marketing is developing its body of knowledge. Within sport studies, these specializations include sport management, sport sociology, sport psychology, leisure management, recreation administration, legal aspects of sport, sports tourism, and sports information. Within business, the specializations include marketing, economics, finance, business law, and consumer behavior. In communications, the areas include journalism, public relations, media studies, advertising, and broadcasting. The areas in the social sciences include human relations, cultural studies, population studies, and labor market studies. Technology includes e-commerce, Internet business, and Web-based marketing.

Table 3.2 presents a list of some areas of study in sport marketing today. As an example of how academicians and practitioners in sport marketing are using other fields of study to develop the theories in sport marketing, let us consider how the social sciences may be used. Yiannakis (1989) suggested that sport marketing could be strengthened through the study and application of sport sociology. This is still true today. Sociology is the study of human behavior. Sport sociology is the study of human behavior and sport. For sport marketing, an understanding of people and sports will help a sport business be successful.

In a study of sport sociology literature, Yiannakis suggested that sport sociology could make significant contributions to sport marketing and management in the following ways:

1. Conceptualization, design, and implementation of good market research;

2. Instrument development;

3. Interpretation of the findings by grounding both a priori and post hoc explanations in existing knowledge bases;

4. Advertising effectiveness by providing essential information bases, especially in the area of lifestyle characteristics;

5. Development of a general marketing information base (target market characteristics);

Sport marketing knowledge is developing from the following fields:

Sport studies:

sport management
sport sociology
sport psychology
leisure management
recreation administration
legal aspects of sport
sports tourism
sports information

Business:

marketing
economics
finance
business law
consumer behavior

Communications:

journalism
public relations
media studies
advertising
broadcasting

Social sciences:

human relations
cultural studies
population studies
labor market studies

Technology:

e-commerce
Web business and marketing

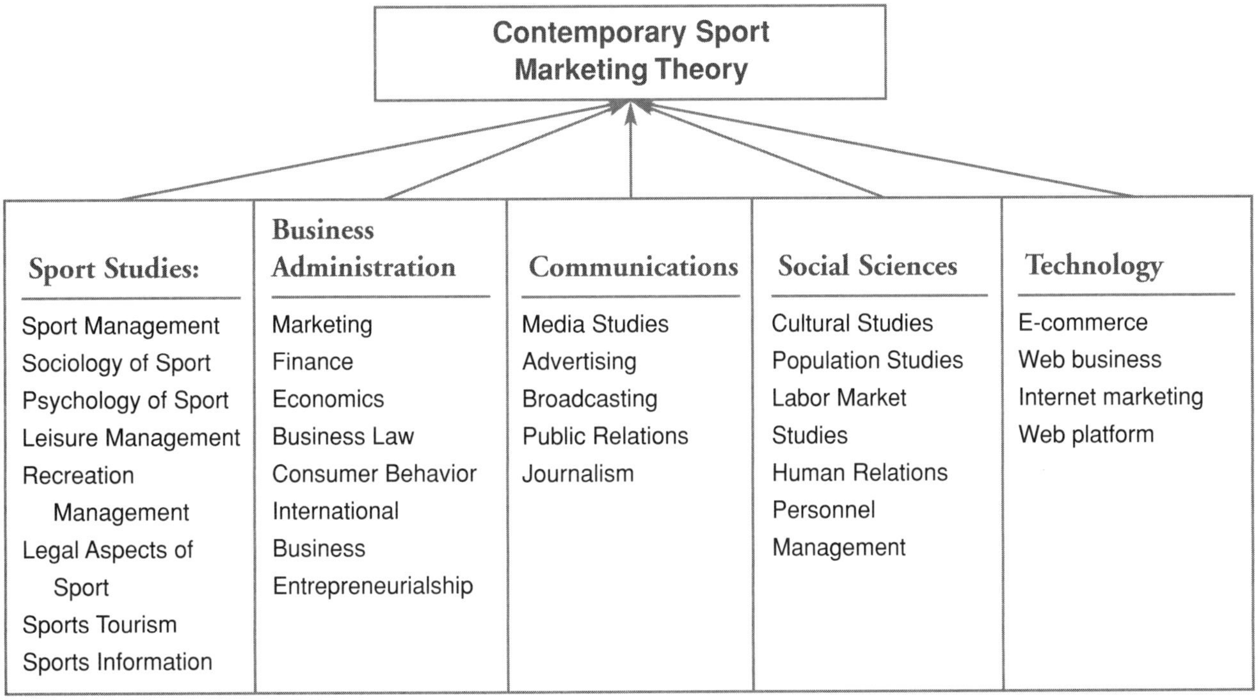

Figure 3.2
Contemporary sport marketing theory. These fields of study are serving as the foundation and framework to build the fundamentals of sport marketing.

Sport Studies:	Business Administration	Communications	Social Sciences	Technology
Sport Management	Marketing	Media Studies	Cultural Studies	E-commerce
Sociology of Sport	Finance	Advertising	Population Studies	Web business
Psychology of Sport	Economics	Broadcasting	Labor Market	Internet marketing
Leisure Management	Business Law	Public Relations	Studies	Web platform
Recreation	Consumer Behavior	Journalism	Human Relations	
Management	International		Personnel	
Legal Aspects of	Business		Management	
Sport	Entrepreneurialship			
Sports Tourism				
Sports Information				

Table 3.2
Examples of areas of study in sport business management.

sponsorship analysis

spectatorial sport

sporting goods

licensing and merchandising

consumer market identification and analysis

web sport business

sport law

sport event management

economic impact

sports tourism impact

sporting goods consumption

commercialization

trends

financial analysis

6. Exploration and identification of new markets; and

7. Introduction of social science orientation to the enterprise.

Yiannakis stated that this involves

> an appreciation of the interactive nature of system forces in the marketing environment and their impact on consumer preferences, underlying patterns and trends and their potential impact on consumer buying readiness, cultural differences and their influence on purchasing decisions, and the role that sport plays in society in terms of influencing values and attitudes, shaping tastes, providing role models, creating new fashions and the like (p. 105).

Another author, Kates (1998), agrees that research and theory in sport marketing literature can be greatly enhanced by using each other's theory, methods, and insights. Kates writes that "some scholarly work within consumer research has focused upon the study of subcultures" in sport, and that this work is providing "theoretical frameworks and substantive findings regarding the enculturation of people into a new set of norms and values while interacting with others." "By linking these discourses, new marketing tactics can be formulated." Kates concludes that "bringing the discourses of consumer behavior, sport sociology, and sport marketing together, new research agendas and new marketing insights will result" (p. 29).

Critical analysis and research of the many different groups of such consumers in the sport industry as the African-American sport market (Armstrong, 1998), the Hispanic sport market (McCarthy, 1998), the gay and lesbian sport market (Pitts,

1998, 1999), and the Generation X sport market (Shoham, Rose, Kropp, and Kahle, 1997) can provide a sport business with the knowledge and understanding needed in today's constantly increasing diverse industry. As a matter of fact, there are vast numbers of sport businesses developed and owned by these markets that offer sport products specifically for these markets, as we learned in chapter one. This new knowledge and understanding can then be used to formulate successful marketing strategies. Therefore, the theories existing in those fields must be used in sport marketing and in studying the sport industry; these theories should continue to be used in the development of a sport marketing theory.

Sport marketing is a process. A process is a continuous cycle. Therefore, marketing is a function that never ends. The *sport marketing management model* is an illustration of the elements and process of sport marketing. It should serve as a guide for

The Sport Marketing Management Model

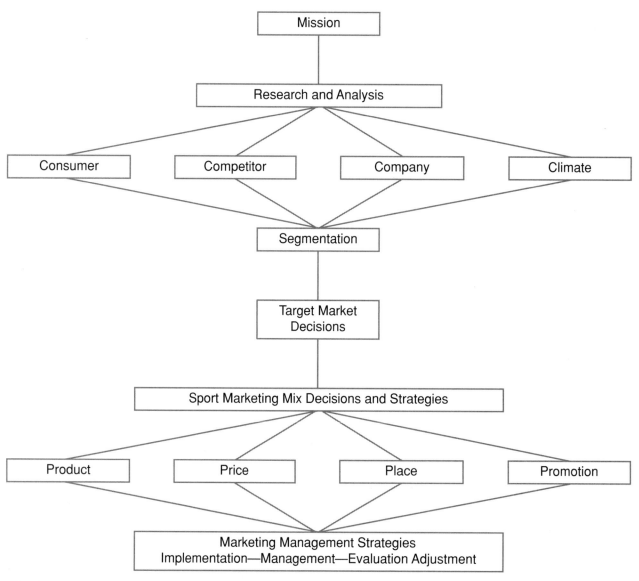

Figure 3.3
The Sport Marketing Management Model.

managing the company's marketing functions. Figure 3.3 illustrates the model. The model illustrates the elements of marketing, the succession of elements and functions, the process of managing, and the interdependency of the elements.

This chapter will present an overview of the model, sport marketing management, each element, and the process. Subsequent chapters discuss each sport marketing element in detail.

The Sport Company's Mission and Objectives

Understanding the company's mission and its current status enables the sport marketer to make key decisions and formulate strategies.

Every business exists for a purpose. Each company strives to stay consistent with its purpose in order to enhance its chances for success. The company's purpose may be found in its stated mission. For example, an intercollegiate athletics program's mission may be "to provide athletic participation opportunities for the college student." In another example, a city parks and recreation department's mission might be "to provide the means for leisure pursuit for the city's population." The company will offer products with the intention of meeting the company's mission. The mission, then, is the reason it exists. All marketing activities must begin with a clear understanding of the company's mission and the company's current situation. The stated mission must be accompanied by the company's objectives. The objectives provide specific and concrete direction whereas the mission statement often may be broad and ambiguous. The objectives should state the exact direction that management wants for the company. For example, whereas the mission of the college athletics department is to provide athletic participation opportunities for the college student, its objectives will be detailed concerning specifically what the athletic department wants to achieve within a given period of time.

All marketing activities must begin with a clear understanding of the organization's objectives.

An example of such an objective might be the following: to win a national championship in track-and-field within five years. The direction is established in the objective, and the college will implement programs and strategies that will most likely achieve the stated objective.

In another example, a professional women's basketball league may have an objective to increase consumer awareness of its existence and to increase attendance by 20% by the end of the regular season. The marketer must now make decisions and implement strategies that will take the league toward attaining the stated objective.

Chapters 4, 5, and 6 cover the details of sport marketing research and managing this information. Information gained from marketing research is a significant element when forming decisions and strategies for the marketing mix. Research will provide vital information in the four key areas the marketer studies that we call the 4 Cs: the consumer, the competitor, the company, and the climate.

> An MIS, or Marketing Information System, enables businesses to handle vast amounts of information by collecting, storing, and retrieving it.

We exist in a world that seems small because electronics, communication systems, and transportation are phenomenal. The amount of information produced and disseminated through communication systems is massive. In fact, the last decade has been labeled the Information Era. Moreover, we are currently in a time that is literally changing the entire face of business. A factor largely responsible for this is the Internet. Business on the World Wide Web has acquired several names, including e-commerce (the e stands for electronic), e-business, Web-based business, and Web malling. It has created a new mode of delivery for business. We can, if we wish, do everything from working to shopping for necessities and never leave the chair in front of the computer. The marketer must achieve the ability to conduct research, obtain information, analyze the results of research and the data gathered, envision uses for the information, and formulate strategic decisions based on the research and information. In addition, the marketer must have or create a system to manage the information and research.

Sport marketing research is a system of gathering and analyzing information. What types of data and how data are gathered is specifically organized and determined by what question is in need of answering. For example, if the company's product isn't selling, the question becomes, "Why isn't this product selling?" Research is then designed to gather and analyze data to try to answer this question.

The sport marketer will need the information gained through research to formulate decisions and strategies concerning every aspect of the company and its marketing plan. Marketing research usually focuses on one problem. At the same time, broad databases may be established and maintained concerning specific aspects of the company or the company's consumer markets and competitors.

The massive amount of information requires a sophisticated information management system. This is usually called a *marketing information system*, or MIS. The purpose of an MIS is to collect, store, and retrieve specific information. An MIS can be as simple as a few index cards or as complex as a state-of-the-art computer system. Some of the determining factors include the company's capability for funding a system, the amount and type of information to be managed, and the ways in which the marketer will need to use the information.

Did you know...?

The average cost to attend a major league game for a family of four in 2005 was $164.43; highest Red Sox, $276.24; lowest Royals, $119.85.

Average price of beer, $5.34 average size, 17 oz

Average ticket, $21.17

Average soda, $2.84 average size, 16 oz

Average hot dog, $3.23

Average parking, $11.05

Average program, $4.06

Average cap, $13.01

Five most expensive: Red Sox, Cubs, Yankess, Giants, Phillies. Five cheapest: Royals, Angels, Brewers, Rangers, Rockies.

teammarketing.com

Everyone in a sport business must possess vast knowledge about many different things. These factors have direct and indirect influence on the company that must be used or referred to when making decisions and developing strategies. The sport business should develop a way to constantly study and analyze them. Most all of these can be categorized into four categories: the consumer, the competitor, the

The Four Cs: Consumer, Competitor, Company, and Climate

Table 3.3
The 4 Cs: what the sport business needs to study.

Consumer:	demographics psychographics lifestyle geodemographics purchase behavior
Competition:	the industry and marketplace product differentiation pricing strategies financial strategies positioning promotion strategies
Company:	mission and objectives financial strength production product management pricing objectives and strategies distribution strategies promotion strategies
Climate:	economic legal social and cultural political ethical trends technological education community corporate

Figure 3.4
The 4 Cs: affecting sport marketing strategies.

company, and the climate. Table 3.3 and Figure 3.4 presents the 4 Cs and their variables that a sport business should constantly study. The following are brief descriptions of each. Thorough details of each are presented in later chapters.

THE CONSUMER

The sport marketer needs to know and understand the people (consumers) who need or want the company's products (see Figure 3.5). This is called *consumer analysis*. With this knowledge the marketer may make educated strategic decisions for the company that will position the company for success. It is also important to identify potential consumers.

> Knowledge of your consumers will guide you and your sport business in making important decisions about product, price, distribution, and promotion.

These are consumers the company might want to attract. For example, you are the owner of a soccer club. You currently offer soccer leagues for two age divisions: 29 and under, and 30 and over. You should consider offering other age divisions as well because you are in the unique position to create a product for a new consumer. That is, you could create a 40-and-over division. All of your 30-and-over players will turn 40 one day. They will probably want to continue to play soccer, but they might not want to continue to play against younger players.

The sport marketer must constantly study and analyze existing consumers and the potential for new consumers. This will afford the sport marketer the knowledge to develop new products, change existing products, set new goals, and make other strategic decisions for the company.

THE COMPETITOR

Studying the competitor involves studying closely related competitors and the particular industry of the business (see Figure 3.6). That is, although it is imperative that you constantly study closely related competitors, it is just as important that you study and understand what is happening in your industry. This is called *competitor analysis,* and it also involves *industry analysis.* For example, let's say that your company is a sport marketing research business. It is important for you to study sport marketing research companies that sell the same products. At the same time, it is important for you to study what is happening in the sport marketing research company industry to help you make informed decisions.

The information about consumers must be analyzed along with information about competitors. As stated earlier, every business operates in a variety of environments and not in a vacuum. What other businesses are doing will affect your business. The sport marketer must continuously study and analyze the competition to gain an understanding of what competitors are doing, what they are capable of doing, and how these activities might impact upon your business. With this information the marketer will be able to change existing strategies, if needed, and formulate new strategies.

THE COMPANY

The study of your own company is vital to success. One example of a method of company study is a SWOT analysis. SWOT is an acronym for Strengths, Weaknesses, Opportunities, and Threats. Other criteria that should be considered are mission and objectives, financial strength, production, product management, pricing objectives and strategies, distribution strategies, and promotion strategies (see Figure 3.7). Further, all of these factors can be compared to competitors.

The information is useful is informing most decisions concerning almost every move the company is considering making. For example, you wouldn't plan to buy another company unless you had a strong financial position, could absorb the other company under current company structure, and could take over the operation of the other company. In another example, your company might be considering entering a market with a product new to the company. A complete analysis of the barriers to entry, competitors, and whether or not your company can afford such a move is vital to this decision.

THE CLIMATE

An important responsibility of the sport business management team is to analyze the climate (see Figure 3.8). *Climate*, also referred to as environment or atmosphere, refers to the current situational factors in a society that can affect the sport business. These include economic, social and cultural, political, ethical, trends, technological, community, education, corporate, and legal aspects of society. With an analysis of each of these in specific relation to its effects on the sport business, the sport marketer must determine how each can influence the company (Gauws, 1997). For example, today there is heightened sensitivity toward civil rights and human-

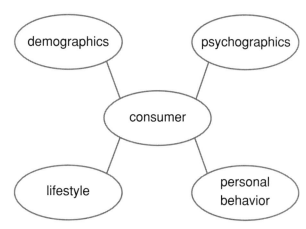

Figure 3.5
The consumer and its factors that affect sport marketing strategies.

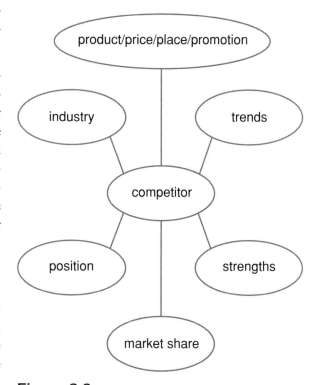

Figure 3.6
The competitor and its factors that affect sport marketing strategies.

Figure 3.7
The company and its factors that affect sport marketing strategies.

ity and thus not offending groups of people. Therefore, titles, names, and logos of some sport businesses have been challenged in relation to their offensiveness to groups. For instance, some sports team's logos that were considered to be offensive and degrading to particular groups of people have been changed.

The economic climate. The state of the economy could impact the sport company. The sport marketer must analyze the current economic situation and determine its effect on the company. There may be opportunities for success and, on the other hand, the possibility for financial disaster for the company. For example, how did the massive hurricane Katrina affect sports in New Orleans? What was the financial impact for professional sports, parks and recreation, or the fitness industry? How will the area rebuild its sport business industry?

The social and cultural climate. Cultural and social traditions and attitudes may affect your company. The sport marketer must grasp the social and cultural structures within which the company exists as well as those that exist within the company and analyze the effects on the company and the effects of the company on society. Some examples include (a) public pressure on private golf clubs that have only white members to allow others, and (b) sport organizations such as professional fishing groups that do not allow women. Present and future social issues may affect your company.

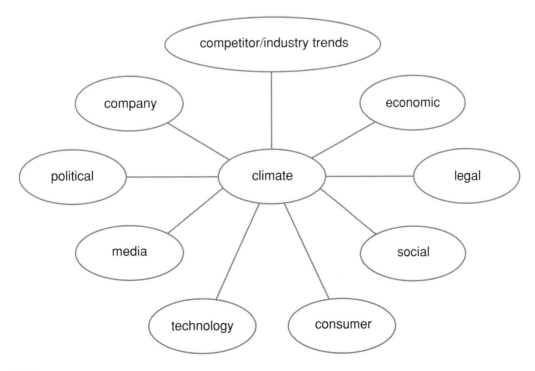

Figure 3.8
The climate and its factors that affect sport marketing strategies.

The political climate. This consists of individuals and organizations that strive to establish tolerance or intolerance within the public sphere for specific business practices. For example, those private golf clubs that do not allow women to reserve tee times on Saturday mornings are under pressure to change that practice. In another example, collegiate athletic programs are under pressure to change many aspects concerning women in athletics such as the number of opportunities to participate, which directly affects the number of sports offered, the number of scholarships offered, and the number of coaching and other staff positions directly involved with the women's athletic program.

The legal climate. "When all else fails, sue." This seems to be the most popular way of handling issues today. However, it has resulted in a great variety of local, state, and federal legislation to protect the consumer. It is important that the sport business knows and understands laws, how they apply to specific products or segments of the sport industry, and how legislation may be used to reveal opportunities and threats for the sport business.

The ethical climate. Society, culture, and business develop certain ethical mores that influence life and business. The ethical climate in the United States was studied intensely during President Clinton's impeachment investigation. People and businesses questioned and discussed their ethical philosophies. The current ethical guidelines will influence the sport business. The marketer needs to know how this is occurring in order to develop strategies.

Trends. Trends can affect the sport business in many ways. We cannot determine if a trend is simply a trend and will be short-lived, or if a trend will become the next commonplace and institutionalized phenomenon. For an example of the influence a trend can have on an industry, just remember that aerobics was once considered a passing trend.

The technological climate. Technology has tremendous effects on the sport business world in many ways. The rise of electronic commerce has reshaped business and marketing. Advances in materials for facility construction, equipment design, and even sports clothing have significant influences on the sport business industry. The sport marketing specialist must study these advances, determine how best to utilize them to maximize success, and capitalize on the competitive advantages they can offer.

The educational climate. The education of sport marketing professionals influences the business world. Imagine a world in which higher education, or any education for that matter, did not exist. It would be stagnant. Education is vital to the sport business industry. Because every segment of the industry constantly grows more complex, education is necessary to prepare individuals for those challenges. The sport business industry should work with sport management education to ensure professors are teaching future industry workers exactly what they need to know to be successful on the job.

Educators in sport management have sport management curriculum standards that were designed based on the minimum knowledge every sport management

Taking advantage of trends can be beneficial to sport businesses, especially if the trend becomes commonplace and exists long-term.

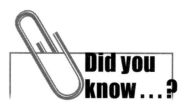

Did you know...?

2004 most marketable MLB players *(Sports-Business Journal)*:

1. Derek Jeter
2. Alex Rodriguez
3. Curt Schilling
4. Roger Clemens
5. Albet Pujols
6. Ichiro Suzuki

student should have to go into any career in the industry. The sport management educator should make every effort to design curriculum modeled on the standards and to attempt to achieve program approval.

Sport management education is proliferating. Every year there is an increase in the number of colleges and universities starting programs in sport management. Unfortunately, most programs have only one or two faculty members, and many times, these faculty members are expected to teach outside of sport management while managing the sport management program. There is a critical need for sport management faculty in general, candidates from doctoral programs designed to appropriately prepare them exclusively for sport management education, and those who are working exclusively in sport management. Moreover, there is a critical need for sport businesses to get involved with sport management education and support the efforts of sport management faculty. Indeed, it will be the sport business that benefits. One day, there just might be colleges or schools of sport business, just as there are colleges of education or business. There will be full departments based on the curriculum content areas such as sport marketing, sport finance, and sport law. The halls will be lined with nicely framed plaques showing sport businesses that have endowed faculty positions, research centers, and department chairs.

The community climate. The local community within which the sport company resides will influence the company. Each area has different climates in relation to economic, legal, environmental, and cultural issues, for example. The sport business in that community must understand the community climate and how it will influence the business. All of these can have influences on the sport business. With that knowledge, the company can make educated decisions regarding its business in the community. For example, one person wanted to start a company with a driving range and lights for nighttime practice. However, people in the residential area that surrounded the new driving range complained that the huge lights would detract from their property values and quality of life. The future driving-range owner ignored the residents and installed the range and the lights. This led the residents to file a formal complaint with the city. The city investigated and sided with the residents. The driving-range owner was only allowed to use the lights one night a week, every other week. The owner learned a hard and expensive lesson. The lights cost several hundred thousand dollars to purchase and install, and it will be many years before the owner will recoup the costs. In addition, the local newspaper ran several stories about the disagreement, and the owner appeared to be insensitive to the needs and desires of the residents, resulting in negative publicity for the company.

The corporate climate. Each company develops what is called its "corporate climate" and is influenced by a regional or national corporate climate. This involves both trendy corporate factors and those that take on a long-time personality. Typically, top administration establishes both the spoken and unspoken rules or limitations and philosophy that govern the way a company conducts business and how it treats its employees. This makes employees believe they must follow the rules in order to stay with the company. Moreover, it creates an atmosphere for business in which an entire industry will operate. For example, it has become corporate practice for large companies to set up manufacturing plants in countries outside the United States because wages are extremely low compared to wages in the United States. This practice has backfired in that Americans have criticized those companies for exporting American jobs and for supporting poor working conditions in poverty-stricken countries. In certain situations, the consequences of this can be boycotting of the company's products, negative press, and a tarnished reputation. These consequences can sometimes be devastating to the company.

In another example, sexual harassment is no longer tolerated as a part of a corporate climate, at least by law. This is not to say that sexual harassment does not continue to take place—it does. However, the issue has been so well addressed that many corporations have stiff penalties for any employee who is found to be sexually harassing another employee.

> Sport businesses must be aware of the climate in which they operate. For example, the corporate practice of establishing plants in foreign countries to take advantage of the relatively low wages has faced heavy criticism by Americans who object to exporting American jobs and to condoning poor and inhumane working conditions in underdeveloped countries. Business practices should not be undertaken without considering their potential effects on other aspects of the business.

The sport business must become aware of corporate climates, how they affect their company, and how the company can make corrections or utilize them to company advantage.

In summary, the sport marketer needs to study and understand the many climates in which the company works and how each affects the company. This knowledge will guide the sport marketer in developing marketing decisions and strategies.

Segmenting, Targeting, and Positioning

Segmenting, targeting, and positioning are essential for every sport business. Without these, the sport business puts itself in serious jeopardy of failing. Segmenting, targeting and positioning enable the sport business to develop strategies appropriate to different sets of consumers. *Segmenting*, also called *segmentation*, is differentiating groups of consumers based on unique characteristics. Through segmentation, the company identifies and understands the common characteristics of the consumers in that segment and can determine how to address their unique demands. *Targeting*, also called *target marketing*, is the selection of consumer segments (also called target markets) for which selective marketing-mix strategies are developed. *Positioning* is the way a company uses its marketing mix to influence the consumer's perception of a product. Such moves may influence what the consumer thinks about the product's quality, value, status, convenience, and many other factors.

The process of segmentation varies. Segmenting strategies can include the division of consumers by, for example, buyer identification, salespeople, purchase location, time of purchase, purchase quantity, product design, product bundling, product tie-ins, and pricing. Other strategies include those that identify consumer segments by sets of demographics, psychographics, and lifestyle. Typically, consumer segments are labeled for identification and definition. Some examples of labeled segments with which you might be familiar include the baby boomers, the senior market, the Generation X market, and the women's market. Some industry segments of the sport industry identify consumer segments according to loyalty. Some examples of these are the hard-core fan, soccer hooligans, and the occasional fan. Some labeled consumer segments in the participant sports segment of the industry include, for example, the thrill-seeker, the adventurer, the competitor, the weekend warrior, the elite athlete, and the recreational participant

Segmentation is used in identifying and understanding the different business segments in the sport industry. These are called *industry segments*. Industry segmentation is used to better identify, define, and understand the common characteristics of those businesses within that industry segment and to help with competitor analysis and competitive advantage strategies. The sport industry can be segmented in several different ways. One example is segmenting the industry by type of business. One industry segmentation study shows the industry segmented into three segments: sport performance, sport production, and sport promotion (Pitts, Fielding, and Miller, 1994). See Figure 1.1 in chapter one. In this model, all sport businesses that are in the business of marketing, promotions, merchandising, and the media are categorized into the sport promotion industry segment. You and your sport business would study this segment, analyzing its strengths and weaknesses, and develop competitive strategies. A sport business must identify its industry segment in order to formulate marketing objectives and long-term company goals. This knowledge allows it to make better decisions about product, price, place, and promotion and to determine positioning strategies.

Target market decisions. Segmentation is used to identify categories, or markets, of consumers and competitors. There can be many segments. The marketer must direct the company in deciding which segments the company is capable of serving. The segments chosen become the company's target markets. A target market is a segment of consumers who are homogeneous and who have purchasing power and the willingness to buy. Target markets should be the basis for all marketing strategies. It is the target market for which a product is produced and offered, a specific price is determined, where to offer the product is selected, and promotion strategies are formulated. Here are a few examples of target marketing:

1. The Women's Basketball Hall of Fame opened in the spring of 1999 ("The Herstory of Basketball," 1999). The target market is the large and growing women's basketball market. The Hall of Fame is based in Knoxville, Tennessee, the home of the hugely successful and popular University of Tennessee women's basketball team and Coach Pat Summitt. Speaking to the market, the advertisement for the hall of fame uses the slogan "Honor the Past. Celebrate the Present. Promote the Future."

2. Targeting Native American Indian people, SNOW-RIDERS.ORG is a website developed to encourage the development of a Native American Olympic Ski & Snowboard Team for the 2010 Vancouver Winter Olympic and Paralympic Games.

3. In 1998, the *SportsBusiness Journal* launched its first issue. Targeting sport business industry management people and sport management educators, the *SportsBusiness Journal* joins the sports industry publications industry segment with an emphasis on trade and business.

4. Targeting the growing NASCAR fan popularity, there are six different fantasy games that a fan can join and play. They are: the Reese's Racing 29 "It's All About

the Cup," Fantasy Cap Challenge, Superstar Fantasy Cap Challenge, Streak to the Finish, Reality Cup Racing, and Nextel Ultimate Fantasy League.

5. The Federation of Gay Games' primary target market is the lesbian and gay sports market around the world. The product is sports participation. The Gay Games is held every four years and are modeled after the Olympic Games with one significant exception: a Gay Games participant does not have to qualify in that individual's sport. Typically, the number of participants is around 15,000, making the Gay Games one of the largest sports events in the world.

6. Targeting the Hispanic population, several professional sports leagues, such as the NFL, WNBA, and MLB, have begun specific marketing initiatives. In addition, sports television programmers have developed channels in Spanish, such as, FOX Sports en Espanol.

In these examples the products were planned and produced specifically for a particular group of consumers—a target market. It is the target market that informs decisions concerning the marketing process, especially the marketing mix.

Sport Marketing Mix Strategies

The *marketing mix* is the strategic combination of the product, price, place, and promotion elements (see Figure 3.9). These elements are typically called the *four Ps of marketing*. Decisions and strategies for each are important for the marketer. Information for making educated decisions involving the four Ps comes from your marketing research involving primarily the four Cs—consumer, competitor, company, and climate. A critical decision and one of the greatest challenges for the sport business is how to strategically combine the four Ps to best satisfy the consumer, meet company objectives, enhance market position, and enhance competitive advantages.

Market position, also called *positioning*, refers to the way a company uses its marketing mix to influence the consumer's perception of a product. Such moves may influence what the consumer thinks about the product's quality and what the consumer is getting for the money, features not found on another similar product, status, convenience, and many other factors.

Figure 3.9
The Marketing Mix: The Four P's.

PRODUCT

The centerpiece of a marketing mix is the product. The product should be understood as a concept and not simply as a singular item. A sport product is any good, service, person, place, or idea with tangible or intangible attributes that satisfy consumer sport-, fitness-, or recreation-related needs or desires. The consumer is looking for functions and benefits. The product is the satisfaction agent for those. The product is something that will satisfy something that the consumer needs or wants. Price, place, and promotion strategies are designed specifically for the product in order to increase the probability that the product will sell.

The sport company must constantly study the consumer in order to discover what the consumer wants or needs. The result could mean developing a new product or changing an existing product in some way. The sport business must use information concerning the competition in making these decisions. For example, if the mechanic for the sailing club discovers that the sailing club members are not buying sailboat hardware at the club's shop because they cannot get what they need, the prices are higher than at other stores, and the quality is not as good, the mechanic should tell the marketer.

The marketer may decide to survey the members to get more information. If the research supports what the mechanic reported, the marketer must determine if action is needed. In this case, the marketer should consider further research to determine what hardware the members need, prices other stores are offering, and if higher quality products are available and can be sold at a specific price level.

The sport marketer will make many critical decisions concerning the sport company's products. One such decision involves the number and types of products to offer. This is called *product mix*, the complete set of all products that the sport company offers.

> The sport business must study the consumer and the competition in order to move its product into line with current trends, wants, and needs.

A sport company will determine what is, or will be, the right combination of products for the company. Product management involves tracking the sales of each product to determine if sales are increasing, maintaining, or decreasing. An analysis will provide the sport marketer with knowledge to make adjustments to specific products or to terminate a product.

The decisions concerning the company's products are important for the company. The product is the company. Any changes, additions, or deletions will have specific effects on the company. It is the sport marketer's job to try to forecast the effects and initiate only those changes that could have positive results for the company and the consumer.

PRICE

Price is the exchange of something for something—that is, one item of value for another item of value. The price of something can have a tremendous effect on a consumer. The consumer's decision to buy something can be affected by many factors. Some of those factors include what the consumer can afford to pay, if what the consumer gets for the money is of value, if the consumer thinks she or he is getting "a good deal," friends' attitudes, family influences, how the product compares to another similar product in terms of features and other factors, and the product's warranty and extended services.

Setting the price for a product is a very important decision for the sport marketer because price affects the product's success, status quo for the product, and the consumer's perception toward the product. The decision should be based on many factors such as knowledge of the consumer and what the consumer will pay, cost to the company to produce and offer the product, profit-making strategies of the company, the competition's prices, and supply and demand within the product market. Although chapter nine offers details regarding price and pricing strategies, here is one example of how setting prices works.

In Center City, USA, there exists one indoor soccer complex, Soccer City, Inc. The city's population is 600,000, and soccer leagues, both recreational and in the schools, are full and growing. Soccer City opened five years ago, and its facility includes one indoor soccer court enclosed by a giant net, a concession bar, and a tiny soccer equipment and apparel store (rented space to a local soccer store). Soccer City enjoys a monopoly on indoor soccer. As the popularity of soccer has grown and proliferated in the city, so has indoor soccer. It offers a place to play soccer during the winter months, which are the off-season in all outdoor soccer venues. The demand is high. All leagues offered fill quickly even though the price has been increased. The adult league fees are $400 for an 8-week session of one game per week. The high school and youth fees are even higher. The fees for these teams are per person. The high school players will pay $75 per person for an eight-week session of one game a week. Although most of the players complain of the high fees, the leagues are always full.

However, within the year, a new indoor soccer facility will open, Pele's Palace. The CEO of Pele's Palace has a choice to make concerning prices. Pele's Palace could charge lower fees compared to Soccer City and probably win quite a few of Soccer City's customers. A second choice is this: Pele's Palace could charge the same fees as Soccer City because it has been established that those prices are what consumers will pay for indoor soccer.

Which would you do? Which is better for the company? Which is best for the consumer? Are there any other pricing strategies you could consider? How much does the product (indoor soccer) cost the company to produce and how will this affect your pricing decisions?

As you can see from the example above, pricing a product is not a simple matter. It involves many factors and critical analysis of those factors before determining marketing mix strategies.

PLACE

Place is where and how a company gets a product from its production or origination point to a place where the targeted consumer can have access to it. Remember that sport industry products include people, places, goods, services, and ideas. Goods that are typically manufactured in a factory must be transported from the factory to the market. Some products such as services must be delivered to the marketplace to the consumer in a different way. Sports activities are very different because a sports event does not exist until a person manufactures it—that is, basketball is an intangible and doesn't exist until someone plays basketball. It is a product like a play in a theater or a live concert by a current famous musician that is manufactured and consumed simultaneously.

In a sports event, the consumer is the participant. The consumer has paid for the product, softball, for example, but does not take possession of it until the consumer actually creates it, or plays softball. In this example, the consumer will probably have to go to a softball field on a given day at a given time to get what he or she purchased. Getting this type of product to the consumer is different from transporting a good from a factory to the marketplace and requires the sport marketer to make specific decisions.

Place, or distribution as it is also called, requires knowledge of type of product, how best to get that product to the consumer, or how to get the consumer to the product, efficient and effective distribution channels, packaging, and other factors. Analysis will lead to better decisions. Chapter Six details the marketing mix variable place.

PROMOTION

Promotion is what the general public thinks is marketing. That is because the promotions are what the public sees. More specifically, promotions are especially designed to get a person's attention. Advertising, one category of promotion, includes TV commercials, radio commercials and announcements, advertisements in magazines, in books, in movie theaters, in video movie rentals, on billboards on every highway, on the sides of buses, trucks and cars, signs on tops and sides of buildings, signs on athletic fields, stadia, arenas, and uniforms. In other words, it is everywhere. People are surrounded by advertising.

> A marketer's message should grab people's attention, educate or convey a message, and entice people to purchase.

Sport businesses lure people to sporting events by incorporating special promotional events, sometimes called promos. Consider these examples: a Leanne Rimes concert the day before a NASCAR race event; a gift such as a coffee mug for the first 2,000 people through the gates; a prize such as a 45-inch television given away at the halftime break at the local college women's basketball game; and the appearance of a sport superstar who will sign autographs after the game. These are just a few of the many promotional methods that sport marketing people use to get the attention of the consumer.

It is no wonder then that the general public thinks that marketing is promotion and promotion is advertising. Promotion, however, involves more than creating advertisements and inventing special events. As you will see in the chapters on promotion and promotional methods and strategies, promotion is multifaceted.

Promotion is the process of promoting. Promoting means raising awareness. Therefore, a simple definition of promotion is: the process of making people aware of something. The process may involve a variety of methods for gaining the attention of potential consumers in order to tell them something and/or to educate them about something. In addition, once the marketer has the consumer's attention, the marketer must keep it long enough to get a message across. Usually the message contains information about a product or a business. The

Promotional methods may include

- direct-mail advertising
- radio and television advertising
- local newspaper or nationally circulated magazine advertising
- billboards advertising
- special limited-time sales
- special financing
- special customer services
- the use of specific colors on a product or its package
- the use of a concert in conjunction with a sporting event
- offering a variety of product packages at various prices
- product giveaways during an event

Companies often turn to well-known athletes to assist in the promotion of their products.

Courtesy of Gary Lake/WVSports.com

marketer's purpose for promotion is to encourage the person to purchase the product. Therefore, the message must be developed in such a way that it serves three functions: First, it gets the attention of people; second, it gets across a message or educates the people; and third, it tempts the people to purchase the product. The promotion may be any one or more of a variety of promotional methods and strategies. The sport marketer may choose any one or a combination of promotional methods and strategies. The promotional message and strategies are put together to speak to a specific kind of person—a market segment. The sport marketer uses research data about the consumer and the competition to create strategies and the promotional message.

Marketing Management Strategies: Implementation, Management, and Evaluation

The sport business must have a system for managing the process of sport marketing. This system includes the implementation, management, and evaluation of all sport marketing components. Management is a multidimensional step that involves setting objectives for the sport marketing strategy, developing the sport marketing plan, selecting and managing sport marketing personnel, establishing a financial plan, establishing and managing an organizational structure, establishing and overseeing deadlines and scheduling, acting as the liaison between sport marketing personnel and top management, and coordinating all sport marketing functions.

The development of the sport marketing plan is an important task. Strategic planning functions to strengthen relationships between sport marketing and other management functional areas in the company. The sport marketing plan is the written, established plan of action for the company or for an element (or product) of the company. It drives the company.

The plan contains the marketing objectives, identified target markets, financial strategies, and details of the marketing mix strategies. The marketing plan can be written for a single sport product, a group of products, a new promotional strategy, or the entire sport company.

The sport marketing management model, illustrated in Figure 3.3, is a graphic representation of most of the components of a marketing plan and should be used as a guide in the development of a plan.

The sport marketing plan should not be taken lightly. It requires time, research, and critical analysis. It should be the culmination of this effort during which every possible task, angle, financial analysis, and every function of the company and the product have been thoroughly studied and analyzed. The final plan should reflect informed decision making and strategy formulation.

Implementation involves establishing a system for planning and managing the implementation of the sport company's marketing strategies. Evaluation involves establishing a system for analyzing marketing strategies to determine if the strategies are accomplishing the established objectives.

Chapter Summary

In this chapter we presented the concept of sport marketing theory, defined sport marketing, presented the sport marketing management model, and briefly discussed the components of the model. Subsequent chapters will provide specific details, methods, and strategies of each component. We encourage you to refer to the sport marketing management model (Figure 3.3) throughout your study and practice of sport marketing. It will remind you of the total picture of marketing and where each component fits.

Theory is built from a foundation of research and knowledge. Sport marketing theory is in the process of being developed as it is a new field of study when compared to many other fields of study. To study the developing theory of sport marketing, one must study the foundation from which it is being built. The foundation of sport marketing comes from several fields of study.

Sport marketing is the process of designing and implementing activities for producing, pricing, promoting, and distributing a sport product to satisfy the needs or desires of consumers and to achieve the company's objectives. Sport marketing is one of many management functions. It has become, however, one of the most important functions because the sport industry continues to grow at a phenomenal rate. The growth means competition and the sport industry is a highly competitive industry.

The sport marketing management model illustrates the elements of sport marketing, the succession of elements and functions, the process of managing, and the interdependency of the elements. The model should be used as a guide for the sport management or sport marketing professional.

QUESTIONS FOR STUDY

1. What is theory?
2. What is marketing?
3. What is sport marketing?
4. What is sport marketing theory? What fields of study serve as the foundation of sport marketing fundamentals and theory? What are some of the areas of research in sport marketing?
5. What is the sport marketing management model? What are the components of the model? Define and describe each one.
6. What are the research journals for the field of sport marketing?
7. What are the different climates within which a sport business exists? Describe each one and how it affects the business.

LEARNING ACTIVITIES

1. (a) Select a list of people who work in the sport industry in different types of sport businesses across the United States. Interview them about sport marketing at their company. Ask them what their theory of sport marketing is. (b) Now do the same with college professors of sport marketing. Interview them about teaching sport marketing. Ask them what their theory of sport marketing is. (c) Compare and analyze your results. Give a presentation in class.
2. Go to the university library and check out textbooks in marketing. Look for the definitions, fundamentals, and theory of marketing. Compare these to the definition, fundamentals, and theory of sport marketing in this book. Analyze your results. Give a presentation in class.
3. Take this book to some people who work in the industry. Ask them to look at the sport marketing management model and to tell you if it matches the marketing activities they perform (or someone performs) in the company. Compile their answers. Give a presentation in class.

Chapter Four

SPORT MARKETING RESEARCH

The Importance of Sport Marketing Research

As you learned in the previous chapter, knowledge is the foundation of all sport marketing and sport business activity. All decisions in a company should be made based on the information and knowledge gained from research. Good information that is timely, accurate, interactive, flexible, and accessible is the lifeblood of the sport company. Among many other reasons, good research can help maximize a company's sales, identify future product and market opportunities, identify potential threats to the company, provide information for understanding consumers, help in the advertising development process, provide consumer feedback on product improvements, and assist in determining prices.

Marketing research is a vital element of marketing. Marketers attempt to know what the consumer wants and what that consumer will exchange for it. The significantly primary method for determining what the consumer wants is to communicate with the consumer or study the consumer's needs, wants, and desires in other ways. With this information, a sport business professional can make decisions that will greatly boost the success of that business.

Okay, so you are thinking: Do I have to constantly conduct research to acquire all this information that I need to make decisions? The answer is yes, but it is not a simple yes. That is, you can conduct the research yourself, or you can acquire research that someone else has worked to collect. Some of this research is free, and some you will have to purchase. The important thing to remember is that making smart decisions comes from having information to guide you to a decision or strategy that will most likely be successful.

Additionally, more successful businesses subscribe to the philosophy of the *marketing concept*. A prominent marketing professor, Philip Kotler, has defined the marketing concept as follows:

"The **marketing concept** is a business philosophy that holds that the key to achieving organizational goals that consist of the company being more effective than competitors in creating, delivering, and communicating customer value to its chosen target markets."

This is also helpful in understanding the typical terms of "customer oriented" and "market driven." The key point is that a successful sport business marketer takes the time to find out what the customer wants and provides it. More than just the right product, however, the marketer can determine the right price, the right place (distribution points), and the right promotional strategies. This provides the sport business with the right *marketing mix strategy*.

Accomplishing getting customer information requires research. Moreover, this research must be *good* research. That is, the research must be as accurate as possible.

Good research helps answer key questions such as the following:

- Who are our competitors? Where are they? What is their market share? How do their products and prices compare to ours?

- Who are our consumers? Are they changing? How are they changing?

- What are the emerging consumer markets that our company could begin to target?

- Can our company get into e-commerce, create a Web-based store, and sell our logo merchandise through the website?

- What new product can our company produce for a new consumer market?

- What do consumers like and dislike about our new sports facility?

- How can we upgrade our manufacturing process without having to add too much to the price of our product?

- Which sport businesses could benefit from our sport marketing research services?

- Do spectators at a major sporting event recognize that our company spent over $12 million to be a major sponsor for this event? Will they be more likely to buy our product because of our sponsorship?

- How does our company compare to others regarding employee benefits?

- Why are some consumers protesting our new advertising campaign? What do we need to do now?

- What is the hottest, newest sport? Can our company be involved in some way?

- If the national weather offices are predicting a warm winter, how can our snow ski resort lessen the potential financial damages and make up potentially low profits?

- What are the largest markets today, and how will they change in 10 years? How can our company plan for the change?

- What is the true economic impact of our marathon and 10K?

- How do our consumers perceive our new promotional gimmicks?

At first glance, the questions seem like common, simple questions. But, try this: start with the first question and develop a thorough answer. How would you answer this question? What kind of information do you need? Does this informa-

Did you know...?

Ad spending by most money spent on sports

- Anheuser-Busch
- Chevrolet
- Cingular
- Ford
- Coca-Cola

Anheuser-Busch spent 293 million on advertising on sports alone in 2004.

12 compaines spent over 100 million on advertising on sports in 2004.

(SportsBusiness Journal)

tion already exist? If so, where can you get this information? Will the information be accurate? Will it be current? Is it specific to your company, your product, and your part of the industry?

If it doesn't already exist, how can you collect the information you need? Do you need to conduct a study? What kind of study? What kind of measurement instrument do you need? Does an instrument already exist, or do you need to develop one? Will the instrument collect the right kind of information? Will it be accurate? Will the information be useful when it is collected, or will you need to manipulate it somehow? How do you analyze the information you collected? Will your analysis be accurate for your needs?

How will you be able to use the information for the company? Won't you need to now study the company with the new information and determine how it will work within the company?

After doing this little exercise, you can see how what appears to be a simple question must be treated with a professional, organized, and calculated approach. That professional approach is research.

In this chapter you will learn what sport marketing research is, how sport marketing research is conducted, and how it is used in the analysis and development of marketing decisions and strategies in the sport industry. In chapter five you will learn how sport marketing research is the basis for segmentation, target marketing, and positioning, and in chapter five you will learn how to manage all of this information gathered through research.

Sport Marketing Research

Sport marketing research is the process of planning, collecting, and analyzing data (a) to gain relevant information or solve a problem to enhance decisions in the sport business exchange process and (b) to enhance the body of knowledge in sport marketing as a field of study.

In the first instance—to gain information or solve a problem—research is a fundamental tool for the sport company to obtain information or solve a problem. Information is necessary for formulating decisions concerning the sport company's financial aspects, product development, pricing strategies, distribution strategies, promotional strategies, and all other functions and operations within the company. This information comes from research.

> **Sport Marketing Research:**
>
> is the process of planning, collecting, and analyzing data to (1) gain relevant information needed or solves a problem to inform decision in the sport business; and, (2) to enhance the body of knowledge in sport marketing as a field of study.

In the second instance—to enhance the body of knowledge in sport marketing—research is conducted to add to and further the level of knowledge about a topic in sport marketing. This type of research is typically developed based on a conceptual framework. That is, it should be based on theory. This textbook, for instance, is based on the theories of marketing as they apply to the sport industry.

Research adds to the body of knowledge that tests theories and forwards the body of knowledge. Theories lead to the development or improvement of practice. Research can be applied. Both theoretical and applied research can help answer questions, solve problems, test theories, or lead to new ideas for theories or practices. In the end, theory leads to practice, and practice leads to theory. For instance, the information and theories in this book are what you, the student, will need to know in order to practice sport marketing on your job—hence the bridge between theory and practice.

Sport marketing research can range from a very simple task to a complex and time consuming job. Figure 4.1 illustrates the sport marketing research continuum. The type of research conducted is based on what information is needed. For instance, if the sport marketer of an indoor soccer club needs to know the addresses of current consumers in order to send direct-mail promotional flyers, the information may be gathered easily from membership application forms. If the publisher of a wakeboarding sports magazine wants to know what's happening in the sport, the company can read and study information published in industry trade publications. At the other end of the continuum, if the management of the LPGA (Ladies Professional Golf Association) needs to know how many people are attending each event, who they are, and why they attend, a study will need to be designed and conducted over a long period of time in order to collect the appropriate data.

Research conducted by sport management academicians and scholars can also range from rather simple methods to more formal and complex methods. The appendix at the end of this book contains examples of research conducted by academicians that enhances the body of knowledge in sport marketing and can be used by the sport business executive. For instance, many academicians—professors—have worked as consultants to sport businesses and conducted research for them. For example, each author of this textbook has served as marketing and marketing research consultants to sport industry for over 20 years—see Table 4.1. This research is used by the sport business for industry purposes. For example, Carl Atkins, the General Manager of the Georgia Dome in Atlanta, Georgia, and Khalil Johnson, COO of the Dome and Georgia World Congress Center, use the market research of Dr. Brenda Pitts and sport marketing students to make informed decisions about sports events at the Dome. Dr. Pitts works with Carol Lucas, the Marketing Research Manager of the Georgia Dome and Georgia World Congress Center, in planning, development, and performance of the studies. Some decisions

SIMPLE   **COMPLEX**

Examples:

Simple—Reading a newspaper, magazine, or sport management journal.

Results: learn about a new sport business opening; a new technology being used in sporting equipment; a study on the demographics of fans of the LPGA.

Complex—The design and conduct of a study that involves, for example, (a) a new metal for a new softball bat, (b) a longitudinal study of children with disabilities in sports activities to determine their sports activity choices in adulthood, or (c) a study of arena advertising to determine its effects on spectators over a long period of time.

Figure 4.1
Sport Marketing Research Continuum.

Table 4.1

Examples of Sport Market Research by Dr. Brenda Pitts (coauthor of this textbook).

- Visitor Spending and Economic Impact of the 2006 NCAA Men's Division I Basketball Regionals
- Factors that Affect Attendance: A Consumer Behavior Study of a SuperCross Event
- Visitor Spending and Economic Impact of the 2005 Professional Bull Riders, Inc. Event
- Sponsorship Recognition: Gay Games VI, Sydney, Australia, 2002

Table 4.2
Examples of Academic Research Journals.

Sport Business

Sport Marketing Quarterly
European Sport Management Quarterly
Sport Management Review
Journal of Sport Management
International Journal of Sport Management
Sport Management and Other Related
    Topics Journal
Journal of Sport and Tourism

Sport Studies

Journal of Sport Behavior
Journal of Sport History
Journal of Sport and Social Issues
International Sport Journal
Women in Sport and Physical Activity
    Journal
Sociology of Sport Journal

Business Administration

Journal of Marketing
Journal of Advertising
Journal of Vacation Marketing
Academy of Management Journal
e-Review of Tourism Research
Journal of Website Promotion
Journal of Product and Brand Management

have included changing seating charts, changing pricing structures, enhancing customer service, and enhancing client services.

Some research is published in journals such as those presented in Table 4.2 and in the appendix to this book. Some research is presented at academic conferences such as the annual conference of the Sport Marketing Association (SMA), the Sport Management Association of Australia and New Zealand (SMAANZ), the Sport Management Council of the National Association for Sport and Physical Education, and the European Association for Sport Management (EASM). Often, summaries (abstracts) of these research presentations are published in the conference proceedings of the association.

Purposes of Sport Marketing Research

Why do we need to do research? What are the purposes of research? Without research and analysis, decisions and strategies can be risky. When a decision is not based on real and accurate information gained from research, the sport company risks making a wrong decision. Wrong decisions can adversely affect the company. Therefore, decisions should be based on information and knowledge gained from research. Some of the purposes of sport marketing research can be found in definitions of marketing from the American Marketing Association (AMA). One definition states that "marketing research links the consumer, customer, and public to the marketer through information—information used to identify and define marketing opportunities and problems; generate, refine, and evaluate marketing actions; monitor marketing performance; and improve understanding of marketing as a process. Marketing research specifies the information required to address these issues; designs the methods for collecting information; manages and implements the data collection process; analyzes the results; and communicates the findings and their implications" ("New Marketing," 1987, p. 1). A second definition states: "is an organizational function and a set of processes for creating, communicating, and delivering value to customers and for managing customer relationships in ways that benefit the organization and its stakeholders" (http://www.marketingpower.com/mg-dictionary-view 1862.php). Using the AMA definitions, let us apply it to the sport industry and identify some of the purposes for sport marketing research.

To Form a Link between the Consumer in the Sport Industry and the Sport Company

The marketers and managers within the sport company can use the information about the consumer to get to know existing and potential consumers and what they want. The consumer receives messages from the sport company that it is trying to meet the consumer's needs. The following are examples of how this works.

1. Puma North America created sports shoes with the extreme generation in mind. For that, Puma received "the cool factor" rating from teens. The shoes are "cool" and "hip" according to alternative kids. Sales of the shoes have boosted profit an amazing 20-fold in a few years—to just over a billion dollars. By comparison, Nike sales grew less than 10 per cent and adidas increased by only 5 per cent. To continue their 'coolness,' Puma teamed with Fader Magazine, a music and culture magazine targeting the "Gen F" market,

> One way to use the increased availability of media to the consumer is to create a media package that offers a variety of ways to access the information and then cross-promote and sell all the parts.

   to support a live music tour. Puma used research on youth and teens to develop a product and promotional strategies to reach the market. The tour, called Gen F Live, involves several cities in the US. Both companies hope to cash in on the cool factor, attracting new fans—and consumers—of their products.

2. In 1970, the National Sports Center for the Disabled (NSCD) was started. It was a one-time ski lesson for children with amputations for the Children's Hospital of Denver. The NSCD has developed into one of the largest outdoor therapeutic recreation agencies in the world. From the NSCD website: "Each year, thousands of children and adults with disabilities take to the ski slopes, mountain trails and golf courses to learn more about sports—and themselves. With specially trained staff and its own adaptive equipment lab, the NSCD teaches a variety of winter and summer sports and activities to individuals with almost any physical, cognitive, emotional, or behavioral diagnosis. The mission of the National Sports Center for the Disabled (NSCD) is to provide quality outdoor sports and therapeutic recreation programs that positively impact the lives of people with physical, cognitive, emotional, or behavioral challenges." (http://www.nscd.org)

Targeting individuals of all ages with nearly any disability, the National Sports Center for the Disabled reaches a market that is growing in both numbers and in the attention it is getting from more and more industry. Numerous companies and organizations offer sporting goods as well as sports activities. Using research conducted by several organizations now about individuals with disabilities, this organization and others develop their products and strategies.

The link between the consumer and the company is the consumer's need or desire for something. That is, the company must know and understand what the consumer needs or desires in order to create products that will meet those needs and desires. To know the consumer requires research and constant monitoring. To do this research, the company must have contact with the consumer. This contact is done through formal research methods such as surveys and interviews and informal methods such as conversations and spending time together. In these ways, the company can learn about the consumer and can then make better decisions in relation to product, price, place, and promotion.

To Identify and Define Marketing Opportunities, Problems, and Threats

A *marketing opportunity* is a chance for a sport company to capitalize on a new idea or new product, move to a new location, gain a specific consumer market, take advantage of a financial management technique, or engage in other activity that will most likely prove a positive activity for the company. A *marketing problem* occurs when something is not quite right in the company. A *marketing threat* is usually more serious for the company. It means that something could have a serious adverse affect on the company. Only through research can the sport marketer discover opportunities, problems, or threats for the company. Let us consider some examples.

A Marketing Opportunity:

is a chance for a sport company to capitalize on something that will most likely be positive for the company.

A Marketing Problem:

occurs when something is not quite right.

A Marketing Threat:

occurs when something will most likely have a negative effect on the sport company.

Customized soccer. Through interviews and casual conversations, both of which are types of research, a soccer league player, Laura Reeves, discovers there is no summer soccer league for women in Louisville, Kentucky, and that there is a group who want to play in the summer. This is a marketing opportunity: Here is a group of consumers who want something that does not exist. In further interviews—more research—Reeves gathers information about what type of league the women would like. Some of the data gathered included the following information:

1. Consumers wanted a shorter-than-regulation game. A regulation game is two 45-minute halves, or $1^1/2$ hours of running. In the summer months in Louisville, the average temperature is hot, and the humidity is very high, which makes it very uncomfortable. A game that lasts around an hour with breaks would be desirable.

2. They wanted teams to consist of fewer players than regulation. Regulation requires 11 players on the field. Fewer players would allow the teams to be flexible in recruiting players and not have to worry about getting enough to show up. The summer months are used for vacations, which means that many players will be absent from games. It is easier to find 10 players who will commit to a team in the summer than for 16 to 18 players commit to a game every week.

3. They wanted the game to be fun and not as structured as the highly competitive and structured fall and spring leagues.

4. They wanted the games to be held in the evening when it is not as hot as during the day.

Using the information gathered, Reeves invented a game and started the league. The new game is played on a small field 70 yards long and 40 yards wide, whereas a regulation field is 110 yards long and 60 yards wide. The new game is a 7-on-7 game with a goalie. Hence, Reeves named the league "Seven-Up Soccer." (There are actually 8 players, but Seven-Up Soccer is a catchy name.) Laura incorporated a "you must have fun" rule to create an atmosphere of lightness and sportswomanship. To keep the price down, Reeves uses no officials. This is probably the most unusual and interesting aspect of the product: There are no officials; hence, every player can officiate. Any player can make a call when there is an infraction of a rule or a foul has occurred. This was the toughest part of the game for the players to get used to because, in a regular game, part of a team's game strategy is to figure out which violations and infractions the official will catch and to work around that. When everyone can officiate, a player cannot get away with anything. This results in a very clean and almost foul-free game.

In the first year, the league was offered on a Sunday evening. However, teams had problems with players showing up because they were gone on summer vacation. After more research, the league was offered on a Wednesday evening the following year. Wednesday was selected because it is the night most players were available from other summer activities such as softball and vacations.

Most of the rules developed were based on the summer heat factor and include unlimited substitutions at any time, including when play is taking place; and the game consists of four 12-minute quarters with 1 minute between quarters and 2 minutes at halftime. The first rule allows the player to get off the field to rest and cool down at any time during play. The second rule keeps the game short and includes breaks for rest, water, and cooling.

In the first year of the league, there were three teams. Four years later, there were ten teams, and Reeves has plans to extend the league to two women's divisions and is considering offering a coed or a men's division.

Through research, Reeves discovered a marketing opportunity. With continuous research, she changed and molded the product to meet the consumer's needs and has a successful product.

Fitness foe. Research can reveal threats. Let us consider fitness centers as an example. Today there are fitness centers everywhere. During the 1970s and 1980s when the number of fitness centers was growing rapidly, the increase was a problem and a threat to the few existing fitness centers. For example, if the Downtown Fitness Center (DFC) is the only fitness center within a 20-mile radius, the DFC feels safe, knowing that competition is at least 20 miles away. When the owner of the DFC discovers through research that three companies are making plans to open within the 20-mile radius, the owner becomes aware of a threat to the DFC. With this information, the owner is in a position to do something so that the new fitness centers will have either no effect or minimal effect on the DFC's business. Without the research effort, however, the owner of the DFC never would have known that competition was about to increase substantially.

Baseball bargains. Stacy Cavanaugh is a sales representative for a large baseball bat manufacturing company. The professional baseball leagues, which currently allow only wood bats, are considering allowing bats made of other materials. Spectator attendance has been slowly declining in the last four years, and leaders in the baseball leagues believe that bats made of other materials will result in more hits, and thus more excitement for fans, and thus increased attendance. There are currently 12 professional baseball leagues in this particular country—4 men's leagues, 4 women's leagues, and 4 minor leagues. Changing the bat-material rule could have significant impact on the bat manufacturing companies, especially those companies whose sole product is wood bats and who sell only to the professional leagues.

Stacy's company, the Acme Baseball Bat Company, manufactures bats from two materials: wood and aluminum. The wood bats are all produced on machines that

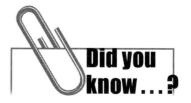

Did you know . . . ?

The National Women's Football Association (professional tackle football league) has 36 teams in two divisions. Demographics of fans include the following:

Male 48%
Female 52%
Single/Divorced 56%
Married 44%
HH Income 30K 37%
HH Income 30–40K . . . 34%
HH Income 41–100K . . . 24%
HH Income 100K 5%
College Educated 58%
Technical Degree 37%
Executives 49%
Self-Employed 28%
Lower/Middle Mgt 17%
Retired 6%
Internet Users 93%
Pet Owners 68%
Fitness Enthusiasts 96%
Camping/Fishing 56%
Extreme Sports 37%
Runners 48%

individually produce bats one at a time according to the specifications of each player who orders bats. The aluminum bats are mass produced in a factory in another country and shipped. The aluminum bats, however, are children's bats and much smaller than an adult's bat. The Acme Company started producing these bats as promotional items—autograph models of some of the professional players. Children using these bats choose according to the name. For example, a child whose favorite professional players include Kelly Powers, Mike Star, and Jay Jay Homer can use the aluminum bats named for the players and dream of becoming that player one day.

Stacy figures that it ought to be easy for the company to make the transition and stay in business if the leagues decide to allow bats of materials other than wood because the company already makes bats out of materials other than wood. So, Stacy proposes this idea to the company's top administration. Stacy is assigned to research the idea.

Stacy makes a trip to the aluminum bat factory to talk to the director and discovers that their aluminum-bat-making machines will not make bats large enough for an adult. The company would have to purchase all new machines. Stacy's research into this leads to the discovery that each new machine, along with reconfiguring the existing factory, will cost $1.2 million. There would also be additional expenses including personnel, extra space, and numerous overhead costs. Further research reveals that the company would have to have a factory with 30 of these machines in order to produce enough bats to sell to be efficient and cost-effective.

After presenting the research to the company's top administration, it is determined that the cost of start-up and production is a problem—one that will require major, long-term commitment from the company in order to effectively produce this new bat. The administration also decides that the problem warrants further research, especially because they are the only wood bat company that already produces bats of other materials. However, more research is needed regarding how many companies currently produce adult-size bats of other materials that could more quickly meet the professional players' demands and perhaps corner the market.

> Research can reveal marketing opportunities, potential threats to businesses, and the work involved in the development of a new product.

In this situation, start-up costs to enter a product market present a problem for this company. Unless further research is conducted, it is not known if a cost-effective solution might be found.

To Generate, Refine, Evaluate, and Monitor Marketing Actions

Marketing actions include such actions as determining the company's products and all of their characteristics, determining pricing strategies, developing promotional methods, and deciding on distribution. Research is needed in order to first generate and design those actions. Decisions about what product to offer and how to offer it can only be made after the research is conducted. Once those decisions and actions are in place, they should be monitored constantly in order to evaluate effectiveness and performance. The following situation illustrates one way this works.

It is no secret that the average spectator of many professional sports is being squeezed out of the prime seating areas of the sports venue. But who would have predicted that spectators would cease to be the prime target of sponsorship advertising? A growing trend in some professional sports, where sponsorship is a form of advertising, is business-to-business sponsors (Owens, 1999). That is, corporate sponsors whose products are only manufactured for and sold to other companies are targeting businesses with their advertising rather than spectators. The trend is not hard to spot. For example, which fans recognize the consumer products being touted by a chemical company such as Dupont? Only those who either work for or do business with Dupont. Dupont doesn't need the fans to recognize their product—their target is corporate. Constant research involving trends of con-

Companies that have rarely been sponsors for sporting events are now taking advantage of the ability to market to a target audience.

sumers of many professional sports reveals the changing nature: the number of corporations that purchase box seats and tickets and also purchase (rent) the pricey spaces around the sports venue for a corporate party tent is increasing.

The tent space is, of course, an extra cost and can range from a small amount to hundreds of thousands of dollars. The increasing number of corporate consumers is causing sponsors to take notice. Companies who had never been sponsors for sports events are taking advantage of the opportunity to market to a target audience. Although most sponsors are still producers of consumer products, a growing number of companies whose consumers are businesses are getting involved. For instance, in NASCAR, many sponsors are not companies whose consumers are end consumers—they are retailers. That is, businesses who do business with other businesses. A sponsor in NASCAR can spend $8 million annually to support a

race car and team. That sponsor will most likely spend another $8 million for promoting the sponsorship and using it to entertain and enhance business with clients and potential clients.

Many events now have enormous areas in which to create hospitality villages for sponsors. Although the average fan at the event may wander through the village and benefit from promotional giveaways or drawings, the village exists for the corporate sponsor executives and their business partners. The sponsors' focus is on the businesses that buy their products in huge quantities. In other words, a train shipment of sales is worth much more than an individual sale to one consumer. The retailers and wholesalers are being courted for their attention and their wallets.

Constant research and monitoring of the existing and potential consumer and their needs and desires are the only ways the sport marketing professional can discover these needs and desires and then plan to meet them. In this instance, sports event executives should study the changing needs of current sponsors in order to best serve them. This will require changes in the product offered—the sponsorship deal, sponsor's needs, and sponsors' areas—in order to meet the desires of the new market—the business-to-business sponsorship.

To Monitor Marketing Performance

Every sport business must determine if its marketing efforts are performing according to the established goals. That is, if one goal of a particular marketing effort was to increase brand awareness, how can the sport business determine if that goal was met? Of course, the answer is research. The sport marketing professional can use brand-awareness research tools to determine if consumers are aware of and recognize the company's brand.

As you will learn throughout this textbook, there are many different marketing efforts. For promotion, for instance, there are numerous promotional methods. Some are advertising in newspapers, television commercials, promotional giveaways, licensed promotional merchandise, and sponsorship promotions. All of these efforts should be monitored—studied—in order to determine if they are working and if they are meeting the objectives set for them.

It's my turn. In a study of the WNBA's marketing tag line "We Got Next!" researchers found that only a small number of fans know what the phrase actually means (Shoenfelt, Maue, and Hatcher, 1999). The researchers studied basketball spectators and a generic group of undergraduate students and found that more basketball spectators than students had watched a WNBA game and could link the tag line to the WNBA.

However, very few of both groups knew the meaning of the phrase. The phrase is one used in basketball pick-up situations where players or groups line up for their time in the game or on the court. The phrase essentially means that the speaker is the next in line. The WNBA wanted to convey to the basketball world to move over, it's time for the women to shine. The slogan also refers to the season scheduling. The NBA season is played "first," and the WNBA season is "next."

If the WNBA now knows that its consumers don't really know what the phrase means, they can make some decisions to effect a change. For instance, they could mount a campaign to attempt to educate consumers as to the meaning of the phrase, or the WNBA could decide to develop a new phrase.

To Improve Understanding of Marketing as a Process

A process can be the routine execution of a method. To understand marketing as a process, research can provide answers to questions concerning why and how the process works. For instance, the sport marketing academic journals, the *Sport Marketing Quarterly*, *International Journal of Sports Marketing and Sponsorship*, and *International Journal of Sport Management and Marketing*, provide outlets for the publication of sport marketing research conducted by people in both the academic and practitioner worlds of sport management. All of the studies and other materials published add to improving our understanding of sport marketing and its process. Table 4.2 provides a representative list of sport marketing, sport management, sport law, sport studies, and business administration journals in which sport marketing research can be found. Examples of this type of research are presented in the appendix at the end of the book. These are brief summaries of the research. You should find the source and read the full study to gain a full understanding of the research. In addition, all of the information presented in the "Sport Business Fact Book: Did You Know . . . " boxes throughout this book are examples of bits of information discovered through research.

The new knowledge and understanding gained through research leads to theory. Theory is the basis of sport marketing practice. The material in the field of sport marketing has changed and been enhanced over the last twenty years because of the research

---

Table 4.3
Sport marketing research.

Consumer classification data and sponsorship effect that were measured in the nine papers.

1. Sponsored property consumer profile
   - demographics
   - buying habits
   - image of sponsored property
   - attitude towards sponsorship
   - attitude towards sponsors
   - perception of sponsored property symbols
   - size
   - frequency of sponsored property consumption
   - perception of fit between sponsor and the sponsored property

2. Exposure
   amount of exposure
   - number of people who were exposed to the sponsor's message
   - number of seconds signage was on TV
   - number of mm of print (newspapers, magazines)

3. Effects on consumer
   on awareness
   - Unaided awareness (compared with competitors)
   - aided awareness (compared with competitors)
   - share of voice/mind—% of total mentions compared with other sponsors/non-sponsors
   - recall by viewing weight—i.e., by frequency of exposure
   - signage recall
   - high- versus low-profile brands share of voice analysis
   - awarenss of current and past sponsor
   - association of sponsor with the sport generally (i.e. soccer, rugby)
   - association of sponsor with the sponsored property (i.e., World Cup)
   - change in share of voice/mind (compared with competitors)
   - change in recall (compared with non-sponsors)
   on image/attitude towards the company
   - degree of image change (compared with non-sponsors)
   - effect on company image (compared with non-sponsors)
   - effect on product image (compared with non-sponsors)
   - general image of sponsor (compared with non-sponsors)
   - on attitudes among business decision maker (compared with non-sponsors)
   - on employee satisfaction
   on behavior
   - effect on brand preference (compared with non-sponsors)
   - rate of growth of brand preference (compared with non-sponsors)
   - on buying intentions

4. Multimedia effects
   - synergy with other communication mediums
   - relative value return of sponsorship versus advertising
   - awarenss by means of message—advertising, sponsorship, product placement, spot advertising
   - relative ability of sponsorship isolated from other communication efforts

Source: Brooks, 1998.

both in the academic field and in the industry. As new and more research is conducted, it adds to the body of knowledge helping it grow and mature. As this happens, it is the student and the practitioner in the industry who will benefit from the information. For instance, Table 4.3 presents research from nine studies on sport sponsorship. The table summarizes the type of consumer information studied and the sponsorship effects that were measured in the research. Students, practitioners, and educators can benefit from this information, which can be used, for example, in designing sponsorship studies.

To Analyze and Understand the Sport Company, Its Industry, and Its Competition

Within this should be the typical journalist's questions: who, what, when, where, why, and how. The sport marketer should seek to understand the answers to these questions concerning the sport company, its consumers, its competitors, and the climate—the 4 Cs discussed throughout this text. Examples of the many questions

Table 4.4
Questions for the sport marketer.

	CONSUMER	COMPANY	COMPETITOR	CLIMATE
WHO ...	... are our consumers? ... consumes the competitor's products? ... could become our next 1,000 consumers?	... works for us? ... is making key decisions?	... is our competitor?	... can influence the economy, law, etc.?
WHAT ...	... do our consumers like/dislike? ... are they willing to pay?	... does our company do? ... can our company do? ... is our financial status?	... does our competitor do? ... is their advertising like? ... is their financial status? ... are their prices?	... is the future of our economy? ... are the laws that affect my company?
WHEN ...	... does the consumer want this product? ... can the consumer pay? ... should we advertise?	... can our company offer a product? ... does the company need to be paid? ... should the company advertise?	... does the competitor offer its products?	... do the new laws go into effect?
WHERE ...	... are our existing consumers? ... are our potential consumers?	... is our company located?	... is the competitor located?	... will the economic setbacks hit hardest?
WHY ...	... does the consumer want a product? ... does the consumer want to pay a particular price?	... does our company offer this service? ... doesn't our company offer this service?	... does the competitor offer a particular service?	... is the economy hit hardest in this area?
HOW ...	... can the consumer use this product? ... can the consumer pay for this product?	... can our company offer a product? ... does our company track sales of its products?	... do we compare with our competitor? ... are we different? ... does our competitor offer the product?	... will the economy be in three years? ... will the new law affect my company?

the sport marketing professional should constantly ask and monitor are shown in Table 4.4. Marketing decisions and strategies should be formulated based on real information and an accurate understanding of the company, the consumer, the competition, and the climate. Again, making uneducated and uninformed decisions is risky.

Consider the information presented in Table 4.5. This chart shows the most popular sports activities participation by people in different countries. If you were in the sporting goods business and looking to get into international markets, how would you analyze this information? Try to answer the following questions by analyzing the information from the various positions:

- If you are a sporting goods retailer, how would you view this information in relation to your specific business?

- If you are a sport shoe manufacturer's sales representative, how do you think this information would affect your product and company?

- If you work for a computer company and you are head of a team to seek sports activities events for sponsorship possibilities, how would you use this information?

In another example of research from the National Sporting Goods Association (NGSA), Table 4.6 shows data concerning prices and price changes in sports footwear. If you had the perception that sports shoes prices have been increasing, would this information change your mind? With this information, consider the following question: Your company manufactures tennis, soccer, softball, basketball, and running shoes. How can you use the data presented in Table 4.6?

Right away, you can see that even a simple survey can reveal interesting and sometimes surprising information and that the information will be viewed and analyzed differently depending on the type of company that is studying the research. Each one of the different companies can use the information provided, but each needs it for different reasons. The new knowledge could affect the company. Therefore, the information must be considered in the company's planning.

Table 4.5
Top 10 Participation Sports by Country.

	Japan	USA	Tasmania/Australia	Taiwan
1st	Bowling	Soccer	Walking	Walking
2nd	Gymnastics (no equipment)	Exercise	Swimming	Jogging
3rd	Jogging, Marathons	Golf	Golf	Basketball
4th	Swimming (pool)	Softball	Aerobics/Fitness	Hiking
5th	Catchball, Baseball	Baseball	Fishing	Excursion
6th	Training	Basketball	Cycling	Mountain Climbing
7th	Cycling, Cycle sports	Walking	Tennis	
8th	Fishing	Snowboarding	Running	
9th	Table Tennis	In-line Skating	Netball	
10th	Badminton	Roller Hockey	Cricket	

Table 4.6
Sports and Athletic Footwear/Shoes Average Prices and Changes.

Shoe Type	Years: 2004	2005	+%	2000	+% to 2005
Aerobic Shoes	42.35	41.54	2.0%	41.25	2.7%
Baseball/Softball	40.53	39.59	2.4%	40.65	-0.3%
Basketball	52.58	53.11	-1%	57.16	-8%
Boat/Deck	29.96	30.25	-0.9%	31.03	-3.4%
Bowling	37.92	37.92	0.0%	31.74	19.5%
Golf	61.48	60.34	1.9%	60.97	0.8%
Hiking	48.95	47.83	2.3%	47.54	3.0%
Jogging/Running	53.55	51.40	4.2%	50.36	6.3%
Skateboard	42.70	44.41	-3.8%	42.27	1.0%
Soccer	34.68	33.97	2.1%	34.22	1.3%
Tennis	34.54	35.14	-1.7%	33.19	4.1%
Volleyball	54.04	54.04	0.0%	54.67	-1.1%
Walking	43.02	42.02	2.4%	42.16	2.0%

Source: National Sporting Goods Association.

A Basic Process for Designing Research

There are some specific models and methods for research design and activity. Figure 4.2 illustrates a basic process for designing sport marketing research. This illustration outlines the process and a series of questions to guide the sport marketer through the process. Each step in the process should be carefully and thoughtfully developed and planned so that the research produces good, truthful, and useful results.

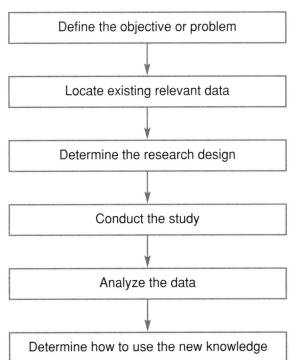

Figure 4.2
A basic process for designing sport marketing research.

Step 1: Define the Objective or Problem

The first step is to define the objective of the project or specify the problem. What does the company need to know? What is the problem? Refer to the list of questions at the beginning of the chapter. Defining the objective or problem can be as simple as knowing the question. Once the objective or problem has been identified, the development of the research will be guided by what is needed.

Step 2: Locate Existing Relevant Data

The second step is to locate information that might answer your question or solve your problem. If this can be done, there might be no need to conduct further research. That is, if you can find information that is accurate, specific, and timely enough to address the objective or solve the problem, then this might be as far as you will need to go. If not, then further research is needed.

Determine what information you need and where it might be available. Typically, information is available in two sources: primary and secondary. *Primary sources* include those sources from which information is gathered directly. Gathering information about your consumers directly from your consumers is using the primary source—the consumer.

Secondary sources are those that contain information that is already compiled or published. A marketing report purchased from a sport marketing firm is a secondary source. The information comes to you secondhand. There are several secondary sources available to the sport marketer.

Determine the Kind of Information Needed

Typically, most information needs fall into the 4 Cs categories as previously discussed in an earlier chapter—the consumer, competitor, company, and climate. For each one of these areas, there are numerous elements that must be studied. The following are descriptions of some of the kinds of information needed concerning each of the 4 Cs and the most common types of research methods used to study them.

The consumer. The sport business must know and understand its consumers and potential consumers. The chapter on segmentation presents specific information needed concerning the consumer and how that information is analyzed and used. Kinds of information studied include

- demographics such as age, gender, disabilities, sexual orientation, income, ethnicity, and education;

- psychographics such as lifestyle preferences, favorite color, household, employment, purchase behavior, brand preferences, class, culture, reference groups, personality characteristics;

- consumer behavior such as consumer values, lifestyles, perceptions, purchase decisions, purchase decision process, problem recognition, perceived value, postpurchase behavior, and factors affecting purchase involvement level; and

- business consumer segments such as producers, retailers, service providers, resellers, governments, vendors, business-to-business buying behavior.

The competitor. Studying the competition is necessary in order to ascertain what your competitors are doing and how those actions will possibly affect your own company.

Additionally, thorough knowledge of the competition can reveal much information that might be helpful. That is, one company can learn from another company's successes. Sometimes, those successes have to do with hitting on a promotional idea that becomes popular. For example, the use of animals in advertising has been rising in popularity. Would you agree that the GEICO Insurance Company's gecko is one of the most highly recognized animals in advertising? Sometimes these popular advertising themes take on a life of their own. The popularity of the gecko spawned a full complement of licensed merchandise.

> **Primary Sources:**
>
> are those sources from which information is gathered directly.

> **Secondary Sources:**
>
> are sources that contain information that someone else compiled and reported, published, or collected.

Study of the competition includes study of an industry segment and the industry as a whole. In an industry as enormous as the sport industry, it is essential to remember that oftentimes, one industry segment can affect another. This requires industry analysis. Sometimes this research can be found in industry trade magazines. It is important to read and study these publications because they record and reveal what's happening in an industry.

Research may indicate that a company would benefit by advertising its product via stadium signage.

The company. Monitoring and studying your own company is essential to making decisions regarding every area of the company. This type of research conducted depends on what is needed to know. For instance, a general overall study of the company can be done with a SWOT (Strengths, Weaknesses, Opportunities, Threats) analysis. Using a SWOT analysis, the company can attempt to critically and objectively determine its strengths and weaknesses, for example, and use this information for strategic planning.

The climate. The environmental considerations outlined and discussed in the previous chapter must be studied, both internally and externally. These include economic factors, the social and cultural climate, and corporate, political, legal, and ethical climates. For instance, it is important to know what is happening in the economy. The economy can affect everyone, and sport businesses are not excluded.

Sources of Information and How to Get Them

There are two categories of information sources: primary and secondary. As you learned before, *primary information* is information collected directly from the consumer via personal interview, phone surveys, or consumer questionnaires. *Secondary sources* are those sources from which you may obtain information that has been reported, published, or collected. There are also internal and external sources of information. *Internal sources* are those sources inside the sport company. *External sources* are those sources outside the sport company. There are primary internal and external sources, and there are secondary internal and external sources. A *primary internal source* is an interview conducted with one of the sport company's employees. A *primary external source* is an interview conducted with consumers. A *secondary internal source* is a report by one of the departments in the company. A *secondary external source* is a report issued by the United States Census Bureau.

Primary sources are those sources from which you collect the information directly. That is, when you collect data directly from your consumers, that is primary information. To do this, you design a study for the collection of data. Designing a study is presented in the next section.

Here are some ideas on where to find secondary information. You can collect a wide array of information from local government offices and other nonprofit agencies. Some of these are the local chamber of commerce, department of health, city planning and zoning offices, city census offices, local colleges and universities, and local real estate or homebuilding offices.

Table 4.7
Examples of Research from the National Sporting Goods Association.

SPORTS PARTICIPATION IN 2004: SERIES I

"Sports Participation in 2004: Series I" repeats the highly successful participation study done by NSGA the past 19 years. It provides data on total 2004 participation, frequency of participation, and average number of participation days by gender and age. Single-time participation, which is not counted in the total, is included separately. Correlation tables relate each sports activity to every other activity in the survey.

Demographic data on participants includes gender, age, gender by age, household income and education of male and female head of household. Geographic analysis includes nine census regions and participation data by metro area size. Presence of children is also noted.

Internet usage by participants (percent using and hours per week) for each sport is reported by gender and age of participants.

The 25 activities covered in "Series I" are: aerobic exercising, backpacking/wilderness camping, baseball, basketball, bicycle riding, billiards/pool, bowling, camping (vacation/overnight), exercise walking, exercising with equipment, fishing (fresh and salt water). Also included are football (tackle and touch), golf, hiking, hunting with firearms, martial arts, running/jogging, soccer, softball, swimming, t'ai chi/yoga, tennis, volleyball and weightlifting.

"Sports Participation in 2004: Series I" is based on a sampling of 10,000 U.S. households. The study, conducted for NSGA by Ipsos-Insight, Uniondale, New York, had a response rate of 67%.

SPORTS PARTICIPATION IN 2004: SERIES II

Identical in sample size and methodology, "Sports Participation in 2004: Series II" surveys 21 additional sports and recreational activities.

The 21 activities in Series II are: archery (target), boating (motor/power), canoeing, cheerleading, hockey (ice), hunting w/bow & arrow, inline roller skating, kick boxing, mountain biking (off road), muzzleloading, paintball games, sailing, scooter riding, skateboarding, skiing (alpine), skiing (cross country), snowboarding, target shooting, water skiing, and work-out at club. The Series II study had a response rate of 69%.

SPORTS PARTICIPATION IN 2004: SERIES III

In conjunction with Irwin Broh & Associates, NSGA has launched a participation survey of sports with lower incidences of participation. Using a 40,000 household (HH) sampling versus the 10,000 HH sampling in the above studies, this survey provides a more reliable picture of participants in these sports.

The 20 sports included in the survey are: badminton, boxing, croquet, dart throwing (soft tip & metal tip), horseshoe pitching, mountain/rock climbing, pilates, racquetball, roller skating (rink), scuba diving (open water), snorkeling, snowmobiling, snowshoeing, squash, wakeboarding, surfboarding, table tennis, wakeboarding, wind surfing, wrestling.

Demographic data on participants includes gender, age, gender by age, HH income, HH type (family vs. non-family), HH size, type of residence and socio-economic status. Geographic analysis includes nine census regions and participation data by metro area size.

SPORTS PARTICIPATION IN 2004: STATE-BY-STATE

"Sports Participation in 2004: State-by-State" projects sports participation on a state-by-state basis for 33 sports. It provides data on total participation, frequency of participation and total participation days.

The 36 activities covered in the survey are: aerobic exercising, backpacking/wilderness camping, baseball, basketball, bicycle riding, billiards/pool, boating (motor), bowling, camping (vacation/overnight),canoeing, exercise walking, exercising with equipment, fishing (fresh and salt water), football (tackle and touch). Also included are golf, hiking, hunting with firearms, in-line skating, mountain biking (off road), paintball games, running/jogging, scooter riding, skateboarding, skiing (alpine), snowboarding, soccer, softball, swimming, target shooting, tennis, volleyball, water skiing, weightlifting and work-out at club.

Sports Participation in 2004: State-by-State" is based on a sampling of 20,000 U.S. households. Only those sports which project at least six million participants nationally are included in this study. The data can be useful in determining marketing strategies, sales expectations, potential regions for growth and similar activities that require a state-by-state analysis.

SPORTS PARTICIPATION IN 2004: LIFECYCLE DEMOGRAPHICS

Advancing beyond traditional demographics, this report uses the LifeCycle segmentation system developed by Ipsos-Insight to analyze sports participation in the continuum from affluent singles to seniors. Households are classified into various life stages using demographic criteria. Sports analyzed are those in "Series I."

Households are classified into one of five mutually exclusive segments, with each segment divided into two or more subgroups. The 12 classifications are: Affluent Singles; Low/Middle Income Singles; Double Income/No Kids (DINKS); Working Parents; Single Parents; Affluent Traditional Families; Low/Middle Income Traditional Families; Affluent Empty Nesters; Low/Middle Income Empty Nesters; Single Active Seniors; Married Active Seniors; 75+ Seniors.

For each group/subgroup, a frequency distribution, an index of participation vs. lifecycle segment and selected demographics are provided. Demographics include age, gender, region and market size. This analysis is particularly useful in examining income-household structure relationships.

SPORTING GOODS MARKET IN 2005

Based on a consumer study of 100,000 U.S. households, "The Sporting Goods Market" is the most comprehensive original research available on consumer purchases of sports equipment and footwear. The footwear section includes 24 styles of athletic and sport footwear. For equipment, the report provides retail sales for 2004 and estimates for 2005 for specific products in more than 20 sport categories, including cycling, camping, fitness, fishing, hunting, golf, wheeled sports and team. Brand share data on most products may be purchased separately.

Purchaser demographics include annual household income, age and gender of major user, education of household head, and region of the country. A 10-year history of sales allows the analysis of long term trends. Place-of-purchase (including Internet) data allows analysis of industry channels of distribution. Average price point for eight types of retailing is provided. The 88-page report is prepared by NSGA by Irwin Broh & Associates, a research company nationally recognized for its work in the leisure field.

Table 4.8
Examples of Sport Business Industry Trade Publications.

Bicycle Retailer & Industry News

Boating Center Management

Boating Industry International

Classic Golf Marketing

Club Industry

Desertsports & Recreation Enthusiast

Fitness Product News

Golf Course News

Golf Retailer

Golf Times Media

Outdoor Retailer

Powersports Business

Sporting Goods Business

Sporting Goods Dealer

Sports Executive Weekly

Street & Smith's Sports Business Daily

Trade or industry-specific associations also can provide information. For almost every career, there is a professional association. Many of these associations track demographic and other data concerning their industry. The National Sporting Goods Association (NSGA), for example, tracks sporting goods sales and sports participation and publishes the information. Tables 4.7 and 4.8 present a few of these. More are listed in appendixes B and C.

> From the NSGA: "Every year NSGA does its research study "The Sporting Goods Market" as a service to its members. The study, prepared by the independent research company of Irwin Broh & Associates, delineates the size and scope of the sporting goods market. At the same time, we gather brand share data on certain products. Each brand share report shows product sold by type of outlet, retail price range, major geographic regions and household income. It includes data on age and sex of major user. Reports include graphs showing year-to-year changes. The brand share data is based on a representative sample panel of 20,000 US households for equipment, 40,000 households for footwear. This panel is maintained by NFO, one of the most respected research companies in this field.

> Types of outlets covered in the report include: sporting goods stores, specialty sport shops, pro shops, discount stores, department stores, catalog showrooms, warehouse clubs, mail order, on-line/internet and other outlets. Brand data is reported specifically for K mart, Target and Wal-Mart in the discount store category and Sears in the department store category. "On-line/Internet" purchases, which are showing significant growth in both sports equipment & footwear, were added three years ago.

> For footwear, specialty athletic footwear stores, family shoe stores and factory outlet stores replace catalog showrooms and warehouse clubs in types of outlets. For fitness equipment, TV shopping is reported."

Professional associations are another source of information. For example, the American College of Sports Medicine (ACSM) is a professional association for a variety of professionals and practitioners in areas such as sports medicine, athletic training, orthopedic medicine, and exercise physiology. The ACSM tracks and collects information about these areas. There are two outlets for the information: (a) annual conferences and meetings and (b) newsletters and journals. Appendix B contains a list of some sport business trade associations.

Publications are another source of information and consist of, for example, magazines, newsletters, newspapers, reports, and journals. Some of these sources are available on newsstands, some in bookstores, some by subscription, and others by membership in an organization. Consider, for example, the many sports magazines. To get an idea of how many there are, walk into any bookstore and look at the magazine section. On average, the section will contain over 50% sports and sport-related magazines. Each magazine holds information about that sport and its participants, equipment manufacturers, retailers, and other types of information. *Boating World* magazine, for example, publishes water sports participation data. *Golf World* magazine even publishes stock information (see any issue)! Appendix C contains a list of some sport business trade publications.

Step 3: Determine the Research Design

If the information collected cannot answer your questions, then you will need to conduct further research and collect primary data. You have several research methods from which to choose. However, specific ones must be selected and matched to your research needs. This must be done to be sure you are conducting the right type of research in order to collect the right data.

Determining the research design includes identifying the right research method and determining the right sampling procedures. The following sections describe these procedures.

Sport Marketing Research Methods

A research method is a procedure, usually an established and tested one. That is, several research methodologies have been developed, tested, and perfected through the years. These methods have higher degrees of reliability and validity. *Reliability* is a measure of the level of consistency of the method. That is, will the method and the results it produces be consistent? *Validity* is a measure of the level of correctness of the method. That is, does the method actually test what it claims it will test? The higher the reliability and validity of a method, the more accurate the resulting data will be.

The research method a sport business or organization selects depends on the purpose of the research. Research methodology is determined by the research question or need. In some instances, research is conducted to enhance understanding and knowledge. That type of research is called *basic* research. In other instances, research is done try to solve a practical problem. That is called *applied* research. Sport businesses typically conduct both basic and applied research, depending on need. Most businesses, however, more often conduct applied research because of their need to solve problems, answer questions, develop solutions, create products, test promotional strategies, increase sales, and address other practical needs.

Examples of the more commonly used sport marketing research methods include the following:

- *Survey research.* The most popular technique used for gathering primary data is survey research. In this method, a researcher interacts with people to obtain information such as facts, attitudes, perceptions, and opinions. Some of the forms of the survey research include personal interviews, mall-intercept interviews, telephone interviews, focus groups, mail surveys, and Web surveys. Sample surveys and questionnaires are given in Appendix F. The survey can be in a printed form, or it can be done in interview format. Either way, development of a list of interview questions or the survey questionnaire is essential to the research. All survey research requires that the questionnaires be consistent so that each person in the study will be asked the same series of questions. Questionnaires consist of three types of questions: closed-ended, open-ended, and scaled-response. *Closed-ended questions* require the respondent to make a selection from a limited list of responses such as a multiple choice exam. *Open-ended questions* ask the respondent to give an answer in essay form. *Scaled-response questions* require the respondent to select from a range of usually intensive related answers such as most to least, higher to lower, strongly agree to strongly disagree. Closed-ended and scaled-response questionnaires are used most often. They are easier to analyze, but they are also more objective in nature. In contrast, open-ended responses are subject to the researcher's interpretation.

- *Focus Group.* A focus group is a method in which a small group of individuals are brought together and guided through a discussion about a topic. The goal of a focus group is to bring out the ideas, opinions, and views of the individuals. The marketer then uses this information to guide decisions about the business or product for adjustments toward improvement.

    The use of focus groups has become popular in marketing research. In many cities, there are a number of companies that specialize in focus group research. You can be sure that as a marketing person in a sport business you will most likely use focus group research at some point.

    The goals of focus groups include generating ideas, revealing consumer needs and perceptions, and understanding consumer vocabulary. Generating ideas means that you will use this information to brainstorm ideas. Revealing consumer needs and perceptions means that you are seeking to adjust your current beliefs about the consumer or to be exposed to and learn about what they are thinking. Understanding consumer vocabulary means that you want to stay current about words and phrases that consumers are using.

- *Telephone Survey.* As you sit at home enjoying an evening of pizza and a movie, the phone rings. Your caller ID shows the words "Out of Area" or "Unknown." You know, however, that the caller is likely a telephone marketer. Still, the telephone is a viable method for conducting some marketing research. The method requires, however, that the sample be a true representative of your population.

    In recent year, cell phones, caller ID systems, voice mail, no-call lists, and general time constraints have worked against the successfulness of the telephone survey interview.

- *Mail Survey.* "Snail mail," as it is called today, continues to be a good method for collecting information about your consumers. The mail survey can be a postcard insert or part of any other type of mailing to the customer.

- *Online Research.* Conducting research via the Internet is the newest method for collecting data about the consumer. Information can be obtained either through customer self-reporting survey, or through hidden measures. Research methodology problems associated with this method include that information is only attained from those individuals who have Internet access. However, as the percent of the population with Internet access increases, so will the projectability rates. That is, the negative aspect of Internet research is that Internet users do not currently reflect all segments of the population. Internet users are primarily younger, more affluent, and better educated segments of the population. Still, as computer and Internet access prices continue to drop, more individuals in all segments of the population will begin to make these purchases and gain access to the Internet, thus making them accessible segments of the population for the marketer.

- *Observation research.* Observation research calls for observing people's behavior. This type of study is usually conducted when a company wants to determine buyer behavior. It is also used in studying consumer's reactions to products.

- *Purchase Behavior.* This is a method of studying what consumers do when making a purchase. There are several methods, but one we will introduce here is a tracking system when a customer is in a retail store. The system will track consumers and develop trends of movement. This information then allows the marketer to strategically design the placement of everything inside the retail store. To learn more about this type of research, visit a company website that specializes in this system: http://www.sorensen-associates.com.

    This system could also be used in sports stadia and arenas to track the movements of consumers as they move around inside and outside the facility. This information would help marketers make better decisions about arranging services and purchase points in and around the facility.

- *Test Marketing.* Test marketing is the term used when you are conducting an experiment or test in a field setting. Your company may use a group of individuals, a city, or a set of cities to test either the sales potential for a new product or to test differences in the marketing mix for a product. In an example, a baseball bat manufacturer will select a number of college baseball teams to test a new bat. The test might last for a full baseball season. At the end of the season, the company will gather the opinions of the baseball players about the bat and use that information for the production of the bat. In a different example, a large sports facility, such as the Georgia Dome in Atlanta, will test the offering of a new promotional item during sports events. The Dome marketing research staff can conduct interviews with people who bought the item about their reasons for purchasing the item. If it is determined that the item has potential for sustainable sales, then that information can be used in the decision for keeping that item.

- *Scientific research.* Research of a more formal and involved nature is typically labeled scientific research. It includes, for example, laboratory research for new product development such as the study and testing of new materials for sport apparel, research to design and increase the aerodynamics of a racing bike or a racing wheelchair, and physiological studies of elite athletes to improve a sport technique for enhancing performance.

Sampling Procedures

A research sample is a representative group of people from a whole population. For instance, if there are 2,000,000 people in a city from which you would like to collect data, you could try to collect the data from all two million or select a sample of the population from which to collect. The sample could be 1,000 people of the total population.

To do this, the population must be identified first. This is the group from which the sample will be drawn. The researcher must also decide what kind of sample to select. That is, the researcher can choose a random sample or a convenience sample. A *random sample* is a way to select the members of a sample so that every member of the population has an equal chance of being selected. For example, if

A convenience sample allows the researcher to use nearby or established contacts to glean information.

you want to survey a population of 20,000 season ticket holders but don't have the time or money to survey every one, you can use random sampling to get a smaller group. You can select the sample number to be 400. Then you can select every 50th person listed on an alphabetical list of all season ticket holders. Thus, you obtain a random sample.

A *convenience sample* comes from using respondents who are convenient, or readily available/accessible to the researcher. For instance, if you elect to use a convenience sample of the season ticket holders, you select a sample because of its convenience for you. One way to do this is to assume that all people seated in luxury boxes are season ticket holders. They are easily available and convenient for you to access. You simply distribute surveys to all the people seated in the luxury boxes.

Most sampling procedures have weaknesses. It is important to know what these are and to analyze the data within those limitations. Refer to research design books in order to determine the best sampling method for your work.

Step 4: Conduct the Study

Plans must now be made for conducting the study. The research design selected will usually call for procedures on conducting the study and collecting the data. The plans for conducting the study should include logistical procedures such as time frames, dates, times, places, and people involved. The plans should also include arrangements for collecting the data and storing it. For example, if the study is a study on sponsorship recall, this type of research methodology calls for the survey/interview technique. Usually, a mall-intercept approach is used. The researcher stays in one area and approaches people wandering by to participate in the study. Researchers must obtain permission to conduct surveys from the site management, decide how many surveys and researchers will be needed at the study site, determine what materials will be needed, and decide what to do with the completed surveys.

Step 5: Analyze the Data

The fifth step is to analyze the data. In other words, ask the question "What does this information mean?" The purpose of data analysis is to interpret the information and draw some conclusions. Of course, the data analytical methods will have already been decided when the research method is chosen because the data must be collected in a specific way according to data-analysis methodologies.

Interpretation of the data can consist of running the data through statistical procedures. If the data collected are numerical, some simple statistics applied to the data may help. Ask others in the company to study the information and tell you what they see. Compare the information to other studies and look for similarities and differences. Another idea is to take the informa-

tion to a research expert such as a sport marketing professor who conducts research, a sport marketing research company, or a general marketing research company.

Step 6: Determine How to Use the New Knowledge

The final step is to determine how you can apply the new knowledge to the business. The information may be used according to why you needed the information in the beginning. Why did you need the information? If you needed the information to understand why your indoor tennis club is losing consumers during June and July, the new information will help you decide what you need to do to retain consumers during these months. Let us say that the reason the club loses consumers in June and July is that they go to play tennis on outdoor courts so that they can be outside during the summer. What can you do? Your club has no outdoor courts. Can you afford to build outdoor courts? If not, is there another way to compete with the outdoor courts? In the next chapter, there are several examples of consumer research and how the information from the research can be used.

Chapter Summary

Research is very important for the sport business. Every sport marketing person should know how to conduct research. The sport business needs information that is accurate, timely, interactive, and flexible in order to enhance success. Information and new knowledge come from research. This information is used in formulating decisions and strategies in the sport marketing elements.

CASE STUDY CHAPTER 4

An 8-second Sport With 7-digit Returns: Here's the Dirt on the PBR

In a research partnership with a major sports facility, the Georgia Dome, Dr. Brenda G. Pitts and students of the Georgia State University Sport Management master's program conduct a variety of market research. The results are very important to the managers of the Dome, who take the information from the research and use it for strategic management and marketing formulation. The research includes such market data as visitor spending variables, factors that affect attendance, customer satisfaction levels of the facility, and consumer perceptions of the host city, Atlanta.

One of the organizations and events studied involves the Professional Bull Riders, Inc (PBR). The Georgia Dome contracted with the PBR to host three annual events. The first of the three was held in February, 2003.

In a relatively short amount of time, the PBR has positioned itself as an exciting sport and has a loyal fan base in several areas of the country.

"With a television viewership of 90 million, a multi-network contract, a world championship ending in Las Vegas, large corporation sponsorship, and a growing fan base, the sport of bull riding has come a long way since its professional start a mere 10 years ago. From a socially accepted stereotype of the poor, lonely cowboy, cowboys and cowgirls today can reap hundreds of thousands and even millions of dollars in professional rodeo circuits. The professional rodeo industry even has the attention of ESPN and NBC Sports. Within the industry, one of the most popular events, the bull riding event, has become a stand alone professional league—the Professional Bull

Riders Inc. Started in 1992 by 20 accomplished bull riders who each invested $1,000.00, the PBR is very popular, with each event bringing in 20,000 to 30,000 spectators and winnings beginning to hit the million dollar mark" (Lu, Pitts, Ayers, & Lucas, 2004).

In one of the studies, Pitts' research team revealed that a number of consumers at a PBR event were extremely upset about their seating assignments. These sets of consumers had been sold tickets to seats that were situated behind television cameras and their crew members, and behind the raised stage of the in-arena officials and announcers. These spectators had a very limited obstacle-free view of the arena ring in which the bull riding was taking place.

With further research, the team discovered that this was the first time that the Georgia Dome had staged a PBR event and had obviously made some mistakes in facility arrangement and seat sales. With this new information, Dome management was able to make decisions about the configuration of the event ring as well as which seats should or should not be included in ticket sales.

The following year, armed with a new staging and ring configuration and specific seat sales, the PBR event was a success with satisfied fans whose every seat was in a position to see the full ring and its activities.

Case Activity

To better understand the PBR, its events and activities, and its fans, conduct your own research and collect as much information as possible. Develop a SWOT analysis of the PBR. Based on the SWOT analysis, develop an informed strategic marketing plan with your recommendations for a five-year period of time. Table 1 below presents the demographics of the fans attending the event in 2003.

Table 1.
Descriptive Statistics for the Demographic Variables (n = 54)—2003 PBR Event.

Variables	Category	n	%	Cumulative %
Gender	Female	27	50	50.0
	Male	27	50	100.0
Age	Under 18	5	9.4	9.4
	18–24	15	28.3	37.7
	25–34	14	26.5	64.2
	35–44	14	26.4	90.6
	45–54	3	5.6	96.2
	55-plus	2	3.8	100.0
Marital/household Status	Single	27	50.9	50.9
	Married	23	43.4	94.3
	Divorced	0	0	94.3
	Living with a partner	3	5.7	100.0
	Other	0	0	100.0
Highest Education Level	Some High School	2	3.8	3.8
	High School Graduate	20	38.5	42.3
	Vocational/Technical School	1	1.9	44.2
	Some College	3	5.8	50.0
	College Degree	23	44.2	94.2

Continued on next page

Variables	Category	n	%	Cumulative %
Highest Education Level *(continued)*	Some Post-Graduate Studies	0	0.0	94.2
	Master's Degree	2	3.8	98.1
	Doctoral Degree	1	1.9	100.0
Ethnicity	African American/Black	13	25.5	25.5
	Caucasian	37	72.5	98.0
	Asian/Pacific Islander	0	0.0	98.0
	Hispanic/Latino	0	0.0	98.0
	Others	1	2.0	100.0
Annual Household Income	$10,000 and under	0	0.0	0.0
	$10,001–$29,999	5	11.9	11.9
	$30,000–$49,999	11	26.2	38.1
	$50,000–$69,999	4	9.5	47.6
	$70,000–$89,999	5	11.9	59.5
	$90,000–$109,999	10	23.8	83.3
	$110,000–$129,999	4	11.9	95.2
	$130,000–$149,999	1	2.4	97.6
	$150,000 or more	1	2.4	100.0
Numbers of children in the house (under 18)	0	15	36.6	36.6
	1	7	17.1	53.7
	2	11	26.8	80.5
	3	6	14.6	95.1
	4	2	4.9	100.0
Companion	Family only	12	22.6	22.6
	Partner only	8	15.1	37.7
	Friends only	19	35.8	73.5
	Alone	1	1.9	75.4
	Family, friends, and partner	12	22.7	98.1
	Others	1	1.9	100.0
People in the party	1	1	2.6	2.6
	2	12	30.8	33.3
	3	4	10.3	43.6
	4	5	12.8	56.4
	5	4	10.3	66.7
	6	7	17.9	84.6
	7	4	10.3	94.9
	8 and plus	2	15.5	100.0
Previous attended	Yes	43	81.1	81.1
	No	10	18.9	100.0
Zip code	Georgia area	50	96.0	96.0
	Other	2	4.0	100.0
How did you find out?	Radio	24	34.8	34.8
	Newspapers	4	5.80	40.6
	TV	12	17.4	58.0
	Friends	17	24.6	82.6
	Website	3	4.3	87.0
	Mail	1	1.4	88.4
	Local sports organization	1	1.4	89.9
	Other	7	10.1	100.0

QUESTIONS FOR STUDY

1. What is sport marketing research? Why is it important?
2. What are the purposes of sport marketing research?
3. List and describe some types of sport marketing research.
4. What are the sources of information? Give examples of each.
5. What are the primary areas of sport marketing research? Give examples of each.

LEARNING ACTIVITIES

1. Interview people in a variety of sport businesses, organizations, or other enterprises in your city or community and ask them what kind of marketing research they conduct and why.
2. Identify at least 10 different places you could obtain existing information in your city or community. Go to the places and research the types of information available at these places. Create a notebook of these resources and save this material for the future.
3. With a group of other students, and with the supervision of your instructor, develop a research study to determine sponsorship recognition (see Appendix F). Conduct the study during a local sports event. Analyze the results and present your analysis to the class.
4. See Appendix F. With the supervision of your instructor, design a study using one of the examples of surveys, conduct the study, analyze the results, determine how the information can be used by the sport business, and share the results with the class and the business.

Chapter Five

SEGMENTATION, TARGETING, AND POSITIONING IN SPORT BUSINESS

Overview

The world population reached 2 billion in 1999 (Population Reference Bureau, 2000). It was estimated that the next billion people to arrive will do so by 2012. Yet, although the number of people is incredible, the world is growing smaller in many respects. In relation to communications, travel, movement, news, and culture, for instance, the world's peoples meet, exchange ideas, influence each other, and are changed forever.

There are advantages and disadvantages to merging peoples and cultures. For instance, as one measure of diversity, there are about 6,000 languages spoken around the world (National Geographic, 1999). Yet, as people and cultures merge, it is predicted that that number could drop to 3,000 by the year 2100. We live in an ever-growing multicultural society, and the fact remains that is merging, mixing, and changing.

Just when marketing gurus thought they had the mass marketing theories and models completed and working well, the world started changing. Today, with ever increasing numbers of populations and cultures in any given country, a marketing professional must constantly monitor the population, known in business language as *consumers*.

The United States is undergoing a transformation from a primarily mono-cultural society to a multicultural one. The total population of the United States is predicted to increase from 297 million in 2006 to 404 million in 2050 (Population Reference Bureau). Since the 1950s, the country has been shifting from a society dominated and controlled by whites to a society characterized by several groups, particularly Black, Asian, Hispanic, lesbian and gay, Jewish, disabled, and Native American. It is predicted that the white population will drop to 64% of the population by 2020. The Hispanic population is expected to realize the greatest growth from 10% to 15%, whereas the African-American population will grow from 12% to 14%, the Asian-American population will grow from 4% to 7%, and the lesbian and gay population will continue to be about 10% of all populations (U.S. Census Bureau).

Businesses are using new marketing tactics such as relationship marketing, cause marketing, niche marketing, and e-marketing to communicate with these emerging markets. *Relationship marketing* is the attempt to development a relationship with the consumer by trying to be more to the consumer than just a company from whom the consumer buys products. *Cause marketing* is the development of marketing tactics designed to recognize and support the cause of a group or organization. *Niche marketing* is targeting specific niches, or groups, that no other company targets. *E-marketing* is the attempt to reach a market through electronic media, specifically, the Internet. As groups proliferate and cultures emerge, marketing professionals will need to stay knowledgeable about the changes and continue to develop marketing strategies to ensure success.

> Marketing professionals will need to stay knowledgeable about the changes and continue to develop marketing strategies to ensure success

Marketing professionals in the sport business industry are in the same boat. It is not an industry existing in a vacuum as though untouched by the outside world. As noted in chapter one, the sport business industry is as multicultural as any population. Therefore, sport marketing professionals must continuously monitor growth and changes in consumers and develop sport marketing strategies to enhance success.

As the population and its many different groups proliferate, the importance of and need for segmentation, targeting, and positioning increase. Segmentation is the marketer's tool to make sense of these numerous and various groups of people in order to make changes in product, price, distribution, or promotion strategies. Targeting, positioning, and brand-awareness management are ways to determine a specific consumer segment to attract.

Segmentation

Segmentation is the division of a whole into parts. Putting things in order helps arrange them so that we can make sense of them. It helps make order out of chaos. For example, products in a sporting goods retail store are arranged by categories: Tennis goods are found in the tennis department; soccer goods are found in the soccer department; boating equipment is found in the water sports department; and sports shoes are all found in the shoe department. The purposes for doing this are to make it easy for customers to find something, to make it easy for workers to stock the shelves, and to group similar items in a practical manner. This categorization is a method of segmentation—the division of a whole into relatively similar segments.

> Segmentation of the consumer market allows sport businesses to understand and target specific groups that share characteristics and behaviors.

In sport business, the work of segmentation is done primarily in two broad areas: the industry and the consumer market. The industry is divided and grouped in a number of ways to make practical order of it. The consumer market is divided and grouped in a number of ways to study consumers, to reach them, and to meet their needs, wants, and desires. The division of a consumer market into relatively homogeneous segments is *sport consumer market segmentation*. The division of the sport industry into relatively homogeneous segments is *sport industry segmentation*.

> **Segmentation:**
> is the first step toward understanding consumer groups, determining target markets, and informing marketing mix and positioning strategies.

Sport consumer market segmentation involves consumer analysis. Consumer analysis is the process of studying a total market or population and dividing the population into groups that have similar characteristics.

Sport companies want to know and understand the people who purchase their products, and companies also want to learn about the people who do not purchase their products. These data help the sport marketing professional make decisions concerning the company's product, price, distribution, and promotional strategies. You will learn more about consumer segmentation in the section titled "Sport Consumer Market Segmentation."

Sport industry segmentation involves industry analysis (also called competitive analysis). Industry segmentation is the process of studying an industry to divide it into industry segments that have similar characteristics. The sport marketing professional uses this information to analyze the segments, analyze which segment the company is in, and develop decisions and strategies for the sport company based on the knowledge about the industry segments. You will learn more about industry segmentation in the section entitled *Sport Industry Segmentation*.

In Sport Business:

segmentation involves dividing and grouping consumers and the industry into relatively similar segments for varying purposes.

Sport Consumer Market Segmentation

THE IMPORTANCE OF MARKET SEGMENTATION

Until the 1950s, few companies practiced market segmentation. Before that time, most of the country consisted of a fairly homogeneous population that could be described easily—historical patriarchal family structure of white male, wife, three children, a dog and a cat; the man worked outside the home, the wife worked at home as a housewife.

Sport Consumer Market Segmentation:

the division of total markets into relatively homogeneous segments.

Sport Industry Segmentation:

the division of the sport industry into relatively homogeneous segments.

Today, the population is very different. Businesses must constantly monitor consumers to determine marketing mix strategies. Today's population is distinctively different in relation to race, ethnicity, or national origin as evidenced by consumer groups of Hispanic Americans, Asian Americans, Latin Americans, Irish Americans, and African Americans. The population also comprises numerous different groups of people with different characteristics such as age, gender, race, ethnicity, religion, disability, national origin, sexual orientation, household status, lifestyle characteristics, cultural factors, social factors, class, income, education, and attitudes. For instance, today we hear about groups called the Baby Boomers, the Silver Fox market, the Pink Market, Generation Y, yuppies, guppies, Generation X, the Lost Generation, DINKS, and e-Gen.

Segmentation is the first step toward understanding consumer groups, determining target markets, and informing marketing mix and positioning strategies. The determination of target markets is essential to the business. Target markets are those specific groups of consumers for whom the company produces its products and to whom the company tries to sell its products.

Sport organizations such as NASCAR should practice market segmentation in order to better target specific groups of consumers.

PURPOSES OF SEGMENTATION

The primary purpose of market segmentation is specialization. Using consumer market analysis and segmentation, the sport company can select one or more consumer market segments on which to concentrate and specialize in meeting the segment's needs. Products, prices, services, advertising, and other promotional methods are developed for specific consumer market segments and with the competition in mind.

Take a look at the information in Table 5.1, and think about how just these few data are going to affect how we market a product to the world and the United States today, in 10 years, and in 20 years. Businesses must monitor the many new, changing, or emerging population segments. More and more businesses are redesigning their products, prices, and promotional methods for these new markets. In pursuit of these markets, many companies are relying less on traditional forms of mass marketing and more on specialized media (cable-specific television, ethnic-centered magazines, and specific-topic magazines).

> Industry analysis and segmentation can reveal how a company compares to the competition or determine if it can compete in a particular segment. This allows the company to concentrate its efforts on particular segments and thus use its resources most efficiently.

> Targeting specific populations is the future of marketing in sport business.

Companies in the sport industry are also paying attention. As pointed out in chapter one, there are sports, events, sporting goods, and other sport products and types of sport management and marketing companies specifically designed for and offering products to the many different markets.

Table 5.1
Some Population Information.

- In 2010, four states (New York, California, Florida, and Texas) will have approximately one-third of the nation's youth. More than 50% of them will be "minority." This means that the new minority will be white.

- The population of the United States is aging rapidly. In 1992 there were 30 million people over the age of 65. In 2020 that number is expected to be 65 million. Most of them will have one year of retirement for every year of work.

- Children under the age of 18, who were 34% of the population in 1970, will be only 25% of the population is 2010.

- In 1990 the population of the United States was 76% Anglo, 12% Black, 9% Latino, and 3% Asian. It is estimated that by 2050, the population will be 52% Anglo, 16% Black, 22% Latino, and 10% Asian.

- There are more than 100 languages spoken in the school systems of New York City, Chicago, Los Angeles, and Fairfax County, Virginia.

- Ethnic minority shoppers, predominantly African Americans, Asians, and Hispanics, spent $600 billion in 1992. This is an increase of 18% since 1990. By the year 2010, minority populations may account for more than 30% of the economy.

- Over 32% of the Asian American households earn an income of $50,000 or more. That is contrasted with 29% of Caucasian households.

- Sixty-four percent of Asian American families are linked to the Internet, compared to 33% of all U.S. families.

- Africa's population will increase from 13% of the world's population in 2000 to 16% by 2025 and 20% by 2050.

- During the same time, Europe's population will decrease from 12% to 7% by 2050. Asia's population will decrease from 61% today to 58% by 2050.

- India's population reached 1 billion on May 11, 2000. One third of its population is under 15 years of age.

- USA ranks third largest in population in 2000 at 276 million and is expected to rank third in 2050 with a population of 404 million.

Sources: Hodgkinson, 1992; *National Geographic*, 1999; The New Face, 1993.

Targeting specific populations is the future of marketing in sport business.

As the years have gone by, businesses in the United States have changed. There are many more industries than ever before, and the new ones are different. The newest industries are high technology such as computers, electronics, cable TV, and space study. Some other new industries are in human services such as travel agencies, consulting, therapy, management services, and fitness consulting. All are consumer driven—developed to meet the needs of new consumer segments.

The sport industry has grown partially because most of the newest segments, which may be the fastest growing segments, are consumer driven. Take, for example, sporting goods and equipment. There are such a variety of people participating in sports activities that equipment is becoming more customized. Golf clubs come in a variety of sizes, weights, materials, colors, and lengths. Tennis rackets are also offered in a variety of sizes, weights, materials, and other factors. Clothing comes in a variety of sizes, styles, and colors. Sport shoes are offered in a variety of sizes, sport-specific styles, and materials. Camping equipment is varied based on consumer preferences, geography, and types of camping. There is a booming variety of water-sports goods and equipment: The air-jet engine is revolutionizing the boat industry; for powerboat enthusiasts, there is a constant new variety of water toys such as the wakeboard; knee board; the ski seat; the skurfer; single, double, and triple-person tubes; the ski board; and barefoot skiing equipment. It is apparent that the new equipment is popular because any Saturday on any lake reveals that people using these new toys outnumber traditional water skiers by four to one.

Sports and other activities, sport organizations, and sport businesses developed and designed by and for specific consumer segments are a fast-growing area of the sport industry. As pointed out in chapter one, many populations in the United States are very busy developing sport organizations, businesses, clubs, leagues, Olympics, and facilities specifically for their population.

Another growing area in the sport business industry includes those sport businesses whose products are service and support. Some of those services include such products as consulting, management, legal work, financial management, research, and marketing services. Here are some examples. If you are a professional athlete and you desire legal and financial help, there are individuals and companies that provide this service. If your sport business needs research on why sales of its product are decreasing, there are companies that will do this work. If your business wants to know if it should put a newly designed hockey stick on the market, there are companies that will study this for you. If your company wants to find a sponsor for a beach volleyball event, there are companies that specialize in sport sponsorship management. They will not only find a sponsor, but they also will negotiate the contract and manage the entire process.

> The sport industry is growing to meet new consumer needs and to provide new support and services.

IMPORTANT MARKET SEGMENTATION CRITERIA

Sport marketing professionals use segmentation for several reasons. Segmentation helps identify groups of consumers with similar characteristics and purchase behaviors. Segmentation provides the sport marketing professional with valuable information that guides marketing mix decisions and strategies specifically customized for the consumer group. Segments can be of any size and mix of characteristics. To be useful, however, segmentation methods should produce segments that meet certain criteria. The most useful criteria include identifiability, substantiality, accessibility, and responsiveness (see Table 5.2).

Table 5.2
Important segmentation criteria.

Identifiability: segments must be identifiable and measurable.

Substantiality: segments must be of a size large enough to justify marketing mix attention.

Accessibility: segments must be reachable with the customized marketing mix.

Responsiveness: segments must respond to a marketing mix customized to that segment.

Identifiability

Segments must be identifiable and measurable. For instance, it is fairly easy to identify segments using different ages in a high school population. However, the segment must also be measurable in its response to a marketing mix. That is, the group and number of high school 15- to 18-year-olds are identifiable and measurable. Say we want to know how many will attend all the high school's football games. We must find a way to measure that segment so that it is both identified and measured. Otherwise, we will have trouble determining if that segment is worth developing a marketing mix for.

Further, each market segment should be homogeneous within itself. That is, those within a segment should be as similar as possible. Segments should be heteroge-

Did you know...?

Royal Phillips Electronics pays 9.3 million dollars for naming rights to Phillips Arena in Atlanta.

America West pays 866 thousand dollars for naming rights to America West Arena in Phoenix.

Source: ESPN.com

neous between groups. That is, a segment should be distinguishably different from all others. These guidelines help the marketer determine like and different characteristics within and between segments.

Substantiality

Segments must be large enough to justify marketing mix customization and attention.

Otherwise, the time and money spent on the marketing mix may never realize a return on investment or a profit. On the other hand, a population can be segmented using so many variables that each segment contains only one individual. The sport marketing professional must determine if and when the segment is large enough to justify customizing a marketing mix.

Accessibility

Segments must be reachable with the customized marketing mix. Some segments are easy to reach, and others are hard to reach. For instance, hard-core baseball fans are easy to reach because they watch a lot of baseball. Therefore, we know where to find them and how to market to them. On the other hand, full-time RVers are hard to reach because they do not live at permanent addresses. An RVer is a person who has purchased an RV, or recreational vehicle, also known as a camper trailer. A full-time RVer is a person (or a couple) who has sold everything in order to live full time in the RV. These people are constantly traveling, camping at RV parks, and enjoying life as RVers.

Responsiveness

Segments must respond to a marketing mix customized to it. Otherwise, there's no use having the customized marketing mix. If the segment does not respond to the customized product, price, distribution, or promotion efforts, maybe that segment need not be considered as a separate segment.

BASES FOR SEGMENTATION

Sport marketing professionals use bases or variables to divide a total market into segments.

The object of market segmentation is to develop useful data about a particular group. Segmentation using one base selects members from a group that share a particular characteristic, while multiple base segmentation selects for a variety of characteristics. The latter method is increasingly popular as the culture becomes more multi-faceted.

These are characteristics that are divided into several categories. The choice of bases is crucial because an inappropriate group of bases will not be successful in relation to response to marketing mix. The key is to identify bases that produce a right mix of identifiability, measurability, substantiality, accessibility, and responsiveness in that segment.

Markets can be segmented using one or more bases. For example, a segment can be created using just gender. WNBA season-ticket holders can be segmented by gender. Markets can be segmented using multiple bases. For example, the WNBA ticket holders can be segmented into groups by gender, age, income, race, household status, zip code, favorite color, favorite movie, and so forth. The disadvantage of using multiple-base segmentation for this market is that it will create too many segments that are small in number and will probably not be of a substantial size to justify a customized marketing mix for each group. However, today's trend is toward the use of more bases rather than fewer because of the multicultural, multifaceted population: More segments want their differences recognized.

As mentioned earlier in this chapter, this trend has led to the development and increased use of relationship, cause, and niche marketing tactics. After all, these marketing strategies meet the most basic of marketing fundamentals—give the customers what they want.

In the sport industry, companies commonly use one or more of the following five bases to segment markets: demographics, psychographics, geography, purchase behavior, and product use and benefits sought (see Figure 5.1). Within each base are several individual characteristics or variables that must be considered. A more detailed description of these bases follows.

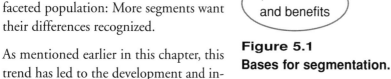

Figure 5.1
Bases for segmentation.

Table 5.3	
Some demographics and typical breakdowns.	
Typical Demographics	**Some Typical Breakdowns**
Age	under 12; adolescent; teen; 18–24; 25–29; 30–34; 35–39; 40–44; 45–49; 50–54; 55–59; 60–64; 65+; 18–24; 25–39; 40–54; 55–69
Gender	female; male
Household status	single; married/partner; divorced
Income: individual or household	under $10,000; $10,000–20,000; $20,000–30,000. $30,000–40,000; $40,000–50,000; $50,000–60,000; $60,000–75,000; $75,000–100,000
Occupation	clerical; sales; craftsman; technical; manager; professional; official; teacher
Education	grade school; some high school; high school; some college; college; graduate work; doctoral
Race	White, Black, Asian, Hispanic
Nationality	American, French, German
Social class	lower-lower; upper-lower; lower-middle; middle; upper-middle; lower-upper; upper; super-rich
Religion	Catholic, Jewish, Protestant, other

Table 5.4

Example of demographics from a study.

Variables	Category	N	%	Cumulative %
Household income	above $200,000	59	6.9	100.0
	$150,000–199,000	37	4.3	93.1
	$100,000–149,000	101	11.7	88.8
	$80,000–99,000	131	15.2	77.1
	$60,000–79,000	151	17.5	61.9
	$40,000–59,000	168	19.5	44.4
	$20,000–39,000	147	17.1	24.9
	below $20,000	67	7.8	7.8
Gender	Male	533	61.9	100.0
	Female	328	37.1	37.1
Ethnicity	Caucasian	617	71.7	100.0
	Hispanic	103	12.0	28.3
	African American	62	7.2	16.3
	Asian	23	2.7	9.1
	Others	46	6.4	6.4
Marital Status	Married	460	53.5	100.0
	Single	291	33.8	46.5
	Divorced	46	5.3	12.7
	Widowed	14	1.6	7.4
	Others	50	5.8	5.8
Education	College Graduate	270	31.4	100.0
	High School Graduate	189	22.0	68.7
	Advanced Degree	129	15.0	46.7
	School Student	114	13.2	31.7
	College Student	73	8.5	18.5
	Others	86	10.0	10.0
Occupation	Professional	207	24.0	100.0
	Management	141	16.4	76.0
	Sales	75	8.7	59.6
	Technical	59	6.9	50.9
	Education	59	6.9	44.0
	Skilled Worker	39	4.5	37.1

Descriptive Statistics for the Demographic Variables ($N = 861$)   Source: Zhang, Pease, Hui and Michand, 1995.

Demographic Segmentation

Demographics are those data about a person that might be called hard-core data. That is, it is information that is not necessarily changeable such as age, education level, and income. Table 5.3 illustrates some of the many demographic variables. Demographic segmentation is used commonly in sport business. As you can see in Table 5.3, demographic information includes basic information about a person that can present a partial picture of the personality and characteristics of that person. Using a few examples from sport marketing research, Tables 5.4 and 5.5 show the demographics of the people who participated in those studies. Note that each example shows some of the commonly used demographical data such as gender, age, ethnicity, sexual orientation, income, and education. By analyzing these data, the sport marketing professional can describe the consumers in these studies and use this information to help with decision making in marketing strategies. Study Tables 5.4 and 5.5 and develop information based on the data there.

Age

Two things are happening in the sport business industry in relation to age segmentation. First, increasingly, current businesses in the sport industry are recognizing a greater variety of age segments as serious consumers of a variety of products in the industry.

Second, new companies and organizations have been started whose sole focus and product is age-specific segmentation. In the first instance, numerous existing sport businesses and organizations that offer sports activities and other sport-related products are recognizing more age groups as consumers and offering an increasing variety of products for those markets. The age groups range from the very young to the very old. Soccer organizations are offering leagues for age segments that range from the under-five-year-old division to the 50-plus division. In tennis, some tournaments offer age divisions such as the women's 60, 70, and 80 national clay court championships (United States Tennis Association, 1999). Swimming and track-and-field are two sports in which age, used as age-group divisions or leagues, are offered as age-related products. More recently, however, those age groups now include higher age brackets and are typically called the master's divisions. More sports organizations and businesses are doing the same.

In the second instance, more recently, a number of sports businesses and organizations have begun whose sole focus and products are age groups, primarily for the upper ages. For instance, annually, there is a senior's softball national championship with

Table 5.5
Example of Demographics from a Study at a SuperCross Event.

Variables	Category	N	%
Age	18–24	192	35%
	25–34	172	31%
	35–44	151	27%
	45–55	32	6%
	Over 55	5	1%
Gender	Male	388	64%
	Female	205	35%
Household	Single	281	48%
	Married	267	46%
	Partner	20	3%
	Divorced	15	3%
Ethnicity	African American	31	7%
	Caucasian	397	88%
	Asian/Pacific Islander	1	0%
	Hispanic	7	2%
	Other	14	3%
Household Income	Under $15,000	34	9%
	$15,000–19,999	3	1%
	$20,000–29,999	44	11%
	$30,000–39,999	60	15%
	$40,000–49,999	62	16%
	$50,000–74,999	98	25%
	$75,000–99,999	40	10%
	$100,000–149,999	34	9%
	$150,000 & above	20	5%
Education Achieved	High School	82	13%
	College	221	37%
	Advanced	114	19%
	College Student	87	14%
	Other	93	15%
Occupation	Trade	101	17%
	Professional	226	38%
	Student	119	20%
	Education	24	4%
	Law Enforcement	18	3%
	Medical	24	4%
	Home	31	5%
	Retired	12	2%
	Other	42	7%

Source: Class project on sport market research 2006; B. G. Pitts, C. Lucas, S. Henderson, K. Wasco, M. Hossler, R. Lightner, M. Lisac, L. Smith, J. Turner, and W. Jones.

Table 5.6
Spectatorship/Viewership Facts about Women's Sports.

- Danica Patrick is credited with being the reason for a massive 40% leap in the overnight Nielsen ratings for the Indy 500, compared with 2004. The 6.6 rating was the highest overnight for the race since 1997 (7.6).

- LPGA reports that the average attendance per tournament is 65,000 people.

- The WTA boasts more than 4 million viewers with more than 825 matches being broadcast worldwide in 2005.

- The Women's Professional Football League (WPFL) average regular-season attendance ranges from 1,000 to 4,500 per team.

- The Women's Professional Billiards Association (WPBA) will have 10 tournaments televised on ESPN in 2005. In addition, between 1,000 and 1,200 fans attend each tournament.

- The LPGA received 251.5 hours of tournament coverage in 2005. All four majors are being televised on network television. There were 53 tournaments televised on The Golf Channel, 32 on ESPN2, 6 on ABC, 4 on CBS, 2 on ESPN, 2 on NBC, 2 on TNT, and 2 TBD.

age divisions of 50–54, 55–59, 60–64, 65–69, and 70-plus. The PGA offers the Senior Tour, and more recently announced was the Women's Senior Golf Tour by The Jane Blalock Co. of Boston (Broughton, 2001).

Gender

Long ago, most spectator sports were limited to a few men's professional sports whose owners and marketers promoted to the male market. Today, however, with an incredible number of hours of sports programming in a 24-hour period on dozens of sports television channels, and with more sports and other fitness and recreational activities televised or offered otherwise at an entertainment event, the sports spectator market has grown exponentially. In addition, contrary to popular belief, sports spectators are not only males; and it's not only women who watch women's sports. In addition, it's not just a few men's sports that we see on television anymore. The number of women's sports and mixed-

Table 5.7
Participation Facts about Women's Sports.

- Over 43 million women play sports each year.

- In the 2004–2005 school year, 1,557 girls played football, 4,334 wrestled and 1,015 played baseball on high school teams in the United States.

- Participation in college athletics for both men and women for the 2003–2004 school year decreased by 1,790 students from the previous year to 375,851. In the last 23 years (1981–2004), overall women's participation in collegiate athletics has increased 137% across all three divisions from 68,062 to 160,997. Men's participation grew from 156,131 to 214,854, an increase of 38%.

- The most popular NCAA women's sport by percentage of schools offering teams in 2004 were: basketball (98.3%), volleyball (94.6%), cross country (88.8%), soccer (88.6%), softball (86.4%), tennis (85.2%), track & field (67.4%), golf (48.7%), swimming (48.7%) and lacrosse (28.5%).

- According to the National Sports Goods Association, the most popular sports for women over the age of 7 in 2004 were exercise walking, swimming, exercising with equipment, camping and aerobic exercise. Over 52.4 million women participated in exercise walking more than once in 2004.

- According to the National Sports Goods Association, women constitute the majority of participants in four fitness activities: aerobic exercising (74%), walking (62%), working out a club (56%) and exercising with equipment (54%).

- Nearly one in five (19%) fitness club members in 2002 was aged 55 or older. The number of members aged 55 or older increased from about 1.6 million in 1987 to 6.9 million in 2002.

- At the 2004 Olympic Games, U.S. female participation as a percentage of total U.S. athletes was at an all-time high. Women were 47.9% of all U.S. athletes.

- In 2005, prize money in women's tennis increased to $61.5 million for 64 events in 34 countries from $58.7 million for 64 events in 33 countries in 2004.

Source: Women's Sports Foundation.

gender sports, some of which are setting records for spectatorship, is increasing. For instance, Table 5.6 provides several notes of numbers of spectatorship for women's sports in 2005.

In sports offered as a participant product, it is also a gender-bending period. Women's participation in sports, fitness and recreational activities is at an all-time high and shows no signs of slowing. Table 5.7 presents some facts about women's participation in sports.

The women's market is being felt across the sport industry in a number of ways. For example, Table 5.8 illustrates several instances. As girls and women have become serious participants, athletes, spectators, managers, owners, manufacturers, and consumers in a variety of ways in the sport industry, their consumerism and commercial value have risen dramatically.

Disability

Disability, or handicap, no longer restricts an individual's access to, or participation in, sports, fitness, recreation, or leisure activities or in sport business. The Paralympics, World Games for the Deaf, U.S. National Wheelchair Games, National Wheelchair Basketball Association Championships, and Special Olympics are some of the events that have been leaders in paving the way for the full participation in sport and sport business of people with disabilities. In addition, the Americans with Disabilities Act has helped open the door for many more opportunities in the sport industry for people with disabilities.

Disability sport is defined as "sport that has been designed for or specifically practiced by athletes with disabilities" (DePauw and Gavron, 1995, p. 6). These sports competitions are not as new as many of us think. For example, the First International Silent Games was held in 1924. The First U.S. National Wheelchair Games were held in 1957. The First International Games for Disabled were held in 1960. Many well-known marathons such as the Boston Marathon have wheelchair divisions, the first of which was established in the 1970s.

Many sports, fitness, recreational, and leisure activities today are modified in relation to rules and equipment for an individual or group according to disability. For example, for people with vision impairments to play softball, there is a softball with a chime inside so that the players can utilize their sense of hearing to compensate. In track, people with vision impairments use their hands to follow a string around the course or track. In water skiing, people with leg impairments have water skis

---

Table 5.8
Women's Consumerism and Commercial Value in the Sport Industry.

- Women make up 70% of all purchases of NFL licensed merchandise.

- A survey of 232 NCAA tennis coaches found that most coaches felt that school Web sites and online Prospective Student-Athlete Forms were useful tools in the recruiting process. The results indicated that Division II and Division III coaches are more likely to use online tools more than Division I coaches.

- 11-year contract with ESPN, worth $160 million, expanded coverage of the NCAA Division I women's basketball tournament to include every game beginning in 2002. The deal also includes coverage of Division II basketball, women's soccer, softball, swimming, volleyball and indoor track.

- Serena Williams has earned an estimated $17.5 million on endorsements including tennis winnings and appearance fees throughout this past year. American Express has agreed in principle to sign Venus Williams to a global, multi-year, seven-figure endorsement contract.

- As of August 1, 2005, three tennis women have topped the $20 million amount in career prize money: tennis players Steffi Graf ($21,895,277), Martina Navratilova ($20,527,874) and Lindsay Davenport (20,398,784).

Source: Women's Sports Foundation.

Table 5.9

Strategies for sport marketers about the Black sports consumer market.

Key Findings about Black Consumers	Strategies for Sport Marketers
1. The Black consumer market is a challenging segment with many cultural nuances that influence their thoughts and behaviors.	Involve individuals with expertise in the Black consumer market in the designing of marketing strategies.
2. Black consumers have unique media consumption patterns.	Use Black media outlets (particularly Black radio) to promote events.
3. Blacks respond more favorably to culturally based approaches of marketing communications.	Advertisements and promotional messages should contain a theme and content that offer a reference point for Black audiences.
4. Blacks often seek a means of identifying with organizations as they decide whether or not to support their business.	Engage in activities that allow Blacks to find a self-reference link to identify with the organization.
5. Black consumers often have an allegiance to patronize Black businesses.	Conduct business with Black vendors to provide organizational needs, and involve them as corporate sponsors.
6. Black consumers often seek a cultural experience in their leisure activities.	Amend the product/service with extensions that are culturally salient to Black consumers.
7. Black consumers are socially conscious individuals.	Demonstrate a respect for the Black community through socially responsible/cause-related marketing.
8. Black consumers may have personal and structural difficulty accessing the existing channels of distribution.	Distribute tickets through outlets that are easily accessible to Black consumers. Also, find creative ways of exposing the product to the Black communities.
9. Sport behaviors are often a result of socialization occurring during childhood.	Invest in programs to include Black youth to nurture their involvement.
10. Just as any other community, the Black community also has opinion leaders.	Form a support group of Black constituents from various realms of the community to serve as staff multipliers.

Source: Armstrong, 1998.

modified so that the skier can sit on the skis. These are just a few of the numerous adjustments made to activities and equipment so that people with disabilities can participate.

Race and Ethnicity

Some groups in the United States have a single characteristic that places them in one market—race or ethnicity. People who are of Hispanic origin might all be categorized into the Hispanic market segment. People who are Asian might all be categorized into the Asian market segment. These segments, and a few others, are increasing as a proportion of the population in the United States while the proportion of whites is declining. These segments are also increasingly exercising their consumer and commercial value as sport businesses target them and as they create their own sport businesses and organizations to serve their sporting demands.

Articles appearing in the *Sport Marketing Quarterly* offer good advice concerning marketing to the African-American and Hispanic American sports markets. Tables 5.9 and 5.10 illustrate the points from those articles. Sport businesses wanting to target these segments would use this information to develop marketing mix strategies. With these segments, it would also be wise marketing to use cause-and-relationship marketing strategies.

Gay and Lesbian Sports Market

The lesbian and gay population comprise approximately 10% of the population, or 29.5 million. It is estimated that almost half, or 11–13 million, people who are gay or lesbian participate in sports, recreation, leisure, and fitness activities and that this market spends an estimated minimum average of $2,000 each per year, or a total estimated $22 billion in the sport industry (Pitts, 1997, 1999a; Simmons Market Research Bureau, 1996). Of course, those numbers might be higher or lower if more accurate research were conducted. Moreover, that study is ten years old. A current study might reveal that the numbers are higher today.

Similar to race or ethnic segments, the lesbian and gay sport market also have organized and started their own sport businesses. It is estimated that there are approximately between 3,000 and 15,000 sports events each year organized by, and targeted primarily to, the gay and lesbian market.

Like other groups, the lesbian and gay sport segment has its own Olympics—the Gay Games, held every four years. The Gay Games is an incredible success, having grown at a rate of 275% since the first games were held in 1982 (Pitts 1999b). Table 1.14 in Chapter One presents some interesting facts about the Gay Games.

After identifying this market, the sport business should then develop marketing mix strategies customized for it. Further, it would be a good idea to develop relationship and cause marketing strategies similar to those suggested for race and ethnic segments. Table 5.11 presents a list of 10 strategies that a company might consider.

Table 5.10
Strategies for sport marketers about the Hispanic sports consumer market.

1. The Hispanic market is a rapidly growing market.

2. The Hispanic population is young.

3. Hispanics tend to locate in urban areas.

4. The market is financially stable.

5. Advertising in the Spanish language is more effective than advertising in the English language.

6. Hispanic culture provides a basis for successful marketing strategies.

7. Community marketing strategies are effective means of penetrating the market.

8. Using cultural icons of the Hispanic community is an effective means of marketing.

9. Successful spokespersons tend to be "average-looking" Hispanic people.

Source: McCarthy, 1998.

Table 5.11
Strategies to Reach the Gay and Lesbian Sports Market.

1. Your company must become a "gay friendly/lesbian friendly" company. This will gain the attention and establish the trust of the lesbian and gay market.

2. Become a member of the IGTA (International Gay Travel Association) and be sure the IGTA logo is displayed in your ads.

3. Develop a strategy specific to the lesbian and gay population.

4. Use market-specific advertising, imagery, and direct marketing copy.

5. Select appropriate media.

6. Stay informed about the dynamic gay and lesbian market in general, and the gay sports industries and market specifically.

7. Form partnerships with local, national, and international lesbian/gay sports organizations and governing bodies.

8. Support gay/lesbian rights organizations and causes.

9. Be sure your company offers equal employment benefits for your lesbian and gay employers.

10. Sponsor lesbian/gay sports events.

Source: Pitts, 1999b.

Income

Income is divided into two categories: disposable income and discretionary income. *Disposable* income is all money, after taxes, at your disposal. *Discretionary* income is all money, after necessities, to be used at your discretion. Of course, it is discretionary income that sport marketing professionals study. The national average expenditure on recreational activity is now about 8% (Kelly and Warnick, 1999). Therefore, if a person's discretionary income is $30,000, then the average amount of actual dollars spent for recreational and leisure activity is about $2,400. As the amount of income increases, so does the amount spent on recreational activity: An income of $50,000 yields about $4,000; an income of $75,000 yields about $6,000; and an income of $100,000 yields about $8,000. Anglers each spent an average of $1,046 for their sport.

PERSONAL INCOME:

DISPOSABLE INCOME—
money, after taxes, at your disposal

DISCRETIONARY INCOME—
money, after necessities, to be used at your discretion

According to the Encyclopedia of American Industries:

> "Americans entertain themselves with a broad spectrum of amusements and recreations that include participatory and spectator sports, tourism, and other activities. Members of this broad industry range from athletes to bowling instructors and from fortune tellers to fireworks operators. The US population's traditional interest in a rich and varied range of recreational activities has supported the growth of an enormous, sprawling industry to capitalize on the continued popularity of such activities.

> Spending on recreational activities has grown dramatically since 1990, even in the absence of more free time. It was projected that spending by Americans on recreational activities would increase more than 30

Table 5.12
Total Number of Snow Sports Participants.

Year	Alpine	Snowboarding	Cross Country	Snowshoeing
2004	5,903,000	6,572,000	2,352,000	1,423,000
2003	6,772,000	6,309,000	1,935,000	1,424,000
2002	7,402,000	5,589,000	2,202,000	N/A
2001	7,660,000	5,343,000	2,337,000	N/A
2000	7,392,000	4,347,000	2,338,000	1,014,000

Gender of Skiers and Snowboarders—2004 calendar year

Gender	Alpine	Snowboard	Cross Country	Snowshoe
Male	55.6%	73.4%	57.8%	53.6%
Female	44.4%	26.6%	42.2%	46.4%

Source: National Sporting Goods Association, *2004 Sports Participation Study.* These figures represent participants who are 7+ years old and participated in a sport more than once during the calendar year 2004. For questions on participation, please contact NSGA at (847) 296-NSGA or info@nsga.org.

Table 5.13
Sales in the Snow Sports Industry.

Total Dollar Sales	2005/06	2004/05	Percent Difference
Specialty Stores			
Alpine Equipment	$348,467m*	$349,693m	-0.35%
Nordic Equipment	$27,365m	$31,588m	-13.37%
Telemark Equipment	$4,920m	$5,822m	-15.48%
Randonee/AT Equipment	$1,358 m	$1,523 m	-10.85%
Snowboard Equipment	$196,936m	$186,894m	5.37%
Total Equipment	**$579,045 m**	**$575,520 m**	**0.61%**
Alpine Apparel	$449,913m	$422,354m	6.53%
Snowboard Apparel	$90,407m	$78,811m	14.71%
Total Apparel	**$540,320m**	**$501,165m**	**7.81%**
Accessories	**$549,082m**	**$510,565m**	**7.54%**
Total Specialty Stores	**$1,668,447b**	**$1,587,250b**	**5.12%**
Total Chain Stores	**$496,556m**	**$464,360m**	**6.93%**
Total Industry	**$2,165,003b**	**$2,051,610b**	**5.53%**

*m = million; b = billion.
source: Snow Sports Industries of America.

percent between 2000 and 2005. Entertainment spending was dramatically higher in affluent and well-educated households." (Encyclopedia of American Industries; http://www.referenceforbusiness.com/industries/Service/Amusement-Recreation-Services-Elsewhere-Classified.html)

Income has long been a demographic used readily in the sport industry. For instance, to which income segment do sports such as polo, sailing, yachting, scuba, snow skiing, and golf seem to be targeted? Although more income groups can afford golf today, there are still many golf clubs to which only the wealthy can belong. Table 5.12 illustrates the participation demographics of snowboarders and skiers. As you can see, the sport of snowboarding has grown while the other winter sports have not. In addition, you can see that in 2004, snowboarding was dominated by males, while the other sports were relatively even in gender representation. As indicated in Figure 5.2, the largest segments are those whose household incomes are in the $50,000 to $74,000 and $75,000-and-over categories. Table 5.13 illustrates how much money is spent on snowboards, snow ski equipment, and apparel. As you can see, these are not inexpensive sports.

Table 5.14 illustrates how consumer market information is used to determine which sub-segments within a market primarily constitute the segment. In this example, we can see that the segment labeled "The Core" is the largest segment—56%—of all snowboarders and that it accounts for $9.5 million in buying power whereas "Beginners" are close at 45%. A sport marketing professional working in the snow-sports industry segment would use this information to make decisions on product, pricing, and promotion and in establishing competitive strategies.

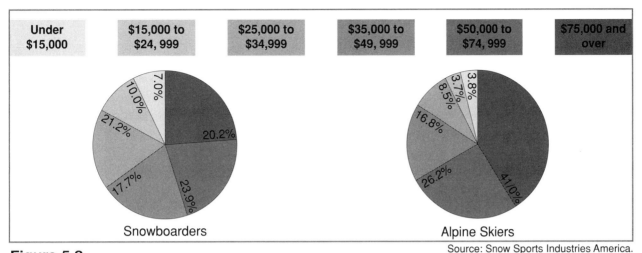

| Under $15,000 | $15,000 to $24,999 | $25,000 to $34,999 | $35,000 to $49,999 | $50,000 to $74,999 | $75,000 and over |

Snowboarders (20.2%, 23.9%, 17.7%, 21.2%, 10.0%, 7.0%)

Alpine Skiers (41.0%, 26.2%, 16.8%, 8.5%, 3.7%, 3.8%)

Source: Snow Sports Industries America.

Figure 5.2
Household income of snowboarders and skiers.

Table 5.14					
The snowboard consumer market breakdown.					
	Kids (Ages 7–11)	The Core (Men 14–24)	The Employed (24 or older)	Women (All ages)	Beginners (all ages)
Growth Trendline	Modest	Substantial	Substantial	Modest	Moderate
Percent of Snowboard Population*	17%	56%	30%	24%	45%
Buying power	$3.47 million (30% more than in skiing)	$9.5 million (200% more than in skiing)	$6.6 million	unknown	unknown (but believed to be significant)

*Some overlap doesn't add up to 100 percent.   Source: Snow Sports Industries America.

Lifestyle, Life Cycle, and Life Course

Earlier in this chapter we mentioned different lifestyle segments identified in the US population, such as the baby boomers. For each identifiable segment, there are specific demographic and psychographic information concerning life course variables such as household characteristics concerning marriage or domestic partnership, divorce, and children.

Other marketing information presents life-cycle information as actual cycles as though moving from point A to point B. For example, Figures 5.3 and 5.4 illustrate some of the possible life situations in one's life cycle.

> Sport marketing research reveals interesting information about people's lifestyles, life cycles, or life courses that can be used to determine markets and develop market strategies.

Sport marketing professionals should monitor such demographics pertaining to their existing markets and potential markets. In today's world, it is a mistake to assume that everyone's life cycle follows the old traditional route of young-single, married, married—with-children, and retired. For instance, in establishing membership categories, most fitness center and sports club businesses are moving away from the old traditional categories of "single" and "family" to more contemporary categories

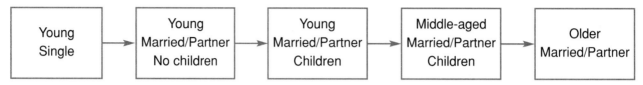

Figure 5.3
Some other possible life situations during a life cycle.

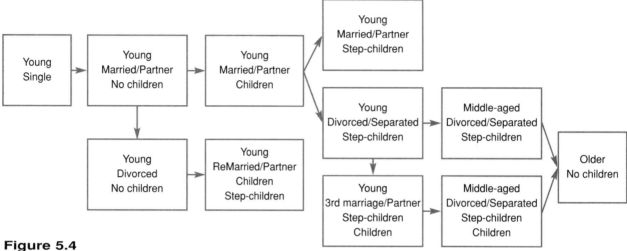

Figure 5.4
A few of many possible life situations during a life cycle.

of "individual" and "household." In those businesses that might continue to use "family" designations, for instance, the definition is contemporary, and the member is given full control to define the family group. For example, the traditional definition of "family" was "married man, wife, and children." Today's definition includes several variations in order to be inclusive and more accurately reflect today's family groups.

Psychographic Segmentation

Demographic information is a good start in describing and developing segmentation strategies, but demographics don't paint the full picture. Personality charac-

Table 5.15
Some psychological factors used in segmentation.
Personality: values, beliefs, habits
Physiological: food, drink, sleep, shelter
Psychological: affiliation, beauty, belonging, curiosity, esteem, independence, love, motive
Lifestyle: household style, parent style, importance of life comfort, culture, financial resources, occupation and education, community
Desire for: acceptance, achievement, comfort, fame, happiness, identification, prestige
Freedom from: anxiety, depression, discomfort, fear, harm, pain, sadness
Source: Walthorn, 1979; Liebert & Splegler. 1978; Kelly & Warnick, 1999.

Table 5.16
Maslow's Hierarchy of Needs (1954).
Self-actualization Needs   self-fulfillment, self-expression
Esteem Needs   self-esteem, self-respect, recognition
Social Needs   love, appreciation, fun, belonging
Safety Needs   security, freedom from pain
Physiological Needs   food, water, shelter

teristics, favorite color, motivation factors, desires, attitude, and beliefs are some of the many other types of information that describe and define a person. These are called psychographics. Partially deriving from the word *psychological*, psychographic information is psychologically related characteristics about a person. Table 5.15 presents a list of several psychographic variables. Note that many of these kinds of information are psychological and preference based such as favorite color, favorite drink, prestige, happiness, and beliefs. Thus, they are subject to change as circumstances and situations in a person's life changes. For example, the way a people spend leisure time can change when they become a parent. At the most basic level of psychographic information are basic human needs, wants, and desires. As Maslow's hierarchy of needs shows, in Table 5.16, people are driven by particular needs at certain times (Maslow, 1954). The most basic human needs are physiological—the needs for food, water, sleep, and shelter. These needs must be satisfied first because they are necessary for survival. Recent sports drink advertising, for example, attempts to appeal to the need to survive and thrive while participating in sports events.

Safety needs are second and include the need for security and protection and freedom from fear, pain, discomfort, ridicule, and harm. Sport marketing professionals often attempt to exploit the human's fear for safety and freedom from pain, for instance, by attempting to show, in ads, potential harming effects if certain actions are not taken. For example, an ad showing bones of extreme osteoporosis in someone who has not been active versus the healthy bones of someone who is active is an attempt to play on fear.

The human's social needs are commonly exploited in advertising. These include such needs and desires as love, acceptance, achievement, prestige, recognition, respect, satisfaction, appreciation, happiness, identification, sensual experiences, and status.

Many sport marketers use these in a variety of ways to reach consumers. These can be seen in, for example, such advertisements as promotions to encourage tailgating activities at sporting events such as football games, car races, and boat races. The ad for a softball bat that tells readers that the bat will make them the envy of the team and will give them more home runs is attempting to appeal to the need and desire for prestige and status, in the first instance, and achievement and satisfaction, in the second instance.

Esteem needs are those that include self-esteem and external esteem, or respect from one's group. These needs include self-respect and a sense of accomplishment, for instance.

The highest human need is self-actualization, which involves reaching a point in life where the person believes he or she should be. This includes self-development, self fulfillment, self-expression, self-identification, and self-realization. To reach this need, the marketer attempts to speak directly to the individual about her or himself. Typically, in these ads you will find such phrases as "you've reached that point in life where you've accomplished everything you wanted" or "you've made it; now you can sit back and enjoy the good life." These tend to be directed more often at the mature markets.

Typically, psychographic information is categorized in three areas: personality, motives, and lifestyle. Personality characteristics are those traits, attitudes, and behaviors that make us "who we are." Many sport products are marketed on the basis of personality segments. In one area of the sport industry in which sporting events are marketed to spectators as consumers, this is most noticeable. The NFL markets primarily to certain male segments based on personality characteristics. Typically, those commercials show male groups with distinct personality characteristics such as the "serious couch potato fan," or "the crazy painted in-the-stands fan." The WNBA markets primarily to certain female personality segments. With slogans such as "We got next," the WNBA is attempting to reach those girls and women whose attitude toward male basketball players and fans is, "You've had your time. Move over, now. It's our turn."

Motives are those needs or desires that give humans a need for action, or motivation.

Fitness center advertising usually always centers on motivation. In those ads are slogans and phrases such as "Summer's coming—can you fit into your bikini?" or "Body check—how do you look in the mirror naked?" These phrases are meant to motivate the human into wanting to get into great shape.

In a study looking at the motivations of sports participants and sports spectators, Milne and McDonald (1999) categorized motivation variables and Maslow's hierarchy of needs. Table 5.17 presents those motivational factors along with a brief description of each. In studying these, it is easy to see how a sport marketer could

| **Table 5.17** |
| **Sport Participation Motivation Factors.** |
| **Physical Fitness**—desire to being in good physical condition and improving health |
| **Risk Taking**—desire to participate in risky, thrilling, and extreme activities |
| **Stress Reduction**—desire to reduce anxiety, apprehension, fear, and tension |
| **Aggression**—desire to inflict aversive stimulus on another person, either in an attempt to reduce or increase aggressive levels |
| **Affiliation**—desire to be connected to associated with something; confirms sense of identity |
| **Social Facilitation**—desire to be with others who enjoy the same activity |
| **Self-Esteem**—desire to enhance one's positive regard of self |
| **Competition**—desire to enter into a rivalry, or contest with another, usually as a test of skill |
| **Achievement**—desire to accomplish a specific goal |
| **Skill Mastery**—desire to positively enhance performance |
| **Aesthetics**—desire to be near or part of the beauty, grace, artistry, and creative expression of sport |
| **Value Development**—desire to develop values such as loyalty and honesty through sport |
| **Self Actualization**—desire to fulfill potential |
| Source: Milne & McDonald, 1999. |

Table 5.18
VALS 2 Psychographic Segments.

Actualizers—people who are successful, sophisticated, active, leader-oriented, have high self-esteem and abundant resources, growth-oriented; seek to develop, explore, and express; and have a cultivated taste for the finer things in life.

Fulfillers—people who are mature, satisfied, reflective, comfortable, value order, knowledge, and responsibility; are well-educated, well-informed, professionally employed; tend to be conservative, are practical consumers, concerned about value, quality, and durability.

Believers—people who are conservative, conventional, traditional about family, church, community, and country; conservative and predictable consumers.

Achievers—people who are success-oriented in work and play, value control, live conventional lives, conservative, respect authority; favor established goods that demonstrate success.

Strivers—people who are self-defined, seek motivation and approval from the world around them, easily bored, impulsive, believe money means success, emulate those who have more possessions.

Experiencers—people who are young, vital, impulsive, enthusiastic, seek excitement and variety; dislike authority and conformity; avid consumers especially on clothing, fast food, movies, music, and videos.

Makers—people who are practical, down-to-earth, value self-sufficiency, traditional in family, work, and play.

Strugglers—people who are poor, ill-educated, low skilled, lack social bonds, live for the moment, immediate satisfaction and gratification; are cautious consumers.

use them to segment consumers and to develop successful promotional campaigns in a number of sport industry businesses. For instance, people who exercise at a fitness center might be categorized in a "physical fitness" segment. This would be used as part of the message, slogans, or tag lines in advertising for fitness centers. In another example, those "achievement" segment. This need to achieve would then be used by the sport marketer in promotions to enter and participate in the event.

Lifestyle, life-cycle, and life-course factors are those characteristics concerning life situations.

Although also used as a demographic, and described earlier in this chapter, lifestyle characteristics can be viewed as preferences and, as such, can be considered beliefs and attitudes.

Psychographic segmentation can include individual variables or can be combined with other variables in order to more accurately describe market segments. One such system, offered by Stanford Research International, is called VALS—Values and Lifestyles program (VALS 2, 1990). This system categorizes consumers by their values, beliefs, and lifestyles. Table 5.18 presents the segments as developed by VALS.

When this system is studied, it's easy to see how many different consumer groups in the sport industry can be segmented into these categories. For instance, those who participate in risky sports such as skydiving might be segmented into the "Experiencers" segment. Those who participate in polo might be categorized into the "Actualizers" segment. Then, using this kind of psychographic information, the sport marketer can develop promotional and advertising campaigns that have a higher chance of success.

Geographic and Geodemographic Segmentation

Geographic segmentation involves dividing or describing a population according to geographic regions or areas. Geodemographic segmentation involves using demographics, psychographics, and lifestyle information to segment a geographic region.

The United States can be segmented according to purely geographic lines. The simplest division is North, South, East, and West. Beyond that, however, geodemographic segments can be developed. For instance, there are segments with such labels as Westerner, Texan, New Yorker, Midwesterner, Yankee, Snowbird, and Southerner. Truthful or not, descriptions of people who live in these areas have been developed.

In sport business, there are sports that must take place in northern climates and sports that are better suited for southern climates. Snow skiing and water skiing are examples. This also means that a company whose products are either snow skis and equipment or water skis and equipment will want to distribute them primarily to those regions closest to where those sports take place—hence, geographic-segment marketing decisions.

Combining demographics and geography, most cities have areas that are segmented by income. There are neighborhoods and subdivisions in which the lower classes cluster and in which the upper classes cluster. This information could be used, for instance, in determining where to locate a private membership, high-priced golf and tennis country club.

Geographic segmentation is used to make distinctions between local, regional, national, and international markets or market segments. A sport company might be more successful at a local level than at a national level. On the other hand, a different sport business might be developed to compete specifically at the national or international level.

In many sports, sport marketers have developed levels of geographic-based competition to which participants can strive. Within a sport, such as boat racing, a team must first complete or win local events, then regional competitions, in order to compete at the national race. In softball, as sponsored by ASA, for example, in order to be able to compete in the national championship, a team must first win at the local, state, and regional levels.

Purchase Behavior Segmentation

Consumers approach purchasing products based on a number of influencing factors. An obvious one is income: a wealthy person might have little regard for the price of a set of golf clubs, whereas a lower-middle-class person will probably seek to buy a set of golf clubs on the secondary market. Income will also affect where and when each consumer shops. The wealthy person is likely to purchase at the country club's pro shop or directly from the manufacturer, whereas the other person will seek clubs through secondary outlets such as yard sales, ads in bargain paper classifieds, or previously owned sports equipment sporting goods stores.

Table 5.19
A typical consumer decision-making process.

All are affected and influenced by personal and social factors.

    Step 1—Problem Recognition

    Step 2—Information Search

    Step 3—Evaluation of Alternatives

    Step 4—Purchase

    Step 5—Postpurchase Behavior

Table 5.20
Promotion, teams, and schedule factors that affect the consumer's decision to attend NBA games.

Direction: Please rate the following variables that may have generally influenced you on making decisions to attend the NBA games. Please circle only one answer (5 = very much, 4 = much, 3 = somewhat, 2 = a little, 1 = none).

Game Promotion (6 items)

1. advertising	5 4 3 2 1	.86
2. publicity	5 4 3 2 1	.84
3. direct mail and notification	5 4 3 2 1	.76
4. good seats	5 4 3 2 1	.66
5. giveaway/prize	5 4 3 2 1	.56
6. ticket discount	5 4 3 2 1	.45

Home Team (4 items)

7. win/loss records	5 4 3 2 1	.88
8. league standing	5 4 3 2 1	.87
9. superstars	5 4 3 2 1	.54
10. overall team performance	5 4 3 2 1	.46

Opposing Team

11. overall team performance	5 4 3 2 1	.90
12. superstar	5 4 3 2 1	.88

Schedule Convenience (2 items)

13. game time (evening)	5 4 3 2 1	.44
21. day of week (weekend)	5 4 3 2 1	.40

Solution of Factor Analysis by Principal Component Extraction and Orthogonal Rotation (N = 861)

Source: Zhang, Pease, Hui & Michaud, 1995.

Many other influencing factors, of which most are demographics, psychographics, geography, location, and product use, affect a person's purchasing behaviors. These factors affect the consumer's decision making process toward a purchase—a step-by-step process used when buying products. The typical process involves problem recognition, information search, evaluation of alternatives, purchase, and post-purchase behavior (see Table 5.19).

One area of study in sport marketing that helps the sport marketer understand consumers is in the area of participant satisfaction and is based on the question of why people participate in sports activities. Gaining an understanding of why people participate in a sports activity helps the sport marketer develop marketing strategies aimed at attracting new consumers and keeping current consumers.

A growing area of study within sport marketing concerning consumer behavior involves the study of spectators. Most of this research involves studying the factors that affect the spectator's decision to attend the event. In a study of why people attend NBA (National Basketball Association) games, researchers studied 14 factors categorized into four groups (Zhang et al., 1995). Table 5.20 presents the information from that study. You can see that the factors listed have to do with promotions, facts about the teams involved in the event, and the game schedule. These groups of factors are still used today in studying consumer behavior. Many other factors influence the purchase behavior of spectators of sports events. Tables 5.21, 5.22, 5.23, and 5.24 present information from studies on factors that influence the purchase behavior of spectators for soccer, golf, and ice hockey events. Figure 5.5 presents a compilation of all of several factors from sport marketing studies (Lu, 2000). As you can see, there are many factors that play a part in the consumer's decision-making process concerning whether or not to attend an event. The sport marketing professional can use this type of purchase behavior information to develop or modify marketing mix strategies.

Table 5.21
Level of involvement of other factors that affect the consumer's decision to attend soccer games.

	Total	Preboom	Boom	Postboom		Total	Preboom	Boom	Postboom
Favorite team					**How to purchase tickets**				
Don't have	11.5%	8.2%	6.7%	26.9%	Through ticketing agency	37.1%	34.1%	35.6%	46.5%
Have	88.5%	91.8%	93.3%	73.1%***	Through supporter's clubs	39.2%	40.9%	43.0%	25.0%
Favorite player					At game	11.3%	14.0%	9.3%	13.3%
Don't have	34.7%	31.1%	31.0%	47.7%	Others	12.3%	11.0%	12.0%	15.2%***
Have	65.3%	68.9%	69.0%	52.3%***	**Transportation time (min.)**				
Understanding rules					Mean	75.0	73.9	74.3	78.1
Well	24.8%	45.6%	19.7%	13.1%	SD	52.4	52.8	52.8	51.2
Enough	57.7%	49.8%	63.0%	53.7%	**Size of party**				
A little	15.5%	3.7%	16.5%	26.7%	Go alone	13.0%	17.4%	11.8%	10.7%
Not at all	2.0%	0.9%	0.7%	6.6%***	Go in a pair	52.6%	50.0%	52.8%	55.4%
Experience of soccer					3 persons	12.8%	12.6%	13.5%	10.7%
Don't have	64.2%	43.9%	70.0%	73.6%	4 persons	12.4%	8.9%	14.0%	12.8%
Have	35.8%	56.1%	30.0%	26.4%***	More	9.2%	11.1%	7.8%	10.4%***
When decide to go					**Who to go with**				
Day of game	5.2%	6.1%	3.8%	7.0%	Friends	36.6%	39.9%	35.5%	36.6%
Before day of game	20.1%	17.3%	17.5%	29.4%	Work Friends	10.6%	10.5%	9.9%	12.8%
and after pregame					Social contract	4.8%	5.6%	4.0%	6.1%
Before previous session	74.7%	76.6%	78.7%	63.7%	Family/Relatives	42.8%	37.9%	46.6%	37.4%
How to get information (M.A.)					Others	5.2%	6.1%	4.1%	7.1%***
Newspaper	19.7%	24.0%	21.1%	11.3%***	**Belonging to supporter clubs**				
TV/Radio	8.7%	8.7%	9.6%	6.4%	I am a member	45.0%	50.7%	50.1%	19.2%
Soccer magazines	25.5%	31.5%	27.6%	14.0%***	I want to be	17.0%	14.6%	17.1%	20.7%
General magazines	7.2%	6.7%	6.6%	9.5%	I do NOT want to be	37.9%	34.7%	32.7%	60.1%***
Friends/Acquaintances	23.4%	18.3%	19.2%	39.4%***	**Frequency of attendance (games)**				
Posters	4.3%	3.8%	5.3%	2.4%**	Mean	4.4	6.0	5.1	1.7***
Club newsletters	29.1%	31.0%	34.7%	13.5%	SD	5.3	6.0	5.2	3.3
Others	19.3%	18.0%	19.3%	21.3%	**Watching games on TV**				
How to get tickets					Often	67.0%	77.9%	71.2%	44.4%
Purchase tickets in advance	57.8%	56.3%	62.4%	48.3%	Sometimes	25.7%	19.3%	23.3%	38.4%
Purchase tickets at stadium	9.0%	11.0%	7.6%	10.0%	Seldom	4.6%	2.0%	3.8%	9.4%
Purchase with package tour	1.8%	1.7%	2.0%	1.5%	Almost never	2.7%	0.7%	1.7%	7.7%***
Receive as a gift	21.1%	19.9%	17.9%	29.8%	**Watch other sports**				
Others	10.3%	11.1%	10.0%	10.3%***	Don't	56.2%	36.9%	47.8%	41.4%
					Do	43.8%	63.1%	52.2%	58.6%

Notes: *p < .05, **p < .01, ***p < .001

Source: Nakazawa, Mahony, Funk & Hirakawa, 1999.

When compared to other types of products, sports events present a complex sport business problem for the sport management and marketing professional. This is perhaps unique in the universe of selling products. It is certainly different from factors that influence the purchase behavior and decision-making process of a consumer's decision to purchase such products as laundry detergent, a DVD movie, or property. Yet, selling sports events is similar to such products as a Broadway play, a circus, or a trip to Disney World. These are all entertainment products, and sports events fall into this category of product. Therefore, sport marketing professionals working for sport businesses selling sports events can use research and information from studies in entertainment.

Step 1: Problem recognition. Do you feel thirsty after your soccer game? Did you break your softball bat? Does your sport company need research? These questions describe situations in which you might find yourself. In order to solve the prob-

Table 5.22
Entertainment options that affect the consumer's decision to attend a minor league hockey game.

Entertainment Option	% of Response to the Likert Scale					Mean	SD
	1	2	3	4	5		
Professional & Amateur Sports							
Attend pro football games	44	26	16	6	7	2.7	2.5
Attend pro indoor soccer games	83	8	5	2	2	1.4	3.0
Attend pro basketball games	31	27	22	11	9	2.4	1.3
Attend pro baseball games	23	26	25	15	11	2.6	1.3
Attend intercollegiate games	40	21	18	10	11	2.3	1.4
Attend other sport shows	25	23	32	13	8	2.0	1.3
Recreational Participation							
Play recreational sports	16	15	24	18	27	3.3	1.6
Work out/Exercise	11	16	23	21	29	3.4	1.4
Travel	8	13	27	24	28	3.5	1.3
Arts							
Attend concerts	18	27	27	16	12	2.8	1.4
Attend movies	7	15	26	26	26	3.5	1.8
Television							
Watch sports on TV	7	11	17	25	41	3.9	1.6
Watch nonsports programs on TV	5	12	21	25	38	3.8	1.2
Dining and Night Clubs							
Attend bars/restaurants	8	7	20	28	37	3.8	1.3
Attend night clubs	35	23	18	12	12	2.5	2.5

*1 = Never; 2 = Occasionally; 3 = Sometimes; 4 = Often; 5 = Always

Source: Zhang, Smith, Pease & Jambor, 1997.

Table 5.23
Factors that affect the consumer's decision to attend a golf event as a spectator.

Number of Professional Tournaments Attended (Past 5 years)	0	1	2–5	6–10	Over 10
	22.3%	8%	50.3%	12.6%	6.9%
	n = 39	n = 14	n = 88	n = 22	n = 12

Number of Professional Tournaments Viewed on Television (Past year)	0	1	2–5	6–10	Over 10
	1.7%	2.9%	14%	18.3%	62.3%
	n = 3	n = 5	n = 26	n = 32	n = 109

Years of Golf Played	Under 10	11–20	21–30	31–40	41–50	Unknown
	50%	21%	12%	9%	4%	4%
	n = 88	n = 37	n = 21	n = 15	n = 7	n = 7

Rounds of Golf Per Year	0	1–10	11–25	Over 25	Unknown
	13.7%	17.1%	18.3%	50.3%	.6%
	n = 24	n = 30	n = 32	n = 88	n = 1

Source: Lascu, Giese, Toolan, Guehring & Mercer, 1995.

Table 5.24
Level of involvement factors that affect a consumer's decision to attend a golf tournament.

Variable	Involvement		t-Value	Prob.
	Low	High		
Motivation for Attendance				
Proximity to golfers	3.99	4.39	140.94	.017
Live action	4.36	4.70	132.41	.007
Fitness motivation	3.07	3.44	138.73	.070
Personal love of golf	3.79	4.67	117.46	.000
Support for charity	3.47	3.93	139.98	.016
Golfing tips	3.07	3.86	135.44	.000
Excitement of the final round	3.78	4.33	140.00	.002
Promotions associated with event	2.49	3.10	133.65	.004
The company of friends	3.35	3.89	140.95	.005
Exposure to advertisements	2.45	2.95	136.31	.022
Ticket value	2.60	3.03	138.07	.055
Excitement of first two rounds	2.47	3.25	125.66	.001
Commitment to Golf				
Golf tournaments attended	2.45	3.07	142.41	.001
Golf tournaments watched	4.08	4.60	127.32	.001
Rounds of golf played	2.58	3.57	125.34	.000
Number years playing golf	11.75	17.92	138.65	.007
Golf Digest	.37	.56	142.74	.025
Use of golf for business	.19	.33	137.92	.053
Money spent last year	1.40	3.14	132.91	.003
Likelihood of attending similar event	4.04	4.72	101.22	.000
Ability to identify Cellular One as a sponsor	.14	.04	115.97	.045

(Source: Lascu, Giese, Toolan, Guehring & Mercer, 1995).

lem, you first must recognize it. Therefore, you have learned that you will get thirsty at your soccer game and so will determine that you need a sports drink to take to the game. You need a new softball bat because you broke the one you have. Your sport business needs to know how consumers think about the new stadium, so you might need to hire a sport marketing consulting firm to do this research and solve the problem.

All of these are situations in which a problem has been recognized. The need for a solution develops.

Step 2: Information search. The first step toward finding a solution is seeking information to help develop the best solution. A person will consider such factors as money available, time available, and memory. These are internal factors that influence the knowledge or decision to purchase a particular product. Other variables that will influence this decision are external factors. External factors include information that a person receives from friends, family, advertising, and sales people.

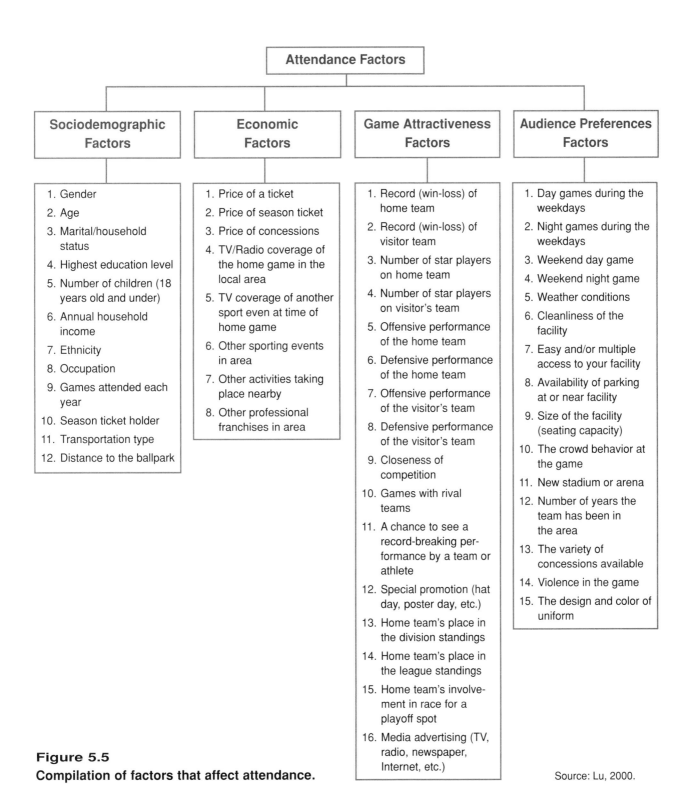

Attendance Factors

Sociodemographic Factors

1. Gender
2. Age
3. Marital/household status
4. Highest education level
5. Number of children (18 years old and under)
6. Annual household income
7. Ethnicity
8. Occupation
9. Games attended each year
10. Season ticket holder
11. Transportation type
12. Distance to the ballpark

Economic Factors

1. Price of a ticket
2. Price of season ticket
3. Price of concessions
4. TV/Radio coverage of the home game in the local area
5. TV coverage of another sport even at time of home game
6. Other sporting events in area
7. Other activities taking place nearby
8. Other professional franchises in area

Game Attractiveness Factors

1. Record (win-loss) of home team
2. Record (win-loss) of visitor team
3. Number of star players on home team
4. Number of star players on visitor's team
5. Offensive performance of the home team
6. Defensive performance of the home team
7. Offensive performance of the visitor's team
8. Defensive performance of the visitor's team
9. Closeness of competition
10. Games with rival teams
11. A chance to see a record-breaking performance by a team or athlete
12. Special promotion (hat day, poster day, etc.)
13. Home team's place in the division standings
14. Home team's place in the league standings
15. Home team's involvement in race for a playoff spot
16. Media advertising (TV, radio, newspaper, Internet, etc.)

Audience Preferences Factors

1. Day games during the weekdays
2. Night games during the weekdays
3. Weekend day game
4. Weekend night game
5. Weather conditions
6. Cleanliness of the facility
7. Easy and/or multiple access to your facility
8. Availability of parking at or near facility
9. Size of the facility (seating capacity)
10. The crowd behavior at the game
11. New stadium or arena
12. Number of years the team has been in the area
13. The variety of concessions available
14. Violence in the game
15. The design and color of uniform

Figure 5.5
Compilation of factors that affect attendance.

Source: Lu, 2000.

An information search can occur internally, externally, or both. The type of product needed or desired and its uses and functions will influence the extent to which the consumer uses internal, external or both factors. Additionally, price can have a fairly significant influence. As presented in the price chapter, the price of a product can affect consumers in a number of ways such as influencing the consumer's willingness to spend, expectation of quality and performance, and post-purchase anxiety or comfort.

The type of product and its uses and functions will trigger an internal or external search, or both. For example, athletic tape needed to wrap a sprained ankle is

a necessity. Most people are not trained in sports medicine. Most retail stores such as Walgreen's and Eckerd's carry only one or two brands, and they are practically identical to the general consumer. Therefore, there is very little, if any, information needed to make this purchase. However, if the consumer is considering purchasing a boat for skiing and other water sports, the consumer is much more likely to employ a major external information search. The purchase of a boat requires some knowledge of the following: how you will use the boat (product uses and functions); how often you will use the boat; where the boat will be used; what size boat you need or want; how many people you expect to have on board on a typical outing; the activities you plan while on the boat and using the boat; the kind of towing vehicle you have; will you have to tow (trailer) the boat for each use; how far you will have to trailer the boat; the kind of terrain you will have to cover in trailering the boat; the amenities you want or need in the boat such as stereo, toilet, water, built-in cooler, kitchen, built-in wet bar, and trolling motor; the kind of engine you want, outboard, inboard, stern drive, or jet drive; the kind of water sports equipment you want or need—skis, kneeboard, skurfer, wakeboard, tubes, or barefoot skiing equipment; and the kind of safety equipment do you want or need. As you can see, to purchase a boat, a consumer will need to collect much information that will help answer those questions and many more.

Consumers with prior knowledge or experience with a product are less needy of external information searches. They will rely primarily on the knowledge gained from the experience with the product from the previous purchase.

Steps 3 and 4: Evaluation of alternatives and purchase. After collecting information concerning the targeted product, the consumer will consider all alternatives, develop a set of criteria, weigh advantages and disadvantages, consider internal and external information again, and then begin to narrow decision to finalist products. Again, as you can see in Tables 5.21, 5.22, 5.23, and 5.24, there can be many factors to consider. Some of those factors are alternative products. If the product is attending and watching a sports event, you can see in the example in Table 5.22 that there are a number of alternative things to do that compete for the consumer's attention or purchase.

Step 5: Post-purchase behavior. Your consumer may exhibit post-purchase behavior. This involves how the consumer feels and what the consumer thinks about the purchase and whether or not the consumer is satisfied or dissatisfied in regard to the consumer's expectations about how the product is performing. In other words, if the consumer went into the purchase with a certain set of expectations (product uses and benefits) and those expectations are being met, then the consumer will probably be satisfied and feel comfortable with the purchase. If, however, the product does not perform to the consumer's expectations, then the consumer will probably be dissatisfied and feel uncomfortable about the purchase. For example, if a consumer buys tickets to a Super Bowl game and expects to have an enjoyable experience with a game that is exciting and close, yet the game turns out to be a large margin-of-victory game, then the consumer would be dissatisfied with the purchase. If, however, a consumer bought tickets to the final of the 1998 Women's World Cup, was a United States team fan, and expected to find a fair-sized crowd and an exciting game, that consumer was probably happily surprised to find that the US team won the World Cup, crowd numbers were well above anyone's expectations, and the game was an exceptionally exciting game. This consumer will conclude that the purchase was above expectation and will be satisfied.

Post-purchase behavior is another area of concern for any sport business and should be considered as part of the company's customer service department.

> Sport businesses must avoid over-broad promises about their products to ensure that consumers receive what they expect.

Sport business management and marketing professionals must take care not to promise too much in a product, lest that product does not meet the claims made and thus adds to the consumer's dissatisfaction with the product. Too much post-purchase dissatisfaction can lead to the development of a negative image for the company. Consider, for example, the image problem facing several professional men's sports today in relation to some public opinion that the players are overpaid and get away with anything, that the league is a haven for criminals and encourages violence, and thus that the games are not worth watching and do not serve as a good role model for our youth. Sport marketing professionals are making attempts to counter some of these claims in order to maintain a supportive consumer base.

Product Use and Benefits Segmentation

A consumer needs a product in order to satisfy a need or desire. Therefore, the product is the tool for the consumer to perform certain functions and realize certain

> **A Consumer Needs:**
>
> a product in order to satisfy a need or desire. Therefore, the product is the tool for the consumer to perform certain functions and realize certain benefits.

benefits. A softball bat is a tool for the player to hit the ball, but a well-selected bat is what the player chooses in looking to improve hitting percentage, have more control, get more home runs, and enhance status among teammates and fans. A fitness center provides the potential for the consumer to get in shape, become physically fit, enhance health, lower blood pressure, control weight, meet people, sweat, grow stronger, lose those holiday-gained pounds, be a part of the cool crowd, fit into certain clothes, and/or get ready for the swimsuit season. As a matter of fact, the sport marketer uses these exact words in advertising for these products. Knowing how the consumer wants to use the product, the functions the consumer expects the product to perform, and the benefits the consumer expects to receive from the product is important for the sport marketing professional in developing marketing mix strategies that are well informed. This enhances the chances for success.

Product usage information can be used in a number of ways in the marketing mix. For example, there is a theory called the 80-20 rule. This means that 20% of all consumers generate 80% of consumption. This can be seen in fitness centers, for example, where a small group of consumers (about 20%) are responsible for the core (about 80%) of the consumption of the product. The rest of the consumers do not use the facility as much or as often. Sport marketing professionals have developed categories for these kinds of groups. Some of those include heavy users, medium users, light users, and non-users; high involvement and low involvement; hard-core fan and fan; and high loyalty, spurious loyalty, latent loyalty, and low loyalty. These kinds of segmentation categories can be used by the sport marketing professional to study consumers and develop appropriate marketing strategies. The information presented in a product in order to satisfy a need or desire. Therefore, the product is the tool for the consumer to perform certain functions and realize certain benefits.

Tables 5.23 and 5.24 provide information from a study on sports participation and its influence on sports spectators. That is, the researchers were studying the relationship between a person's involvement as a participant in a sport and his or her involvement as a spectator of that sport. In general, the researchers found that high-involvement consumers—those who participate more frequently in the sport—are more likely to attend more of the sport's events in person, watch more on TV, pay more attention to activities offered at the live event, pay more attention to promotions associated with the event, and such consumers are more capable of correctly identifying the event sponsors (Lascu et al., 1995).

Business Consumers, B2B Marketing, and Business Consumer Segmentation

If your business produces products for businesses, then your consumers are business consumers. Business-to-business marketing involves the marketing of products to individuals and organizations for purposes other than personal consumption (Lamb, Hair, & McDaniel, 1996). These consumers acquire products and services for purposes of manufacturing, production, resale, operations, enhancement of a company's position, or other business-related reason. For example, if your company manufactures T-shirts to sell directly to a licensing and merchandising company for a sports event such as the national rodeo, then your consumers are business consumers. If your company conducts studies of sponsorship advertising and its effects for companies who are the sponsors or the companies who manage the event, then your consumers are business consumers.

Segmenting and targeting business consumers are similar to segmenting end consumers (those who purchase products for personal consumption). Business consumer segmentation involves categorizing into groups with similar characteristics. Most business consumers can be categorized into the following groups: manufacturers, resellers, sports-governing bodies, institutions, and media sports enterprises. Manufacturers are those businesses that purchase products that are used to manufacture or produce products or that are used for the daily operations of the company. For example, Hillerich and Bradsby (H and B) is a producer of baseball bats and ice-hockey equipment. To manufacture these, H and B must purchase materials such as wood and plastics. Therefore, H and B is a business consumer. H and B also sells primarily to business consumers. Such companies as sporting goods retailers, distributors, and wholesalers who purchase H and Bs products such as their bats and golf clubs do so for resale purposes. Therefore, H and B must study, segment, and target business consumers.

Resellers include those businesses that purchase products for the purpose of reselling them for a profit. Sporting goods retail stores, for instance, are resellers: They purchase many products from many different companies in order to resell them for profit. Another example includes promotion and sponsorship management companies. For instance, a company that consults and manages sponsorship contracts must purchase signs for signage from a sign manufacturer. Therefore, they are a business consumer. Also, their products are targeted primarily to business consumers—those companies who want their sponsorship management products. In another example, a college licensing and merchandising company is a business-to-business company and therefore both a business consumer and a company that targets business consumers. This type of company will purchase merchandise from manufacturers and producers and sell them to their business customers.

Governing bodies include numerous organizations whose business is to govern various sports, recreational, and leisure activities, events, and organizations as well as equipment and facilities. The International Olympic Committee, for instance, governs everything involved in the Olympics enterprises. Its business-to-business product is primarily to stage, or produce (sell), a multi-sports event to end consumers, yet its transactions involve primarily selling the rights to broadcast the event to media sports enterprises such as TV and radio, rights to produce the event to a host organization, and sponsorship products to sponsorship companies. Thus, the IOC practically never directly sells the event to the end consumer.

Institutions are usually non-profit entities that include such organizations as schools, colleges and universities, faith-based sports clubs, city sports commissions, sports foundations, youth sports organizations, and city sports and recreation offices. They purchase such business products as facilities, office equipment and supplies, sporting goods, equipment, apparel, and promotional merchandise.

Media sports enterprises are those for-profit businesses that seek to broadcast, or distribute, sports events, sports-related shows, sports news, and sports-related material via media such as television, radio, magazines, video, DVD, and the Web. Sports events broadcast on TV and radio are a common product. As pointed out earlier in this chapter, there are 235 hours of sports programming every 24 hours on 48 sports channels. Although many sports magazines, video, DVD, and Web products target end consumers, the companies that manufacture these products must transact with several businesses to purchase such products as the rights to the sports event for publications purposes, paper, videotapes, DVD disks, Internet website providers, and satellite distribution companies. Some of these companies also target businesses consumers with some of their products. For instance, trade publications are targeted to businesses.

BASES FOR BUSINESS CONSUMER SEGMENTATION

Business consumer segmentation variables are a little different from end consumer variables. Whereas end consumer bases focus on human characteristics, business consumer bases must include business characteristics. Although it will be humans who make particular purchase decisions for the company, the company most likely has purchase criteria or policies that the buyer must follow. The following are brief descriptions of bases for business consumer segmentation (from Lamb, Hair, & McDaniel, 1996).

Sport Business Consumers:
Manufacturers
Resellers
Sports Governing Bodies
Institutions
Media Sports Enterprises

Geographic location. As presented earlier in this chapter, consumers can be segmented according to geographic location variables. Common variables using simply geographic locations include local, state, and region. For instance, often various regions of the United States are known for certain sports: The West is associated with rodeo events; coastal regions are associated with ocean-related sports; the Rocky Mountain states are associated with winter sports and mountain-climbing sports; certain states such as Indiana are known as basketball states, and certain states such as Texas are known as football states. Companies that sell to industries that are concentrated geographically would benefit by locating close to those markets. For instance, surfboard companies will enhance efforts if they locate in coastal areas. In another example, sports agents might enhance efforts if they locate in large city areas that can sustain several professional and semi-professional sports organizations.

Customer type. Segmenting by type of customer has benefits because the seller can concentrate marketing mix strategies. For instance, manufacturers of sports equipment can focus on retail stores, specialty stores, or distributors. Thus, marketing mix strategies would be developed specifically to one or more of these.

Customer size. This base is similar to segmenting end consumers based on product usage such as heavy, medium, and light. This base involves volume. Your company might decide that its best strategy is to target those companies that purchase in large volume only.

Product use. Many products can be used in different ways, especially raw materials such as wood, plastics, and steel. How your customers will be using these products will determine how much they buy and other criteria. For instance, if a golf club manufacturer produces steel shafts, then the company will probably need to purchase a particular type of steel and a certain amount of steel. In another example, if a licensing company needs T-shirts for a very large sports event, such as the Kentucky Derby, then their use of the product for a once-a-year event will affect their purchase.

Purchase criteria. A company might purchase based on specific criteria such as price, quality, reputation, or delivery. If your company can deliver what the company needs when they need it, then you might want to use this as a reason to target this company.

Industry Segmentation

Industry segmentation is the process of dividing or categorizing an industry into logical and/or similar parts, or industry segments. It involves industry analysis—the study of an industry. The sport marketing professional needs to know and understand the whole sport industry and, more specifically, its segments. This will help in determining where an individual sport business fits into a particular segment and into the whole industry. It helps in determining how events in the industry, or in a segment, will affect an individual sport business. This knowledge will help in marketing strategy.

Understanding the entire sport industry and its segments allows the sport marketing professional to determine where to position the business in the industry and what type of competitive strategy is needed.

Industry segmentation may be conducted in a manner similar to consumer segmentation: one whole group divided into categories of smaller groups based on homogeneous characteristics. The primary purpose for industry segmentation is competitive strategy formulation. Other reasons include identifying marketing opportunities and threats within a specific segment, to develop an appropriate marketing mix, and to inform resource allocation (Pitts, Fielding, and Miller, 1994).

BASES FOR INDUSTRY SEGMENTATION

Segmenting an industry is typically done primarily using two variables: products and buyers. An industry can comprise one product and one buyer. More typically, an industry segment comprises multiple similar products and buyers. The following are some of the ways the sport business industry has been segmented.

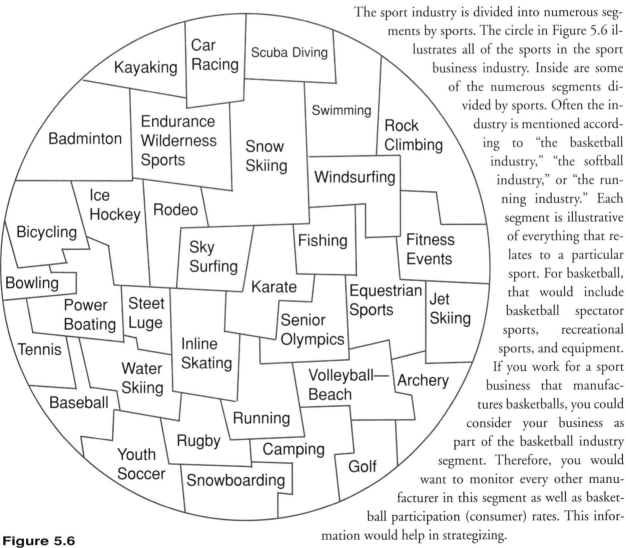

The sport industry is divided into numerous segments by sports. The circle in Figure 5.6 illustrates all of the sports in the sport business industry. Inside are some of the numerous segments divided by sports. Often the industry is mentioned according to "the basketball industry," "the softball industry," or "the running industry." Each segment is illustrative of everything that relates to a particular sport. For basketball, that would include basketball spectator sports, recreational sports, and equipment. If you work for a sport business that manufactures basketballs, you could consider your business as part of the basketball industry segment. Therefore, you would want to monitor every other manufacturer in this segment as well as basketball participation (consumer) rates. This information would help in strategizing.

Figure 5.6
The sport business industry and some of its numerous segments as divided by sports.

Figure 5.7 is an illustration of the Pitts et al. (1994) sport industry segmentation model, which categorizes the whole industry according to product function. Figure 5.8 shows the full model. If your company offers products whose function is promotion, then your company is categorized into the sport promotion segment. In this segment, you would want to monitor your competitors and all consumers of these products. This knowledge will help with competitive strategy development.

Figure 5.9 divides the industry according to career fields (Parks and Zanger, 1990). Within each area might be different sports and different products, but each is similar by area. For instance, there are numerous different professional sports. Those might be further subdivided by each sport, or by season such as winter sports and summer sports. However, what makes them all similar is that they are all professional sports.

Figure 5.10 illustrates the sport industry as divided by financial size (Meek, 1997) with the largest segment at the top.

As in all other studies on the financial size of the industry, sporting goods and participant sports are always in the number one and two positions. It certainly makes sense. Participant sports contains all those millions of average (nonprofessional) sports people participating in all those recreational sports

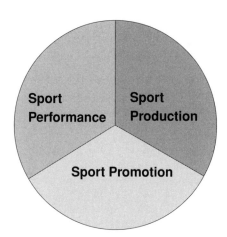

Figure 5.7
The sport industry and its segments as divided by product function in the Pitts, Fielding & Miller Sport Industry Segmentation Model (1994).

Sport Industry: All Sport-Related Products— Goods, Services, Places, People & Ideas— Offered to the Constumer

SPORT INDUSTRY SEGMENTATION
BY PRODUCT AND BUYER TYPE

SPORT PERFORMANCE SEGMENT	SPORT PRODUCTION SEGMENT	SPORT PROMOTION SEGMENT
Definition: Sport performance as offered to the consumer as a participation or spectatorial product	**Definition:** Those products needed or desired for the production of or to influence the quality of sport performance.	**Definition:** Those products offered as tools used to promote the sport product.

SPORT PERFORMANCE SEGMENT
1. Athletics
   a. Amateur Sport
   b. Professional Sport
2. Private Business Sport
3. Tax-Supported Sport
4. Membership Supported Sport Organizations
5. Non-Profit Sport Organizations
6. Sport Education
7. Fitness & Sport Firms

SPORT PRODUCTION SEGMENT
1. Outfitting Products
   a. Equipment
   b. Apparel
2. Performance Production Products
   a. Fitness Trainer
   b. Medical Care
   c. Sport Facilities
   d. Governing Bodies & Officials

SPORT PROMOTION SEGMENT
1. Promotional Merchandising Products
2. Promotional Events
3. The Media
4. Sponsorship
   a. Single Event Sponsorship
   b. Multiple Event Sponsorship
   c. Single Team Sponsorship
   d. Individual Sponsorship
   e. Circuit or League Sponsorship
   f. Shared Sponsorship
5. Endorsement
   a. Individual Endorsement
   b. Team Endorsement
   c. Full Organization Endorsement
   d. Nonspecific Sport Use

Figure 5.8
The Sport Industry Segment Model.

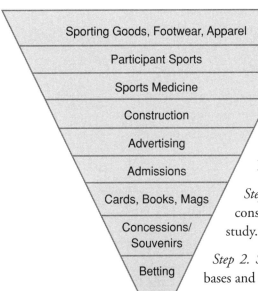

Source: Parks, Zanger, and Quarterman, 1998.

Consulting	Sport Marketing
Sports Club Management	Sports Information
Intercollegiate Sports	Physical Fitness
Athletic Training and Sports Medicine	Campus Recreation
Community Sports	Facility Management
Professional Sport	Aquatics Management
Entrepreneurship	Sports Journalism

Figure 5.9
The sport business industry as divided by career fields.

on a daily basis, and all those people must have equipment and apparel in order to participate. So, their financial importance should come as no surprise.

Other methods include segmenting the industry by product. For example, baseball bat manufacturers study the "baseball bat industry;" athletic shoe manufacturers study the "athletic shoe industry;" golf course construction companies study the "golf course industry;" and a boat manufacturer studies the "boat-building industry." Each company needs to know what is going on in its specific area.

Industry Segmentation Information

Industry segment information is readily available. Appendixes B and C offer information on sport business trade organizations and trade publications. *Trade* refers to a particular vocation, skill, knowledge area, profession, or business type. These businesses and publications offer information regarding industry information, research, and market events.

Segmentation information can also be found in numerous places on the internet. Try doing a search through any Internet search engine, such as *Google*, and see what you can find.

Sporting Goods, Footwear, Apparel
Participant Sports
Sports Medicine
Construction
Advertising
Admissions
Cards, Books, Mags
Concessions/ Souvenirs
Betting

Figure 5.10
The Sport Business Industry as Divided by Economic Size According to Meek (1996)

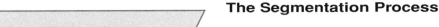

The Segmentation Process

Now that we know what characteristics to use in segmenting markets and an industry, let's look at a simple step-by-step process in segmenting a market. Table 5.25 illustrates the steps in such a process. Remember that the primary purpose of segmentation is to understand specific groups of consumers or an industry segment to inform marketing mix strategies.

Step 1. Select a market or industry. Determine which set of consumers or industry your company wants to consider and study.

Step 2. Select one or more segmentation bases. Determine which bases and variables your company wants to use.

Step 3. Select specific variables. Within the bases, determine which variables your company wants to consider.

Step 4. Analyze the segment. Study, analyze, and determine conclusions about the segment(s) chosen. Which will be most beneficial to the company?

Table 5.25
A Typical Segmentation Process.

Step 1—Select a market or industry	Step 4—Analyze the segment
Step 2—Select one or more segmentation bases	Step 5—Select one or more target markets
Step 3—Select specific variables	Step 6—Develop appropriate marketing mix strategies

Step 5. Select one or more target markets. Determine which specific market or industry segment your company wants to target.

Step 6. Develop appropriate marketing mix strategies. Develop marketing mix strategies based on your information about the target market(s) or industry segment.

> When segments are very similar to each other, an undifferentiated targeting strategy—much like mass marketing—may be used, whereby all consumers receive the same marketing treatment.

Target Market(s) Selection Strategies

From the segments, your company will select which one or more to target. These become the company's target markets or industry segments. These groups are the ones for which the company will develop specific marketing mix strategies. The following are typical target market strategies (from Lamb et al., 1996).

Undifferentiated targeting strategy involves making no distinctions between any of the segments. Therefore, this is similar to mass marketing. This approach will work if the segments are so similar in characteristics that a distinct differentiation cannot be made. Marketing mix strategies will concentrate on the entire market.

Niche targeting strategy involves the selection of one segment on which to focus. Typically, niche marketing will work if the company is the only one selling the only product to its consumers. This strategy will be successful as long as the situation stays the same. However, once another company begins to offer the product, your targeting strategy will be changing.

Multi-segment targeting strategy involves the selection of two or more segments to target. Usually, this strategy can be the most successful in terms of efficiency and effectiveness. Even if there is very little difference between segments, people feel special when showered with attention.

Positioning the Sport Business and/or Product

"Positioning" is what a consumer thinks about a product in comparison to other products. Positioning refers to the development of specific marketing-mix elements to influence the consumer's perception of a product, brand, or company. For instance, a consumer might think that the golf clubs made by the Red Brand Company are better than those made by the Blue Brand Company because the Red Brand clubs are lighter, stronger, give more control, give more distance, and are higher quality clubs because they are more expensive. The Red Brand Company's product carries a particular place, or position, in the consumer's thinking.

> Positioning establishes the image of a product or company and becomes the consumer's base of reference when deciding which company's product to purchase.

Courtesy of Bigfoto.com

Positioning is important for products such as road bikes, which are produced by numerous competing companies.

The consumer could have developed this perception with no input. However, it might be more likely that the marketing tactics and strategies of the Red Brand Company influenced the consumer. For instance, the Red Brand Company can use the phrase of "lighter, stronger, longer" so much in all of its advertising that the consumer can be influenced by the words.

Positioning assumes that a consumer will compare products produced by different companies and could be influenced by the company's positioning tactics. Of course, if a product has been positioned to target a specific market, then that market will be more readily influenced because it already possesses the demographics and other segment variables to which the product was customized. For example, if a golf club company wants to target a wealthy segment and position the club to be the club for the wealthy, then the consumers in this segment are more likely to be influenced by the marketing mix strategies and are more likely to be attracted to that club.

Positioning is a critical element for the sport marketing professional. Most sport businesses have more than one market. Many products therefore have more than one market, and some products have more than one function (use). The sport business must develop the image of the product that it wants the consumer to hold concerning that product. If there is more than one consumer market for a product, and if the product has more than one function, then the sport business must develop a position for each market and each

Table 5.26
A Simple Positioning Process.

Step 1—Identify the target market's product attribute preferences

Step 2—Identify current positioning strategy

Step 3—Analyze current position and the market's preferred product attributes

Step 4—Determine a positioning strategy

function. The following steps outline a simple process for developing a positioning strategy for a product (see Table 5.26).

Step 1. Identify the target market's attribute preferences. A market wants or needs a product for a specific function—the attributes of the product (refer to the product chapter for further study). Study the market for those attributes. If the product and its consumer market are known, study the current market. If the product is new and the consumer market is not yet known, determine the potential consumer market.

Step 2. Identify current positioning strategy. How is the company currently positioning the product? How do competitors position their product? Typically, positioning can be found in the advertising for a product because advertising is where the company communicates to a market. So look there first.

Step 3. Analyze current position and the market's preferred product attributes. Study the current positioning strategy and the consumer market's preferred product

Table 5.27

Examples of Positioning Strategies Based on Multiple Markets.

Sample 1: Manufacturer of personal watercrafts (commonly known as jet skis).	**Sample 2:** An indoor soccer arena and club.
Overall: We offer a fantastic line of personal watercrafts. We have PWCs of all sizes, for ever need, or for fun. No company has more variety.	*Overall:* We offer the most flexible indoor soccer facility for any of your needs—practice, fun, or competition—our arena can serve your every need.
Business market: Our line of working PWCs are all you need for emergency, rescue, or waterway control. Our PWCs are built tough to give you more years of service and dependability, ready to serve in the line of duty when you need them. Traditionally or custom rigged, your company can have a fleet of the most rugged and dependable PWCs on the water today.	*Business market:* We offer the best practice facility for soccer or field hockey in the area. Just call and talk to our friendly staff today and schedule your practice. And if you need the coaching room, just let us know! We have a fully equipped coaching room just waiting for you and your team—the place where you can plan your winning strategy.
Recreational market: The (name) is built with your fun in mind! No company offers the variety of PWC that we do. No matter what your fun requirements, we've got the PWC for you—fun, fast, and safe.	*Recreational market:* The best soccer fun in town! Looking to play indoor soccer for fun? Or is your team looking for some serious competition? We have both! Every session includes recreational and competitive divisions. We also have age-group divisions from under 16 to 40 plus. Register your team today—the next league starts soon.

attributes, and determine if they match. If the positioning strategy matches the consumer market's preferred product attributes, then the current positioning strategy is a match. If the current positioning strategy and the consumer market's preferred product attributes do not match, then it may be time to reposition the product.

Step 4. Determine a positioning strategy. Using the research collected in steps 1, 2, and 3, determine a positioning strategy to meet the consumer market's preferred product attributes.

Positioning statements. Table 5.27 presents some examples for positioning statements for one product to target different consumer markets. Note how the statements for each different consumer market are specific to that market's preferred product functions.

Chapter Summary

With constantly changing markets and industries, the sport marketing professional must constantly monitor and develop marketing mix strategies that will be beneficial for the company. Segmentation involves the study of markets and industries to divide a whole into parts in order to develop customized marketing mix strategies.

In the sport industry, sport marketing professionals study primarily two broad categories: sport consumer markets made up of end consumers and business consumers, and the sport industry, made up of a variety of industry segments.

Segmentation is the first step toward understanding consumer groups, determining target markets, and informing marketing mix and positioning strategies. Segmentation bases and variables are used to segment a consumer market or an industry. The choice of bases and variables is crucial because an inappropriate group of bases will not be successful in relation to responding to a marketing mix.

Target marketing involves the development of marketing mix strategies customized for one or more target markets or industry segments. These groups are the ones for which the company will develop specialized marketing-mix elements, strategies, and promotional campaigns.

Positioning involves communicating to the consumer what the company wants the consumer to think about the product. It is a critical element in marketing because it positions the product, or company, with a particular image about the product's functions in the consumer's mind.

CASE STUDY CHAPTER 5

Golf: A Game for Everyone

Golf events seem to be growing recently. Golf is increasing in popularity due in large part to media exposure of the women's and men's tournament events and the global exposure of Tiger Woods and Annika Sorenstam. In 2005, *Golf Digest* magazine reported that there were nearly 32,000 golf courses worldwide and that nearly half of those courses were in the United States.

Who is reaping the benefits of the growing number of courses? Golf players. Who is reaping the profits? Golf equipment manufacturers. With an increasing number of players comes an increasing variety of player styles and performances. Individual players want equipment that performs to their liking. Over the years, golf balls have changed from feather-filled leather sacs to complex composite materials. Golf clubs have changed from wooden shafts and club heads to carbon fiber shafts and precisely engineered club heads. Today's golf equipment manufacturers are producing an increased variety of each piece of equipment to meet consumers' demands.

Technology and engineering have had a major impact on design and performance of golf equipment. Computerized systems measure the golf ball's spin and speed, the golf club's movement and weighting factors, and the player's movement during the swing of the club and contact with the ball. The results are used by the player to make adjustments and improvements; and research results are used by the equipment manufacturers to make modifications to their designs.

Competitive analysis of strengths and weaknesses of the largest companies such as Callaway Golf, Taylor-Made-adidas Golf, Cleveland Golf, and Adam's Golf show that the growing success of these companies is due in large part to their segmentation research. Although golfers can be categorized into three basic segments—beginner, intermediate, and advanced—golf is a game of intricate movements that can have major influence on the simple performance of hitting a ball with a club. Couple that with the large variety of body shapes, sizes, strengths, weaknesses, and even quirks, and all factors together add up to thousands of variables that affect getting a tiny ball from point A to point B.

Continued on next page

In a major research undertaking, Golf 20/20, the National Golf Foundation, and the NFO studied golf in the United States in an attempt to identify and understand golfers. Among the findings, it was reported that there are 36 million golfers Researchers segmented them into the markets as shown in Table 1.

Sources

http://www.Golf2020.com; http://www.golfdigest.com.

Table 1
Golf 2020's Report: The Segments.

- Occasional Golfers: 11.8 million—played 1 to 7 rounds of golf
- Core Golfers: 7 millionplay 8 to 24 rounds
- Avid Golfers: 6.6 million—play 25-plus rounds
- Junior Golfers: 12–17 years of age
- Range Users: 4.9 million—did not play a round of golf, but hit golf balls at a driving range
- Alternative Facility Users: 1.7 million—did not play on a driving range

Case Activity

Go to the website http://www.golf2020.com/reports_2001Segmentation.asp and download and study the report. Using this report as a basis, conduct a market segmentation study in your home town. This can be done using a select number of golf facilities. Write a market segment report about your study and findings.

QUESTIONS FOR STUDY

1. Describe how the population of your country has changed over the last 25 years and how it is going to change in the next 25 years. How will this affect the sport business industry?
2. What types of marketing strategies are sport businesses using more often for emerging markets? Describe each one and how they work.
3. What are segmentation, sport consumer market segmentation, and sport industry segmentation?
4. What are bases for segmentation? Describe how they are used.
5. What is target marketing? Describe how to determine one or more target markets for a sport business.
6. What is positioning? Describe how to develop a positioning strategy for a product and a consumer market.

LEARNING ACTIVITIES

1. Using students in your class, conduct a study of demographics, psychographics, and other segmentation bases and variables using sporting goods as a basis. What did you learn about the class? How could this information be used if your company is a sporting goods retail company?
2. Write down a sports product that you purchased recently, one that is sold by more

than one company. Create two columns. Label one column "My Buy" and the other column "Didn't Buy." In the "My Buy" column, create a list of all of the reasons you bought the product. In the "Didn't Buy" column, create a list of all of the reasons you did not buy the product from other companies. On another sheet, try to consider all the information you gathered to help you decide on your purchase and list them (family, friends, advertising).Write down all the things the people told you or that you remember from the advertising. Now compare all your notes and see if there is a relationship between any of them. Why do you think you found a relationship between, for example, the reasons you bought the product from a specific company and the company's advertising for that product?

3. With a group, determine a way to segment the sport industry. First, determine a reason for segmenting the industry such as pretending that your group is a television broadcasting company that focuses on extreme sports events. Develop bases for segmentation. Determine an appropriate marketing mix strategy for your company.

4. Pretend that your company is a team of the WNBA. You want to increase spectator attendance numbers for each game, but you also want to increase the number of games that many of your fans attend during a season. Develop a list of the factors that have an influence on attendance and design a study that will answer the questions you have for your fans.

5. Identify some different sport businesses such as a manufacturer and a sport facility. Identify different consumer markets for the products. Develop positioning statements for each consumer market.

Chapter Six

MARKETING INFORMATION SYSTEMS

The growth and expansion of information that sports organizations generate daily are staggering. The major problem is that our thinking and skills have not developed quickly enough to accommodate this tremendous onslaught of data. It has been estimated that sport managers spend 80% of their time on information transactions (Horine & Stotlar, 2004). This phenomenon demands the development of systematic methods to process the abundance of information that is available and use it in marketing our sports products and services.

Marketing information systems are about information management. They have been referred to by many names—marketing information systems (MIS), computer information systems (CIS), and information asset management (IAM). Although no one title is singularly appropriate, the development and use of systems that can manage information for your sport organization or company is essential. Mullin (1985) said, "The MIS provides the link between the market and the marketer, and it is therefore the lifeline of marketing" (p. 210). Unfortunately, marketing information systems and database marketing in particular are not as well developed in the sport industry as they are in other business segments (Fielitz & Scott, 2003; Lefton, 2003).

> Marketing information systems—known as MIS, CIS, and IAM—deal with large amounts of information and are essential to the success of your sport organization or company.

Marketing information systems are generally characterized as a collection of data that are utilized by management in the operation and development of marketing programs and market-related decisions. In past decades, former coaches and athletes have managed many sport organizations. Marketing and management choices were often intuitive judgments rather than logical decisions based on data. The time has long passed when organizations can remain competitive in with yesterday's decision making styles. In today's environment, successful sport marketers must develop skills and abilities to interact with technology in making data-based decisions for marketing their products and services.

> MIS allows companies to establish channels of communication in order to maintain a relationship with consumers. These relationships allow marketers to increase consumer loyalty and thus encourage repeat purchases.

Hughes (2000) noted that each contact a company has with customers represents an opportunity to acquire customer information. Examples of these interactions include sales transactions, warranty cards, coupon redemption, and credit applications.

Advances in technology have enhanced corporate utilization of information. Typically, this information is used to develop a customer database. Hughes (2000) identified several benefits that this information can provide for marketers. First, the information allows marketers to access basic customer information such as name, address, and email; information that could facilitate direct marketing. More importantly, these data open channels of communication through which marketers can establish and maintain a relationship with consumers. Through these relationships, marketers are able to increase consumer loyalty and thus encourage repeat purchases (Aaker, Kumar & Day, 2000; Bonvissuto, 2005; Javalgi and Moberg, 1997). Most sport executives realize that repeat purchasers are essential for producing a higher lifetime value from each customer.

Sports organizations have access to a considerable amount of information on their customers. Some use it; some do not. Mullin, Hardy, and Sutton (2000) indicated that much of the information available to the sport marketer is either lost or not retrievable. Therefore, the purpose of this chapter is to assist sport marketers in the development and utilization of an effective marketing information system.

Obtaining Information

The first step in building an effective marketing information system is to collect or generate useful data. But, you may ask, where do you obtain the data? Traditionally, sports organizations have not been as sophisticated as many other business operations in collecting and using marketing data, so it is important to improve in this area of operations. Managers of sport organizations receive various kinds of information (i.e. sales reports, membership data) from within their organization and from other sources with which they must interact on an ongoing basis (Stotlar, 2005). These must be clearly identified and become main sources for marketing data.

Sources of MIS data are typically identified as being either primary or secondary (Mullin et al., 2000; Mullin, 1985; Stotlar, 2005). Primary research is research conducted with, or collected directly from, your customers.

Sports organizations can, through technology, keep very accurate records of all their clients and all people doing business with the organization. This includes both those who have purchased from the organization and those from whom the organization buys goods and services (Stotlar, 2005).

Health and fitness clubs have access to considerable amounts of information about their clients. They all filled out application forms that included not only their name and address, but also typically their occupation and income. Many clubs also have an extended system that can track the programs and equipment used in the club by each member and can generate reports detailing individual and club usage. This information can be quite useful to the marketing manager in tracking renewals and future marketing campaigns.

> The most popular methods for primary data collection for sports organizations are direct-mail surveys, telephone interviews, and personal interviews.

In one study, Chen (2005) found that by examining data from a fitness center, managers could accurately predict which members where most likely to drop their

Courtesy of Tempe Convention and Visitors Bureau

Many universities scan student IDs upon entrance to football games, which gives the school reliable and useful information.

membership. He analyzed the club's database across variables of gender, payment methods, residence, club visits, account status, and membership type. Chen was able to predict with 82% accuracy which members failed to renew their memberships. With national retention rates of only about 55%, club managers could certainly benefit from being able to forecast members who have a high potential to drop out.

The University of Northern Colorado Athletic Department implemented an MIS to better track the students attending athletic contests. Prior to implementation, students would just show their ID to access gate entrance; however, with the new system, the ID was scanned at the entry gate. The athletic department now had current and reliable information on student attendance. These data were used successfully to push forward plans to locate a new stadium closer to the main student housing areas. These data could also be cross-referenced with basketball attendance to see if the consumers were the same as for football or different and appropriate marketing efforts could then be initiated. As a side benefit, former students who had been accustomed to flashing their out-of-date IDs and proceeding through the gate were stopped and referred to the ticket window because the system could quickly check their enrollment status.

Another innovative method for collecting marketing and consumer information was introduced at Colorado ski resorts. Several of the major ski resorts implemented computerized systems for validating and tracking skiers. The systems included scanners located at all lift locations across the resort. When skiers lined up for transport up the mountain, the lift operators scanned their lift tickets or season passes. Information collected through the process could then be analyzed and evaluated by resort managers. Specific information that would be valuable would be the types of terrain skied by the most skiers, the frequency and duration of runs, and the typical ski pattern for the majority of skiers on the mountain as well as the price and location of ticket purchase. These data could also be tabulated from week to week throughout the season, and individual reports could be generated for day-pass and season-pass holders. One interesting advantage of the system was discovered when two young season-pass skiers were reported lost at the end of a day skiing. Resort personnel were able to use the scanned data to locate the last ski lift accessed by the skiers, and a rescue was launched in the most likely areas where the boys would have skied. One boy was rescued though the other unfortunately died.

However, the rescue of the lone survivor would most likely not have been successful without MIS data.

The most popular methods for primary data collection for sports organizations are direct-mail surveys, telephone interviews, and personal interviews. Data generated through client questionnaires or surveys can be valuable sources of information about customers' attitudes toward your products and services, as well as short-term demand trends (Stotlar, 2005). Primary data can also enhance a sound quality-control system by eliciting feedback to be used in refining product and service offerings.

Primary data collection can also take the form of pilot testing and product experiments. Those companies that manufacture sporting goods are continuously involved in this type of research, specifically in product development.

Unfortunately, many sport organizations discard valuable consumer information. Mullin (1985), a former marketing executive with several MLB teams and at NBA headquarters, said that some "franchises that make it to the playoffs throw away the names and addresses of unfilled ticket applications, when these individuals clearly should be added to the mailing list" (p. 205). Spoelstra (1997) also found that when he joined the front office of the NBA New Jersey Nets, they were throwing away valuable data. When customers called the Nets to obtain a copy of the season schedule, the ticket office staff simply grabbed an envelope, wrote down the caller's name and address, and mailed the schedule. Because these people had expressed an interest in the Nets' product, Spoelstra felt that their names should be placed into an MIS for additional direct-mail marketing. Needless to say, Spoelstra changed the system. The development of this line of thinking could be seen through actions utilized by the Cleveland Cavaliers when they used data from Ticketmaster to place follow-up phone calls to recent ticket buyers in hopes that they would purchase tickets for future games (Bonvissuto, 2005).

A similar oversight in many organizations is failure to record information when clients pay by check. These people may not be regular customers, but they could be included on special mailings designed to attract new business. Another technique often used with fitness clubs is to capture data when guests of current members register at the front desk. The office staff is trained to enter the visitors' names into a "prospects" file that can be used in future marketing activities.

In the late 1990s, many sport organizations began to realize the value of collecting information and designed programs similar to the airline industry's frequent flyer programs. One of the first teams to initiate such a program was the San Diego Padres of MLB. In 1996, the Padres introduced the Compadres Club. In their first year of operations, they signed up 90,000 members. Forty-six percent of the club members increased their game attendance over the previous season. Other clubs (Anaheim Angels, Mighty Ducks of Anaheim, San Francisco Giants) quickly followed the model established by the Padres. With their long-overdue World Series Championship in 2004 the Boston Red Sox worked with Relizon (a database marketing company working with many MLB teams) to implement the Red Sox Nation fan loyalty program. For $9.95 fans can become official citizens of the Red Sox Nation and receive preferential access to ticket sales and special edition commem-

Did you know...?

Men are more likely to purchase exercise equipment that stresses muscular development/toning, while women are more likely to purchase equipment that focuses on cardiovascular well-being.

Source: NSGA.com.

orative souvenirs. In fact, the Red Sox sold all of their 2005 spring training tickets in six hours. They also increased sales of team hats by 200% and brought in $225,000 for the sales of commemorative World Series rings (Hiestand, 2005). Thus, for many MLB teams, database marketing is finally playing a part in their marketing strategies.

It's not just the professional sport teams who recognized the benefits of database marketing. NASCAR implemented their fan club in 2005 with a stated purpose of promoting a "direct connection between NASCAR, its drivers, teams, tracks, sponsors and its loyal fans" (Dyer, 2005).

Barlow (1992) detailed three models of consumer loyalty programs. The first model is the points and prizes model. As you would expect, consumers earn points for purchases and eventually achieve point levels appropriate for prize redemption. A second, more structured model allows customers to continually accumulate points for awards. When specified point levels are attained, predetermined awards are distributed. This plateaus, perks, and prizes model has proven successful in numerous business segments. The third and least complicated loyalty program is the membership program. Customers are encouraged to join a corporate club that entitles them to special benefits and discounts. This model has been used as the basis of many sport fan clubs.

> The three models of consumer loyalty programs are the points and prizes model, the plateaus, perks, and prizes model, and the membership program model.

The Padres, and (with some variation) the other professional teams noted above, adopted the plateaus, perks, and prizes model. Padre fans were encouraged to join the Compadres Club by completing a club application. Huang (1999) investigated the types of data collected by these teams through their application forms. He found that the teams collected vast amounts of consumer information, more information than did other business-sector loyalty programs. The data collected included personal data, demographic background, and purchase behavior. The personal information requested included name, address, phone and fax numbers, and date of birth. The demographic variables encompassed gender, age, marital status, ethnicity, number of children, education, household income, and occupation. In addition, some information was collected regarding the customers' lifestyle interests. Finally, application forms requested data relating to the applicants' purchase behavior. Factors such as where tickets were purchased, previous and future purchases, seating location, and media influences were also recorded. Collectively, these data would be of significant benefit to sport marketers if used properly.

Collecting email contact information opens the channels of communication between the company and its customers. However, email marketing has become so prevalent that many people have installed "spam blocking" software on their personal computers. The best method to avoid being blocked by consumers is to have the consumer request information from you. Thus, the key to effective communication with your consumers is not by interrupting them, but rather obtaining their permission to pursue a relationship. This is commonly called "permission marketing." Getting the customer to ask for information about products is much more effective than bombarding them with advertising asking for money.

Permission marketing starts with the contact. It provides the opportunity for the consumer to contact you for information. While this concept is not totally new, it has emerged with the growth of the Internet. Typically, the sport organization has a section of their web site available for fans to sign up for club membership or for permission to receive special email notices. When sport organizations and corporations collect email addresses in their database it is important to remember that the email address belongs to the customer, not to you. So, if you want to use them for subsequent marketing activities, developing trust with the consumer is critical. The best ethical position is to have a section of your email communication that would allow the consumer to "unsubscribe" with a click of the mouse if you violated their trust or if they decide to terminate the relationship.

McConnell and Huba (2004) note that sports teams should begin the development of a database by gathering as much feedback from their fans as possible. Teams like the Dallas Mavericks, Portland Trailblazers, and the New Orleans Saints have established systems to gather input by creating "Fan Advisory Boards." The Miami Heat (NBA) developed a "buddy program" where members of the Heat staff were assigned to contact season ticket holders several times during the season. Many times the contact was initiated to notify the person of an upcoming event; sometimes it was just to ask if there was anything that the team could do for them. One Heat executive said, "there is nothing more important than our season ticket holders and it has brought our entire organization together to humanize this" (Migala, 2003).

Permission marketing was also implemented by English Premier League club Arsenal. CAKE Communications developed a downloadable program for the team's web site that would provide team-related stories and information based on a customized profile supplied by the fan. This involved a "Skinker," a desktop icon (in this case an animated figure of the manager) that would pop up on the fans computer screen with instant match results, video highlights, and news items. The results for Arsenal were impressive. In the first 12 weeks of the program, they had 50,210 downloads and 131,579 click-throughs to the team's web site, an increase of 44.9% (Arsenal Case Study, 2005). The US Olympic Committee uses a similar tactic sending notices to their US Olympic Fan Club members including news stories and human interest pieces on select athletes and sports. Because club members have a special interest in Olympic sport, they welcome this information.

The practice of permission marketing is not confined to professional and Olympic level organizations. Colleges and universities have also used the strategy. Sports Information Directors traditionally send press releases to media outlets from their database. The question arises, "Why not add season ticket holders and fan club members to the distribution list?" The University of Oregon used their database to allow selected preferred customers to order single game tickets 48 hours before they went on sale to the general public (Migala, 2005). These practices can make your best customers feel special and increase their identification with the team.

Many sports retail companies ask customers to complete customer profiles when they order from the web site. Then, when special promotions area available, the consumer gets an email notice based on the consumers identified preferences or

previous purchasing patterns. The key is to make sure that the offer is really special and not just an advertisement for regular merchandise.

Sport organizations are also consumers; therefore, every supplier to the organization should also be considered as a potential consumer. A wide variety of products and services are purchased by your organization and represent another possible marketing opportunity. These companies could be contacted for ticket purchases, product donations, and sponsorship opportunities (Stotlar, 2005).

Secondary research is characterized by the fact that it is not conducted directly by the sport organization. According to Shaw (1991) the information-vending business was one of the fastest growing areas of the information business in marketing information.

Several major companies are in the business of market research, including sport market research. A considerable amount of data can be obtained from these organizations, which collect and publish data about the sport industry.

Probably the most comprehensive data are available through Simmons Market Research Bureau, which produces volumes of marketing research for all industries, including sports and fitness. Their data are presented in a variety of areas, and an entire volume is devoted to sports and leisure. Sport marketers will be most interested in the data on sports participation, attendance at sporting events and sports equipment sales. Simmons details consumers by age, income, geographical location, occupation, education, marital status, and size of family. Access to Simmons Market Research Bureau is available at most public libraries. Specifically related to sports is the Super Study of Sports Participation published by American Sports Data. This company also works with the Sporting Goods Manufacturers Association and the International Health, Racquet and Sportsclub Association in producing quality data for the industry. Although the data can be expensive, it is typically cheaper than conducting the analysis independently.

For example, the Sporting Goods Manufacturers Association in association with American Sports Data conducted a study of 10,000 children aged 10–18 regarding their participation, attitudes, and opinions surrounding sport. These data would be quite valuable in defining both market size and potential for sport retailers. The International Health, Racquet and Sportsclub Association (IHRSA) conducts an annual analysis of the fitness and exercise club industry. These data would certainly be helpful to fitness clubs in designing and correctly positioning their products and services. For example, IHRSA data indicated that for all health and fitness centers in the United States, average revenues per club member was $653 per year. The mean revenue per square foot of floor space was $47 whereas revenue for tennis-only facilities was $63 per square foot. These data would be essential when assessing operating efficiency of your business. They would also be critical in making decisions regarding which business sector to enter (Wallenfels, 2005). Thus, professional and trade associations also publish information represent crucial secondary data and MIS sources for sport marketers.

Manufacturers have become ingenious in ways to build MIS data. For example, Nike placed a hand-tag on their Air Jordan youth apparel. This tag was an application form to join the Air Jordan Flight Club. Membership in the club included a poster, membership card, and special T-shirt, but most important, Nike obtained critical contact information of a young sports consumer. The Phoenix Coyotes of the NHL held an on-line scavenger hunt for their young fan who had recently attended a Coyotes games. Through customer log-on, the Coyotes were able to capture email and other pertinent data from their fans.

The sources for information are almost unlimited, but finding the information takes a little time, imagination, and effort. For example, a national governing body such as US Swimming could easily access information from sporting goods retailers (or perhaps one of their sponsors like Speedo) detailing purchase information for recent customers. This information could in turn be entered into a database and included in future membership or marketing efforts.

As sport manufacturers and sport organizations collect market data, sport marketing professionals need a marketing information system to manage the data necessary for making informed decisions. The accuracy and availability of marketing data are vital for sports organizations because their fans, clients, participants, and consumers change rapidly (Mullin et al., 2000). Therefore, the MIS must be designed to store, retrieve, and assimilate the data in meaningful ways.

Designing Information Systems

The MIS does not make decisions, but merely makes information available quickly, accurately, and in a form that marketers can interpret. In fact, sport icon Mark McCormack, founder of IMG, noted "we can always find what we are looking for, despite all evidence to the contrary" (McCormack, 2000, p. 229). Refer to the model of marketing information systems for sport organizations presented in Figure 6.1. It should be noted that although not every MIS is computer based, the microcomputer and an MIS function well together. The advantages of a computer-based MIS are that information can be retrieved much faster than through old-fashioned paper filing methods and computers are more accurate than manual methods (Stotlar, 1987).

Marketing information systems must be integrated so that fragmented data can be fused into composite pictures of individual consumers and specific sport markets (Shaw, 1991). It is imperative that when sport marketers are required to make decisions, they make informed decisions based on the best and most current information. All sport marketers can make decisions, but the success of the marketing decision often depends on the quality of the information on which it is based (Stotlar, 1987). It is the function of the MIS to provide that information.

Mullin (1985) was one of the early sport marketers to recognize the value of a well-managed MIS. He indicated that "the full value of an MIS is realized only when data from various sources are integrated into a common database" (p. 207). Mullin (1985) and Grantham, Patton, York, and Winick (1998) describe the essential characteristics of an effective sport marketing database as follows:

1. A protocol must be established to collect data needed for the system.

2. It must be linked to a central processing unit. An organization needs to have all of its data located in one centralized system.

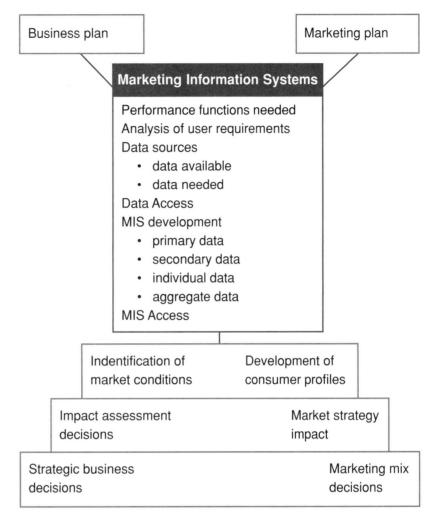

Figure 6.1
Integration of marketing information system for sport organizations.

3. Storage capacity must be planned into the system through a thorough analysis of anticipated data volume and characteristics.

4. The various databases (consumer files, accounting records, sales records, etc.) need to be fully integrated so that the data from one source can be contrasted and/or combined with data from another source.

5. The data must be retrievable in a form that the sport marketer can use for decision making.

6. Control mechanisms should be designed into the system to facilitate data security.

Maintaining Data Security

Two distinct types of security problems accompany the use of microcomputers. The first problem involves the software used to perform the various tasks. Because the information on the software program and the information that has been entered by the staff are stored on a disk, the characteristics of that disk are important. Almost all microcomputers use combinations of flash drives and CD-ROMs. Larger computers will use removable hard drives and other storage systems. Although storage systems are relatively durable, they can be erased through exposure to any magnetic object. This totally destroys any information on the disk, program, and/or files. Disks have also been known to "crash" on their own. Therefore, one of the most important aspects of data security is "backing up." This involves making a duplicate of all stored programs and information. This may seem

> Watch for two potential security problems with using microcomputers to help manage data—the erasure of a disk's content upon exposure to magnets or general disk failure and the availability of data to unqualified people.

like extra work, but the penalty for failing to back up work is that someone must reenter all of the information that was lost.

The second problem regarding security involves access to restricted information. Sport organizations consider their marketing information confidential. It is important that this information be reserved for viewing only by appropriate people. This restricted access is often accomplished through the password system (Westmacott & Obhi, 2001). The user must enter a predetermined password to gain access to MIS files. New developments in security are constantly evolving. Systems that evaluate the user's eye geometry are currently being used in some corporations. These security measures are critical when any unauthorized access could cause severe problems for the organization.

Getting the System to Work

Two common mistakes are often made in the application of computers in sport organizations. First, managers buy a computer with the idea that a job will be found for it to do. Second, the people who will be using the computer are often not involved in the testing and purchase of the system (Danziger, 1985; Stotlar, 1987). On many occasions, a well-intentioned administrator has purchased a computer to assist staff, only to discover that the computer will not perform the functions that the staff needs it to perform. The computer and the software should be purchased with specific requirements in mind, and the staff should be involved in the decision from the very beginning of the process.

Two basic types of programs are available, custom programs and commercial "off-the-shelf" business applications. Commercial software packages are readily available to create and manage marketing information, and they can handle the majority of information storage and retrieval needs of sport marketers. Each program has unique strengths and weaknesses, and many of them will let you create custom forms for storing and retrieving your marketing information. Another advantage is that many office workers will be familiar with the operation of the more well-known software programs.

In the event that your organization has special needs, you may need to have a software program written especially for your applications. Although these programs will fit your needs, they are generally expensive, and any future modification that is required will often mandate hiring the same person (or company) that designed the original program. It goes without saying that this situation would not leave you in the best position to negotiate the cost of any needed changes.

A commercial database usually allows for individualized category ("field") names to be developed by the end user. The computer manages pieces of information by these "fields;" therefore, each piece of information by which the marketer may wish to sort, list, or search must have its own field, so it is important for the sport marketer to carefully review the ability of the program to handle files by fields. When considering either a custom-programmed package or a commercial one that allows for individualized fields for each file, the sport marketer must determine the exact information that will be needed.

Many commercial programs have companion software that will allow you to create and move information from one application to another. Thus, a marketing director in a fitness center could have a memo written on the word processor, have the MIS select the addresses of all members who had not been in for a workout in the past month, and merge the mailing list with the memo.

Considerable attention has thus far been devoted to the various tasks and programs for the accomplishment of those tasks. One more type of program must be addressed: integrated database-graphics programs. These programs can combine word processing, graphics, spreadsheets, database, and telecommunication. Use of this type of software facilitates sales reports, marketing projects, and communication with both clients and staff, enabling the user to purchase one piece of software that will do just about everything. Integrated software is more expensive, but the convenience of a "one-system" package is often worth the expense.

A well-designed database system can also perform many standard business tasks. Some MIS applications can perform accounts-receivable functions such as preparation of invoices, maintenance of customer accounts, and production of sales and other reports. In sports organizations, this function is often applied to ticket sales or membership payments. The accounts-payable segment of the program would generally enjoy a wider application through the organization detailing all vendors with whom business is transacted. The features that often appear in this function are purchase-order control, invoice processing, check writing and control, cash-requirement forecasting, and vendor-information analysis. Programs may be designed for specific accounting and data management, but a truly integrated MIS can be adapted for a variety of uses in sport marketing activities.

In the sport setting, these features may surpass the needs and desires of the average sport marketer, but they should be fully compatible with the associated needs of the entire sport organization. The business computer industry has expanded so fast in the past decade that it is difficult to believe that a commercially available package cannot be found that could meet all of your MIS needs.

Working With the System

It should also be pointed out that an MIS cannot be expected to solve problems efficiently as soon as the computer comes out of the box. It takes about 40 hours for a person to become fully acquainted with the operation of any hardware system and about 20 hours to be become familiar with a specific software package (Danziger, 1985). According to Shaw (1991), an MIS must be designed "with a view to the people who will use them, and with an understanding of how the business in which they work operates. [An MIS] must deliver the right information to the right people at the right time" (p. 60).

With the right system, access to the information is quick, and updating the material is much simpler than with conventional methods. Printouts of data should be available by any combination of factors selected by the sport marketer. This will allow for effective sales and market planning.

Producing Results

The point of marketing research and data analysis is to better identify segments of the market that are most likely to purchase your goods and services. The individual pieces of data in your MIS can tell you who bought what and when. However important that may be, what you really want to know is who will buy what and when. This is the aspect of sport marketing called *forecasting*. Forecasting is a distinct advantage provided by computerized MIS systems.

> The main goal of conducting marketing research and analyzing data is to determine who will buy what goods and when.

Exactly what is forecasting and why is it necessary? Forecasting is the ability of the market manager to see how the future will be affected by anticipated or hypothetical decisions, the playing of "what if?" This can be very beneficial to sport marketers because hypothetical figures can be entered into the MIS for such items as sponsorship revenues, ticket prices, or membership fees. The program could then be manipulated to perform calculations detailing the financial and market consequences of those decisions.

Conducting marketing research and data analysis would allow a company to determine whether it would be beneficial to advertise its product at an event such as a tennis tournament.

Although MIS information is entered into the system piecemeal, sports marketers need to be able to look at that organization's data as a whole. There is a need for aggregate information to develop business and general marketing strategies, yet there is also a demand for synthesizing data to project individual consumer profiles. Sport marketers must clearly see the macro and micro perspectives of their consumer base. Therefore, both individual and aggregate information is needed for intelligent marketing mix decisions.

Chapter Summary

All sport organizations deal with consumers and consumer information is ideally suited to the storage and retrieval capabilities of the MIS. Having discovered the broad range of applications for a marketing information system, it should be clear that such systems will not immediately make a poor sport marketer competent or an inefficient sales person good. An MIS is a tool that can be used by skilled employees and managers to assist in the performance of sport marketing tasks and decision making. Typical information contained in MIS files would include the consumer's name, address, age, occupation, and purchasing activity. It is precisely this type of information that is particularly well-suited to MIS and a computer-managed database because of the need to continually update and change entries. Sport marketers can combine these data with other information in the corporation's database to facilitate decisions on target markets and consumer profiles. Remember that the quality of your decisions reflects the quality of the information upon which they were based.

CASE STUDY CHAPTER 6

MIS in a Fitness Center: Marketing Implications

Chen-Yueh Chen, Ph.D.

Yi-Hsiu Lin, Ph.D.

David K. Stotlar, Ed.D.
   University of Northern Colorado

Overview

The fitness club industry continually faces a significant problem in high attrition rates of club members. In an effort to reduce attrition, many club managers utilize Management Information Systems (MIS) via a database to identify the demographic characteristics of members who are likely to leave. The input in this case extracted information from the membership database of a moderately sized multi-service fitness center in Colorado. Data analysis is presented and students are asked to develop marketing implications linked to the results.

Background

The demand in the health & fitness club industry continues to grow across the U.S. generating gross revenues of $14.8 billion as of January 2006. The number of people joining fitness centers increased from 17.4 million in 1987 to 41.3 million in 2006. The prospects for this industry look very optimistic for the ensuing decade. However, the attrition rate in the fitness industry is also very high. According to International Health, Racquet and Sportsclub Association (IHRSA), the membership attrition rate in the industry is approximately 40%. Thus a typical fitness center would have totally replaced its membership every 3 years. In the current market, many fitness club managers focus on acquiring new memberships and neglect the importance of retaining their existing members. Yet, if fitness center managers could lower the attrition rates, even slightly, they could save a substantial amount of money. Therefore, understanding how MIS can assist mangers in retaining fitness club members has become a critical marketing issue.

Managers have implemented various initiatives to address member retention. They include: adding innovative programs, increasing interaction with members, focusing on the staff training, better facility maintenance, member care programs, and creating significant first impressions of the fitness club. Although some of these tactics have been successful in boosting membership retention, attrition rates in this industry were still high. Therefore, another approach seems warranted.

Unfortunately, many fitness centers fail to build a database and identify the demographics of the members who have a tendency to leave. If fitness centers could identify the characteristics of the members who are most likely to leave, they could better communicate with those members and develop tailored tactics to meet their needs. While discussions about why members leave may be helpful, quantifying the likelihood of members' leaving by analyzing members' actual behavior (stay or leave) along with demographic information in the membership database is more accurate. This necessitates the creation of a consumer database and MIS. Because of advancements in Information Technology, building a customer database in order to improve the performance of business operation is quite feasible. Managers can purchase a commercial database program from a variety of sources.

One of the best examples of database utilization in marketing is Amazon online bookstore. They use database marketing to provide their consumers with customized services to meet their needs and interests. For example, if a customer searches for a specific some book on Amazon's website, the website provides you with a list of books that others who bought the book in question also purchased. This has been achieved by utilizing customer database, i.e., purchase records of online customers, an analysis with the data collected and then generating customized recommendations to customers. Database marketing has not only been adopted by many retail compa-

Continued on next page

nies, but has been implemented by many sports teams. The Phoenix Suns and Denver Nuggets of the NBA (among others) have successfully used database marketing to identify their best customers and then increase their season renewal rates. They expand the concept using the database to provide a profile of their best customers and then use that profile to seek new customers. Unfortunately, this approach has not yet been commonly applied across the sport industry. This is especially true in the fitness industry even though many fitness centers or have established a membership database comparable to professional sport teams.

Therefore, it seems that increased profits would result if fitness center managers could extract relevant information from their membership database and subsequently reduce member attrition. The data that follows is from a medium-sized (more than 3000 members) fitness center in Colorado.

Methodology

The a regression model (Logit) was used on the data set to group membership by using independent variables and a binary response variable (e.g., renew fitness center membership or leave). The data set consisted of 4,304 members. This purpose of the analysis was to identify the demographic characteristics of fitness club members who are likely to leave by calculating that probability. The independent variables were as follows:

- Member visit counts represented the visit counts of members per week.
- Membership enrollment fees represented the amount of money members paid in the beginning of their enrollment.
- Member year-to-date sales amount was the cost of services purchased by each member this year.
- Membership type were coded on five membership types including; regular membership, student membership, temporary membership, dependent and spouse membership, and other membership.

- Whether members were charged a service charge or not. This variable indicated that whether members were charged a rebilling fee when their account was past due.
- Members' zip code was included to distinguish members who lived in the site city from those who lived outside the site city.
- Payment methods were coded via two methods of payment for members, i.e., annual payment and monthly payment.
- Personal demographic data were also analyzed.
- Whether members were delinquent on their payment on individual accounts.

Results

The Logit statistical analysis of the database revealed the following;

- Members who had fewer visit counts per week were found to be more likely leave the fitness center.
- No significant differences were found on membership enrollment fees.
- No significant differences were found regarding member year-to-date sales.
- Regular Membership individuals were less likely to leave compared with Temporary Membership customers. Dependent and Spouse Memberships were less likely to leave compared with Other Membership types.
- Members who had incurred a service charge were more likely to leave than those who had not incurred the fee.
- No significant differences were found on members' zip code between members who lived in the site city from those who lived outside the site city.
- Annual Payment members were less likely to leave compared with Monthly Payment customers.
- No significant differences were found on other personal demographic data.
- On the average, the probability of leaving was lower if the member was delinquent in their payment compared with not-delinquent individuals.

Discussion & Case Questions

1. What explanations can be provided for the findings noted above?
2. What should the marketing response be based on the MIS data?

QUESTIONS FOR STUDY

1. What are the essential characteristics of a well-designed marketing information system?
2. What MIS sources would be available for an intercollegiate athletic program, and how would you go about setting up an MIS?

LEARNING ACTIVITIES

1. Select your favorite sport and consult a copy of Simmons Market Research Bureau. See where you fit in the demographic segments presented.
2. Take a trip to your local fitness center or health club, and inquire about the types of information they have on their clients. Also look at their application form if they are uncooperative with your first request.

PROFESSIONAL ASSOCIATIONS AND ORGANIZATIONS

Sporting Goods Manufacturers Association
  200 Castlewood Drive
  North Palm Beach, FL 33408

SUGGESTED READINGS

Hughes, A. M. (2000). *Strategic database marketing: The master plan for starting ad managing a profitable, custom-based marketing program.* 2nd ed. New York: McGraw-Hill.

Mitchell, S. (2003). The new age of direct marketing. *Journal of Database Marketing, 10*(3), 219–229.

Chapter Seven

THE MARKETING MIX AND THE SPORT INDUSTRY

Overview	This chapter presents a brief overview of a significant element of the sport marketing management model called the marketing mix. The marketing mix is crucial because it defines the sport business, and much of the sport marketer's time is spent on various functions within the marketing mix.

The marketing mix comprises four elements: product, price, place, and promotion. In this chapter we will define the marketing mix, present a description of its place in the sport marketing management model, provide a brief description of each of the elements of the marketing mix, and describe how the elements are combined to create the marketing mix for the sport company.

The Marketing Mix	The *marketing mix* is the strategic combination (mix) of four elements called the 4 Ps. These are product, price, place, and promotion. At the heart of the decision-making process regarding your mix are the research and knowledge gained about the consumer, the competition, the company, and the climate (see chapters four, five and six). All factors must be given careful attention. If the sport marketer ignores one or the other, this increases the chances of making wrong decisions.

The development of the marketing mix involves determining the optimal combination of product, price, promotion, and place. Reaching the optimal combination depends on developing and manipulating each of the 4 Ps until each one is right for a particular product—and for the business. For the business, "optimal" means the combination that will sell; thus this mix meets consumer needs. There are many variables of each of the 4 Ps that can be manipulated by the sport marketer.

> Creation of the marketing mix involves the process of discovering or developing the right combination of product, price, place, and promotion.

They are manipulated to meet the consumer's desires or needs or for competitive strategy, according to what the company can do within ethical, political, economical, and legal constraints and considerations. The 4 Cs—consumer, competitor, company, and climate—constantly change, and therefore require constant monitoring and research. When any one of these elements changes, it can have an impact on one or all of the 4 Ps. A change has the potential to be positive or negative.

This could be considered an opportunity or a threat to the company. The important thing is that you know about the change, study it and its possible consequences—opportunities or threats—and make decisions necessary to optimize or minimize those consequences.

Product. The product is what the sport company is trying to sell. The challenge is to produce the *right* product for the consumer. Products can be goods, services, people, places, and ideas. There are many products in the sport industry. There are many consumers and competitors also. As you learned in chapters four and five, the sport marketer must determine exactly what consumers want as well as analyze its competitors to learn what already exists in the market. As you will learn in chapter eight, the process for developing the right product can be very involved.

The product can be manipulated, or differentiated as it is called in marketing. A tennis racket may be produced with a new shape or a new color. The sport center can offer new divisions in a volleyball league based on age, gender, or skill level. The same sport center could offer a new form of volleyball by simply changing some rules, court size, or number of players. As an example, beach volleyball can be played in a 2-player, 3-player, or 4-player format.

Price. Price is the exchange value of a product. The challenge for the sport marketer is to determine the *right* price for the consumer. The price of a product can be manipulated many ways. Promotional pricing can be used: 2-for-1 tickets to the game or 2-for-1 memberships to the fitness club, special sale prices on sports clothing for during a holiday period, special sale prices on sporting goods equipment for seasonal sports, or price breaks as the quantity purchased increases. There are also long-term price-planning strategies that the sport marketer can use. Refer to the chapter on price and pricing strategies for detailed information.

Place. Place is the process of getting the sport product to the consumer. It is also called distribution: distributing the sport product to the consumer. The sport marketer will analyze the types of distribution methods available and select those that will deliver the product to the right place. The right place means: where the consumer is, shops, or will travel. There are two types of distribution in the sport industry because of the types of products offered. *Hard goods* are those products that must go from a manufacturing plant to a retail outlet and therefore involve their distribution by means of actually moving product from one point to another. There also are products that cannot be moved in the sport industry. For example, a basketball game is not a product that can be moved to a retail outlet. The consumer must go to the place in which the game will be played (manufactured) in order to consume it.

Marketing Mix:

the strategic combination of product, price, place, and promotion decisions and strategies.

Marketing Mix Elements:

The 4 Ps
- Product
- Price
- Place
- Promotion

Change in the Marketplace Requires:

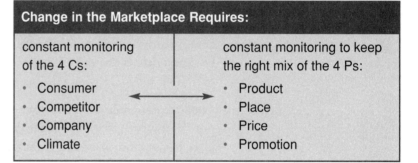

constant monitoring of the 4 Cs:	constant monitoring to keep the right mix of the 4 Ps:
• Consumer • Competitor • Company • Climate	• Product • Place • Price • Promotion

If the consumer believes that a product is overpriced or even underpriced, there is a good chance that the consumer will not purchase the product.

Courtesy of Tom Campbell/Gold & Black Illustrated

Associating legendary college basketball coach John Wooden and his name to a basketball tournament is a method of promoting the event.

The distribution (place) of a product can be changed. One can now purchase tickets to various sporting events through many different ticket outlets because they are distributed through many outlets. Sport facilities are becoming a one stop shopping facility: many new arenas include hotels, shopping malls, and other attractions like fitness centers and amusement parks. Sport sold as a spectator product can change other factors in the way it is distributed to the consumer. For example, there are over 60 official Kentucky Derby Festival events prior to the actual Derby race, a sporting event that lasts about two minutes! Refer to the chapter on distribution for detailed information.

Promotion. Promotion is the element of marketing that the general public thinks IS marketing. That's because promotion is the element that the general public sees and relates to as marketing. Promotion includes advertising and other promotional methods. These are designed to attract the consumer's attention. Therefore, the consumer believes that promotion covers the scope of the marketing effort.

There are many promotional methods and tricks available for the sport marketer to use, and there are some used in the sport industry that are rarely used in other industries. In one extreme example of trying to get the attention of the consumer and the media, when the first Super Bowl (at that time it was called the AFL-NFL World Championship Game) was played in 1966, organizers were so worried that the event would be ignored by the nation, that they planned to create interest by staging a kidnapping of the silver trophy (Carucci, 1994)!

Promotional methods include television commercials, print advertisements in magazines, direct-mail advertising, promotional pricing, "giveaways" at sports events, and press guides. See chapters 11, 12, 13, 14, and 15 for the detailed information concerning promotion in the sport industry.

Though the public is often under the impression that promotion is strictly advertising, it is actually a process—the goal is to create enough interest in a product to convince a consumer to purchase it.

> Though the public is often under the impression that promotion is strictly advertising, it is actually a process—the goal is to create enough interest in a product to convince a consumer to purchase it.

All of the marketing mix elements are manipulated by the sport marketer for two reasons: first, to stay in business and, second, to be successful. The only way to do this is to offer products that will sell, at a price that will be paid, offered through a place where they can be bought, and made attractive to the consumer. In other words, the sport marketer needs to develop the right product at the right price offered at the right place and promote it with the right methods.

> Research is the foundation upon which all marketing decisions are made.

The sport business professional uses the listed elements to develop the optimal combination for target markets and in response to changes in the market. It is the responsibility of the sport marketer to control and manage the marketing mix. Although each of the elements is developed through a specific planning process, they are not planned in a vacuum. The elements are interrelated. As such, all decisions regarding one element must be done in conjunction with decisions regarding all other elements. In addition, decisions concerning the elements in the marketing mix must be made in relation to what the consumer wants, compared to what the competitor has, considered for its fit for the company and considered against legal, ethical, social, cultural, and political climates.

The Interrelationship of the Elements

The marketing mix elements are interrelated. This means that each element affects each other element. The sport business professional must develop the optimal combination. Decisions should be made based on the information gained in the marketing research.

The consumer is looking for the right product, at just the right price, and that can be purchased at the right location. As you will learn in the chapter on product, the consumer does not arbitrarily buy products—the consumer is looking for something to satisfy a need or desire. From that perspective, the product and everything about the product take on characteristics beyond the intended function of the product. This notion must be understood by the sport businessperson and used during the development of a marketing mix. For example, let's look at a consumer who wants a new pair of running shoes. The consumer's existing shoes are not quite worn out, but this consumer is becoming a "serious runner." A serious runner is a different person than a "recreational runner" and therefore has different product needs and beliefs about those needs. This runner believes that the shoes must be thought of in the running community as "serious-runner" shoes. This is in marketing terms what can be described as a consumer who is image conscious, perhaps brand loyal, has high product knowledge, wants to fulfill a desire, and price is not really a factor. The sport marketer, having studied the running market, understands the serious-runner consumer and recognizes what this particular consumer wants. Therefore, the sport marketer will produce a serious-runner shoe, and most likely, price will be no factor. The shoe will be advertised in serious-runner publications only, and the advertisements will carry the message and image that this shoe is only for the serious runner. In addition, the

> Consumer purchases are not arbitrary—the consumer is looking for a product that satisfies a need or desire.

shoe will be sold only through serious-runner stores. This will add to the notion that the shoes are for serious runners only.

In this example, the sport marketer studied and understands this particular consumer. A product is produced specifically for this consumer; the price is set at what

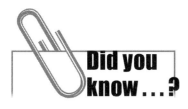
the consumer is willing to pay; the promotional methods imply the type of product for this particular type of consumer; and the product is offered for sale in specific places. This process and the decisions about the combination of the four elements are indicative of the interrelationship and impact of the elements. The primary strategy for the sport business in designing a marketing mix is to customize the marketing mix for a specific consumer market until the optimal mix is found. As the sport marketer identifies consumer market segments and selects target markets, the marketing mix elements are designed specifically for the consumer.

For example, if the sport marketer determines from research that the typical consumer of memberships in fitness centers is female, aged between 28 and 46, single, with one child; has an income range of $32,000 to $98,000; has an education level of at least a bachelor's degree; and their favorite sport and fitness activities are weight training, working out on the stair climbing machine, aerobics, tennis, and volleyball, then the sport marketer can design the product—a fitness and sport center—for the consumer, price it for the consumer, develop promotional methods designed to attract the consumer, and place the facility in an area of the city in which a high percentage of those types of consumers live.

Also affecting the decision to open a fitness center is information concerning the industry and the competition. For example, if a fitness center already exists that offers exactly what the consumer wants, at the desired price, and in the right location, the sport marketer must determine if it will be feasible to open a fitness center. If reports of the fitness industry nationwide show that fitness center membership purchase is increasing, how does this compare to the local fitness industry?

In addition, the marketing mix should change as markets change. You have learned earlier in this chapter that the product, price, place, and promotional methods can be manipulated. Here is where constant research is needed. If it has been eight years since your company conducted any marketing research, the decisions and strategies are riskier as every year goes by. Most assuredly, the information of the 4 Cs (consumer, competitor, company, and climate) has changed. In fact, it is more important that you **constantly** monitor the 4 Cs and make changes as needed on a consistent basis.

A good example of the kind of constant research a company should do is the research done on the baby boomer market. This is most likely a market you've heard about because they are mentioned in relation to practically everything in this country, from politics to retirement to toys to sports utility vehicles (SUVs). The baby boomer market has been given credit for making or breaking the success of many products, companies, and even whole industries, some of which are the fitness industry and the SUV industry.

Other examples of groups you have most likely heard about are the X-Generation, Techies, and Dead Heads. Each of these is a market—a group of people (consumers) with some like characteristics or interests. They are studied and monitored constantly because their purchasing decisions and product needs and desires affect a company's marketing mix.

The information gained from research should be current. Therefore, research should be an ongoing process within the company. With a flow of current and accurate information, the sport marketer's decisions and strategies for the marketing mix can be much more successful.

The marketing mix is the strategic combination of four elements: product, price, place, and promotion. It is the component of the sport marketing management model on which the sport marketer will spend a great percentage of time. It is a crucial element because it involves decisions and strategies concerning the product, price, place, and promotion. The marketing mix is designed based on information concerning the consumer, the competition, the company, and the climate. The remaining chapters in this book are devoted to the 4 Ps of the marketing mix and detail the intricate functions within each element.

Chapter Summary

Chapter Eight

THE PRODUCT IN THE SPORT INDUSTRY

Defining Product

People seek to satisfy needs or desires. To do this, they seek goods, services, people, places, and ideas—products. It could be said that people do not buy products. They are looking for something that will satisfy specific needs, wants, or desires. Products perform as the satisfaction agent. Consider the following examples:

1. A softball player *desires* to improve hitting and enhance batting average. The player will search for the product that will fulfill those desires: the right bat. What the person *wants* is to hit better and to attain a better batting average. The bat is the implement that might meet the consumer's desires.

2. Someone wants to lose weight and get into shape. This person decides that the product to fulfill those desires is a fitness center. In order to get into the fitness center, the individual must purchase the opportunity to do so: a fitness center membership. The fitness center is offered as the opportunity for the person to fulfill those desires: the place to exercise.

3. A bicycle manufacturing company wants to increase sales and reach more markets. After much research, the company executive determines that the Internet would be a good choice as an outlet store for sales. The Internet is the product for this company—it will purchase an Internet domain and hire someone to design and manage a website. The bicycle company has sought services to meet needs.

4. While someone is playing tennis, the strings of his or her tennis racket snap. This person wants to continue playing tennis. In order to fulfill that desire, the racket's strings must be replaced. The service of stringing the racket provides the opportunity for the racket to be repaired so that the individual can fulfill the desire to once again play tennis.

These examples serve to partially explain why and how a person purchases a product—people are actually purchasing functions and benefits. The product is the satisfaction agent for those functions and benefits.

A definition of product should represent the breadth of the term. Therefore, *product* should be understood as a *concept* and must be used as an umbrella term that includes goods, services, people, places, and ideas

> **Product:**
>
> should be understood as a concept and must be used as an umbrella term that includes goods, services, people, places, and ideas with tangible or intangible attributes.

with tangible or intangible attributes. The softball player wants the softball bat for what it will *do*, the function it will fulfill, and not because it is simply a softball bat.

A sport marketer should strive to understand exactly *what* the consumer wants in order to offer just that. As stated before, products provide benefits and fulfill functions.

For instance, a fitness center is a "place" that provides the opportunity to fulfill desires for fitness, weight loss, socializing, fun, relaxation and other benefits. In the example of replacing the broken tennis racket strings, the consumer gets both a "service" and a "good" new strings and the job (service) of putting the strings on the racket. The bicycle company's need to increase sales and reach new markets was fulfilled by the creation of an Internet site.

Benefits of products include intangibles such as the guarantee of quality. The consumer purchases a product with the company's promise of "satisfaction or your money back." The seller is promising that the product will satisfy the consumer's desires or needs. If satisfaction is not realized, whether real or perceived, the consumer may return to the seller, who will give the consumer a refund or satisfy the consumer in some other way. For example, the tennis racket stringing was guaranteed. If the strings were to break, the consumer may return to the company, which will resolve the situation.

The fitness center example is somewhat different. The fitness center may guarantee satisfaction. In this case, satisfaction may be measurable only by the consumer's perception. This is different from the tennis racket stringing. If the strings break, the materials or the service was faulty. If the fitness center consumer is not losing weight and getting into shape, at least according to the consumer's definitions, where does the fault lie—with the consumer or the center? In this situation, the consumer must perform—exercise—in order for the product—weight loss and fitness—to work. The fitness center can only provide the opportunity—*place*—and the means (exercising equipment, classes, and other). Hence, if the consumer does not perform, there will most likely be no weight loss or fitness gain. In this case, is there an obvious opportunity for consumer satisfaction and a money-back guarantee? For instance, a fitness center in Arizona offered a 30-day money-back guarantee. However, the offer was based on an agreement between the club and the consumer: The consumer promised to visit the club three times a week for a four-week period and included the establishment of fitness goals. This resulted in only three of 3,000 members asking for a refund.

Toward developing an understanding of a *concept* of product, let's first consider some definitions of product from a variety of marketing textbooks.

> A product is everything, both favorable and unfavorable, that one receives in an exchange. It is a complexity of tangible and intangible attributes, including functional, social, and psychological utilities or benefits. (Pride and Ferrell, 1991, p. 240)

> A product is a bundle of physical, service, and symbolic attributes designed to enhance consumer want satisfaction. (Boone and Kurtz, 1989, p. 271)

A product is a set of tangible and intangible attributes, including packaging, color, price, quality, and brand, plus the services and reputation of the seller. A product may be a tangible good, service, place, person, or idea. (Stanton, Etzel, and Walker, 1991, p. 168–169)

A product is "the sum of the physical, psychological, and sociological satisfactions that the buyer derives from purchase, ownership, and consumption" and includes "accessories, packaging, and service." (Tarpey, Donnelly, and Peter, 1979)

> A tangible product is a concrete, physical object while an intangible product is indefinite. To buy a baseball is to receive a tangible product; to attend a baseball game is to receive an intangible product.

Some words can be found in most of the definitions. To reach an understanding of the concept of product, is important to first understand these terms.

TANGIBLE AND INTANGIBLE

A tangible product is something that is concrete, definite, discernible, and material. It is a physical object. A softball bat is a tangible product. It physically exists. An intangible product is something that is indefinite, indiscernible, indistinguishable, and imperceptible. It is not a physical object. When the broken tennis racket strings need to be repaired, the task of replacing the strings is an intangible product, in this example, a service. Further, a tangible object is involved in this purchase. The consumer gets new strings, a tangible product, and the broken strings are replaced, an intangible product.

Professional sport events provide us with examples of intangible products. A professional men's basketball game is an intangible product. One can only watch the game. Benefits realized include entertainment, socializing, fun, and a number of other personal satisfactions.

It is important that sport marketing decision makers understand the concepts of tangible and intangible. This knowledge guides decisions concerning product strategies and influences other marketing variables as well.

UTILITY AND BENEFITS

"Utility may be defined as the attribute in an item that makes it capable of satisfying human wants" (Stanton, Etzel and Walker, 1991, p. 16). There are four types of utility: form, time, place, and ownership (possession). *Form utility* is the production of a product—using raw materials to create finished products.

Time utility is getting a product to the consumer *when* the consumer wants it. *Place utility* is getting the product to the consumer *where* the consumer shops. *Ownership utility* is the ability to transfer ownership or possession of a product from seller to buyer (Boone and Kurtz, 1989).

Using our previous examples, let's consider utility. The consumer who wants a specific softball bat (form utility) to improve bat-

Four Types of Utility

Form—using raw materials to produce a product

Time—making a product available when the consumer wants it

Place—getting the product to the venues where the consumer shops

Ownership—transferring ownership or possession of a product from seller to buyer

ting average wants the bat *before* the softball season begins (time utility) *from* a reputable sporting goods store *close to* where the consumer lives (ownership and place utilities). The sport marketer's job is to produce the bat from specific raw materials (form utility), get it on the market in advance of softball season (time utility), and in reputable sporting goods stores and other outlets (ownership and place utilities). It is only when the sport marketer completely understands the consumer's specific needs—what, when, how, why—that the marketer may make informed decisions concerning form, time, place and ownership utilities.

For the bicycle company that needs a website to increase sales and reach new markets, every utility is met. The company is getting a website through which to sell their products; they are getting it when—immediately—they need it; they are getting it from a well-known and respected company (an Internet service company); and they are getting it close to where they want it—the Web designer they hired works in the main office suite.

The *benefits* of a product are everything the consumer derives from the product. In other words, benefits may include functions of the product and intangible benefits such as status, quality, durability, cost effectiveness and others. For example, the consumer who wants to improve his or her batting average expects that the selected bat will improve batting average. The sport marketer, based on an understanding of what the softball player wants, promotes the bat as a bat that will give the player a better batting average. Promotion messages such as "this bat has a bigger sweet spot," "the only bat for champions," or "the home-run hitter's dream bat" are strong suggestions to the consumer that this bat will give the consumer what he or she wants, a better batting average.

You should now have a good understanding of product. It is not simply a good or a service. It is something that functions in some capacity to fulfill a consumer's desire or need. The sport marketer must know what the consumer wants the product to do—its benefits—and guide the company toward meeting those demands—utility. The sport company produces a product *after* learning what the consumer wants.

Sport Product Defined

There is a vast array of products in the sport industry. Based on the definition presented in chapter one, we recognize the sport industry as broad and comprised of industry segments such as fitness management, recreation and professional sports, any product that fulfills the sport, fitness, or recreation-related needs or desires of a consumer is considered a sport product. This requires a broad concept definition of sport product. Drawing on the definition of sport and the sport industry in chapter one and the general definitions of product in this chapter, the definition of sport product is "any good, service, person, place, or idea with tangible or intangible attributes that satisfies the consumer's need or desire for sport, fitness, or recreation related products."

> **Sport Product:**
>
> Any good, service, person, place, or idea with tangible or intangible attributes that satisfies the consumer's need or desire for sport, fitness, or recreation related products.

Return to chapter one and reread the section on what exists in the sport industry. Using our definition of sport product, those are all sport products offered to fulfill consumer sport-related needs or desires. With so many sport products in this industry, it is necessary for the sport marketer to identify differing consumer needs and desires in order to create and offer products that will fulfill those needs and desires. The most common method is product classification.

Sport Product Classifications

An initial step in developing products is to determine what type(s) of product(s) to offer. This task involves studying a particular product category, also known as a product market or an industry segment. The reasons for studying product categories or segments are similar to the reasons for studying and segmenting consumers. A thorough understanding of your product, its benefits and functions, and its utilities, along with understanding the same about your competitor's product, is critical to product management. Constant study of your product and all products like it will guide decisions concerning product development or diversification, pricing strategies, distribution tactics, and promotional strategies.

> A product category is a group of products that are either exactly alike or have homogeneous characteristics. Studying these categories enables marketers to fully understand and market their product.

This information provides the basis for the sport company to define its product(s), make decisions concerning opportunities or threats, develop appropriate marketing plans, develop a successful product mix, and determine the right time for product differentiation and deletion.

One method of classifying products is based on the consumer. In this method, products are traditionally classified in two very broad categories: consumer products and business products. *Consumer products* are those products offered to the final consumer for personal or household use (Evans and Berman, 1987). *Business products* are those products offered to businesses or organizations for use in the production of other goods and services, to operate a business, or for resale to other consumers (Stanton et al., 1991).

The sport industry offers a wide diversity of products targeted to both business consumers and end consumers. In each category, products can be goods, services, people, places, or ideas. In relation to service products, they can be classified into one of three categories: rented-goods service, owned-goods service, and non-goods service

A *rented-goods service* is the renting of a product for a period of time. Some examples in the sport industry include the following: a fitness center rents a fitness video to clients; a tennis center rents tennis rackets to members; a tennis center rents court time; a park near a lake rents jet skis on an hourly basis; a snow ski resort rents skis for a day or a week; a marina rents a houseboat for a weekend or for a week.

Owned-goods services include those services to repair or alter something that the consumer owns. Some examples of owned-goods services in the sport industry are replacing broken strings on your tennis racket; getting your golf clubs cleaned at the club; getting numbers, names, and logos put on your softball uniform; having your boat's engine repaired; getting your wheelchair repaired in order to play a wheelchair basketball game.

Non-goods services do not involve a good at all. This category includes personal services offered by the seller. In the sport industry some examples are tennis lessons, golf lessons, or summer basketball camp; a fitness center offers childcare service on site. This category also includes those services offered by sport management or sport marketing companies that specialize in managing and/or marketing a sporting event for you. For example, you hire a sport marketing company to market and manage every aspect of a large marathon in your city.

Business products. Business products in the sport industry are those products offered to sport businesses for use in the manufacture of sport products, to operate a sport business or for resale. Hillerich and Bradsby, manufacturers of the famous Louisville Slugger bats, purchases wood as a material used to make wood baseball bats (Pitts and Fielding, 1987). Consider the following variety of other types of business products offered to business consumers:

- A golf club manufacturer purchases graphite and other materials to produce golf clubs.

- A running shoe company purchases a variety of rubber, leather, and other materials in order to make running shoes.

- A bicycle manufacturer purchases aluminum to use in the manufacture of lightweight bicycles.

- A sport sponsorship management company purchases research services in order to help analyze sponsorship effectiveness.

If the sport marketer understands these types of classifications, the marketer will understand consumer type and what the consumer is looking for. Another method used in marketing to classify products is industry segmentation.

Industry Segmentation

Industry segmentation is another method used by marketers to classify products and buyers. *Industry segmentation* is defined as the division of an industry into subunits (industry segments) for purposes of developing competitive strategy.

An *industry segment* is a combination of a product variety and a group of consumers who purchase it.

Some industries contain just one product. More typically, an industry contains a variety of product items sold to many existing or potential consumers who vary in many ways.

The sport industry contains a wide variety of products offered to a great variety of consumers—final and business. Trying to keep up with every product in the sport industry would be practically impossible. It becomes important and even necessary that the sport marketer focus on a section or segment of the total industry. This guides the sport marketer in the identification of marketing opportunities and threats within a specific product market and the development of an appropriate marketing mix (Day, Shocker and Srivastava, 1979; McCarthy and Perreault, 1984; Porter, 1985).

> Industry segmentation is the division of an industry into industry segments in order to develop a competitive strategy. The sport industry can be divided into the sport performance segment, the sport production segment, and the sport promotion segment.

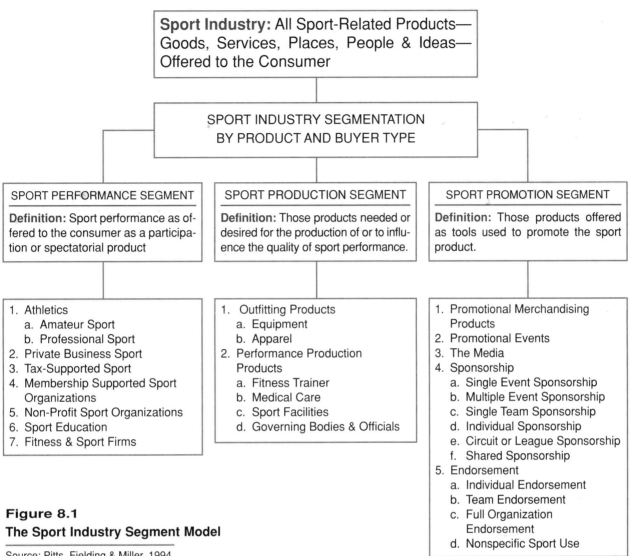

Sport Industry: All Sport-Related Products—Goods, Services, Places, People & Ideas—Offered to the Consumer

SPORT INDUSTRY SEGMENTATION BY PRODUCT AND BUYER TYPE

SPORT PERFORMANCE SEGMENT

Definition: Sport performance as offered to the consumer as a participation or spectatorial product

1. Athletics
   a. Amateur Sport
   b. Professional Sport
2. Private Business Sport
3. Tax-Supported Sport
4. Membership Supported Sport Organizations
5. Non-Profit Sport Organizations
6. Sport Education
7. Fitness & Sport Firms

SPORT PRODUCTION SEGMENT

Definition: Those products needed or desired for the production of or to influence the quality of sport performance.

1. Outfitting Products
   a. Equipment
   b. Apparel
2. Performance Production Products
   a. Fitness Trainer
   b. Medical Care
   c. Sport Facilities
   d. Governing Bodies & Officials

SPORT PROMOTION SEGMENT

Definition: Those products offered as tools used to promote the sport product.

1. Promotional Merchandising Products
2. Promotional Events
3. The Media
4. Sponsorship
   a. Single Event Sponsorship
   b. Multiple Event Sponsorship
   c. Single Team Sponsorship
   d. Individual Sponsorship
   e. Circuit or League Sponsorship
   f. Shared Sponsorship
5. Endorsement
   a. Individual Endorsement
   b. Team Endorsement
   c. Full Organization Endorsement
   d. Nonspecific Sport Use

Figure 8.1
The Sport Industry Segment Model

Source: Pitts, Fielding & Miller, 1994.

The sport industry segmentation model (Pitts, Fielding and Miller, 1994; presented in Figure 8.1) is a unique study of products in the sport industry. The authors used a portion of the Porter (1985) model for industry segmentation and used product function and buyer types in segmenting the sport industry. Three sport product industry segments were identified. These are the sport performance segment, sport production segment, and sport promotion segment. The information is important to the sport marketer in developing an understanding of the product segment within the sport industry in which the company's product(s) fits, identifying and monitoring the competition, and determining product management strategies (Table 8.1).

The *sport performance industry segment* consists of sport performance as a product. Sport performance is offered to the consumer in two ways: as a participation product and as a spectatorial product. Each of these may even be considered

Table 8.1
Three Reasons for Understanding Sport Industry Segments.

1. To understand the company's product.
2. To identify and monitor competitors.
3. To determine product management strategies.

Table 8.2
Products in the Sport Performance Industry Segment.

SPORT PERFORMANCE INDUSTRY SEGMENT		
EXAMPLES OF SETTING	PARTICIPATION Collegiate athletics Pro sports Recreational leagues	SPECTATORIAL Collegiate athletics Pro sports Recreational leagues
FORMAT	League Seminar Event Camp Tournament Lab Lessons Olympics Clinic Matches Rehabilitation	Games/matches/meets/contest
MARKETS	By age groups By gender and mixed By race By disability By sexual orientation By religion By skill level	By age groups By gender Special groups such as Girls or Boys clubs By race
FUNCTIONS AND BENEFITS	Fun Fitness gain Skill development Knowledge gain Weight loss Competition Stress management Entertainment Rehabilitative	Entertainment Fun Stress management Activity Support

Source: Pitts, Fielding & Miller, 1994.

separate segments as the marketing of participation and spectatorial products is different. However, they were placed in one category due to their similarities in function and benefit.

Functions and benefits include working out, stress management, fun, activity, competition, and entertainment. Examples include basketball, hiking, boating, swimming, jogging, camping, Frisbee throwing, martial arts, and many, many more. These activities are offered in a variety of settings, to a variety of consumer markets, and in a variety of formats (a tournament, a league, a one-day event, a single event, a weekend event, lessons, clinics, seminars, and many more). Table 8.2 shows some examples of the variety of sport performance segment products.

As a spectatorial product, sport performance is offered primarily in two ways: attendance at a sport event and spectating via television or video. Sport spectating has changed dramatically over the last few decades. The spectator is offered plush skyboxes, restaurants, and even a hotel in the sport facility; entertainment before, during, and after the event; and even spectator participation events during the sport event. These have become an integral part of the sport event spectator's package.

The *sport production industry segment* is defined as including those products necessary or desired to produce or to influence the quality of sport performance. Most sport participation requires specific equipment and apparel before it can be properly performed. The equipment and apparel afford the production of the sport performance. Further, in an effort to enhance performance, specific products or services may be desired. This creates a demand for a variety

Table 8.3 **The Sport Production Industry Segment Examples.**
1. Sport-specific equipment
2. Safety and protective equipment
3. Apparel: Clothing, shoes
4. Facility
5. Performance enhancing products: <ul><li>personal fitness trainer</li><li>fitness equipment</li><li>sports medicine care</li><li>equipment and supplies</li><li>coaches</li><li>other staff</li></ul>
6. Governing organizations: <ul><li>rules committees</li><li>officials: referees, umpires</li><li>governing associations</li><li>statisticians</li><li>scorekeepers, announcers, and other officials</li></ul>
Source: Pitts, Fielding & Miller, 1994.

Table 8.4 **The Sport Promotion Industry Segment Examples.**
1. **Promotional Merchandise:** Merchandise with a logo, might include caps, cups, key chains, bumper stickers, decals, mugs, hats, t-shirts, dress shirts, ties, napkins, sweaters, jackets, clocks, shorts, sweat shirts and pants, blankets, stadium seats, pencil holders, stationary holders, pens and pencils, checks.
2. **Promotional Events:** Offering an event or activity along with a main sport event to bring attention to the product. Examples include holding a Beach Boys concert after a Major League Baseball game; offering a golf tournament to promote pre-game, half-time, and post-game events that surround the Super Bowl.
3. **The Media:** The media provide vast exposure for some segments of the sport industry. Sport marketers negotiate with television, radio, and print media for coverage of sporting events. The coverage promotes the sport event.
4. **Sponsorship:** Sponsorship is a two-way promotional tool. The sponsorship company provides funding for a sport event, which is a form of advertising for the company. Sport marketers use the funding to produce and manage the event. The company providing funding gains exposure and promotional benefits. Examples: Almost all college football bowl games have sponsors; many of the women's and men's professional golf tournaments have sponsors; the auto racing industry is practically driven by sponsors; the Olympics, Special Olympics, Gay Games, and Maccabiah Games all have sponsors.
5. **Endorsement:** Similar to sponsorship, endorsement is also a two-way promotional tool in the sport industry. Some examples: Mary Lou Retton's picture on Wheaties cereal boxes suggests her endorsement of that product; Michael Jordan's endorsement of Nike products.
Source: Pitts, Fielding & Miller, 1994.

of products and product quality for the production of sport and to enhance the quality of performance.

For example, Venus Williams can probably play tennis with any tennis racket. However, she prefers custom-designed rackets in order to enhance performance. She also purchases a number of other products that influence her tennis performance such as a personal fitness trainer, weight training equipment, a sports medicine person and sports medicine equipment and supplies, and a professional tennis coach. Table 8.3 presents examples of products in the sport production industry segment.

The *sport promotion industry segment* is defined as those products used in the promotion of sport industry products. Refer to Table 8.4 for examples of products in the sport promotion industry segment. For example, college women's basketball can exist without promotion. However, it is enhanced, promoted, and in some situations, partially funded by promotional tactics. The competitors in all segments of the industry use a variety of promotional products and techniques. This creates a demand for promotional products, events, methods, and people who specialize in promotion, marketing, public relations, and other related areas.

With a thorough understanding of the sport company's product, the sport marketer increases chances for successful sport product management strategies. However, sport products come and go. Sometimes, the product can be labeled a fad. In other cases, the product was simply not a good idea. If the sport marketer can identify the success level of a product, decisions can be determined that may save the life of the product or, at a minimum, save the company. This product analysis is called the *product life cycle*.

The Sport Product Life Cycle

Just as people go through changes and stages throughout their lifetime, so do products. A person is born and then goes through childhood, adolescence, teenage years, young adulthood, adulthood, middle age, the senior citizen stage, and eventually death. A product begins life as an idea. It is then introduced onto the market, experiences a period of growth, a time of maturity, and will eventually decline in sales and then be taken off the market. One major difference between the person's stages and the product's stages is this: The person's stages may be measured using years of age. Death is certain. Although a product's stages may be measured using several factors, some of which are sales and profits, the amount of time in each stage can vary markedly. For example, a human's life span is estimated at approximately 74 years whereas a product's time on the market can range from just a few short days to hundreds of years (for example, religion).

> Studying, understanding, and managing products and their life cycle stages can have considerable influence on the success of a company.

The product life cycle is a concept popularized by Levitt in 1965 and is still applicable to and an important factor in today's market place (Levitt, 1965). It is a way to define and understand a product's sales, profits, consumer markets, product markets, and marketing strategies from its inception until it is removed from the market. Studying your company's products and understanding the product life cycle stage in which each product exists is imperative to planning marketing strategies. Through research, it is now known that (a) product lives are shorter now than in the past; (b) higher investment is presently required for new products; (c) the marketer may use the product life cycle to adjust marketing strategies; and (d) the marketer may strategically establish a more successful product mix in relation to the product life cycle concept—planning to establish products in each stage of the cycle so that, as one product declines, another product is introduced. As an example, let's look at fitness centers.

In the 1960s and early 1970s, fitness centers were known as health spas. The typical spa offered only a few products: a small weight room, a small pool, rolling machines, and locker rooms with a sauna and steam room. Typically, no exercise classes

Determining the stage of a product's life cycle will affect marketing strategy decisions.

were offered as the "instructors" were hired only to look good and sell memberships. With the "fitness boom" of the late 1970s, a new crop of fitness centers entered the market, and existing spas found themselves in the decline stage of the product life cycle. The new health-conscious consumer wanted more, and the new companies jumped into the fitness product market and offered much more in their facilities. Some of the existing spas changed, but some did not. Those that did not eventually lost out to the new multipurpose fitness centers.

Today's fitness centers offer a much greater product mix. In most, you will find a very large weight room, large pool, indoor running track, and a variety of exercise classes such as aerobics classes, swimming or pool exercise classes, fitness and nutrition classes. There will usually be a few sports such as tennis, racquetball, wallyball, volleyball, and basketball. The locker rooms are large, clean and airy with a full service of towels, shampoo, hair dryers, toothbrushes and toothpaste, and deodorants as well as plush carpeting, beautiful lockers, big-screen television sets complete with a VCR for your convenience in viewing specific videotape programs also supplied by the center. In addition, you will probably find nice, large whirlpool baths, saunas, and steam rooms. There will be a number of other services such as a childcare service—sometimes a child-size fitness center itself, laundry service, full clothing services, sporting goods and apparel shops, restaurant and lounge, and a small business office area complete with phone, computer, fax and copy machines so you can conduct business while at the center.

The stages of the product life cycle are introduction, growth, maturity, and decline. The stages are shown in Figure 8.2. Sport management executives or marketers must be able to recognize in which stage of the product life cycle a product is at any given time. This determination will affect marketing strategy decisions.

The *introduction stage* is the period when a sport product is put on the market (offered to the consumer) for the first time. During this time, it is likely that no one knows that the product exists. The sport marketer must promote aggressively to make distributors and consumers aware of the product. Typically, sales are practically zero and profits are negative.

The sport company has invested in manufacturing and promoting the product but has not begun to receive profits from sales. The product that is offered is one that probably went through many stages of refinement such as idea generation, research and development, test marketing, and pilot trials. Investment during this period, for some products, may reach into the millions of dollars.

As Figure 8.2 indicates, sales are low and losses are common. There is also a high percentage of product failure during this stage. The sport company may have marketing research to show that there is a market for this product, but when the product finally hits the marketplace, many things could have happened:

The market may be no longer interested; consumer needs or wants may have changed; or another company might have already entered the market and established share. The sport company must promote aggressively during this stage to create demand for the product.

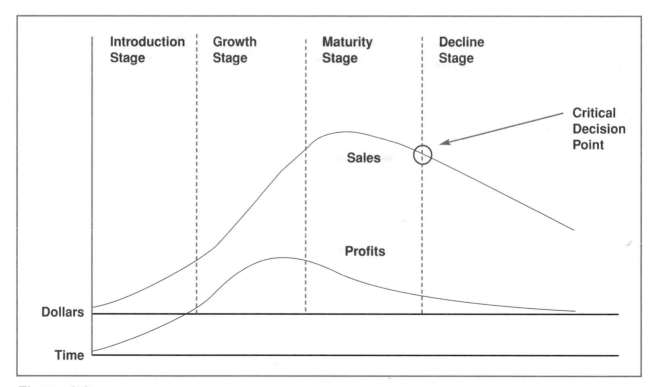

**Figure 8.2
The product life cycle stages.**

As demand for the sport product begins to develop and the product begins to sell, it enters the next stage in the product life cycle, *the growth stage*. As Figure 8.2 indicates, it is during this stage when sales and profits rapidly and steadily increase. Although sales and profits soar, the company may still be in danger. It is during this stage that competitors will enter the product market with identical or similar products. This competition will drive prices down, and profits will decline. Aggressive pricing promotions, adjustments in costs, legal action against imitators, and other marketing strategies will help to stabilize profits.

> Product promotions stress information about a product, as well as its features and, perhaps most important, what it does for the consumer.

After the bumpy road, the sport product may finally reach *the maturity stage*. It may have found a steady place in the market. However, during this stage, there still are many competitors, and this keeps prices low, which keeps sales and profits down. It is also during this period that the product has been changed enough to finally meet the consumer's needs. Differences among competing products diminish. It is at this point, however, that companies will begin to promote any difference in their product that they believe will gain some market advantage. Usually, pricing wars begin and continue until one or more companies are driven out of the particular product market. Critical marketing decisions must be made at this point.

During *the decline stage*, sales fall rapidly. There may be many reasons, some of which are new products on the market, a shift in trend, or new technology. Now the sport marketer is faced with the decision of terminating production of the sport product or making changes, sometimes drastic, to revive it. Of course, the sport marketer may also wait and see which companies drop out of the market. This can be a successful strategy because if a large number drop out, your company may become one of a few making the product and the cycle can be stopped. This tactic is risky as always when one plays a wait-and-see game.

It must be understood that the length of each stage can vary for any given product. The challenge to the sport marketer is to be able to recognize each product's life cycle stage and make marketing decisions accordingly. For example, let's say

Table 8.5
Examples of sport products in the product life cycle stages.

	Participant Sport	Sporting Goods	Spectator Products
Introduction Stage	Slam Ball Ski Dancing Wakesurfing	Speed suits Wakesurfing	Slam Ball
Growth Stage	Snowboarding Wakeboarding	Snowboards Wakeboards	Snowboarding WNBA
Maturity Stage	Basketball Soccer	Golf Clubs PWC (Jet Ski)	PGA/LPGA NBA
Decline Stage	Field Hockey Croquet	Croquet Water skis	Ice Hockey?

that you are the manager/marketer for a multi-sport club. You are experiencing an unusual, sharp decline in participants in the adult tennis leagues. Upon investigation, you find that most of those clients are now playing tennis at a different club because it is offering childcare services all the hours that it is open. You are faced with a decision: Change what you offer or lose consumers to another company. Table 8.5 shows a variety of examples of sport products in various product life-cycle stages.

> By the time a product reaches the maturity stage, all the companies producing it have most likely discovered the successful product, price, and other marketing strategies that keep the product selling.

The Product Mix and Product Management

Product management and product mix are critical elements of a sport company's business plan and marketing strategy. It is the sale of products and services that makes a company successful or may bring about failure.

Product mix is the complete set of all products that the sport company offers to the consumer. It consists of all of the company's product lines and all related services.

Table 8.6
Examples of Product Mix, Lines, and Items in the Sport Industry.

SPORT COMPANY	Product Assortment (Mix)		Product Line	Product Items Offered in the Product Line

FITNESS CENTER	fitness
	weight loss
	restaurant and
	  lounge
	aerobics
	weight training
	tanning
	massage
		testing-fitness;
		  cholesterol
		sports leagues:
		  tennis
		  volleyball
		  swimming
		pro shop
			aerobics classes . . . .
			
			weight training . . . .
			
			tennis . . . .
				low impact aerobics
				kid aerobics
				elderrobics
				advanced aerobics
				body building
				free weight training
				sport-specific
				strength events
				classes
				beginner's league
				intermediate league
				advanced leagues
				club tourney

COLLEGE ATHLETICS	women's sports men's sports		women's individual . . . . . sports women's team . . . . sports	track field swimming cross country tennis basketball volleyball soccer
SPORTING GOODS MANUFACTURER	golf equipment tennis equipment		golf . . . . tennis	golf clubs: 4 different sets golf balls golf umbrellas tennis rackets tennis string tennis balls tennis ball retriever

For instance, a collegiate athletic program offers 12 women's and men's sports and promotional merchandise. A sporting goods manufacturer offers 10 different sport equipment products. The local fitness center offers a variety of fitness and sport-related products, including a full range of exercise classes, tennis classes and leagues, volleyball leagues, swimming classes and open swim time, a clothing and sporting goods shop, childcare services, equipment repair, laundry service, towel service, a restaurant and lounge, and many others.

The product mix may be measured by its product lines and items. A *product line* is a set of closely related products. For example, as Table 8.6 shows, a fitness center offers fitness, sport, clothing, and equipment as four of its product lines. Within each product line, there are product items. A *product item* is a specific product within a product line. Aerobics classes are a product item in the fitness center's fitness product line. Tennis, volleyball, and swimming are product lines. Each of these may consist of a variety of classes, leagues and other items. In another example, a sporting goods manufacturer offers three product lines: softball equipment, baseball equipment, and tennis equipment. The softball equipment line consists of a variety of items: bats, gloves, batting gloves, softballs, and equipment bags. In a different example, a professional women's golf league offers two lines: golf spectation and souvenir merchandise.

The product mix of a sport company may be described by its width, depth, and consistency. The fitness center has a narrow width for it offers product lines that are primarily of a fitness or sport nature. There are a wide variety of products offered within each product line, which means that the fitness center may be described as having depth. For example, the tennis line contains the following items: (a) classes: classes for age-groups of 5–7 years old, 8–12, 13–15, 16–18, 19–21, 22–25, 26–30, and in five-year increments after 30; (b) classes for skill levels: beginner, intermediate, and advanced; (c) individual instruction; (d) leagues consisting of the following categories: skill groups ranging from beginner through advanced and within each are categories for women, men, and coed singles, women, men, and coed doubles (see Table 8.7). There may most likely be other items such as special clinics or seminars, league tournaments, special tournaments, and competition with another center. The fitness center would be considered consistent as its product mix is focused on products of a similar nature.

The product mix has three aspects:

Width is the number of product lines offered.

Depth is the number of items within a line.

Consistency refers to the similarity of product lines.

Table 8.7
The Center's Tennis Line.

1. Classes Segmented By:	Age Groups
	Skill Levels
2. Instruction:	Individual Lessons
	Lessons for Double Play
3. Leagues Segmented By:. . . .	Skill Levels: beginners to advanced
	Gender: women's, men's, mixed
4. Clinics, Seminars:.	for coaching, for individuals, for play strategy, for rules knowledge
5. Tournaments:	—Intramural
	—Extramural

Product management presents a major challenge for the sport company. Products are what your company produces, if the company is a manufacturer, or what your company selects and buys, if your company is a wholesaler or retailer, in order to fulfill needs and desires of consumers. Effective management of the product is crucial to success. The remaining sections of this chapter are devoted to product management strategies.

Product management involves deciding which products to offer, what type of a product line to carry, when to keep or delete a product, when to add new products, and other product management strategies. In marketing terms, this includes management of the product life cycle, positioning of the product, new product development, product diversification, line extension, product identification, and product deletion. Decisions concerning these areas make up *product mix strategies.*

Product positioning involves trying to position a product appropriately in the market. A product's position is the image or perception that the consumer holds about the product's attributes, quality, uses and other functions as these compare to other similar products. As was pointed out in the opening paragraphs of this chapter, a consumer does not simply purchase a product. The consumer is looking to satisfy needs or desires. Products perform as the satisfaction agent. Consumer perceptions are measured through marketing research. The research will show what the consumer thinks about a product and how it compares to another company's product. This information is important in making changes to the product or to the image of the product.

New product development as a strategy is the addition of a new product to a company's product line. There are many reasons a company might consider developing a new product, including a need to stimulate sales, a desire to capture a new consumer need, a desire to improve the company's reputation, or a desire to expand.

New products are a constant event in the sport industry. In chapter one, we discussed many factors that have positively influenced the growth and development of the sport industry. Some of those factors are the consistent offering of new sports, new activities, new leagues, new sport organizations for all populations, and new sport equipment.

There are, perhaps, more sport equipment and clothing products than sports when considering that most sport activities require a few pieces of equipment, special clothing, and footwear for each participant.

In the sport industry, it can be quite confusing when trying to determine which comes first: the sport or the equipment. In some cases, ideas for a new sport develop first. James Naismith developed some rules for a new sport and used a soccer ball. That sport today is basketball and requires very different equipment than was first used.

Every year the Sporting Goods Manufacturers Association (SGMA) stages exhibitions of new sporting goods, apparel, shoes, and equipment. The SGMA has two exhibits: the SGMA Spring Market and the SGMA Fall Market. Thousands of sporting goods manufacturers and businesses are involved. They bring their most current products for display. People attending are buyers for retailers, wholesalers, distributors, and resellers.

Did you know...?

The Home Depot is the top hardware store among loyal NBA fans. According to Scarborough Sports Marketing, a division of Scarborough Research *http://www.scarborough.com*, loyal NBA fans shopped the following hardware stores in the past 30 days: the Home Depot, 42%; Menard's, 30%; Ace Hardware, 26%; Target, 19%; and Wal-Mart, 19%.

For more information, visit Scarborough Research online at *http://www.scarborough.com*.

Of course, not every new product introduced is successful. As a matter of fact, most new products fail. The failure rate is estimated to range between 33 and 90 percent. Companies spend tremendous amounts of money during the process to get a new product to the market. There are many elements involved in new product development. Some ideas require years of research, which can involve scientists, technology, testing, manufacture of the new product, and promotion. However, with all the money and time invested in producing the new product, there is no guarantee that the product will sell.

There are some common reasons that new product offerings fail. The primary reason is failure to match the product to the consumer's needs. If the product will not do what the consumer wants, the consumer will not buy it. Further, this may be the result of poor consumer research, the company's failure to stick to what it does best, and failure to provide a better product at a better value than the competition.

Good product management and planning can increase your chances of new product success. As was pointed out in the chapter on research and earlier in this chapter, information and research are primary keys in making decisions.

As pointed out earlier, there are many reasons that a company offers a new product. Sometimes, a new product isn't a totally new product. It is a product that has been modified as a means of offering a differentiated product or an improved product. For example, consider the variety of aerobics type classes offered today. Some examples are hard aerobics, soft aerobics, water aerobics, elderobics, jazzercise, and step aerobics.

None of these are brand-new products. Rather, they are variations of the original aerobics product. In another example, arena football (football played in a small, indoor field with fewer players and a variety of rule modifications) might be considered a brand-new product because it is different from the original football sport. However, arena football is a variation of the original product. It is marketed as a different product—different from the regular 11-player game.

How many ways might one offer a new product? There are at least nine (Peter and Donnelly, 1991). Following are the nine ways with examples in the sport industry (also see Table 8.8).

Table 8.8 **Nine Ways to Offer a New Product.**
1. A product that performs an entirely new function.
2. A product that offers improved performance of an existing function.
3. A product that offers a new application of an existing one.
4. A product that offers additional functions over an existing product.
5. When an existing product is offered to a new consumer market.
6. Offering a lower cost on a product can attract new buyers.
7. A product offered as "upgraded" or an existing product integrated into another product.
8. A downgraded product or the use of less expensive parts or components in the manufacturing process.
9. A restyled product.
Source: Peter & Donnelly, 1991.

1. *A product that performs an entirely new function.* When the snowmobile was introduced, it performed a new function: motorized transportation across snow-covered areas in a small personal-sized vehicle.

2. *A product that offers improved performance of an existing function.* As an example, consider the introduction of new materials for wheelchairs. Aluminum and other composite materials offer the possibility for wheelchairs to be light and durable. This provides wheelchair athletes the capability to enhance performance in athletic feats.

3. *A product that offers a new application of an existing one.* Personal watercrafts (more commonly known as jet skis) were first introduced to be used as recreational vehicles: new toys for play on the water. Today, personal watercrafts are used by police, emergency water rescue services, and Coast Guard operations for law enforcement, safety, and rescue functions.

4. *A product that offers additional functions over an existing product.* In one example, a fitness center may offer more sports and services than does another fitness center, thereby offering more functions to the consumer. In another example, weight-training equipment, one product is a single unit that allows the consumer to perform up to 12 exercises whereas another product is a single unit that offers only one exercise.

5. *An existing product that is offered to a new consumer market.* This may be done either by repositioning the product or offering the product in new markets (market development). In an example of the latter, the National Football League (NFL) is trying to gain market development by offering its product—football games—in European and Asian countries.

6. *A product that can attract new buyers with lower prices.* When a new material is used for golf clubs, the existing clubs may be offered at a lower cost. Softball bats are offered in a wide range of prices. A fitness center may offer special priced memberships to first-time consumers for a limited period of time.

7. *A product that is offered as "upgraded" or an existing product that is integrated into another product.* In one example, fitness centers offer a variety of possibilities for "upgrading" a consumer's membership. The consumer may purchase one level of membership with the possibility of upgrading it to another level. In another example, computers have been integrated into a variety of sport equipment as a method of upgrading the equipment. Playing a round of golf indoors in a small room is possible with the use of a computerized golf course system. Through the use of video, screens, displays, sensors and other equipment, the consumer uses real golf clubs and golf balls to play a round of 9 or 18 holes of golf without leaving the room.

Table 8.9
Growth Vector Components.

| Markets | Products | |
	Present	New
Present	Market Penetration	Product Development
New	Market Development	Diversification

Source: Ansoff, 1965.

8. *A product that has been downgraded or that uses less expensive parts or components in its manufacture.* Many sporting goods and equipment manufacturers use plastics and other less expensive materials, parts, or components in their products. This changes the cost to produce the product and is sometimes promoted to the consumer as "new low price" or "we pass the savings on to the consumer" item.

9. *A restyled product.* Examples include the almost annual changes in sport clothing, running shoes, and other sporting equipment.

In another approach to offering new products, Ansoff (1965) developed *growth vectors,* which are used by most businesses today (see Table 8.9). These are product strategies involving present or new consumer markets and present or new products, and they include market penetration, market development, new product development, and product diversification.

Market penetration is a strategy in which a company tries to sell more of its present products to its present consumer markets. *Market development* is a strategy in which a company tries to sell its present products to new consumer markets. *New product development* is the creation of new products. *Product diversification* is a strategy in which new products are added in an attempt to meet the needs of new consumer markets.

New Product Development Planning and Process

How does a sport company organize for new product development? The type of company and the products it offers will influence the eventual organization, planning, and process the company will use to develop new products. A fitness center that offers a variety of products must make a decision concerning the addition of new products such as new sports, fitness activities, or even a new line of tennis clothing in the pro shop. A tennis racket manufacturer will study the possibility and feasibility of manufacturing a new tennis racket. These are different types of companies: One is a manufacturer and the other a retailer. However, each must have and manage a new product development process. The process will involve hours, sometimes years, of analyzing information concerning factors such as consumer markets and product markets, cost of producing the product, cost to the consumer, capability of the company to produce the product, distribution possibilities and cost, as well as promotion possibilities and cost.

Consider another, very different example—the National Basketball Association (NBA). For the NBA, a new product might be an additional team in the league or a modification of the rules of the game of basketball. The addition of a new team to the league requires analyzing consumer markets and product markets, production (startup) costs, price (ticket prices) to the consumer, and many other decision factors. Modifying, adding, or deleting rules can change the game—the product—dramatically.

There have been many modifications to the game of basketball since it was invented. Some of those changes were instituted specifically to make the game more attractive to the consumer. For example, dunking was not allowed until the late 1970s primarily for safety reasons: Rims and backboards were not made for dunking and would break. Another reason was that the dunk was not considered to be a skill. A stiff penalty was levied against a player who dunked either during the warm-up period before a game or during a game: The player was ejected from the game. Dunking became a tactic.

Coaches realized that a dunk motivated the team and excited the crowd. Specific players were instructed to dunk at key moments: during the warm-up period before the game or during the game. It wasn't long before coaches, athletic directors, and others involved in selling the game realized that the crowds loved to see someone dunk the ball. Soon the rules were changed, and rims and backboards were modified to be safe for dunking. The dunk changed the game. Today there are even slam-dunking contests with large amounts of money, prizes, and titles involved.

There are some common stages in the new product development process within most companies. These are idea generation, screening and analysis, product research and development, test marketing, and commercialization (Boone and Kurtz, 1989; Peter and Donnelly, 1991; Stanton et al., 1991). Figure 8.3 represents the stages a sport company might utilize within a new product development process

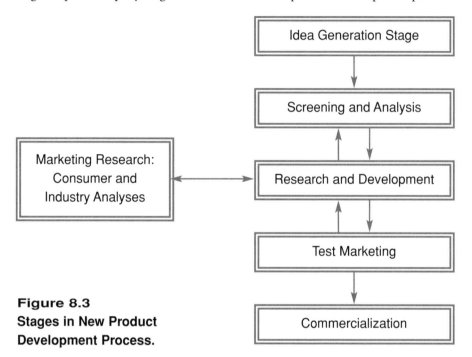

Figure 8.3
Stages in New Product Development Process.

The *idea generation stage* involves generating ideas for new products, product modification, or other types of product changes. Ideas may come from a multitude of sources. If the company has the resources, it may have a product research and development department, commonly known as a "R and D" department. It is the responsibility of the "R and D" people to generate product ideas, research them, and present feasible product ideas to company management. In other companies, product ideas must originate from employees. In either situation, the company management must create an atmosphere that supports idea generation.

Some companies offer incentives for those employees whose ideas eventually result in a successful product. Eventually, a decision will be made to take the next step and study the feasibility of a product.

The next stage is *product screening and analysis*. This involves determining the feasibility of a product. This process includes determining if the company can market a product

> Idea generation should utilize information obtained through marketing research concerning the consumer and product markets.

profitably, if the product fits with the company's mission, if the company has all the necessary resources or technology, or if it might be beneficial to form partnerships with other companies. Based on the conclusions drawn from the research, a decision will be made, and the product could move into the next stage.

In the *product research and development stage*, product ideas with potential are converted. The type of product and its conceived functions determine the type of testing.

If the product is a tangible item, a model can be produced. The model will undergo a number of tests in an effort to develop the best possible product.

Type of product requires further discussion here because there are many different types of products in the sport industry. Remember our definition of product earlier in the chapter. Product is a concept that includes goods, services, people, places and ideas. Also, remember that consumers are looking for a specific function—what the product will do. With this in mind, let's consider examples of each type of product and how it may be developed through testing.

Tangible good. Softball bats provide a good example. The research and development department in a bat manufacturing company is considering the idea that aluminum might be a good material for bats. The purpose or function of a bat is to hit a softball.

However, what the softball player wants is a bat that will hit a softball farther, consistently, and with control. The question, then, the company should consider is this:

- Will an aluminum bat meet the needs of softball players? Other questions are

- Can aluminum bats be made?

- What kind of aluminum can be used?

- How much will it cost the company?

- What kind of machinery and other equipment are needed to construct an aluminum bat?

- Where might the company get the aluminum?

- Will the aluminum bat function?

- How can it be tested?

- What will the consumer think about the idea of an aluminum bat?

- Will the consumer accept—and purchase—a bat made of metal instead of wood?

- Are any other companies considering making aluminum bats? If not, can this company possibly be the first with this product?

If most of these questions can be answered positively, the company's next move is to produce some bats made of aluminum and test them in the company's laboratories. A variety of aluminum would be used in a variety of models. The bats would be put through a battery of tests. The company could also test the models by providing them to some softball players, teams, and/or leagues. The company would follow the players throughout the league and receive feedback from them. The information is used to make changes in the bat until reaching a point at which the players seem to be satisfied with the performance of one or more models. Further test marketing would include placing the bat on the market in a region and waiting for the results. If specific outcomes are reached, the company would consider going into full-scale production, getting the bats into more markets, and going into full promotion status.

Service product. The testing of a service product could follow the following process. A fitness instructor at a fitness center overhears customers discussing why the center does not offer childcare services. The customers say that they would come to the center more often if they did not have to spend the extra amount of time, effort, and money finding a sitter. The instructor thinks offering childcare might be a good idea and takes it to the center's manager. The manager also thinks it might be a good idea and organizes a committee, headed by the instructor, to study the idea. The committee, after studying the idea and surveying their members, concludes that the center has the space needed and could charge a small fee to cover the addition of an employee to manage the childcare center, and that the fitness center ought to offer the service for at least six months to test the idea.

Person. What might a company do if the company's products are people? As an example, consider a sport marketing and management company that specializes in managing and promoting professional athletes. The company's task is to try to find the best contracts and jobs for the athletes. The company uses the athletic and personal characteristics of the athlete as selling points. When the company considers the addition of a new product (adding another athlete) to its line of products (athletes already under contract), it will research many factors. Some of these factors are popularity of the individual, consumer markets (the variety and extent of demand for the athlete), cost to the company, and possible profitability. Further, the company might add the athlete for a one-year trial basis (test marketing).

Place. When the product is a place, research and development are contingent on factors such as the type of place (facility) and whether or not it exists. Let's look at an example of a facility that does not exist. The local state university has announced that it would like to have a new facility to house the women's and men's basketball and volleyball teams. The programs are very successful and have been nationally ranked in the top 25 for more than eight years. The existing facility was built in 1936. The process for determining the feasibility of this product can be very complicated. The university is a state-supported institution, which means that tax dollars are involved. The process might include the development of a committee to study the idea. The committee needs to gather information such as facility needs, the cost of such a facility, if resources exist or where the university might obtain the resources, if space (land) is available and obtainable, ticket price structure, who will use the facility, how many ways the facility might be used, expenses involved, consumer surveys, and other. This will involve working with contractors, architects, the state education department, state government, and many other agencies and individuals. The committee could perform all the research or hire a marketing company to do the work. In this type of situation, the university usually hires a marketing company to do the research. Be careful to hire a marketing company with experience in the sport industry and with specific experience in sport facilities and sport facility research.

When the testing is complete and test results yield information, conclusions may be drawn about the product. The information from the research will guide decisions pertaining to moving to the next stage.

Did you know...?

OLN is the leader in competitive and adrenaline-charged content. Now in 63.4 million homes, OLN is the cable home of the National Hockey League and best-in-class events like The Tour de France, The America's Cup, Professional Bull Riders (PBR), the Boston Marathon and USSA Skiing. The network offers unique programming in four primary areas: Action Sports, Field Sports, Bulls & Rodeo and Awe-Inspiring Series, and is the exclusive home of Survivor in syndication.

The *test marketing stage* is the next step in the new product development process. Test marketing involves selecting a specific market area in which to offer the product. It is usually offered with a specialized marketing campaign. The primary reason for test marketing is to determine how the product performs in a real market. In selecting the test market area, some factors to consider are size, control of selected promotional media, cost, the consumer markets, and the product markets.

A sports wheelchair manufacturing company has developed a wheelchair for basketball. The company offers the chairs in two large cities (test markets). The company's plan is to promote the wheelchairs in the two cities for a one-year period. If the wheelchair sells well in the two test markets, the company will expand to additional large cities.

You may decide to skip this stage because it can be very expensive. The decision to skip test marketing should be based on the conclusion that the new product has a very high possibility of selling and success.

The final stage is *commercialization*. Full marketing strategies are planned, and the entire company gets ready to make the necessary adjustments for the new product. Complete business and marketing plans are developed, implementation plans are identified, plans for production are developed, personnel considerations are established, and promotional efforts are determined. The product is finished and goes on the market.

Each sport company should organize its new product development process and attempt to manage the process for success. Management must remember, however, the high rate of unsuccessful new products and make a commitment to support the investment necessary for new product development.

Product Identification, Branding, and Brand Management

Product identification involves establishing an identity for your product through the use of some identifying device. The primary purpose of product identification is to differentiate your product from other relatively homogeneous products. It may also be used as a strategy to increase the strength of the company or product image, to establish or to use an established reputation, and to facilitate market and product development strategies.

The most commonly used methods of product identification are branding and packaging. Branding is accomplished through the use of a brand, brand name, or trademark.

A *brand* is a name, symbol, term, and/or design intended for the identification of the products of a seller. It may consist of any combination of a name, word, letter, number, design, symbol, and color. A *brand name* is the word, letter, or number that can be vocalized. The symbol, design or coloring is the *brand mark*. It can be recognized by sight and not expressed vocally. For example, the brand mark of NIKE includes the word NIKE and a mark that looks like a

> The establishment of a brand—a name, symbol, term, or design that represents a product—is important because it allows the idea of a product to exist in a consumer's mind even when the product itself isn't visible.

well-rounded checkmark. NIKE calls it a "swoosh." One would never know that the symbol actually has an identifying name, however, until looking into Nike's legal papers that describe the NIKE brand name and mark. It is at this point that the brand name and mark may become what is commonly called a *trademark*.

Trademark is essentially a legal term. It is a brand that has legal protection; that is, it is protected from being used by other companies. Why would a company want to use another company's trademark instead of developing its own identity? The reason is to confuse and trick the consumer. The consumer purchases the product thinking that the product is from a well-known company. What the consumer actually purchased is a copy—an imitation of another company's product. These products have become known as "clones." For example, the consumer sees a mark that looks like the NIKE swoosh on a pair of sneakers. The consumer purchases the product because the price is very low (compared to the price for the real NIKE product) and believes it is a deal too good to pass. In reality, the consumer purchased an imitation product.

The establishment of a brand is important for products such at tennis racquets because it allows the product to be clearly identified by consumers.

Success in branding lies in selecting a good brand name and mark. The company should select something short, easy to pronounce and spell. A great brand suggests something about the product, and is unique. Other factors to be considered are ethics, market segments, and current events. A company can do harm to its image and its product if its brand name or mark is insensitive to cultures, populations, or specific current events. For example, in 1993 Converse intended to release a basketball shoe called the "Run 'N Gun" until community groups in Boston, where Converse is located, protested the implications of the name. The name is derived from a basketball term used to describe a specific type of play. The protesting groups, however, pointed out that in today's society the word *gun* means a gun. Further, youths have actually been robbed and even murdered for their clothing and popular name brand shoes. Converse recognized its responsibility to young people, the impending bad press, and the possibility of a boycott and decided to change the name of the shoe. (Its new name is "Run 'N Slam") (Moore, 1993).

> Consumers react to branding on three levels: brand recognition, brand preference, and brand insistence. Companies aim for brand insistence, the level at which consumers will buy only their brand and no other.

There are three levels through which a consumer might progress in relation to branding. In the first level, brand recognition, a consumer is only aware of the existence of a particular brand. At the second level, brand preference, the consumer has developed a preference for a specific brand and will select it for purchase over other brands. At the third level, brand insistence, the consumer will purchase only a specified brand. It is, of course, the third level that is the goal of most companies. This level, however, is difficult to achieve due to the speed at which competitors can enter the market.

Packaging is the activity of enclosing a product. It involves designing and enclosing the product in some type of package or container in an attempt to differentiate the product from others. In addition, the package should protect the product, should be a convenient size, be easy to open and attractive so that it can be used as a promotional tool, and it should be honest. Although the sport marketer has many decisions to make concerning packaging, information guiding these decisions must also include consumer data. Because design and package costs are included in the final price of the product to the consumer, the marketer must know the price that a consumer is willing to pay for the product. Final decisions on packaging usually mean compromise when final cost becomes a major factor.

In the sport business industry, there are products for which packaging takes on a slightly different meaning. Sport marketers have developed a way to "package" sporting activity events in an attempt to make the event more attractive to a greater diversity of consumer segments. Packaging a sport event involves enveloping the event with an array of activities, benefits, and products. In one example, sport marketers trying to sell season tickets to collegiate women's basketball games create a variety of ticket packages.

> It is important to remember that sport event packaging includes not only the product or services themselves, but also certain elements of presentation such as the cleanliness of facilities, the attitude of the staff, and the amount of attention paid to the consumer during the event.

The lowest cost season-ticket package might contain just the tickets and nothing else. The highest cost ticket package might include VIP valet parking, a parking space, seats on or near the 50-yard line, admission to a pre-game and half-time reception, admission to a post-game party with the coach, and admission to the end-of-the-year banquet.

One of the shortest events in sport is surrounded by a month of activities. The event is a racing event over a distance of one mile and a quarter (*Derby winners 1875 to 1992*, 1993). The race lasts just a few seconds over two minutes. The event is the Kentucky Derby—a horse race. The Derby's first race was in 1875, and since that time, it has grown to a major money sport event with an attendance of over 120,000 (McMasters, 1993). In 1971, there were 12 events and activities surrounding the Derby (Harris, 1993). In 1993, there were 63 official Kentucky Derby Festival events and activities and countless unofficial events, parties, socials, and other activities. Today, there are even more events and many of them are sports events, such as the

* adidas Derby Festival Basketball Classic,

* BellSouth Derby Festival Volleyball Classic,

* Don Fightmaster Golf Outing for Exceptional Children,

* Fifth Third Bank Derby Festival $1 Million Hole-in-One Ladies Day,

* Fifth Third Bank Derby Festival $1 Million Hole-in-One Contest,

* King Southern Bank Derby Festival Foundation Pro-Am Golf Tournament,

- Meijer Derby Festival Marathon/miniMarathon, and

- U.S. Bank Derby Festival Great Balloon Race.

The Kentucky Derby race is held every year on the first Saturday in May. The official Kentucky Derby Festival events and activities in 1993 were held beginning on April 7, and the last event was held on May 14. The events surround the Derby race providing a multitude of activity and entertainment for the consumer. Hence, the Kentucky Derby is a packaged sports event.

Sport event packaging goes beyond events and activities to include often-overlooked factors such as facility cleanliness, friendliness of workers and staff, and prompt attention to a variety of consumer needs while attending the event. Everything included in the package is designed to create an atmosphere in which the consumer believes that she or he is getting plenty more than just viewing the event.

Making the Decision for Product Deletion

For some products, the time will arrive when it no longer fulfills a consumer need or desire. The sport marketer must be able to identify that time and make the decision to eliminate the product. The decision should be based on an analysis of the product's situation: sales and sales trends, profits trends, cost analysis, and product life cycle stage. There are also indirect factors to be considered such as the effect of eliminating a product on the company and employees, the effect of eliminating a product on other companies, and the effect of eliminating a product on the consumer.

If the sport company has decided to eliminate a product, there are some techniques that may be used in order to decrease the many effects that its elimination could have. For example, the product could be *phased out* over a period of time. This will allow everyone involved in the production of the product and the consumer to begin to make the transition toward the day that the product is no longer offered.

Chapter Summary

Products are the company. Products provide benefits and fulfill functions. The sport consumer looks for products that will satisfy specific needs or desires. In the sport industry there is a vast array of products. Product needs to be understood as a concept because a product involves tangible and intangible characteristics.

The wide variety of sport products available to the consumer in the sport industry requires some method of classification. Product classification typically involves an analysis of the consumer and, in particular, consumer needs and desires. It is the function of the product for the consumer that is the reason for its existence.

The product life cycle is a concept that must be understood by the sport marketer. Product management strategies are influenced by the stages in which the company's products might be categorized in the product life cycle. Product mix and product development strategies are also influenced.

New product development is important to the sport marketer as new products are a constant event in the sport industry. When the sport marketer understands the industry segment in which the company's products exist, informed decisions and strategies may guide the company to the successful addition of a new product.

The sport company must establish an identity for the product through product identification. This can include branding and packaging. Packaging is the activity of enclosing a product. There are some products in the sport industry that require a different kind of packaging—surrounding the product with an array of other products, activities, and events.

Product deletion is also a sport management and marketer's responsibility. A time will come when a product no longer fulfill the needs or desires of the consumer. At this critical point, a decision must be made concerning the elimination of the product.

CASE STUDY CHAPTER 8

Professional Women's Soccer League: Kicking up Success Through Sport Marketing Planning

In the US, women's soccer has been fast to grow in rates of participation and in spectatorship. Estimates reveal that there are 40 million girls and women playing soccer around the world, and the number of women will equal the number of men by the year 2010. Perhaps one of the most singular factors that can be attributed as having an enormous influence on its success was the popularity of Team USA in the 1990s and early portion of the 21st century. This team had players that are recognized around the world, such as Mia Hamm, Brandy Chastain, Tiffeny Milbrett, Kristine Lilly, Michelle Akers, Joy Fawcett, Kate Sobrero, Julie Foudy, and Brianna Scurry.

The popularity of the team's players is coupled with its tremendous success in the US and globally. Team USA won the gold medal at the 1996 Olympics, silver at the 2000 Olympics, and gold at the 2004 Olympics. In women's World Cup competition, Team USA has captured two of the four championships. The first women's World Cup championship was held in 1991—61 years after the first men's World Cup.

More than 650,000 spectators attended the FIFA women's World Cup in 1991 in the US and nearly one billion viewers from 70 countries tuned in to watch 16 countries compete for the title.

With many accolades to her credit, Hamm holds the world record—female or male—for international goals scored with 150. In addition, Hamm and Akers are the only two women, and the only two Americans (male or female),

named to the FIFA 100—a list of the 125 greatest living soccer players as selected by Pele and commissioned by FIFA. Hamm has played in 259 international matches; only Lilly, her Team USA teammate, has played in more.

The WUSA was the first women's professional soccer league in the US. In its inaugural year in 2001, the WUSA had the best players from around the world as members of its eight teams. The league was popular, with average attendance per game of more than 8,000. This exceeded projections by about 1,500 per game.

Sponsors of the first season in 2001 included major corporations such as Hyundai and Gillette. Subsequent seasons saw additional companies join as sponsors of the league.

In television, the WUSA was shown PAX-TV in a Sunday afternoon time slot. This targeted the demographic of soccer families that would be free from their typical Saturday youth games. This worked. But a mere three years after its inception, the WUSA closed its doors with the statement that it was only suspending play, not ending it.

There are many critics of the league, as is typical with any new sport attempting to become a major professional league. New leagues ostensibly, although unfairly, get compared to the current professional leagues, such as the NBA, WNBA, NFL, LPGA, and Major League Baseball. There's always the question of why wouldn't the league start small, build a fan base over many years, and eventually, through sustained growth, go big. For example, it has

continued on next page

(continued)

taken decades for each of the current big-time leagues to grow into the product they are today. Each one started, failed, started, failed, and typically continued this trend until it finally caught on—and "catching on" means that there is a sustainable fan base with enough loyalty and or curiosity to warrant the level of the product, the level of sponsorship, its commercialism, and its level of media coverage.

For example, the NFL didn't keep attendance figures for its first dozen years. After competing against the popularity of college football, the NFL began keeping these numbers around 1934. The average attendance was just around 8,200—slightly better than the average attendance recorded by the WUSA.

In comparison to the NBA, during the decade between 1952 and 1962, average attendance at NBA games in-

creased from 3,200 to 4,600. It took another decade before the NBA averaged more than 8,000 fans at its games.

Women's professional basketball began in 1978. After several start-ups and closures of different leagues by different individuals, it has taken nearly three decades to build to its current level of success. The WNBA's all-star and playoff games are televised worldwide in nearly 200 countries.

Sources

Orton, K. (2001, September 4). WNBA is facing growing pains. *The Washington Post*.

Wikipedia. WUSA. http://www.wikipedia.org.

Wylie, J. P. (2002, May). The people's choice: Attendance exceeded expectations. *Soccer Digest*.

Wylie, J. P. (2003, June-July). The bottom line: In the worst economic climate for a startup company in decades, the WUSA re-tinkers its financial structure and remains optimistic about its future. *Soccer Digest*.

Case Activity

If the WUSA was such an instant success in its initial three years, where is it today? What happened to the fans, the TV contracts, and the sponsors? What is the WUSA doing to bring women's professional soccer back to the market? What would you do to bring it to the market? What business model would you follow?

QUESTIONS FOR STUDY

1. What is a product? What is a sport product? List examples of sport products.
2. Why do people purchase sport products?
3. Define these terms: form utility, time utility, place utility, and ownership utility. Give an example of each.
4. What is product classification?
5. What is the product life cycle? What are the stages in the product life cycle?
6. Give examples of sport products in each product life cycle.
7. Why is it important for the sport marketer to know in which stage of the product life cycle each of the sport company's products may be categorized?
8. What is the product mix? Why is it important?
9. How many ways might a sport company offer a new product?
10. What is the new product development planning process? What are the stages?
11. What is product identification? Why is it important? How is it used in the sport business industry?

Chapter Nine

PRICING STRATEGIES FOR THE SPORT BUSINESS INDUSTRY

"What do I get for my money?!"

This is a question asked by every consumer everywhere. What a consumer pays for something and what that individual believes they get for their money varies from one consumer to another. As an example, let's consider a conversation between two individuals about two boats. Consumer A believes that Boat #1 is the better buy because the boat has more features and instruments than Boat #2. Consumer B believes that Boat #2 is a better buy because the engine has more horsepower. Consumer A points out that the price of Boat #1 is slightly lower than the price of Boat #2. Consumer B replies that the reason the price is slightly higher is that Boat #2 has a larger engine and engines are expensive. Consumer A argues that Boat #1 has more safety features such as a built-in automatic fire extinguisher in the engine compartment. Consumer B argues that Boat #2 has a good-looking color combination and that a more powerful engine is necessary to produce the speed and power needed when pulling water skiers. Consumer A states that water skiing isn't fun anymore and everyone's favorite toys are tubes, kneeboards, and wakeboards.

This discussion can go on for hours, days, or even weeks. Which consumer is right? Both are right insofar as each is willing to pay a particular price for what each believes is the best buy. Which one is the best buy? The consumer defines "best buy" according to needs and desires. In addition, the definition will change from situation to situation and from product to product.

Determining the price of a product in the sport business industry is the sport marketing mix element that is most difficult to determine. The sport marketer must consider that price is perhaps the most sensitive element of a product for the consumer. The price, from the consumer's perspective, is the amount of money the consumer must sacrifice for a product. In addition, money is relative. Every consumer has a unique amount of money to spend and only a specific amount to spend for sport products. Further, many other factors affect the consumer's decision to buy. These and other factors that affect the determination of price, pricing objectives, pricing methods, and pricing strategies will be discussed in this chapter.

We will first define price, consider it as a concept, and look at the many ways it is presented to the consumer. Second, we will discuss the 4 Cs and their relationship to price determination. Third, we present the concept of elasticity of demand.

Fourth, we discuss determining pricing objectives for the sport business. Finally, we present pricing methods and strategies that can be used in the sport industry.

Simply stated, price is something a consumer exchanges for a product. There are two terms to understand in these definitions: exchange and value. *Exchange* is the trading of something for something. The form of exchange may be money, services, or other forms for the exchange of products from the seller to the buyer. The first system of exchange was bartering, or trading. If you wanted corn, you might expect to trade wheat for it. If you wanted a little boat, you might have to trade a couple of cows for it. Eventually, something called money became the trading means of choice. Today, currency is the most common means in the process of exchange used by the consumer to obtain wanted or needed products.

Value is not an easy term to define. One definition states that value is a "quantitative measure of the worth of a product" (Stanton, Etzel, and Walker, 1991). Where do we begin to determine the quantitative worth of a product? In the above example of trading two cows for a boat, the individuals involved would negotiate over the exchange. If the individual who wants the boat—the buyer—believes that two cows are too much to trade for the boat, that means that two cows are worth more than the boat. The individual with the boat—the seller—believes that the boat is worth two cows. The bartering, or negotiating, will continue until an agreement can be reached. If an agreement cannot be reached, we can conclude that the buyer believed that the VALUE of the boat was not worth two cows. The buyer might decide to not make the trade. The seller has lost a deal.

This is exactly what takes place in today's marketplace. Buyers and sellers negotiate over price. Negotiation takes place in more than one form—verbal and nonverbal. For example, negotiation over some products might be realized through nonverbal communication when the consumer decides not to purchase a particular product because of the price. This can force the seller to set a different price—or not make any sales. In the negotiation over some other products such as cars or boats, verbal negotiation takes place. The buyer and seller negotiate until

> Price is the exchange value of a good or service and fluctuates according to its exchange value in the marketplace, or its market value.

an agreement can be reached. As a matter of fact, negotiation over price is expected for some products in the United States. In some other countries, negotiation over prices, sometimes called bargaining or haggling, is expected and part of the culture. For example, anyone who has been to certain cities in Mexico will agree that negotiation is commonplace among street vendors. If the buyer does not haggle over the price and pays the asking price, the buyer is considered foolish and an easy target by the seller. The seller will pass the word to other vendors. Some vendors consider the buyer rude if the buyer does not negotiate, and other vendors are insulted if the buyer does not negotiate.

A consumer's perceived value of a product such as golf clubs can be influenced by many factors.

There can be many factors involved in the determination of value, and it can have several meanings. This is because each individual involved in determining the value of a product has a unique perspective. For example, let's revisit our discussion concerning two consumers discussing two boats. Each individual holds attitudes, preferences, values and beliefs, a certain amount of expendable money, an amount of money each thinks should be spent on a boat, and other ideas that will affect what each believes ought to be the price, or value, of the boat. In other words, many factors besides price affect the establishment of the value of a product. Hence, we can suggest that price is a reflection of value.

Price:

is the exchange value of something.

Value:

is the quantitative measure of the worth of a product.

Perceived Value:

is what the consumer thinks something is worth.

Price is presented to the consumer in a number of ways, and this is also true in the sport industry. One reason for this is to give identification to the product through the price title. Another reason is to soften the blow: Other words are easier on the ear than the word *price*. Take a look at the following examples of words used in place of the word *price* that can be found in the sport industry:

- A licensing fee is the price a sports apparel company pays a university for the right to sell a T-shirt with the university's logo on it.

- The ticket charge is the price you pay to enter a facility and watch a basketball game.

- Membership fee is the price you pay to use a fitness center's facilities.

- Admission is the price you pay to enter the water sports park.

- Rental is the price you pay to use a water tube at the water sports park.

- A league fee is the price your softball team must pay to play in a softball league.

- A sponsorship fee is the price the local bank pays to be the sponsor of a Special Olympics event. (What the bank gets for its money is advertising and goodwill exposure.)

- Registration fee is the price you pay for your daughter to attend the summer basketball camp.

- A signing bonus is part of the price a professional basketball team pays to assure the services of a player.

- A salary is the price a professional baseball team pays for the services of coaches and players.

- Commission is the extra bonus-oriented price a sports marketing company would pay its sales people for their services.

- Shipping and handling is the price a sporting goods company pays to have its products moved from one place to another.

- The purse is the price a professional golf organization pays the golfers who place in money-winning finishes in a tournament.

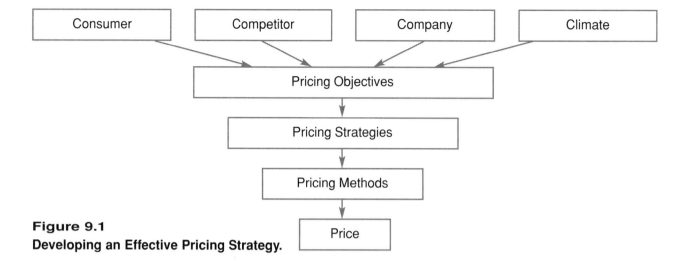

Figure 9.1
Developing an Effective Pricing Strategy.

- A bid is your offered price for an item at a sport art collection auction.

- An endorsement fee is the price a sport shoe company pays to have a famous athlete like Mia Hamm or Danica Patrick state that she endorses—believes in, favors, prefers, and supports—the products of that company.

- Broadcasting rights is the price a television station company pays to televise the local women's volleyball match.

- A consulting fee is the price a company pays a sport marketing research company to analyze the effectiveness of their sponsorship of a sports event.

- A franchise fee is the price that an organization or individual pays to enter a team in a professional sports league.

These are some of the terms used in place of the word *price* in various segments of the sport industry. The words give definition and identification to the product. This creative use of language is also part of the company's promotional efforts: Price is used as a promotional tool. This illustrates the inter-relatedness of marketing mix elements. Price can be a complex element of marketing for the sport marketer. Figure 9.1 is a model for developing pricing decisions and strategies. Each of the parts of the model will be discussed in the following sections of the chapter.

The Four Cs of Price Determination

The sport marketer must consider many factors that affect price and pricing strategies. However, most of these factors can be organized in order to consider them in a manageable manner. They fall primarily into four categories: the consumer, the competitor, the company, and the climate (environment). Each of the four Cs, is presented here with a brief description of how it relates to pricing.

THE CONSUMER

Although the price for something is a sensitive factor for the consumer, the consumer considers much more than the price in making a purchase decision. The consumer also considers factors such as product quality, warranty, company serv-

ice agreement, refund policy, the consumer's image and reputation, and product bargain. Each factor is weighed in the consumer's analysis according to what the consumer will obtain of each one for the price. For example, if the consumer is considering the purchase of a fitness center membership, he or she will consider services included in the membership package. Because this package costs more than another, how many services are included, and will the consumer use them?

In addition to the factors mentioned, the consumer's buying decision is also affected by the decision-making pathway to reach conclusion. Along the path, the consumer's decision process could be affected by the opinions of friends, family members, a significant other, and salespeople. The consumer could also be affected by age, income, education, geographic location, race, sexual orientation, and gender. Other factors include the consumer's personality, favorite activity, religion, and lifestyle. In addition, some consumers will research a product and its price to inform the decision to be made. There is information available through consumer product reports, product research labs, and government and private product testing organizations. The study of the consumer's consideration of price is an element of a specialized field of study called consumer behavior. We recommend that the sport marketer read extensively in this area.

THE COMPETITOR

There is another factor the sport business cannot ignore: the competitor. More specifically, the sport marketer cannot ignore the competitor's prices and pricing strategies. When determining the price to place on a product, you should give serious consideration to the price in the marketplace—prices being used by the competitors. For example, let's say that you are planning to build and manage an indoor soccer facility. Presently, there are three indoor soccer facilities in the same city. You decide, without investigating the competitor's prices, that you will establish the price, or league fee, for two of your products as follows:

1. Women's advanced league—$400.00

2. Men's advanced league—$400.00

When your facility opens, you get no entries in either league. Upon investigation, you discover that the consumers—soccer players—are buying the product—playing—at the other three facilities. You approach some of the players to ask why and find that they believe your price is too high. You investigate the prices of the other facilities and find the following:

FACILITY A: WOMEN'S ADVANCED FEE—$300.00

MEN'S ADVANCED FEE—$300.00

FACILITY B: WOMEN'S ADVANCED FEE—$280.00

MEN'S ADVANCED FEE—$300.00

FACILITY C: WOMEN'S ADVANCED FEE—$295.00

MEN'S ADVANCED FEE—$295.00

The amount that the consumers of indoor soccer are willing to pay has been established. The consumers have been paying a specific amount for soccer for quite a few years, and they are not willing to pay more. Finally, you decide that there is a simple solution. You will set the price below your competitors' prices. You set the fee at $100.00 for each of the leagues. This time, a couple of teams register and pay the $100.00, but there are not enough teams to fill the eight slots needed. Therefore, you have to cancel them and return the money to those who had registered.

Once again, you investigate by talking to the consumers. This time you discover that the consumers thought that the price you set was some kind of a hoax with plenty of other hidden charges that would eventually add up to the $400.00 you originally wanted to charge. In addition, some of them tell you that they were concerned with what they would get for only $100.00. In other words, they think that a price of $100.00 is too low to pay for soccer and that they will not get a quality product. This situation reflects two factors in price consideration: first, the consumer's perception of the value for a product; second, careful analysis of the competitor's prices.

THE COMPANY

Another important piece of the puzzle is your company. What are the factors in your sport company that will affect setting the price of a product? Some of these are materials, equipment, rent or mortgage payment, payroll costs, maintenance, renovation, promotion, and dividends to stockholders. If the company is a manufacturer, it cannot put a price on a product that does not, at a minimum, cover the cost of producing the product. If it is a retailer or wholesaler, the price must at least cover the purchase of the product.

The type of sport company will also affect price determination. Generally, there are two types—nonprofit and for-profit. Nonprofit sport companies include those that are supported by government funding such as community recreation facilities and nonprofit sport companies supported by membership fees such as a YMCA. Usually, these are tax-exempt. For-profit sport companies are the opposite—companies owned by individuals, groups, or large conglomerates that do not receive government funding support and are not tax-exempt.

There is a difference in the costs associated with producing similar products in nonprofit and for-profit enterprises. For example, a nonprofit community fitness center receives a variety of tax breaks. Therefore, the total cost of producing the sport product is less than is the total cost for a for-profit fitness center. This allows the nonprofit sport company to set decidedly lower prices for the same products that the for-profit sport company offers. Hence, for-profit sport company owners complain that this is unfair competition.

Nonprofit sport enterprises gave special attention to raising prices, however, in the early 1990s. The reason was decreasing government and charitable funding. As state governments struggled to balance budgets during the early 1990s, the proportion of funding to recreation and sport facilities decreased. Nonprofit companies reported a decrease in charitable giving in the early 1990s due to the recession and the change in tax laws governing charitable giving—less of a given amount is deductible on a person's income tax calculations. As a result, some companies implemented higher fees. As government changes tax laws and these changes affect charitable giving, the sport marketing professional must become aware of these changes and how they will affect their business.

Raising fees will affect consumers and the companies. It will be up to the sport marketer to carefully analyze and estimate the effects of higher prices. As you will learn later in this chapter, the company might lose some consumers if prices are increased, but may make a greater profit.

THE CLIMATE

The climate includes those factors that are primarily external and that the sport marketer cannot directly control. These include factors such as laws pertaining to pricing, government regulations, the political climate, the economic situation, and local public attitude.

The economy can have perhaps the most direct effect on the sport company's pricing strategies. For example, since the terrorist attack event on September 11, 2001, the United States has been experiencing a recession involving high unemployment rates, which slows economic growth. Consumer spending has been low. When consumers are not buying, the consumer price rate—known as inflation—falls. Therefore, if a company cannot raise prices to cover costs and company objectives, it is forced to change pricing strategies.

The sport marketer cannot afford to develop something referred to as "tunnel vision." Tunnel vision means that the person has stopped paying attention to or studying all factors affecting a situation and has become lazy or egotistical, paying attention to only one or a few factors. The sport marketer must constantly study all factors involved in order to make educated decisions.

Elasticity of Demand

The sport marketer must understand a marketing concept called the elasticity of demand. Here is a simple definition: changes in the market (sales) when there is a change in price. *Elasticity* is a measure of how consumers react—consumer sensitivity—to changes in price. The following questions can help you understand this concept:

1. What will happen if we raise the price of a sport product? If fewer consumers purchase the product, how many is "fewer"? How will that affect revenue, profit, and sales?

2. What will happen if we decrease prices? Will more consumers purchase the products? How will this affect revenue, profit, and sales?

3. Is there any guarantee that any change in price will result in a change in consumer purchasing pattern?

The sport marketer can answer these questions only through estimation or experimentation. The sport marketer can attempt to estimate what will happen when a change is made to the price. The following example illustrates the concept of estimating elasticity of demand.

WILD ADVENTURES WATER SPORTS PARK

The cost of admission to the Wild Adventures Water Sports Park is $8.00 for a full day pass. If the price is increased to $10.00, our first analysis is that there will probably be an immediate drop in attendance. This drop may level off, and the final effects will be minimal when we consider this situation over a long period and if the increase in revenues from sales equals or is greater than current revenue from sales.

If the attendance number decreases, we can conclude that the demand for this product is relatively inelastic. Refer to Figure 9.2 in which the graph illustrates the two-dollar increase and attendance figures. The graph shows that although the attendance number decreased from 320,000 to 300,000, total revenue increased from $2,560,000 to $3,000,000—an increase of $440,000, although there was a decrease of 20,000 buyers. This means that this situation is relatively inelastic because the change in price results in a parallel change in revenue.

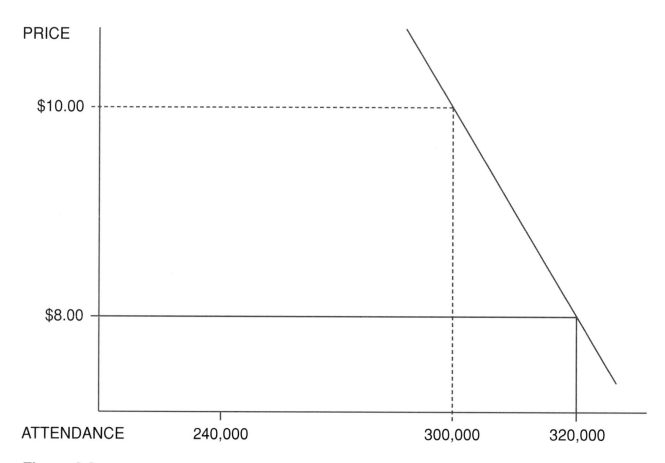

Figure 9.2
Elasticity of Demand at the Wild Adventures Water Sports Park. This situation is considered relatively inelastic.

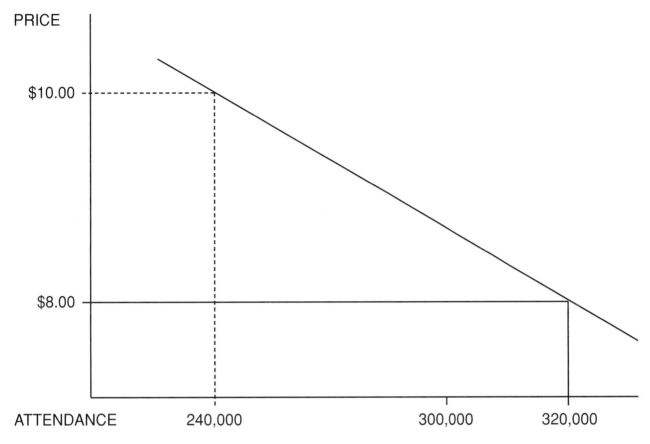

PRICE

$10.00

$8.00

ATTENDANCE   240,000   300,000   320,000

Figure 9.3
Elasticity of Demand at the Wild Adventures Water Sports Park. This situation is considered relatively elastic.

Figure 9.3 illustrates the estimate of what could happen if there were a drastic change in consumers. If the number of buyers drops from 320,000 to 240,000—a difference of 80,000 buyers—and this decrease results in a loss in revenue, demand is relatively elastic: A change in price causes an opposite change in revenue. The higher price and fewer buyers resulted in a $160,000 decrease in revenue.

Determinants of Elasticity

What causes elasticity and inelasticity of demand? First, consider the situation at the beginning of the chapter: the consumers comparing two boats. Many factors affect their decision to buy. One factor is what they would "expect" to pay for a specific boat with a specific set of features. This "expected price" is what the consumer thinks the product is worth (R. E. McCarville, Crompton, and Sell, 1993). The expected price usually is one somewhere within a range of prices with relative minimum and maximum limits: a price most frequently charged, price for similar products, price of the brand usually purchased, or the price last paid (Winer, 1988). For example, the consumer might expect to pay between $100 and $300 for a one-year membership in a fitness center because that is the range of prices for that product in today's market. In another example, a consumer might believe that a fair price for a new pair of running shoes is "not over $80." If a consumer has "shopped around," this means that the consumer has compared prices of a product at two or more places. This is also precisely what the sport marketer should do. As one means of estimating setting a price, shop around—compare prices of the same or a comparable product. If the product seems to sell well within a specific range of prices, this is a fairly accurate estimate of "expected price," or what the consumer expects to pay and is paying. Some of the other factors that affect elasticity are presented in Table 9.1. They are discussed here next.

Necessity or luxury product. Price can be relatively inelastic if the product is a necessity and elastic if it is a luxury. For example, football pads are a necessity, and there are no substitutes. Therefore, the buyers must pay the set prices. On the other hand, going on a sports adventure trip is a luxury, and there are plenty of substitutes. Therefore, prices must be set specific to consumer markets because the consumer does not have to spend money for a trip.

Product Substitutability. Have you ever seen or heard these advertising words: "There is NO substitute," "Accept no substitute," or "No other product compares"? The availability of substitutes for products can have a strong affect on elasticity. Those sport products or

Table 9.1
Some Factors That Affect Elasticity of Demand.
product necessity or luxury
product substitute availability
frequency of purchase
proportion of income available for a specific product
economy
brand loyalty
competition (quantity and quality)
quality of the product
product specialization
time frame of demand

Sources: Boone & Kurtz, 1989; Burnson & Shelby, 1993; Howard & Crompton, 1980; Pajak, 1990; Peter & Donnelly, 1991; Raju, Srinivasan & Lal, 1990; Stotlar, 1993; Stotlar & Bronzan, 1987; Stotlar & Johnson, 1989; and Tarpey, Donnelly & Peter, 1979.

other products that can meet the consumer's needs, wants, or desires are direct competition for the consumer dollar. In research on recreation and leisure, *substitutability* has been defined as "an interchangeability among activities in satisfying participants' motives, needs and preferences" (Hendee and Burdge, 1974). More recently, Brunson and Shelby (1993) offered the following definition: The term recreation substitutability refers to the interchangeability of recreation experiences such that acceptably equivalent outcomes can be achieved by varying one or more of the following: the timing of the experience, the means of gaining access, the setting, and the activity. (p. 69)

Using this definition, the sport marketer must study two factors: what the consumer is looking for and the potential substitutes for their product. With this knowledge the sport marketer can incorporate pricing and other marketing-mix strategies to try to keep the consumer from selecting the substitute.

Frequency of purchase. The frequency with which the consumer must purchase a product affects elasticity of demand. Frequency can be linked to necessity. For example, if a consumer has a consistent need for athletic tape to stock the sports medicine clinic, pricing strategies can be set according to the frequency of purchase. In another example, if the sport product is such that there is a very low frequency of purchase such as the need for a sport marketing study on building a new student recreation center for the university, price will likely be much higher.

Income. An individual's income limits the amount of money a consumer has available to spend on discretionary products after all the bills are paid. As income increases, the percent of income a consumer has to use for food and bills decreases.

This means that the percent of income available for discretionary purposes will increase. An individual with a lower income spends a larger percentage on food and bills and is therefore left with a smaller percentage for discretionary spending. For example, consumer A's take-home income is $25,000 and consumer B's take-home income is $50,000. Both use approximately 40% of their income for necessities such as mortgage, food, vehicles, insurance, utilities, phone, and cable TV. Forty percent of each income is:

$25,000.00 \times 40\% = \$10,000$

$50,000.00 \times 40\% = \$20,000$.

Now calculate how much money each consumer has left for discretionary spending:

$25,000 - \$10,000 = \$15,000$ or $1,250 per month

$50,000 - \$20,000 = \$30,000$ or $2,500 per month.

Consumer B has more discretionary income than consumer A has even though each uses the same percentage of income for necessities.

The economy. The economy affects elasticity of demand. For example, how does recession impact consumer spending and setting prices? The early 1990s were labeled the "Age of Disinflation" (Farrell and Schiller, 1993). Inflation is the rising

Courtesy of The Georgia World Congress Center Authority

Changes in the economy affects consumers' spending patterns and a struggling economy could lead to a low turnout at a sporting event.

price level measured in percentages over a period of time, usually annually. Inflation in the United States reached double-digit proportions in the late 1970s and early 1980s and eventually reached 13.6% in 1980. Between 1990 and 1993, the inflation rate decreased from an annual 5.4% to a 1993 rate of 2.7%. Forcing this period of "disinflation" were recessionary factors such as high unemployment, slow economic growth, increased fierce global competition, and worldwide overcapacity. What this means to the sport marketer is that when the consumer has less money to spend due to unemployment or is spending less money for reasons due to the fear of losing employment, the company will begin to feel the effects. The sport marketer must either redesign pricing strategies or implement significantly radical ones.

On the other hand, sports activities seem to be sustained as compared to many other product markets during times of recession. It seems that Americans love their sports, recreation, and fitness activities, and they are more willing to forego the purchase of a washer and dryer in order to continue participating in their favorite activity. Moreover, these activities are thought to be therapeutic and stress-relief activities, adding to justification for not giving them up.

Brand loyalty. A consumer can become brand-loyal, meaning that the consumer will purchase only products of a certain brand. As an example, Consumer A believes the running shoes of the Smith Company are the best and only shoe that fits everything the consumer is looking for in a running shoe and, more important, that the Smith Company is the only company in which the consumer believes. The consumer will buy shoes and probably other products from the Smith Company. Consumer B will buy running shoes from any company as long as they fit and the price is right. In this example, Consumer A is loyal to one brand.

> Changes in market demand are important to the sport marketer because they affect consumer spending patterns.

Most companies strive to create brand loyalty within its consumers. It will even use this as part of its advertising. Have you ever seen or heard the advertising slogans presented here: "Our customers always come back" and "Once a S _____ customer, always a S _____ customer"?

Brand loyalty applies to the sport industry in another unique way: something called the "hard-core fan." A hard-core fan is someone who picks and supports a particular team, or sport, and will stick with it through good times and bad. For example, a hard-core fan of a university basketball team whose college colors are gold and white may be heard to exclaim, "My blood runs gold!"

The competition. The prices of products of the competition will affect elasticity of demand. Sometimes "price wars" evolve between two or more companies or between companies within an entire industry. For example, the fitness center industry experienced such phenomenal growth in the late 1970s and throughout the 1980s that the market became saturated with fitness centers. Almost all fitness centers offered the same set of products to the consumer. Therefore, the only difference between centers was the price. If the manager of a fitness center wanted to stay in business, prices had to be lowered—some prices were below the cost of the product.

Did you know...?

The loyal NASCAR fan shops for sports apparel at retail stores, 80%, at sporting goods stores, 32%; at other stores, 6%; and online 3%. (According to Scarborough Sports Marketing, a division of Scarborough Research. For more information, visit Scarborough Research online at *http://www.scarborough.com*.)

To be able to make educated decisions and to set marketing strategies that will compete best with the competition, the sport marketer must study the competition's prices and pricing strategies.

Product quality. A sport product's quality will affect consumer purchasing and hence elasticity of demand. If the consumer knows, or even suspects, that a sport product is of poor quality, demand will be relatively elastic. Thus, if prices are increased, the consumer simply will not buy, believing that the product is not worth the increase.

Product specialization. The specialization of a sport product will affect elasticity of demand. For example, a softball player must use a softball glove to participate in softball. A softball glove is a specialized sport product. There are over 30,000,000 estimated softball participants over the age of six in the United States today. All of them must have this specialized piece of sport equipment to participate in softball. Therefore, the consumer (the softball participant) will purchase this product because it is the only product to perform the function he or she needs. However, there are many softball glove manufacturers and retailers. The consumer has a wide range of choice. This keeps the price down.

Time frame of demand. Another factor affecting elasticity of demand is the time frame of demand: the amount of time a consumer has or is willing to take in the process of making a purchase. Following are three examples. If a soccer player needs athletic tape to wrap an ankle before a game and forgot to purchase the tape in plenty of time before the day and time of the game, the player will be under pressure and will pay almost any price for the tape. The player must stop at the closest store to purchase the tape and does not have time to shop around for the best price. In another example, consider the consumer who wants to buy a new softball bat. This individual currently owns a bat and is fairly satisfied with it. The new bat purchase is a consideration for the future. Therefore, this consumer is under no time pressure to purchase and can shop around for exactly what she wants and for the price she wants. In another example, a college athlete is pursued by several athlete-agents trying to persuade the athlete to retain their services if and when the athlete ever wants or needs an agent. The athlete can be under great time constraints as the senior year approaches.

Pricing Objectives for the Sport Business

One of the most fundamental management skills necessary for positively affecting success is objective setting. Objectives give direction to determining the price and pricing strategies. Pricing objectives should derive from the established marketing objectives that were established in line with the sport company's objectives and mission. A question the sport marketer must always ask first is "What results does the company expect to occur as a result of the price?" The objectives should be clear, forthright, quantitative, realistic, and achievable; and they should establish vision for the future. Table 9.2 shows some examples of a variety of pricing objectives categorized by type based on the 4 Cs.

Objectives are general aspirations toward which all marketing activities are directed. An objective is declared; then goals are formulated to meet the objectives.

Table 9.2
Pricing Objectives Categorized by the 4Cs.

Consumer	Competition	Company	Climate
• price sensitivity	• meet competitive	• image	• legal restraints
• purchase decision	prices	• cost	• sensitivity
• fairness	• be price leader	• efficient use	
• image	• stabilize the market	• return on investment	
• maximize opportunity	• discourage entrants to	• profit margin	
• targeted markets	the market	• increase market share	
		• survival	
		• growth	

Objectives are open-ended statements. Goals are concrete and usually quantitative; goals have specific timelines. Further, company objectives and goals often involve more marketing elements such as promotion and production than pricing. For example, if a running-shoe manufacturer has an objective to become the largest market shareholder, then more than pricing strategies will be involved.

The sport marketer and management of the sport company have the responsibility for establishing pricing objectives. Each objective has potential positive and negative consequences for the company and its consumers. The sport marketer and all of management must analyze the consequences and make decisions based on this knowledge and on the direction in which they want the company to go. Once they have identified the objectives, the next step is to plan the methods and strategies that have the best potential in achieving the objectives.

Pricing Methods and Strategies for the Sport Business

After you have established pricing objectives, the next step in setting prices for your sport products is deciding on specific methods and strategies. In this section we will present some common pricing methods and strategies that may be used in the sport industry with a brief description of each.

Going-rate pricing (also called status quo pricing). This method is applied when the company wants to keep prices at the going rate—the average price of your competitors for same or equivalent products. For example, if you were working with a fitness center, a check of all membership prices charged at fitness centers will be used to determine the going rate.

Demand-oriented pricing. Using this pricing method, the sport marketer ascertains the price that potential customers are willing to pay for a particular product. The price that potential customers are willing to pay can be determined through consumer surveys or studying the competition.

Price discrimination. In this pricing method, different prices are charged for the same sport products (Berrett et al., 1993; Walsh, 1986). This method uses consumer demographics and other factors. For example, sport companies use variables such as the following:

> A strategy is a detailed plan of action by which an individual or company intends to reach objectives and goals.

- Age—senior citizen discounts; special rates for children

- Income—a sliding-scale pricing method according to income

- Facility use—peak prices for peak-use times

- Corporate rate—skyboxes sold to companies for luxury suites at the arena.

Peak-load and off-load pricing. This is the method of charging different prices for the same products demanded at different points in time. It is very similar to demand oriented pricing. The peak-load method involves charging higher prices during times when product sales will have a peak time. For instance, the primary selling time for softball bats is in March, April, and May just prior to softball season. Prices for softball bats during this period will be a little higher than they will be during December and January.

Off-peak pricing involves setting prices lower during off-load times. Some fitness centers use this method. Because the high-use times are those times just before work (6:30–7:30 A.M.), lunch hour, and just after work (5:00–6:30 P.M.), fitness center management wants to encourage more use during the low-use times by offering price incentives. For example, the center can offer a membership discount price to those who promise to only use the center between those high-use times.

Seasonal pricing. This pricing strategy is used when a sport product is affected by the seasons and usually relies on specific seasons. Snow ski resorts charge higher prices during winter when there is plenty of snow and skiers want to go skiing. Lower prices are charged during summer months. During the summer, houseboat rental fees are almost twice the amount charged during winter.

Average cost pricing. This method utilizes the following formula (Howard and Crompton, 1980):

Average Cost Price = Average Fixed Cost + Average Variable Cost

where

Average Fixed Cost = Total Fixed Costs ÷ Number of Participants

and

Average Variable Cost = Total variable Costs ÷ Number of Participants.

The first step in average cost pricing is to determine which fixed costs and variable costs you will use in the formula. Fixed costs are those expenses within the sport company that are constant such as mortgage or rent, payroll, utilities, and phones. Variable costs are expenses such as short-term loan payments, temporary staff, short-term facility rental, and equipment purchases or rental. Once these have been determined, the formula can be used. Howard and Crompton (1980) give the following example:

IF Total Fixed Costs = $1,000

Total Variable Costs = $500

Projected Number of Participants = 100

THEN the Average Cost Price (ACP) = $1,000 ÷ 100 + 500 ÷ 100

THUS ACP = $15.

Penetration pricing. This pricing strategy is used when the sport company wants to penetrate a market by using price as a primary marketing tactic. Prices are relatively lower than other prices for the same products on the market. Penetration pricing is typically used as a first-time offering of a product. For example, a sport marketing company will be opening for business. They decide their pricing strategy will be penetration pricing. To try to secure consumers, they set prices for their services much lower than those of other companies. The company must use a promotion message that speaks to product quality. You'll remember we discussed the problem of setting price too low. Once the product achieves some market recognition, prices can be slowly increased over a period of time.

Cost-plus pricing. In this pricing method, the price of the sport product is based on the cost of the product plus a desired profit (Stanton et al., 1991). If the cost to produce one game of indoor soccer is $40, the price for a game will be $40 plus any amount of profit desired. Therefore, if the indoor soccer facility wants to make $60 of profit from each game, the price of one game will be $100. This will be multiplied by the number of games in a league round of play (usually 8–10 games). If there are 10 teams in the league and the schedule is a round-robin schedule, each team plays each other team once, a schedule that gives each team nine games. Apply the round-robin formula for determining how many games will be played (Byl, 1990):

N × (N−1) ÷ 2 = Total Number of Games*

(*N is number of entries)

In this example we find that 10 × 9 ÷ 2 = 45 games.

Hence, there will be 45 games in the league. If the price per game is established at $100, the total price for all 45 games is $4,500.

Your next step is to determine what to charge each team. The common method is to charge a league fee: Divide the $4,500 by the number of teams entering. Thus, $4,500 ÷ 10 = $450. At this point in the formula, each team will pay a league fee of $450. Now add the "plus" amount to the $450. This amount can be any amount needed or desired, provided, of course, that the "plus" amount won't put the price out of reach for the consumer. The "plus" amount can be added according to goals and objectives for the company. For example, the company wants to start saving for the purchase of some equipment and wants to be able to purchase the equipment at the end of 2 years. Use the cost of the equipment divided over two years and divided among all teams in all leagues in all sports to determine the "plus" amount to add to the cost.

Break-even analysis. This method for pricing is determined through an analysis of costs and revenue, more specifically, when the costs of producing the product equal the revenue taken from the sales of the product. If Central College sold $200,000 worth of tickets to its sports events and the events cost the college $200,000 to produce, the college broke even. In this example, however, Central College didn't make any profit. Break-even analysis will determine how many tickets need to be sold at what price to first break even, and every ticket after that point is profit.

Table 9.3
Calculating the breakeven point using different prices.

Ticket Price	Quantity to Sell	Revenue	Event Cost	Breakeven Point (Units that must be sold to break even)
$2.00	100,000	$200,000.00	$200,000.00	100,000
$5.00	40,000	$200,000.00	$200,000.00	40,000
$7.50	26,666	$200,000.00	$200,000.00	26,666
$10.00	20,000	$200,000.00	$200,000.00	20,000
$15.00	13,333	$200,000.00	$200,000.00	13,333

If Central College sports events average 200 paying attendees and there are 100 events, the total number of paying attendees to all events is 20,000. The breakeven price is $10.00 and the breakeven point is 20,000. Thus, if the ticket price is set at $10.00, Central must get 20,000 paying attendees to break even. In this example, Central will not make any profit at $10.00 per ticket. Central should consider raising the price to make a profit. At $15.00 per ticket, with 20,000 paying attendees, Central will profit $100,000.00.

Short-term pricing methods:

- Quantity discounts (the more you buy, the lower the price per unit)
- Special sales
- Allowances
- Rebates
- Clearance sales
- Promotional sales

To use break-even pricing effectively, the sport marketer first determines the break-even point for a product using several different prices. This allows the sport marketer to determine total costs and revenue for each price being considered. Table 9.3 illustrates this method using different prices for tickets to Central College's events.

Short-term pricing methods. The many short-term pricing methods all involve selling a product at a discounted rate for a limited period of time.

Product line pricing. This method involves setting specific price minimums and maximums for each product line. Acme Tennis Racket Company can carry three lines of rackets differentiated by price: the $500 line, the $300 line, and the $100 line.

Single price. This method involves setting just one price for everything the company offers.

Secondary market pricing. This method involves determining the secondary market value of an item and establishing price. For example, the popularity and growth of the Play It Again, Sports store is proof that there is a desire and a market for previously owned sports equipment. The management of the store establishes the value (price) of each item based on its condition and what it might sell for.

Chapter Summary

In this chapter we outlined and discussed pricing for the sport marketer. We discussed the broad conceptual definitions of price, exchange, and value. We looked at the 4 Cs of price determination and discussed each in relation to its effect on price and the pricing strategy. We discussed the concept of elasticity of demand and its effect on price. The determinants of the elasticity of demand were presented. Last, we looked at several pricing objectives, methods, and strategies that can be used by the sport marketer. The decision-making process for pricing for the sport marketer is not an easy one. Before establishing the price for a sport product, sport marketers must consider, study, and understand many factors. The sport marketer will be making educated decisions and decisions that will have increased positive potential when all factors have been analyzed and the pricing decisions are based on research.

CASE STUDY CHAPTER 9

Sports Businesses Will Score with Pricing Strategy: Who Scores with Scalping?

Setting price is a critical element for sports businesses. Determining the right price level, strategies, and structure are important aspects of effective pricing. Setting ticket prices for events can be a major role in meeting and/or creating demand. For a super-demand mega event such as American football's Super Bowl, setting prices is more an art than science. Factors affecting pricing tickets for the Super Bowl includes variables that are dependent on the teams that will be playing and other individual event factors such as the host city for that year, the record of the two teams that will play for the championship, the popularity of individual star players and their performance for that individual season, each team's Super Bowl history, and the match-up of the coaches of the two teams.

The 2007 Super Bowl proved to be a case of two teams with very interesting Super Bowl histories. The Chicago Bears had not been to a Super Bowl in 21 years. For the Indianapolis Colts, it had not been to the Super Bowl since 1985 (22 years), when the organization was in Baltimore. Both Chicago and Indianapolis fans had a significantly strong demand for tickets.

The price for the 2007 Super Bowl game was $700.00—if you bought it through an official ticket seller outlet. But if you bought it from a secondary source, you could have paid as much as between $4,000 and $10,000. Why? Demand.

Who owns the tickets? The original seller? The secondary source—also called a ticket gouger or ticket scalper? No, says the NFL—the teams own the tickets. If you purchase tickets from the original seller and then resell the tickets at a profit, that profit actually belongs to the teams.

Scalping is against the law in many states and exists for many reasons. One of the reasons against scalping is that access to events should not be affordable to only the wealthy. Even in a capitalist free economy, laws are in place to attempt to keep fairness at play. Therefore, scalping is against the law as a means of helping keep economies fair to people in all classes.

Additionally, the teams, owners, and promoters of events are concerned about scalpers harassing fans and spectators as they shop for tickets to an event. And, they are worried about the real possibility of counterfeit tickets. In today's high-tech age, it is highly likely that even tickets with built-in security measures can be reproduced; or, at least, reproduced to a degree that can fool the fan's untrained eye. In that case, a fan could pay out thousands of dollars for two counterfeit tickets that prevent the fans from entering the stadium, while the scalpers have left the vicinity.

The 2007 Super Bowl was held in a state (Florida) that recently removed restrictions on resell prices of tickets. So, couple that with the excited fans and some ticket sellers were reporting sales as high as $10,000.

StubHub reported eight tickets sold for more than $10,000 each and other tickets averaged a price of $4,500. RazorGator reported sales of tickets at $8,000 for some and an average ticket price of $4,400. The face value—original sales price—of all 2007 Super Bowl tickets, other than luxury box suites, was either $600 or $700.

In fact, it has been the explosion of online ticket sales through e-ticket sellers that has been a major factor in ticket sale growth and increasing ticket prices. Online ticket sales have increased *annually* an estimated $3 billion.

Sources

http://www.CNNMoney.com; http://www.StubHub.com; http://www.RazorGator.com; http://www.intellectualcapital.com

Case Activity

How would you price the product? Invent a local sports event and conduct market research to help you determine pricing for the tickets.

QUESTIONS FOR STUDY

1. How does the consumer perceive "price"?
2. Discuss the concept of price.
3. List some examples of words used in place of the word *price* that can be found in the sport industry. Explain why these words are used.
4. What are the 4 Cs of price consideration? Discuss each and give examples.
5. Discuss the concept of the elasticity of demand. Give some examples.
6. List some examples of pricing objectives for sport.
7. List and describe some pricing strategies for the sport industry.

LEARNING ACTIVITIES

1. Identify sport businesses, organizations, or other enterprises and their products in your city or community that use these pricing strategies: going-rate pricing, demand oriented pricing, price discrimination, seasonal pricing, short-term pricing, and product line pricing.
2. Identify in your city or community some of the sport businesses, organizations, or other enterprises that use the price titles as presented in this chapter such as licensing fee, admission, and purse. Develop a list of those businesses and the price titles. Describe each one and how it is used.

Chapter Ten

MARKETING CHANNELS AND DISTRIBUTION DECISIONS IN THE SPORT BUSINESS INDUSTRY

Overview

A sport business has to get its product to the consumer, or, in some instances, get the consumer to the product. This is called *distribution* (also called *place*). There are many different ways this can be done. For example, there are tangible and intangible products, and each has to be delivered or transported in unique ways. There are many categories of consumers such as the end consumer and the business consumer. Some distribution channels work best for different types of consumer, and there are different marketing channels with different costs involved. For example, the cost to ship one product in one package for next-day delivery for one consumer is much more expensive than the cost of shipping a large truckload of thousands of the product with a three-week delivery period to a retail store.

> The best method of distribution is contingent upon the type of product as well as other factors such as cost, time, laws, and promotional possibilities.

In this chapter you will learn about distribution in the sport business industry, the role of distribution in marketing strategy, the selection of a distribution network, and the types of distribution intermediaries available for moving and/or offering sport business industry products.

Distribution Defined

The sport business must determine how to get its products from the manufacturer or producer to the consumer. Additionally, in this industry, there are products produced at a point where the consumer must be present at its production to consume the product. These products are sports events, such as a professional basketball game, a soccer match, or a super cross race. In these types of products, the event—the product—is staged at a facility where fans will gather to watch. The sport business will have made decisions regarding the facility in relation to location and other factors that will make the facility attractive to the consumer as a place in which to consume these types of products.

> Distribution is the process of getting the product to the consumer.

Distribution involves identifying distribution channels or intermediaries and determining the cost of distribution, the best distribution process for a specific product, and the distribution intensity. The distribution system is contingent on the type of product, the best interests of the sport company, the consumers, and other factors.

A *distribution system,* also called a *marketing channel,* includes the methods and channels used to deliver products from producer to consumer. An *intermediary* is an individual or organization through which products move from producer to consumer.

Distribution and Marketing Channel Decisions in the Sport Industry

Distribution decisions in the sport industry depend on the type of product and consumer, among many other factors. In this section, you

A Distribution System:

is the methods and channels used in delivering products from producer to consumer.

An Intermediary:

is an individual or organization through which products move from producer to consumer.

Table 10.1
Examples of Distribution and Channel Types Based on Consumer and Product Types.

Product Type	Consumer Type	Product Examples	Distribution Type	Channel Examples
Sports Activities	End Consumers: Sports Participants	events & activities, such as leagues, tournaments, meets, races	Direct	Producer/Provider: Sports Complex or Organization
Sport Business Goods: 1. Sporting Goods 2. Business Goods 3. Promotional Goods	1. End Consumers, such as sports participants. 2. Business Consumers 3. End Consumers: fans, participants	1. bowling ball, snow bike 2. astroturf 3. logo t-shirt; keychain	1. Complex 2. Direct 3. Complex	1. sporting goods retailer 2. direct sales: business-to-business 3. retailers, vendors
Sports Business Services: 1. sporting 2. business	1. End Consumers: sports participants 2. Business Consumers: corporations	1. racket stringing 2. marketing research; sponsorship management	1. Direct 2. Direct	1. Producer—a person set up in a pro shop 2. Producer: business-to-business
Sports Entertainment: Spectator Sports	Two Types: 1. End Consumers: sports spectators 2. Business Consumers: corporations	WNBA, NASCAR, Olympics, X-Games, American Gladiators, PGA/LPGA, NFL	1. Complex 2. Direct	1. ticket retailers and brokers 2. direct sales
Media: 1. Sports Magazine 2. E-sports business 3. Industry Trade Magazine	1 & 2. End Consumers, readers of sports information 3. Business Consumers: retailers, producers, advertisers	1. Snow Boarding Magazine, Outdoors, Runner's World 2. CBS Sportsline 3. Sporting Goods Business, WinterSport Business, Sportstyle	1. Direct & Complex 2. Direct 3. Direct	1. subscription; retail stores 2. online 3. subscription

will learn about five different types of products in the sport industry and the kinds of distribution channels typically used for them. Those five product types are sports activities, sport goods, sport services, sports entertainment, and sport media. Refer to Table 10.1.

Product Types

There are two broad categories of products in the sport business industry: those products that must be manufactured and then moved from the manufacturer to retail points for purchase by end consumers; and those that are produced in a place where the consumer must be present to consume. In the first category, products such as basketballs, tennis rackets, and motorcycles must be manufactured at a place of production, then moved from there to a location where the consumer will shop for that product. In the second category, these products are comprised of those types of products that must be staged at a fixed facility. For example, the consumer will be either watching a sports event at an arena, or participating in a sports activity such as hiking, skydiving, basketball, or working out.

SPORTS ACTIVITIES

Sports activities are participation products such as participation in basketball, bowling, scuba, hiking, sky diving, running, weight training, sailing, water skiing, golf, and snow-boarding. The consumers of these products are people who want to participate in these activities. Numerous sports, fitness, recreation, leisure, and sports tourism activities are offered to millions of different consumers today. Participatory sports activities are the largest segment of the sport business industry in the United States.

The activities are offered to the consumer in a number of ways such as leagues, tournaments, championships, races, meets, regattas, outings, and adventure travel packages. These are further delineated by using a number of different demographical, psychographical, or lifestyle segment elements to customize the events for different target markets. For example, softball may be offered by gender, age, skill level, company, sexual orientation, religion, race or ethnicity, geographic region, and climate.

Consumers of sports activities are end consumers, although there can be some business-to-business transactions surrounding the activity such as sponsorship. The type of distribution for these products is direct: from producer to consumer. Examples of producers include city parks and recreation departments that offer basketball leagues; a privately owned sports complex that offers snow skiing; a sports organization that offers a roller hockey tournament; and a sports club that offers yachting tournaments, sailing races, or scuba outings. The exchange is directly from producer to consumer.

SPORT BUSINESS GOODS

These are tangible goods such as sports equipment and apparel, artificial turf, facilities, and trophies. This type of product must be manufactured or produced in factories, shops, or plants and must be transported from the factory to a place where the consumer can purchase the good. Consumers include both end consumers and business consumers, depending on the product. As you can see in Table 10.1, some of these kinds of goods include sporting goods, business goods, and promotional goods.

The distribution system for these products will be either direct or complex, depending on the product type. Most sports equipment, for example, is manufactured in a factory and must be transported from that factory to where the consumers can purchase the product. For example, snowboards are manufactured in a factory in Delaware. Snowboard consumers are in several states and towns. Therefore, the snowboards must be transported from Delaware to places where the consumers can obtain them. Typically, snowboards are sold in sporting goods retail stores. The manufacturer must decide how to move the snowboards from Delaware to the stores. There are many marketing channel options available such as transporting by truck, plane, or train. Usually, some combination is required.

SPORT BUSINESS SERVICES

Many of those millions of sports participants are going to need their sports equipment cleaned, repaired, and/or maintained. This, of course, sustains a fairly large industry segment of services such as tennis racket stringing, golf club cleaning, pool maintenance, and equipment repair. For these products, which are primarily intangibles, the distribution is usually a direct exchange. For example, a tennis player with a racket in need of new strings and stringing takes the racket to a person who can perform this service.

> The cleaning, repair, and maintenance of sports equipment alone makes up an important part of the sport service industry.

Other products are business service products. These consumers are business consumers. Therefore, typically the exchange is a business-to-business exchange. For example, a sport company needing sponsorship management services will work directly with the provider of these services.

SPORTS ENTERTAINMENT

Some sports events are produced and sold as entertainment products. In the United States, some sports events such as the X-Games have been created specifically as entertainment products, and some sports events such as college athletics were slowly developed as entertainment products. Consumers of sports as an entertainment product include both end and business consumers. End consumers are those who are typically called "spectators." Spectators go to the event to watch the event and be entertained.

> The development of sports as an entertainment product is a fast-growing segment of the sport business industry.

Business consumers can be one of two types: those corporations that purchase the box seating (skyboxes or corporate luxury boxes) or those companies that purchase advertising, sponsorship, or other similar space at the event.

Distribution depends on the type of consumer. Distribution to end consumers usually occurs through a complex system of ticket retailers and brokers. Sales to the corporate business are usually direct. The cleaning, repair, and maintenance of sports equipment alone makes up an important part of the sport service industry.

SPORT MEDIA

Some examples of sport media are sports magazines (print), electronic sports businesses (Internet-based businesses), and industry trade magazines. The consumers of these can be either end or business consumers. Consumers of sports magazines are end consumers: those who want to see and read about sports, fitness, and recreation activity. Distribution can be either complex or direct. For industry trade magazines, however, the more typical distribution is direct.

There are a number of Internet-based sports businesses today. These businesses use one distribution channel—the World Wide Web—as a point of purchase. However, the delivery of the actual product requires transporting the product to the consumer. In many cases, the product is shipped through a company such as Federal Express directly to the consumer.

Distribution of Products

Tangible products are physical objects. Most are manufactured in mass quantities at a factory and must be moved—distributed—to a place of purchase—retailer or wholesaler. For example, running shoes are manufactured in a factory and must be moved to a retailer to be sold.

Intangible products are not physical objects and include products such as services, places, and ideas. In addition, entertainment is included in this category. Most intangible products are not produced until ordered by the consumer. In a fitness center where laundry services are offered, the consumer must order the service, then simply leave dirty laundry in a bag in a certain spot. The center will perform the service and return the clean laundry to the locker area. Entertainment, however, is scheduled for a specific date, time, and place and the consumer must be available at that time and be able to go to the place where the event is offered. A basketball game, for example, can be offered as an entertainment product. The game will be scheduled at a specific date and time and in a sports facility. To consume the product, the consumer must travel to the facility and watch the game. In addition, the game is not produced, or manufactured, until the players play the game. Therefore, the consumer must be present when the game is played.

The distribution of sporting goods such as golf balls can utilize several intermediaries.

Another significant difference between the tangible running-shoe product and the intangible laundry service or basketball game is something called shelf life. The running-gear product has a long shelf life—it is manufactured and can exist for quite a long period of time until sold. The laundry service has a long shelf life. The service is produced and then awaits the consumer to take possession. The basketball game, however, has no shelf life. The game cannot be manufactured and put on the shelf until a consumer purchases it. As a matter of fact, the game is not manufactured until the players play the game. In other words, the game is simultaneously manufactured and consumed. The game must be consumed at the same moment it is being produced. If not, it is not consumed and perishes. That game will never be manufactured again. There is, however, through the use of video and audiotape, a secondary product that the consumer may purchase to watch the game: videotapes of the game sold to the consumer.

> Shelf life is the amount of time that a product can remain in a good and consumable condition after being manufactured.

Because of the perishable shelf life of spectator sports events, today's spectator sports marketers take great pains to increase what consumers receive for the amount of time and money spent at the game. Hence, most spectator sports events offer a variety of sideshows, concessions, services, souvenirs, and rewards in the form of door prizes or fourth-quarter drawings.

In a different sport product, some providers of participation sports are offering the consumer more than participation for their money and time. To attract more runners, management and marketers of many marathons and 10K runs offer much more than just the race itself. Many offer the consumer t-shirts, concessions, pasta dinners, door prizes, rewards for every entrant and every person who crosses the finish line, childcare services, changing and shower services, medical care services, insurance, souvenirs, and photographs of the runner crossing the finish line. Some of these are included in the price of entry, and some are sold separately.

For some types of products in the sport industry, *how* and *when* the product is packaged and offered to the consumer are important parts of distribution. Almost all running events are held on Saturday mornings. Professional football games are held on Saturday, Sunday, or Monday evenings. Softball leagues are offered during the summer months and on weekday evenings. College women's and men's basketball games are played in evening slots. These are important elements of distribution called time, place, and possession utility. These are described in detail in the following section.

Time, Place, and Possession Utility Through Distribution

Distribution offers time, place, and possession utility to the consumer. The product must be accessible to the consumer, in the desired form, when it is needed. For example, a softball player needs to be able to purchase a softball bat before the season starts, usually in the summer; to buy the bat close to home; and to take possession of it when wanted.

Time utility is getting the product to the consumer when the consumer wants it. *Place utility* is getting the product to the consumer where the consumer wants it. *Possession utility* is creating possession of the product for the consumer. The distribution system is the channel through which the producer gets the product to the consumer when, where, and how the consumer wants it. For example, women's basketball fans want women's basketball at prime times (evenings, weekend evenings, prime-time slots such as 7 or 8 p.m.), in a great facility (in the same arena used by the men's team), and on a major broadcasting station (the major broadcasting networks, not the hard-to-find stations), and they want season tickets (giving them rights to specific seats for the entire season instead of "admission-at-the-door and no reserved seating"). Spectator sports marketers are listening, and more women's basketball is being offered in prime-time slots on major broadcasting stations, and pre-sold tickets and season tickets are being offered. This offers the product to the consumer when, where, and how the consumer wants it.

In another example, a manufacturer of sporting goods must distribute the goods to places where the consumer is most likely to purchase the goods. For example, Hillerich & Bradsby Co. (H & B), manufacturer of the famous Louisville Slugger baseball and softball bats, has a manufacturing plant in Louisville, Kentucky. Their bats, however, are sold around the world. Therefore, H & B must decide on the methods they will use to move the bats from the plant to places around the world where the consumer is most likely to purchase them. Those places are usually sporting goods retail stores and department stores with a sporting goods department. Some of the methods involved in moving the goods include moving them by truck, plane, ship, or train.

The Distribution System

The truck, plane, ship, and train mentioned above are examples of distribution intermediaries. Others include wholesalers, retailers, agents, brokers, distributors, sales agents, and shippers. *Distribution intermediaries* are those individuals or organizations through which products are moved from producer to consumer. They are the links through which products move on the route from manufacturer to consumer. The sport business management, as part of the overall marketing plan for a product, should have decided before a product is manufactured which intermediaries will be best for the company, the product, and the consumer. The determination of distribution intermediaries is a part of the development of a distribution plan.

Types of Distribution Intermediaries

There are a variety of distribution intermediaries available to the sport marketer. Some of these are listed and briefly described here.

Wholesaler—a company that buys goods in large quantities specifically to resell to retailers or final consumers (Peter and Donnelly, 1993).

Retailer—a company that buys goods to resell to consumers (Peter and Donnelly, 1993).

E-tailer—an Internet-based retail store.

Agent—a person or a company who "moves" products (facilitates the sale) by taking orders for a buyer and placing the order with the producer.

Mail order—a company that buys direct from a manufacturer or producer and offers the products through a catalog or electronic system.

Distributor—a wholesale intermediary.

The distribution plan is called the distribution system (also sometimes called a distribution network, distribution channel, or marketing channel). The *distribution system* is the system developed for moving products from producer to consumer (Peter and Donnelly, 1993).

There are many differences between the distribution of tangible products, such as sporting goods, and intangible products, such as a swimming meet.

Courtesy of Isaiah Sellers III/U.S. Navy

How does one construct a distribution system? There are many different systems because there are many types of companies, many different types of products, and many different consumers with different needs. The distribution system selected must be one that is effective and efficient for the manufacturer or producer, the intermediaries, the product, the company, and the consumers. In addition, the company must give serious consideration to the environment. The management must not be fooled into thinking that the fastest or most economical method for moving products is also automatically environmentally friendly. A question a sport marketer or sport management executive will always face is one of ethics: If something is good for the company, is it okay for the environment, and is it ethical to proceed?

DISTRIBUTION SYSTEM

A distribution system can range from direct (also called simple) to complex. A *direct distribution system* is one in which only the manufacturer and the consumer are involved as depicted in Figures 10.1 and 10.2 In a direct system, the sport product moves from the manufacturer or producer directly to the consumer. There is no intermediary involved. A few examples include the following:

1. A sport sponsorship management company that sells services directly to a client,

2. A tennis pro who sells lessons directly to a student,

3. A sport facility construction company that sells directly to a college athletic department,

4. A city parks and recreation department that sells basketball leagues directly to teams, and

5. A professional football championship game that sells directly to the spectator.

A *complex distribution system* is one in which one or more intermediaries are involved in the movement of the sport product from the pro-

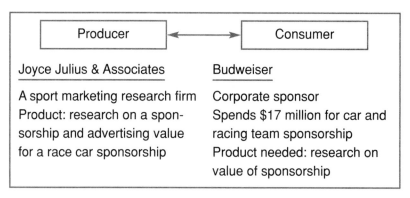

Figure 10.1

Example of a direct distribution transaction, from producer to consumer. This is a business-to-business transaction. The consumer is a business consumer.

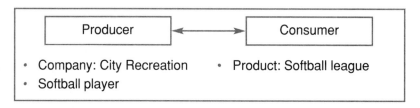

Figure 10.2

Another example of a direct distribution transaction. Here, though, the consumer is the end-consumer.

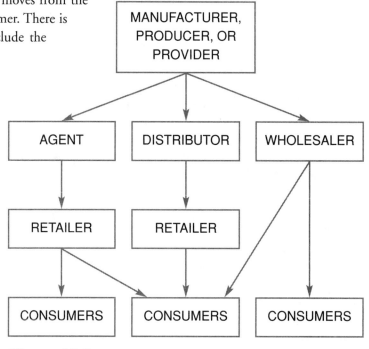

Figure 10.3

A complex distribution system in the sport industry.

Table 10.2 Example of a sport product's increasing cost as it moves through a distribution system.	
Cost to Manufacture Bat	3.75
Packaging	1.25
Shipping Charges to Distributor	.50
Other Expenses Such as Advertising	3.50
Manufacturer's Total Cost	9.00
Manufacturer's Profit Margin	+3.50
Manufacturer's Price to Distributor	12.50
Shipping Charges to Retailer	.50
Other Expenses	.50
Distributor's Cost	13.50
Distributor's Profit Margin	+5.00
Distributor's Price to Retailer	18.50
Retailer's Expenses	2.00
Retailer's Profit Margin	+19.45
Retailer's Price to Consumer	$39.95

ducer to the consumer. Examples of routes of a complex system are illustrated in Figure 10.3. In one network, the product moves from the producer to an agent to a retailer and then to the consumer. In another network, the product moves from the producer to a distributor to a retailer and then to the consumer. In a third network, the product moves to a wholesaler and then to the consumer.

In most instances in which intermediaries are involved, the final price of the product to the consumer is higher—hence, the popularity of a phenomenon called the "outlet store" or "factory-direct" store. No intermediaries are involved, which keeps the cost of moving the sport product very low. This results in a lower price to the final consumer and an increased profit margin for the manufacturer. When intermediaries are involved, the price of the product to the final consumer is driven up. For example, the manufacturer sells the sport product to a distributor who sells it to a retailer who sells it to the final consumer. Each entity involved must make a profit. Therefore, an aluminum softball bat that costs $3.75 to manufacture will be sold to the consumer for $39.95. Table 10.2 illustrates this process and what happens to the price of the product along the way to the consumer.

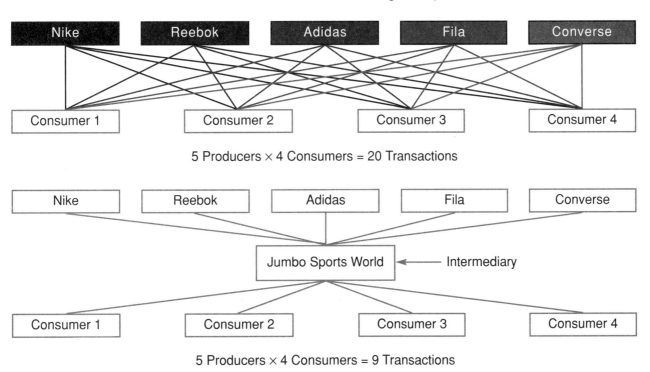

Figure 10.4
How an Intermediary Reduces the Number of Required Transactions.

However, intermediaries are necessary for many products. Although the costs of intermediaries drive up the final price of the product, many products would not be available to consumers if intermediaries did not exist. For example, it is not practical for a consumer who lives in Central City, Michigan, to travel to a running-shoe manufacturing plant in another country to purchase needed running shoes. Therefore, the manufacturer must move the product from the factory to Central City. To hold down cost, the manufacturer sells many products to retail stores in Central City. The running shoes are transported as part of a large shipment of goods to the stores in the city. To get the running shoes, the consumer simply shops at one of several sporting goods and shoes stores in the city. Figure 10.4 illustrates how many manufacturers use these intermediaries to distribute products, to reduce the number of transactions between consumers and manufacturers, and to increase effective and efficient transportation of goods from producer to consumer.

Selection of a Distribution System

At first glance, the task of selecting a distribution system might seem overwhelming because there are so many options. However, if the sport marketer will first consider the factors that will affect the final selection, this will help guide the sport marketer's decision-making process.

An important element to remember is that the distribution system should be consumer driven. After all, it is the consumer who will purchase the product. Therefore, the product must be offered to the consumer when, where, and how the consumer wants it—time, place and possession utility. One idea is to begin with the consumers of the product and trace the path from the consumer to the manufacturer.

Another important question to consider is which distribution options are available to you. Some sport marketers spend hours designing elaborate distribution systems only to discover that intermediaries do not exist or will not serve their needs.

FACTORS AFFECTING SELECTION

The many factors that affect the final selection of a distribution system, or channel, are presented in Table 10.3. It is important that the sport marketer analyze each factor, and understand how each one is interrelated to others, and how the distribution system considered fits with the overall marketing objectives. Notice that the 4 Cs come into play again in distribution with the important element of product.

> The considerations of the consumer should be the deciding factor in the selection of a distribution system.

The consumer. Consumers want a product when, how, and where they need or desire it. This must be studied and understood by the sport company in order to know when, how, and where to distribute products. *The sport company.* The position of the sport company will influence distribution. For example, the company might not be able to afford the higher-priced distribution channels or intermediaries and will have to select less expensive ones. The location of the company might be a barrier. If the company is in a city with no airport, distribution intermediaries will be limited to other forms of transportation.

Table 10.3
Factors to consider in the selection of a distribution system.

The Consumer
Characteristics: number, geographical location
Needs: purchase behavior, when needed, how needed, where needed
Psychographic Characteristics: promotion

The Sport Company
Strengths: financial, location, availability of distribution options and weaknesses

The Sport Product
Type of Product: tangible, intangible, shelf life, packaging and shipping requirements

The Competitors
Characteristics: number, geographic location, distribution methods

The Climate
Legal: laws, regulations, policy
Political: who is in office; what is "politically correct & incorrect"
Economic: cost, inflation, and other economic factors
Ethical: rights, issues, and other ethical considerations

Distribution Channels/Intermediaries
Availability of Channels: what intermediaries exist and are available to you?
Characteristics: types, location, cost, strengths and weaknesses, acceptance of product, ability to handle product

Distribution Intensity
Positioning the product

Adapted from Evans & Berman(1987), Boone & Kurtz (1992), Cravens & Woodruff (1986), and Peter & Donnelly (1993).

The sport product. The type of product will influence how it is distributed. Shelf life, for example, is the amount of time a product can last before it loses quality. Of course, most of us know that fresh vegetables must be consumed before rotting, but what about sport products? What products are there that have a long shelf life or a short shelf life? Here is an example of each. A Super Bowl game has a short shelf life. The game must be consumed at the moment it is produced. A basketball has a long shelf life. It can remain in a sporting goods store for a long time until consumed. Products that are services require different distribution channels. A good is usually transported from producer to consumer through intermediaries. A service is usually sold directly to the consumer without the use of intermediaries.

The competition. Unless the sport company has the only product of its kind, the sport company has competitors. To stay in business, the company must take its competitors into consideration when making almost all business decisions. This information could help with ideas or could shed light on why the competitor always gets its product to the consumer first.

The climate. Laws, politics, the economy, ethical considerations, and environmental concerns will all have an influence on decisions about distribution. These should be constantly monitored so that the information gained can be used in determining distribution systems.

Determining Distribution Intensity

One of the elements of distribution on which the sport marketer must decide is the intensity of the distribution of the product. The degree of distribution intensity will affect sales of the product and is linked to positioning the product. *Distribution intensity* is the amount of distribution selected for a particular sport product. Distribution intensity ranges from intensive to exclusive and is contingent on most of the same factors that affect the sport marketer's decisions on distribution channels. Table 10.4 illustrates the range of intensity.

A company should study what its competitors are doing before making any sort of business decision.

Table 10.4
Continuum of Distribution Intensity and Some Sport Product Examples.

	INTENSIVE	SELECTIVE	EXCLUSIVE
WHERE DISTRIBUTED:	everywhere possible	a few places	a few select places
EXAMPLES:			
Basketball Game	• TV & cable channels • radio taped for later broadcast • taped for sale in-person	• in-person • only one TV channel • two radio stations	• in-person • only one TV channel
Softball Bats	• every sporting goods outlet possible • stores and department stores	• only half of all sporting goods stores	• only one select sporting goods store

The type of distribution intensity selected becomes part of the advertising message to the consumer primarily to let the consumer know where the product is available and to establish status quo for the product or company. An advertising message used to let the consumer know might be "widely available" or "available at all local sporting goods stores."

Intensive distribution. If the sport marketer chooses an intense distribution strategy, then the product will be offered in as many places as possible. In the examples given in Table 10.4, softball bats would be offered everywhere possible: all sporting goods stores, pro shops, department stores with sporting goods departments, and other outlets. A basketball game would be offered through as many outlets as possible: many television channels, many radio stations, in-person viewing, taped-for-later broadcast, and videotaped or captured digitally for later sale.

Selective distribution. If the sport marketer chooses a selective distribution strategy, the product will be offered in a limited amount of places. The softball bats will be offered only in sporting goods stores. The basketball game will be offered through one local television station, one local radio station, and in-person viewing.

Exclusive distribution. With exclusive distribution as a strategy, the sport marketer will offer the product in one or a small number of outlets. The softball bats will be offered in only one sporting goods store. The basketball game will be offered only through one television station or in-person viewing.

Another factor affecting the decision on distribution intensity is advertising dollars. In intensive distribution, much of the advertising effort is handled by the place of distribution. In exclusive distribution, much of the advertising effort lies with the producer, although the outlet selected can claim to be the exclusive outlet for the product.

Another factor to be considered is image. Exclusive distribution creates an image of prestige. The advertising message will sometimes include the words "available only at S _____ 's Sporting Goods."

Exclusive distribution also allows for price increases. If your company is the only company with a product that has high demand, you can take advantage of the situation and assign higher prices than normal. For example, some television broadcasting companies pay for the rights to exclusively broadcast certain sports events. In this situation, the broadcasting company can increase the cost of advertising during the event. In some cases, the broadcast can go to a pay-per-view status in which consumers must pay specifically to view that particular event on television.

Chapter Summary

A sport business must decide how to get its product to the consumer through a distribution system and strategies. The selection of a distribution system is affected by many factors including the consumer, the company, the product, product positioning, the climate, and distribution systems available to the sport company. Distribution intensity will determine how extensively the product will be made available to the consumers. Different distribution channels work best for different types of products and different types of consumers. Each distribution channel has unique costs involved that should be given serious consideration in the selection process.

There are many different products in the sport business industry. Distribution decisions depend on the type of product, the consumer, the company, the climate, and the competitor, among other factors. The ultimate decision is to find the most appropriate way to get the product to the consumer, or the consumer to the product, when and how the consumer needs it, and in a way that meets the company's objectives.

CASE STUDY CHAPTER 10

Dome, Destination, Delivery: Competitive Distribution Strategies of a World-Class Sports Arena

The Georgia Dome, which opened in 1992 and is located in downtown Atlanta, is the largest cable-supported domed stadium in the world. The Georgia Dome offers sports and entertainment fans a unique and spectacular venue. It has a seating capacity large enough to host political conventions, major concerts, and even the Super Bowl. The Dome can seat 71,250 in permanent seating, yet it still has an intimate feel due to extraordinary architectural planning. The stadium is oval and seats are close to the arena floor. The Teflon/fiberglass roof gives a sense of closure, yet still allows sunlight into the facility for natural illumination.

The Dome serves as the home venue for the NFL's Atlanta Falcons. In addition, the Dome is a multi-sport, multi-purpose facility. Such varied sports events as gymnastics, basketball, SuperCross, and Professional Bull Riding are staged in the Dome. Events such as conventions, confer-

ences, major concerts, trade shows, marching band competitions, and even tryouts for American Idol are staged in the Dome.

In sports, the Dome hosts the annual events of the Atlanta Football Classic, the SEC football championship, and the Chick-fil-A Bowl.

The Structure

The Dome consists of the following materials:

- A total of 8,300 tons of reinforced steel was used to construct the Dome. That is more than the total weight of iron and steel used in the Eiffel Tower.
- A 437-mile sidewalk, from Atlanta to Cincinnati, could be built from the 110,000 cubic yards of concrete used at the Dome.
- The building covers 8.9 acres and contains 1.6 million square feet on all seven levels.

Continued on next page.

- The 290-foot high roof is composed of 130 Teflon-coated fiberglass panels—covering 8.6 acres. The roof's supporting cable totals 11.1 miles and the Dome is as tall as a 27-story building.

The Utilities

The Dome contains super-sized numbers of needed utility works:

- 798 lighting fixtures in the roof structure provide lighting.
- Four 1,250-ton air conditioning units in the Georgia Dome that generate enough power to cool 1,666 homes.
- More than 600 television monitors scattered throughout the stadium.
- To supply soft drinks to dispensers, thousands of liquid lines wind through the stadium. These include 32,952 feet of lines (the length of 109 football fields) to feed liquids to hundreds of dispensers throughout the building.

The Capacity

The Dome can accommodate a lot of people:

- There are 203 executive suites, 4,600 club seats, and the Penthouse Suite. The Dome's permanent seating capacity is 71,250.
- The Dome has three times the code-required number of restrooms—and all are accessible to guests with disabilities.
- A pair of C-5 military transport planes could fit on the Georgia Dome's floor, which contains 102,000 square feet of space.

Attendance Records

The Dome holds some attendance records:

- Chick-fil-A Bowl: 75,406 on December 30, 2006
- SEC football championship: 74,913 on December 6, 2003
- NCAA men's basketball Final Four: 53,406 on April 1, 2002
- Professional Bull Riders, Inc (PBR): 33,000 on February 8, 2003
- Motorsports Monster Jam: 66,162 on January 12, 2002

Other Records Set in the Dome

- **Longest paper airplane flight:** The level flight duration record for a hand-launched paper airplane is 27.6 seconds, set by Ken Blackburn of the US, in the Georgia Dome on October 8, 1998.
- **Fastest men's indoor 400 meters:** Michael Johnson (US) ran the 400 meters in 44.63 seconds, in the Georgia Dome on March 4, 1995.
- **Most yards gained passing in a Super Bowl game:** Kurt Warner threw a record-breaking 414 yards for the St Louis Rams in Super Bowl XXXIV on January 30, 2000.
- **Dome's largest hot dog:** Sara Lee Corporation made a 1,996-foot wiener for the 1996 Olympics. It took more than 2,000 buns to hold the huge hot dog that wrapped twice around the Georgia Dome field.

Destination: Atlanta, Georgia

A major draw for the Georgia Dome is its location in a world class city—Atlanta. As a destination, Atlanta is a tourist magnet for its multiculturalism, arts, and its many media, shopping, sports, festivals, museums, and entertainment possibilities.

Atlanta is also home of the following:

- Georgia Aquarium: Opened in November, 2005, contains the largest aquarium in the world at 800,000 gallons
- "Beverly Hills of the East": shopping in the legendary Buckhead area
- Fifteen Fortune 500 companies, a ranking of 3rd nationally
- The world's largest theme park company: Six Flags, Inc.
- The King Center: established in memory of Dr. Martin Luther King, Jr.
- The Fernbank Museum of Natural History: the first museum to display the world's largest dinosaur in 2001
- The Atlanta Motor Speedway: 870 acres of top sports facility
- The World of Coke Museum: the world's largest collection of memorabilia about the refreshment beverage created in Atlanta in 1886
- The High Museum of Art: the leading art museum in the southeastern United States

- The Fox Theater: a nationally known theater and a protected and preserved landmark
- Turner Field: host of ceremonies for the 1996 Olympics and home to the Atlanta Braves
- CNN Atlanta: first 24-hour all news network that has changed the way the world views news
- Zoo Atlanta: an annual average attendance of over half a million and a member base of the same size
- Hartsfield-Jackson Atlanta International Airport: the world's busiest airport
- World class hotels and restaurants
- The state of Georgia is home to more than 450 golf courses, some of which are among the nation's finest and play host to significant annual amateur and professional tournaments.

Delivery and Distribution:
Georgia Dome Competes

The Georgia Dome competes in a highly competitive market of public assembly facilities. Others around the country include such facilities as the Verizon Center in Washington, DC; Air Canada Centre in Toronto, Ontario; San Diego Sports Arena in San Diego, California; Staples Center in Los Angeles, California; the Pepsi Center in Denver, Colorado; the Toyota Center in Houston, Texas; Target Center in Minneapolis, Minnesota; FedEx Field in Washington, DC; Giants Stadium in East Rutherford, New Jersey; the Superdome in New Orleans, Louisiana; and the Metrodome in Minneapolis, Minnesota.

The Georgia Dome aims to deliver a multi-sports, multi-purpose facility capable of producing any event in a fan-friendly environment. The directors, managers, and all other staff are highly knowledgeable and experienced in the area of public assembly facility management, and event and sports event management with degrees in specialized fields such as facility management, sport management, marketing, and research.

Sources

Georgia Dome. http://www.gadome.com.
Lucas, C. (2007). Personal communication. Carol Lucas, Marketing Research Manager, Georgia Dome and Georgia World Congress Center.
Stadiums of the NFL. http://www.stadiumsofnfl.com/nfc/Metrodome.htm

Case Activity

In such a highly competitive segment of the industry, what competitive advantages delivery strategies would you incorporate into a five-year plan?

QUESTIONS FOR STUDY

1. What is distribution?
2. Describe the different kinds of distribution in the sport industry.
3. What are distribution intermediaries? Give some examples.
4. What is a distribution system? Give some examples of systems in the sport industry.
5. What are the factors that affect the selection of a distribution system?
6. What is distribution intensity? Why is it linked to promotion and positioning the product? Give some examples of each type.
7. What are some examples of different types of products found in the sport business industry? Develop what you think would be some appropriate distribution channels for these products.

LEARNING ACTIVITIES

1. List some sport products offered in your city or community. Create a distribution system for each. Research the real costs of the systems. Give a presentation in class.

2. For a tennis racket manufactured in Taiwan, develop a distribution system based on the fact that the tennis racket will be a high priced high end product targeted to very serious amateur tennis players. Use as much real information as you can find to develop a full distribution plan.

Chapter Eleven

PROMOTION IN THE SPORT INDUSTRY

People will not buy a product if they do not know it exists. The purpose of promotion is to tell people about a product. From an academic standpoint, Irwin, Sutton, and McCarthy (2002, p. 5) defined promotion as "the deployment of a fully integrated set of communication exchanges intended to persuade consumers toward a favorable belief or action as a tactical component of the overall marketing campaign."

> Promotion is a critical part of the marketing mix for a sport company.

Promotion is such an important marketing variable that companies have been formed for the sole purpose of selling promotional products. It is also critical for the service sector. According to Delpy, (2000) "event organizers can no longer just open their gates and expect spectators to attend" (p. 8). Similarly, few clients will just "drop by" a sport business without prompting.

So many companies have been formed for the purpose of providing promotional support to sport organizations that "sport promotion" is considered an industry. There are marketing firms and sport marketing firms, advertising firms, and agents who specialize in promoting sports people or teams, and companies that specialize in producing promotional products such as logo t-shirts, bags, cups, mugs, hats, towels, key chains, watches, jackets, flags, banners, trinkets, and drink coolers. Further, within the promotion industry there is specialization. One company, Multi-Ad Services (http://www.multi-ad.com) in Illinois specializes in the production of media guides, newsletters, scorecards, game programs, brochures/catalogs, and logo design. If you need inflatable displays, there's a company for that too. For example, IDG (Inflatable Design Group, http://www.inflatabledesigngroup.com) created a 25-foot inflated Spalding Basketball for a WNBA promotion. Other products have included inflatable display structures with customized team logos, used around the stadium for children.

There are companies that specialize in managing the logos, licensing, and merchandising for sport properties (Pitts, Fielding, and Miller, 1994). For example, the Collegiate Licensing Company (http://www.clc.com) represents a prestigious base of universities, bowls, and athletic conferences. One of their tasks is to develop a base of licensees and retail outlets to successfully market licensed products. Their efforts are intended to target consumers of collegiate products and facilitate their purchase of licensed products. They also assist the marketing directors of their member institutions in establishing goals and a marketing strategy.

As in other industries, promotion is a very important communication tool in the sport industry. Again, people will not buy a product if they do not know it exists. In the sport industry, promotional communication is used to inform, educate, remind, and persuade.

Promotion and Sport Promotion Defined

The word *promotion* brings many concepts to mind—some good, some bad. Similar to the Irwin et al. (2002) definition above, Boone and Kurtz (1992) defined promotion as the function of informing, persuading, and influencing the consumer's purchase decision. Promotions include all corporate activities aimed at influencing consumers' purchasing attitudes and behaviors (However, to some, promotions have come to mean some shady practice where misrepresentation and inaccuracy are used to sway the public into unwanted or unnecessary purchases.) In a sport marketing perspective, promotion applied to the sport industry is defined as the function of informing or influencing people about the sport company's products, community involvement, or image. In this definition the many segments of people to whom the sport company promotes are a significant factor when developing promotion strategies. The sport company promotes to the end consumer, the business consumer, the general community, the business community, and the media. To inform means that the sport company wants to tell them something. To influence means that the sport company wants a specific action from the person. Usually, the final action wanted is a purchase action.

According to Ries and Trout (1986), consumers screen and reject a considerable amount of the product and marketing information delivered via traditional communication sources. Thus, consumers may not be conscious of wants until their wants are stimulated by the sport marketer through an array of well-selected and designed promotional activities. Creating new concepts and ideas about consumer desires as well as products or services to fulfill them is difficult; therefore, sports marketers must be proficient in their promotional strategy to move the consumer to purchase.

One innovative idea was set in place at the opening of the 57th Street Niketown store in New York City. The store utilitzed virtual reality, sport memorabilia, and computerization to showcase Nike technology. Shoe sizing was not performed with the standard Brannock device. Instead, customers just put their foot on the NGAGE digital sizing system, and the computer prepared a 3-D image of their foot. Although the true benefit of this new system is unproven, it was shown to be an effective promotion and convinced many consumers that Nike was on the cutting edge of technology.

Promotions are an integral part of all communication efforts. As Irwin et al. (2002, p. 22) noted, "Communication is the foundation of all buying behavior." One of the objectives of promotion is the acquisition and retention of public acceptance of an idea, product, or service. This can be accomplished through effective communication with consumers.

The general literature on communication theory suggests that there are four essential ingredients in pro-

> It is incumbent on the marketer to develop communications that are socially responsible and ethically sound.

motional communication: the sender, the message, the medium, and the receiver. For messages to convey clear and succinct meanings, the sender must accurately create the message and put it in an appropriate media form. When the receivers encounter a message, it must be decoded and interpreted. Interpretation of the message is influenced by the receiver's emotional status, perceptions of the sender, and cultural disposition, among other factors. The people to whom the sport company will communicate are existing and potential consumers. In addition, the sport company communicates to the general community, the business community, and the media. As a result, sport marketers use promotional communications to influence or change the attitudes, opinions, and behavior of consumers in the sport industry.

For example, many sport companies want the general community to know that they care about the community. One way this is accomplished is through the financial support of local children's recreation leagues. Companies often select a billboard in the community to disseminate the message. Companies may choose to have a message emblazoned on the billboard such as "We care. We are the proud supporter of the Central Children's Sports Leagues—Southland Sporting Goods—where your family shops for all your sporting needs." Companies may use more than one method to reach the audience. They may choose to post signs around the children's ballpark, send flyers through direct mail to everyone in the community, and hold a special sale in recognition of their involvement in the children's leagues. Each company must decide which methods will be most effective in gaining the attention of its audience and imparting the message.

Rationale for Promotion

There are other reasons for promotion because there are a variety of different messages a sport company wants to communicate to the people about its product or company. Effective promotions can facilitate a variety of marketing functions.

Promotion establishes an image. The sport marketer has a reason for being in business and a mission for the company. The company was designed based on a specific market segment. Therefore, the sport marketer wants to communicate to the consumer and the community a specific image. According to Ries and Trout (1986), a company's image is the sum of beliefs, ideas, and impressions held by consumers about the company and its products. The image may be luxury, prestige, convenience, cost savings, one-stop shopping, or creativity. The message of the promotion will communicate the company's image. For example, if the company is a marina and the objective of the marina is primarily to service and house large, expensive yachts, the promotional mix and message should communicate luxury and prestige. The marina's name might be "Class One Yacht Club." The communication through promotional methods such as advertising might be a slogan like "Your home is our home at Class One Yacht Club" or "Yachting is your luxury and your luxury is our business." Through the name of the company and the communication message in the slogan, the consumer is told that this marina is for the upper-class consumer who owns a yacht and that this company will take care of consumers in the fashion to which they are accustomed.

If a product has gained a poor reputation, the sport marketer can use effective promotions to reverse consumers' image of the product.

Promotion can reposition the image of a faltering product. For example, personal watercraft (PWCs), more commonly known as jet skis, began to develop a poor reputation because of the loud noise level of the engine, the recklessness of the drivers, the increase in accidents, and the increase in numbers invading previously quiet water areas without PWCs. The Personal Watercraft Industries Association (PWIA) and several PWC manufacturers have rallied to create a variety of promotional methods they hope will facilitate control of the reputation and turn it around. Their activities are directed at the end consumer, manufacturers, PWC rental businesses, and state and local water-governance organizations. Some of their activities include educational programs on safety (posters, videocassettes, brochures), research to decrease the noise produced by the PWC, rescue and education loan programs in which manufacturers lend PWCs to area Coast Guard offices or rescue units for their use and lend PWCs to lake and beach lifeguard stations for rescue operations. The cooperative promotional effort was successful in improving the reputation of the PWC and positively affected sales.

Promotion creates awareness for new products. As stated earlier, if people do not know your product exists, they will not buy it. If the sport company is planning to release a new product, no one will know unless the company implements an appropriate approach. Various sport companies orchestrate product launches using celebrity endorsers and press conferences. Many times, these promotional activities are coordinated through sport trade shows. An array of methods is integrated to publicize the offering.

Promotion alerts the consumer to sales. The consumer will not know that the company will be having a sale unless the company tells them. The sport marketer must identify promotional methods and design a communication message that will tell the consumer about the sale: dates, times, type of sale, purpose of sale, and any other information the consumer might need. If your company is a sporting goods retail store and you are planning a Thanksgiving sale, you must create the promotion to tell the consumer. Another important factor is your decision on when and where to promote. For example, your Thanksgiving sale will be the Friday, Saturday, and Sunday after Thanksgiving. Perhaps the best promotion is an advertisement in the local newspaper, and the best time to run the ad is in the Sunday paper before Thanksgiving.

Promotion tells the consumer where your business is located. Although this sounds like a simple message, it is very important. If the information is provided, the consumer does not have to spend extra time trying to find the business. This communication is usually handled within the promotion as a map depicting the location or as directions to the business. Sometimes a business will refer to a well-known landmark as a locater. For example, a well-known landmark in the city of Louisville, Kentucky, is the Water Tower—an historic city waterworks facility situated on the Ohio River. Businesses in the area use the Water Tower as a locater. A boat retailer's advertisements include the words "next to the Water Tower." A restaurant uses the same words. An indoor soccer facility uses the wording "located close to the Water Tower." The purpose of the message in the promotion is to establish the location of the business. For Web-based companies, clearly presenting the Internet address serves the same purpose.

Promotion Planning

Figure 11.1 illustrates the steps to be taken in promotion planning. Promotion planning is the process of developing all aspects of the company's communication effort. Many factors should be considered that will affect decisions concerning the promotion elements of the company's marketing mix. Some of these factors are the consumer, the competitor, money and other resources, product life cycle, and mission and objectives of the sport company. The following sections discuss the steps in the promotion planning process.

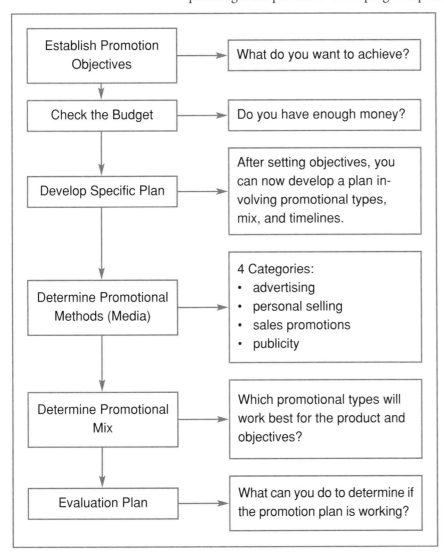

Figure 11.1
Promotional Planning Model.

SET PROMOTION OBJECTIVES

In the promotion planning process, the first step is to establish promotion objectives. The establishment of promotion objectives is based on this question: What does your company want to achieve through promotion? The promotion objectives should emerge from the marketing objectives, which should emanate from the company objectives.

Promotion objectives are statements that specify exact results desired by the company. They are based on what the company wants to accomplish. Usually the objectives are demand-oriented, education-oriented, or image-oriented. The overall objective is to affect behavior, knowledge, or attitude. Each promotional action selected must be based on the objectives of the promotion. Therefore, a sport company should select the specific type of promotion, or form of communication, based on carefully crafted objectives. Table 11.1 illustrates these objective types, purpose, outcome desired, message, and an example of each.

If the sport company wants to affect behavior, demand-oriented objectives will be established. The behavior that the company wants to affect is purchase behavior. The company wants the consumer to purchase its products and wants to persuade the consumer to do so. With this as an

Consider the following when designing promotion goals:
• stage of product life cycle
• reasons for considering a promotion plan
• available resources

Table 11.1
Sport Promotion Objective Types.

TYPES OF OBJECTIVES:	DEMAND	EDUCATION	IMAGE
PURPOSE	To affect behavior	To affect knowledge	To affect attitude or perception
OUTCOME DESIRED	Consumer purchases the company's product	To educate or inform the consumer about the company or its products	Consumer thinks of company in specific terms: good, positive, brilliant, creative, fun, serious, etc.
MESSAGE	• persuasive • demand oriented	• informative • reminder	• informative • persuasive
EXAMPLE	A sport shoe manufacturer uses a famous male basketball player to persuade the consumer to buy its shoes.	A new sport marketing firm is opening. It places an ad in a local business paper that tells story of company, what it does, its products and services, where it is located, and its hours of business.	A women's professional golf association uses TV and billboard ads to tell about its disadvantaged-youth golf-with-the-pros day held once a year. The association and the players pay for the youth to spend a day with the players golfing and participating in other events.

objective, the company must design a promotional method and message that persuade the consumer to buy.

If the company wants to educate or inform the consumer about something, education-oriented objectives are developed. Usually, the company wants to educate the consumer about something about the company, its products, services, or other information. Typical information includes the location of the company, information on sales taking place and the company's offerings, or details about the company's products.

If the sport company wants to affect attitude or perception, it will develop image-oriented objectives. The company wants to assist consumers' formation of positive attitudes toward the company and its products. Marketers must strive to ensure a consistent image across all promotions.

REVIEW THE BUDGET AND OTHER RESOURCES

During the process of developing the objectives, it is wise for the sport marketer to know how much money is available for promotion and whether the company has other necessary resources available. This information will certainly have an impact on decisions made for promotional planning. Some promotional methods are expensive whereas others are inexpensive, and still others are free. Television advertising can be very expensive. On the other hand, staging an open house is relatively inexpensive. Realistically, the sport marketer must determine if there is enough money and other resources to pay for and follow through with the promotional methods selected.

Ideally, the sport marketer must determine what promotional methods are available that are most effective for the objectives set within available resources.

A promotion plan of action should include

- promotional objectives
- a budget
- personnel assignments
- promotional mix strategies
- a schedule with deadlines and time lines
- an evaluation plan

The primary components of promotion in the sport industry include advertising, publicity and public relations, personal selling, and sales promotion. These components exist in conjunction with each other and can be used by the marketer in consort or separately to accomplish marketing and sales objectives.

After checking the budget and other resources needed for the promotional methods selected, you must develop a detailed plan of action that involves selecting the most appropriate and effective promotional types, determining a promotional mix, and developing an evaluation plan.

UTILIZE PROMOTIONAL METHODS

As noted above, there are four general categories of promotional methods: advertising, publicity, personal selling, and sales promotions. Table 11.2 illustrates the four categories and specific promotional methods available for the sport marketer in each category.

Advertising. Hiebing and Cooper (1990) define advertising as a message that informs and persuades consumers through paid media. We are all aware of effective and ineffective advertising. Think for a minute about ads that you have seen and enjoyed, but for which you cannot remember the product; in contrast, other ads

Table 11.2
Four Categories of Promotion Methods and Some Examples.

ADVERTISING	PERSONAL SELLING	SALES PROMOTIONS	PUBLICITY
• newspaper ad • magazine ad • television • radio ad • direct mail • billboard ad • ads on buses, grocery carts, walls, etc. • sponsorship • merchandising • the logo	• sales force • public speaking	• telemarketing • price • point of purchase display • newsletter • giveaways • target market specials • sponsorship • special events • open house day dinner, parties, etc. • exhibitions • merchandising	• press conference • press release • articles in local or other newspaper • coverage on TV or radio

immediately bring a specific product to mind. All advertising firms plan for success, but it is not always achieved. Consider the short-lived Reebok campaign of "U.B.U." and Nike's long-running "Just Do It" advertising.

Advertising is a controlled medium. That is, the message delivered to the consumer is carefully crafted and controlled by the organization so that its content consists of only information that the organization wishes the consumer to receive. However, because the company controls advertising, its credibility with consumers may be low.

In sport, advertising can take many forms. There is advertising of sport products and services and advertising through sports events. The advertising of sport products and services is a multimillion-dollar industry. Advertising through sport is also a sizable segment of the industry. As much as $15 billion of the total amount spent per year on all advertising is spent on sport-related advertising and sponsorship (Irwin et al. 2002: "Sponsorship Spending," 2004).

A new form of sport advertising has developed around sport video games. If television advertising developed because people were spending hours watching TV, then consider that the average video game player spends 60 hours on each game they purchase. Data project that by 2008 spending on video game advertising will total $1 billion a year (Advancing to the next level, 2005)

A primary motive for advertising in sport is that sports present a wholesome image and a wide demographic profile from which specific segments can be targeted. Advertising through sports events can also take the form of a sponsorship, as will be detailed in Chapter 14. Research on sponsorship through stadium advertising has shown that it is an effective media purchase producing an effective return on investment (ROI) (Ukman, 2004).

A popular advertising-related promotional activity conducted by many sport organizations is the trade-out, also known in the industry as VIK (value-in-kind). This process is seen most often when a sport organization gives something of value (complimentary seats, stadium advertising space, program ads) to the sponsor in exchange for products needed by the organization. With media sponsorships, the exchange is typically for advertising space or airtime that can be used by the sport organization for promotional activities.

Media trade-out programs within the university segment seek to do two things: increase the attendance at athletic events and increase overall support of the school's programs. Radio seems to be a viable choice as one of the media selected for trade-out campaigns. Many sport organizations trade out radio time for tickets at a cash-value ratio of about 4 to 1 favoring the organization (Spoelstra, 1997). Using coveted football or basketball tickets as barter, some universities have negotiated deals with major TV markets. Newspaper and billboard space can also be included in this strategy. This area presents a variety of issues. Many media sources always quote "full rate card" prices in the negotiations. On the other hand, the sport organizations occasionally inflate the prices printed on tickets that are included in trade-out and sponsor packages.

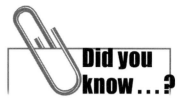

Did you know...?

The Sporting Goods Manufacturing Association sponsors an annual Super Show. The Super Show is an exhibition event for the sporting goods industry trade, including retailers, manufacturers, and distributors. Starting in the year 2007, SGMA split the event into two events: a Spring Market and a Fall Market event. The Spring Market event presents product and market segments including running, racquet sports, fitness, accessories, licensed merchandise, athletic footwear, performance apparel, team uniforms, soccer, baseball/softball.

Some universities use TV and radio networks to blanket their region including critical consumer areas in adjoining regions. During the summer and early fall, tapes can be made by players and coaches discussing their upcoming season. In this setting, you need to make sure that all of your activities are in compliance with collegiate rules. These plans have been particularly successful in encouraging advertisers who have rejected more traditional appeals for direct advertising. Additional coverage of this topic is offered in Chapter 13 in dealing with leveraged media sponsorships.

Publicity. Publicity, although not identical to advertising, is often considered in discussion of the topic. Irwin et al. (2002) indicate that publicity differs from advertising in that, although it informs and affects consumer attitudes, it is free. This includes the promotion or communication that comes from being mentioned

> Publicity is any form of unpaid promotion.

in a magazine or being the subject of an article in the local newspaper. It has several benefits over advertising. First, because the information comes from a third party, it is seen as more credible and trustworthy. Secondly, it may also be consumed more readily by consumers that may avoid direct advertising. The disadvantage of publicity is that the company usually has no control over the content. This means that if the local paper wants to write an article about your company, the reporter can write almost anything. Additional coverage of this topic is found in Chapter 12.

Sport marketers must realize that publicity alone will not sell tickets, raise funds, win supporters, retain members, or sell merchandise. Nevertheless, publicity can be helpful in conveying ideas to people so that these ends can be more easily attained.

Publicity efforts should be planned with these guidelines in mind:

1. Too much publicity can be poor public relations, because at a given point, people tend to react negatively to excessive publicity.

2. The amount of publicity absorbed is important, not the amount printed.

3. The amount of publicity disseminated does not necessarily equal the amount used.

4. The nature of the publicity eventually tends to reveal the character of the institution or department it seeks to promote, for better or worse.

5. Some publicity an institution or department receives originates from outside sources.

6. Not all promotional activities result in publicity.

A successful publicity program depends on the development of an effective plan. This plan should incorporate the following elements:

1. Identification of publicity needs,

2. Recognition of appropriate media sources,

3. Development of goals for each source,

4. Creation of a specific methodology for targeted sources,

5. Implementation through selected promotional materials, and

6. Assessment of publicity outcomes.

Personal selling. Personal selling is defined as an oral presentation with potential customers for the express purpose of making a sale. Irwin et al. (2002, p. 8) expand the concept of personal selling with the term Personal Contact to "convey the breadth of promotionally oriented personal interaction that transpires within the sport industry."

Commitment to personal selling and personal interaction is key to effective promotions. There is an understanding among those in sales that communicating how a product or service can benefit the consumer is paramount. Within this approach is the belief that without the salesperson, consumers would not be capable of realizing the benefits of consumption and that personal selling therefore is the most important aspect in the promotional mix.

You may not personally adhere to that philosophy, but there are many in personal selling who do. They see their role as providing the link between the organization and consumers, so that consumers' lives may be enhanced by the product or service to which they were introduced.

Personal selling is direct promotion between the seller and a potential consumer. The initial stage of personal selling has been termed the *approach phase*, "creating a favorable impression and building rapport with potential clients" that sets the stage for all subsequent interaction between the salesperson and the prospective customer (Pride and Ferrell, 2003, p. 444). Several authors (Miller, Shaad, Burch, and Turner, 1999; Pride and Ferrell, 2003) have noted the importance of establishing a relationship with the consumers before activating sales-related dialog. Personal selling also includes selling face-to-face as well as via the telephone, videoconferences, and interactive computer links (Boone and Kurtz, 1992; Miller et al.). In addition, considerable selling is done through television. Consider those television channels dedicated to bringing into your home hundreds of thousands of products. Professional salespeople host these, and a simple phone call to the company completes the purchase of any product offered on the show. Personal selling is a major element in the sport industry. There are salespeople in the sporting goods stores, salespeople for sports apparel manufacturing companies to sell their products to retailers, promoters whose job is to sell a sporting event to television and sponsors, telemarketers whose job is to sell tickets for the team, and salespeople whose job is to sell advertising space in the Super Bowl program. In the sport industry, individuals who are not trained as salespeople also become salespeople. For example, in men's college basketball, the players and coaches become salespeople for the program. They are scheduled to speak at local banquets and other activities. The coach usually has local radio and/or television shows and the coach usually is hired by local businesses as a "pitch person" in advertisements for their products.

> Sport marketers should not draw extra attention to negative publicity by trying to explain or excuse it.

Success in personal selling depends heavily on locating potential consumers (Miller et al., 1999; Pride and Ferrell, 2003). Connor (1981) said that "if you can

Did you know . . . ?

In the world of motorcycling, you can take lessons from a professional racer? The Kevin Schwantz Syzuki School offers only 10 dates a year for two-day workshops on riding. The course costs either $1200 or $1600 (the extra cost covers bike and equipment rental if you don't have your own) and is held at Road Atlanta.

Source:
http://www.schwantzschool.com

master one skill in selling, become a master prospector. It will guarantee your future success" (p. 14). Two questions arise, "What exactly is a prospect?" and "What exactly is prospecting?" Irwin et al. (2002, p. 108) define a prospect as "a targeted individual or group with the potential (interest, need or want: and time/money resources) to purchase or utilize your products or services." Prospecting is building a viable portfolio of potential clients and customers that positions the salesperson for work. Just as many executives go to the office, the person in sales consults the prospects' database. The question arises, just how do you go about creating a client base with potential customers? For the sport marketer, this often leads to the marketing information system discussed in Chapter 7. You should also remember the traditional 80-20 business adage where 80% of your sales usually result from 20% of your customers.

A substantial amount of interaction with consumers occurs through the Internet. For 2005, total Internet retail sales were estimated at $172 billion ("Click on this," 2005). The Internet serves as an effective communication tool for interacting directly with consumers. Although a bit atypical from personal selling in that the consumers search for the company, rather than vice versa, the promotional methods most closely resemble personal selling. Yet, as with other advertising, the consumer must be able to find your company and products. One study indicated that 43% of customers came from search engine marketing. In order to get the best results, most retailers actually pay the owners of the search engines (i.e. Google) on a performance basis to direct traffic to their company's site. Some have argued that websites are simply advertising offered through an alternative media; however, because customers can almost always engage immediately in purchasing products or services, this characterization does not fit.

Tucker (1997) noted that the Internet is "a useful part of today's marketing and communication mix" (p. 29). He noted that for fitness clubs, the Internet provides excellent opportunities to promote club services, sell merchandise, and communicate with existing members. In particular, the Internet was effective in publicizing "up-to-date information on club events" (Tucker, p. 29). Sport organizations are also using websites for promotional activities. The Snow Industries Association, the Outdoor Recreation Coalition of America, and the Sporting Goods Manufacturers Association are among the organizations that use the Internet to gain name recognition and explain organizational services. Almost all of the professional sports teams use their websites to communicate with fan clubs (as discussed in Chapter 7). Through this medium, they typically offer special deals to club members and occasionally run trivia contests and other interactive activities. Fan Clubs are particularly helpful in activating many of the promotions identified in this chapter.

Ski resorts have also begun to use the Internet for promotional activities. The method seems to be particularly effective in this industry. Because snow conditions change quite literally overnight, resorts are quick to promote fresh snow and great skiing conditions via the Internet. In market research from Vail (Colorado), marketers found that 30% of their customers preferred the Internet as a source for gathering information about the resort (Gonzalez, 1998).

The Internet offers other promotional advantages over advertising. The mere fact that it is the consumer who seeks the information is powerful. Research has indicated that only 6% of upscale, highly-educated consumers (exactly those using the Internet) trust advertising a credible source for product information ("10 Steps," 1998). The objective is almost always to develop meaningful relationships with customers that enhance overall company sales.

Sales promotion. The term *sales promotion* has been characterized as "a catch-all for all communication instruments that do not fit into advertising, personal selling or publicity categories" (van Waterschoot and Van den Bulte, 1992, p. 87). In their review of contemporary definitions, van Waterschoot and Van den Bulte indicate that sales promotions are activities of short duration that are intended to move consumers to an immediate exchange. Sales promotions often consist of those promotional activities other than advertising, publicity, or personal selling; and they are designed to affect consumer attitude or behavior. Some sales promotions include telemarketing, price promotions, point-of-purchase display, newsletter, giveaways, sponsorship, merchandising, and special events. In the sport industry, several examples exist that can be categorized as sales promotions. Point-of-purchase displays are particularly effective. In retail sporting goods stores, displays of products are often used to tie the product with previous advertising. The phrase "as seen on TV" should be familiar to most sports consumers. Point-of-purchase displays can also initiate recall of sponsorship. A cardboard cutout of Lindsey Davenport in front of the tennis racket section could stimulate the consumer's memory of Davenport's recent victory and move the consumer to purchase the racket that sponsors her tournament play.

Many sales promotions in sport center on selling season tickets. The Dallas Stars' ticketing department recently created a DVD for season ticket holders as part of the annual renewal campaign. In the past, the Stars had sent a nicely worded letter and invoices to season ticket holders asking for renewal. However, after the 2004 work stoppage, the Stars decided a new approach was necessary. Their Vice President of Ticket Sales said "You can't capture emotions on paper. You need the video to show it. People have not seen us play for a year and we wanted to touch on their emotional attachment to the team." They mailed out over 3,000 DVDs featuring highlights of the team including their 1999 Stanley Cup Championship season at cost of $0.83 for each DVD. Their VP continued "If it saves one season ticket account, it is worth it" (Video Killed the Renewal Letter, 2005).

Trade shows have also been effective sales promotions for sporting goods companies. The Sporting Goods Manufacturers Association has conducted a nationwide trade show for many years with the express intent of motivating large-scale retail chains to order merchandise "hot off the line." The International Health and Racquet Sportsclubs Association (IHRSA) has organized and run trade shows in the fitness industry for more than 25 years with great success. For 2006, the IHRSA trade showed hosted over 8,000 visitors, and 650 industry suppliers. It enabled the suppliers to meet face-to-face with their customers in a relaxed and festive environment. Many club managers place orders directly at these shows because they have been able to compare equipment from different companies firsthand and, based upon what they see, initiate the purchase. As you can see, that makes this type of activity crucial to marketing success.

Discount coupons have been a popular promotion for many years. McCarville, Flood, and Froats (1998) noted that over 7 billion coupons per year were redeemed in the United States. Today, coupons available through corporate websites provided an alternative to the traditional direct mail coupons. Coupon popularity has been attributed to four factors: "(a) the monetary (or discount) effect, (b) the advertising effect (the coupons provide the consumer with product information), (c) a reminding effect (they enhance awareness through repeated exposure to the coupon), and (d) a utility effect (satisfaction is gained through the redemption process" (p. 54).

Sports organizations can also serve the sales promotions of non-sport businesses through incentives. Situations in which purchasers receive free tickets to a sporting event with the purchase of a particular item may move that person to purchase. Store appearances of a sport celebrity at point of purchase can also stimulate immediate sales.

Although sales promotions have been referred to as a "catch-all" category, they strike at the heart of marketing, consummating the exchange. Sales promotions must be incorporated with other elements in the promotional mix.

DETERMINE THE PROMOTIONAL MIX

After establishing the promotion objectives, developing the budget, and considering promotional methods that will work best for the company, product, and consumer, the sport marketer must determine its promotional mix. The promotional mix is the combination of promotional methods that will help the sport company meet its objectives in the most effective way. It is rare that a sport company will use only one method—for example, a college athletic program use only direct mail, a sport marketing company use only journal advertising, a sporting goods retailer use only newspaper advertising, or the Special Olympics use only merchandising. It is more typical and much more effective for the company to use a mixture of these methods.

The decisions about which methods to use are contingent on many factors. Table 11.3 illustrates many of the factors that affect the decision on promotional mix. Each of these is discussed briefly here.

Each promotional method serves a different function. Advertising on television can reach a large number of consumers, but it is expensive. Publicity can reach a large number of consumers but cannot be controlled by the company. Personal selling is effective if the salesperson is knowledgeable and

Table 11.3
Factors Affecting Decision on Promotional Mix.
1. A different function for each method
2. The company
3. Stage of product life cycle
4. Access to promotional methods
5. Channels of distribution
6. Target markets
7. The competition
8. Geographic dispersement of the consumer market
9. The product
10. Push or pull strategy
11. Laws
12. Sport company resources

influential, but it serves a very small number of consumers. Sales promotions are effective in different ways, depending on the type of sales promotion. Each sales promotion attracts a different consumer and a different number of consumers.

The stage of product life cycle will affect decisions concerning the promotional mix (Stotlar, 2005). During the introductory stage, the company should aggressively promote the product. This means that the promotion budget will need to be extensive. During the growth stage, sales will increase. This means that revenue will increase. Promotional methods and aggressiveness will change, and money put into promotion will typically decrease. In the maturity stage, the pace of sales may slow and will eventually plateau. During this stage, however, the product is established and promotional objectives and methods change. If a product is approaching the decline stage, promotional objectives and methods must change to avoid disaster. If the product is allowed to continue in this direction, eventually all sales will cease. Typically, promotional objectives and methods become more aggressive and sometimes the product is repositioned and treated like a new product.

Channels of distribution will impact decisions on the promotional methods used (Irwin et al. 2002). Managers of specific channels may have requirements that the sport company cannot or will not support. Based on their marketing experiences, many marketing managers often favor specific channels of distribution.

In one example, stadium signage—a form of billboard advertising—has been found to be an effective promotional method for many companies (Stotlar, 2005). Although many of the companies using stadium signage are not sport companies, some are. Footwear companies who sponsor teams are very likely to include signage in their packages. Stadium signage has as its roots outdoor billboards. However, whereas a billboard has space and location limitations, and captures the attention of the consumer for a few seconds as the consumer drives by, a sign in a stadium is in front of the consumer as long as the event lasts, which can range from 1 to 5 hours. That amounts to a lot of impression time.

> Impression time is the length of time an ad or message is displayed within the consumer's line of vision.

During an event such as the Indy 500, which lasts approximately 5 hours, signage can make a significant impact on impression time. The Indy 500 event is televised and attracts a large viewership. The signage is not confined to the facility walls, it's everywhere, including on the cars and the drivers' suits and helmets (Ruff, 1992a,b). The spectator attending the event is surrounded by the signage, and the consumer watching the event on television also will be impacted by the advertising. As the camera captures and focuses on a specific car, the television viewer will see the advertising on the car. As the camera follows the cars around the track, various signs come in and out of view. As the research shows, nearly 70% of spectators could correctly identify advertising seen during an event (Stotlar and Johnson, 1989).

One popular promotional method for businesses is taking advantage of signage space for sale by sport organizations.

Impression time was also generated at the dramatic conclusion of the 1999 Women's World Cup soccer match when the USA's Brandi Chastain ripped off her jersey in celebration after scoring the winning goal. This act displayed her Nike sports top. Nike immediately began negotiating for video footage and still photos. According to one expert, "that ten second piece of film is all Nike needs to sell more sports bras than it can produce" (Wells and Oldenburg, 1999, p. 1A).

The data showed that Tiger Woods' victory in the 2005 Masters accounted for $10 million of television exposure for Nike based on logos visible during the telecast for Nike, Nike One Ball, and Nike's Tiger Woods Collection.

Target markets of the sport company will influence promotional methods. The promotional methods will need to be effective for each target market identified by the sport company. Target market factors to consider include geographic location and size as well as the associated demographic and psychographic characteristics. Some promotional method factors to consider are listed below in the form of questions:

1. Which method will catch the attention of the market? Only sport marketing consumer research can answer this question. A true understanding of the consumer will guide the sport marketer to decisions concerning the method to which the consumer will positively react.

2. What kind of message will attract the consumer, and will the consumer be able to understand it? Again, consumer research will guide the sport marketer to the answer to this question. The sport marketer should develop the promotional message so that the consumer can relate to it and understand it. In other words, the sport marketer should consider writing the advertising message in the consumer's language.

3. Can the promotional method reach the intended target market? If a sport magazine is being considered as an advertising medium, does the target market subscribe to the magazine? For example, the Gay Games uses promotional methods that reach its specific target market: the lesbian and gay population around the world. Some of these methods are direct mail using mailing lists of prior Games participants and from lesbian and gay magazine publishers; merchandising advertisements in mail-order catalogs such as Shocking Gray; and advertising in lesbian and gay targeted magazines such as *The Advocate, Deneuve*, and *Out*.

The competitor will affect the promotional method selected for the sport company. Although the promotional methods must be selected and designed for the consumer, equal attention must be given to the competitor (Schnaars, 1991). Promotional methods selected can impact sport marketing strategies with increased market share and the outmaneuvering of a competitor in a specific area such as price, market penetration, and advertising message.

> The sport company must spend time gaining an understanding of the consumer and what the consumer wants while simultaneously studying the competitors.

Geographic dispersal of the consumer market will affect the promotional methods selected. Personal selling may be best for localized markets. However, as the location of the sport company's consumers spreads geographically, the company will have to consider promotional methods that will reach the new consumers.

The product and its elements will affect the promotional methods selected. The type of product and the characteristics and elements of the product will impact the method and message of promotion. Some of the characteristics include product type (good, service, person, place, idea), customized versus standardized, differentiation, quality, features, performance, design, and product life-cycle stage.

The decision to use a push or a pull promotion strategy will affect the promotional method used (Cravens and Woodruff, 1986; Peter and Donnelly, 1991). The objective of both strategies is to get the product into the consumer's hands. A *push strategy* involves trying to move the product into the channels of distribution and encouraging sellers to increase sales volumes. The strategy usually involves offering a variety of awards and enticements to the channelers. Many sporting goods manufacturers use this strategy. A company will offer incentives or price breaks to a wholesaler or retailer that increases sales volume. A *pull strategy* involves strong promotion directed toward the end consumer in order to affect the consumer's demand for the product. The consumer's demand for the product acts to "pull" the product through the channels. The sport company's promotional methods are designed to target the consumer and create demand. The consumer in turn asks for the product. For example, if a sporting goods retailer does not carry a specific product, a motivated consumer may ask the retailer to carry the product.

> Sport product characteristics should guide the sport marketer in selecting the best promotional method for the product.

Laws governing promotion will affect selection of promotional methods. Local, state, and federal government agencies and consumer protection agencies have enacted laws, guidelines, and restrictions that affect a sport company's promotional efforts. Some of these include the Federal Trade Commission, the Food and Drug Administration, the Securities and Exchange Commission, the United States Patent Office, and the Department of Justice. Other organizations and groups also work to control promotions. Some of these are the National Association of Broadcasters and the Better Business Bureau. Further, individual companies exercise ethical decision making in selecting and developing promotional methods.

Sport company resources will impact the promotional methods decision. There are two types of resources within a sport company—material and nonmaterial. Material resources include money, supplies, equipment, and the like. Nonmaterial resources include human resources. Does the sport company have the resources necessary to accomplish the promotional methods it is considering? The critical bottom line may be the ultimate factor affecting the company's decision concerning promotional methods.

As you can see, the sport marketer must consider and analyze many factors in the process of selecting the promotional methods and activities for the company.

CREATE PROMOTIONAL ACTIVITIES

Based on the marketing mix, business enterprises create special activities to promote their programs, products, or purposes. Hiebing and Cooper (1990) indicated that promotions, as marketing tools, provide activities and incentives directly to consumers. One of the most notable names in sport promotion is

Veeck. Bill Veeck Jr., one of baseball's most famous (and outrageous) promoters, is perhaps best known for sending a midget to bat in Major League Baseball. More noteworthy contributions included adding names to player uniforms and designing lighted, graphic scoreboards. His son, Mike Veeck seems to have followed in the family tradition when he served as the marketing and promotions director for the MLB Tampa Bay Devil Rays (see side bar for Veeck's promotional activities). Perhaps Veeck's (Williams, P., 2000) most disastrous promotion was his 1979 Disco Demolition Night for the Chicago White Sox. The intent was to signal and end to the Disco era. Spectators were asked to bring old disco records to be piled up between the games of a doubleheader to be blown up on the field. However, fans smuggled extra records into the stadium and began a "Frisbee" riot that resulted in the eventual forfeiture of the game.

Intercollegiate athletics and interscholastic sports must likewise engage in promotional activities. The University of Texas started a promotion in 2005 with the online magazine program. Their online video magazine gave Texas fans exclusive, behind-the-scenes content about the Texas football program. It included text, images, web links and full-screen, broadcast-quality video. Issues were automatically downloaded to a fan's computer and could be viewed an unlimited number of times at the fan's convenience. Fans from almost every state and many foreign countries downloaded the magazine. In addition, 53.2% of viewers clicked through to the Longhorns Store generating incremental revenue. Incidentally, many subscribers were not season ticket holders or Longhorn Foundation members which gave The University of Texas a whole new list of fans for their database (Plonsky, 2005).

Traditional promotions such as the "hat day," "bat day," and "poster day" events continue to be popular with both fans and sports organizations. The research on the effectiveness of such promotions varies. Boyd and Krehbeil (2003) found that in general about 40% of MLB teams used these types of promotional items. Interestingly they found that if "Give-Away" items were used for a game against an arch rival, attendance did not appreciably increase. On the other

As a marketing tool, fun and unique promotions prove to be effective in attempting to attract more consumers.

hand, when a give-a-way item was used in a contest against a non-rival, attendance was positively affected. Overall, their research found that promotions in general increased attendance by about 20%. Liberman (2004) found that the most successful give-away item, producing a 20.7% increase in attendance, was the jack-in-the-box toy (where a mascot or team player would pop out of a small box). A long-time favorite, the bobblehead toy produced increases of 15.3%. An interesting perspective was forwarded by Texas Rangers (MLB) Chief Operating Officer when he said that "the team doesn't view give-aways as inducements to buy tickets; they're rewards, and the team gives them out at high attendance games throughout the year" (Liberman, 2004, p. 21).

This also brings forward the aspect of protocol. Many teams have found that consumers "cherry pick" the games that have give-away items. That is, they scan the teams schedule and chose to purchase only tickets to games where there is a give-away item. Many times this defeats the purpose of the promotion (selling more tickets). In response, some teams have decided not to publicize the give-away until closer to game day. Those who chose to use the give-away as reward also have some choices with protocol. The typical method involves giving the item to the first 1,000 number of fans into the stadium. However, many times season ticket holders, your most valued customer, is not among the first 1,000 into the stadium. Thus, your best customer does not get the reward that other fans receive. One method that solves this problem is to provide coupons for season ticket holder to use for item redemption at the stadium's customer service booth. An interesting side benefit is that oftentimes fans in the stadium may ask "Where did you get that?" and the response is "I am a season ticket holder." While there does not appear to be any research on this specific topic, it seems that this may be effective in both rewarding your best customer and increasing ticket sales.

The mid-1990s brought very popular Beanie Baby promotions to many sporting events, including the 1998 Major League Baseball All-Star Game. Dave Coskey, former President of the NBA 76ers commented on special edition beanie babies offered by the team saying "We saw fans line up at 8:00 a.m., and subsequently we brought in 18,000 fans for the game" ("Better to give", 2005)

Research studies into the effectiveness of these activities vary. In some cases, they produced large increases in overall attendance, whereas at other times they produced increases only for those specific events where people attended primarily to obtain the free novelty. Sport marketers should not jump to the conclusion that it is detrimental if a person attended an event for the express purpose of obtaining a free product. Sport can serve an effective (and profitable) role in linking consumers with products from sponsors.

The University of Tennessee launched some nontraditional promotions for their women's basketball contests. They had a face-painting night, balloon-making nights, and a petting-zoo night. At the petting-zoo promotion, animals were brought into the arena from local animal shelters for fans to pet and possibly adopt (Fechter, 1998.). This type of promotion, which connects the university with a community-based organization, is often referred to as "cause-related." Cause-related promotions can be effective in drawing positive attention to sport

Did you know...?

In the motorcycling industry, consumer statistics (of American Motorcyclist Association members) show that riders/owners have an average household income of $91,500, which is about double the national average.

Source:
http://www.AMAdirectlink.com

programs. The University of Arkansas women's athletic marketing staff created a program called "Read with the Lady 'Backs" for children in grades K-6. The participants earned points, and prizes were awarded in various categories. The event produced significant public goodwill and helped form the image of the women's sport program as one concerned about the academic performance of children. NASCAR also had a "Race to Read Program" sponsored by Ford Racing.

Promotional activities that involve high school, collegiate, or amateur players require the exercise of considerable caution. Many sport-governing bodies have restrictive guidelines regulating the appearances of athletes in commercial activities. In some instances, if an athlete is associated with a specific product or company, he or she may be declared ineligible for amateur competition.

Some promotional activities seek to draw attention to the team/event/product by awarding prizes to those in attendance. Several sports teams have sponsored contests where spectators' ticket stubs were drawn at random for chances to win prizes by scoring goals (soccer, hockey), kicking field goals, or shooting baskets. These events usually are scheduled prior to the contest or between periods of play. The cost to the sport organization is minimal because the prizes often can be secured from sponsors as a trade-out for name recognition during the event or covered by relatively inexpensive insurance policies. These policies are offered through a myriad of companies that specialize in sport event promotions and contests. However, as with any business decision, you should investigate the company managing the promotion.

> You must make sure that your marketing practices conform to all regulatory standards and professional ethics.

Several years ago, what seemed like a typical promotion went horribly wrong. During halftime of a Chicago Bulls NBA game, a 23-year-old office supply worker sank a 73-foot shot to win a million dollars. However, shortly after the event, it was discovered that the contestant had recently played college basketball, a violation of contest rules. With the payout in jeopardy, the Bulls held a press conference the following day and laid blame on the insurer. The insurer noted that the player had signed a waiver (which the Bulls administered only AFTER the shot) in which the stipulation was clear. Unfortunately, this promotion did not produce the intended result of positively impacting attendees (Cohen, 1993). Just one year later, a similar controversy erupted in Miami where the Florida Panthers (NHL) conducted a contest in which a fan could win a million dollars by shooting a puck the length of the ice toward a small opening in a template across the goal. The contestant shot the puck into the slot on the template, and an immediate celebration began. However, contest officials began to claim that the puck had not passed "completely through" the opening as required. This promotion generated lengthy litigation rather than the intended promotional benefit. The oldest and largest company that handles promotions like these is the National Hole-In-One Association (http://www.hio.com). Based on a fee paid by the team, the company sets up the rules of the contest and guarantees the payout if the prize is won. Sports teams using this company include the Orlando Magic, Milwaukee Bucks and the Big East Conference.

Some of the many possible promotional activities associated with sport events that have proven successful are presented below:

1. Banquets to honor the participants of various sport teams through tributes to coaches, players, and support staff. These can be effective as award ceremonies where special acknowledgment and honors are accorded either employees or prominent citizens. To obtain the maximum promotional value, you should prepare personal stories, pictures, and awards.

2. Exhibitions of new products, protective sports gear, or the latest in sport and fitness fashion. These have also proven to produce positive media coverage.

3. Team reunions in conjunction with a reception, dinner, and game.

4. Events, including guest days or nights for senior citizens, disadvantaged youth, Boy Scouts, Girl Scouts, and other groups who attend games. Often these programs are enhanced by coordinating the event with a civic or service club where the members of the club provide transportation and supervision.

5. Sports clinics for various age-groups in popular sports. These can expose and profile your staff for the media. Clinics also can be conducted on prevention and care of injuries, new fitness programs, or a myriad of other sport-related subjects.

One of the reasons that promotions are so popular is that they are relatively inexpensive and often do not cost the sport company at all. Other examples of successful promotional ideas include the following:

- Hosting a fun-run

- Hosting a celebrity tennis or golf tournament

- Holding a wellness fair

- Holding an open house at your sport organization

- Holding a live concert before or after a game

- Getting a famous athlete to make an appearance in your store to sign autographs

- Encouraging tailgating for events and contests

- Giving out "buy-one-get-one" coupons for future contest

- Hosting a holiday tournament

A unique aspect of many sport programs is the desire of the public to associate with players, coaches, or employees. This can take many different forms: Colleges and universities offer their coaches, fitness centers provide their instructors, and many corporations offer their leading salespeople for inspirational and informative talks. Many sport organizations circulate lists of speakers available to various organizations

> Successful organizations often play on consumers' desire to associate with players, coaches, or employees by making them available through a speakers' bureau.

that may have the desire for guest speakers, whereas more aggressive organizations actively seek speaking engagements for their employees.

DEVELOP PROMOTIONAL PUBLICATIONS

Every sport organization will produce some type of promotional publication at one time or another. The purpose of organizational publications is usually to transmit knowledge or information to the public. A publication also communicates various aspects about the sport organization, style, approach, attitude, and image. For the publication to be effective, it must also be consistent. Herein lays the dilemma for managing promotional publications in many sport organizations. Do you create one single office that is responsible for all publications, or do you allow each department to produce its own publication to fit its individual needs?

Because publications are so crucial in the promotion and marketing of a company's goods and services, most sport organizations have one central unit that is responsible for the organization's publishing. Centralization of this promotional function reduces several publishing problems that have been encountered by sport organizations.

> Businesses must understand their weaknesses and not undertake projects that they aren't qualified to do—such as publishing their own promotional literature.

A major problem for many sports organizations is the dreaded desktop publisher. With the popularity of computer-based publishing programs for personal computers, everyone thinks they can be in the publishing business, and they can.

According to Herman (1992), the "freedom of the press belongs to the person who has one" (p. 25). For your organization, this means that you can have untrained people creating and disseminating material to the public about your products and services. The pitfalls here are tremendous. Poorly written, poorly designed, and inaccurate information may be presented to consumers without your knowledge or control.

Three different methods of addressing this problem have been presented. Herman (1992) suggests that you have a centralized system, a franchise process, or an "official" publications policy. In the centralized system, one office handles all of the printing and publishing for the entire organization. This system affords the greatest amount of control and consistency and is very effective in protecting the organization from unprofessional or inaccurate publications. The limitations with this system are that it requires a relatively large staff and the demands on one unit often fluctuate during different times of the year, which may create ineffective staffing patterns.

The franchising of publication operations can be effective because individual units are allowed to produce their own promotional materials. The franchise allows a representative from each unit to approve any publications from that unit. To qualify as a unit representative, a person has to undertake special training from a publication specialist. Not only do the units often have a better idea of exactly what they need, but they also often have a better idea of the unique benefits of the product or service in which the consumer may be interested. This option retains some of the advantages of having the centralized system in control, yet it decentralizes responsibility and workload.

The official publication method provides the least control of the three options. This policy limits the central publishing unit to the official publications of the organization (catalogs, brochures, advertising copy, etc.). All other units are free to produce their own (unofficial) newsletters or internal releases. This does eliminate the "publications police" that exists in the two previous systems; however, it also allows for the uncontrolled production of promotional literature. There is also a high probability that unofficial publications will find their way into the public eye, creating confusion and occasionally crises.

Regardless of the administrative structure, special brochures about your sport organization are effective in increasing exposure and publicity. Most commercial sport organizations use an annual report for communicating with both internal and external audiences. As a controlled medium, this document can be effective in creating favorable impressions about the organization in the minds of employees, clients, and prospective investors. In sport, these have been used by sporting goods companies, professional and collegiate teams, fitness centers, and commercial recreation enterprises.

Sports teams have, for many years, prepared and distributed game programs as promotional publications. Boeh (1989) indicates that although sports teams have many advertising and promotional opportunities, game programs are still the most popular and reliable.

Irwin and Fleger (1992) found that the game program could be effective as a promotional tool through providing team history and contest information and also as a source of revenue. Data from their research indicate that although attendance figures over the past few years at collegiate events have declined, program sales increased significantly. The average sales data showed that currently 1 in 10 football fans and 1 in 13 basketball spectators purchased a program.

The philosophy surrounding the production and pricing of ads in the game program is of significant importance. If you are going to be competitive with other advertising media, then you are in the advertising business. If you cannot, you are really asking for philanthropy and contributions. This position/philosophy needs to be established early.

If you decide you are in the philanthropy business, you must recover enough advertising revenue to offset printing costs. These advertisers must know that they will not receive the same exposure for their dollar as they would with other media. This does not, however, automatically mean that they will not purchase an ad. In many small towns, the advertisers are willing to support your organization through the purchase of an ad, irrespective of the cost-benefit ratio. Boeh (1989) advises that

> the sponsor should not be led to believe that he or she will receive the same advertising impact that other mediums offer. Rather, advertising in your game program should be explained as a way for the sponsor to support the athletic program with a donation and receive recognition in the form of an ad. (p. 53)

The way to determine if you are truly in the advertising segment is to calculate a CPM (cost per thousand impressions). In doing so, you present the cost of advertising in your program on the same basis as other media sources such as the local newspaper. Although your ad costs are typically higher, few people keep newspapers as souvenirs.

Irwin and Fleger (1992) presented several ways for sport marketers to manage game programs (see suggested readings). The options they cite for producing profits and exposure provide valuable information in the area.

EVALUATE THE PROMOTIONAL PLAN

The sport marketer must determine if the promotional plan is effective. The sport marketer must therefore establish a method to determine if the plan or parts of the plan are accomplishing the company objectives. The promotion objectives outlined what the company expects to achieve with the promotional plan. Did the plan accomplish these objectives? To answer that question, the sport marketer must assess the outcomes of the plan. Typically, this is performed through marketing research. Although Chapter 5 details marketing research, the following is a brief look at how it can be used for determining promotional effectiveness.

Some types of marketing research are good for determining if the promotional plan is working. If the sport company wants to determine if certain forms of advertising are effective, it can conduct a consumer survey. The survey will provide answers for the sport marketer to analyze. In the analysis, the sport marketer must assess whether or not the advertising is accomplishing its goals. For example, the Blue Ridge Ski Resort wants to determine the effectiveness of direct mail advertising its special two-for-one ski week. The sport marketer prepares a special skier check-in form that will be used for that week only. Questions on the form ask the skiers to identify where and how they found out about the special. If 50% state that they found out about the special in the direct mail they received, the sport marketer can make a subjective judgment about whether the promotional method was successful. If 12 people came for the special, 50% is 6. Does an increase of six skiers who found out about the special through the direct mail mean that it was an effective method? Before we can answer that question, we must ask, "How many direct-mail pieces were sent to potential buyers?" If the answer is 1,000 pieces, 6 out of 1,000 could be determined unsuccessful. If the answer is 20 pieces, perhaps 6 out of 20, or 30%, may be considered to be a successful method.

STUDY PROMOTION LAWS AND REGULATIONS

There are laws, guidelines, regulations, policy, and perception that affect promotion. The primary reason for regulation is consumer protection. The sport marketer must study and understand all of the regulations in order to produce a legal and ethical promotional plan. These areas are discussed in the following sections.

Laws. The sport marketer must know, understand, and apply any applicable laws to the promotional plan. Federal regulation involves two primary laws: the Federal Trade Commission (FTC) Act and the Robinson-Patman Act. The FTC Act prohibits unfair methods of competition. One area of unfair competition is false, misleading, or deceptive advertising. The Robinson-Patman Act outlaws price discrimination and has two sections on promotional allowances. These sections state that promotional allowances must be fair and equal.

Regulation by other organizations. There are many organizations that affect promotional activities. For example, the Better Business Bureau is a nationwide company that works as a consumer advocate and works to control unfair promotion practices.

Industry control. Many industries and individual companies work to affect promotional activities of their counterparts. These controlling mechanisms, although they are not law, are very effective in regulating ethical and tasteful promotional practices of companies.

Promotion and Ethical Issues. Every aspect and function of the sport business must follow ethical guidelines usually determined partially by the company and partially by the public. Ethical consideration should be given serious attention in areas including sociocultural issues and environmental issues. The sport marketer cannot afford to assume that the population of the United States or even other countries is of a similar culture and lifestyle. Serious attention to socioeconomic factors, cultural factors, and other such factors will exert a responsible and leadership role for the business. In other words, it is critical that the sport marketer always "do the right thing" ethically and in socially responsible ways to position the company as people friendly and earth friendly.

Let us look at an example of how the entire process might work. Management of the Ship Shape Fitness Center has decided to target senior citizens. Their objective is to sell memberships to those senior citizens defined as 60-plus. Some products designed for and to be offered to this group are customized aerobics classes, one-on-one training, partner walking, water shaping, and a 60-plus tennis league. T-shirts will be specially designed to give as awards for milestones and league winners. The company develops the following message to be used as its primary promotion slogan: Fitness is good for you no matter how young you are! Management believes that this message is positive and keys on the 60-plus person thinking of her- or himself as young, not old. Promotional activities will include a one-week open house that will include activities designed to educate the 60-plus person about fitness. There will be exhibitions to show how fitness can be fun and an attainable goal. Management decides that the center will get 50, 60, or even 70-year-olds to perform the exhibitions. The objective is that the 60-plus person can see someone of his or her age exercising. The target group can relate to this much better than watching a very young and fit person exercising. The methods for communicating the message are selected based on the best method for reaching the audience.

From their marketing research, management learns that this market most likely does not work, they are busy people and are not at home very much, and they do not watch much television or listen to radio. Therefore, management concludes that the best way to reach the audience is through direct-mail advertising. The piece will be informative and simple, and will include information about the open house and the center. Other promotional methods will include coupons for two free days at the center, a special half-price membership fee for the first year, and special membership fee discounts for every year after that.

> A successful marketer will identify the target market, select a message, and develop specifically tailored strategies for the market.

The sport marketer in this example has identified a target market, selected a positive message, and developed promotional methods specifically for the market. The products added were designed for the market, and the prices were identified based on the market's income. Communication is the tool used in getting the message to the consumer.

In conclusion, creating and managing promotion as a marketing element are difficult. Therefore, it is essential to unify all of the organization's executives on the role of promotions, the desired results, and the specific strategies to employ. Competition between specialists in various areas of the corporation can defeat the purpose of the promotional mix. For example, the advertising department may claim that it can do more to produce results than can the sales force. On the other hand, the public relations department may assert that its activities are more effective than advertising is. Therefore, a marketing manager must clearly understand the role of each component and be able to integrate promotional functions into the organization's overall business and marketing plan.

Chapter Summary

Promotional systems are central to effective sport marketing because they relate directly to the consumer's decision to purchase. As the various promotional activities described in this chapter indicate, no single approach suits every situation. Promotions are limited only by one's imagination and, more often than not, by budget. Sport marketers must carefully analyze a particular setting, become knowledgeable about ideas tried by others, and create a promotional mix that best fits their specific organization and market conditions.

People will not buy a product if they do not know it exists, and promotion is the sport marketer's tool for communicating to the market about the company and its products. Sport promotion is the function of informing people about the sport company's products and influencing their purchase behavior. Promotion can shape a company image, reposition a product, create awareness for a new product, alert the consumer to sales, tell the consumer where the sport company is located, and inform the consumer about where a product can be purchased. The critical steps involved in promotion planning include establishing objectives, determining promotional methods deemed best for achieving those objectives, and developing a promotional mix. The sport marketer must know and understand the many factors that impact the development of the promotional mix. A master plan for all promotional activities should be developed, executed, and evaluated. Finally, the sport marketer must know the laws and the legal and ethical issues surrounding promotion in today's society.

Fundamental to the success of all promotional activities is the confidence of the manager. Oftentimes, those who succeed are those who believe they will. Although it is highly unlikely that any sports organization can implement all the promotional methods outlined in the chapter, a complete study should be made of available opportunities. It is hoped that this chapter has provided some basic principles, guidelines, and practices that will improve your confidence and ultimately your chances for success.

Promotion in the Sport Industry

Rationale

The data for the industry show that many sports teams and leagues teams use "Give-Away" promotional items to increase attendance. Research finding discussed in the chapter showed varying effects resulting from the use of promotional items. The decision to use give-away items depends on the sport, the fan characteristics and the opponents. Additional consideration needs to be given to the type of items and its popularity.

Charge

The purpose of this case/exercise is to evaluate the appropriateness of a give-away promotion at the college or university where students are enrolled. Each group of students is assigned a sport where attendance is reasonable, but neither dismal or near capacity. Each group will then evaluate the situation, select and price a promotional item (through web research), project changes in attendance, and determine if the use of a promotional item is warranted.

Teaching points:

- Discuss current practices in professional sport.
- Discuss the characteristics and unique nature of the sport assigned to each group and the impact on the use of promotional items.
- Discuss the process and rationale for the selection of the promotional item.
- Analyze the methods utilized to determine the return on investment and the groups decision to use or not use a promotional give-away item.

QUESTIONS FOR STUDY

1. What is promotion?
2. What is sport promotion?
3. Why is promotion important to the sport marketer?
4. What is the process of communication?
5. What are promotional methods? Give some examples in the sport industry.
6. What is the promotional mix?
7. What are the factors that affect decisions about the promotional mix?
8. What are legal issues affecting promotion?
9. What are ethics, and what are some ethical issues the sport marketer should use in determining promotion strategies?

LEARNING ACTIVITIES

1. Conduct a study of three different sport businesses, organizations, or other enterprises in your city or community. Determine the promotional methods used by each.
2. Collect print advertising of a variety of sport products from numerous sources. Conduct a study of the ads and determine the target market(s) and the promotional message.
3. What are some populations recently objecting to the use of certain promotional messages and logos? In discussion groups, discuss the reasons and the ethical responsibility of the sport marketer.
4. Visit a local media outlet (radio, television station, or newspaper) and talk with a producer or editor about their relationships with sports organizations. Prepare a contact

sheet for that outlet complete with the names, position titles, and phone numbers of important people.

5. Investigate an advertising purchase for an athletic program or stadium scoreboard sign and determine if it is an equitable media buy compared to other advertising outlets.

PROFESSIONAL ASSOCIATIONS AND ORGANIZATIONS

National Association of Collegiate Marketing Administrators (NACMA)
24651 Detroit Road, Westlake, OH 44145

SUGGESTED READINGS

Helitzer, M. (2000) *The dream job: Sports publicity, promotion, and marketing,* 3rd Ed. Athens, OH: University Sport Press.

Irwin, R. L Sutton, W. A. & McCarthy, L. M. (2002). *Sport Promotion and Sales Management.* Champaign, IL: Human Kinetics.

Chapter Twelve

MEDIA RELATIONS IN SPORT

Marketing communication cannot be limited to annual reports, advertising, and brochures. Interaction with the media is both a necessary and a valuable endeavor. Historically, businesses interacted with the public mostly through face-to-face encounters. However, today perceptions of your organization are delivered though multiple communication channels. Media and communication theorists have suggested that the expanded nature of communication in the global community and the speed with which information is transmitted mandate an understanding of media relations (Thompson, 1994). Irwin, Sutton & McCarthy (2002) note the importance of fulfilling the needs of the media. In fact, they say that the media should be treated like any other customer. The media need information and stories that are both interesting and newsworthy and fit the target market of the media's consumers. It is the sport marketer's job to create and distribute information for the media that meets those criteria. "For example, NASCAR significantly increased its coverage in USA Today by demonstrating that the race fan demographics characteristics matched those of the publisher's readers" (Irwin, et al., 2002, p. 174).

> The two most important aspects of media relations are the development of media relationships and media competencies.

Media relationships form a basis from which all marketing and promotional strategies are launched. From the competency standpoint, the sport marketer must be knowledgeable about the specific formats, terminology, and personnel employed by the media. In the sports community, the title of the person who dealt with the media was "Sports Information Director." However, with the expanded role and the explosion of duties many sport organizations are titling the person "Director of Communications."

Media is a broad term when used as a noun. It generally includes two categories, print and electronic. Within these categories, print media refer to newspaper and magazine professionals whereas electronic media typically include television and radio. Although the classification system has worked well for many years, technology is rapidly blurring the lines of distinction. Many television stations are owned by publishers; publishers are producing vignettes for television and with electronic computer bulletin boards, some newspapers are never printed. Regardless of the labels placed on media professionals, sport marketers must develop sophisticated skills and nurture productive relationships.

The media must be considered as clients. Effective relations with media outlets will provide significant opportunities for communicating marketing concepts and product information with other clients and customers. Radio, television, and newspapers are the traditional media sources with which the sport marketer must become familiar. By providing a high-quality service to the media, all marketing functions can be enhanced.

One example of how not to build positive media relations occurred in 1999 immediately following Michael Jordan's retirement from basketball. Nike offered company chair Phil Knight to ESPN for an interview related to Jordan's announcement. However, Nike demanded that Bob Ley be replaced as the interviewer. Ley had served as the principal reporter on ESPN's documentary critical of Nike's labor practices in Asian shoe factories. ESPN refused, and Nike received additional negative publicity rather than the positive exposure originally sought.

Building Media Relationships

Sport marketers can develop confidence and respect by adhering to some basic principles or guidelines. According to Fox and Levin (1993) and Helitzer (2000), these include the following:

Principles of Good Media Relations

1. Know the players. A thorough understanding of the titles and responsibilities of media personnel will contribute greatly to your success. In the television environment, you will encounter executive producers, senior producers, talent (on-air hosts and reporters), and other production personnel. With the print media, you will come in contact with editors, reporters, staff writers, and occasionally stringers (those who write for the publication on a part-time basis).

2. Be accessible. Everyone has tight schedules and more work to do than time in which to do it. However, if you want media coverage, you will have to make yourself available on their terms. The only time when the media want you and are willing to wait for you is during a crisis in your organization.

3. Be cooperative and non-combative at all times. You will never win an argument with a reporter or writer. Even stupid questions deserve an answer. Remember, they do the editing and they will always have the last word.

4. Appearance is critical. Although you might think that this aspect of media relations applies only to television, this is not accurate. Your attire projects an image to all reporters. A person in formal business attire is almost always afforded more respect and credibility than a person in shorts and a golf shirt.

5. Don't use jargon. Instead, use words with which the public is familiar. In the sport industry, it is easy for us to use words and phrases that are unique to the field. Although we may believe that everyone should know the meaning of our words, which is not typically the case. Think before you speak, and rehearse the vocabulary that will be most effective with every audience.

6. Use facts, not rumors, and be precise. Gather as many pertinent facts as possible prior to talking to reporters. Although facts in some stories may initially be more detrimental than a rumor, specific examples confine a story whereas ru-

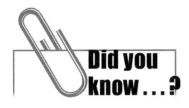
mors tend to remove all boundaries. Good reporters will verify facts through alternate sources prior to airing and/or printing a report. Eventually all of the facts will surface and you do not want to be labeled a liar. Honesty and trust are critical to the survival and success of your organization.

7. Don't stress or depend upon off-the-record accounts. If you can see a camera, microphone, or reporter's notebook, assume your words are recorded. Remember, the job of the media is to get facts and report the story; asking a reporter to abide with off-the-record requests is unfair. Never say anything that you would not like to see in the media (i.e., there is no "off the record," and "the microphone is always on").

8. Give as much service to the media as possible. When news occurs, get the story out expeditiously. All reporters desire "hot" news, so you must be willing and able to supply the stories, pictures, and statistics they wish, in the form they need and on time.

9. If a reporter uncovers a story, do not immediately give the same story to other reporters. Treat it as an exclusive. Many reporters pride themselves on finding sensational news stories and believe that they should have the right to be the first to break the story.

10. Because news is a highly perishable commodity, timing is critical. Breaking stories have a very limited shelf life and, if you want the publicity, you must provide all of the necessary information quickly and in a format that the media outlet needs. Remember that the media need news, not publicity.

PERSONNEL

Most college athletic departments employ a full-time person, typically called a sports information director (SID), to coordinate and manage the press and public relations activities for the college. The SID may have a staff ranging from one intern to a corps of employees, including an assistant SID, graduate assistants, secretaries, and several work-study students. It is the job of the sports information office to manage all of the public relations, media relations, and publicity activities for the athletic office.

This office develops the media guides, manages press day and the pressroom, develops the press packets, and makes available up-to-the-minute statistics and general information. Although these activities are sales promotion activities, the target market includes the media and the activities are designed to influence attitude and perception.

In most sport corporations, media relations are managed by the communication directors or marketing managers. These companies also engage in media relations activities in an attempt to garner positive publicity through the media. Specifically, retail sporting goods companies engage in many of these strategies. For example, Reebok's running division seeks to maintain close trade relations with leading running-enthusiast magazines like *Runner's World*. Rohm (1997) reported that Reebok's objectives are to "ensure critical editorial coverage and proper running-product reviews" (p. 22). This does bring to question some ethical issues with regard to the relationship between publicity and advertising. It has been hypothesized that some magazine advertisers put a considerable amount of pressure on trade publications to provide favorable reviews or risk losing their advertising revenues. Regardless of the type of sport organization, the personnel engaged in media relations must be highly trained and exhibit the highest of ethical standards.

PRESS CONFERENCES

One essential aspect in providing service to your media clients is identical to the basic concept of marketing: Provide what your client needs. Press conferences can provide that service, but should occur only when circumstances warrant their use. Too often, a media relations director will call press conferences to disseminate information that should have been in a news release. This causes the press to be wary of conferences. A press conference takes up a great deal of a reporter's day; therefore, if the press conference is to be a success, the information must warrant its occurrence.

Helitzer (2000) provides several considerations for planning a successful press conference. He recommends that you assess the value of calling a press conference. Irwin et al. (2002) and Heliter (2000) discuss some of the more common reasons for calling a press conference.

- A major change in personnel including players, coaches, owners, or management

- Scheduling of an important event such as a title bout, championship game, or interstate rivalry

Conducting a press conference to release information to the media should only be done when circumstances warrant the event.

- A change in facility location or name

- Introduction of a new or revised product

- Presentation or display of award

- Announcement of a new rule or policy

- Announcement of a major sponsorship/partnership agreement

- Crisis development

> **Press conferences are most appropriate when the information must be distributed to all outlets at the same time.**

The timing of the press conference is also important. You must make sure that the key media people are available at the scheduled time. Although it is not always possible to check everyone's schedule, the media do have some times that are better than others based on the media source (morning paper vs. afternoon, radio vs. television).

If the decision has been made to conduct a press conference, the effected media must receive invitations. The invitation can be delivered to the media sources through the mail or in person. The former is the most efficient, with the latter being more effective. The key decision factors often revolve around the number of media invited and the time of the organization to issue the invitations. If the decision was made to send the invitation through the mail, it is also advisable to place a reminder call a few hours before the conference.

The preparation and selection of the site are also important considerations. Here, Helitzer (2000) has some specific criteria. Ample space must be assured for the anticipated number of attendees. Parking, seating, telephones, refreshments, and the amount of materials available must also be designed around this factor. Attention should be given to the electrical facilities present at the press conference site. All communication media, including the public address system, the podium height and lighting, projectors, and multimedia equipment, must be checked before the conference.

First impressions are critical with the press conference. The agenda or program for the press conference should be distributed along with any particular rules about the process of addressing the speakers.

> **There should be a registration table at the press conference where press kits are available for all attendees.**

Some sport companies work hard to influence the kind of publicity they receive through the media. For example, most university athletic departments will stage a press day to which they invite reporters, journalists, and sports broadcasters. They are encouraged to interview and photograph the athletes and coaches. Packets of material are offered to each individual. The packets contain information about the athletes and coaches, such as their records in high school, past season's records, highlights, hometown information, human-interest information, and expectations for the upcoming season. There will also be plenty to eat and drink. The purpose of press day is to treat the press positively in the hope that the press will return the favor through their stories, reports, articles, and broadcasts. The treatment doesn't stop here. At every sport event during the season there is a special room for the press. The pressroom will again contain packets of information, pictures, and current statistics about the season.

Although the primary objective of your media relations program is to draw attention to a person, organization, or event, sometimes attention is directed to the sport organization in negative situations. Accusations, accidents, and indiscretions can occur in any sports organization and unfavorable publicity often results. One of the worst mistakes that a media relations practitioner can make is to give additional publicity to bad news by attempting to deny or explain the problem (Helitzer, 2000). In one-to-one communication, a dialogue can exist and a general conclusion as to the truth can be reached. However, mass media do not operate on a one-to-one basis.

It is certain that only part of the audience who saw or heard the original story will hear or see the rebuttal. Thus, the part of the audience who received only the rebuttal will begin to seek additional information and add impetus to the "crisis." Furthermore, those who received only the original story often remain unaffected by the rebuttal.

Too often, sport organizations attempt to use media for free advertising. If you want to serve the media, provide what they need: news. Your task as the sport marketer is to make the information you have, look and sound interesting and newsworthy. This could be a new product being introduced, announcements of new sales records, or even promotions and awards for company personnel. Traditionally, sport marketers provide much of their information to the media in the form of press releases.

PRESS RELEASES

Used by commercial, amateur, and collegiate sport organizations for many years, the press release has become a familiar tool for dealing with the media. It has become the most common form of communication in the sport industry. Several authors (Fox and Levin, 1993; Helitzer, 2000; Irwin, Sutton & McCarthy, 2002; Yudkin, 1994) have presented criteria regarding successful press releases.

The press release must be written in a style that conforms to the style of the particular media even though releases are generally not used exactly as received. The journalist must present the information in a way that attracts audience attention. For electronic media, it is crafted into a usable form by the media, and for newspapers it is redesigned to fit the specific space allotted. In both situations, the release should be written in a style commonly referred to as the "inverted pyramid" (Helitzer, 2000; Yudkin, 1994).

> A good news release has three parts: the significance (headline), the essence (lead), and the details (tail).

When scanning a newspaper, people want to see if a story is important to them prior to spending the time to read it. A headline is the first thing the reader will notice. There is some disagreement about whether a press release should have a headline attached. A recommendation would be to supply the headline and allow the reporter to make an editorial decision. In the electronic media, the people listen to the lead-in and make decisions about the relevance of the topic.

A standard element with all press releases is to identify the name of your organization, phone number, and an appropriate contact person in the upper left-hand corner of the first page. The piece must include the essentials of who, what, when, why, where, and how. This should be accomplished in the first paragraph. The media can then decide if the story is worth attention. The first paragraph also may account for all the space the story is allotted in the paper. Thus, the news release must include the details of the story or event in descending order of importance. Writing in this style (inverted pyramid) will more closely match the style of the reporter and will make it more likely that the information will appear in the media.

It is clear that simply grinding out releases is a costly waste of time and money. Helitzer (2000) and Irwin et al. (2002) report that only about 10% of the information received by daily publications through press releases is ever used. These data clearly indicate that most press releases never appear in print, and many are never even read as the news media sort through daily stacks of releases in order to select those stories they believe to be of most interest or benefit to their clients.

The quality of presentation has a bearing upon whether or not a release is used, and competition is intense. One method of improving the chances that a release will be used is to meet the standards expected in preparing and delivering the story. Some of the most critical areas in meeting these standards are the following (Helitzer 2000; Irwin et al., 2002; Yudkin, 1994):

1. All news releases should be double-spaced on white paper; use $8\,^1/_2$ by 11 inch paper; use only one side of each sheet of paper (Helitzer, 2000; Yudkin, 1994). If the information is sent via electronic transfer, spacing is unimportant as the information will be reformatted upon receipt.

2. Minimum margins of one inch on the sides and two inches at the top and bottom should be provided on each page (Helitzer, 2000).

3. The organization's name, address, and telephone number should appear on the release. Corporate stationary is acceptable, but the information can also be included in the upper left-hand corner of plain paper (Helitzer, 2000; Yudkin, 1994).

4. It is essential that the release contain the name of a "contact" person in the sport organization. This should include full name, position title, address, e-mail address, and phone number. News is a 24-hour business, and timely follow-up is an important feature for reporters and editors (Helitzer, 2000; Yudkin, 1994).

5. The words "For Immediate Release" and the date should appear on the upper right-hand corner of the first page on almost all releases. An exception would be stories on future events or quotes from a yet-to-be-presented speech (Helitzer, 2000; Yudkin, 1994).

6. There is considerable debate over whether or not you should write a headline for the release. Helitzer (2000) indicates that a good headline assists the news organization with routing the information and can catch the attention of an editor, spurring more reading. However, both Helitzer (2000) and other

authorities (Mullin, Hardy, and Sutton, 2000) indicate that headlines supplied by the sports organization are rarely used.

7. Arrange paragraphs in their descending order of importance. This is known in the trade as the "inverted pyramid." Each succeeding paragraph should contain information that is less crucial than the preceding one. This style facilitates editorial decisions and enables the newspaper to cut the story to meet its space needs (Helitzer, 2000; Yudkin, 1994).

8. The essential facts and story line must be included in the first paragraph (Yudkin, 1994). According to Helitzer (2000), the editor will only read the first two paragraphs in making preliminary decisions about running or rejecting your release. Therefore, the first paragraph must include the five Ws: who, what, when, where, and why. This is part of the lead for the story and is used to bring the editor (and readers) into the remaining part of the story.

9. Use short sentences because they are more readable and understandable than longer ones. Depending upon the classification of words used, the length of the sentence should seldom exceed 17 words. Sentences that incorporate technical terms, figures, unusual names, or places must be short to ensure clarity and understanding. Paragraphs should be "purposely" short for easier reading (Helitzer, 2000).

10. All pages should be numbered at the top, and at the bottom of every page except the last one, use the word "More." You should also mark the end of the story by the word "End" or a series of encircled ### marks (Helitzer, 2000; Irwin et al., 2002; Yudkin, 1994).

Other useful tips for getting press releases into the media have been provided by both authors. When distributing press releases to the Sports Editor, the editor's name should also be included so that the person performing those functions will open it. Distribution times are very important because the print/broadcast deadline of the receiver can affect whether the release is available for use. If you personally deliver a news release, try to avoid the front desk and present your release directly to the person who will make the decision on its use. Sports marketers must become familiar with the specific needs of different media outlets and their preferred method of receiving information. With advances in technology, most press releases are distributed electronically through e-mail distribution lists. With one click of the mouse, a press release can be sent to hundreds of media outlets simultaneously. The following section examines of the needs of the various media sources that may be used in the sport marketing field.

> A file of contacts should be formulated and kept in the media relations office so that essential information can be sent to an appropriate publication at any time.

NEWSPAPERS AND MAGAZINES

Media Outlets

Although newspapers have continued to be a mainstay of American culture, magazines in sport, health, and fitness and other publications that carry featured sports stories have experienced phenomenal growth in the past several decades. Almost

Sport marketing directors should become acquainted with the local media.

all segments of the sport industry have specialized publications. Newspapers and magazines are not imposed upon readers; the reader purchases or reads one that someone else has purchased. Thus, at the outset, there is some assurance of readiness to accept or expose oneself to the content. Generally, readers are interested in the content, and most influential citizens make it a practice to read current newspapers and sport magazines (Irwin et al., 2002). Because these publications often are read at leisure, readers generally have time to digest the content of the items read and to formulate at least tentative opinions.

Sport marketing directors should make a point to get to know the publishers, the CEO, the editor, the editorial page editor, and finally the managing editor. This personal contact is critical to your long term relationship.

You also want to determine which day or days are best for particular stories. Most authorities suggest that you chart the calendar for appropriate and inappropriate days based on the daily content of a publication and plan accordingly.

If possible, provide photographs to accompany press releases.

As a rule, magazines usually devote more space to stories than do newspapers. Furthermore, magazines provide more specific material for the reader, so the impact of any story may be enhanced. Magazine articles also have a longer life than that of newspaper stories. Most people throw their newspapers away after reading them whereas they tend to keep magazines longer and often pass them on to colleagues and friends, thus prolonging the impact.

A common complaint from newspaper and magazine editors is that the purpose of some sport organizations is to seek free advertising. Experienced media personnel are quick to recognize this tactic, which severely strains relationships. Another familiar complaint is that sport marketers often attempt to color or censor the material. Editorial personnel, on the other hand, rightly believe that it is their duty to the readers to remove any bias that may have been included. Finally, the sport marketer must never attempt to use influence or pressure tactics to get an item in or out of the paper. Although this has been attempted where event sponsors have threatened to withdraw advertising from publications that did not give substantial media coverage to a sponsored event, the practice is considered unethical.

Many sport teams and events utilize the media to enhance their properties. In this process, sport managers often secure media outlets (newspapers and television stations/networks) as sponsors. This allows the sport organization to "leverage" the media for coverage. Because media coverage is vital to sport organizations, sponsorship benefits (i.e., on-site signage, tickets) are often provided to media outlets in exchange for advertising space in their paper or on their network. This exchange (often called "value-in-kind") benefits the sport organization because it offsets the cost of advertising and it benefits the media outlet through preferential access to event or team coverage (Irwin, et al., 2002). In some situations, the sport manager may also extend the advertising options to other sponsors (sometimes called a pass-through).

Many stories and releases are printed because they include an exciting photograph. Sports are action-packed activities, and high-quality photographs can catch the attention of editors and readers alike. A glossy-finish picture with no more than two or three persons in the picture is preferred. You should identify photographs by typing the information about the event and all people in the picture on the lower half of a standard sheet of paper; then paste the upper half of the paper to the back of the photograph so that the caption material will drop down below the picture when it is withdrawn from the envelope. Although "sticky notes" have become standard office fare, they often fall off photographs and render the information useless. For digital photos, the information can be included with the image or on a separate attachment.

Yudkin (1994) indicated that the major causes of rejection can be traced to common errors or omissions. She felt that many stories were poorly written and contained "inconsistencies in tense, person and voice" (p. 167). If stories or press releases are continually rejected, arrange to have a conference with the editor, reporter, or others involved to determine any problems that may exist. The stated purpose of this meeting should be to improve your service to the media, and it is hoped that the conference will result in a more positive relationship between your organization and the print media.

Yudkin (1994) continued to point out problems with many press releases. She noted that companies often overuse meaningless superlatives such as "best" and "newest" (p. 166). These materials cannot be distinguished from advertising and therefore usually conflict with traditional editorial policies. On occasion, some materials are obviously exaggerated or contain apparent inaccuracies.

Did you know . . . ?

Golf is the fastest growing sport in America today with women constituting 49% of all new golfers. At a recent women's business seminar, it was suggested that any woman working toward an advanced career in the corporate world should consider taking up golf at the same time she starts her graduate studies.

Of course, newspapers and magazines are also valuable in calling attention to other forms of communication such as forthcoming speeches, event, radio, or television programs. It is through this avenue that many sport marketers encounter the electronic media. Because radio and television are instantaneous communication media, they present special needs to which the sport marketer must attend.

RADIO

Sport marketers can use radio in a variety of ways. Probably the most common is for a team to broadcast its games over an official radio network. These distribution outlets are important in providing the game to fans who cannot attend in person or to those who enjoy the casual atmosphere of listening to sports events without visual cues or while traveling to the event site.

As an example, ESPN Radio Network provides 24 hours of sport programming per week, 7 days per week through 700 affiliates. They also have introduced Podcasting with downloadable MP3 formatted content.

TELEVISION

From the Olympic Games to a local coach's show, sport marketers will encounter television in many aspects of their work. Competition in the television industry increased markedly in the 1990s with over 150 new cable networks were established, and 400 new stations came into existence. From the addition of the Fox Sports Network as a competitor to ESPN to ESPN's addition of ESPN 2, the competition is fierce in the sport broadcast industry. Cross-ownership of cable and networks has produced some interesting programming choices. For example, Disney owns ESPN (and the entire sector of ESPN outlets) and ABC television. In this environment, viewers could see the first two rounds of golf's US Open on ESPN and the final two rounds on ABC. Australia's Rupert Murdock owns News Corp. and its vast media outlets in Australia, Star Network in Asia, Fox Sport Network and the Speed Channel in the US, Britain's cable network BSkyB in addition to a multitude of European sports networks sport properties. Thus, doing extensive background research in this environment is essential.

Regular network distribution is also changing. Pay-per-view has become available for regional broadcast of sports events. All of the major networks produce and telecast a variety of games on any given day. However, the local affiliates of the network select the contest that they feel will have the broadest appeal in the area. Yet because the other games are also available, the viewer can, for a fee, view other games via cable with a few flips of a switch. All of the professional leagues have per-per view options and in 2003 the NFL launched its own network. After two years of operation, the NFL Network was distributed in the US, Canada, and Mexico reaching 58 million households. DirecTV (also owned by Rupert Murdock) added its "Super fan" platform to its existing Sunday Ticket in 2005 which allowed for real interactive viewing of NFL games. The system allows viewers to watch up to eight games simultaneously with switchable audio and provides real-time statistics. The increase in this

> To get your sport event on television, contact the programming director and present a proposal for your event's coverage.

format has occurred because there are few, if any, additional costs to the producer, and a limited hassle for the distribution; the consumer gets the desired product at a reasonable price.

Sports programming has increased 500% over the past 15 years primarily due to the increase in the available program sources (Stotlar, 2000). The types of programming that are traditionally available include regularly scheduled contests (NFL, NHL, MLB, NBA, college games, motor sports, and horse racing), made-for-TV events (X Games, WWE, and celebrity sport events), and sport anthology or talk shows (NFL films, ESPN's *Outside the Lines*, etc.). The New York Jets, Pittsburgh Steelers and the Philadelphia Eagles (NFL) have developed television programming (either wholly owned or leveraged with their media partners) aimed directly at the youth market. Their programs seek to create the new generation of fans by targeting kids with animated players and contests linked to through their web site. The programs are not positioned as profit centers but rather investments in growing future market share and brand building (Kaplan, 2004). The clear trend in the industry is for media outlets to "develop an equity position" in (read that—own) sporting events ("Steve Risser: The Interview," 1997). ESPN controls all of the details of the X Games and therefore can shape the content to provide the best programming. Companies like the International Management Group own their own television production companies as well as events so that they can protect the interests of their sponsor and athlete clients.

If you want to have your event covered on television, the process is quite complicated. However, an overview may be helpful. To obtain coverage, you have to make the content you have look like what the networks need. Television stations must pay for all programming; even reruns of *Friends* cost approximately $1 million per episode. What you can do is demonstrate to them that your event may be better and cheaper. Remember, your task is to prove it.

The first step is to contact the programming director, not the sports person. When the contact is made, you will need to present a proposal for the coverage of your event. In general, you there will be a lead time of approximately 6 to 8 months, 12 if you are trying to obtain coverage on a network affiliate. As with most sport marketing areas, the sport marketer must be prepared. Some of the information that you will need to know includes data about television programming. For instance, you must know the difference between *ratings* and *share*.

The Nielsen ratings have long been the benchmark for measuring television-viewing patterns across the United States. The system is based on a selection of 4,000 households equipped with a "people meter." This device records the viewing patterns of the household. The resulting data are transformed into ratings and shares. *Ratings* represent the percentage of the total television households (approx. 93 million in the United States) that are tuned to a particular program. *Share*, on the other hand, is the percentage of those sets in use [at that specific time] which are tuned in to a given program. To be successful, your event must be able to deliver competitive ratings and share for the station.

The outline of your proposal should include the following points:

- Explanation of the event;

- Benefits to the station—previous rating/share;

- Level of involvement—production, wild footage, telecast only;

- Your facilities—camera hookups, knowledge of staff; and

- People and organizations in control—time/date, during event timing and running.

Although the number of programming and outlet sources has increased, so has the competition across sport. However, with a lot of hard work, it is possible to present your event on television.

Media Relations During a Crisis

Although the scope of this chapter does not allow complete coverage of how to work with the media during a crisis, some attention seems warranted. Sport organizations must manage the flow of information during a crisis to protect the reputation that the company has worked diligently to create. Mangers must direct both the actual crisis and the public's perception of the crisis. The first step in this process entails the establishment of a crisis management team (Young, 1996). This team should have one designated person who will have the ultimate responsibility to control all information provided for the public and serve as the conduit for all information coming in to the organization. In some instances, this person is referred to as the "gatekeeper" (Caywood and Stocker, 1993; Young, 1996). Depending on the team director's public speaking skills and media savvy, this person may or may not be the spokesperson for the group. The crisis management team comprises the top management within the organization. For example, the USOC "Controversy" team for the Olympic Games included the USOC president, executive director, *chef de mission* (head of the US delegation), director of public relations, and other staff as specified (United States Olympic Committee, 1996). Essentially, the role of the crisis management team is to "plan, execute, and then evaluate" (Caywood and Stocker, 1993, p. 411).

The crisis management plan should be more than a list of policies, procedures, and actions; it should reflect the full scope of organizational considerations regarding a potential crisis. Once the members of the team have been designated, the team director should select the spokesperson. Depending on the background and experience of this person, some additional training would most likely be appropriate. This training can assist the person in remaining calm, fielding and responding to questions from reporters, and crafting answers that will best serve the organization while simultaneously accommodating the media.

One of the responsibilities of the team director is to prepare and distribute the actual crisis plan. The plan should include the tasks for each member of the team and the sequence of actions required. Implementing the plan depends heavily on the equipment and facilities accessible. For dealing with a crisis in close proximity to corporate headquarters, Caywood and Stocker (1993) have suggested that following: the "command center should be equipped with computers, modems, fax machines, copier, tape recorder, numerous telephones, pads of paper, pens, pencils, stationary, envelopes and a paper shredder" (p. 416). Other information that would be beneficial would be an organizational chart; a corporate contact sheet with names, addresses, and phone numbers of all key employees; and a copy of the updated database of media contacts. Consideration should also be given to creating a crisis kit that could be carried by key personnel who might be required to travel off-site to handle company problems. In this case, the computers should be portables with e-mail and fax capabilities as well as a small printer.

Once the crisis has been defused, a thorough evaluation should be conducted immediately. "It is critical that all elements of the plan area [be] analyzed to determine the effectiveness of each in resolving the situation" (Caywood and Stocker, 1993, p. 14). These actions have been found to be extremely constructive in preparing for and managing future crises.

Chapter Summary

Media relationships are one of the most important factors in designing marketing communications. While the primary goal is the provision of accurate information for all media sources, the trend in the sport environment is for the media relations director to take a lead role in shaping the corporate image and brand. In describing the new role of an NFL Communications Director, Schoenfeld (2005) said that a decade ago the role of the PR director in the league was to provide news stories, statistics and injury reports; but today's Communication Director takes a more proactive approach and helps shape the image of the franchise with the fans and the media.

Productive media relationships require sophisticated skills and the highest of ethical standards. This mandates a high level of service, well organized press conferences, professional quality written material, and the development of personal relationships across all media outlets. Internet, radio and television programming are evolving in new directions, and top sport marketers will need to be current with technology and trends. As programming and outlet sources change, so will the competition across sport. Yet, with hard work, your marketing functions can be enhanced through effective media relations.

CASE STUDY CHAPTER 12

Media Relations in Sport

Rationale

Interaction with the media is critical for every sport organization. In collegiate sports, the athletes are amateurs and just learning the power of the media. As a sport marketer in the collegiate ranks it may be part of your responsibilities to assist athletes in handling situations involving the media. Several instances occur each year where athletes are interviewed by the media and make a less-than-positive impression. The purpose of this case/exercise is for students to develop a training module that could be used in the college setting to assist athletes in dealing with the media.

Continued on next page

(continued)

Charge

Several instances occur each year where college athletes are interviewed by the media and make a less-than-positive impression. As a sport marketer your role is to utilize the media to make favorable impressions. The purpose of this case/exercise is for your team to develop a training module that could be used in the college setting to assist athletes in dealing with the media.

Teaching points

- Defining the elements to be included
- Athlete appearance
- Addressing the media by name or proper salutation
- Balance between the camera and the interviewer
- Vocabulary choice
    Think before you speak
    Silence is better than "um"
    Be positive; do not make negative remarks about teammates/program
- Deflecting controversial questions
- Deferring to University officials or coaches
- Practice sessions with cameras
- Critiques by athletes and department personnel

QUESTIONS FOR STUDY

1. What are the essential steps in obtaining electronic (television or radio) coverage of your sport event?
2. What are some of the differences between the impact of newspaper and magazine articles that would affect sport marketing?

LEARNING ACTIVITIES

1. Contact a sport organization and obtain permission to attend a press conference. Take notes and compare them with material in the text.
2. Working with a local high school and city newspaper, attend a sport event and write a press release after the event. Contact the local newspaper and deliver your release. Go over the content with a local college Sport Information Director and discuss the quality of the release.

PROFESSIONAL ASSOCIATIONS AND ORGANIZATIONS

College Sports Information Directors of America/ COSIDA
    http://www.cosida.com/

SUGGESTED READINGS

Irwin, R. L., Sutton, W. A., & McCarthy, L. M. (2002). *Sport promotion and sales management.* Champaign, IL: Human Kinetics.

Chapter Thirteen

MARKETING THROUGH ENDORSEMENTS AND SPONSORSHIPS

Overview

The purpose of this chapter is to describe how sport organizations can enhance their marketing efforts through athlete endorsements and sport sponsorships. Although non-sport companies have long used sport personalities and sports events to sell products, the contents of this chapter will be confined to the use of such endorsements and sponsorships by sport organizations. James (2002) noted that "people don't usually distinguish between sponsorships and endorsements and they are very different. Sometimes they can serve the same purpose, but a lot of times they don't. It all comes down to what your company's objectives are."

As explained in the sections of the text on marketing and promotional mix, the sport marketer must incorporate all available resources to satisfy the sport consumer. That process can be expedited through opinion leaders, individuals who have specialized knowledge of your sport product or service and who can influence others in the purchasing process. Poole (2005) found that 88% of consumers make product recommendations to their friends. Pride and Ferrell (2003) noted that opinion leaders are most effective when consumers in the target market share values and attitudes similar to those of the opinion leader. While one age group may find golfer Arnold Palmer trustworthy, a younger group may trust skateboarder Tony Hawk. The athlete must connect with and be readily recognizable by the target audience.

This has been one of the main forces for the successful use of action athlete-endorsers in sport. The growth of action sports across the globe has been tremendous and many companies have followed the trend by signing niche athletes to promote their products. Sports such as inline skating, skateboarding, climbing, and even paintball have all seen double-digit increases in participation. The average snowboarder spends more than $400 per year on equipment and accessories (Extreme Sports, 2005).

Sport marketers have used individual athletes through sport product endorsements with the hope that their endorsement will result in increased sales. For example, Australian Olympic swimming star Ian Thorpe helped push sales of adidas swimming suits on a global basis after gold medal performances in both the 2000 and 2004 Games (Clark, 2004). This can be an effective component of sport marketing when matched to target markets and appropriately implemented with consumers.

The use of sponsorship marketing by sport corporations as a component of their corporate brand-management strategy is also prevalent in the sport industry. US spending on sponsorship exceeds $12 billion per year with worldwide spending over $30 billion ("Sponsorship Spending," 2004). Clearly, this represents an effective marketing element for sport and non-sport companies alike. This chapter will provide an overview of the use of both endorsements and sponsorship in accomplishing corporate marketing objectives.

Opinion Leaders and Endorsements

Many sport companies use endorsers and opinion leaders because of their knowledge and power within certain groups. Brooks (1998) indicated that companies could use athletes as endorsers in four fundamental modes:

Explicit Mode—the athlete directly endorses the product.

Implicit Mode—the athlete exhibits product use.

Imperative Mode—the athlete recommends the product.

Co-present Mode—the athlete simply allows his or her image to appear conjointly with the product.

Research showed that sport celebrity endorsements positively affect Gen Y market word-of-mouth marketing and brand loyalty (Bush, Martin & Bush, 2004). Skateboarder Tony Hawk brings in over $10 million in endorsements most significantly from his Pro Skater video game. In 2003, it was the #1 sports video game and #3 seller of all video games. Hawk obtained his fame principally through the X-Games, an event developed by ESPN and broadcast in 145 different countries. All of the major shoe companies use coaches as opinion leaders. College coaches have been paid as much as $1,000,000 per year to outfit their team in specific shoes. The considerable economic value generated from the national television coverage of college football and basketball games provides the incentive. The exposure achieved through this endeavor comes not only in the arena but also through a company's support of the coach's summer sports camps where clothing for the coaching staffs, T-shirts, posters, and related merchandise can influence the impressionable youth market.

Youth programs represent the grass roots of the sport shoe market. If you want to move shoes, the youth market is the place to be. Establishing the purchasing patterns of customers early in their lives is a powerful tool in marketing. Both Nike and adidas selected this tactic in the late 1990s when they entered into agreements with several high school basketball programs. Typically, each school would receive about $2,500 in sport product for players and the coaches would be outfitted in company apparel. The companies' strategy centered on the hope that not only would the players influence their peers, but they would also accessorize with additional company products.

It is not just the coaches and athletes of organized team sports who can be incorporated into endorsement as part of sport marketing plans. In the cheerleading and performance-dance industry, specialty companies often provide free shoes and apparel to the leading groups in the nation in an effort to influence the style selection and purchasing of other participants.

The manufacturers typically put the coaches under contract to guarantee specified actions and to protect the value of the endorsement. A typical contract calls for the following:

1. Give the company use of their name, nickname, initials, autograph, voice, video or film portrayals, facsimile signature, photograph, likeness and image.

2. Make the company shoes available to players and assistant coaches as well as cheerleaders, game personnel, and the team mascot.

3. Film a TV commercial and participate in two photo sessions the results of which may be exploited by the company throughout the world in any manner determined by the company.

4. Make eight promotional appearances in the United States and one abroad, designated by the company

5. Attend a company party and/or annual retreat.

6. Assist in the production of a promotional video on topics such as basketball fundamentals, physical conditioning, nutrition, academics, drug and alcohol education and preparation for the real world.

7. Comment favorably upon the use of company products whenever possible.

8. Wear a sport jacket, sweater, or shirt bearing the company logo prominently displayed during all college basketball games and at other appropriate public activities.

9. Give the company four complimentary tickets to each game.

10. $5,000 will be deducted from the contract if team members do not achieve a 2.25 mean grade-point average each year. (Brubaker, 1991, p. A1)

Other tactics of using opinion leaders in sport have included product sampling and prototype testing as additional ways to receive input. Golf is one of the areas where this is quite visible. One of the best reasons to sign an endorsement with a PGA player is to get feedback on product performance. You want to "get a player that can give you the right feedback in R&D and wants to be involved in R&D. The information you get from a pro is so different from what you get from a robot" (Seligman, 2005, p. 10). Product testing always generates a great deal of interest in the product and can be tracked to indicate the overall effect on sales. According to Seligman (2005, p. 10) "Tour presence justifies a company's product in the eyes of the consumers." Often a product new to the market or even a prerelease prototype is distributed to key opinion leaders within an industry. In another example, Reebok often provides prerelease shoe models to top sales personnel in selected sporting goods stores to seed sales and generate product interest. This develops loyalty and can provide the company with reliable feedback on its products with minimal costs.

The use of individual athletes to endorse products has been a marketing practice in sport for decades. As early as the 1936 Berlin Olympics, adidas provided track star Jesse Owens with free shoes. Historically, the line between professional and amateur athletes was finely drawn. If an athlete was paid or received money from sport, he or she was a professional; if the athlete received nothing, he or she was an amateur. All of this has changed in Olympic sports, and although the Olympic Games offer no prize money, the athletes certainly collect from their endorsement deals. In 1981, the Olympic rules were modified. The International Olympic Committee (IOC) changed its regulations and allowed each international federation to establish its own standards on the receipt of monies and the effect on eligibility. At this time, the IOC no longer even refers to athletes as amateurs, but as eligible athletes. Many of the shoe and apparel companies provide cash incentives tied to medals won at the Olympic Games.

Probably one of the best lessons about individual athlete endorsements for a sports company was the 1992 "Dan and Dave" campaign initiated by Reebok prior to the Barcelona Olympic Games. Shoe manufacturer Reebok used potential US Olympic decathletes (Dan O'Brien and Dave Johnson) to promote new models of their Pump training shoe. The ad copy ("To be settled in Barcelona") attempted to predict who would win the gold medal. However, O'Brien failed to make the US team because of a disastrous performance at the US Olympic trials. With over $30 million in the ad campaign, Reebok reworked their strategy with a sympathy-centered theme on the gallant efforts of athletes who sometimes fall short of victory. The result was a bonanza of publicity worth several times the advertising costs. Incidentally, a Reebok-sponsored athlete, Robert Zmelik from the Czech Republic, did win the 1992 decathlon gold medal. O'Brien not only made the 1996 Olympic team, but also set several world records in the interim and won the gold medal at the 1996 Atlanta Olympic Games. In 2003, Reebok signed Yao Ming, the Shanghai 7' 6" Chinese star to a multimillion dollar contract. Reebok's VP of marketing stated "We see Yao as the key to unlocking growth in China" (Playing the global game, 2004). These moves provided Reebok with substantial media exposure and maximized Reebok's marketing campaign with more "authentic" marketing and endorsements.

For many years, shoe companies engaged in bidding wars in an attempt to secure the next Michael Jordan. As a result, endorsement contracts for some players, particularly those in the NBA, escalated into the millions of dollars. However, weak shoe sales and a change in fashion trends to "brown shoes" (Doc Martins, Vans, Sketchers, etc.) caused a decline in athletic footwear sales in the late 1990s (Hofman, 1999, p. 33–36). In response, many shoe companies substantially curtailed their player endorsements. Reebok went from having over 130 NBA players under contract to having fewer than 10 during the 1999 season. Nike and adidas followed those tactics (Bernstein, 1998). However, a reemergence of the shoe market and the NBA in the early 2000s saw Nike sign rising star LeBron James for over $90 million and the "urban influence" of Allen Iverson (Reebok) reversed the decline.

In some instances, athletes may be able to earn more from endorsements than from salary. The leading endorser in world motor sports is Michael Schumacher. The seven-time Formula 1 driving champion reportedly earns a salary of $48 million from Ferrari and another $96 million from endorsements and merchandising. It may be of interest to note that Formula 1 drivers own the sponsorship rights to their helmet, whereas the team owner has the rights to signage on the car and the driver's uniform. Several of the F1 drivers make as much as $500,000 from their helmet sponsorships (East, Ronchin & Smith, 2000; "The Celebrity 100," 2004).

Late NASCAR driver Dale Earnhardt won seven Winston Cup Championships and in 1996 accumulated $2.5 million in winnings. However, by licensing his own name and likeness, he was able to generate an additional $8 million in endorsements earnings (Hagstrom, 1998). In a 1998 personal appearance on shopping channel QVC, Earnhardt sold $741,266 in licensed merchandise in a single evening (Spanberg, 1998). Earnhardt's sales accounted for almost 40% of 1998 NASCAR sales (Hagstrom). With his untimely death at the 2001 Daytona 500, Earnhardt merchandise became the sport's most coveted merchandise. NASCAR's youngest champion, Jeff Gordon, was able to generate $5 million in licensing profits after his 1998 Winston Cup Championship (Spiegel, 1998).

Michael Jordan established the benchmark for endorsement earnings. In his last year of NBA play, Jordan earned $47 million from product and company endorsements. Even with his retirement from basketball, Michael Jordan continues to derive profits from licensed merchandise. A cable-based TV channel, the Home Shopping Network, interrupted its programming to air Jordan's retirement announcement and proceeded to offer Jordan-related merchandise ranging from autographed basketballs to limited-edition trading cards. This event, which immediately followed his press conference, grossed over $1 million.

Tiger Woods, arguably the successor to Jordan, signed a contract with Nike immediately following his final amateur match. The Nike contract (5 year, $40 million) was one of the highest in sport endorsement history (Lombardo, 1998). Tiger Woods renegotiated his Nike contract to 5 year, $100 million after the 2000 season which featured wins in the PGA Championship, US Open, British Open, and Canadian Open. Current annual salary and endorsements earnings for Woods include: $25 million with Nike, $7 million from General Motors, appearance fees of $9 million, Accenture $8 million, EA Sports $7.5 million, Upper Deck $7 million, American Express $7 million, On-course earnings for 2004 of $6.4 million, Disney $5 million, TLC Laser Eye Centers $3 million, Warner books $2.5 million, and TAG-Heuer $2 million for a total of $89.4 million (Sirak, 2005).

The question remains, does the sponsorship of an individual athlete provide an adequate return on investment? Tiger's success on the tour helped push sales of Nike golf equipment from $100 million in 2000 to $300 million in 2003. When he switched to a Nike golf ball their market share went from 1% to 3% in three months and the following year to 10% (James, 2002). Trek's sponsorship of Lance Armstrong resulted in significant increases in sales of their $4000 tour model bike after Armstrong's 6th Tour de France win and in fact pushed the total market for the sale of road bikes to record levels (Company cashes in on Lance, 2005) Electronic Arts signed Woods for a video game bearing his name after his victory at the 1997 Masters and has had considerable success with the product for many years.

It has been more difficult for women to secure equivalent levels of individual endorsements. Only Reebok's commitment to Venus Williams in 2001 for an estimated $40 million over five years has approached the level secured by her male counterparts. There is, however, a trend for companies seeking women athletes as product and service endorsers. According many executives, women athletes are far less likely to generate negative publicity and are more accessible and personable with consumers. They will actually sign autographs and spend time with fans. In a 2003 study, Stone, Joseph, and James found that "endorsement opportunities for female athletes are growing and that elite female athletes may now be able to effectively compete with male athletes for some of the lucrative endorsement deals that have traditionally gone to men" (2003, p. 101). Leading women in the endorsement field include tennis stars Venus & Serena Williams, WNBA standout Lisa Leslie, golfer Annika Sorenstam and Anna Kournikova, a cross-over tennis-fashion celebrity who earns $14 million from her endorsement deals even though she never won a WTA tournament. Most corporations play down the "sex sells" controversy surrounding some women endorsers and instead portray their female endorsers as role models and athletically talented representatives of the company who can connect with consumers.

Unfortunately, some companies devalue women as athletes and focus on their physical attractiveness. According to Kaufman, "How a woman looks still matters in endorsements and just about everything else. It's not right, but it's reality" (Kaufman, 1998, p. 48). Golfer Natalie Gulbis created a similar controversy with her 2005 calendar and layout in FHM magazine. Many considered the calendar to be too risqué but the LPGA was also pushing the attractiveness of many of its top players. Former LPGA commissioner Ty Votaw said if Natalie was comfortable posing, they would support that decision. Research has shown that the more "feminine" and more attractive women endorsers received more endorsement opportunities than their less attractive colleagues. However, recent studies have shown that highlighting the female athlete's skills and level of expertise correlated positively with consumer attitudes and purchase intentions (Fink, Cunningham, & Kensicki, 2004).

There is also a significant credibility problem with many athlete endorsers. Research indicated that over 79% of consumers thought athlete-endorsers added no value to the products they endorsed (Poole, 2005). Furthermore, Veltri's (1996) research indicated that most people believed the athletes were endorsing products just for the money and few people were able to match an athlete-endorser and the products that she or he endorsed. In general, basketball players were more often accurately recognized than were athletes in other sports, and male endorsers were more likely to be recognized than were female athletes.

Another phenomenon that has proven to be successful in the sport marketing industry is cross-promotion. If your sport enterprise sponsors an individual athlete and that athlete obtains other, non-sport endorsements, your company can receive increased exposure. Take for example, Nike's sponsorship of Michael Jordan. When Michael Jordan appeared on a Wheaties box, he was wearing Nike shoes and holding a Wilson basketball. In 1999, *Golf Digest* signed an agreement with Kmart Corporation to establish Golf Digest Accessory and Training Centers in all

Did you know . . . ?

The three major networks—ABC, NBC, and CBS—together showed 1,500 hours of sports in 1985, double what they programmed in 1960, with about 8 minutes of commercials an hour.

Kmart stores. Kmart agreed to sell licensed Golf Digest products including instructional videos and training aids, and Kmart agreed to purchase advertising in Golf Digest publications.

Endorsements with individual athletes do not exist without danger and controversy. One question that continues to cause controversy is "Who controls the rights?" Do team players have the right to select their own shoes, or do coaches have the power to demand that specific shoes be worn? Currently, the rights battle has been going to the player, but it will remain an issue for some time to come.

Another issue relates to organizational control. This has been particularly evident in the Olympic Games. During the 1992 Barcelona games, the US men's basketball team had uniforms sponsored by Champion, and individual players each had their own shoe contracts. However, the United States Olympic Committee had an agreement with Reebok for the medal presentation uniforms. Because the players had not signed the USOC agreement (requiring participants to wear the USOC-designated presentation apparel) and because wearing a Reebok logo conflicted with their shoe contracts, a serious problem arose. In the end, the players agreed to wear the Reebok uniforms, but unfolded the collar or otherwise covered the manufacturer's logo. Similarly with Formula One racing, the car owner has the rights to signage on the car and driver's suit yet, as mentioned above, the drivers own the rights to the helmet. Thus, conflicts can arise when drivers pursue sponsors that may conflict with the car's primary sponsor.

Almost all sports organizations (NCAA, the NFL, the NBA, Major League Baseball, and the IOC) have so-called "billboard rules" (Woodward, 1988). These rules limit the size and number of logos that can appear on uniforms and equipment. Even with the tight rules, many sport marketers find loopholes. At the Tour de France, the rules control the riders, but not their equipment cars; as a result, sponsors have literally covered the cars with logos and advertising.

Choosing an Athlete-Endorser

As noted earlier, the principle rationale for selecting an athlete-endorser is that person's status as an opinion leader. Martin (1996) noted, "The central issue for the manager is to pick an athlete spokesperson with the right set of characteristics who will best be able to produce the most favorable response from consumers" (p. 28). His research found that best endorsement value was generated from situations in which a high level of congruity existed between the image of the athlete and the image of the product. Moreover, for some products, certain sports would be more effective in producing positive consumer response than would others. This determination can only be made through extensive market research.

Martin (1996) suggested several steps needed for marketers to determine the right athlete for a product endorsement:

1. The image of the product must be assessed through market research with customers.

2. Marketers should then measure the image factors associated with a variety of sport activities.

3. Once the images of the product and the sport have been assessed, the marketer should select an athlete(s) from the sport that most closely matches the images of the product.

4. The final step would be to evaluate the athlete's ability to enhance the consumers' perception of the product.

According to Martin's (1996) research, "careful consideration of the perceived degree of fit between images of the product and images of the sport can significantly increase the positive evaluation of the endorsement by an athlete from the chosen sport" (p. 37).

Endorsement Trends

Although sport marketers can still benefit from individual athlete endorsements, the risk is high (e.g., Kobe Bryant, Latrell Sprewell, Mike Tyson). As noted earlier, Veltri (1998) indicated that the power of athletes in endorsing products has faltered. As a safeguard, many endorsement contracts have special clauses to cover instances in which a player or coach is involved in some horrid scandal. Converse's contract includes a special termination clause that indicated that Converse could terminate the agreement at any time if the person wears another manufacturer's product, commits any act that "tends to shock, insult or offend" the community, violates any league rule, or becomes "disabled/incapacitated and unable to perform." Thus, Converse terminated its relationship with Latrell Sprewell after he attacked his coach at a practice session in 1998. Players can recover from negative incidents. Sprewell went on to a successful career and a subsequent shoe endorsement after being traded to a different team. In 2004, NBA player Kobe Bryant was accused of sexually assaulting a women resulting in his endorsements being cancelled or simply not renewed. Once the case was settled, his major sponsors once again began using Kobe in their advertising.

As a result of the problems and risks associated with individual athlete endorsements, many sport organizations are considering sponsoring more events.

Sport marketers must consider both the rewards and the risks involved in selecting an athlete as an endorser.

Event Sponsorships

The initial question that must be addressed is whether a sport organization should use sponsorship in lieu of traditional advertising. Sponsorship offers a number of distinct advantages over more conventional advertising techniques. Sponsorship spending has grown at a rate three times that of advertising. Worldwide advertising increased at 6.4 percent in 2005 and US spending on advertising increased at a slightly slower pace of 5.3 percent reaching $200 billion. Advertising delivers a straightforward commercial message, whereas sponsorships connect with people through a different source. Within the sport industry, marketers must understand the role of sponsorship as a marketing tool.

Sponsorship involves a company being prepared to make a commitment and support an activity; it says the company is going to be more people oriented than advertising suggests. In several ways, sponsorship is longer lasting in the terms of its commitment. (International Events Group, 1992c, p. 7)

Sponsorship has been defined as "a cash and/or in-kind fee paid to a property (typically sports, arts, entertainment, or causes) in return for access to the exploitable commercial potential associated with that property" (Ukman, 2004, p. 154). Essentially, the primary goal of sponsorship is to augment marketing communication (Ferrand and Pagés, 1996). The sponsorship of sports activities ranges from local beach volleyball tournaments and fun runs to the Olympic Games. Deals range in scope from a $2,500 sponsorship of youth sport to the $85–100 million sponsorship of the 2008 Olympic Games. Collectively, these events can provide sport marketers with an array of opportunities to market their products and services. As outlined at the beginning of this chapter, this discussion of sponsorships will be limited to their use as marketing tools for sport organizations. Although they have been extremely successful and widely used by non-sport companies, that treatment will not be included in this text.

> Team and event sponsorships are becoming more common than individual-athlete deals.

Worldwide, corporate spending on sport sponsorship increased dramatically during the 1980s and 1990s. 2005 US spending on sponsorship was predicted to total $12.09 billion, up 9.6% over 2004 ("Sponsorship Spending," 2004). Contributing to this total were more than 80 companies that spent over $15 million each on sponsorship programs. Among the top 10 companies the only sport company was Nike at $190 million per year ("Sponsorship Spending," 2004). European corporations contributed $8.4 billion, followed by Pacific Rim countries with $5.8 billion, and Central/South America spent an additional $2.5 billion. Various other regional spending accounted for $1.6 billion, bringing the worldwide spending total to $30.4 billion ("Sponsorship Spending," 2004). This figure represents an increase of 8.8% above 2004 revenues ("Sponsorship Spending," 2004).

Numerous companies engage in sport sponsorship activities in almost every sport organization from local fitness centers and high schools to the Olympics and professional sport leagues. As the number of sports organizations desiring an affiliation with sponsors has grown, the leverage in the industry changed. This created a situation in which the sponsor could weigh the offers from competing organizations keep sponsorship prices down. As a result, during the early part of the decade, the momentum shifted from the sport organizations to the sponsoring corporations. In today's environment it is increasingly important for sport managers to be skilled in the methodologies and techniques of sponsorship as a marketing component. A successful sponsorship arrangement can serve as a positive marketing vehicle for any sport organization.

Similar to the research cited with individual athlete endorsements, McDonald (1998) evaluated perceptual fit between the image of a sport and that of a sponsoring company. His research investigated consumer reaction to terms such as sophisticated, rugged, exciting, and wholesome in relation to both companies and the sports considered for sponsorship. His research concluded that creating a good perceptual fit between the sport and a sponsor could contribute to brand equity for the sponsor (McDonald). Thus, the prevailing research (Martin 1996; McDonald, Fink et al., 2004) confirms that both sponsorships and endorsements are more effective if there is a high level of congruence between the image of the sport/athlete and the image of the corporation.

Stotlar (2004) provided a model that would serve sport marketers in the evaluation and implementation of sponsorship programs. The author recommends that the sponsorship be considered as part of the comprehensive assessment of corporate objectives. All too often question marketers ask is "What can sponsorship do for us?" A better question is "What do we need to do and can a sponsorship accomplish that objective?" As such, sponsorships should be selected with attention to specific criteria.

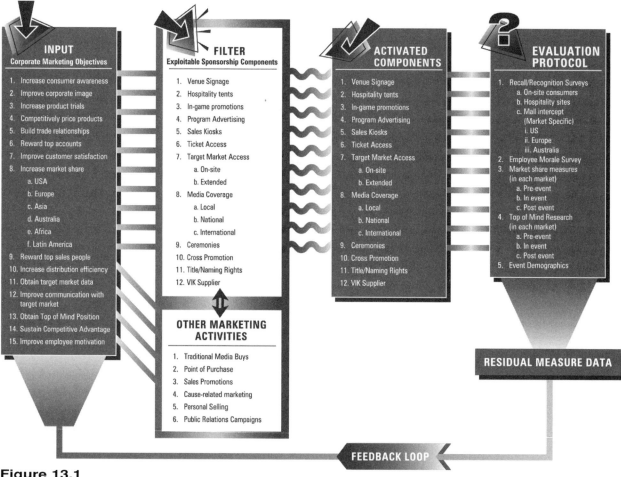

Figure 13.1
Sponsorship Evaluation Model.

From Stotlar, David K. "Sponsorship Evaluation: Moving from Theory toPractice". *Sport Marketing Quarterly*. Vol. 13, 1, March 2004.

Rationale for Pursuing Event Sponsorships

Sport organizations can buy into event sponsorship for a variety of marketing reasons. In the past, many organizations were attracted to sport properties to cultivate the social benefits. Sport executives could associate with star players; play in celebrity golf tournaments (FYI: the current price tag for a top PGA player to appear in a pro-am event is $100,000), and host parties for their friends in conjunction with the event. Although these reasons may still exist, their prominence has clearly decreased. In today's business environment, shareholders and boards of directors demand measured return on investment from sponsorship activities.

Thus, decisions to sponsor sport-related properties must be linked to business-related objectives of the company. You must "look at an event to help meet a marketing objective, then make sure it meets sales promotion, PR, and internal employee morale needs" (Ukman, 2004, p. 6). There must be a match between the organization's target market and the property's audience (or participation base). An obvious example of this can be seen in adidas' sponsorship of the Boston Athletic Association that owns and operated the Boston Marathon. In their deal ($400,000–900,000 per yr. –2010), adidas supplies 12,000 jackets and shoes for staff & volunteers, they get the right to put flyers in all participant race packets, display on-course signage, distribute logo blankets for the top finishers, and have exclusive sales of logo apparel at race headquarters. Because of its historical ties with soccer, adidas signed a sponsorship agreement with FIFA and the World Cup through 2014 for an estimated $351 million (Woodward, 2005). adidas executives estimate that their sales of World Cup-related products will increase their 2006 revenues by $135 million over 2004 earnings.

The participants and fans of those events clearly represent the core customers for adidas' many products. Sport companies must also look for direct product sales at sponsored events. Thus, adidas would be more inclined to sponsor a road race if it could access the participants through on-site sales points or obtain the event's database for future marketing initiatives. For the 2006 World Cup, adidas secured the rights as sole supplier of official merchandise.

Sponsorships have also been effective in promoting the image of the sponsor. Thus, Reebok, through its sponsorship of the NFL, NBA, and NHL could generate consumer impressions and further position the brand through "authentic" association with the leagues. Ferrand and Pagés (1996) proposed that sponsorship can be effectively used in image management. Companies can use sport sponsorship to (a) establish an image in the consumer's mind, (b) solidify an existing image, or (c) modify the consumer's image of the company. Companies must select rationally the appropriate event or group to sponsor in order to maximize the communication potential. Then, "the sponsor must consider the image of the event, the sponsor's present image, and the desired future image of the sponsor or its brand" (Ferrand and Pagés, 1996. p. 279). This was clearly evident when the Chief Marketing Officer of the PGA tour was asked about their sponsorships. Tom Wade noted that "companies are judged by the company they keep" [a slogan also used with the IOC TOP program some years ago] (IEG, 2004, p. 4). Wade went on to discuss the importance of a partnership between the organization and its sponsors. "Corporate relations are our life and blood" (p. 4). This is reflected in the fact that the PGA tour staff is 75% in service and 25% in sales. Wade said that with "more than 100 major companies as sponsors, we can't afford a lot of turnover because there aren't another 100 companies to replace them" (p. 4). The PGA also established a dedicated web site (http://www.pgamarketingcenter.com) to service their sponsors and attract new sponsor business. Along with Wade, many other industry experts support the aspect of relationship building in sponsorships. The Baltimore Ravens put a similar emphasis on sponsorship service at about 80% of their duties (Rocklitz, 2005).

However, changes in corporate expectations have mandated more utility from sponsorship associations. One company's director of sponsorships stated this point clearly when he said, "We are no longer satisfied with enhanced image; give us opportunities for on-site sales, well-developed hospitality packages and dealer tie-ins and we'll listen" (qtd. in International Events Group, 1992d, p. 5)

The key trend in today's sponsorship environment is activation. As a corporation seeking sponsorship opportunities, you must look beyond signage to strategies that connect with the consumer in meaningful ways. Activation has taken on many forms over the years, but it essentially means that the sponsorship connects the product directly with the consumer. Gatorade has been seen prominently on the sidelines for sports activities for more than 30 years. Their sponsorship of professional and college teams has provided them with an authenticity that would be impossible to replicate through traditional advertising.

Sport-related businesses, like most corporations, desire to be seen as community citizens with a responsibility to contribute to the well-being of the communities where they do business. In support of this concept is the message delivered by a special events manager, "Customers want companies that care about them, that give back to the community" (qtd. in International Events Group, 1992d, p. 5). As an example, a local bicycle shop could sponsor a triathlon to influence competitive riders and also could sponsor a child's bike safety class. These strategies are often tabbed "cause-related marketing." While there are many examples of sports companies supporting worthy causes, one of the most successful was Nike's support for the Lance Armstrong Foundation (cancer research). Many cause-related efforts fail because the company is really trying to use the cause for its own self-interest. Consumers can typically see through this rather easily. In Nike's case, the yellow bracelets (sold for $1 each) did not include the Nike swoosh or other marketing logos. Rather, Nike subtly showed their support by selling more than 50 million bracelets.

A close examination of the reasons your business should become involved in sport sponsorships is essential. Understanding how sponsorship activities can help accomplish your business goals is one of the key elements in selecting successful sponsorship opportunities. These must be specific to each event that the sport marketer intends to approach.

Did you know . . . ?

ESPN was launched in 1979 and by mid-1980 reached 4 million homes. By 1986, 37 million households subscribed.

Developing a Winning Strategy

The sponsorship relationship between your sport entity and event owners must include advantages to both parties whereby your product's market value and profits are increased and their event benefits as well. A key component in the success is the measurement of return on investment (ROI). Sport managers must be fully cognizant of the data with which to demonstrate the accomplishment of specified corporate objectives. For example, data indicate that 73% of NASCAR fans choose products of their sport's sponsors over others (Ukman, 2004).

These data should be provided by the event owner, but are occasionally collected by the sponsor. Sport organizations that use sponsorship as a marketing tool must be prepared to evaluate sponsorship in the same manner as other marketing efforts. "The general measurement mentality has been to simply transfer advertising metrics [the criteria against which objective are measured] and process to sponsorship without considering either the differences that the sponsorship environment requires" (Ukman, 2004, p. vii). Her four step approach includes, 1) setting objectives and baseline measures, 2) creating the measurement plan, 3) implementing the plan, and 4) calculating the return on the sponsorship.

You can also have professional market research firms collect the data for you. One such company is Joyce Julius and Associates, which conducts research in sponsor exposure and publishes the results in a publication titled *The Sponsor's Report* that measures logo time on televised sports broadcasts. The data showed that Tiger Woods' victory in the 2005 Masters garnered more than $10 million of television exposure for Nike during CBS' telecast. According to their research, logos for Nike, Nike One Ball, and Nike's Tiger Woods Collection were clearly seen on screen for a total of 30 minutes and four seconds. When compared to the estimated cost of a 30-second commercial during the CBS broadcast, Nike was credited with $10,824,000 of in-broadcast exposure value. Table 13.1 details the exposure earned by the corporate sponsors of Woods during the CBS final-round telecast.

One of the aspects of sponsorship that attract sport-related companies are its ability to reach consumers by breaking through the clutter in advertising. Marketing managers have used sponsorship as an avenue to present their message to consumers in a more relaxed atmosphere and to support their other marketing efforts. Sport events are also attractive because they can provide a cross-sectional exposure when compared to other marketing avenues available to the sport marketer (Stotlar, 2004).

Media attention is another important factor in selecting an event to sponsor. Good events have the potential to generate considerable media coverage. This type of message can be particularly effective because consumers typically see this in a different light than they see traditional advertising. Another related facet of media coverage and sponsorship is that if an event has a media sponsor, you can often obtain discounted or free coverage by tagging their promotional messages. Such a

Table 13.1
Calculated On-Screen Exposure Value.

	On-Screen Time	Exp. Value	Appearances
Buick	1:22	$492,000	34
Nike	18:46	6,756,000	08
Nike One Ball	:35	3,090,000	161
Tiger Woods Collection	2:43	978,000	58

Source: Joyce Julius and Associates, Ann Arbor MI.

situation exists with the annual Bolder Boulder road race in Boulder, Colorado. The local NBC affiliate and New Balance shoes sponsor the event. Not only does New Balance get sponsorship of the race, but it also receives logo presentation on all TV spots promoting the race. Similarly, New Balance can benefit from the televised coverage of the race, which will of course have several prominent sponsor banners strategically located for the cameras. Media coverage also provides a reliable and measurable method to calculate return on investment.

Although the number of times the sponsor's name was mentioned by the announcers, the column inches of print devoted to the event, and the number of times the corporation's banner was seen on national television are important, the raw data do not always reflect the whole picture. Take for example an announcer who, in the middle of a race, says, "Her Nike shoes have fallen apart, and she'll have to finish this race barefooted." What is the economic value of that? Other sport marketing research firms such as the Denver-based Bonham Group indicated that some of the calculations are based on rate-card advertising costs. Most major corporations purchase advertising at a substantial discount. Thus, some of the reported value assessments may be inflated.

Before undertaking a sponsorship, you should develop criteria for evaluating possible opportunities. This process has been discussed extensively (Irwin and Assimakopoulos, 1992; Mullin, Hardy, and Sutton, 1993; Stotlar, 1993). Irwin, Assimakopoulos, and Sutton (1994) provided an inventory detailing the typical factors to be considered as companies deliberate engaging in sponsorship activities:

- Budget—affordability, cost effectiveness, tax benefits

- Event management—past history, organizing committee

- Image—match to products and services offered

- Target market—demographics, geographical reach

- Communications—media exposure, audience size, and demographics

- Sponsor mix—match with other sponsor's products and image

- Level of involvement—title sponsor, in-kind supplier, exclusivity

- Other Opportunity—wholesaler tie-ins, on-site displays, signage, product sampling, merchandising.

It is critical that all of the components of the sponsorship agreement be detailed in a written contract. Many of the terms and elements provided in a sponsorship lack industry-wide standards, and any confusion must be minimized. If an event owner offers a sponsorship that can meet your criteria, is ethically grounded, and gives you service and data with which to justify continuation, sport sponsorships can be a successful marketing tool for sport organizations.

As with other sports organizations "marketing as a basic function and central dimension of the Olympic enterprise requires specific planning and the performance of distinct activities" (Stauble, 1994, p. 14). Olympic and amateur sport

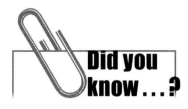

Did you know . . . ?

Attendees at the annual LPGA Kraft Nabisco Championship in California are 63% female and 37% male; 86% aged 36 and older; 78% married; 72% combined household incomes range upward from $50,000 (17% of these earn over $125,000); 51% college graduates or advanced professional degrees.

The Olympic Games and Sponsorship

organizations have, over the past several years, become very dependent upon sponsorship income. Stauble views Olympic organizations as resource-conversion machines. These organizations obtain resources from sponsors and convert them into specific products and services that are provided to the public. To accomplish this, Olympic organizations must create an exchange with the sponsor (Stauble). Typically, these have been in the form of signage, logo presentation, hospitality opportunities, and identification with high-level teams and athletes.

> There are plenty of opportunities for sale in the five ring circus: television, commercials, product licensing, product exclusivity at the Games, team sponsorships, Olympic movement sponsorships, awards presentations, training center support, product endorsements, and almost anything a marketing [person] could devise. (Marsano, 1987, p. 65)

Sport sponsorships between Olympic organizations and corporations have existed for many years. In 1896, Kodak had an ad in the official program of the first modern Olympics, and by 1928, Coca-Cola had begun its long-standing relationship with the Olympic movement (Pratzmark and Frey, 1989). Sponsorship and the Olympics have a prolonged relationship and one that has increased significantly in complexity.

In 1985, the IOC hired ISL Marketing to create a program to facilitate corporations interested in sponsoring the Olympic Games (Marsano, 1987). The Olympic Programme (TOP) was the creation. According to ISL, TOP "brings together the rights of the IOC as owner of the Olympic Games, the two Games Organizing Committees, and the National Olympic Committees throughout the world as partners in one four year sponsorship programme" (ISL Marketing, 1993, p. 3). This process also accomplished another major goal of any sport marketer—make it easier for consumers to buy your product. Another factor in this formula was the IOC's restructuring of the games so that an Olympic Games (Summer or Winter) would occur every two years instead of both Games occurring in one year with a four-year cycle. This would allow for sponsors to gain more long-term benefits and would spread the payments over an extended period.

The system was designed to allow a limited number of sponsors to receive special treatment and benefits on a worldwide basis and achieve exclusivity and protection in their Olympic sponsorship activities (Pratzmark and Frey, 1989). Specifically, TOP Sponsors would receive the following benefits (ISL Marketing, 1993; *Olympic Fact File*, 1998; Pratzmark and Frey, 1989):

1. Product Exclusivity—Only one sponsor would be allowed for any product category. This meant that if Coca-Cola

Sponsorship between Olympic organizations and corporations has existed for many years.

and Visa were members of the TOP, then Pepsi and American Express would not be allowed to become involved with Olympic sponsorship on any level, International, National, or with the Organizing Committee.

2. Use of Marks and Designations—Each participant was granted the right to use the solitary Olympic rings and their use in combination with all NOC designations. This gave them worldwide and local impact. Companies could also use the "Official Sponsor" and "Official Product" designations. All Organizing Committee logos were also available to sponsors.

3. Public Relations and Promotional Opportunities—Sponsors were given special tie-ins and media events to increase their exposure.

4. Access to Olympic Archives—The IOC made articles from its archives in Switzerland available to sponsors for special exhibits and displays. Film and video archives were also available.

5. Olympic Merchandise and Premiums—Clothing and apparel could be used bearing the Olympic logos for sales incentives and marketing activities. Visa had to reorder company shirts five times in 1996.

6. Tickets and Hospitality—Sponsors received priority access to seating at both the Winter and Summer Games.

7. Advertising Options—Each participant in TOP was given first chance at souvenir program ads and the option (where possible) to television commercial purchases.

8. On-Site Participation—Point-of-purchase and product display were included in the package. Companies would also have certain rights to concession areas and space for product sampling. For example, Kodak provides each athlete in the Games with a disposable camera and supplies the 900 photojournalists with 175,000 complimentary rolls of film.

9. Research—Each sponsor would receive a full research report on the public's reception of their participation and an assessment of the valued-added benefits. Research after the 1998 Games showed significant improvements in product image for TOP participants.

10. First Right of Negotiation for the Next Quadrennial—Those who were satisfied with TOP would have the option to continue in their product category. (Pratzmark and Frey, 1989, p. 20–21)

Data shows that the money sponsors pay to display an event or property's logo on their products or packaging is a good investment—consumers are more likely to buy the product with the logo than one without.

For the 2004 Summer Olympic Games in Athens, 11 TOP sponsors were secured paying about $65 million each for TOP sponsorship status (*2004 Marketing Fact File*, 2004). Since the 1985 development of TOP, sponsorship has become an integral part of the Olympic movement. Over the last two decades, TOP served two major goals of the IOC: It made the IOC less dependent on television revenues and it assisted all countries in the world with sport development through a shared-revenue system.

Trends in Grassroots Sponsorship

One of the most important issues that sport marketers should consider is how their corporation can benefit from sponsoring at the grassroots level. Many sport-related companies are realizing that speaking to consumers in a local environment may be more persuasive than nationwide involvement. However, some caution should be exercised when working with grassroots events. Event personnel are often largely composed of volunteers with unproven success. Thus, when you choose to sponsor their event or property, your corporate reputation is in their hands.

The movement to event sponsorship and away from individual endorsement should continue as consumer data show that the credibility of individual endorsers is low. Events can be successful for the sponsor regardless of who wins, and they are less likely to become entangled in controversy (i.e., Mike Tyson theory). However, the scandal surrounding the Salt Lake City 2002 Olympic bid showed that events are not immune to controversy that could adversely affect sponsors. The very nature of the event can also cause trouble for sponsors. For instance, animal rights activists have threatened to boycott products from the sponsors associated with the Iditarod dogsled race because of alleged cruelty to animals. The Professional Rodeo Cowboys Association moved to diminish the possibility of controversy through the publication of a brochure detailing the methods employed to safeguard animals used in rodeo events.

Another interesting sponsorship trend appeared when sport computer game manufacturer Electronic Arts began selling sponsorship on outfield walls and other signage in its video games. These proved to be very effective in targeting youth markets.

Sport marketers can certainly look toward including the arts and social issues in their marketing campaigns (Greenwald and Fernandez-Balboa, 1998). Consider these three noteworthy examples. The Denver Nuggets of the NBA had a very successful program exchanging game tickets for handguns. For many years, the United States Sports Academy used various sponsors to support a sport art museum housed on its campus. In relation to social issues, an event was started in 1996 to honor the late college basketball coach Jim Valvano and raise money for cancer research. The college basketball tournament entitled "Coaches vs. Cancer" raises over $1,000,000 annually.

The power of the Internet has also made it possible to expand your dominion for securing candidates for endorsements and events for sponsor partnering. Many sport organizations post a Request for Proposals (RFP) on their websites in order to facilitate a wide range of companies looking to partner through sponsorship. Shoe manufacturer Airwalk also used its website to attract potential endorsees through an on-line application form. Airwalk's Internet strategy seemed particularly appropriate given the lifestyles of its primary clientele.

In the dynamic worlds of sport and finance, new trends will certainly emerge. The challenge for sport marketers is to keep abreast of the industry and creatively seek opportunities to use sponsorships and endorsements to market products and services.

Chapter Summary

This chapter was to describe how sport organizations could enhance their marketing efforts through athlete endorsements and sport sponsorships. Because of their knowledge and power within certain groups, sport companies can effectively use opinion leaders to increase product sales. Opinion leaders can also be used in product sampling and prototype testing. Endorsement of products by individual athletes has been a marketing practice in sport for decades, yet its popularity has been waning. A credibility problem with individual endorsements exists because many consumers believe that sports celebrities were endorsing products only for the money. The scope of all marketing strategies and tactics must also include attention to the organization's social responsibility and ethical business practices.

A trend that appears to be successful is cross-promotion, whereby several companies band together around an athlete or event to gain additional exposure. The objectives for sponsorship center on market communication. James (2002) suggests that event sponsorship can provide companies and opportunity to interact with clients and customers on a large scale whereas choosing an individual athlete as a spokesperson can enhance brand awareness and consumer loyalty. The company can use sport sponsorship to communicate to the market that it is a successful and socially responsible firm that produces and sells quality products (Ferrand and Pagés, 1996). The concerns for the future are whether the sport sponsorship and endorsement field are saturated and whether sponsors will switch to other areas like the arts and regional festivals to accomplish their objectives.

CASE STUDY CHAPTER 13

Marketing Through Endorsements and Sponsorships

Rationale

As noted in the chapter, there are a multitude of issues over who has control of corporate logos, licensing rights and personal assets. A few years ago some controversy immerged in professional golf. The PGA had developed agreements with their tournament sponsors enabling them to use photos of the winning athlete in one advertisement following the sponsored tournament. This was part of the agreement for signing up as a title sponsor. Players, on the other hand did not benefit financially from the agreement, yet their image was being used in association with the title sponsor's product. Although the sponsors was not allowed to imply that the player endorsed it's products or services directly, the implication was there even when the players image appeared in the company ad (see Co-Present Mode in the chapter).

The issue came into the media spotlight when Daimler-Chrysler's Mercedes line sponsored a PGA tournament won by Tiger Woods. One of Tiger Woods' primary sponsors in Buick, a General Motors brand. Having Tiger appear in a Mercedes advertisement undermined the value of Buick's investment.

Charge

The purpose of this case/exercise is for your group (PGA group vs. Players group) to negotiate a policy that is acceptable to both constituents.

Teaching points

Negotiation groups should be allowed to investigate their position and engage in web and library searches for data to support their position.

Key elements for the negotiation;

- Did the PGA have the right to grant player images to its sponsors?
- Did the players agree to the PGA's position by entering the tournament?
- What power does the PGA have to regulate post-tournament activities?
- What role do players agents have in the final outcome?
- What actions could/did the players take to leverage their position?

QUESTIONS FOR STUDY

1. Describe the advantages and disadvantages of having an individual athlete as a product endorser.

2. Compare and contrast the sponsorship rights available through each level of Olympic sports: IOC, NOCs, NGBs, IFs.

LEARNING ACTIVITIES

Attend a local sport event where sponsors have signage displayed in the venue. After exiting the event, ask patrons which, if any, of the sponsors they can remember.

PROFESSIONAL ASSOCIATIONS AND ORGANIZATIONS

IEG Sponsorship Report
> International Events Group
> 640 North LaSalle, Suite 600
> Chicago, IL 60610-3777
> www.sponsorship.com
> 1-800-834-4850

Sports Market Place
> Franklin-Covey
> 7250 N. 16th Street
> Phoenix, AZ 85020
> http://www.sportscareers.com

SUGGESTED READINGS

Reed, M. H. (1990). *Legal aspects of promoting and sponsoring events.* Chicago: International Events Group.

Stotlar, D. K. (2001). *Developing successful sport sponsorship plans*, 2nd ed. Morgantown, WV: Fitness Information Technology.

Chapter Fourteen

USING LICENSING AND LOGOS IN THE SPORT INDUSTRY

Overview

Licensing is the act of granting to another party the right to use a protected logo, design, or trademark (Griffith, 2003). Although trademark licensing may be traced back hundreds of years, dramatic growth occurred in the 1980s and 1990s. Comic book heroes, cartoons, schools, professional teams, clubs, causes, characters, and many other subjects became featured designs on clothing. However, sales of sport-related merchandise subsided in the late 1990s due in part to changes in fashion trends. Regardless of fluctuations in market conditions, licensing can be an effective component in branding strategies for many sport entities.

Historically, sport organizations have found it desirable to initiate efforts to protect the investment in their name and marks through trademark licensing (Irwin, 1990). Through such programs, sport organizations receive name recognition and substantial revenue. In 1963, the National Football League established its licensing program to bring the protection of team names and insignia under central control. On the collegiate scene, the University of California at Los Angeles (UCLA) began its licensing program in 1973 (Irwin and Stotlar, 1993). Other sport organizations such as the International Olympic Committee, Gold's Gym, ABC's *Monday Night Football* and ESPN have also established strong licensing programs.

On the revenue side, about $17.9 billion is attributable to the US professional leagues plus NASCAR (Freifeld, 2004). In 2004, each NFL team received over $4 million from the league's licensed product sales of over $3 billion (Kaplan, 2003). The other professional leagues reported significant revenues as well. The National Basketball Association realized $4.3 billion in sales, followed by Major League Baseball at $3.3 billion (Sosnowski, 2005), and the National Hockey League earned more than $1.5 billion. NASCAR brought in $2.1 billion in licensing revenues in 2005 (Warfield, 2005).

The industry has not been devoid of turmoil. Sales of licensed professional sport apparel declined 30–40% in 2000–2001. And the NHL suffered tremendously from the player lockout of 2004. The significant declines in the late 1990s pushed three of the biggest companies producing licensed sports wear into bankruptcy. Pro-Player and Starter went bankrupt in 1999, and in 2000, Logo Athletic also filed for bankruptcy.

This situation has led many of the professional leagues to re-examine their licensing programs. The move has been to reduce the number of licensees and work on partnerships between the league and the licensee.

The profits generated from licensing are not limited to professional teams completing in league play. NASCAR is able to generate over $1 billion annually in licensed product sales ("NASCAR Merchandising," 2001). An analysis of their merchandising indicated that 50% of sales came from apparel, 25% from collectible die-cast cars, 10% from trading cards, and 15% from other products (Bhonslay, 1999b; Hagstrom, 1998) with $247 in average annual merchandise expenditure per fan. Individual events have also been capable of deriving significant revenues from licensed products. The 2006 World Cup (soccer) revenues from licensing are estimated at $2 billion in worldwide sales (Phillips, 2005). World Cup managers set up 330 official World Cup shops in Germany and a total of 75,000 outlets for licensed merchandise. Data from the 2002 World Cup showed that 80% of their business came from 20% of their outlets. Thus, some may question the concept of attempting to manage all of those retailers (Phillips, 2005).

If you think that this effort is not worthwhile for collegiate institutions and amateur sports, consider that sport organizations such as the United States Olympic Committee receive revenues that account for approximately 25% of their budget from their licensing programs (USOC Board of Directors, 2005). Several collegiate sport entities profit measurably from the sale of licensed products. The 2002 Salt Lake Winter Games and 2004 Athens Summer Games brought in $81 million from licensed merchandise based on royalty rates of between 10%–15% (IOC, 2004).

The Collegiate Licensing Company (CLC) originated in the 1980's to assist colleges and universities across the US in strengthening the market for licensed apparel through leveraging retailers. Through their assistance, universities would be

NASCAR annually generates billions of dollars in licensed product sales.

better able to secure shelf space in the market and establish a defined protocol for dealing with organizational licensing and merchandising. Furthermore, their clients could work to set more uniform royalty fees and payment schedules. Typically, royalty rates for colleges and universities run about 8% of the price at wholesale. CLC, the leading company in the college market, represents $3.5 billion in retails sales and about 200 universities. Michigan's deal with Nike is reported worth $28 million over its seven year contract (Lee, 2003). In 2005, the top selling universities were: 1.) University of Michigan 2.) University of Texas—Austin 3.) University of Georgia 4.) University of North Carolina and 5.) University of Oklahoma, all generating over $1 million in licensing revenues.

In a new licensing twist, CLC has also contracted with EA Sports, the nation's leading producer of sports video games to offer games linked to the most popular college teams in the country (Ryan, 2005).

The current trend in collegiate licensing is to broaden their distribution channels and to maximize their brand exposure across multiple markets (Freifeld, 2005). Several large companies, including CLC, entered the business to assist sport organizations in the management of their licensing programs. In these organizations, the licensing agent helps in the protection of an organization's logo or marks. CLC developed seven basic goals with short-term and long-term strategies (Battle et al., 1991; Bhonslay, 1999b; Conklin, 1999; Freifeld, 2005). The consortium not only affects its members (over 180 in 2005), but it also directly and indirectly affects nonmember schools. Their goals include the following:

1. To attract, maintain, and strengthen a prestigious base of universities, bowls, and athletic conferences.

2. To attract and maintain a base of licensees sufficiently large enough to cover all potential market segments and distribute all marketable products.

3. To identify retailers that are current or potential carriers of collegiate merchandise and show them the requirements and opportunities of collegiate licensing.

4. To identify consumers of collegiate products and encourage them to buy licensed products.

5. To improve the effectiveness of current methods of enforcement and to develop new methods.

6. To establish marketing programs that can expand the market for "Officially Licensed Collegiate Products" and take advantage of synergistic marketing, advertising, and promotional programs.

7. To provide unparalleled services to member institutions and licensees and to develop a database and reports to give management the information needed to analyze, evaluate, and manage progress toward the goals previously listed.

In sport licensing, four factors led to the development of organized sport licensing (Irwin, 1990). One of those factors was the increased popularity of sport and the resulting media coverage. Successful athletic teams, especially in football and basketball, have, for many years, been a rallying point for the public. Increased popularity led to greater attendance at games, leading to increased media coverage. This, in turn, led to increased popularity, higher attendance figures, and even more media coverage. Stadiums and arenas were enlarged, front pages of major newspapers carried the outcomes of major sports contests, and television magnified sports and multiplied their popularity. Today, sporting events receive headline coverage virtually year round.

Another development during the 1970s was the technology involved with screen printing or silk-screening, which greatly expanded the licensing industry. Blank garments were easily acquired from a number of mills and could be printed to meet any demands. Printed T-shirts became a communications medium during the 1970s. Adults, as well as children, were part of a market that grew dramatically throughout the 1980s.

In sport, the demand for imprinted goods was advanced through fan pride, loyalty, and desire to support the team by wearing team colors and designs. Anyone who has attended major events knows the emotions that fans generate in support of their teams or favorite player. People found themselves extremely attracted to their favorite school, team, or player and desired a means to express their feelings. As the market for imprinted products expanded, fans sought licensed goods as a method of expressing their support.

During the 1980s, the costs of running competitive sport programs increased dramatically. As a result, the sale of imprinted sport merchandise was activated to help build revenues. Parallel with the increases in sales, problems began to occur with logo abuse and counterfeit merchandise. In 1998, losses to counterfeiting were estimated to be $200 million (Bernstein, 1998). During the Major League Baseball 2000 "subway series," 24 federal marshals confiscated items from 80 bootleggers. After the final World Series Game, the NYPD raided one factory and retrieved $1 million in counterfeit goods and an official MLB logo-disk containing all of the League's protected marks. With these levels of abuse, sport managers quickly decided that they needed greater control over the use of their marks to prevent the obnoxious designs, poor-quality merchandise, and product liability risks that they were beginning to face.

In a sport licensing program, the marketer typically grants a manufacturer the right to use the organization's logo (or indicia) in producing and selling merchandise. The licensee is required to sign a contract, pay royalties, and adhere to strict licensing regulations. Royalties for licensed goods typically run about 8 to 15% of the price for which an item is sold.

As a marketing vehicle, licensing enables sport organizations to generate consumer awareness and interest through logoed products, all with minimal capital outlay (Irwin and Stotlar, 1993). The established protocol for licensing revenues in most professional sport leagues is to engage in profit sharing. All of the major professional leagues collect royalty payments through league subsidiaries normally called "Properties" (e.g., NBA Properties, NFL Properties). These entities collect all licensing revenues and then distribute them equally across all teams in the league.

> Products that carry an organization's logo provide a relatively inexpensive way to increase consumer awareness and interest.

Although teams and events have profited from licensing, sport leagues have also entered the market. The NBA, PGA Tour and NASCAR began to open retail outlets to sell not only team and player/driver items but also organizational apparel. These sport organizations believed that they could build strong brands around their own logo (NBA, PGA Tour, NASCAR). The USOC also initiated similar brand-building activities in the late 1990s. The market for sport-logoed items is no longer limited to the team's home city, campus, or a local market, but extends around the globe.

> Licensing is extremely important to the sport organization because it provides control over the way the company name and indicia are portrayed on merchandise.

To ensure standardization and quality, many souvenirs such as clothing, mugs, or novelties bearing sport logos are put through rigorous marketing and approval processes. Each item is checked for both quality and design. Products of inferior quality can be rejected, and strict labeling requirements can be enforced so the consumers can identify the merchandise as authentic. In addition, the product manufacturers can be required to carry product liability insurance, which protects the organization if legal action is filed because of an incident involving a licensed product.

Because of the popularity of sport licensing and trademarks on manufactured items and the potential revenue, commercial, professional, intercollegiate, and amateur sports organization marketers must develop a significant knowledge base in this area. There has also been an increasing amount of litigation in this field, and the

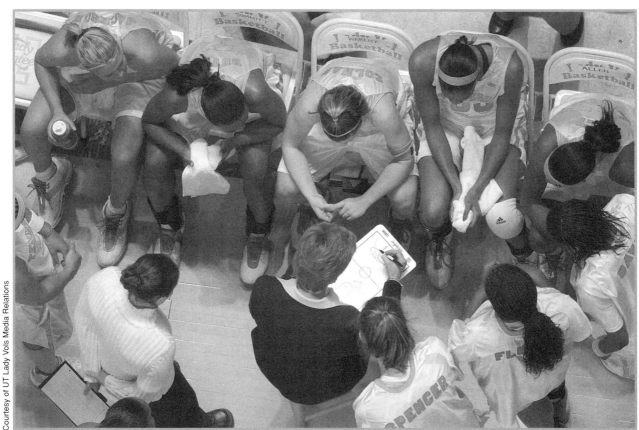

Courtesy of UT Lady Vols Media Relations

College athletic teams can make millions through licensing agreements with apparel and shoe companies.

guidelines governing the use of sports trademarks are still being established in the courts (Wong, 2002). As the national and international markets for merchandise bearing sport logos, names, and indicia develop, sport administrators will be required to seek legal avenues to protect their market, products, and marks. However, most sport organizations know little about how to protect their marks or how to license legally protected properties to second parties for commercial use (Irwin, 1990).

Another aspect of licensing involves licensing a business name to other businesses. This is similar to a concept with which you may be familiar, franchising. Under licensing agreements, sport organizations such as fitness clubs (e.g., Powerhouse Gyms) purchase the right to use an established name, but are free to operate the business in any manner they wish. However, in a franchise arrangement, the proprietor must purchase the franchise rights and typically agree to relinquish some operational control. Included with the purchase are restrictions on business practices often relating to facility size, mandated equipment, and audits/inspections by corporate officers. Although many of the benefits associated with franchise and licensing are best suited for start-up businesses, a recent trend has been for existing businesses to switch over to a recognized industry name through this process (Shaffer, 1997).

The Legalities of Trademark Licensing in Sport

The case law governing sport licensing is sparse but has developed rapidly based on traditional trademark law. Sport organizations therefore must develop a firm legal basis for requiring that users of their trademarks obtain permission to use the trademarks and for requiring that the users pay royalties for the privilege. In order to more fully understand trademark licensing, you need to be familiar with the following principles, terms, and definitions surrounding trademark law (A weighty matter, 2004).

TRADEMARK PRINCIPLES

The Federal Trademark Act of 1946, Lanham Act 45, 15 U. S. C. 1051–1127 (1946), commonly known as the Lanham Act, governs the law of trademarks, the registration of trademarks, and remedies for the infringement of registered trademarks (Griffith, 2003; Wong, 2002). The Trademarks Law Revision Act, which went into effect in 1989, was Congress's first overall revision of the Lanham Act since 1946. The revised Lanham Act created major changes in federal trademark law that are highly relevant to sport trademark registration and licensing. Sports Edge magazine suggest that manufacturers that encounter problems with trademark infringement email the US Commerce Department ipr.hotline.mail.doc.gov for help. The fundamental aspects in the use of trademarks are (Irwin, 1990):

1. Trademark: "Any word, name, symbol, or device, or any combination thereof used to identify and distinguish the goods of one person from those manufactured or sold by others."

2. Service mark: "Any word, name, symbol, or device, or any combination thereof used to identify and distinguish the services of one person from the service of others."

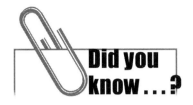

3. Collective mark: "A trademark or service mark used by members of a cooperative, association, or other collective group or organization."

4. Mark: "A shorthand reference to any type of mark, including trademarks, service mark, and collective marks."

5. Registered mark: "A mark registered in the United States Patent and Trademark Office, as provided under the Act." (United States Department of Commerce, 1993, p. 1)

INFRINGEMENT OF A TRADEMARK

The Act defines trademark infringement as the reproduction, counterfeiting, copying, or imitation, in commerce, of a registered mark "in connection with the sale, offering for sale, distribution, or advertising of any goods or services on or in connection with which such use is likely to cause confusion, or to cause mistake or to deceive without consent of the registrant" (Basic Facts . . ., 1993, p. 7).

Secondary meaning. Secondary meaning is a mental recognition in the buyer's mind, associating symbols, words, colors, and designs with goods from a single source. It tests the connection in the buyer's mind between the product bearing the mark and its source (Wong, 2002). Certain terms that are selected or invented for the express purpose of functioning as trademarks may be classified as inherently distinctive. Such marks are protected and can be registered immediately on use. One such example would be the swoosh created by Nike. However, some potential marks describe products or services, geographic designations, or personal surnames. To qualify for protection as a mark, the courts require evidence that such a term has acquired secondary meaning; that is, consumers associate the products or services under the term with one particular source (Wong). The example here is that one shoe company produced a football shoe called Montana. They claimed that it was a generic reference to a geographical region. Football player Joe Montana, his agent, and eventually the courts disagreed.

Laches. Laches may arise when a party fails to assert a right or claim within a reasonable time, and the other party relies on this inaction to claim use to the other party's mark (Battle, Bailey, and Siegal, 1991). An example of just this case arose when the University of Pittsburgh tried to stop Champion from producing sweatshirts with the Pitt logo. The court in this case said that because Pitt had previously allowed Champion to use its logo, it could not now prevent its use by Champion.

Each of the types of marks described earlier is protected equally under the Lanham Act. Sport organization names, team names, and logos may be described as trademarks, service marks, or collective marks (Wong, 2002). Any of these marks used on items such as clothing and novelties as well as services is entitled to protection. Registered marks are not always confined to team names and indicia. In the not-too-distant past, sports facilities registered their names, including the 1988 Olympic Oval in Calgary, Wrigley Field in Chicago, and Fenway Park in Boston.

Because of the complexity of managing a sport-licensing program (integrating financial, promotional, and legal responsibilities), there have been organized efforts to control the use of sport organizations' logos, trademarks, and copyrights. As a result, organizations have been faced with a serious dilemma: internal versus external management (Irwin and Stotlar, 1993). Irwin's (1990) research and subsequent publications shed considerable light on this decision.

Another twist of the licensing setting occurred in 2000 when Nike signed an arrangement with British football club Manchester United for $432.3 million (10 years beginning in 2002) to manage its licensing program. Not only did Nike obtain exclusive worldwide sales of merchandise, but they also were authorized to run the worldwide merchandising program for the team. Previously, Manchester United had established stores in China, Singapore, Kuala Lumpur, Dubai, Kuwait, Dublin, and Cape Town. Manchester United and Nike formed a joint-venture business controlled by Nike, Manchester United Merchandising Limited (MUML) (Kaplan, 2001; Phillips, 2005).

Research by Irwin (1990) examined the pros and cons of internal versus external management and found that most organizations are better off handling their own programs. Specific factors in program design were established against which sport organizations could judge their programs. A review of these operational factors seems appropriate (Irwin 1990; Irwin and Stotlar, 1993).

The advantages and disadvantages assignable to internally and externally managed licensing programs must be reviewed within the context of the organization's resources. Generally, internally managed programs are more expensive to run, but they yield higher profits. External or agency-managed programs usually offer easier access to wholesale and retail networks and may have better nationwide success.

Bhonslay (1999b) indicated that many sport organizations utilize agencies to initiate a licensing program. The agencies typically have a higher level of expertise, more manufacturing contacts, and understanding of all of the management factors that must be addressed. Once the licensing program is operating efficiently, the sport organization can bring the program in-house and obtain greater control. Furthermore, profits can be maximized by avoiding the 30% commissions normally charged by agencies.

Sport licensing is a journey, not a single destination. All factors affecting the program must be considered. Irwin's (1990) conclusions prescribed a licensing paradigm. The major components of a licensing system should include

1. An examination of the feasibility of assigning a full-time licensing administrator.

2. An evaluation of the cost-effectiveness of internal versus

Operational Protocol Factors in Sport Licensing

Program Governance and Leadership

- Designated internal licensing authority
- Principal licensing assignment full-time
- Direct report to central administrator
- Licensing policy committee assembled
- Professional licensing agency assistance

Program Protection and Enforcement

- Legal specialist consultation
- Majority of logos registered as trademarks
- Licensee application and screening process
- License issuance and renewal procedures
- Basic agreement nonexclusive
- Execution of joint-use agreements
- Execution of international licenses
- Product sample required for quality control
- "Licensed product" identification required
- Counterfeit logo detection procedures
- Counterfeit logo reduction procedures

Program Promotions and Public Relations

- Proactive recruitment of licensees
- Proactive recruitment of retailers
- Licensee/retailer public relations program
- Advertising used to promote products/program
- Publicity used to promote products/program
- Licensing program information published

Revenue Management

- Advance payment required
- Uniform royalty charged on all products
- Written royalty exemption policy
- Royalty verifications routinely conducted
- Royalty verifications conducted by specialist
- Written royalty distribution policy

external management of the program based on internal resources and potential markets and profits.

3. Identification of a single administrative authority for licensing agreements.

4. The development of policy for the issuance of exclusive and nonexclusive license agreements.

5. The design of specific royalty and exemption policies.

6. Application procedures for issuance/renewal of licenses.

7. A process whereby licensees must disclose financial stability, distribution intent, and licensing references.

8. A request for advance payments from licensees as earnest money to be applied to future royalties.

9. The establishment of a uniform royalty rate calculated on the net cost of the licensed item sold.

10. The requirement to furnish finished samples of the licensed merchandise.

11. The requirement to furnish certificates of insurance pertaining to licensed merchandise sold.

12. The federal registration of at least one of the organization's marks.

13. The required use of licensee identification on all merchandise distributed (hang tag, label, etc.).

14. A plan for the allocation of royalties received by the organization.

15. An enforcement policy including the responsibility to police merchandisers and issue cease and desist orders.

16. Consultation with trademark law specialists as needed.

17. The performance of compliance review with licensees.

18. The recruitment and recognition of licensees on a sustained basis.

19. The development of licensing brochures or guidelines for distribution to prospective licensees.

20. The reporting structure for the licensing administrator within the organization (p. 151).

Many of the professional baseball teams (Chicago Cubs, Atlanta Braves, San Francisco Giants, and New York Yankees, among others) have developed methods that borrowed strengths from both systems. Although MLB administers the licensing program for all baseball clubs, these clubs aggressively began to sell their own merchandise through specialty catalogs, corporate-owned retail stores, and on-line sales. Not content with collecting only the 10% royalty provided by MLB, these organizations began selling the merchandise directly to their fans to bring retail profit margins to the team. These profit margins averaged 50% after expenses were taken from the typical 350% markup from wholesale cost. By 1999, 40 major professional sport teams operated off-site retail stores. Some teams have opted to establish "single-team stores" like the MLB Colorado Rockies chain of Rockies Dugout stores. Other organizations like the NBA Utah Jazz, began with Jazz-related souvenirs in 4 stores and expanded to 28 full-line shops (Fanzz). In Phoenix, corporately owned shops sell merchandise for all three of their professional franchises, the NBA Suns, the MLB Diamondbacks, and the NHL Coyotes (Bernstein, 1998). The San Francisco Giants opened their first on-line store in 1998 and found that sales quickly grew to equal that of a traditional mall-based shop (Goldfisher, 1998). With the increased use of the Internet by many sport organizations, about 50% of all US licensed product sales in 2000 were accomplished through e-commerce.

Regardless of the system employed, the major objectives of any sport licensing program are threefold: (a) Protection—to protect the trademarks of the organization, (b) Public Relations—to create a favorable image and positive exposure for the organization, and (c) Profit—to maximize revenues (Irwin,1990).

TRADEMARK LICENSING AGREEMENTS

Program enforcement procedures include all methods of securing and exercising protection of the sport organization's property rights in its name, logo, seals, and symbols. As sport licensing programs are constructed and policy parameters are established, licensing administrators typically develop contractual relationships with licensees as a part of the program enforcement protocol (Irwin, 1990). The primary legal base for this contractual relationship has been the licensing agreement. This agreement should provide for controls, checks, and balances regarding the exclusivity of mark, usage, royalty management, and quality control (Irwin, 1990). Previous empirical data have indicated the authority to grant and execute licensing agreements on behalf of the organization came primarily from upper-level administration. Gaston (1984) found that 42% of respondents identified the financial vice president as the source of authority for executing most licensing agreements.

According to experts in the industry (Baghdikian, 1996; Reed, 1989), the elements that should be examined in a licensing agreement include, first of all, the parties entering into the agreement. The pertinent definitions in the agreement must also be detailed. Service marks and trademarks should be defined with attention to the level of protection through either federal registration or common law use.

The contract should also describe the specific products to be licensed, the duration of the agreement, and terms under which the agreement can be terminated or modified. It is also imperative that the royalty and payment structure be addressed, complete with details providing for audits. Specifically, the contract should define the royalty on net sales without deduction for shipping, advertising, or even returns or uncollectible accounts. The agreement should prescribe the reporting procedures and the payment methods and schedule. Other areas traditionally covered would include the types of products to be licensed, the rights for approval, ownership of artwork and designs, insurance and indemnification, and the territory governed by the agreement. Finally, it is crucial for the organization to restrict the ability of the licensee to assign the license to subcontractors (Baghdikian; Reed).

Although licensing contracts are intended to control the use of registered marks, the situation may be spinning out of control. Battles are continually fought over who has the right to control. This issue has surfaced most frequently in professional sports. The NFL recently instituted a program to capture what seemed to be lost revenues. Although the league obtained royalties from the sale of team-logoed items, the players were attracting sponsorship dollars from corporations for displaying corporate logos on shoes, gloves, and sideline hats. In a move to profit from these images during the game, the NFL established the Pro Line program. This program required companies who wished to have their logo visible during an NFL game to pay a fee to the league. In some instances, depending on the scope of the license, the fees surpassed $50 million per year.

To many, this action seemed like extortion. The league was restricting the rights of player to wear shoes and other items that were not specified as "uniforms" under the collective bargaining agreement. Therefore, if a player wanted to wear a shoe from a company that had not paid the fee to the league, he would have to tape over (spat) the logo. The league even went so far as to hire former players to police the sidelines looking for unauthorized logos. Two Denver Bronco players filed grievances after they were fined for wearing unauthorized logos in a locker room interview after a game. In 2001, the NFL changed its process and contracted with a single company (Reebok) to produce its on-field apparel. Reebok also secured the uniforms rights for the NBA through a similar exclusive agreement and with its 2005 acquisition of The Hockey Company will leverage control on the ice in the NHL.

This appears to be the trend across US professional sports. Five years ago, the NFL had 250 product licensees and 50 apparel licensee. They have reduced that number to 100 and 6 respectively. This reduction in licensee is a defined strategy of the league to assist their licensing partners by allowing "strategic exclusivity" in particular segments of the market and "maximize the value of the brand" (Freifeld, 2004, p. 44). MLB also entered into an exclusive licensing agreement with Majestic Athletic to serve as the official supplier of on-field uniforms for all MLB teams (Ryan, 2005). In a sense, fewer is better, more manageable, and more profitable.

Defining control and the limits of licensing agreement is critical in the industry. As noted previously, Majestic Athletic was selected to serve as the official supplier of on-field uniforms for all MLB teams (Ryan, 2005) yet the New York Yankees have a deal through 2013 with adidas as the "Official Athletic Apparel and Footwear Company of the New York Yankees." The deal gives adidas the right to supply club personnel with warm-up and practice apparel, shoes and also gives them signage in Yankee Stadium and a suite for client entertainment, yet Majestic still has the right to on-field competition uniforms (Ryan, 2005).

In another situation involving control, during the 1998 US Open (tennis), the WTA fined Venus Williams $100 for refusing to wear the Corel WTA Tour patch on her clothing. Williams indicated that the language in her Reebok contract "prohibited any other logo" on her dress (Kaplan, 1998, p. 9). Interestingly, William's attorney discovered that the WTA rules provided an exemption for Nike logos. Williams threatened to sue, but ultimately abandoned her challenge. Saying that Williams could do whatever she wanted to do, Reebok stayed above the fray (Kaplan, 1998). Ultimately, the players in both cases prevailed, but it seems that greed has irreversibly contaminated this aspect of sport.

Sage (1996) has also suggested that many of the professional leagues engage in hypocritical trade practices. Although they have gone to "great lengths" to tie licensed merchandise to an all-American image, the vast majority of merchandise is manufactured by exploited foreign labor. The NFL, MLB, and the NBA all used red, white and blue colors predominantly in their logos and garment hang tags. According to Sage, the leagues are fervently selling the American image and pushing patriotism through these products. Yet, in their quest for profits, it seems that the leagues are increasingly exploiting men and women of color from economically disadvantaged countries. In many cases, these workers labor in unsafe and unhealthy work environments. "It is their low wages and long hours that make manufacturers of licensed merchandise commercially successful, and that provide a significant revenue stream to professional team sports" (Sage, 1996, p. 8). It is imperative that these issues be mitigated and eliminated through the contractual language between sport organizations and licensees.

Chapter Summary

As evidenced by the financial data presented earlier, sport licensing has (since its inception) achieved substantial commercial success. The development of this industry has obviously had a substantial impact on manufacturers, retailers, and consumers. The future of sport licensing seems very bright and appears to be on solid legal ground. A good foundation has been laid, and the present multi-billion-dollar market should easily expand. However, styles and trends can change as quickly as they evolve. There seems to be some disparity over the strategy in the market place. The trend in collegiate licensing to broaden their distribution channels and sign as many as 380 different licensees is in stark contrast to the trend in professional sports to minimize licensees and maximize each licensee's exclusivity and profitability (Freifeld, 2005). In the author's opinion, the pro sports team approach seems to represent a better partnership which will, in the long term, serve both organization and licensee better. With a clear focus on all three elements of a sound licensing program, Protection, Profit and Public Relations, sport organizations can continue to manage successful licensing programs.

Licensing and Logos in the Sport Industry

Rationale

The practice of protecting sports logos through registration and copyright is relatively recent in the history of sport. Only for about the last 25 years have colleges and universities become actively involved in licensing. The practice has yet to make significant inroads in the high school sports setting. However, with diminishing budgets and greater sophistication of high school sports, many sport marketers are examining the concept more closely.

Charge

The purpose of this case/exercise is for each class member to contact a high school athletic director (suggest their own high school or one in the local area) to ascertain if the school has formally protected their logos. If they have, ask for how long the practice has been in place; and if not, ask why they have not done so. Subsequently, examine area stores that sell school-logoed merchandise and discuss with the store manager the practice of licensing as it relates to high school apparel.

Teaching points

- Discuss reasons cited by ADs for engaging or not engaging in licensing.
- Discuss the points of view of store managers about the practice.
- Debate the idea that revenues are lost if royalties are not collected vs. the right of the public to use public school logos.

QUESTIONS FOR STUDY

1. What are the laws that affect licensing and trademarks?
2. What factors led to the development of organized sport licensing?

LEARNING ACTIVITIES

1. Investigate the origins of NFL Properties, Inc. Who was their first licensing director?
2. Develop a sport logo and determine the procedures and costs for registering that mark in your state.
3. Contact a sport organization with a registered mark(s) and request a copy of its graphic standards manual.

References

1999 sponsors spending: 7.6 billion. (1998, Dec. 21). IEG Sponsorship Report, 1, 4–5.

2004 Marketing Fact File (2004). Lausanne: International Olympic Committee.

A weighty matter, (2004, September). *Sports Edge, 14*(9), 14.

Aaker, D. A., Kumer, V., & Day, G. S. (2000). *Marketing research*, 7th ed. New York: John Wiley & Sons.

A.R.C. (1998, May). Park and roll. *Athletic Business*, 23, 18.

ABC Evening News. (2000, September 14). Report on ABC Evening News.

ABC Evening News. (2000, September 22). Report on ABC Evening News with Peter Jennings.

Adelman, M. L. (1986). *A sporting time: New York City and the rise of modern athletics, 1820–1870.* Urbana, IL: University of Illinois Press.

Advancing to the next level (2005, June 27– July 3). *SportsBusiness Journal*, 17–20.

Andrew Peck, Pioneer. (1916). *Sporting Goods Dealer, 34*(4), 55–56.

Armstrong, K. L. (1998). Ten strategies to employ when marketing sport to black consumers. *Sport Marketing Quarterly, 7*(3), 11–18.

Arsenal Case Study (2005). Retrieved February 2, 2005, from http://www.CakeCommunications.com

Arthur, D., Scott, D., Woods, T., & Booker, R. (1998). Sport sponsorships should . . . A process model for the effective implementation of sport sponsorship programs. *Sport Marketing Quarterly, 7*(4), 35–48.

Ashland personnel. (1916). *Sporting Goods Dealer, 34*(1), 78–81.

Athletic promotions: Ways to generate revenue and increase attendance. (1997, April) *Athletic Administration*, 6, 12–14.

Axtell, R. E. (1991). *Gestures: The do's and taboos of body language around the world.* New York: John Wiley and Sons.

Baghdikian, E. (1996). Building the sports organization's merchandise licensing program: The appropriateness, significance and considerations. *Sport Marketing Quarterly, 5*(1), 35–41.

Bairner, A. (2003) Globalization and sport: The nation strikes back. *Phi Kappa Phi Forum, 83*(4), 34–37.

Ball, A. (1989, November 13). Here's who's living with whom. *Adweek's Marketing Week*, HM 11.

Barlow, R. (1992, March). Relationship marketing: The ultimate in customer service. *Retail Control*, 29–37.

Barney, R. K. (1978). Of rails and red stockings: Episodes in the expansion of the national pastime in the American West. *Sport and Recreation in the West*, 61–70.

Bartels, R. (1988). *The history of marketing thought.* Columbus, OH: Publishing Horizons.

Battle III, W. R., Bailey, B., & Siegal, B. B. (1991). Collegiate trademark licensing. In B. L. Parkhouse (Ed.), *The management of sport: Its foundation and application* (pp. 245–263). St. Louis, MO: Mosby.

Bean, R. B. (1997, December). Business-to-business database marketing: The future is now! *Direct Marketing*, 60(8), 43–45.

Berlin, E. (1996, July). Just a fantasy. Internet World, 7(7), 102–104.

Bernstein, A. (1998, August 10–16). Coalition targets $2 billion-a-year counterfeiting trade. *SportsBusiness Journal, 1*, 29.

Bernstein, A. (1998, November 23–29). Reebok's future not in the stars. *SportsBusiness Journal, 1*, 7.

Berrett, T., Slack, T., & Whitson, D. (1993). Economics and the pricing of sport and leisure. *Journal of Sport Management*, 7, 199–215.

Berthon, P., Pitt, L., & Watson, R. T. (1996a). Marketing communication and the world wide web. *Business Horizons, 39*(5), 24–32.

Berthon, P., Pitt, L., & Watson, R. T. (1996b). Re-surfing w3: Research perspectives on marketing communication and buyer behavior communications on the world wide web. *International Journal of Advertising, 15*(4), 287–301.

Berthon, P., Pitt, L., & Watson, R. T. (1996c). The world wide web as an advertising medium: Toward an understanding of conversion efficiency. *Journal of Advertising Research, 36*(1), 43–54.

Better to give—Better giveaway items to drive ticket sales (2005). Retrieved September 1, 2005, from http://www.migalareport.com/sep05_story3.cfm

Betts, J. R. (1974). *America's Sporting Heritage, 1850–1950.* Reading, MA: Addison-Wesley Publishing Company.

Bhonslay, M. (1999a, February 8–14). Women's goods don't score with fans. *SportsBusiness Journal, 2*, 28.

Bhonslay, M. (1999b, February 8–14). You did a great job for us—You're fired. *SportsBusiness Journal, 2*, 24.

Blumenstyk, G. (1996, April 19). Money-making champs. *Chronicle of Higher Education*, A49–51.

Boeh, T. (1989, October). A program for selling. *Collegiate Athletic Management, 3*, 53–55.

Bonham, D. (1999, February). *Sport marketing in the new millennium.* Presentation at the University of Northern Colorado, Greeley, CO.

Bonvissuto, K. (2005). Cavaliers forge fans friendships with strategic database use. *Crain's Cleveland Business, 26*(8), 1.

Boone, L. E., & Kurtz, D. L. (1989). *Contemporary marketing.* Orlando, FL: The Dryden Press.

Boone, L. E., & Kurtz, D. L. (1992). *Contemporary marketing.* Fort Worth, TX: The Dryden Press.

Borden, N. (1942). *The economic effects of advertising.* Chicago, IL: Irwin, Inc.

Bourdon, S. (2000, December). Glass cutter. *Trailer Boats, 30*, 30–33.

Boyd T. C., & Krehbeil, T. C. (2003). Promotion timing in Major League Baseball and the staking effects of factors that increase game attractiveness. *Sport Marketing Quarterly, 12,* 173–183.

Bradbury, M. (1990). How club life cycles affect strategy. *Club Business International, 11*(7), 16, 35, 37.

Bradley, S. (1996, April 15). D. mail is becoming email: Direct marketers are getting interactive. *Brandweek, 37*(16), 44–45.

Branvold, S. E. (1992). Utilization of fence signage in college baseball. *Sport Marketing Quarterly, 1*(2), 29–32.

Branvold, S. E., & Bowers, R. (1992). The use of promotions in college baseball. *Sport Marketing Quarterly, 1*(1), 19–24.

Briggs, R., & Hollis, N. (1997, March/April). Advertising on the web: Is there response before click-through? *Journal of Advertising Research, 37*(2), 33–45.

Briner, R. A. (1992, April). *European sports business opportunities.* Paper presented at the 1992 International Conference on Sport Business, Columbia, SC.

Brooks, C. M. (1998). Celebrity athlete endorsement: An overview of the key theoretical issues. *Sport Marketing Quarterly, 7*(2), 34–44.

Broughton, D. (2001, January 1–7). Events up for bid. *SportsBusiness Journal, 3*(37), 27.

Brown, M. T. (1998, January). An examination of the content of official Major League Baseball team sites on the world wide web. *Cyber-Journal of Sport Marketing, 2*(1).

Brubaker, B. (1991, March 11). In shoe companies' competition, the coaches are the key players. *Washington Post,* A1.

Brunson, M. W., & Shelby, B. (1993). Recreation substitutability: A research agenda. *Leisure Sciences, 15*(1), 67–74.

Bucklin, L. P. (1972). *Competition and evolution in the distributive trades.* Englewood Cliffs, NJ: Prentice-Hall, Inc.

Bunn, D. (1997a, December 1). Online shopping boon for retailers. *Rocky Mountain News,* 1B, 14B.

Bunn, D. (1997b, December 7). Truecount counts times ad seen on Net. *Rocky Mountain News,* 13G.

Bush, A. J., Martin, C. A., & Bush, V. D. (2004). Sports celebrity influence on behavioral intentions of generation Y. *Journal of Advertising Research, 44*(1), 108–119.

Byl, J. (1990). *Organizing successful tournaments.* Champaign, IL: Leisure Press.

Byrd, A. (1999, September 27–October 3). Extreme publications take aim at sport—and lifestyle. *SportsBusiness Journal, 2*(23), 27.

Carpenter, K. (1999, March 8). On edge: The snowsports industry has no need for more challenges these days. *Sporting Goods Business, 32*(5), 30.

Carucci, V. (1994). Touchdown south: Super Bowl XXVIII in Atlanta. *Sky Magazine, 23*(1), 36–40, 43–44, 46.

Caywood, C., & Stocker, K. (1993). The ultimate crisis plan. In J. Gottschal (Ed.), *Crisis response* (pp. 409–427). Detroit: Gale Research Inc.

Chalip, L., & Thoma, J. (1993). *Sport governance in the global community.* Morgantown, WV: Fitness Information Technology.

Chandler, A. D., Jr. (1977). *The visible hand: The managerial revolution in American business.* Cambridge, MA: Harvard U Press.

Chen, C. Y. (2005). *Membership retention: A database marketing approach.* Unpublished research project, University of Northern Colorado.

Chudacoff, H. P. (1981). *The evolution of American urban society.* Englewood Cliffs, NJ: Prentice-Hall.

Clark, G. (2004). Global sports brand is born. Retrieved July 21, 2005, from http://www.rockymountainnews.com/drmn/business/article/0,1299DRMN_4_3143895

Clay, B. (1995). 8 great careers in the sports industry. *Black Enterprise, 25*(12), 158–166.

Click on this. *Sports Edge, 5*(4), 12.

Coast to coast. (1998, November 2–8). *SportsBusiness Journal,* 36.

Cohen, A. (1993, July). How not to run a promotion. *Athletic Business, 17,* 14.

Company cases in on Lance (2005, July 21). *Greeley Tribune,* C1.

Comte, E., & Stogel, C. (1990, January 1). Sports: A $63.1 billion industry. *The Sporting News, 208*(28), 60–61.

Conklin, A. (1999, April). Licensing renewal. *Athletic Business, 23,* 32–34.

Cravens, D. W., & Woodruff, R. B. (1986). *Marketing.* Reading, MA: Addison-Wesley Publishing Company.

Danziger, G. (1985). Computer applications in sport. In G. Lewis & H. Appenzeller (Eds.), *Successful sport management* (pp. 215–241). Charlottesville, VA: The Michie Company.

DeBrock, L. (1991). Economics. In B. Parkhouse (Ed.), *The management of sport: Its foundation and application* (56–73). St. Louis: Mosby-Year Book, Inc.

Delpy, L. (2000, January). Winning contests. *Sports Travel, 4*(1), 8–9.

Delpy, L., & Bosetti, H. (1998). Sport management and marketing via the world wide web. *Sport Marketing Quarterly, 7*(1), 21–27.

Dénes, F., & Misovicz, K. (1993, October). *Changes and contradictions: Sport market in Hungary.* Paper presented at the 4th International Conference on Sport Business, Paris, France.

DePauw, K. P., & Gavron, S. J. (1995). *Disability and sport.* Champaign, IL: Human Kinetics.

Dick, R., & Sack, A. L. (2003). NBA marketing directors' perception of effective marketing techniques: A longitudinal study. *International Sport Journal, 7*(1), 88–99.

Dodd, M., & Pearson, B. (1997, November 21). Big-time matchups underscore the big business of college ball. *USA Today,* 1C, 4C.

Donahue, M. D. (1998, February 2). Adapting the internet to the needs of business. *Advertising Age, 69*(5), 26.

Doyle, B., Modahl, M. A., & Abbott, B. (1997, May 5). What advertising works. *Mediaweek, 7*(18), S38–S41.

Ducoffe, R. H. (1996, September/October). Advertising value and advertising on the web. *Journal of Advertising Research, 36*(5), 21–35.

Dyer, M. (2005, July 13). Fans race to join NASCAR membership club. *Seaver Marketing Newsletter, 4*(12), 1.

East, W., Ronchin, F., & Smith, N. (2000, October). The highest earners in European sport. *EuroBusiness,* (24), 106–123.

ESPN Radio Network: One year later. (1993, Winter). *Between the lines: Ernst and Young's financial newsletter for the sports world,* 10–11, 13.

ESPN Sportzone. (1998, January 14). Retrieved October 13, 2001, from http://www.espnet.sportzone.com

ESPN. (2000). *ESPN Insider* Retrieved October 13, 2001, from http://espn.com

ESPN.com wraps up 2000 with record-breaking traffic. (2000, December 29). *Business Wire.* Retrieved October 13, 2001, from http://www.businesswire.com

Evans, J. R., & Berman, B. (1987). *Marketing.* New York: Macmillan Publishing Company.

Extreme sports: Ranking high in popularity (2005). Sporting Goods Manufacturers Association. Retrieved June 13, 2005, from http://www.sgma.com/press/2005/press1117636042-19826.html

Fahri, P. (1997, November 4). As women take the field, firms deliver pitches. *Washington Post*, A1.

Falk, H. (1983). *Handbook of computer applications for the small or medium-sized business*. Radnor, PA: Chilton Book Company.

Fan-favorite endorsers. (2000, September 9–15) *Sport Business Journal, 3*, 35.

Farrell, C., & Schiller, Z. (1993, November 15). Stuck! How companies cope when they can't raise prices. *Business Week*, 146–155.

Farrell, P. V., & McCann, D. J. (1997). Computers, the internet, and marketing college athletics. *Sport Marketing Quarterly, 6*(3), 12–13.

Fechter, S. (1998, September). Fun for fans. *Athletic Management, 10*, 48–52.

Feigenbaum, R. (1996, September 9). Garbage in—and in and in. *Business Week, 3492*, 110.

Ferrand, A., & Pagés, M. (1996). Image sponsoring: A methodology to match event and sponsor. *Journal of Sport Management, 10*, 278–291.

Fielding, L. W., Pitts, B. G., & Miller, L. K. (1991). Defining quality: Should educators in sport management programs be concerned about accreditation? *Journal of Sport Management, 5*(1), 1–17.

Fielitz, L., & Scott, D. (2003). Prediction of physical performance using data mining. *Research Quarterly for Exercise and Sport, 74*(1), 25.

Fink, J. S., Cunningham, G. B., & Kensicki, L. J. (2004). Using athletes as endorsers to sell women's sport: Attractiveness vs. expertise. *Journal of Sport Management, 18*(4), 350–367.

Fitzgerald, M. (1997, March 8). Web cash lies in entertainment. *Editor & Publisher, 130*(10), 46.

Forrester Research. (1998a). *The forrester report: Entertainment & technology strategies*. Retrieved October 13, 2001, from http://wysiwyg://20/www.forrester.com/cgi-bin/cgi.pl

Forrester Research. (1998b). *Forrester research finds internet business trade to jump to $327 billion by the year 2002*. Retrieved October 13, 2001, from http://www.forrester.com/press/pressrel/970728BT.htm

Foskett, S. (1996, November). Online technology ushers in one-to-one marketing. *Direct Marketing, 59*(7), 38–40.

Fox, J., & Levin, J. (1993). *How to work with the media*. Newbury Park, CA: Sage Publications.

Fram, E. H., & Grady, D. B. (1997, January). Internet shoppers: Is there a surfer gender gap? *Direct Marketing, 59*(9), 46–50.

Freedman, S. (1978). The baseball fad in Chicago. *Journal of Sport History, 5*(1), 42–64.

Freifeld, L. (2004, January). Licensing round table. *License!*, 42–51.

Freifeld, L. (2005). *School spirit*. Retrieved July 21, 2005, from http://www.licensemag.com/licensemag/content/printContentPopup.jsp?id=98091

Frickey, E. (1947). *Production in the United States, 1860–1914*. Cambridge, MA: Harvard University Press.

Fried-Cassorla, A. (1995, March). Successful marketing on the internet: A user's guide. *Direct Marketing, 57*(11), 39–41.

From the field. (1997, September 17). *Reebok, International*, (12).

Fullerton, R. A. (1988). How modern is modern marketing? Marketing's evolution and the myth of the production era. *Journal of Marketing, 52*(1), 108–125.

Gaston, F. P. (1984). *Administrative decision making: A study of collegiate trademark licensing programs*. Unpublished doctoral dissertation, University of Alabama, Tuscaloosa, AL.

Gauws, J. S. (1997). *Sport management theory and practice*. Pretoria, South Africa: Sigma Press.

Gibson, H., Attle, S. P., & Yiannakis, A. (1998). Segmenting the active sport tourist market: Life-span perspective. *Journal of Vacation Marketing, 4*(1), 51–64.

Global Sport Equipment: Industry Profile (2004). Datamonitor. Retrieved November 14, 2005, from http://www.datamonitor.com

Godin, S. (1996, December). When stamps are free—Using email and the internet for direct response. *Direct Marketing, 59*(8), 46–49.

Going global: The challenges of letting go (2004, October). *Sportsedge, 4*(10), 11.

Goldfisher, A. (1998, August 10–16). Cyberselling delivers global marketplace. *Sport Business Journal, 1*, 25.

Goldstein, W. (1989). *Playing for keeps: A history of early baseball*. Ithaca, NY: Cornell University Press.

Gonzalez, E. (1998, March 9). Marketing ski resorts on Internet a slick idea. *Rocky Mountain News*, 1B.

Gorn, E. J. (1986). *The manly art: bare-knuckle prize fighting in America*. Ithaca, NY: Cornell University Press.

Graham, J. R. (1996, October). How to market and sell in a cyberworld. *Direct Marketing, 59*(6), 26–27.

Grantham, W., Patton, R., York, T., & Winick, M. (1998). *Health fitness management*. Champaign, IL: Human Kinetics.

Graphic, Visualization, & Usability Center. (1997). *GVU's 8th www user survey*. Retrieved October 13, 2001, from http://www.gvu.gatech.edu/user_surveys/survey-1997-10/

Graphic, Visualization, & Usability Center. (1999). *GVU's 10th www user survey*. Retrieved October 13, 2001, from http://www.gvu.gatech.edu/user_surveys/survey-1998-10

Greenwald, L., & Fernandez-Balboa, J. (1998). Trends in sport marketing industry and in the demographics of the United States: Their effect on the strategic role of grassroots sport sponsorships in corporate America. *Sport Marketing Quarterly, 7*(4), 35–48.

Greim, L. (1997, October 26). Internet users gagging on spam. *Rocky Mountain News*, 1G, 5G.

Griffith, C. C. (2003, September). Sports licensing: Creation and protection of logod. *The Licensing Journal*, 26–27.

Griffin, J. (1996, November). The internet's expanding role in building customer loyalty. *Direct Marketing, 59*(7), 50–53.

Gunther, M. (1996, March 4). Web + sports = profit. Right? *Fortune, 133*(4), 197–198.

Hagstrom, R. (1998). *The NASCAR way*. New York: Wiley.

Handel, C., & Forrester, S. (1997, Spring). Database marketing: Increasing participation in recreational sports. *NIRSA Journal, 21*(3), 46–48.

Harada M. (1993, October). *Development and structural changes in sport business in Japan*. Paper presented at the 4th International Conference on Sport Business, Paris.

Hardy, S. (1982). *How Boston played: Sport, recreation, and community, 1865–1915*. Boston: Northeastern University Press.

Hardy, S. (1986). Entrepreneurs, organizations, and the sport marketplace: Subjects in search of historians. *Journal of Sport History, 13*(1), 21.

Hardy, S. (1990). Adopted by all the leading clubs: Sporting goods and the shaping of leisure, 1800–1900. In Richard Butsch (Ed.), *For fun and profit: The transformation of leisure into consumption* (pp. 71–101). Philadelphia: Temple University Press.

Hawkins, D. T. (1994). Electronic advertising: On online information systems. *Online*, 15–25.

Helitzer, M. (1995). *The dream job: Sports publicity, promotion, and public relations,* 2nd ed. Athens, OH: University Press.

Helitzer, M. (2000) *The dream job: Sport publicity, promotion and marketing,* 3rd ed. Athens, OH: University Sport Press.

Hendee, J. C., & Burdge, R. W. (1974). The substitutability concept: Implications for recreation research and management. *Journal of Leisure Research, 6,* 157–162.

Herman, J. T. (1992, April). From chaos to control. *Case Currents,* 24–28.

Hiebing, R. C., & Cooper, S. W. (1990). *How to write a successful marketing plan.* Lincolnwood, IL: NTC Business Books.

Hiestand, M. (2005, January 20). Red Sox nation buys big into team's success. *USA Today.*

Higgs, R. (1971). *The transformation of American economy, 1865–1914: An essay in interpretation.* New York: Cambridge University Press.

Himelstein. L. (1997, January 27). The game's the thing at Nike now. *Business Week,* 88.

Hodges, J. (1996, October 28). Direct marketing. *Advertising Age, 67*(42), S1–S2.

Hodgkinson, H. L. (1992, June). *A demographic look at tomorrow.* Washington, DC: Institute for Educational Leadership.

Hofman, M. (1999, December). Searching for the mountain of youth. *Inc. 21*(18), 33–36.

Holland, M. (1992, May). International opportunities. *Fitness Management,* 39–43.

Holland, S., Pybas, D., & Sanders, A. (1992). Personal watercraft: Fun, speed—and conflict? *Parks and Recreation, 27*(11), 52–56.

Horine, L. (1995). *Administration of Physical Education and Sport Programs, 3rd Ed.* Madison, WI: Brown and Benchmark.

Horine, L., & Stotlar, D. K. (2004) *Administration of physical education and sport programs.* St. Louis: McGraw-Hill.

Hounshell, D. A. (1984). *From the American system to mass production, 1800–1932.* Baltimore, MD: The Johns Hopkins University Press.

How China runs the world (2005, July 31, D6). *Seattle Post-Intelligencer.*

Howard, D. R., & Crompton, J. L. (1980). *Financing, managing and marketing recreation and park resources.* Dubuque, IA: Wm. C. Brown Company Publishers.

Huang, Y. (1999). *An investigation of the current practices of relationship marketing programs within professional baseball through a content analysis.* Unpublished doctoral dissertation, University of Northern Colorado, Greeley, CO.

Hughes, A. M. (2000). *Strategic database marketing: The master plan for starting ad managing a profitable, custom-based marketing program,* 2nd ed. New York: McGraw-Hill.

Hughes, D. (2005) *The Collegiate Licensing Company names top selling universities and manufacturers.* Retrieved July 21, 2005, from http://www.clc.com/Pages/home2.html

IEG Forecast: Sponsorship spending growth will slow in 2001. (2000, December 18). *IEG Sponsorship Report, 19,* 1, 4–5.

IEG, Inc. (1995). *IEG SR briefing: Computer industry sponsorship.* Chicago: Author.

IEG, Inc. (1996). How properties price internet benefits. *IEG Sponsorship Report, 15*(7), 1–3.

IEG, Inc. (2004). Online content summary and industry update 3Q 2004. Chicago: International Events Group

IMG (2005). Retrieved August 1, 2005, from http://www.imgworld.com/

Infoseek Corporation. (1999). *Driving the growth of the internet.* Retrieved Oct. 12, 2001, from http://www.info.infoseek.com

International Events Group (1992a, September 7). Centerfold. *IEG Sponsorship Report, 11,* 4–5.

International Events Group (1992b, November 2). Assertions. *IEG Sponsorship Report, 11,* 2.

International Events Group (1992c, November 2). Industry news. *IEG Sponsorship Report, 11,* 7.

International Events Group (1992d, December 21). Centerfold: The bottom line on sponsorship. *IEG Sponsorship Report, 11,* 4–6.

International Events Group (1994, December 6). Assertions. *IEG Sponsorship Report 13,* 2.

International Health, Racquet and Sportsclub Association. (1998). *IHRSA: State of the industry report.* Boston: Author.

International Olympic Committee (2004). *2004 Marketing Fact File.* Lausanne: International Olympic Committee.

Internet population reaches 56% of U.S. adults. (2001, February 19). *USA Today.* Retrieved October 13, 2001, from http://www.usatoday.com

InterZine Productions, Inc. (1997a, May 2). ESPN Chilton sports poll: Online sports information. *The Sports Business Daily, 3*(143), 11.

InterZine Productions, Inc. (1997b, September 30). The daily follows MLB's postseason via the air and web. *The Sports Business Daily, 4*(13), 4.

InterZine Productions, Inc. (1997c, October 22). Online news & notes: One more record for dean at UNC. *The Sports Business Daily, 4*(26), 10.

InterZine Productions, Inc. (1997d, October 23). Online news & notes: NHL puts the puck in audionet. *The Sports Business Daily, 4*(27), 5.

InterZine Productions, Inc. (1997e, October 28). NBA.com included increased game coverage and new sponsors. *The Sports Business Daily, 4*(30), 5, 8.

InterZine Productions, Inc. (1997f, October 29). MJ's website takes to the air at jordan.sportsline.com. *The Sports Business Daily, 4*(31), 10.

InterZine Productions, Inc. (1997g, November 7). Throwing copper: Here's some insight on AZ bowl plans. *The Sports Business Daily, 4*(38), 2.

InterZine Productions, Inc. (1997h, November 21). ESPN Chilton sports poll: Internet usage among NFL fans. *The Sports Business Daily, 4*(48), 11.

InterZine Productions, Inc. (1997i, November 24). Big blue connects with NFL for Super Bowl sponsorship. *The Sports Business Daily, 4*(49), 1.

InterZine Productions, Inc. (1998a, January 5). Insight's Copper Bowl sponsorship not a fan favorite. *The Sports Business Daily, 4*(67).

InterZine Productions, Inc. (1998b, January 7). Media notes. *The Sports Business Daily, 4*(69), 8.

InterZine Productions, Inc. (1998c, January 22). Media notes. *The Sports Business Daily, 4*(79), 12.

InterZine Productions, Inc. (1998d, February 12). Online news & notes: Will NFL be shopping internet rights? *The Sports Business Daily, 4*(94), 6.

InterZine Productions, Inc. (1998e, February 25). Nfl.com looks to major players for next online partner. *The Sports Business Daily, 4*(102), 5.

InterZine Productions, Inc. (1998f, March 26). Online news & notes: Is Disney-Starwave deal near? *The Sports Business Daily, 4*(123), 8.

InterZine Productions, Inc. (1998g, April 9). MLB online notes: Yankees sign three-year deal with Audionet. *The Sports Business Daily, 4*(130), 8.

InterZine Productions, Inc. (1998h, April 17). Sportsline USA reports record first quarter performance. *The Sports Business Daily, 4*(134), 20.

Irwin, D. L., & Fleger, B. (1992). Reading between the lines. *Athletic Management, 4*, 15–18.

Irwin, R. L. (1990). *Development of a collegiate licensing administrative paradigm*. Unpublished doctoral dissertation, University of Northern Colorado, Greeley, CO.

Irwin, R. L., Assimakopoulos, M. K., & Sutton, W. A. (1994). A model for screening sport sponsorship opportunities. *Journal of Promotion Management, 2*(3/4), 53–69.

Irwin, R.L., & Asimakopoulos, M. (1992, December). An approach to the evaluation and selection of sport sponsorship proposals. *Sport Marketing Quarterly, 1*, 43–51.

Irwin, R. L., & Stotlar, D. K. (1993). Operational protocol analysis of sport and collegiate licensing programs. *Sport Marketing Quarterly, 2*, 5, 7–16.

Irwin, R. L., Sutton, W. A., & McCarthy, L. M. (2002). *Sport promotion and sales management*. Champaign, IL: Human Kinetics.

Isaacs, G. A. (1931). *The story of the newspaper printing press*. London: Cooperative Printing Society.

ISL Marketing (1993). *The Olympic programme*. New York: Author.

J. Walter Spalding original ledger (1947). *Sporting Goods Dealer, 96*(3), 128–129.

James, D. (2002). Athlete or competition? How to choose. *Marketing News, 36*(15), 4.

Javalgi, R., & Moberg, C. (1997). Service loyalty: Implications for service providers. *Journal of Services Marketing, 11*, 3, 165–179.

Jensen, J. (1995, April 3). Shooting to score on the 'net. *Advertising Age, 64*(14), 24–25.

Jizhong, W. (1997, June). *The potentiality of sports in the Chinese market*. Paper presented at conference on Marketing of Sports in the 21st Century, Hong Kong.

Johns, R. (1997). Sports promotion & the internet. *Cyber-Journal of Sport Marketing*. Retrieved May 5, 2000, from http://www.cad.gu.edu/market/cjsm/johns.htm

Joyce Julius and Associates. (1991). *The sponsor's report almanac*. Ann Arbor, MI: Joyce Julius and Associates.

Julian W. Curtiss: Master of arts in sporting goods merchandising (1928). *Sporting Goods Dealer, 58*(4), 139.

Jupiter Communications. (1998a). *European online ad markets: Strategic overview*. Retrieved May 5, 2000, from http://www.jup.com/briefs/oa43_02.html

Jupiter Communications. (1998b). *Jupiter model defines online ad/direct marketing convergence*. Retrieved May 5, 2000, from http://www.jup.com/jupiter/release/9708/online.shtml

Kaplan, D. (1998, September 7–13). Venus patches rift with WTA. *SportsBusiness Journal, 1*, 9.

Kaplan, D. (2003, December 1–7). NFL pushes growth category: Holiday sales. *Sport Business Journal*, 4.

Kaplan, D. (2004). Eagles plan kids' TV show in bid to hatch next generation of fans. *SportsBusiness Journal, 17*(38), 9.

Kaplan, D. (2006, September 6) 500M homes outside the US to get NFL games. *SportsBusiness Journal, 8*(17), 4.

Kapoor, A., & McKay, R. J. (1971). *Managing international markets*. Princeton, NJ: The Darwin Press.

Kates, S. M. (1998). Consumer research and sport marketing: Starting the conversation between two different academic discourses. *Sport Marketing Quarterly, 7*(2), 24–31.

Kaufman, M. (1998, May 11–17). Women take their place at the table. *SportsBusiness Journal, 1*, 48.

Kelly, J. R., & Warnick, R. B. (1999). *Recreation trends and markets: The 21st century*. Champaign, IL: Sagamore Publishing.

King, B. (1998, October 12–18). Primo premiums: Beanies, beach towels. *SportsBusiness Journal*, 34–35.

King, B. (1998a, August 17–23). Earnhardt wants to tune up your engine. *SportsBusiness Journal, 13*, 9.

King, B. (1998b, May 18–24). NASCAR: It ain't just racin'. *SportsBusiness Journal, 1*, 48.

Kirsch, G. B. (1989). *The creation of American team sports: Baseball and cricket, 1838–1872*. Urbana, IL: University of Illinois Press.

Klein, D. (1997, October 27). Advertisers should invest in sites, not just banner ads. *Advertising Age, 68*(43), 52.

Kogan, R. (1985). *Brunswick: The story of an American company from 1845 to 1985*. Skokie, IL: Brunswick Corp.

Koranteng, J. (1998, January). Reebok finds its second wind as it pursues global presence. *Advertising Age*, 18.

Koranteng, M. (1999, May). Huge response for Olympic licensing. *The Sydney Spirit*, (10), 4.

Kotler, P. (2000). *Marketing management: The mellenium edition*. Upper Saddle River, NJ: Prentice Hall, p. 19.

Kotler, P. (1988). *Marketing management: Analysis, planning, implementation, and control, 6th Edition*. Englewood Cliffs, NJ: Prentice Hall.

Laessing, U. (2005). Adidas to buy Reebok. Retrieved August 8, 2005, from http://news.yahoo.com/news?tmpl=story&u=/nm/20050803/bs_nm/retail_adidas_reebok_dc

Lamb, C. W., Hair, J. F, & McDaniel, C. (1996). *Marketing*. Cincinnati, OH: South-Western College Publishing.

Lascu, D-N., Geise, T. D., Toolan, C., Guehring, B., & Mercer, J. (1995). Sport involvement: A relevant individual difference factor in spectator sports. *Sport Marketing Quarterly, 4*(4), 41–46.

Lee, J. (2003, Dec. 22–28). College deals build brand and relationships. *SportsBusiness Journal*, 25.

Lefton, T. (2001, February 18). Fourth and long. *The Industry Standard*.

Lefton, T. (2003, November 17). NFL flexes database marketing muscle to sell tix, boost viewership. *SportsBusiness Journal*.

Legergott, S. (1946). *Manpower in economic growth: The American record since 1800*. New York: McGraw-Hill Publishing.

Leonard, D. (2001, February 5). Madison avenue fights back. *Fortune*. Retrieved October 13, 2001, from http://www.fortune.com

Levine, P. (1985). *A. G. Spalding and the rise of baseball: The promise of American sport*. New York: Oxford University Press.

Levitt, T. (1965, Nov. - Dec.). Exploit the product life cycle. *Harvard Business Review, 43*, 81–94.

Liberman, N. (1999, April 19). TV partners provide juice to net sites. *SportsBusiness Journal, 1*(52), 21.

Liberman, N. (1999, September 27–October 3). Publishers cross over to the Web, TV. *SportsBusiness Journal, 2*(23), 27.

Liberman, N. (2004, October 18–24). Top give-a-ways in sport. *SportsBusiness Journal*, 17–24.

Liebert, R. M., & Splegler, M. D. (1970). *Personality*. Homewood, IL: Dorsey Press.

Lombardo, J. (1998, May 4–10). "Team Tiger" takes Woods to the top. *SportsBusiness Journal, 13*, 22–23.

Lu, D. (2000, October). *Factors affecting spectator attendance in professional baseball: A comparison of Taiwan and USA*. Paper presented at the Florida Association for Health, Physical Education, Recreation, and Dance conference, Orlando, FL.

Lucas, J. A., & Smith, R. A. (1978). *Saga of American sport*. Philadelphia: Lee and Febiger.

Maddox, K. (1997, October 3). Banner quarter for web ad sales, IAB study finds. *Advertising Age, 68*(40), 34.

Maddox, L., & Mehta, D. (1997, March/April). The role and effect of web addresses in advertising. *Journal of Advertising Research*, 47–59.

Madsen, H. (1996, December). Reclaim the deadzone. *Wired, 4*(12), 206–220.

Mainardi, J. (1997, February). Match the media to the message. *Best's Review*, 88–91.

Mangalindan, M. (1997, December 1). Holiday shoppers beat the bustle by booting up pc. *Rocky Mountain News,* 13B.

Marsano, W. (1987, September). A five ring circus. *Northwest, 1*, 64–69.

Martin, J. (1996). Is the athlete's sport important when picking an athlete to endorse a non-sport product? *Journal of Consumer Marketing, 13*(6), 28–43.

Maslow, A. (1954). *Motivation and personality*. New York: Harper and Row.

McCarthy, E. J., & Perreault, W. D., Jr. (1984). *Basic marketing: A managerial approach*. Homewood, IL: Irwin, Inc.

McCarthy, E. J., & Perreault, W. D. (1990). *Basic marketing: A managerial approach*, Homewood, IL: Richard D. Irwin, Inc.

McCarthy, L. M. (1998). Marketing sport to Hispanic consumers. *Sport Marketing Quarterly, 7*(4), 19–24.

McCarville, R. E., Flood, C. M., & Floats, T. A. (1998). *The effectiveness of selected promotions on spectators' assessment of a nonprofit sporting event sponsor*, pp. 15–62.

McCarville, R. E., Crompton, J. L., & Sell, J. A. (1993). The influence of outcome messages on reference prices. *Leisure Sciences, 15*, 115–130.

McConnell, B., & Huba, J. (2004). Creating customer evangelists: How loyal fans can become a volunteer sales force. Retrieved July 2, 2005, from http//:www.mialiareport.com/jul04_story5.cfm.

McCormack, M. H. (2000). *Staying street smart*. New York: Viking Press.

McDonald, M. (1998). *Sport sponsorship and the role of personality matching*. Buffalo, NY: Conference of the North American Society for Sport Management.

McMasters, L. (1993, March 29). Then there was the time a thrown shoe held up the Derby. *Call to the Post*, 62.

McMurray, S. (1998, January). The web's three-way tug of war. *SportsSense: The Journal of Sports Business, 1*(1), 5.

Meek, A. (1997). An estimate of the size and supported economic activity of the sports industry in the United States. *Sport Marketing Quarterly, 6*(4), 15–21.

Microsoft Corporation. (1996). *Getting started with Microsoft Frontpage 97: Professional website publishing without programming*. Redmond, WA: Author.

Migala, D. (2003). My buddies: Heat and Suns use internal marketing program to improve relations with season ticket holders. Retrieved December 2, 2005, from http://www.migaliareport.com/dec03_story4.cfm

Migala, D. (2005). You've got mail: How to use email more effectively to sell tickets. Retrieved May 5, 2005, from http://www.migaliareport.com/apr05_story4_pfcfm

Millar, S. (1999, June 28–July 4). X Marks the Spot—On Center Stage. *SportsBusiness Journal*, 23–30.

Miller, L. K., Fielding, L. W., & Pitts, B. G. (1993). The rise of the

Louisville Slugger in the mass market. *Sport Marketing Quarterly, 2*(3), 9–16.

Miller, L., Shaad, S., Burch, D., & Turner, R. (1999). *Sales success in sport marketing*. Wichita, KS: Events Unlimited.

Miller, L. K., Fielding, L. W., & Pitts, B. G. (1993). The impact of the Americans with Disabilities Act of 1990. *Clinical Kinesiology, 47*(3), 63–70.

Millican, M. (1985, July). Direct marketing response mail. *Ski Area Management, 24*(4), 52–54.

Milne, G. R., & McDonald, M. A. (1999). *Sport marketing: Managing the exchange process*. Sudbury, MA: Jones and Bartlett.

Moore, M. T. (1993, February 17). Converse makes fast break to rename shoe. *USA Today*, 1B.

Morganthau, T., Barrett, T., Dickey, C., & Talbot, M. (1992, June 22). Piling up the gold. *Newsweek*, 56–58.

Morris, R. (1999, September 27). 3 giants dominate sports publishing. *SportsBusiness Journal*.

Morrison, T., Conaway, W., & Borden, G. (1994). *Kiss, bow, or shake hands*. Holbrook, MA: Bob Adams, Inc.

Mott, F. L. (1957). *A history of American magazines, 1885–1905*. Cambridge, MA: Harvard University Press.

Mrozek, D. J. (1983). *Sport and American mentality, 1880–1910*. Knoxville, TN: The University of Tennessee Press.

Mullen, E. (1998, August 10–16). Asian flu hits sports industry. *SportsBusiness Journal, 1*, 46.

Mullen, L. (1998, August 31–September 6). Adidas ties up UCLA deal, said to be worth $18 million. *SportsBusiness Journal*, 10.

Mullin, B. (1985). An information-based approach to marketing sport. In G. Lewis & H. Appenzeller (Eds.), *Successful sport management* (pp. 201–214). Charlottesville, VA: The Michie Company.

Mullin, B., Hardy, S., & Sutton W. A. (1993). *Sport marketing*. Champaign, IL: Human Kinetics.

Mullin, B., Hardy, S., & Sutton W. A. (2000). *Sport marketing*, 2nd ed. Champaign, IL: Human Kinetics.

Murphy, G. G. S., & Zellner, A. (1959). Sequential growth, the labor safety-valve doctrine, and the development of American unionism. *Journal of Economic History, 19*(3), 402–419.

Nakazawa, M., Mahony, D. F., Funk, D. C., & Hirakawa, S. (1999). Segmenting J. League spectators based on length of time as a fan. *Sport Marketing Quarterly, 8*(4), 55–65.

NASCAR merchandising on a roll. (2001, Feb 20) *Sport Business Daily*, 7.

National Basketball Association. (1998). *NBA international facts*. New York: Author.

National Handicapped Sports. (1993). *Registration pamphlet of the National Handicapped Sports Adaptive Fitness Instructor Workshop*. Rockville, MD: Author.

NBA and Russell Corporation enter into largest equipment deal in sports (2005). Retrieved January 3, 2005, from http://www.sponsorship.com/news/contenet/6294.asp?source=iotw121604

NBC gets Olympic TV deal. (1993, July 28). *Greeley [CO] Tribune*, B2.

NCAA internet survey. (1998, January 19). *The NCAA News*, 2.

NCAA to create website for all championships. (1998. April 13). *The NCAA News*, 1, 8.

New Gotham headquarters opened by A. G. Spalding and Bros. (1924). *Sporting Goods Dealer, 50*(4), 85–87.

New marketing research definition approved. (1987, Jan. 2). *Marketing News*, 1.

Nike reaps $10 million of TV exposure during Tiger's triumphant final round at The Masters. Retrieved July 24, 2005, from http://www.joycejulius.com/

Noack, D. R., (1996, August). The sporting world. *Internet World, 7*(8), 48–52.

Noack, D. R. (1998, February 21). The secrets of web advertising sales. *Editor & Publisher*, 32–33.

Norris, J. D. (1990). *Advertising and the transformation of American society, 1865–1920.* New York: Greenwood Press.

Ober, E. (1992, August 5). Interview with David Stern, Commissioner NBA. New York: Columbia Broadcasting System.

Official IAAF partners. (1999). Retrieved January 16, 1999, from http://www.IAAF.org

Olympic fact file. (1998, Spring) Lausanne: International Olympic Committee.

Oriard, M. (1993). *Reading football: How the popular press created an American spectacle.* Chapel Hill, NC: University of North Carolina Press.

Owens, J. (1999, August 23–29). Strength with retailers powers NASCAR. *SportsBusiness Journal*, 10.

Ozanian, M. K., & Taub, S. (1992, July 7). Big leagues, bad business. *Financial World*, 34–51.

Pajak, M. (1990). Every fly ball is an adventure. *Athletic Business, 14*(3), 26.

Parks, J. B., & Zanger, B. R. K. (1990). *Sport and fitness management: Career strategies and professional content.* Champaign, IL: Human Kinetics Books.

Parks, J. B., Zanger, B. R. K., & Quarterman, J. (1998). *Contemporary sport management.* Champaign, IL: Human Kinetics Books.

Paul, P. (1996). Marketing on the internet. *Journal of Consumer Marketing, 13*(4), 27–39.

Paulin, C. O. (1932). *Atlas of the historical geography of the United States.* Washington, DC: Carnegie Institution.

Peter, J. P., & Donnelly, J. H. (1991). *A preface to marketing management.* Boston: Richard D. Irwin, Inc.

Peter, J. P., & Donnelly, J. H. (1993). *A Preface to marketing management.* Boston, MA: Irwin, Inc.

Pfaffenberger, B. (1996). *Publish it on the web.* London: Academic Press, Inc.

Phelan, M. (1850). *Billiards without a master.* New York: D. D. Winant.

Phoenix Suns. (1996, November 23). Personal correspondence to David Stotlar.

Pickle, D. (1997, October 20). Volleyball video goes on net. *The NCAA News*, 3.

Pitts, B. G. (1997). From leagues of their own to an industry of their own: The emerging lesbian sports industry. *Women in Sport and Physical Activity Journal, 6*(2), 109–139.

Pitts, B. G. (1998). An analysis of sponsorship recall during Gay Games IV. *Sport Marketing Quarterly, 7*(4), 11–18.

Pitts, B. G. (1999a). Sports tourism and niche markets: Identification and analysis of the growing lesbian and gay sports tourism industry. *Journal of Vacation Marketing, 5* (1), 31–50.

Pitts, B. G. (1999b, March). *The $11.8 billion dollar gay and lesbian sports tourism market: Defining, targeting, and competitive advantage strategies for corporate America stakeholders.* Paper presented at the 1999 conference of the Snow Sports Industries of America, Las Vegas.

Pitts, B. G., & Ayers, K. (1999, June). *An economic analysis of Gay Games V.* Paper presented at the annual conference of the North American Society for Sport Management, Vancouver, B.C., Canada.

Pitts, B. G. (1993). Interviews with soccer players: The Louisville Women's Soccer Association, Inc. Unpublished raw data.

Pitts, B. G., & Fielding, L. W. (1987, May). Custom-made bats and baseball players: The relationship between form utility and promotion—J. A. Hillerich's contribution to sporting goods marketing. *North American Society for Sport Management Conference Proceedings.*

Pitts, B. G., Fielding, L. F., & Miller, L. K. (1994). Industry segmentation theory and the sport industry: Developing a sport industry segment model. *Sport Marketing Quarterly, 3*(1), 15–24.

Playing the global game. (2004, January 12). *FN*. Retrieved March 29, 2005, from http://0-web.lexis-nexis.com.source.unco.edu/universe/document?-m=6083e8fce31b541b3

Plonsky, C. (2005). *Long Horns lead the herd.* Retrieved August 15, 2005, from http://www.sports-forum.com/sellingit/univtex.htm

Polsky, N. (1969). *Hustlers, beats, and others.* New York: Anchor Books.

Pope, N. K. L., & Forrest, E. J. (1997, April). A proposed format for the management of sport marketing websites. *Cyber-journal of sport marketing, 1*(2), 43–49.

Poole, M. (2005, May 16– 22). Why try to reach consumers in ways that will only annoy them? *SportsBusiness Journal*, 11.

Porter, G. (1973). *The rise of big business, 1860–1910.* Arlington Heights, IL: Harlan Davidson, Inc.

Porter, M. (1985). *Competitive advantage.* New York: The Free Press.

Porter, M. E. (1985). *Competitive advantage: Creating and sustaining superior performance.* New York: The Free Press.

Pratzmark, R. R., & Frey, N. (1989, January). The winners play a new global game. *Marketing Communications*, 18–27.

Presbrey, F. (1929). *The history and development of advertising.* Garden City, NY: Doubleday, Doran and Company, Inc.

Pride, W. M., & Ferrell, O. C. (1991). *Marketing concepts and strategies.* Boston: Houghton Mifflin Company.

Pride, W. M., & Ferrell, O. C. (1997) *Marketing,* 10th ed. New York: Houghton Mifflin Company.

Pride, W. M., & Ferrell, O. C. (2003). *Marketing: Concepts and strategies,* 12th ed. Boston: Houghton Mifflin.

Quelch, J. A., Buzzell, R. D., & Salama, E. R. (1990). *The marketing challenge of 1992.* New York: Addison-Wesley.

Rader, B. G. (1990). *American sports: from the age of folk games to the age of televised sports.* Englewood Cliffs, NJ: Prentice Hall.

Raju, J.S., Srinivasan, V., & Lal, R. (1990). The effects of brand loyalty on competitive price promotional strategies. *Management Science, 36*(3), 276–305.

Reasons for Spalding success. (1915). *Sporting Goods Dealer, 32*(2), 40–49.

Reed, M. H. (1989). *IEG legal guide to sponsorship.* Chicago, IL: International Events Group.

Reed, M. H. (1990). *Legal aspects of promoting and sponsoring events.* Chicago, IL: International Events Group.

Reiss, S. A. (1989). *City games: The evolution of American urban society and the rise of sports.* Urbana, IL: University of Illinois Press.

Resnick, R. (1997, April). The case for "opt in" marketing on the internet. *Direct Marketing*, 52–53.

Reynolds, M. (1998, June 22–28). Women's sports: A growth industry. *SportsBusiness Journal*, 30.

Rich, L. (1997. September 22). A brand new game: Does new research prove the branding value of banners? *Brandweek, 38*(35), 55–56.

Ries, A., & Trout, J. (1986). *Positioning: The battle for your mind.* New York: McGraw-Hill.

Rocklitz, K. (2005, February 2). *A view from the top*. National Sports Forum presentation Seattle:

Rodin, S. (1998, May 11–17). Shrewd marketers can share in boom. *SportsBusiness Journal*, 34.

Rofe, J. (1999, February 8–14). Winning record makes a sales slump. *SportsBusiness Journal*, 7, 23.

Rohm, A. (1997). The creation of consumer bonds within Reebok Running. *Sport Marketing Quarterly*, 6, 2, 17–25.

Rosner, H. (1996, March 4). Will email become j-mail? *Brandweek*, 37(10), 30.

Ruff, M. (1992a). The driving force. *AutoWeek*, 42(22), 37.

Ruff, M. (1992b). What's in a name? *AutoWeek*, 42(22), 37.

Ruibal, S. (1998, June 5). Participation grows by leaps and bounds. *USA Today*, 3c.

Ryan, T. J. (2005, May). License and registration please. *Sporting Goods Business*, 23–24.

Sage, G. (1996). Patriotic images and capital profit: Contradictions of professional team sports licensed merchandise. *Sociology of Sport Journal*, 13, 1–11.

Schmetterer, R. (1997, May 5). Meeting the measurement challenge. *Mediaweek*, 7(18), S72–S73.

Schnaars, S.P. (1991). *Marketing strategy: A consumer-driven approach.* New York: The Free Press.

Schoenbachler, D. D., Gordon, G. L., Foley, D., & Spellman, L. (1997). Understanding consumer database marketing. *Journal of Consumer Marketing*, 14(1), 5–17.

Schoenfeld, B. (2005). PR playbook. *SportsBusiness Journal*, 18(8), 35.

Schoenfelt, E. L., Maue, A. E., & Hatcher, E. B. (1999). "We Got Next"—Next what? An evaluation of the effectiveness of the WNBA tag line and a case for sport marketing research. *Sport Marketing Quarterly*, 8(3), 31–38.

Seligman, B. (2005, March 21–27). Do PGA player endorsements really sell? *SportsBusiness Journal*, 7(45), 10.

Semich, J. W. (1995, January 15). The world wide web: Internet boomtown? *Datamation*, 41(1), 37–41.

Seymour, H. (1989). *Baseball: The early years.* New York: Oxford University Press.

SGMA International (2005). SGMA International: 2004 U.S. Sporting Goods Report. Retrieved January 28, 2005, from http://www.smga.com

Shaffer, A. (1997, March). What's in a name? *Club Industry*, 2, 17–24.

Shatzkin, C. (1996, September). Opportunity knocks. *Panstadia International*, 3(4), 78–80.

Shaw, R. (1991). *Computer-aided marketing and selling.* London: Reed International Books.

Sherwin, G. R., & Avila, E. N. (1997). *Connecting online: Creating a successful image on the internet.* Grants Pass, WA: The Oasis Press.

Silverstein, B. (1996, January). The internet: It's not a proven direct marketing medium . . . yet. *Direct Marketing*, 58(9), 30–33.

Simmons Market Research Bureau. (1996). *Market report.*

Sirak, R. (2005). The golf diget 50—On and off the course. *Golf Digest*, 56(2), 99–101.

Smith, M. L. (1998, January). One to one: Put the customer in the information driver seat and build better relationships. *Direct Marketing*, 37–39.

Snider, M. (1997, February 19). Growing online population making internet 'mass media.' *USA Today*, D1.

Solomon, S. D. (1994, November 15). Staking a claim on the internet. *Inc. Technology*, 16, 87–92.

Somers, D. A. (1972). *The rise of sports in New Orleans, 1850–1900.* Baton Rouge, LA: Louisiana State University Press.

Sosnowski, T. (2005, June). Batter up. *Platythings*, 25.

Spain, W. (1996, October 14). Ad impressions cause headache for web 'zines. *Advertising Age*, 67(42), S2.

Spanberg, E. (1998, June 8–14). The intimidator's empire. *SportsBusiness Journal*, 1, 17.

Speer, T. (1999, March 16). Avoid gift giving and cultural blunders in Asian locales. *USA Today*, 3E.

Spiegel, P. (1998, December 14). Heir Gordon. *Forbes*, 189–197.

Spoelstra, J. (1997). *Ice to the Eskimos.* New York: Harper Business.

Spoelstra, J. (1997*). Ice to the Eskimos: How to sell a product nobody wants.* New York: Harper Business.

Sponsors reveal how to bring deals to life. (1999, March). *IEG Sponsorship Report*, 18, 7.

Sponsorship spending to see biggest rise in five years. (2004) Retrieved January 3, 2005, from http://www.sponsorship.com/iegsr/2004/12/27/printable.asp

Sport and television. (1996, July 20). *The Economist*, 17–19.

Sporting Goods Manufacturers Association. (January 20, 2000). Retrieved October 13, 2001, from http://www.sportlink.com/research

Sports information bulletin. (1992, June). Brussels: Sport for All Clearing House.

Sports licensed products: Who wins at the cash register (2005). Retrieved July 12, 2005, from http://www.sgma.com/press/20051118078382-31157.html

Sports Media Challenge (1991). *Pocket guide to media success.* Charlotte, NC: Sports Media Challenge.

Sports participation trends 1999. (1999). *The SGMA Report.* Retrieved May 5, 2000, from http://www.sportlink.com

Standeven, J., & DeKnop, P. (1999). *Sport tourism.* Champaign, IL: Human Kinetics.

Stanton, W. J., Etzel, M. J., & Walker, B. J. (1991). *Fundamentals of marketing.* New York: McGraw-Hill, Inc.

Starwave Corporation. (1997a). *Nascar online advertising rate card.* Retrieved May 5, 2000, from http://www.starwave.com/saleskit/nascar.html

Starwave Corporation. (1997b). *Nba.com online advertising rate card.* Retrieved May 5, 2000, from http://www.starwave.com/saleskit/nba.html

Starwave Corporation. (1997c). *Nfl.com advertising rate card.* Retrieved May 5, 2000, from http://www.starwave.com/saleskit/nfl.html

Starwave Corporation. (1998). *ESPN sportszone advertising rate card.* Retrieved May 5, 2000, from http://www.starwave.com/saleskit/sz.html

Stauble, V. (1994). The significance of sport marketing and the case of the Olympic Games. In Graham, P. (Ed.), *Sport business* (pp. 14–21). Dubuque, IA: Brown-Benchmark.

Steve Risser: The interview. (1997, April*). Sport Travel*, 2, 30–31.

Stevens, T. (1996, April 1). Increasing net worth. *Industry Week*, 245(7), 54.

Stewart, J. (1999, March 8–14). Formula one finds roar bumpy with EU. *SportsBusiness Journal*, 34.

Stipe, S. E. (1996, April). Selling on the internet. *Best's Review*, 96(12), 44–48, 96.

Stone, G., Joseph, M., & Jones, M. (2003). An exploratory study on the use of sport celebrities in advertising: A content analysis. *Sport Marketing Quarterly*, 12(2), 94–102.

Stotlar, D. K. (1987). Managing administrative functions with microcomputers. In J. E. Donnelly (Ed.), *Using microcomputers in physical education and the sport sciences* (pp. 117–132). Champaign, IL: Human Kinetics.

Stotlar, D. K. (1989). *Successful sport marketing and sponsorship plans.* Dubuque, IA: Wm. C. Brown.

Stotlar, D. K. (1993). *Successful sport marketing.* Dubuque, IA: Brown-Benchmark.

Stotlar, D. (2001). *Developing successful sport marketing plans.* Morgantown, WV: Fitness Information Technology.

Stotlar, D. K. (2005). *Developing successful sport marketing plans, 2nd ed.* Morgantown, WV: Fitness Information Technology.

Stotlar, D. K., & Bronzan, R. T. (1987). *Public relations and promotions in sport.* Daphne, AL: United States Sports Academy.

Stotlar, D. K., & Johnson, D. A. (1989). Assessing the impact and effectiveness of stadium advertising on sport spectators at Division I institutions. *Journal of Sport Management, 3*(1), 90–102.

Swerdlow, Joel L. (1999, August). *National Geographic.* Global Culture issue.

Tarde, J. (1997, August). The PGA's cup overfloweth. *Golf Digest,* 4.

Tarpey, L. X., Donnelly, J. H., & Peter, J. P. (1979). *A preface to marketing management.* Dallas, TX: Business Publications, Inc.

Tedesco, R. (1996a, September 30). Internet panel sees big marketing pull: Full-motion video on 'net could fuel consumer interest. *Broadcasting & Cable, 126*(41), 31–32.

Tedesco, R. (1996b, October 14). Widening the world of sports. *Broadcasting & Cable, 126*(43), 85.

Tedesco, R. (1996c, October 26). Internet business is a waiting game. *Broadcasting & Cable, 126*(45), 36–37.

Tedesco, R. (1996d, December 2). ABC sports scoring with 'Monday night football' site. *Broadcasting & Cable, 126*(50), 60.

10 Steps to build better brands and where sponsorship fits in. (1998, March 30). *IEG Sponsorship Report,* 4–6.

The answer: $213 billion. (1999, December 20–26). *SportsBusiness Journal.*

The Celebrity 100 (2004, July 4). *Forbes, 174*(1), 47.

The herstory of basketball [Advertisement for the Women's Basketball Hall of Fame]. (1999, February 1–7). *SportsBusiness Journal,* 18.

The new face of America: How immigrants are shaping the face of the world's first multicultural society. (1993). *Time, 142*(21).

Thomas, J. W. (1998, January). The brave new world of internet marketing. *Direct Marketing, 60*(1), 40–41.

Thompson, J. (1994). Social theory and the media. In D. Crowley & D. Mitchell (Eds.), *Communication theory today.* Stanford, CA: Stanford University Press.

Tips to make your internet advertisements more effective. (1997, May 5). *Mediaweek, 7*(18), S46–S49.

Top 25 female athlete endorsements. (1998, May 11–17). *SportsBusiness Journal, 1,* 25.

Tucker, R. (1997, November). Clubs on the web. *Fitness Management, 13*(12), 29–32.

2001 World Population Data Sheet. (2001). Population Reference Bureau. Retrieved October 13, 2001, from http://www.prb.org /pubs/wpds2000

Tucker, R. (1997, November). Clubs on the Web. *Fitness Management, 13,* 29–32.

Tuller, L. W. (1991). *Going global.* Homewood, IL: Business One Irwin.

Ubois, J. (1997, January). Eye on the storm: Marketing guru Geoffrey Moore plumbs the turbulent currents of the internet market. *Internet World, 8*(1), 74–81.

Ukman, L. (1995). *IEG's complete guide to sponsorship.* Chicago: International Events Group.

Ukman, L. (2004). *ROS: How to measure, justify and maximize your return on sponsorships and partnerships.* Chicago: International Events Group.

United States Department of Commerce (1993, September). *Basic facts about registering a trademark.* Washington DC: Patent and Trademark Office.

United States Olympic Committee. (1996). USOC controversy preparedness plan. Colorado Springs, CO: Author.

United States Olympic Committee. (2005). USCO Board of Directors approves 2005 operating budget. Retrieved July 21, 2005, from http://www.usoc.com

United States Tennis Association. (1999, June). Spotlight: Women's 60, 70 and 80 National Clay Court Championships. *USTA Magazine,* 30–31.

VALS 2: Your marketing edge for the 1990s. (1990). Menlo Park, CA: SRI International.

van Waterschoot, W., & Van den Bulte, C. (1992, October). The 4P classification of the marketing mix revisited. *Journal of Marketing,* 82–93.

Vavra, T. (1992). *Aftermarketing: How to keep customers for life through relationship marketing.* Homewood, IL: Business One Irwin.

Vavra, T. (1994). The database imperative. *Marketing Management, 2*(1), 47–57.

Veltri, F. (1996). *Recognition of athlete-endorsed products.* Fredericton, NB: Conference of the North American Society for Sport Management.

Video killed the renewal letter: *How the Dallas Stars are using video to drive renewals.* Retrieved September 1, 2005, from http://www .migalareport.com/reports.cfm?report=aug05_story3_pf.cfm

Wallenfels, S. (2005). *The demand for spa services is exploding, and clubs are helping to meet the need.* Retrieved August 23, 2005, from http://cms.ihrsa.org/IHRSA/viewPage.cfm?pageId=2144

Walsh, R. G. (1986). *Recreation economic decisions.* State College, PA: Venture Publishing, Inc.

Walthorn, C. G. (1979). *Consumer behavior.* Homewood, IL: Richard D. Irwin.

Walzer, E. (2005, March). The Globalization of women's sport. *Sporting Goods Business.* Retrieved July 7, 2005, from http://www.sbr-net.com.source.unco.edu/sbr/publication-search.cfm?function

Warfield, S. (2005). NASCAR's new deal: Rare and well done. *SportsBusiness Journal, 8*(18), 4.

Warner, B. (1997, March 3). Brewers tapping the web, at last. *Mediaweek, 7*(9), 38–39.

Webster's II New Riverside Pocket Dictionary. (1978). Boston, MA: Houghton Mifflin Company.

Wells, M., & Oldenburg, A. (1999, July 13). Sports bra's flash could cash in. *USA Today,* 1A.

Welz, G. (1996, July). The ad game: Industry analysts and agencies see the web advertising market exploding. *Internet World, 7*(7), 50–57.

Westmacott, P., & Obhi, H. (2001). The database right: Copyright and confidential information. *Journal of Database Marketing, 9*(1), 75–76.

Why internet advertising. (1997, May 5). *Mediaweek, 7*(18), S8–S12.

Williams, P. (1999, April 12). Company's links make it a direct line to virtual ticket window. *SportsBusiness Journal, 1*(52), 33.

Williams, P. (2000). Marketing your dreams: *Business and life lessons from Bill Veeck*. Champaign, IL: Sports Publishing, Inc.

Winer, R. (1988). Behavioral perspective on pricing: Buyer's subjective perceptions of price revisited. In T.M. Devinney (Ed.), *Issues in pricing: Theory and research*. Lexington, MA: Lexington Books, 35–7.

Wong, G. M. (1994). *Essentials of amateur sports law*. Westport, CT: Praeger Publishing Company.

Wong, G. M. (2002) *Essentials of Amateur Sports Law*, 3rd ed. Westport, CN: Praeger Publishers.

Woodward, S. (1988, May 29). Teams foresee war brewing keeping "billboard rules" in place. *USA Today*, 2C.

Woodward, S. (2005, March 21–27). This cat is red hot. *SportsBusiness Journal*, 7(45), 1, 42–43.

Yang, X. S. (2005, March 11). The future of the sport industry in China. ASPESD Conference, Seoul, Korea.

Yeh, K. T., & Li, M. (1998, Winter). Globalization of sport: What sport management professional should know. *ICHPER-SD Journal*, 29–32.

Yiannakis, A. (1989). Some contributions of sport sociology to the marketing of sport and leisure organizations. *Journal of Sport Management*, 3, 103–115.

Young, D. (1996). *Building your company's good name*. New York: AMACOM.

Yudkin, M. (1994). *6 steps to free publicity*. New York: Penguin Group.

Zarkowsky, D. (1997, July 21). Cardinals keep score on web, blues also at bat. *St. Louis Business Journal*. Retrieved October 13, 2001, from http://www.sbj.com

Zhang, J. J., Pease, D. G., Hui, S. C., & Michaud, T. J. (1995). Variables affecting the spectator decision to attend NBA games. *Sport Marketing Quarterly*, 4(4), 29–39.

Zhang, J. J., Smith, D. W., Pease, D. G., & Jambor, E. A. (1997). Negative influence of market competitors on the attendance of professional sport games: The case of a minor league hockey team. *Sport Marketing Quarterly*, 6(3), 31–39.

Appendix A

SPORT BUSINESS ORGANIZATIONS CONTACT INFORMATION

Contents

Age-Related Organizations and Businesses

Amateur Athletic Union
AAU National Headquarters
PO Box 22409
Lake Buena Vista, FL 32830-1000
407-934-7200
407-934-7242 (Fax)
http://www.aausports.org

American Youth Soccer Organization
12501 S. Isis Avenue
Hawthorne, CA 90250
800-872-2976
http://www.soccer.org

AUSSI Masters Swimming
148A Ferguson Street,
Williamstown VIC 3016
Australia
Telephone: 03 9399 8861
Fax: 03 9399 8863
http://www.aussimasters.com

Boys & Girls Clubs of America
1230 W. Peachtree Street, NW
Atlanta, GA 30309
404-487-5700
http://www.bcga.org

Charlie Tarricone's American Basketball Consulting Services
1305 Campus Drive
Vestal, NY 13850
607-724-8155

Moreno Valley
14177 Fredrick Street
Moewno Valley, CA 92552
909-413-3000
909-413-3750 (Fax)

National Adult Baseball Association
NABA
3609 S. Wadsworth Blvd., Suite 135
Lakewood, CO 80235
800-621-6479
303-639-6605(Fax)
http://www.dugout.org

National Alliance for Youth Sports
2050 Vista Pkwy
West Palm Beach, FL 33411
561-684-1141
561-712-0119 (Fax)

National Senior Games Association
PO Box 82059
Baton Rouge, LA 70884-2059
225-766-6800
225-766-9115 (Fax)
http://www.nsga.com

PrepUSA
PO Box 97427
Tacoma, WA 98497
253-581-5324
253-756-2900 (Fax)

U.S. Budokai Karate Association
100 Everett Road
Albany, NY 12205
518-458-2018

Young American Bowling Alliance (YABA)
800-514-2965 ext. 3158
414-421-4420 (Fax)
http://www.bowl.com

Youth Basketball of America, Inc.
10325 Orangewood Blvd
Orlando, FL 32821
407-363-YBOA
407-363-0599 (Fax)
http://www.yboa.org

Auto Sports Racing Organizations and Businesses

American Rally Sport Group, Inc.
3650 South Pointe Circle, Suite 205
Laughlin, NV 89028
702-298-8171
951-737-5519 (Fax)
http://www.rallyusa.com

Boston Performance Group
18 Fordham Road
Allston, MA 02134
617-787-8035
617-787-6492 (Fax)

Cotter Group
SFX/Cotter Group
6525 Hudspeth
Harrisburg, NC 28075
704-455-3500
Kelley Racing
9350 Castlegate Drive
Indianapolis, IN 46256

NASCAR/National Association for Stock Car Auto Racing (public relations)
PO Box 2875
Daytona Beach, FL 32120
386-253-0611
PacWest Racing Group
4001 Methanol Lane
Indianapolis, IN 46268
317-297-2500
317-297-2100 (Fax)

Pep Boys Indy Racing League
4565 W. 16th Street
Indianapolis, IN 46222
317-484-6526
317-484-6525 (Fax)

Rally School Ireland
Gola Scotstown
Co. Monaghan
047 89098
047 89223 (Fax)

Disabled Sport Organizations and Businesses

American Blind Bowling Association
411 Sheriff Street
Mercer, PA 16137
742-745-5986

Canadian Blind Sports Association
7 Mill Street, Lower Level, Box 1574
Almonte, Ontario, K0A 1A0
Canada
613-256-7792
613-256-8759 (Fax)

Disabled Sports USA
451 Hungerford DR, STE 100
Rockville, MD 20850
301-217-0960
301-217-0968(Fax)
http://www.dsusa.org
International Blind Sports
   Association
http://www.ibsa.es/eng

International Paralympic Committee
Adenauerallee 212-214
D- 53113 Bonn
Germany
Tel: +49-228-2097 200
Fax: +49-228-2097 209

National Foundation of Wheelchair Tennis
940 Calle Amanecer, Ste B
San Clemente, CA 92672
714-361-3663

**National Sports Center
for the Disabled**
PO Box 1290
Winter Park, CO 80482
970-726-1540
303-316-1540
970-726-4112 (Fax)
http://www.nscd.org

**National Wheelchair Basketball
Association**
6165 Lehman Drive Suite 101
Colorado Springs, CO 80918
719-266-4082
http://www.nwba.org

**Skating Association for the
Blind and Handicapped**
1200 East and West Road
West Seneca, NY 14224
716-675-7222
http://www.sabahinc.org

USA Deaf Sports Federation
102 North Krohn Place
Sioux Falls, SD 57103-1800
605-367-5760
605-367-4979 (Fax)
http://www.usdeafsports.org

**U.S. Association of Blind
Athletes**
33 N. Institute Street
Colorado Springs, CO 80903
719-630-0422
719-630-0616
http://www.usaba.org

**U.S. Cerebral Palsy Athletic
Association**
200 Harrison Avenue
Newport, RI 02840
401-848-2460
401-848-5280 (Fax)

Wheelchair Sports, USA
1668 320th Way
Earlham, IA 50072
515-833-2450
http://www.wsusa.org

Fitness Organizations and Businesses

American Council on Exercise
4851 Paramount Drive
San Diego, CA 92121
800-825-3636
858-279-7227
858-279-8064 (Fax)
http://www.acefitness.org

**American Fitness Professionals
& Associates**
PO Box 214
Ship Bottom, NJ 08008
609-978-7583
http://www.afpafitness.com

**Association of Women's Fitness
and Health**
273 South Centerville Road
Ashburn, VA 20147
http://www.association-of-wom
ens-fitness.org

National Gym Association
PO Box 970579
Coconut Creek, FL 33097-0579
954-344-8410
954-344-8412 (Fax)
http://www.nationalgym.com

Nebula Fitness
PO Box 54
1142 North Center Street
Versailles OH 45380
800-763-2852
937-526-9411 (Fax)
http://www.nebula-fitness.com

**Professional Fitness Instructor
Training**
PO Box 130258
Houston, TX 77219-0258
800-899-7348
713-868-8086
713-868-2683
http://www.pfit.org

The Fitness Zone
800-875-9145

International Sports Organizations and Businesses

British Athletics
http://www.british-athletics.co.uk
Canadian Association for the
    Advancement of Women and
    Sport and Physical Activity
N202-801 King Edward Avenue
Ottawa, ON, Canada K1N 6N5
613-562-5667
613-562-5668 (Fax)
http://www.caaws.ca

**Fédération Internationale de
Football Association (FIFA)**
PO Box 85
8030 Zurich, Switzerland
+41-43/222 7777
http://www.fifa.com

**General Association of
International Sports
Federations**
Villa Le Mas 4, boulevard
du Jardin Exotique, MC 98000,
    Monaco
+377 +97 97 65 10
+377 +93 25 28 73 (Fax)
http://www.agfisonline.com

**International Amateur Athletic
Federation**
Stade Louis II—Avenue Prince
    Hereditaire Albert
MC 98000 Monaco
377 92 05 70 68
377 92 05 70 69 (Fax)
http://www.iaaf.org

International Olympic Committee

Chateau de Vidy
Case Postale 356
1007 Lausanne, Switzerland
41.21 621.61.11
41.21 621.62.16
http://www.olympic.org

Irish Surfing Association

Easkey Surf and Information Centre
Easkey, Co. Sligo, Ireland
+353 (0) 96 49428
+353 (0) 96 49020

North American Sports Federation

PO Box K
Drifton, PA 18221
570-454-1952
http://www.nasf.net

Media Organizations and Businesses

CBS SportsLine

http://www.sportsline.com

CNN/SI

http://www.sportsillustrated.cnn.com

ESPN

http://www.espn.go.com

Fox Sports

http://www.msn.foxsports.com

The Sporting News

http://www.sportingnews.com

USA Today

http://www.usatoday.com

Minority Sports Organizations and Businesses

African American Sports

African American Golf Association (AAGA)

309-682-1482
http://www.aagagolf.com

Black Coaches Association

Pan American Plaza
201 S. Capitol Ave. Suite 495
Indianapolis, IN 46225
317-829-5600
317-829-5601 (Fax)
http://www.bcasports.org

Black Entertainment & Sports Lawyers Association

PO Box 441485
For Washington, MD 20749-1485
301-248-1818
301-248-0700 (Fax)
http://www.besla.org

Gay and Lesbian Sports

The Chiltern Mountain Club

http://www.chiltern.org
Federation of Gay Games
584 Castro Street Suite 343
San Francisco, CA 94114
415-695-0222
http://www.gaygames.com

Georgia Gay Rodeo Association

PO Box 7881
Atlanta, GA 30357-0881
770-662-9510
http://www.georgiagayrodeo.com

Hotlanta Volleyball Association

PO Box 8144
Highland Station
Atlanta, GA 31106
770-621-5062

International Gay and Lesbian Aquatics

http://www.igla.org
International Gay and Lesbian
    Football Association
http://www.iglfa.org

Native American Sports

Iroquois Nationals Lacrosse

http://www.iroquoisnationals.com

National Organizations and Businesses

National Association of Intercollegiate Athletics (NAIA)

23500 W. 105th Street
PO Box 1325
Olathe, KS 66051
913-791-0044
http://www.naia.org

National Auto Sport Association

PO Box 21555
Richmond, CA 94820-1555
510-232-NASA
510-412-0549 (Fax)
http://www.nasaproracing.com

National Bicycle League

3958 Brown Park Drive, Ste D
Hillard, OH 43026
800-886-BMX1
614-777-1625
614-777-1680 (Fax)
http://www.nbl.org

National Collegiate Athletic Association

PO Box 6222
Indianapolis, IN 46206-6222
317-917-6222
http://www.ncaa.org

National Golf Foundation

1150 South US Highway One,
    Ste 401
Jupiter, FL 33477
561-744-6006
http://www.ngf.org

National Junior Colleges Athletic Association

1755 Telstar Drive, Suite 103
Colorado Springs, CO 80920
719-590-9788
719-590-7324 (Fax)
http://www.njcaa.org

National Softball Association
PO Box 7
Nicholasville, KY 40340
859-887-4114
859-887-4874 (Fax)
http://www.playnsa.com

USA Basketball
5465 Mark Dabling Blvd.
Colorado Springs, CO 80918-
    3842
719-590-4800
http://www.usabasketball.com

U.S. Specialty Sports Association
215 Celebration Place, Suite 180
Celebration, FL 34747
(321) 939-7640
(321) 939-7647 (Fax)
http://www.usssa.com

Professional Sport Organizations and Businesses

American Bowling Congress
5301 S. 76th Street
Greendale, WI 53129
1-800-514-bowl
http://www.bowl.com

American League of Professional Baseball Clubs
350 Park Avenue
New York, NY 10022
212-339-7600
212-593-7138 (Fax)

Association of Surfing Professionals (North America)
PO Box 309
Huntington Beach, CA 92648
714-848-8851
714-848-8861 (Fax)
http://www.aspworldtour.com

Association of Tennis Professionals
201 ATP Tour Boulevard
Ponte Vedra Beach, FL 32082
904-285-8000
904-285-5966 (Fax)
http://www.atptennis.com

Association of Volleyball Professionals (AVP)
6100 Center Drive, 9th Floor
Los Angeles, CA 90045
310-426-8000
310-426-8010 (Fax)
http://www.AVP.com

American Basketball Association
9421 Holiday Drive
Indianapolis, IN 46260
(317) 844-7502
(317) 844-7501 (Fax)
http://www.abalive.com

Continental Basketball Association
1412 W. Idaho St. Suite 235
Boise, ID 83702
208-429-0101
208-429-0303 (Fax)
http://www.cbahoopsonline.com

International Korfball Federation
PO Box 85394
3508 AJ Utrecht
The Netherlands
http://www.ikf.org

International Shooting Sport Federation
ISSF Headquarters
Bavariaring 21, D-80336
Mynchen, Germany
+49-89-5443550
+49-89-5443554 (Fax)
http://www.issf-shooting.org

Major League Baseball (MLB)
350 Park Avenue
New York, NY 10022
212-339-7800
212-355-0007 (Fax)
http://www.mlb.com

Major League Soccer (MLS)
110 E. 42nd Street, 10 Floor
New York, NY 10017
212-450-1200
212-450-1300 (Fax)
http://www.mlsnet.com

National Basketball Association (NBA)
645 Fifth Avenue
New York, NY 10022
212-407-8000
212-832-3861 (Fax)
http://www.nba.com

National Football League (NFL)
280 Park Avenue
New York, NY 10017
212-450-2000
212-681-7599 (Fax)
http://www.nfl.com

National Hockey League (NHL)
1251 Avenue of the Americas
47th Floor
New York, NY 10020-1198
212-789-2000
212-789-2020 (Fax)
http://www.nhl.com

National League of Professional Baseball Clubs
350 Park Avenue
New York, NY 10022
212-339-7700
212-935-5069 (Fax)

National Bicycle League
3958 Brown Park Drive, Suite D.
HIlliard, OH 43026
614-777-1625
614-777-1680 (fax)

Religion and Faith-Based Sports Organizations and Businesses

Athletes in Action
651 Taylor Drive
Xenia, OH 45385
937-352-1000
http://www.athletesinaction.org/

Fellowship of Christian Athletes
8701 Leeds Road
Kansas City, MO 64129
816-921-0909
http://www.fca.org

Maccabi USA
Maccabi USA/Sports for Israel
1926 Arch Street 4R
Philadelphia, PA 19103
215-561-6900
http://www.maccabiusa.com

National Christian College Athletic Association
NCCAA National Office
302 West Washington Street
Greenville, SC 29601
864-250-1199
864-250-1141 (Fax)
http://www.thenccaa.org

OC International
PO Box 36900
Colorado Springs, CO 80936-6900
719-592-9292

Sport Market Research Organizations and Businesses

Joyce Julius & Associates, Inc.
1050 Highland Drive, Ste E
Ann Arbor, MI 48108
734-971-1900
734-791-2059 (Fax)
http://www.joycejulius.com

Simmons Market Research Bureau
230 Park Avenue South, 3rd Floor
New York, NY 10003-1566
212-598-5400
212-598-5401 (Fax)
http://www.smrb.com

Society for American Baseball Research
812 Huron Road, Ste 719
Cleveland, OH 44115
216-575-0500
216-575-0502 (Fax)
http://www.sabr.org

Sport Business Research Network
PO Box 1417
Princeton, NJ 08542
609-896-1996
609-896-1903 (Fax)
http://www.sbrnet.com

Sport Marketing Agencies

International Management Group (IMG)
IMG Center, Suite 100
1360 E. 9th Street
Cleveland, OH 44114
216-522-1200
216-436-3187 (Fax)
http://www.IMGworld.com

Proserv, Inc.
1401 North Street, Suite 203
Escanaba, MI 49829
906-786-1699
888-598-5208
http://www.proserv-inc.com

R.L.R. Associates, Ltd.
7 W. 51st Street
New York, NY 10019
212-541-8641
212-262-7084 (Fax)
http://www.rlrassociates.net

Sporting Goods and Apparel Manufacturers and Retailers

Sporting Goods Manufacturers Association
200 Castlewood Drive
North Palm Beach, FL 33408
561-842-4100
561-863-8984 (Fax)
http://www.sgma.com

Action & Leisure
45 E. 30th Street
New York, NY 10016
212-684-4470
212-532-6194 (Fax)

Adams USA, Inc.
610 S. Jefferson Avenue
Cookville, TN 38501
800-251-6857
http://www.adamsusa.com

adidas—Salomon AG
Social and Environmental Affairs
World of Sports
Adi-Dassler-Strabe 1-2
91074 Herzogenaurach Germany
+49 (0) 9132/84-0
+49 (0) 9132/84-3242 (Fax)
http://www.adidas-salomon.com

Airwalk Footwear
http://www.airwalk.com
Bike Athletic Company
3330 Cumberland Blvd.
Atlanta, GA 30339
678-742-TALK
http://www.bikeathletic.com

Bolle America
9500 W. 49th Avenue
Wheat Ridge, CO 80033
800-554-6686
303-327-2200
303-327-2300 (Fax)
http://www.bolle.com

Discus Athletic
PO Box 5186
Martinsville, VA 24115
540-632-6459

Hillerich & Bradsby Company, Inc.
800 W. Main Street
Louisville, KY 40202
800-282-2287
502-585-5226
502-585-1179 (Fax)
http://www.slugger.com

Nike, Inc.
PO Box 4027
Beaverton, OR 97005
800-344-6453
http://www.nike.com

Reebok International, Inc.
PO Box 1060
Ronks, PA 17573
800-934-3566
http://www.reebok.com

Scott USA
PO Box 2030
Sun Valley, ID 83353
208-622-1000
208-622-1005 (Fax)
http://www.scottusa.com

Sims Sports, Inc.
888-360-SIMS
http://www.simsnow.com

Skis Dynastar Inc.
PO Box 25
Hercules Drive
Colchester, VT 05446-0025
802-655-2400
802-655-4329 (Fax)
http://www.dynastar.com

Spalding Sports Worldwide
150 Brookdale Drive
Springfield, MA 01104
1-800-SPALDING
http://www.spalding.com

Tecnica USA Corporation
19 Technology Drive
W. Lebanon, NH 03784
800-258-3897
603-298-8032
603-298-5790 (Fax)
http://www.tecnicausa.com

Wilson Sporting Goods Company
8700 W. Bryn Mawr Avenue
Chicago, IL 60631
773-714-6400
773-714-4550 (Fax)
http://www.wilson.com

Sports Logo and Licensed Merchandise Organizations and Businesses

Art's Pro Sports Apparel & Things
http://www.citivu.com
B&J Collectibles, Inc.
801 Corporate Circle
Toms River, NJ 08755
732-905-5000

BestSportsGifts.com
Summit Bldg.
13575 58th Street N
Clearwater, FL 34620
727-593-8692

eCompanyStore
5945 Cabot Parkway Bldg 200,
   Ste 150
Alpharetta, GA 30005
800-975-6467
877-588-8932
678-942-3101 (Fax)
http://www.ecompanystore.com

InstantPromo.com
Executive Graffiti Inc.
361 S. Camino Del Rio
Suite 202
Durango, CO 81303
970-247-8344
970-247-8345 (Fax)
800-255-1334

LogoProducts.cc
The Backyard Store
3419 Northeast Parkway
San Antonino, TX 78214
888-814-7531

Nikco Sports
516 Trade Center Blvd.
Chesterfield, MO 63005
800-345-2868
636-777-4070
636-777-4071 (Fax)

Racing USA, Inc.
228 Commerce Parkway
Pelham, AL 35124
205-985-5280 (fax)
http://www.racingusa.com

Rugby Imports
855 Warren Avenue
East Providence, RI 02914
800-431-4514
401-438-2727
401-438-8260 (Fax)
http://www.rugbyimports.com

Selinda's
PO Box 1732
Suwanee, GA 30024-0973
678-482-8239 (phone and fax)
http://www.selindas.com

Twenty-Four Seven Incentives, Inc.
5435 S. Gibralter Street
Aurora, CO 80015-3767
303-699-5012
303-699-2931 (Fax)
http://www.247incentives.com

Wendy Havins Promotions, Inc.
4060 Palm Street, Suite 604
Fullerton, CA 92835
888-556-9010
714-525-3330
714-525-3495 (Fax)
http://www.whpromotions.com

Sport Sponsorship Management Organizations and Businesses

ACC Properties
412 E. Boulevard
Charlotte, NC 28203
704-378-4400
704-378-4465 (Fax)

AJ Sports Inc.
9229 Sunset Blvd, Ste 608
Los Angeles, CA 90069
310-550-5922
310-274-3280 (Fax)

API Sponsorship
1775 Broadway, Room 608
New York, NY 10019
212-841-1580
212-841-1598 (Fax)

Barnes Dyer Marketing, Inc.
15510 Rockfield Blvd, Ste C
Irvine, CA 92618
714-768-2942
714-768-0630 (Fax)

Marketing Event Partners, Inc.
6075 Barfield Road, Suite 200
Atlanta, GA 30328
404-256-3366

Genesco Sports Enterprises, Inc.
214-237-6945
http://www.genescosports.com

Miramar Sports & Special Events
PO Box 27
El Granada, CA 94018
650-726-3491
650-726-5181 (Fax)
http://www.miramarevents.com

Premier Management Group
919-363-5105
919-363-5106 (fax)
http://www.pmgsports.com

Vantage Sports Management
222 W. Comstock Avenue, Ste 208
Winter Park, FL 32789
407-628-3131
407-628-3121 (Fax)
http://www.vantagesportsmanage
ment.com

State Sports Groups

Florida Sports Foundation
2930 Kerry Forest Parkway
Tallahassee, FL 32309
850-488-8347
850-922-0482 (Fax)
http://www.flasports.com

Water Sports Organizations and Businesses

American Water Ski Association
1251 Holy Cow Road
Polk City, FL 33868
863-324-4341
863-325-8259 (Fax)
http://www.usawaterski.org

American Windsurfing Industries Association
1099 Snowden Road
White Salmon, WA 98672
800-963-7873
509-493-9463
509-493-9464 (Fax)
http://www.awia.org

International Jet Sports Boating Association
3303 Harbor Blvd. Suite E-3
Costa Mesa, CA 92626
714-751-8695
714-751-8609 (Fax)
http://www.ijsba.com

Sail America
850 Aquidneck Avenue, B-4
Middletown, RI 02842-7201
800-817-SAIL
401-847-2044 (Fax)
http://www.sailamerica.com

Super Boat International Productions, Inc.
1323 20th Terrace
Key West, FL 33040
305-296-6166
305-296-9770 (Fax)
http://www.superboat.com

Unlimited Light Hydroplane Racing Association
12065 44th Place
South Tukwila, WA 98178
206-315-1716
206-767-2157 (Fax)
http://www.ulrs.org

U.S. Lifesaving Association
http://www.usla.org
U.S. Windsurfing Association
5009 South Lake Drive
    P.O. Box 99
Chelsea, MI 48118-009
877-386-8708
http://www.uswindsurfing.com

Water Polo Canada
Unit 12-1010 Polytek
Gloucester, ON K1J-9H9
Canada
613-748-5682
613-748-5777 (Fax)

Water-Skiing Federation, International
PO Box 564
6314 Unteraegeri
Switzerland
+41 41 7520099
+41 41 7520095 (Fax)
http://www.iwsf.com

Women's Sports Organizations and Businesses

Canadian Association for the Advancement of Women and Sport and Physical Activity
N202-801 King Edward Avenue
Ottawa, ON, Canada, K1N 6N5
613-562-5667
613-562-5668 (Fax)
http://www.caaws.ca

U.S. Women's Curling Association
c/o Kettle Morain Curling Club
PO Box 244
Hartland, WI 53029
http://www.uswca.org

Women's Basketball Coaches Association (WBCA)
4646 B Lawrenceville Hwy
Lilburn, GA 30047-3620
770-279-8027
770-279-8473 (Fax)
http://www.wbca.org

Women's Basketball Hall of Fame
700 Hall of Fame Drive
Knoxville, TN 37915
865-633-9000
http://www.wbhof.com

Women's International Bowling Congress, Inc. (WIBC)
5301 S. 76th Street
Greendale, WI 53129
414-421-9000
414-421-4420 (Fax)
http://www.bowl.com

Women's National Basketball Association (WNBA)
645 Fifth Avenue
New York, NY 10022
212-688-9622
212-750-9622 (Fax)
http://www.wnba.com

Women's Ocean Racing Sailing Association
PO Box 2403
Newport Beach, CA 92663
714-840-1869
714-846-1481 (Fax)
http://www.worsa.org

Women's Pro Fastpitch (WPF)
4610 S. Ulster Drive, Suite 150
Denver, CO 80237
303-290-7494
303-415-2078 (Fax)
http://www.profastpitch.com

Women's Sports Foundation
Eisenhower Park
East Meadow, NY 11554.
800-227-3988
516-542-4700
516-542-4716 (fax)
http://www.womensportsfounda
    tion.org

Appendix B

SPORT BUSINESS TRADE ORGANIZATIONS

American Association for Leisure & Recreation
Promotes school, community, and national programs of leisure services and recreation education.
1900 Association Dr.
Reston, VA 20191-1598
703-476-3400
http://www.aapherd.org

American Sportfishing Association
Ensures a healthy and sustainable resource (more fish), increases participation in sportfishing through promotion and education (more anglers), and helps member sportfishing companies increase their business (more profits).
*Offers trade shows (ICAST), annual meeting, management conference, Future Fisherman Foundation, Fish America Foundation, American Sportfishing newsletter
225 Reinekers Lane, Suite 420
Alexandria, VA 22314
703-519-9691
703-519-1872 (Fax)
http://www.asafishing.org

American Sportscasters Association, Inc.
Promotes professionalism and enhances the image of professional sport broadcasters.
*Sponsors Hall of Fame, Sportscaster of the Year, Sports Personality of the Year
212-227-8080
http://www.americansportscasters.com

Athletic Footwear Association
Serves to promote the athletic footwear industry.
*Offers generic marketing programs, market research programs, and annual meetings
407-840-1161

Club Managers Association of America
Promotes and advances friendly relations between and among persons connected with management of clubs and other associations of similar nature. Assists club officers and members through their managers to secure the utmost in successful operations.
*Offers annual Assistant Club Managers conference, managerial openings list, club management forums, premier club services, international staff exchange program, publications
1733 King Street
Alexandria, VA 22314
703-739-9500
703-739-0124 (Fax)
http://www.cmaa.org
cmaa@cmaa.org

European Fishing Tackle Trade Association (EFTTEX)
Organizes annual trade show available to anyone involved in the fishing tackle trade.
*Offers newsline, members website page, annual international business reception (EFTTEX Show Report)
71 St. John Street
London EC1M 4NJ
England
+44 20 7253 0777
+44 20 7253 7779
http://www.eftta.com
info@eftta.com

Golf Course Superintendents Association of America

A professional membership organization for golf course superintendents in the United States, Canada, and throughout the world. Advances the art and science of golf management, collects and disseminates practical knowledge of the problems of golf course management and a view toward more economical management of golf courses.

*Offers job listings, seminars, continuing education, certification, *Golf Course Management* magazine, GCSAA News Weekly

1421 Research Park Drive
Lawrence, KS 66049-3859
800-472-7878
785-841-2240
http://www.gcsaa.org
infobox@gcsaa.org

Ice Skating Institute

Provides leadership, education, and services to the ice skating industry.

*Offers annual World Championship competition, ISI EDGE (bimonthly professional journal), *Recreational Ice Skating* (quarterly magazine), education foundation, annual conference, and trade show

17120 N. Dallas Pkwy., Suite 140
Dallas, TX 75248-1187
972-735-8800
972-735-8815 (Fax)
http://www.skateisi.com
ISI@SkateISI.com

International Health, Racquet, & Sports Club Association

Exists to enhance the quality of profitability of its member clubs through education, information, networking, and marketing opportunities, group purchasing, legislative support, and public relations.

*Offers *Club Business International* (CBI) magazine, IHRSA/Boys and Girls Clubs of America Program, passport program, annual trade show, annual conference, annual international convention

263 Summer Street
Boston, MA 02210
800-228-4772
617-951-0055
617-951-0056 (Fax)
http://www.ihrsa.org
info@ihrsa.org

National Association of Charterboat Operators (NACO)

Unifying force for the charterboat industry with more than 3,300 members, realizing major successes in combating and challenging government regulation.

*Offers The NACO Report (bimonthly newsletter), Group Rate Liability Insurance Program, drug testing compliance program, government regulation and lobbying, annual conferences and meetings

PO Box 2990
Orange Beach, AL 36561
251-981-5136
866-981-5136
251-981-8191 (Fax)
http://www.Nacocharters.org

National Association of Sports Commissions

Fosters cooperation and sharing of information and professionalism among local and regional sports commissions and authorities.

9916 Carver Road, Suite 100
Cincinnati, OH 45242
513-281-3888
513-281-1765 (fax)
http://www.sportscommissions.org

National Bicycle Dealers Association (NBDA)

Exists to aid the growth of cycling in America through research, education, and advocacy.

*Offers Bicycle Retail Education Conference (BREC), inter-bike bicycle trade expos, articles, books, and resources

777 W. 19th Street, Suite O
Costa Mesa, CA 92627
949-722-6909
http://www.nbda.com
info@nbda.com

National Scholastic Surfing Association (NSSA)

Promotes the sport of amateur surfing, provides top quality, structured events and encourages the merits of academic achievement for the benefit of its members.

*Offers eight competitive conferences, National Scholarship Program, rulebook, annual National Championships, current news, and news archives

Janice Aragon
PO Box 495
Huntington Beach, CA 92648
714-536-0445
714-960-4380
http://www.nssa.org
jaragon@nssa.org

National Skating Suppliers Association

Provides information, merchandise, and resources to skating manufacturers and distributors.

130 Chestnut Street
PO Box 831
North Attleboro, MA 02760
800-325-1917
http://www.skatingsupplierassoc.org

National Ski and Snowboard Retailers Association (NSSRA)

Develops, improves, and promotes the business of ski retailers, ski shops, ski areas, and other members of the ski industry; improves communication with the ski industry.

1601 Feehanville Drive, Suite 300
Mt. Prospect, IL 60056-6035
847-391-9825
847-391-9827 (Fax)
http://www.nssra.com

National Sporting Goods Association (NSGA)

Consists of retailers, dealers, wholesalers, suppliers and sales agents in the sporting goods industry. Committed to providing members with up-to-date information.

*Offers annual management conference, NSGA newsletter, retail focus articles, industry research and statistics, TeeTeam Dealer Summit

1601 Feehanville Drive, Suite 300
Mt. Prospect, IL 60056-6035
847-296-6742
847-391-9827 (Fax)
http://www.nsga.org
info@nsga.org

Ontario Association of Sport and Exercise Sciences (OASES)

Provides fitness appraisal certification, training, and national CSEP certification for fitness consultants by offering workshops, support to member through certification, and training for personal trainers who promote safe, effective physical activity.

*Offers Fitness Certification Appraisal, courses and conferences, job opening postings, Vanguard newsletter, workshops

http://www.oases.on.ca
info@oases.on.ca

Roller Skating Association International

Promotes roller skating and established good business practices for skating rinks. Represents skating center owners and operators, teachers, coaches, and judges of roller skating and manufacturers and suppliers of roller skating equipment.

*Offers *Roller Skating Business* magazine, annual convention and trade show, insurance services, advertising, and vendor information

6905 Corporate Drive
Indianapolis, IN 46278
317-347-2626
317-347-2636 (Fax)
http://www.rollerskating.org

Sporting Goods Manufacturers Association

Represents manufacturers of sporting goods equipment, athletic footwear, and sports apparel in the areas of legislation, marketing information, market protection and growth, consumer safety, international trade, product liability, and program funding.

*Offers research reports and related studies, annual events, The Super Show, annual conference, advanced management education program, Coalition of Americans to Protect Sports (CAPS), exhibitor manual

200 Castlewood Drive
North Palm Beach, FL 33408
561-842-4100
561-863-8984 (Fax)
http://www.sgma.com
info@sgma.com

Women's Basketball Coaches Association (WBCA)

Promotes women's basketball by unifying coaches at all levels to develop a reputable identity for the sport of women's basketball and to foster and promote the development of the game in all of its aspects as an amateur sport for women and girls.

*Offers annual national convention, WBCA Coaches Poll, and publications including *Women's Basketball Journal, Coaching Women's Basketball, Fastbreak Alert,* and *At the Buzzer*

4646 Lawrenceville Highway
Lilburn, GA 30047
770-279-8027
770-279-8473 (Fax)
http://www.wbca.org
wbca@wbca.org

Women's Sports Foundation

Promotes participation and provides information in the area of sport and fitness to women and young girls.

*Offers job listings, newsletter, resource center, biennial summit

Eisenhower Park
East Meadow, NY 11554
800-227-3988
516-542-4700
516-542-4716 (Fax)
http://www.womenssportsfoundation.org

Appendix C

SPORT BUSINESS INDUSTRY TRADE PUBLICATIONS

Aquatics International
Focuses on design, management, and programming of public and semi-public swimming pools, waterparks, beaches, and other water-oriented facilities.
> Frequency: 11 times per year
> Circulation: 30,000
> 888-269-8410

Archery Business
Archery related trade publication.
> Frequency: 7 times per year
> Circulation: 11,000
> 800-848-6247

Athletic Business
For owners and operators of athletic, recreation, and fitness facilities.
> Frequency: 12 times per year
> Circulation: 42,000
> 505-988-5099

Bicycle Retailer & Industry News
Offers news and features about the bicycle industry for retailers, manufacturers, and distributors of equipment, bike wear, and accessories. Covers in-depth market news and analyzes one of the fastest-growing segments of the golf market.
> Frequency: 18 times a year
> Circulation: 6,500
> 949-206-1677
> http://www.bicycleretailer.com

Black Belt Magazine
Martial arts trade publication.
> 24900 Anza Drive, Unit E
> Valencia, CA 91355
> Frequency: 12 times a year
> 661-257-4066, x. 10
> http://www.blackbeltmag.com

Boxing Monthly
Provides worldwide information and current news on the sport of boxing.
> Frequency: 12 times per year
> Topwave Ltd.
> 40 Morpeth Road
> London E9 7LD
> United Kingdom
> +44 0 181 986 4141
> +44 0 181 896 4145 (Fax)
> http://www.boxing-monthly.co.uk
> bmsubs@mmcltd.co.uk

Club Industry
Business magazine for health club owners and operators.
> Frequency: 12 times per year
> Circulation: 30,000
> 215-643-8100

Fitness Management
For owners and managers of athletic and health facilities.
> Frequency: 12 times per year
> Circulation: 25,000
> 323-964-4800

Fly Fishing and Fly Tying
Provides practical and technical information in the area of fly fishing and fly tying.
> Frequency: 11 times per year
> Rolling River Publications Ltd.
> Aberfeldy Road, Kenmore Perthshire
> Scotland PH15 2HF
> +44 0 1887 830526
> +44 0 1887 830526 (Fax)
> http://www.flyfishing-and-flytying.co.uk

Fly Fishing Retailer
Focuses on the health, development, and success of the fly fishing industry. Covers issues, detailed information, and brings them into focus for retailers, manufacturers, and raw-goods suppliers for this marketplace.
> Frequency: 5 times per year
> Circulation: 4,900
> 949-376-6260
> http://www.flyfishingretailer.com

NCAA News

Primary means of communication for NCAA with its more than 1,100 member institutions, organizations, and conferences, as well as the news media and other persons interested in staying abreast of developments in college athletics.

Frequency: 52 times per year
Circulation: 25,000
317-917-6222
http://www.ncaa.org

Outdoor Retailer

Focuses on specialty sports retailers of backpacking, mountaineering, camping, hiking, climbing, cross-country skiing, padding, mountain biking, adventure travel, snowboarding, snowshoeing, and related clothing.

Frequency: 2 trade shows per year with publications
Circulation: 18,000
http://www.outdoorbiz.com

Poundbury Publishing Ltd.

Magazine publishing company which currently publishes six magazines, four of which are sport related.

Prospect House
Peverell Avenue East, Poundbury
Dorchester, Dorset DT1 3WE
United Kingdom
+44 0 1305 266360
+44 0 1305 262760 (Fax)
http://www.poundbury.co.uk

Procycling

Worldwide voice of international professional road racing, distributed in every country where there are English-speaking fans of cycling.

Frequency: 12 times per year
+44 (0)207 6086300
http://www.procycling.com
feedback@procycling.com

Ski Area Management

Trade publication for the skiing industry conveys event, product, and company information.

45 Main Street North
PO Box 644
Woodbury, CT 06798
203-263-0888
203-266-0462 (Fax)

Sport Business.com

Provides daily on-line information and news concerning sport business.

Frequency: Daily
6th Floor
Elizabeth House
39 York Road
London
SE1 7NQ, UK
+44 (0)20 7934 9000
+44 (0)20 7934 9200 (fax)
http://www.sportbusiness.com

Sport Business Research Network

Provides a fee-based service, focusing on the sporting goods and sports marketing industry including: sports equipment sales, participation, broadcasting, sponsorship, and marketing. Providing sporting goods industry with current news and information concerning the market.

Frequency: 12 times per year
PO Box 2378
Princeton, NJ 08543
609-896-1996
609-896-1903 (Fax)
http://www.sbrnet.com
richard@sbrnet.com

Sporting Goods Business

Over 30 years old, *SBG* covers and analyzes the sporting goods business.

Frequency: 18 times per year
Circulation: 24,700
646-654-4997
http://www.Sportinggoodsbusiness.com

Street & Smith's SportsBusiness Journal

Authority on sports. Business journal devoted to news of the industry.

Frequency: 49 times per year
Circulation: 17,000
120 West Morehead Street, Suite 310
Charlotte, NC 28202
704-973-1410

Appendix D

SPORT BUSINESS ACADEMIC JOURNALS AND ASSOCIATIONS DIRECTORY

CONTENTS

SPORT MANAGEMENT ACADEMIC CURRICULUM STANDARDS

In May, 1993 the first NASPE-NASSM Sport Management Curriculum Standards manual was published through a joint task force of membership involving scholars and practitioners in sport management representing the National Association for Sport and Physical Education (NASPE) and the North American Society for Sport Management (NASSM). The manual and the review council are listed here. More information can be found through the NASSM or NASPE web sites (http://www.nassm.org, http://www.aahperd.org/naspe/template.cfm).

The Manual:
NASPE-NASSM Sport Management Curriculum Standards and Program Review
Published by NASPE, can be purchased through NASPE or NASSM.

The curriculum standards review council:
NASPE-NASSM Sport Management Program Review Council
Made up of six council members, one director, and several reviewers; can be contacted through NASPE or NASSM organizations.

SPORT BUSINESS JOURNALS

Entertainment and Sports Lawyer
Entertainment and Sport Lawyer American Bar Association
321 North Clark Street
Chicago, IL 60610-4714
800-285-2221

European Sport Management Quarterly
Bill Gerrard, Editor
University of Leeds, UK
Business School
3 Henrietta Street
Covent Garden, London
WC2E 8LU, England

International Journal of Sport Finance
Dennis Howard, Editor
Fitness Information Technology
262 Coliseum, WVU-PE
PO Box 6116
Morgantown, WV 26506-6116
304-293-6888
http://www.fitinfotech.com

International Journal of Sport Management
William F. Stier, Jr., Editor
Professor and Graduate Director
Coordinator of Sport Management/Athletic Administration
Physical Education and Sport
State University of New York
Brockport, New York
bstier@brockport.edu
585-395-5331

International Journal of Sport Management and Marketing
Mohammed Dorgham, Editor
Inderscience Enterprises, Ltd.
International Centre for Technology and Management,
  United Kingdom
http://www.inderscience.com
editorial@inderscience.com

International Journal of Sports Marketing and Sponsorship
International Marketing Reports Ltd
7 Greville Road, London NW6 5HY
United Kingdom
+44 (0) 20 7372 6561
+44 (0) 20 7372 6538

International Sports Journal
University of New Haven
UNH Foundation
300 Orange Avenue
West Haven, CT 06516

Japan Journal of the Sports Industry
Japan society of Sports Industry
3-6 Kanda-Jinbo-Cho
Chiyoda, Tokyo 101-0051
Japan
81-3-5276-0141
81-3-5276-0288 (fax)

Japanese Journal of Management for Physical Education and Sports
Japanese Society of Management for Physical Educa-
  tion and Sports
Taiiku Keiei Gaku Kenkyushitsu
Institute of Health & Sport Sciences
University of Tsukuba
Tsukuba, Ibaraki, 305-8574
Japan
81-298-53-6363
81-298-53-6363 (fax)

Journal of Korean Society of Sport Management
College of Education Sciences
Department of Sport & Leisure Studies
134 Sinchondong Seodaemoon-Ku #307
Seoul, South Korea
02-361-3193, 4138
02-363-5952 (fax)
http://www.web.sportkorea.net/kssm

Journal of Sports Economics
Sage Publications
2455 Teller Road
Thousand Oaks, CA 91320
800-818-7243
805-499-0871 (fax)
http://www.sagepub.com

Journal of Sport Management
Official journal of the NASSM; membership includes
  subscription
Human Kinetics Publishers, Inc.
1607 N. Market Street
Champaign, IL 61820-2200
http://www.humankinetics.com

Journal of Sports Engineering
Official journal of the International Sports Engineer-
  ing Association; membership includes subscription
Editorial Office and Subscriptions
Amanda Staley, Department of Mechanical Engineering
The University of Sheffield
Mappin Street, Sheffield, S1 3JD, UK
+44 (0)114 222 7891
+44 (0)114 222 7855 (fax)
a.staley@shef.ac.uk

Marquette Sport Law Review
Marquette University Law School
Sensenbrenner Hall, Room 146
PO Box 1881
Milwaukee, WI 53201-1881
414-288-7090
414-288-6403 (fax)
http://www.Law.marquette.edu

Seton Hall Journal of Sports and Entertainment Law
Seton Hall University School of Law
1111 Raymond Blvd.
Newark, NJ 07102

Sport Management and Other Related Topics Journal (The SMART Journal)
Dr. Jason Lee
Troy University
338C Stadium Tower
Troy, AL 36081
334-670-7563
http://www.thesmartjournal.com

Sport Management Review
Sport Management Association of Australia and New Zealand (SMAANZ)
Sport Management Program
Deakin University
221 Burwood Hwy
Burwood, VIC, Austrailia 3125

Sport Marketing Quarterly
Fitness Information Technology
262 Coliseum, WVU-PE
PO Box 6116
Morgantown, WV 26506-6116
304-293-6888
http://www.fitinfotech.com

The Sports Lawyers Journal
Tulane University School of Law, editors
Sports Lawyers Association, publishers
11250-8 Roger Bacon Drive, Ste 8
Reston, VA 20190-5202
703-437-4377

Villanova Sports & Entertainment Law Journal
Villanova University School of Law
Villanova, PA 19085
http://www.law.villanova.edu/currentstudents/journals
    andmootcourt/sportsandentlj/sportsandentlj.asp
Sports@law.villanova.edu

SPORT INDUSTRY RELATED JOURNALS

This is a sample of the many journals in which you will find sport, recreation, leisure, fitness, and sport tourism related research and material. Additionally, refer to the many journals in the areas of business, such as the *Journal of Marketing*, and law for research and material in foundational and related content areas.

Australian Leisure Management
Karen Sweaney, editor
Nigel Benton, publisher
Australian Leisure Management
PO Box 478
Collaroy NSW 2097 Australia
+61 0 2 9970 8322
+61 0 2 9970 8355 (Fax)
http://www.ausleisure.com.au
leisure@ausleisure.com.au

Carnegie Research Papers
Canegie School of PE and Human Movement Studies
Leeds Polytechnic
Beckett Park
Leeds LS6 3QS

Current Issues in Tourism
Channel View Publications
Mltilingual Matters Ltd
Frankfurt Lodge
Clevedon Hall
Victoria Road
Clevedon North Summerset BS21 7HH, UK
+44 (0) 1275-876519
http://www.multilingual-matters.com

Electronic Journals of Martial Arts and Sciences
PO Box 14361
Tumwater, WA 98511-4361
http://www.ejmas.com

International Review for the Sociology of Sport
2455 Teller Road
Thousand Oaks, CA 91320
800-818-7243
http://www.irs.sagepub.com

Journal of Aging and Physical Activity
Human Kinetics Publishers
1607 North Market Street
Champaign, IL 61825-5076

Journal of Applied Sport Psychology
Vicki Ebbeck
Department of Exercise and Sport Science Oregon
　State University
Corvallis, OR 97331
541-737-6800
541-737-2788 (fax)

Journal of Hospitality and Leisure Marketing
Oxford Brookes University
Gipsy Lane
Oxford OX3 0BP
United Kingdom

International Journal of Hospitality Management
Elsevier Publishing Company
6277 Sea Harbor Drive
Orlando, FL 32887-4800
877-839-7126

Journal of Leisure Research
National Recreation & Park Association
22355 Belmont Ridge Road
Ashburn, VA 20148-4501
703-858-0784
703-858-0794 (fax)

Journal of Park & Recreation Administration
National Recreation & Park Association
22355 Belmont Ridge Road
Ashburn, VA 20148
703-858-0784
703-858-0794 (fax)

Journal of Philosophy of Sport
Nicholas Dixon, Editor
Department of Philosophy
Alma College
614 W. Superior
Alma, MI 48801

Journal of Sport and Social Issues
2455 Teller Road
Thousand Oaks, CA 91320
800-818-7243
http://www.jss.sagepub.com

Journal of Sport Behavior
University of South Alabama
Department of HPELS
Room 1011
Mobile AL 36688

Journal of Sport History
The Amateur Athletic Foundation of Los Angeles
2141 West Adams Boulevard
Los Angeles, CA 90018
323-730-4600
323-730-9637 (fax)
http://www.naash.org

Journal of Sport Tourism
Sports Tourism International Council
Routledge, Ltd.
11 New Fetter Lane
London EC4 P4EE
United Kingdom
http://www.tandf.co.uk/journals/titles/14775085.asp

Journal of Sustainable Tourism
Channel View Publications
Mltilingual Matters Ltd
Frankfurt Lodge
Clevedon Hall
Victoria Road
Clevedon BS21 7HH, UK
01275-876519
http://www.portlandpress.com/pcs/journals/journal.cfm
?product=JOST

Journal of Vacation Marketing
Henry Stewart Publications
PO Box 10812
Birmingham, AL 35202-0812
800-633-4931
205-995-1567
205-995-1588 (fax)

Leisure Sciences
Routledge, Ltd.
11 New Fetter Lane
London EC4 P4EE
United Kingdom
http://www.tandf.co.uk/journals/tf/01490400.htm

NIRSA Journal

National Intramural-Recreation Sports Association

4185 SW Research Way

Corvallis, OR 97333-1067

541-766-8211

541-766-8284 (fax)

http://www.nirsa.org

Quest

Human Kinetics Publishers, Inc.

1607 North Market Street

Champaign IL 61825-5076

http://www.humankinetics.com/products/journals/jour
nal.cfm?id=QUEST

Parks and Recreation

National Recreation & Park Association

22377 Belmont Ridge Road

Ashburn, VA 20148-4501

http://www.nrpa.org/p&r/magazine.htm

Sociology of Sport

Annelies Knoppers, Editor

University of Utrecht

School of Governance & Organizational Studies

Bijlhouwerstraat 6

3511 ZC Utrecht

The Netherlands

http://www.humankinetics.com/ssj

NASSM News

Newsletter of NASSM

http://www.nassm.com

Women in Sport and Physical Activity Journal

National Association for Girls and Women in Sport
(NAGWS)

1900 Association Drive

Reston, VA 20191

703-476-3400

http://www.aahperd.org/wspaj/

SPORT BUSINESS/MANAGEMENT ASSOCIATIONS

American Alliance for Health Physical Education and Dance (AAHPERD)

Publications: JOPERD, Strategies, Journal of Health
Education, Research Quarterly for Exercise & Sport,
Update Newsletter

Conference: annual

1900 Association Drive

Reston, VA 20191

800-213-7193

703-476-3400

http://www.aahperd.org

Association for the Advancement of Applied Sport Psychology (AAASP)

Publications: Journal of Applied Sport Psychology,
Newsletter

Conference: annual

AAASP Home Office

2810 Crossroads Drive, Ste. 3800

Madison, WI 53718

608-443-2475

608-443-2474 or (Fax)

http://www.aaasponline.org

webmaster@aaasponline.org

Division 47 of the American Psychological Association (APA)

Publications: Exercise and Sport Psychology News
(ESPNews), Exploring Exercise and Sport Psychology, Graduate Training & Career Possibilities in Exercise and Sport Psychology, Sport Psychology: A
Guide to Choosing a Sport Psychology Professional

Division Services

American Psychological Association

750 First Street, NE

Washington, DC 20002-4242

202-336-5500

202-218-3599 (fax)

http://www.apa.org

European Federation of Sport Psychology

Publications: Psychology of Sport and Exercise, FEPSAC
monographs, FEPSAC Bulletin, Annual Reports

Conference: every 3 years

http://www.fepsac.org

International Society for Sport Psychiatry (ISSP)
Ronald L. Kamm, President
257 Monmouth Road, A-5
Oakhurst, NJ 07755
732-517-0595
732-517-8585 (fax)
http://www.mindbodyandsports.com/issp

North American Society for the Psychology of Sport and Physical Activity
Publication: Journal of Sport and Exercise Psychology, Motor Control
Human Kinetics Publishers, Inc.
1607 N. Market Street
Champaign, IL 61820-2200
North American Society for Sport Management (NASSM)
http://www.nassm.org

National Association for Sport and Physical Education (NASPE)
1900 Association Drive
Reston, VA 20191
703-476-3400
703-476-8316 (fax)
http://www.aapherd.org

National Collegiate Athletic Association (NCAA)
Publication: The NCAA News
Confernce: annual
700 W. Washington Street
PO Box 6222
Indianapolis, IN 46206-6222
317-917-6222
317-917-6888 (Fax)
http://www.ncaa.org

European Association for Sport Management (EASM)
Publication: European Sport Management Quarterly
Conference: annual
EASM Office
PO Box 213
40101 Jyväskylä
Finland
+ 358 40 58 67493
http://www.easm.net

SPORT MANAGEMENT CONFERENCES

International Society of Sport Psychology
ISSP 11th World Congress of Sport Psychology
Sydney Convention & Exhibition Centre
Sydney, Australia
North American Society for Sport Management (NASSM)
Conference: annual
www.nassm.org

National Golf Course Owners Association
NGCOA Annual Conference and Trade Show
Publications: Marketing research handbooks, marketing manual, annual conference
Conference: annual
291 Seven Farms Drive
Charleston, SC 29492
843-881-9956
843-881-9958 (fax)
http://www.ngcoa.org
info@ngcoa.org

European Association for Sport Management (EASM)
Publication: European Journal of Sport Management
Conference: annual
EASM Office
P.O. Box 213
40101 Jyväskylä
Finland
+ 358 40 58 67493
http://www.easm.org

American Alliance for Health, Physical Education, Recreation, and Dance (AAHPERD)
This is the umbrella organization for several organizations, one of which is the National Association for Sport and Physical Education (NASPE). NASPE consists of groups for several different areas, one of which is the Sport Management Council. AAHPERD has an annual conference at which the Sport Management Council hosts 3 to 4 research sessions. Information can be found by contacting NASPE.

AAHPERD

1900 Association Drive
Reston, VA 20191
800-213-7193
http://www.aahperd.org

Florida State University Conference of Sport Administration

Conference: annual
Department of Physical Education
200 Tully Gym, 4280
Florida State University
Tallahassee, FL 32306-4280
850-644-4814 or 0578
850-644-0975 (fax)

Sport Management Association of Australia and New Zealand (SMAANZ)

Sport Management Program
c/o Dr. John Dodd
Centre for Sports Studies
University of Canberra
+61 (0)2 6201 2986

National Collegiate Athletic Association (NCAA)

Publication: The NCAA News
Conference: annual
700 W. Washington Street
PO Box 6222
Indianapolis, IN 46206-6222
317-917-6222
317-917-6888 (fax)
http://www.ncaa.org

Appendix E

SPORT MARKETING RESEARCH BRIEFS

The following briefs, unless otherwise noted, are from the 2004 Published Proceedings of the North American Society for Sport Management Conference held in Atlanta, Georgia, hosted by Dr. Brenda G. Pitts and the Georgia State University Sport Business Program.

Predicting Participation Frequency and Purchase Behavior: A Commitment Perspective

Jonathan Casper • *University of Northern Colorado*

There is a need in the sport management literature for a testable model of sport participation. According to Kang (2002), "understanding how an individual makes a decision to participate in sport and exercise is critical to sport marketers who want to make customer-oriented marketing plans" (p.173). The purpose of this study was to predict participation frequency and purchase behavior among adult recreational league bowlers.

With 53.2 million participants 6 years of age and older, recreational bowling ranked as the top participation sport in 2002 by the Sporting Good Manufacturers Association (SGMA; 2003). The SGMA statistics are deceiving because the participants in the study only had to bowl once during the 2002 study period. When looking at frequent participants (25 + days a year) the number drops dramatically to 8.2 million (SGMA, 2003). According to SGMA data (2003), frequent participants typically represent 15–30% of all participants for a sport/activity and are a "core" market for sport marketers. In an earlier study of Sports Participation (SGMA SuperStudy, 2002), of the total population of bowlers (55.4 M), the average number of bowling days was 15. Recent trends indicate that there is an increase in the "casual" bowlers activity and a decrease among frequent bowlers. The bowling industry is doing an excellent job in getting individuals to initiate participation in the sport; however, if only 15% of the participants are frequent consumers, it would appear that increasing the number of these participants could dramatically boost the industry in the future.

Based on these SGMA statistics, bowling is an ideal example of a sport that can benefit from a better understanding of participants. The theoretical foundation for this research is the Sport Commitment Model (Scanlan, Carpenter, Schmidt, Simons, & Keeler, 1993). Sport commitment is defined as the psychological state representing the desire and resolve to continue sport participation. There are five antecedents of commitment: sport enjoyment, personal investments, social constraints; involvement opportunities; and involvement alternatives. It has been suggested by Scanlan et al. that the model is open to additional variables. Therefore, two additional variables, bowlers' attitude toward the sport, and perceived behavioral control, were added to the theoretical model. In an analysis of the sport commitment model, Weiss and Ferrer-Caja (2002) stated that a test of this model would be incomplete without an investigation of the actual behavioral consequences of commitment. Therefore, frequency of bowler participation and purchase behavior (the amount of money spent to participate) served as measures of actual behavior in the study.

A 45-item self-report questionnaire was administered to a regional sample of 400 recreational adult bowlers on the variables of interest. Most of the participants were members of a 35-week bowling league. It was predicted that all of the antecedent variables would increase sport commitment with the exception of involvement alternatives, which would have a negative affect. It was also hypothesized that sport commitment would significantly predict participation frequency and purchase behavior. Multiple regression analysis revealed that enjoyment, involvement opportunities, and attitude toward the sport were the strongest predictors of commitment. Commitment significantly predicted both participation frequency and purchase behavior. Theoretical and practical implications are discussed.

Woo Jeong Cho • *The University of New Mexico*

Nancy Lough • *The University of New Mexico*

Seok Ho Song • *St. Thomas University*

An Examination of the Relationship Between Market Orientation and Organizational Performance in the Sport Fitness Industry

As competition has intensified in most industries, the role of marketing has become critical to the success of any organization (Moorman & Rust, 1999). The sport industry is not immune from such a phenomenon. However, marketing myopia has been prolific within sport organizations (Mullin, Hardy, & Sutton, 2000). This suggests that sound marketing efforts be practiced to create customer value by providing products and/or services that customers want and need. Sport organizations that do so can be competitive and thus survive in the challenging sport marketplace.

Market orientation, regarded as the implementation of sound marketing concepts, has been researched in various industries (Deshpande & Farley, 1998; Farrel & Oczkowski, 1997; Slater & Narver, 1994, 2000). Many researchers have attempted to link market orientation to organizational performance, providing evidence that the marketing concept is highly correlated with a variety of performance variables (Chan & Ellis,1998; Deshpande et al. 1993; Hart & Diamontop, 1993; Jaworski & Kohli, 1993; Narver & Slater, 1990, 1998; Pelham & Wilson, 1996; Pitt, Caruana, & Berthon, 1996; Ruekert, 1992; Slater & Narver, 1994).

However, the marketing concept, which is equally important to a sport organization's success, has not yet been explored in the sport industry. Accordingly, this research examined the relationship between market orientation and organizational performance in the sport fitness industry. To this end, a total of 400 sport fitness centers in Korea were randomly selected. The marketing manager within each sport fitness organization was surveyed as a key informant. The questionnaire included a market orientation scale (Narver & Slater, 1990) and an organizational performance scale (Homburg et al., 2002). Evidence on content and construct validity was established through a psychometric scale purification process (Nunnally, 1978). A hierarchical regression analysis was used to statistically control for situational variables, including size, operating type, market turbulence, and market intensity.

Results indicated that a significant relationship exists between market orientation and organizational performance in the sport fitness context. Specifically, each dimension (i.e., customer orientation, competitor orientation, and interfunctional coordination) of market orientation had a unique relationship with business performance. Accordingly, this study validates the applicability of this theoretical framework to general aspects of the industry namely manufacturing and service) that have been the focus of most prior research. This study further provides empirical evidence on organizational dynamics associated with the role of marketing, as well as important managerial implications for strategic marketing. Further findings and implications will be presented along with future research opportunities and study limitations.

The Relationship Between Repeated Attendance Behavior and Socio-Psychological Factors Associated with Attitude Strength, Subjective Norm and Situational Factor

Jae Hyun Ha • *Florida State University*

Richard Hsiao • *Florida State University*

Jinwook Han • *Florida State University*

Krosnick and Petty (1995) proposed that attitude strength affected repeat purchase behavior toward a product or service. Also, attitude strength has been linked to strong attitudes of persistence and resistance. Persistence related to stability and the degree to which an individual's attitude has remained unchanged over an extended period of time, regardless of whether it has been attacked directly or not (Krosnick and Petty, 1995). Thus, strong attitudes are expected to persist more than weak attitudes. Resistance referred to the ability of an attitude to withstand an attack when challenged (Krosnick and Petty, 1995). Thus, strong attitudes are not easily changed. Sebastian and Bristow (2000) conducted loyalty research associated with attitude strength as persistence and resistance across six different product categories to collegiate students. Results indicated for blue jeans, soft drinks, tennis shoes, beer, and delivery pizza, participants changed attitude strength based on persistence and resistance for inferior or low quality products. However, students' attitude strength scores were not negatively impacted for professional sports teams exhibiting low quality or inferior performance.

In addition to attitude strength, Dick and Basu (1994) suggested that subjective norm and situational factor influenced repeat purchase behavior. According to the theory of reasoned action by Ajzen and Fishbein (1980), The subjective norm was the person's perception of the social pressures to perform or not perform the behavior in question.

For example, according to Kim (2003), subjective norm for the watching behavior of the 2003 Women's World Cup was friends family members, and news sportscasters. Results indicated that subjective norm affected the watching behavior intention of 2003 Women's World Cup. Fazio (1990) proposed that the situational factor was the process that mediates the bystander effect, where an assignment affects whether sport fans will attend a game. For example, Zhang et al., (1995) examined the situational factor in terms of negative impact on repeated attendance behavior such as another entertainment like concert and competition by other sport events.

However, in sport domain, little research has been devoted to the relationship between repeated attendance behavior and socio-psychological factors based on attitude strength, subjective norm and situational factor. Thus, the purpose of this study was to identify the relationship among attitude strength, subjective norm, situational factor, and repeated attendance behavior toward a sport team.

Population was the undergraduate students at a large public southeastern university. Sample was 111 students participating in the eight courses of the Lifetime Activity Programs (LAP) using convenience sampling. The survey instrument for this study was self-modified and developed on the basis of information from previous studies (Kim, 2003; Mahony et. al, 2000; Zhang et al., 1995). The survey instrument used a 7-point Likert and open-ended. The survey instrument developed for this study consisted of 15 items concerning attitude strength, subjective norm, situational factor, and repeated attendance factor toward a sport team.

In order to determine whether the initial questionnaire was valid, a face validity test was conducted. The panel for the validity test included two professors and two doctoral students in the sport management program, and three students from the Lifetime Activity Program. Based on the information provided by panel, the initial survey questionnaire was revised. Cronbach's alpha coefficients were calculated for reliability. Cronbach's alpha coefficients ranged from .6767 to .9670. These values indicated that the questionnaire was reliable for measuring the variables. In other word, according to McMillan (2000), if the Cronbach's alpha value was more than 0.6, the items were internally consistent.

The standardized multiple regression was used to determine the relationship among attitude strength, subjective norm, situational factor, and repeated attendance behavior toward a sport team. Thus, independent variable was attitude strength, subjective norm, and situational factor. Also, dependent variable was repeated attendance behavior.

The result ($F = 13.405$, df = 3, $p < .001$) was statistically significant, and indicated that the relationship between the independent variables and the dependent variable in the regression model were linear. A further examination for significance of the beta coefficients was conducted, based on t-tests. The t-tests indicated statistical significance in the two beta coefficients: attitude strength ($b = .332$, $t = 2.738$, $p < .01$), and situational factor ($b = -.204$, $t = -2.265$, $p < .05$). Also, based on the tolerance values, it can be said that there was no significant multicollinearity among the independent variables because all of the tolerance values were greater than .20 (Fox, 1991).

The findings indicated that attitude strength and situational factor except subjective norm were significant predictors of individual's behavior of repeated attendance toward the sport team. In other words, there was positive relationship between attitude strength ($b = .332$, $t = 2.738$, $p < .001$) and behavior of repeated attendance of the sport game while situational factor ($b = -.204$, $t = -2.265$, $p < .01$) had negative value of coefficient. That is, Individuals, which has high repeated attendance behavior was not affected by situational factor but individuals with low attendance behavior, were influenced by situational factor. However, there was no statistically significant relationship between subjective norm and repeated attendance behavior. That is, subjective norm (i.e. friends, family member, and sportscasters on TV) did not influence on repeated attendance behavior.

The Accidental Fan: An Interpretive Investigation Revealing How People Became Fans Of The Hartford Whalers

Craig Hyatt • *Brock University*

Fan loyalty continues to attract the attention of sport marketing researchers. Much fan loyalty research has been inspired by psychologists interested in fan motivation (Sloan, 1989; Wann, 1995). Marketing researchers have noted that fans can have fluctuating levels of loyalty (Sutton, McDonald, Milne, & Cimperman, 1997; Funk & James, 2001), and that fans can switch loyalties from one team to another (Harada & Matsuoka, 1999; Mahony, Madrigal, & Howard, 1999).

Other research has examined how people become loyal team fans to begin with. While dozens of reasons have been identified, three of the most common socializing agents noted involve the intergenerational transfer of team loyalty from parents to children (James, 1997; Hyatt, 2002; Kolbe & James, 2000; Wann, Tucker, & Schrader, 1996), participation in an organized youth sport and cheering for a team in that sport (James, 1997; Hyatt, 2002), and geographic proximity and corresponding access to local media covering that team (James, 1997; Hyatt, 2002; Kolbe & James, 2000; Wann, et al, 1996). An interpretive study of Hartford Whaler fans revealed that comparatively few Whaler fans fit this profile.

The Hartford Whalers played in the National Hockey League from 1979–1997. Twenty-four of their fans were interviewed in-depth in order to gain an understanding of their experience as Whaler fans—including how they first formed an allegiance with the team. Consistent with interpretive assumptions, open-ended questions designed to encourage conversation were utilized, in an attempt to understand the meanings inherent in the fans' lived experience (Glesne & Peshkin, 1992; Putnam, 1983). The interviews were transcribed verbatim and QSR N6 software was used to assist in coding. Themes and theory emerged from their stories in an inductive manner. While many fans cited one of the three socializing agents listed above, only a single fan had all three. When it came to analyzing the stories of how they became fans, few commonalities emerged. It was apparent that many became Whalers fans almost by chance.

This study suggests that the unique context of the Hartford Whalers existence may explain why their fans did not follow the socialization path shown to be typical in other markets with other teams. A team with a relatively short history would seem less likely to create new fans through the intergenerational transfer of loyalty from parent to child. A team in a relatively small city sandwiched between two much larger world-class cities (each having an NHL team for generations before the Whalers were born) would have to fight for media attention at the periphery of its fan region in areas overlapping the cheering hinterland of the neighbouring big city team. In a city where hockey was not one of the most commonly organized participatory sports options for children, it stands to reason that few fans developed an interest in the game through direct participation. With so few fans having the mutually reinforcing package of influences common with fans of other teams, it comes as no surprise to hear story after story of how fans fluked into an interest in the Whalers. Many can be considered accidental fans, and their stories call into question the generalizability of previous theories on how people are socialized into cheering for a specific team.

Jeffrey D. James • *Florida State University*

Pin-Sheng Sun • *Florida State University*

Michael Lukkarinen • *University of Illinois*

The Sport Consumption Experience: Why is Sport Entertaining?

A variety of research has been undertaken to advance our understanding of why people are interested in sports teams and reasons for attending sporting events. Previous work has examined the effect of economic factors, promotions, and residual preference factors (e.g., scheduling of games, new arenas, accessibility) on attendance at sporting events, and has studied the relationship between socio-demographic variables and watching sports (c.f., Baade & Tiehen, 1990; Greenstein & Marcum, 1981; Hansen & Gauthier, 1989; Zhang, Smith, Pease & Jambor, 1997). Related lines of inquiry have focused on identifying the motives or intrapersonal reasons that drive an individual's psychological connection to a sports team (c.f., Trail & James, 2001; Wann, 1995), and the relationship between sports followers and their favorite teams (c.f., Smith, Patterson, Williams & Hogg, 1981; Wakefield & Sloan, 1995; Wann & Schrader, 1997; Wann, Tucker & Schrader, 1996; Cialdini, Borden, Thorne, Walker, Freeman & Sloan, 1976; Mahony, Madrigal, & Howard, 1999; Snyder, Lassegard & Ford, 1986).

Using strength of psychological connection to a sports team, researchers have found that the stronger one's psychological connection, the greater the number of motives that drive a connection to a team (Kolbe & James, 2003; James, Kolbe & Trail, 2003; James & Ross, 2002). Research-to-date has done a good job helping us better understand sport consumers, particularly those with a strong psychological connection to a sports team. Better understanding the motives of sport consumers enables sport marketers to develop more effective marketing strategies, particularly promotional activities and content for advertising.

An area in which additional work is needed is better understanding the motives or reasons why people with little or no psychological connection to a sports team watch or attend games. The explanatory power of various features and motives has been highest for those with a strong psychological connection to a sports team (James & Kolbe, 2003; James et al., 2003). Much less is known about motives of consumers with little or no psychological connection to a team. One conclusion from previous research is that people with little or no psychological connection to a team attend events because the experience is entertaining. What is still unclear is why attending sporting events is entertaining.

The current project sought to (1) identify additional dimensions that help explain what is entertaining about sporting events, and 2) develop a scale to measure the entertaining aspects of sport. The initial stage involved personal interviews with sport consumers at a professional football game to find out what they enjoyed about attending games. Eight dimensions were identified based on content analysis of the interview data. Statements from the interviews were used to develop scale items making up the Sport Entertainment Experience Scale (SPEEC). The SPEEC was tested with a random sample of consumers attending a different professial football game (N = 159). Confirmatory factory analysis was utilized to assess the validity and reliability of the scale. Results indicated a reasonable fit of the data to the model with reliabilities ranging from .73 to .84, RMSEA of .065, RMR of .071, NNFI of .95 and CFI of .96. Suggestions for further scale development and implications for sport marketers will be discussed.

The Effect of Sport Sponsorship on the Sponsor's Brand Image: A Longitudinal Approach Using Panel Data

Joon-Ho Kang • *Seoul National University*

Jong-Eun Lee • *University of Texas, Austin*

Sung-Ho Cho • *University of Connecticut*

Jin-Woo Kim • *Seoul National University*

The effectiveness of sport sponsorship has been examined in terms of sponsors brand awareness, brand image, and consumer characteristics for or response to sport sponsorship (Meenaghan, 2001). Particularly, the effect on sponsors brand images has obtained much less research attention than brand awareness because of the measurement problem for image (Ferrand & Pages, 1996; Hansen & Scotwin, 1995; Rajaretnam, 1994; Rajshekhar, Traylor, Gross & Lampman, 1994; Stipp & Shiavon, 1996; Stipp, 1998). Also, the literature reveals that relatively small number of studies used a longitudinal approach and few relied on panel data to examine the effectiveness of sport sponsorship in a real situation. Self-administrated cross-sectional data or longitudinal data collected from different samples (when each sample is not statistically randomly selected from the population) cannot demonstrate the change of brand images over time.

The purpose of this study is to analyze panel data to test the change of the sponsor's brand image caused by sport sponsorship and to examine the moderating role of selected personality variables (responsiveness and assertiveness). The data were collected at two times for a real sport event: 30 days before the 2002 FIFA World Cup Opening Ceremony and one day after the final. Two hundred thirty five out of 289 participants, who were randomly selected from the panels of an Internet company, completed the same survey twice. The questionnaire consists of (1) Aaker (1997)'s brand personality scale for KTF(Korea Telecom Freetel), an official FIFA sponsor, in the context of 2002 FIFA World Cup Korea/Japan and (2) Merrill and Reid's scales measuring thinking vs. feeling orientation and the degree of self-assertiveness. The data were analyzed using repeated measures two-way ANOVA. The results showed that the sponsor's brand images were changed in all of the five image dimensions of the Aaker's scale: sincerity, excitement, competency, sophistication and ruggedness. Moreover, it was demonstrated that the effect of sport sponsorship on sponsor's brand image was stronger for feeling-oriented people than thinking-oriented people in three image dimensions (excitement, sophistication, ruggedness). Also, the influence of sport sponsorship on sponsor's brand image was stronger for self-assertive people in all the five image dimensions. Discussions and future directions are provided.

Sangho Kim • *Mississippi State University*

Jongback Kim • *Florida State University*

Sunho Mun • *Florida State University*

Since 1998 when Seri Pak won McDonald's LPGA Championship and the U.S. Women's Open titles, the number of Korean recreational golfers have rapidly increased. Also, more diverse people have participated in playing golf in Korea. Accordingly, more strategic segmentation approach is needed to effectively penetrate a golf industry market in Korea. The purposes of this study were to cluster Korean recreational golfers on the basis of recreational golfers' attitude toward purchasing golf clubs, and then to identify the variables that can differentiate the clusters.

Schiffman and Kanuk (1994) have suggested eight approaches to market segmentation. Among them, demographic variables have been prevalently utilized for market segmentation. However, Sherma and Lambert (1994) indicated two problems with the demographical segmentation approach: 1) demographic data is assumed to reflect consumption patterns; and 2) difficulty of formulation of marketing strategy. In this study, psychographics (attitude toward purchasing golf clubs) were considered as a basis for golf industry market segmentation because they can offer greater insights into consumer behavior (golfers' purchasing behavior).

Through a focus group interview (n = 8), total 25 items were generated and used to develop a survey questionnaire: recreational golfers' attitudes toward purchasing golf clubs (15 items) and demographics (10 items). Total 202 usable data were conveniently collected from five different golf ranges located in two provinces (Kyung-Ki and ChungNam) in Korea. Multiple steps were taken to analyze the data: an exploratory factor analysis to explain the 15 items in attitudes in terms of their common underlying dimensions (factors); a cluster analysis to segment Korean recreational golfers based on the identified factor groupings; and a discriminant analysis and a cross-tabulation analysis (chi-square) to determine any significant segment descriptors among the identified factors and the demographic variables.

The results of a principal-component factor analysis with VARIMAX rotation produced a solution of four factors with eigenvalues greater than unity: a) function, b) appearance, c) brand reputation, and d) price. These factors accounted for 67 percent of the total explained variance. In the second step of data analysis, a cluster analysis was used to identify possible segments according to the four factors explaining the Korean recreational golfers' attitudes toward purchasing golf clubs. The number of clusters was determined by using a Ward's clustering analysis on two split-half samples. In results, a three-cluster solution was identified. Having identified the solution, a K-mean cluster analysis was performed on all respondents: cluster 1 (n = 46), cluster 2 (n = 97), and cluster 3 (n = 59). In the third step, a multiple discriminant analysis (MDA) was performed on the three clusters in order to identify which attitude dimension(s) best discriminated among the three clusters. In results, the two functions accounted for 72.8 percent and 27.2 percent, respectively, of the variance in the attitude factors. Of main importance in function 1 were brand reputation and price. The others (function and appearance) were in function 2. In the last step, the demographic profile (10 items) for each cluster was identified using a cross-tabulation analysis. The Chi-square statistics were used to determine whether there were any statistically significant differences among the three segments. In results, the three segments were not significantly different across different demographic variables, except on the number of rounding (c2 = 26.1, df = 12, p < .05), the golf career (c2 = 22.8, df = 10, p < .05), and the average score (c2 = 22.0 df = 10, p < .05).

By using an attitude-based segmentation approach, this study identified three distinct segments, which have different attitudinal perceptions toward purchasing golf clubs in Korea. The segments based on golfers' attitudinal perceptions are likely to provide valuable information for the academics and practitioners because attitude toward an actual behavior has been regarded as a precedent for the behavior. Rather than treating all the golfers as a homogeneous group, the identification of the segments provides opportunities to optimize the use of resources and marketing efforts.

Examining The Attitudes Of Sports Fans Toward The Involvement Of Casinos And Lotteries As Sponsors Of Sport Organizations

Stephen McKelvey • *University of Massachusetts-Amherst*

Jay Gladden • *University of Massachusetts-Amherst*

The image and integrity of professional sport organizations is inextricably linked to consumers' belief that games are not "fixed." As recently as 1991, the commissioners of the major professional sport leagues converged on Congress to decry the potential threat of legalized gambling to the integrity of their sports (Ostertag, 1992). Recently, however, there has been a dramatic shift in the relationship between U.S. professional sport organizations and legalized gambling entities ("LGE's"). Mohegan Sun casino's ownership of the WNBA Connecticut Sun and their numerous other pro team sponsorships, Sycuan Indian Tribe's title sponsorship of the San Diego Padres, and the NBA and NHL's licensing arrangements with state lotteries, provide a sampling of examples of the recent embrace of LGE's as a new source of revenue for sport organizations.

These relationships mirror the unprecedented growth, governmental endorsement and societal acceptance of legalized gambling, a trend that has also extracted increasing socio-economic costs (Clausen & Miller, 2001; Goldin, 1999; Kindt & Asmar, 2002). Drawing upon prior academic research on other "vice" related sport sponsorships, namely tobacco and alcohol (Chebat, 2003; Danylchuk, 2000; Howard & Crompton, 1995; McDaniel & Mason, 1999), this study was the first of its kind to explore the attitudes of sport consumers toward LGE sport sponsorship in general, and the Mohegan Sun/WNBA relationship in particular. To explore consumer attitudes, a mail survey was sent to 3,511 randomly selected subscribers to a popular sport magazine residing in Connecticut, due to their proximity to Mohegan Sun casino and arena (home of the WNBA Suns). Approximately two weeks following the mailing of the survey, a follow-up postcard was sent to respondents reminding them to complete the survey if they had not already done so. The survey instrument was reviewed and approved by the University Human Subjects Committee.

The survey included scaled items to assess attitudes toward the pro team sponsorships by LGE's. It also included a number of variables that might account for the attitudes, including self-interest, proximity to casinos, level of sport fandom, participation levels of gambling activity, religiosity and demographics. Also included in the survey instrument were items to assess the potential harmful effects of LGE sport sponsorships on adolescents, who represent an increasingly disproportionate population of compulsive and problem gamblers (Crary, 2003; Kindt & Asmar, 2002). Of the 3,511 surveys that were mailed out, 59 were returned as undeliverable. Of the remaining 3,452 surveys, 705 surveys were returned for a response rate of 20.4%. From a demographic standpoint, the majority of respondents were male (89.0%), aged 35 or older (81.4%), and had household incomes of $50,000 or more (72.8%). 86.9% of respondents indicated that they were "at least somewhat religious," with 47.0% of respondents indicating that they were either religious or very religious. 61.6% of respondents considered themselves "avid fans" and another 25.0% considered themselves "high-moderate fans." While only 23.7% of respondents were interested or very interested in the Connecticut Sun (WNBA team), 67.5% were at least somewhat interested in the Connecticut Sun.

The vast majority of respondents had either gambled and/or played state lotteries in the past. 39.8% of respondents played the lottery at least once a month and 55.9% of respondents visited a casino at least once a year. 50.3% of respondents had gambled on a professional sports event and 77.5% of respondents had participated in a sports pool

One of the more intriguing results to emerge from a descriptive analysis of the data was that people were more tolerant of casino involvement with pro sports teams than they were of state lottery involvement with sports teams. For example, 35.2% of respondents (i.e. those that answered 5–7 on a 7 point Likert scale where the anchors were strongly disagree and strongly agree) indicated that they were opposed to casinos sponsoring pro sports teams. Meanwhile, 49.6% of respondents indicated they were opposed to state lotteries sponsoring pro sports teams. Similarly, 30.7% of respondents felt that casino sponsorship of pro sports teams was unethical. Yet, 41.9% of respondents felt that state lottery sponsorship of pro teams was unethical.

As it related to the specific case of the Connecticut Sun, the majority of respondents condoned the Mohegan Sun's ownership of the WNBA's Sun. 54.8% felt that it was acceptable for the Mohegan Sun to own and operate a WNBA team and 50.9% felt that it was acceptable for a WNBA team to be named after a casino. Only 32.6% of respondents felt that the Sun's being named after a casino sent the wrong message to children. This was consistent with other responses that indicated the majority of respondents did not feel that casino and state lottery involvement with pro teams had a negative influence on children.

As sport organizations continue to broaden their relationships with LGE's, the results of this and subsequent follow-up studies hold important implications for stakeholders. This research can help sport organizations and LGE's to better understand public opinion, attitudes and effects of LGE sport sponsorship, including the potential impact that such relationships may have on their respective brand images and upon the perceived integrity of sport events themselves. The research may also benefit those involved in pro-social campaigns to understand the resistance they may face.

Consumer Purchasing Behavior Of Sport Merchandise/ Apparel Online: The Who, What And Why

John Miller • *Texas Tech University*

Frank Veltri • *Ball State University*

The Internet has been heralded by marketers and technicians as the most significant and potentially greatest marketing tool ever invented (Solomon, 1994; Griffin, 1996). It has created a rare opportunity for organizations to break through the physical boundaries traditionally placed upon commerce, creating a new way to allow retailers to reach consumers. Online shopping now brings millions of products to consumers without them ever having to leave their homes (Walsh & Vanderkam, 1999). At the end of 2000, the online adult population reached 104 million Americans, or 56% of U.S. adults, an increase of 16 million adults from June 2000. Yet, despite the popularity and prevalence of the Internet very little is actually known about the web-based sports retail-marketing online activities. Therefore, the purpose of this investigation was to better understand the nature of consumer's purchasing behavior of sport merchandise/apparel online.

This study employed an online survey that was posted on the World Wide Web from November, 2002 to March, 2003 and attracted 1035 responses. Demographic information was obtained from the respondents in the first part of the survey to answer who purchases sport merchandise or apparel online. In the second portion individuals were queried regarding their preference in purchasing sport merchandise or apparel online rather than traditional retail outlets. Those answering in the affirmative were to identify the reasons why they preferred purchasing sport merchandise/apparel online. Reasons made available on the survey included: a) ease of online navigation; b) security of transactions online; c) wider range of selections online; d) better economic value online; e) easier to find sport merchandise/apparel online; f) easier to locate specific items online; and g) purchasing convenience online as well as any other the respondent cared to identify. The respondents were also asked to identify what sport merchandise or apparel items they preferred to purchase online on the third part of the survey.

Using frequency of responses, the investigators were able to identify who, why and what individuals most purchase online concerning sport merchandise or apparel. Additionally, the researchers used a regression analysis to study the relation between those that preferred to purchase online as the dependent variable and the demographic information obtained by the survey as independent variables. A regression analysis was also employed to determine the relation between those who preferred to purchase online and the aforementioned reasons as the independent variables. The researchers were then able to predict which of the demographic information of the respondents as well as their reasons for purchasing online would be most significantly related to those that purchase online. Thus, the results reflect information regarding who tends to purchase sport merchandise or apparel, why they tend to do so, and what they tend to purchase. The specific results of each of these findings will be presented to the audience. For the sport marketer, the findings of this study may add significantly to the understanding of who, why and what people purchase sport merchandise/apparel online.

Sport Marketing Pages 87–150

Brian E Pruegger • *Flagler College*

Factors associated with attendance at sporting events have been well documented at two of three levels of spectator sport. Numerous studies have been conducted at 1) the collegiate level (Grant & Bashaw, 1995; DeShriver, 1999; Wells, Southall, & Peng, 2000; DeShriver & Jensen, 2002) and 2) in major league professional sports (Jones, 1984; Marcum & Greenstein, 1985; Hansen & Gauthier, 1989; Baade & Tiehen, 1990; Kochman, 1995; Zhang & Smith, 1997; Zhang, Pease, & Smith, 1998; Boyd & Krehbiel, 1999; Kanters & Wade, 2000). However, few studies to date have specifically investigated factors (e.g., game day promotions) associated with attendance in the minor league professional sport (Muret, 1996; Branvold, Pan, & Gabert, 1997; Zhang, Smith, Pease, & Jambor, 1997).

Based on the absence of some of the potential drawing factors associated with college and professional sports (e.g., superstars, rivalries), promotional activities become of greater interest at the minor league level. If minor league organizations are creative in developing promotions, then these promotions can translate into increased attendance and revenue. Therefore, the objective in the current study is to investigate the use of promotions in the minor leagues, specifically minor league hockey.

The purpose of this study was to investigate factors associated with attendance in the East Coast Hockey League (ECHL) for the 2001–2002 season and specifically game day promotions and their effect on attendance. Data was collected utilizing the feedback from a survey of fourteen marketing personnel of ECHL franchises during the summer of 2002. The survey was adapted from a previous questionnaire (Branvold & Bowers, 1992) and was used to assess factors related to attendance. Other questions were added to the Branvold and Bowers tool in order to address other factors of interest.

Results indicated that several factors including number of promotions were correlated with attendance. A stepwise multiple regression analysis revealed that the factors of city size, ticket price, day of week, winning percentage, season ticket holders and promotions contributed more than 45% of the variance in predicting attendance. Specific promotions such as "Puck Night", "Scouts Night" and "Fan Appreciation Night" were identified by a binomial probability analysis as the most successful in increasing attendance. Weekend promotions were more related to an increase in attendance than weekday promotions and children were the most popular target group. ANOVA analysis exposed that attendance based on promotional games versus non-promotional games varied greatly among the fourteen teams of interest. The findings are similar to previous research on promotions and attendance (Branvold & Bowers, 1992; McDonald & Rascher, 2000). Similar to the current study, promotions in those two studies were associated with a discernible increase in attendance for most markets. Fans seem to be drawn to games featuring special promotions. Therefore, a sport marketing director can offer many creative game day promotions throughout the season and be confident in their ability to generate fan interest.

The Effect of Game-day Promotions on Attendance in the East Coast Hockey League

An Examination of Virtual Signage Exposure on Major League Baseball: Comparing Virtual And In-Stadium Signage by a Content Analysis

Do Young Pyun • *Florida State University*

Jongback Kim • *Florida State University*

Jae Hyun Ha • *Florida State University*

Virtual advertising is the latest developed technology in the area of sport-related advertising. Virtual advertising enables television broadcasters to insert a computer-generated company logo or brand name into the scenery during live sporting events. Experts agree that the market for virtual advertising is rapidly growing, and expect virtual advertising to generate sales of $2.1 billion in the U.S. by the end of 2005 (Ruth, 2002). Normally, in-stadium signage has the advantage of providing high levels of impact on consumers (Harshaw & Turner, 1999). Unlike other outdoor signage that could be easily missed, such as signage on buses passing at high speed or on highway billboards, in-stadium signage at televised sporting events allows viewers to observe sponsors' messages for the entire game telecast. The spectators present at a sports event can see all of the signage in the stadium or arena that they choose to look at; however, TV viewers are unable to see all of the signage. For the advertising to be beneficial to the sponsor during the telecast, the signage must be seen. Therefore, advertising exposure and location of the signage are very important to improve the effectiveness of advertising (Harshaw & Turner, 1999). Using a content analysis, some researchers have examined the actual exposure of logos and brand names displayed during live televised sports coverage (Boa, 1995; Pokrywczynski, 1992). So far, however, the exposure of virtual advertising signage in stadiums has not been studied. At present there are two types of advertising signage in the stadium-virtual and real-and marketers are slowly moving toward a preference for virtual advertising. Thus, an examination of the exposure that logos and brand names receive during televised baseball games through both virtual signage and other in-stadium signage has practical value for advertisers.

Therefore, the primary focus of this study was to investigate and compare exposures of virtual advertising and in-stadium advertising according to locations and the product class advertised during ESPN's Sunday Night Baseball games. Specifically, a content analysis was conducted to answer the following research questions:

1. Is there a difference in exposure frequency between virtual advertising and in-stadium advertising during televised baseball games?

2. Is there a difference in exposure frequency between various locations of advertising signage during televised baseball games?

3. Is there a difference in exposure frequency in the product class between virtual advertising and in-stadium advertising during televised baseball games?

Five of the 14 Sunday Night Baseball games broadcast from May 4, 2003, to August 3, 2003, were chosen and videotaped at random by using a table of random numbers. All in-stadium signage including virtual signage during five entire games was content analyzed. To establish intercoder reliability, an additional coder was selected for this study. The percentage of agreement between the coders for simple agreement was 73.3%, and the coefficient for the Pearson correlation (r) was

.996. According to Riffe et al. (1998), these results of intercoder reliability were considered adequate for the purpose of this study.

A total of 2,215 advertising exposures of 122 brands was coded through five ESPN's Sunday Night Baseball games. An average of 443 exposures of 24.4 brands was exposed per game. Of 443 exposures of 24.4 brands, 298.2 exposures of 11.2 brands on virtual signage and 144.8 exposures of 13.2 brands on in-stadium signage were shown per game. Briefly, on average, each brand on virtual and in-stadium signage was exposed 26.63 and 10.97 times respectively per game. First, results showed the exposure frequencies both virtual and in-stadium advertising. Of a total 2,215 advertising exposures, 1,491 exposures (67.3%) were virtual advertising, and 724 exposures (32.7%) were in-stadium advertising $\chi^2 = 265.593$, df = 1, p < .001). Second, in a comparison of the exposure frequencies among various advertising locations, the location of the most frequent exposure of advertising was rotating signage behind home plate (67.3%), followed by infield fences (13.9%), outfield fences (9.3%), dugouts (6.1%), scoreboards (2.9%), and others (0.5%) $\chi^2 = 4237.617$, df = 5, p < .001). Lastly, chi-square analysis revealed that there was a statistically significant difference in exposure frequencies in the product class between virtual and in-stadium advertising $\chi^2 = 305.895$, df = 2, p < .001). Cramér's V also indicated that the advertising type and product class were significantly related (Cramér's $V = .372$, p < .001). Consequently, consumer and broadcast-related products were more frequently exposed by virtual advertising, while manufacture products were more frequently exposed by in-stadium advertising.

Based on the results of this study, future research could expand exposure of virtual advertising for other sporting events not mentioned in this study, such as National Basketball Association (NBA) and National Football League (NFL) games. Exposure of virtual advertising could also be measured in such big games as the World Series in MLB and the NFL Super Bowl as well as in other broadcast companies using virtual advertising. For example, the 2003 Division Series and World Series in MLB were nationally and internationally televised by Fox, and all signage behind home plate was virtual signage. Moreover, uncertainty of the outcome of this year's postseason games greatly increased fans' interest. This exploratory research can also provide the basis for studying the effectiveness of virtual advertising in future research. Recognition or recall rates could be applied to compare effectiveness between virtual and in-stadium advertising. In addition, the difference between consumers' attitudes toward virtual and in-stadium advertising could be also measured.

Stephen D. Ross • *University of Minnesota*

Hyejin Bang • *University of Minnesota*

The Influence of Identification on Brand Associations of Favorite and Least Favorite Professional Sport Teams

Although sport managers are now viewing their teams, leagues, and properties as brands to be managed (Gladden & Funk, 2002), an understanding of brand associations is still in its developmental stages. Brand associations, which exist in the minds of consumers, have a level of strength and favorability (Aaker, 1991; Keller, 1993). That is, brand associations can take on directional characteristics, both positive and negative.

Past research has shown that team identification strongly influences cognitive responses and subjective knowledge (Murrell & Dietz, 1992; Wann & Branscombe, 1995). One potential subjective response of sport fans are the types of attributes ascribed to fans of a rival team. In fact, research suggests that highly identified fans are especially likely to possess a biased perception of fellow in-group fans and rival fans (Wann & Branscombe, 1993, 1995; Wann & Dolan, 1994). Specifically, highly identified fans are more likely than lowly identified fans to ascribe negative traits to out-group fans (Wann & Branscombe, 1995).

One under examined aspect of this in-group favoritism is the assignment of negative traits not only to rival fans, but to the rival team itself. From a sport branding perspective, these critical traits or the negative thoughts held in the minds of consumers directed at rival fans and teams, can be described as negative brand associations. The intent of this study was to examine the influence of team identification on the brand associations held by consumers not only for their favorite professional sport team, but for their least favorite professional sport team as well.

METHODS

Eighty-three participants completed a paper and pencil thought listing procedure. Subjects were instructed to list their favorite professional sport team, and then to write down the first descriptive thoughts that occurred to them in regards to that team. Similarly, respondents were asked to list their least favorite team, and to then write down the first descriptive thoughts that occurred to them with regards to that team. The presentation of favorite and least favorite team instructions were randomly presented in order to reduce biases. Individual boxes were provided for each one of the thought-listings. In addition, respondents completed four identification items with regard to the favorite team listed.

ANALYSIS

In order to examine differences among identified fans, respondents were categorized as either low or high identified sport fans through an analysis of the completed identification measure. Content analysis was used to categorize each thought-listing into fifteen specific categories of brand associations found to be significant in previous research (Ross & James, 2003). In addition, independent researchers coded the associations as positive, negative or neutral in order to aid in the analysis.

RESULTS

Results of the analyses revealed differences between the responses of highly identified and lowly identified fans. The respondents from the high identification segment had a greater tendency to assign negative traits to their least favorite team as compared to the respondents in the low identification segment. Similarly, respondents from the low identification segment had a tendency to assign positive traits to their least favorite team as compared to those respondents comprising the high identification segment. One interesting result was the tendency for respondents of both identification segments to provide neutral characteristics for their favorite professional sport team.

DISCUSSION

The results of the analysis provided further evidence of the effect of identification on cognitive responses and subjective knowledge of sport fans. While the results pertaining to the positive and negative properties were not surprising, the quantity of neutral associations provided by respondents of both segments highlighted a notable and potentially advantageous marketing opportunity for sport managers. Previous research has revealed that strong, positive brand associations may have a considerable positive influence on the equity of a brand (Aaker, 1996). That is, service providers with "good" reputations have the potential for high levels of customer loyalty (Keller, 1993; Aaker, 1996). The neutral associations provided by respondents indicate an opportunity for organizations to develop additional loyal customers, in addition to strengthening the loyalty of existing customers. If sport marketers could shift neutral associations in a positive direction, there is a greater likelihood that lowly identified fans could be transformed into customers with higher levels of loyalty, and existing highly identified fans could maintain or increase present levels of loyalty.

Jeroen Scheerder • *Katholieke Universiteit Leuven, Belgium*

Marijke Taks • *University of Windsor, Canada*

Wim Lagae • *Katholieke Universiteit Leuven, Belgium*

Youth Sports Participation Styles and Market Segmentation Profiles: Evidence and Applications

Nowadays, youngsters can chose from a broad scope of active and passive leisure-time activities. In the last two decades, competition for sports participation providers has increased markedly. A whole set of passive leisure-time activities, such as watching television, going to the movies, playing computer games, and the internet are mere examples of those available to teenagers (Christenson, 1994; Johansson & Miegel, 1992; Mast & Geuens, 2001; Siongers & Stevens, 2002; Ter Bogt, 1997; Van Wel, 1993; Zeijl, 2001). To successfully compete in the expanding leisure market, sports organisations must develop a thorough understanding of participant consumption behaviour and how it is affected. Researchers agree that sports programs help young people develop physically, psychologically, and socially (e.g. Bouchard, Shephard, Stephens, Sutton & McPherson, 1990; Bouchard, Shephard & Stephens, 1994; Curtis & Russell, 1997; Quinney, Gauvin & Wall, 1994). Sports providers also agree that sports participation helps prepare young people to become responsible, independent, and contributing members to society (Martens, 2003). Every initiative preventing teenagers from becoming sports participation defectors or which helps teenagers to find their way to sports opportunities is, therefore, worthwhile. In order to get youngsters on, or keep them up the 'sports participation escalator' (Mullin, Hardy & Sutton, 2000), sports service organisations have to identify the needs and wants of these consumers. This is the core element of the marketing management process. Effective marketing requires research to reveal different market segments. Smith introduced the concept of market segmentation in 1956 as follows: "Market segmentation involves viewing a heterogeneous market as a number of smaller homogeneous markets, in response to differing preferences, attributable to the desires of consumers for more precise satisfaction of their varying wants" (as cited in Wedel & Kamakura, 1998, p. 3). For each target segment the organisation will have to position its offering. Segmenting, targeting and positioning (STP) represent the organisation's strategic marketing thinking (Kotler, 1999). Following these steps, the organisation can develop its tactical marketing mix (MM).

Although 'encouraging participation in a sport' is recognized as an area of sport marketing (e.g. Chalip, 1992; Mullin et al. 2000; Pitts & Stotlar, 2002; Shank, 2002), marketing active participation has received little attention (Pitts, 2002). Sports marketers have also started to recognise the power of the kids' market, but more so related to 'kids as fans', and to 'kids as purchasers' of sporting goods (Shank, 2002), and much less related to 'kids as active participants' (Burton, Bradish, Stevens, Taks & Lathrop, 2003). This paper fills this gap by focusing on the first two steps of the marketing management process of youth sports participants, i.e. the research phase and the STP phase, with a special focus on market segmentation.

There are different methods employed to segment a market (Brassington, & Pettit, 2000; Wedel, & Kamakura, 1998; Weinstein, 1994). From a sports marketing perspective Mullin et al. (2000) distinguish: (a) the consumer's base of being (demographics); (b) the consumer's state of mind (psychographics); (c) product usage; and, (d) product benefits. Usage, benefits and behavioural segmentation are effective ways to segment the sports market (e.g. the occasion in which young people participate in sports; the level of involvement; heavy versus light 'users'; benefits looked for by youngsters). However, it is common practise to combine segmentation variables to identify groups of consumers with similar needs. Often market segments arise from a manager's conceptualisation of a structured and proportioned market. The foregoing survey, however, brings forward an empirical partitioning of the market based on available data collected on active sports participation and socio-cultural background characteristics of elementary and high school students.

Different models on participant consumption behaviour in sports indicate different sets of factors influencing how and to what extent people become involved with and committed to sports. Mullin et al. (2000) distinguish individual and environmental influences, while Shank (2002) indicates internal, external and situational factors. Shilbury, Quick and Westerbeek (1998) argue that consumer behaviour is as much situation specific as it is person specific. As these models are too complex to study as a whole, the researcher has to impose limits and boundaries in deciding which determinants he/she wants to include analysing the effect of different variables upon the active sports participation behaviour. The data used in the present study allow to developing an understanding of participant consumption behaviour of elementary and high schoolboys and girls. First of all, the sports participation components are described through the basic demographic variables age and gender. Second, the study analyses which environmental and psycho-graphic variables, affect the different components of sports participation behaviour. Third, different sports participation styles are detected, based on the different type of sports practised. Finally, all variables, i.e. all the sports participation behaviour components and all the affecting variables are put into one model, to highlight different sports market segments among these youngsters. Thus, multiple segmentation bases are used to form the segments, including demographic, socio-economic, psycho-graphic, and behavioural characteristics of the participants.

In this study leisure-time sports participation styles and market segments of elementary and high school boys and girls (N = 5,172) are studied based on product usage. Demographic, socio-economic, and psycho-graphic characteristics of the different components of sports participation behaviour, i.e. intensity, diversity, organisational context, and type of sports are analysed using logistic regression modelling. 'Highly intense sports users' are determined by age, sex and parental sports participation, while 'multi-diversity sports users' are influenced by parental sports participation and the respondents' school program. The active sports participation behaviour of the parents is one of the most influential socio-cultural characteristics with regard to the organisational context and the specific sports preferences of teenagers. Using components analysis, five youth sports participation styles can be detected: traditionally organised, family-oriented, aesthetic, exclusive and glide-oriented. To investigate the different market segments, non-linear canonical correlation analysis is used including all variables in the model. This results in a perceptual map consisting of six segments: actives, organised conformists, non-organised conformists, organised progressives, non-organised progressives, and non-participants. The identification of different homogenous subgroups helps marketers from sports service organisations and policy agents to: (a) select their target markets; (b) identify their demographic, socio-economic and consumer characteristics; (c) (re)position their services in the minds of these target groups; and, (d) provide new benefits to attract non-users or neglected segments.

David Sit • *The University of Western Ontario*

Karen Danylchuk • *The University of Western Ontario*

Brand Awareness, Brand Preference, and Brand Loyalty of Sports Apparel: Differences Amongst Select Ethnic Groups

The consumer market in practically every industry has become saturated by choice (Trout & Rivkin, 2000). The sports products industry is no exception. One only has to examine the athletic shoe industry to realize the wealth of choices. A consumer has to choose not only the type, colour, style, and technology of shoe, but also the brand name. With the overwhelming amount of choice, companies are constantly competing for the consumer's awareness, preference, and loyalty of their brand. These companies are attempting to not only attract new customers, but also retain existing ones (McAlexander, Schouten & Koenig, 2002). To accomplish this goal, marketers are responsible for understanding to the best of their ability their potential and current consumers. However, this task may be daunting as marketers discover that understanding today's consumers is becoming more difficult due to such a variety of ethnic and cultural backgrounds. For example, the face of Canada has altered dramatically over the last two decades. Recent statistics reveal that almost one fifth of Canadians are born elsewhere, the highest ratio since 1931 (Statistics Canada, 2001). In fact, more immigrants have arrived in Canada during the 1990s than in any other decade within the past 100 years (Statistics Canada, 2001). As the ratio of foreign-born residents and proportion of visible minorities continues to rise, marketers must avoid the mistake of ignoring the effect such groups will have in influencing the marketplace. Also, marketers in countries such as Canada, with highly ethnic diverse populations, cannot rely on generic marketing strategies if they wish to have people of various cultures identifying with their brand (Yoo & Donthu, 2002). Advancing the knowledge of branding differences of ethnic groups can be useful to sport marketers as the demographics in Canada and other countries become more multicultural.

The purpose of this study was to examine the level of importance that different ethnic groups place on factors related to consumer awareness, preference, and loyalty towards sports apparel brands. Canadians of Chinese, East Indian, and Anglo-European descent were invited to participate in a paper and pencil survey. These three ethnic groups were selected based on the fact that the Chinese and East Indians are currently the top two growing ethnic groups in Canada, while the Anglo-Europeans are the majority group in Canada. The method of recruiting participants was based on Sudman's (1980) shopping mall-intercept approach. The surveys were distributed at the storefront of five different retail outlets throughout the Greater Toronto Area. The first part of the survey asked participants to rate 14 factors related to brand awareness, 14 factors related to brand preference, and 11 factors related to brand loyalty using a five-point Likert scale ranging from one ("definitely not important to me") to five ("definitely important to me"). A multivariate analysis of variance was employed to compare the mean scores of the three ethnic groups. Gender, age, years lived in Canada, occupational status, level of education, and generational status were later factored in along with ethnicity to investigate any within group differences. Part two of the survey elicited consumer profile information focused on purchase habits, market share, and intended product usage. Frequencies and percentages were used to report the results of this section.

A total of 433 surveys were collected. Only participants of the three targeted groups were included in the data analysis. From these surveys, 156 were Anglo-Europeans, 88 were Chinese, and 75 were East Indian for a total sample size of 319. Significant differences were found between the three ethnic groups in several areas. For brand awareness, East Indians rated the factors "newspaper ads" and "internet ads" more important than the Anglo-European group. In terms of brand preference, East Indians were more likely to find "trendy" brands and the factor "people of my ethnic background wear the brand" more important than Anglo-Europeans. In regard to brand loyalty, measured on the likelihood that one would continue to buy the same brand, Anglo-Europeans and Chinese were found to rate the factor "availability" more important than East Indians; and Chinese rated the factor "trust in a brand and company" as more important than Anglo-Europeans. No significant differences were found according to gender, age, years living in Canada, occupational status, level of education, and generational status in the within group analysis. However, when ethnicity was not taken into account, combining the three groups together for the analysis, significant differences were found in the previous categories. The second portion of the study revealed purchase habits and apparel brand market share. Most of the participants purchased their sports apparel from sporting goods chain stores and wore sports apparel for casual purposes and for playing sport. Approximately one-quarter of respondents believed there were specific apparel brands that people of their ethnic background were more likely to wear. Nike and adidas combined to share half of the sports apparel market share for this study and Nike was clearly the favourite shoe brand of respondents.

The results of this study have implications for sport marketers. As many big businesses are waking up to the strength of growing immigrant populations, marketers involved with sport must realize they are not exempt from this trend. Though minimal differences were discovered among the select ethnic groups, sport marketers may find that they can gain a competitive edge by paying attention to ethnic marketing. Because the research involved two ethnic groups that are considered untapped markets, the information gathered will help us gain insight on how to meet their specific marketing needs.

Jennifer A. Sloan • *Seton Hall University*

Larry McCarthy • *Seton Hall University*

Women in Major League Baseball: An Untapped Resource in Marketing Baseball to Women

Despite the fact that, "She is attending games, watching on television, and purchasing licensed product . . . she has been given the chance to play, understands the game and has developed into just as passionate a spectator as her male counterpart" marketing sport to women continues to be identified as a neglected aspect of the sport industry (Branch, 1995; Lopiano, 1993, 1999, 1999; Mullin, Hardy & Sutton, 2000; Sutton & Watlington, 1994; Women's Sport Foundation, 1997). However two major league sport organizations in the United States have undertaken what they perceive to be major marketing initiatives focusing on the women's market, understanding as Horwath (1997) suggested, that women no longer represent the "nice to have" audience but a marketing majority that the sports industry need to grow".

Major League Baseball undertook The Commissioner's Initiative on Women and Baseball while the National Football League undertook a number of educational initiatives which included football 101 and 201, seminars on football strategies and rules. The Baseball Commissioner's Initiative was conducted to determine "what women knew and believed about the game" and how the "sport could build stronger relationships with female audiences" (MLB, 2000). While the Commissioners Initiative looked outside the baseball industry for insight to connecting with the female audience, this study took a decidedly different focus. It focused on women employed in Major League Baseball. Popcorn & Marigold (2000) and Myers (1994) both suggest that such an internal resource can provide valuable insight to marketing to a female audience. The study specifically examined the contribution women in baseball were asked to make to the marketing of baseball to women. It also examined strategies which they felt might be successful as well as the extent to which they their respective organization marketed to women and the obstacles which they saw as impediments to marketing baseball effectively to women.

A total of 255 completed surveys were returned from 535 women working either in Major League Baseball clubs or the Baseball Commissioners Office and drawn from the 2001 Baseball America Directory. This represents a response rate of 49% The survey had been pilot tested on a small sample of women working in the Commissioners Office. Those responding held a variety of positions and represented areas as diverse as ballpark operations, broadcasting, and accounting. The survey research was supplemented by in depth interviews with 5 women, each of whom held Vice President level positions in the Commissioners Office.

The data indicates that 73.7% of the respondents had never been asked their opinion on the matter of marketing baseball to women even though eighty one respondents held positions in either marketing, public relations or advertising in their organizations. The Commissioners Initiative was not a well known document to the women, 57% of respondents had not heard of the study. Among those who had not heard of it were people who held Director and Vice President of marketing positions. Among those who were familiar with the initiative, many were under whelmed. The respondents suggested that educating women about baseball via seminars was an effective way marketing strategy. Surprisingly, the open ended question provided an extensive analysis on the role of women in baseball. The in-depth interviews, with the Commissioner's Office VP's, provided insightful commentary on obstacles which the organization sees as challenging in their attempts to more effective marketing of baseball.

Identification as a Sport Fan: Analysis of Sport Fandom in Season Ticket Holders of a WNBA Team

Laura Burton • *North Carolina State University*

Diana Henderson Gore • *North Carolina State University*

Recent research has recognized differences in sport fan behavior from the perspective of team identification and sport fan identification. Team identification involves a psychological connection to a particular team or player, whereas sport fandom identification involves an individual's self-perceptions as a sport fan (Wann, 2002). Though the two types of identification are likely to be correlated, there may be individuals identifying a connection to a sports team while not perceiving themselves as fans of sport in general. The opposite is also likely to occur, with individuals identifying an affinity to sports but not reporting identification to a particular team or player (Wann, 2002). Additionally, differences in sport fan identification have been found based on gender of respondents, with males reporting greater self-perceptions as sport fans than females (Wann, 2002). These differences have initially been attributed to the historical role of sport fan as a male gender role. Females have tended to equally identify as fans of particular teams, but when moving beyond team identification into sport fan identification female fans may begin to sense hostility among male fans, and subsequently are less likely to identify as sport fans (Dietz-Uhler, End, Jacquemotte, Bentley, & Hurlbut, 2000). Currently there is no research that has explored the concept of sport fandom identification with fans of a women's professional sports team. Much of the sport fan research has focused on fans of collegiate sports, often utilizing college students as the research cohort. Fans of the WNBA provide a different demographic fan base for exploration, most notably including a greater percentage of female fans than noted in previous sport behavior research. Additionally, much of the research in sport fan behavior has also focused on men's sports (James, 2002; Williamson, Zhang, Pease, & Gaa, 2003, noted exceptions).

This research sought to explore the difference in level of sport fandom identification by examining a cohort of season ticket holders of a WNBA team. Those with a higher identification toward the team expend a great amount of time and resources to watch their team play than those who are less identified with the team; season ticket holder status would indicate a higher level of team identification (Wann & Branscombe, 1993). Season ticket holders provide interesting information regarding identification as sport fans as compared to identification toward the team. Wann's (2002) Sport Fandom Questionnaire (SFQ) was included in a larger market research survey distributed via mail to all season ticket holders of a WNBA team (n = 614), with a total of n=214 surveys returned for a response rate of 35 percent. The SFQ scale was altered from an eight-point Likert scale to a five-point scale to maintain consistency in scales throughout the survey.

Data were analyzed comparing mean SFQ scores and each individual question on the SFQ on socioeconomic factors, including gender, race, age, level of education, and income level. A mean SFQ score was calculated (M = 4.03, SD = .87). Overall mean scores on the SFQ for males was 4.05 (SD = .69), for females 4.03 (SD = .90). No significant differences were observed in mean scores of the SFQ across all measures of demographic factors, and no significant differences were observed for all individual questions within the SFQ. Results of this research do not support the differences in gender found in previous research assessing sport fandom identification (Wann, 2002). As season ticket holders with high team identification, this cohort indicates they also consider themselves to be sports fans as assessed by the SFQ. These fans also do not differ in their identification as sports fans based on gender, or any other demographic variables assessed.

Initial indications that females may be less likely to identify as sports fans, as measured by the SFQ, are not supported in this research. Differences in identification as sports fans may not be due to gender role expectations, but perhaps may be attributed to the populations being evaluated. To move toward greater understanding of sport fandom identification, researchers should continue to examine identification of fans from several types of sports teams, including women's collegiate and professional sports.

Herbert Woratschek • *University of Bayreuth, Germany; Department of Services Management*

Guido Schafmeister • *University of Bayreuth, Germany; Department of Services Management*

Assessing the Determinants of Broadcasting Fees for the German Soccer League—Theoretical Foundations and Empirical Evidence

The sale of broadcasting rights is the most important source of income of the German Soccer Clubs, accounting for approximately 40% of their overall income. Other sources of income are also important but on a lower level. Therefore, it is quite surprising that previous research on the demand for sports is mainly focused on the demand and the prices for stadium tickets (Bird 1982; Hart et al. 1975; Jennett 1984; Peel and Thomas 1992 and 1988; Whitney 1988) and that relevant literature on the prices for broadcasting rights is still missing. Moreover, we believe that the ticket market is often a regional monopoly and therefore it is very different from the TV-sports market. Thus, our paper contributes to the existing literature by analyzing the determinants of broadcasting fees.

Before assessing the determinants of broadcasting fees it is necessary to describe the TV-market. The broadcasting fees for the German premier soccer league have risen all the time, except for the year 2002. Nevertheless, two different periods of market development can be identified. The first period from 1965 to 1983 is characterized by a bilateral monopoly. During this monopolistic period, the TV-market consisted of public broadcasting corporations only. In the second period from 1984 to 2002 the market structure became more competitive, as more broadcasting stations came into the market. The market structure now favors the league since the demand side lost bargaining power. However, a further analysis of the different revenue models on the TV-market is necessary to understand the intentions and objectives of the parties negotiating the prices for the broadcasting rights.

The German soccer league organization sells the broadcasting rights jointly to the broadcasting stations, usually via a dealer in broadcasting rights. The broadcasting stations fall into two categories: Free TV-stations and pay TV-stations. Free TV-stations offer their program without any costs to the TV-viewer. These stations generate money from TV-advertisers because the TV-advertisers can show their commercials. Pay TV-stations receive money directly from the TV-viewers, who do not have to accept advertising during the program. Here, the payment is either a subscription fee or a pay-per-view fee. Based on these insights, some theoretical arguments can be derived: Broadcasting fees (p) seem to depend on the bargaining power (b) of the demand side. Furthermore, the expected number TV-viewers can be assumed to influence broadcasting fees. This expected demand of TV-sports broadcastings (yexp.) depends on the entertainment value of the event. People will derive more value from watching sports if they have built up consumption capital (cc) beforehand (Schellhaaá and Hafkemeyer 2002). Here, consumption capital is defined as knowledge about a particular sport. As this analysis is conducted from an aggregated perspective, other factors influencing the expected demand for particular games can be assumed to be constant (const.). Furthermore, TV-advertisers tend to engage more in advertising, if their expectations about advertising revenues (aexp.) are promising. Advertising revenue expectations depend on the expected demand for a certain broadcast (yexp.) and the expected sales opportunities (oexp.).

As the expected demand is already part of the model, the equation can now be changed:

$$p = f^*(b, cc, oexp.)$$

Based on these findings, five hypotheses can be formulated. H1: If the bargaining power of the demand side decreases, the broadcasting fees will increase. H2: The higher the consumption capital, the higher the broadcasting fees. H3: If TV-advertisers have higher expectations of the sales opportunities, the broadcasting fees will be higher. As the German TV-market went through at least two different stages of evolution, it would not make sense to calculate a single model for the whole period. Thus, the above formulated model has to be tested twice, for the monopolistic and the competitive period. During the monopolistic period, companies could not advertise sufficiently because of legal restriction. Thus we derive H4: In the competitive period the influence of expected sales opportunities is stronger, than in the monopolistic period. Furthermore, since the arrival of private broadcasting stations, advertising is the only source of income for a majority of broadcasting stations. At the same time, the consumption capital is sufficiently high and the advertising rights are liberalized. Hence, advertising through TV-sports events has become very interesting for companies. Therefore, H5 postulates: In the competitive period the main determinant are the expected sales opportunities. For the statistical analyses, the following linear regression model was used.

$$p = b0 + b1\ v + b2\ m + b3\ d + E$$

Within the model, the number of TV-stations (v) is used as an indicator of the bargaining power of the demand side. Furthermore, the number of soccer club members (m) is used as an indicator of consumption capital, because the club members are usually interested in that particular type of sport and will have built up consumption capital. The German stock market index DAX (d) is used as an indicator of the expected sales opportunities. H1 could not be tested for the monopolistic period, because the number of TV-stations was constant. H2 and H3 were confirmed for the monopolistic period. The consumption capital and the expected sales opportunities influence the broadcasting fees. For the competitive period, H3, H4 and H5 could be confirmed. H1 and H2 could not be confirmed. Only the expected sales influ-ence the broadcasting fees significantly and that influence was stronger than during the monopolistic period.

From a micro economic perspective, these results are surprising. The market structure, namely the number of broadcasting stations has no significant influence on the broadcasting fees. Furthermore, for the competitive period, we expected that the consumption capital was built up beforehand. Hence, H2 could not be confirmed. This suggests that prices for broadcasting rights are mainly influenced by the sources of income of the TV-stations. As the DAX—representing the expected sales opportunities—is the only significant determinant during the competitive period, it is obvious that the advertising opportunity is the dominating revenue model on the German TV-market. Based on these findings implications for sport management can be derived: Managers of popular sports must consider the economic situation of the advertising market, when they calculate their income and their budgets. Less popular sports, trying to increase income from broadcasting fees, must build-up consumption capital first.

Chia-Chen Yu • *University of Wisconsin-La Crosse*

Paul M. Plinske • *University of Wisconsin-La Crosse*

Shannon M. Weckler • *University of Wisconsin-La Crosse*

Marketer's Perceptions of the Use of Web Advertising on Professional Sport Web Sites

In 2002 the number of Internet users eclipsed 605 million (Nielsen NetRatings, 2002). With the increasing number of sites on the Internet for various purposes, users are now spending more time on the World Wide Web than ever before (The Pew Internet & American Life, 2001). Knowing this has empowered marketers to use web advertising at a rate never seen.

Due to the popularity of sport and the Internet, sport web sites have become one of the more common venues for corporations to place their advertisements. Simultaneously, sport organizations are utilizing their web sites to incorporate additional marketing strategies such as fantasy sports and sport sponsorship (Murphy & Church, 2000). While these organizations are using their web sites as one method to communicate with their customers or fans, there is little information about web advertising on sport web sites. As a result, the major purpose of this study was to explore the professional sport marketer's perception of the use of web advertising among their teams or leagues. The findings of this research will provide practitioners with a greater understanding of web advertising and the factors that attract corporations to professional sport web site advertising.

The respondents of this study were marketers of professional sport teams or leagues from the following United States organizations: Major League Baseball (MLB), National Basketball Association (NBA), National Football League (NFL), National Hockey League (NHL), NASCAR, Professional Golf Association (PGA), United Soccer Leagues (USL), Women's United Soccer Association (WUSA), and Women's National Basketball Association (WNBA). One hundred and seventy-eight marketers were asked to respond to the online survey, which included three sections. Part I addressed site demographics and basic information about professional sport web sites. Information related to the current use of web advertising was collected in Part II. Part III gathered marketers' perceptions regarding the critical factors to attract corporations to the web advertising opportunities on professional sport web sites. Data was analyzed using descriptive statistics, MANOVA, and multiple regression.

The results showed that a small amount of professional sport teams are currently not utilizing web advertising; however these organizations plan to incorporate it in the near future. Also, current web advertising is often used as part of the sponsorship agreement incorporated by most sport teams. Professional sport marketers and corporate sponsors have similar perceptions regarding the factors they use when deciding to place web advertisement on professional sport web sites. These include marketing objectives, team performance, and target market fit (Yu & Mikat, 2003). The finding of this study indicated that the use of web advertising in professional sport is still in the development stage. As a result, future studies related to the evaluation of web advertising effectiveness might serve as a useful tool for sport organizations.

Spectator Satisfaction with Event Operations of an Intercollegiate Women's Basketball Conference Tournament: Congruence Between Expectations and Perceptions

James J. Zhang • *University of Florida*

Eddie T. C. Lam • *Cleveland State University*

Debbie P. Williamson • *Campbell University*

Michelle Gacio-Harrolle • *University of Florida*

Daniel P. Connaughton • *University of Florida*

John O. Spengler • *University of Florida*

Although the overall attendance at National Collegiate Athletic Association (NCAA) women's basketball games has continued to increase in recent years, arenas are usually far from being filled to their capacities. This is particularly problematic for athletic conference tournament games. A conference tournament is usually held in a neutral location, where it is difficult to attract a home school type crowd. To enhance the marketing of women's basketball tournament conference games, it is necessary to identify and study those variables that affect event attendance. Besides the competitiveness of games and increased media coverage, the quality of tournament operations presents an opportunity for the tournament organizers to make the event attractive to current and potential tournament attendants. Numerous researchers have indicated the importance of quality event operations to the overall satisfaction and continued consumption of attendants at sport events. Marketing resources are better spent by keeping and satisfying existing customers than attracting new ones. This requires service quality that meets or exceeds consumer expectations, where it is essential for tournament organizers to identify and study those service variables that affect spectator consumption levels at the tournament. Following the conceptual framework of the "expectancy disconfirmation theory," the purpose of this study was to examine spectator satisfaction with event operations of an intercollegiate women's basketball conference tournament. Through a modified application of the Spectator Satisfaction Inventory (SSI) (Zhang, Smith, Pease, & Lam, 1998) and the Spectator Satisfaction Scale (SSS) (Zhang et al., 2003), a questionnaire was developed that contained three sections: (a) quality of tournament operations with 22 Likert-5-point-scale items in two versions (expectation and perception) under five factors (Arena Presentations, Audio and Visual, Tournament Accessibility, Tournament Staff, and Media Relations), (b) game consumption level with 8 variables (total number of the conference tournament game(s) attended so far this season, total number of the conference tournament game(s) attended last season, total number of the conference tournament game(s) that you intend to attend next season, total number of collegiate women's basketball games attended this season, ticket type of this season for the conference tournament, ticket type of last season for the conference tournament, regular season ticket type of an intercollegiate women's basketball team, and total number of the conference tournament seasons attended so far), and (c) sociodemographic background with 15 variables for the purpose of describing characteristics of the participants. Selected by random cluster sampling procedures, research participants (N = 1,076) were the attendants of an intercollegiate women's basketball conference tournament, who responded to the survey during the halftimes of the three rounds of games (i.e., first round, second round, and championship) that lasted three days. The participants proportionally represented the number of spectators attending the three rounds of the games, with close to 50% from the first round, and 25% from the second round and the championship, respectively. All of the tournament operation factors displayed good internal consistency, with alpha reliability coefficients ranging from .60 to .88. Repeated measure t-tests with adjusted alpha levels revealed that the perception mean scores of three tournament operation factors (Audio and Visual, Tournament Accessibility, and Tournament Staff) were significantly ($p < .05$) greater than the expectation mean scores, respectively, suggesting that the tournament attendants were generally satisfied with these three areas of the event operations. Conversely, two tournament operation factors (Arena Presentations and Media Relations) had the perception mean scores that were significantly ($p < .05$) less than the expectation mean scores, respectively, suggesting that the tournament attendants were generally dissatisfied with these two areas of the event operations. For the purpose of reducing data for the game consumption variables, a factor analysis with principal component extraction and varimax rotation techniques was conducted. Using the criteria of an eigenvalue equal to or greater than 1.0 and a factor loading equal to or greater than .40 without double loading, two factors were determined for the game consumption variables, with all eight variables retained: Attendance Frequency (4 items) and Ticket Type (4 items). These factors also displayed good internal consistency, with alpha reliability coefficients greater than .60. Regression analyses revealed that the congruence scores between the expectation scores and the perception scores for two tournament operation factors (Tournament Staff and Media Relations) were significantly ($p < .05$) predictive of the game consumption factors, suggesting that the more satisfied the tournament attendants, the higher the game consumption level. Overall, the research findings further emphasized the importance and relevance of event management quality for an intercollegiate women's basketball conference tournament, particularly in the areas of Tournament Staff and Media Relations. Tournament organizers should work hard to make improvements in the areas of Arena Presentations and Media Relations.

An Examination of the Effects of Time on Sponsorship Awareness Levels

Brenda G. Pitts • *Georgia State University*

Jennifer Slattery • *Florida State University*

Billions of dollars are invested in sponsorship of sports events and organizations as an advertising tool in the United States and around the world (Pitts & Stotlar, 2002; Quester & Farrelly, 1998). It provides the sponsoring company opportunities for advertising, publicity, selling, influencing attitudes and opinions, and to promote the company, create brand awareness, enhance favorable attitudes toward the brand, align with events or products to enhance competitive advantage, and influence intent to purchase (Knox, 1992; Levin, 1993; Meenaghan, 1991; Nicholls, Roslow, & Dublish, 1999; Pitts & Stotlar, 2002; Wilson, 1997). For the recipient of the sponsorship it provides opportunities to have additional income, provide an enhanced product, align with companies for exchange, and enhance competitive advantage.

While using single event sponsorship awareness research measures an individual's recall or recognition of sponsor company or brand immediately after the event, it does not measure whether the consumer can recall or recognize the sponsor over time. Several researchers and practitioners encourage the use of testing sponsor awareness levels over time in order to study long-term effects (Armstrong, 1988; Parker, 1991; Quester & Farrelly, 1998; Wright, 1988). Indeed, a sizable body of literature reports that the "repeated exposure of an individual to a stimulus will, of itself, enhance that person's familiarity with and liking for the stimulus" (Bennett, 1999; Berlyne, 1997; Zajonc, 1968).

The ultimate evidence of sponsorship effectiveness is often seen as a change in direct sales of a company's brands and products through brand loyalty. Important in this process towards positive sales changes is brand loyalty and an intention-to-purchase. Studies that examine brand loyalty and purchase intent, usually through consumer behavior methods, have been cited as possibly the most powerful predictors of the potential financial impact sponsorship may have on sales (Howard & Crompton, 1995).

PURPOSE OF THE STUDY

The aim of this study was to examine changes in sponsor awareness levels and purchase intent of season ticket holders over a period of time with repeated exposure to sponsor advertising.

METHODS

Participants. The population selected for examination in this study was season ticket holders at a successful and nationally ranked university football organization.

Instrument. A customized sponsorship recognition survey instrument was developed based on previous instruments reported in the sponsorship literature.

Based on the results of this study, the following conclusions were drawn. First, there was some improvement in recognition rates at the post season measure. Participants' recognition rates for six of the nine actual sponsor companies were in the 40% and above range. Moreover, four of the nine were statistically significant. Therefore, recognition of sponsors improved over the period of time measured. However, it should be remembered that these study participants were season ticket holders. Season ticket holders have been shown to be high involvement spectators. Results might be different with non season ticket holders. A future study could involve both groups and examine for differences.

In addition, in the current study, the setting chosen for study was American collegiate football. A typical college football game lasts nearly three hours. This offers the opportunity for a long exposure time while at one game. On the other hand, a typical college football season includes on average six home games, resulting in an average of six opportunities for an average three hours of exposure over a four-month period of time. Results may vary if studies are conducted with spectators at other types of events with differing lengths of exposure time.

Second, the participants in this study were not inclined to support the sponsors through a willingness to purchase their products. Further, that number increased by nearly 20% in the post season measure. This was a surprising finding because it was expected that season ticket holders would be more appreciative of the sponsors' support of the program and would therefore be more willing to support the sponsors by purchasing their products. As noted, the literature reports that the repeated exposure, especially in a pleasant and entertaining environment such as sports events, should result in enhanced awareness and increase liking. This needs further examination.

Appendix F

EXAMPLES OF SURVEYS AND QUESTIONNAIRES FOR RESEARCH

Overview: The purpose of Appendix F is to provide examples of research instruments commonly used in sport marketing. The examples are survey instruments. A brief overview of each instrument is provided offering the topic of study, its purpose, the type of instrument, methodology, and some uses of the information. The survey instruments included are real surveys from actual research in sport marketing.

Activity: Actual studies may be conducted using any of these instruments with appropriate guidance and supervision of the sport marketing course instructor and/or the authors from whom these instruments derived. (Use of these instruments without the supervision of the instructor is NOT recommended and should not be attempted.)

Topic of Study: Sponsorship and Sports Events

Purpose in Sport Marketing: Sponsors spend money as a method of advertising to increase brand awareness. Sponsors of sports events would like to know if this category of advertising is reaping results, such as brand awareness and increased sales of the company's products. With positive results, sponsor company decision makers will most likely continue to use sponsorship as an advertising form.

Sports event managers desire sponsorship to gain business relationships and as a form of funding the event. Managers would like spectators to support the sponsors as a reward and a show of support for the sponsor's support. This would help in the triangle relationship between the event manager, the sponsor, and the spectator.

Purpose of this study: To measure sponsorship recognition.

Instrument: Survey

Survey 1: Sponsorship Recognition

2001–02 (event)

Directions: Please circle your answer or place an X in the spaces provided. All replies are strictly confidential. Thank you in advance for your assistance!

1. Have you noticed sponsor signs or booths at the (event) stadium or surrounding area for the 2000–2001 season? ❑ Yes ❑ No

Below, answer Yes or No if you think there is a company as a sponsor of the (event). If you answer Yes, identify the *one or more companies* you can remember.

Is there a soft drink sponsor?
a. Pepsi   b. Coca-Cola   c. RC Cola   d. Mountain Dew ❑ Yes ❑ No

Is there a bank sponsor?
a. Capitol City Bank   b. Barnett Bank   c. Sun Trust
   d. Government Employees Credit Union   ❏ Yes   ❏ No

Is there an American automobile manufacturer sponsor?
a. Chevrolet   b. GMC   c. Ford   d. Dodge   ❏ Yes   ❏ No

Is there a hotel sponsor?
a. Winn Dixie   b. Bruno's   c. Albertson's   d. Publix   ❏ Yes   ❏ No

Is there a video rental company sponsor?
a. Blockbuster   b. Greg's Video   c. Video 21
   d. Movie Gallery   ❏ Yes   ❏ No

Is there a sports magazine sponsor?
a. Sports Illustrated   b. ESPN—The Magazine
   c. Women's Sport & Fitness   d. College Football Weekly   ❏ Yes   ❏ No

Is there a medical/health facility sponsor?
   a. Tallahassee Memorial HealthCare
   b. Tallahassee Wellness Center
   c. Orlando Orthopedic Clinic
   d. Tallahassee Regional Medical Center   ❏ Yes   ❏ No

Is there an ice cream company sponsor?
a. Ben & Jerry's   b. Baskin Robbins   c. Edy's
   d. Haagan-Daas   ❏ Yes   ❏ No

Is there an internet company sponsor?
a. monstor.com   b. travelocity.com   c. Yahoo! Sports
   d. careerbuilders.com   ❏ Yes   ❏ No

Is there a sports retail sponsor?
a. Jumbo Sports   b. Play It Again Sports
   c. Champ's   d. Finish Line   ❏ Yes   ❏ No

Is there a local television station sponsor (individual)?
a. WTWC-NBC   b. WCTV-CBS   c. WTXL-ABC
d. WTLH-FOX   ❏ Yes   ❏ No

2. Are you more likely to buy the products of sponsor companies
   of this season because they are sponsors of the (event)?   ❏ Yes   ❏ No

3. How long have you been a (event) season ticket holder (in years)? _____

4. Are you a member of the (club) Boosters also?   ❏ Yes   ❏ No

Please offer some information about yourself (all information is kept confidential).

5. What is your gender? ❏ Female   ❏ Male

6. What is your age? _____

7. What city and state do you live in? _____

8. Which category below best describes your total, annual household income?
   - ❏ 0–$10,000   ❏ $10,000–29,999   ❏ $30,000–49,999
   - ❏ 50,000–69,999   ❏ $70,000–89,999   ❏ $90,000–109,999
   - ❏ $110,000–129,999   ❏ $130,000–149,999   ❏ $150,000–over

9. What is your highest level of education attained? _____
   - ❏ grade school   ❏ some high school   ❏ high school graduate
   - ❏ vocational/technical school   ❏ some college   ❏ college degree
   - ❏ some post graduate work   ❏ master's degree   ❏ doctoral degree

When you have completed the survey, please enclose it in the postage-paid, addressed return envelope provided, and drop it in the nearest postal box.

Thank you for participating.

Methodology: As you can see in the example, sponsorship recognition asks the study participant to 'recognize' the sponsor company (or brand) in a particular product category. The typical protocol is multiple choice. (For more specific directions, refer to research methods books and sport marketing literature.)

Surveying takes place during the event away from areas where sponsors' signs would be visible—usually, just outside the arena. The researcher approaches people who attended the event and asks if they would participate in marketing research and complete a survey.

A second surveying technique is to mail the survey to the attendees and ask them to complete it and send it back. This requires gathering a mailing list with names and addresses of people who attended the event. Sometimes, mailing lists are available that contain season ticket-holders, for example.

Sources: (1) Slattery, J., & Pitts, B. G. (2001). Paper presented at the annual conference of the North American Society for Sport Management, Virginia Beach, Virginia, May 29–June 3, 2001. Available from the authors, Florida State University. (2) Cuneen, J., & Hannan, M. (1993). Intermediate measures and recognition testing of sponsorship advertising at an LPGA tournament. *Sport Marketing Quarterly, 2*(1), 47–56.

Topic of Study: Purchase intent; Support of sponsors of sports event

Purpose in Sport Marketing: The purpose of this research is to determine if sports event attendees (spectators) intend to support the sponsors of the event by purchasing the product of that company. Some research is showing that consumers of sports events are more influenced to purchase certain products (of sponsoring companies) and less influenced to purchase others. For example, certain food product companies, such as pizza and sub sandwiches, seem to enjoy more support from attendees than others. The reasons need further investigation. However, if the owner of a more formal restaurant that offers more formal cuisine determines through research that the market (spectators) at certain sports events are less likely to purchase their product, then that owner might decide that advertising (through sponsorship) at this sports event is not producing successful results. This type of research can help answer those questions.

Instrument: Survey

Directions: Please circle your answer or place an X in the spaces provided. All replies are strictly confidential. Thank you in advance for your assistance!

Please rate how likely you are to purchase the products of the following sponsors of 2000–01 (event) due to their sponsorship of this organization.

1 = definitely will not buy
2 = probably will not buy
3 = might or might not buy
4 = probably will buy
5 = definitely will buy

1. Piccadilly Restaurant	1	2	3	4	5
2. Subway	1	2	3	4	5
3. Papa John's	1	2	3	4	5
4. US Airways	1	2	3	4	5
5. U.S. Cellular	1	2	3	4	5
6. Furrin Auto	1	2	3	4	5
7. Comp-U-Wiz	1	2	3	4	5
8. Snookers Billiards Room	1	2	3	4	5
9. Blockbuster	1	2	3	4	5
10. Budweiser	1	2	3	4	5
11. All State Insurance	1	2	3	4	5

Also, please rate your attitude towards these companies as a result of their sponsorship of (event).

1 = more favorable attitude due to sponsorship
2 = somewhat more favorable attitude
3 = doesn't make a difference in opinion about the company
4 = somewhat less favorable attitude
5 = less favorable attitude due to sponsorship

12. Piccadilly Restaurant	1	2	3	4	5
13. Subway	1	2	3	4	5
14. Papa John's	1	2	3	4	5
15. Airways	1	2	3	4	5
16. Cellular	1	2	3	4	5
17. Furrin Auto	1	2	3	4	5
18. Comp-U-Wiz	1	2	3	4	5
19. Snookers Billiards Room	1	2	3	4	5
20. Blockbuster	1	2	3	4	5
21. Budweiser	1	2	3	4	5
22. All State Insurance	1	2	3	4	5

23. Does the type of signage a person has at an event influence your likelihood to purchase something from that company? ❏ Yes ❏ No

24. Have you ever purchased the products of any (event) sponsors in the past? ❏ Yes ❏ No

If yes, which companies? And why?

25. Estimate the number of games you attended last season (1999-2000):
    ❏ 0-10   ❏ 11-20   ❏ 21-over

Estimate the number of games you will attend this season (2000-2001):
    ❏ 0-10   ❏ 11-20   ❏ 21-over

Please offer some information about yourself (all information is kept confidential).

26. What is your gender?
    ❏ Male   ❏ Female

27. What is your age? _____

28. What city and state do you live in? _____

29. Which category listed below best describes your total, annual
    HOUSEHOLD income?
    ❏ 0-$10,000   ❏ $10,001-29,999   ❏ $30,000-49,999
    ❏ $50,000-69,999   ❏ $70,000-89,999   ❏ $90,000-109,999
    ❏ $110,000-129,999   ❏ $130,000-149,999   ❏ $150,000-over

What is your highest level of education attained?
    ❏ grade school   ❏ some high school   ❏ high school graduate
    ❏ vocational/technical school ❏ some college   ❏ college degree
    ❏ some post-graduate work   ❏ master's degree   ❏ doctoral degree
    ❏ law degree

THANK YOU FOR PARTICIPATING!

Methodology: This instrument attempts to determine the level of purchase intention. As you can see in the example survey, the attendee is asked to rank their level of intention as listed from "definitely will not buy" to "definitely will buy." Surveying takes place during the event. The researcher approaches people attending the event and asks if they would participate in marketing research and complete a survey.

A second surveying technique is to mail the survey to the attendees and ask them to complete it and send it back. This requires gathering a mailing list with names and addresses of people who attended the event. Sometimes, mailing lists are available that contain season ticket-holders, for example.

Sources: (1) Slattery, J., & Pitts, B. G. (2000). Purchase intent of attendees of minor league hockey. Unpublished study. Available from the authors. Florida State University. (2) Shannon, J. R., Turley, L. W. (1997). The influence of in-arena promotions on purchase behavior and purchase intentions. *Sport Marketing Quarterly, 6*(4), 53–59.

Topic of Study: Market competitors

Purpose in Sport Marketing: The purpose of this research is to determine the level of influence of the competition in the marketplace for your sport business. This information will be used in determining product differentiation and positioning in promotional efforts.

Instrument: Survey

Marketing Survey Form

Purpose: This survey is for the purpose of providing better service to the Xxxx (professional team name) audience. The collected information will be solely used for research, and your name will not be identified. Your sincere and honest response is greatly appreciated.

Entertainment Options: Please rate how much you participate in the following activities (5-Always; 4-Often; 3-Sometimes; 2-Occasionally; 1-Never).

1. Attend professional indoor soccer game	5	4	3	2	1
2. Attend a concert	5	4	3	2	1
3. Attend intercollegiate games	5	4	3	2	1
4. Attend professional basketball games	5	4	3	2	1
5. Attend a night club	5	4	3	2	1
6. Attend professional baseball games	5	4	3	2	1
7. Watch sports on TV	5	4	3	2	1
8. Play recreational sports	5	4	3	2	1
9. Attend a movie	5	4	3	2	1
10. Watch non-sport programs on TV	5	4	3	2	1
11. Work out/Exercise	5	4	3	2	1
12. Travel	5	4	3	2	1
13. Attend professional football games	5	4	3	2	1
14. Go to bar/restaurant	5	4	3	2	1
15. Attend other sport shows	5	4	3	2	1

ATTENDANCE INFORMATION. Please fill in the blanks.

How may Xxxxx home games have you attended this season? _____

How many total Xxxxx home games do you plan to attend this season? _____

How many Xxxxx games will you attend next season? _____

DEMOGRAPHIC INFORMATION. Please provide the following information.

Age: _____

Gender: _____

Ethnicity (circle one):
a. Caucasian   b. Black   c. Hispanic   d. Asian   e. Other

THANK YOU FOR YOUR COOPERATION AND ASSISTANCE!

Methodology: This instrument attempts to determine which competitors in the area are supported by consumers. The attendee (spectator) is asked to rate their involvement in the competitor's products. The attendee is also asked to provide information about their level of involvement in your product (event). This information can be analyzed and the influence of your competitors can be evaluated. Surveying takes place during the event. The researcher approaches people attending the event and asks if they would participate in marketing research and complete a survey.

A second surveying technique is to mail the survey to the attendees and ask them to complete it and send it back. This requires gathering a mailing list with names and addresses of people who attended the event. Sometimes, mailing lists are available that contain season ticket-holders, for example.

Source: Zhang, J. J., Smith, D. W., Pease, D. G., & Jambor, E. A. (1997). Negative influence of market competitors on the attendance of professional sport games: The case of a minor league hockey team. *Sport Marketing Quarterly*, *6*(3), 31–39.

Topic of Study: Economic impact, sports event

Purpose in Sport Marketing: The purpose of this research is to determine the financial (economic) impact of a sports event (or business). This information is useful in several ways. It can help the organizers of the event determine how much money the event is responsible for bringing into an area and how much of that money is spent on different areas, such as lodging, food, entertainment, transportation, event admissions (the sports event and other connected events), retail shopping, and event souvenirs. These types of information can help the organizers and local businesses involved (called stakeholders) in decision-making for the future of the event. The information can also be used to garner further support for the event from local government offices, current stakeholders, and potential stakeholders. The information is also used to ascertain the commercial value of the event which is sometimes used to inform prices for advertising and sponsorship fees, broadcasting fees, and other aspects of the event.

Instrument: Survey

Survey 4: Economic Impact, Sports Event	**Event Economic Impact Survey** Directions: Simply write your answers or an X in the spaces provided. Thank you in advance!

1. Why are you attending the event?
   - ❏ athlete/participant   ❏ cultural/participant   ❏ exhibitor/sales
   - ❏ spectator   ❏ event worker/staff
   - ❏ media with magazine (which one?) _____
   - ❏ media with film crew (which one?) _____
   - ❏ media with TV (which one?) _____
   - ❏ media with newspaper (which one?) _____
   - ❏ media other (which one?) _____

2. With whom did you come to the event?
   - ❏ family only   ❏ partner only   ❏ friends only
   - ❏ alone   ❏ both friends and family/partner
   - ❏ organization (please fill in): _____

3. How many are in your party (including yourself)?

4. Would you have come to city either now or in the next 3 months if the event were not held?
   - ❏ Yes   ❏ No

5. If yes above, how many days longer was your stay (if any) than it would have been if the event had not been taking place? _____

6. How many nights did you spend in city? _____
   In other cities? _____

7. Where (other cities) did you stay? _____

8. If you stayed overnight, where did you stay in city?
   ❏ hotel/motel   ❏ with friends/relative   ❏ RV   ❏ camping
   ❏ hosted housing   ❏ hostel   ❏ apartment ❏ other

9. Have you attended the event previously?   ❏ Yes   ❏ No
   ❏ 1982   ❏ 1986   ❏ 1990   ❏ 1994

10. Do you plan on attending the event again in (Year)?   ❏ Yes   ❏ No

11. Where do you live?
    Country _____ City _____ State _____ Postal Code _____

12. What is your source of information about the event?
    ❏ radio   ❏ newspaper   ❏ TV   ❏ friends
    ❏ website   ❏ direct mail from the event
    ❏ local (city) sports organization   ❏ other

13. How many event SPORTS events did you attne/participatein? _____

14. How many event CULTURAL/ARTS events did you attend? _____

15. Please estimate (in even US dollars) how much you spent on each of the following items during your entire stay for the event in city. Your responses are very important to the study. if you can not covert to US dollars, note what currency you are listing:

    food & beverages (restaurants, concessions, grocery stores, etc.) $ _____

    fees (to participate in the event) $ _____

    admission fees (sports events and other shows) $ _____

    night clubs, lounges, & bars (coverage charges, drinks, etc.) $ _____

    retail shopping (clothing, gifts, etc.) $ _____

    event souvenirs $ _____

    loding expenses (hotel, motel, etc.)   _____

    private auto expenses (gas, oil, repairs, parking fees, etc.) $ _____

    commercial transportation (airlines, bus, train, rental car, etc.) $ _____

    any other expenses (please identify) $ _____

16. What is your age? _____

17. What is your gender?
    ❏ female   ❏ male   ❏ other

18. What is your sexual orientation?
    ❏ lesbian   ❏ gay   ❏ bisexual   ❏ heterosexual

19. Please describe your household, "I live . . ." (check one and fill in the blanks):

I am the only adult in my household. I have _____ children.

I live with my spouse/partner/lover of years. We have _____ children.

I live with a friend/roommate. I have _____ children.

Other: Please describe: _____

20. Which category listed below describes your total, annual HOUSEHOLD income in US dollars? (or specify currency)
  - ❏ 0–$10,000
  - ❏ $10,001–29,999
  - ❏ $30,000–49,999
  - ❏ $50,000–69,999
  - ❏ $70,000–89,999
  - ❏ $90,000–109,999
  - ❏ $110,000–129,999
  - ❏ $130,000–149,999
  - ❏ $150,000–plus

21. What is your highest level of education?
  - ❏ grade school
  - ❏ some high school
  - ❏ high school graduate
  - ❏ vocational/technical school
  - ❏ some college
  - ❏ college degree
  - ❏ post-graduate work
  - ❏ doctoral degree

22. What is your occupation? (If retired, please check "retired" and list former occupation.)
  - ❏ professional/tehnical
  - ❏ clerical/office worker
  - ❏ homemaker
  - ❏ craftsperson
  - ❏ retired
  - ❏ salesperson/buyer/agent
  - ❏ service worker
  - ❏ other:

Methodology: This instrument attempts to determine several aspects of economic impact of the event, such as how much money the attendee spends on transportation, lodging, food, and other items by simply asking the attendees to report on the amount of money they spent. Further, the instrument gathers information concerning length of stay, future plans to attend, how many people in the group, how they learned about the event (tells the event marketer which advertising media were effective), in what other activities the attendees participated while in the area, and what other cities were visited by the attendees. Surveying takes place during the event. The researcher approaches people attending the event and asks if they would participate in marketing research and complete a survey.

A second surveying technique is to mail the survey to the attendees and ask them to complete it and send it back. This requires gathering a mailing list with names and addresses of people who attended the event.

Source: (1) Pitts, B. G., & Ayers, K. (2001). An analysis of visitor spending and economic scale on Amsterdam from the Gay Games V, 1998. *International Journal of Sport Management, 2*(2), 134–151. (2) Turco, D. M. (1997). Measuring the economic and fiscal impacts of state high school sport championships. *Sport Marketing Quarterly, 6*(3), 49–53.

Topic of Study: Consumer behavior; level of involvement

Purpose in Sport Marketing: The purpose of this research is to study the consumer. The area of research in this study focuses on the influence of an individual's level of involvement with a product as a determinant of level of consumerism. More specifically, how does the consumer's type and frequency of involvement with a particular sport affect their consumption? In this particular study, the authors focused on the spectators at a golf event and attempted to determine if their commitment to play golf, watch golf on TV, attend golf events, money spent on golf, and even use of golf for various activities (such as business and networking) affected their level of involvement as a golf spectator. This type of research can help determine if high level or low level of involvement consumers are more or less likely to attend more similar events. (Typically, research shows that high level involvement consumers of a sport are more likely to attend events.) This information is useful in studying markets, which is then used in making decisions on a number of sport marketing elements concerning the company and product.

Instrument: Survey

Personal Involvement Inventory

important	— — — — — — —	unimportant*
of no concern	— — — — — — —	of concern to me
irrelevant	— — — — — — —	relevant
means a lot to me	— — — — — — —	means nothing to me*
useless	— — — — — — —	useful
valuable	— — — — — — —	worthless*
trivial	— — — — — — —	fundamental
beneficial	— — — — — — —	not beneficial*
matters to me	— — — — — — —	doesn't matter*
uninterested	— — — — — — —	interested
significant	— — — — — — —	insignificant*
vital	— — — — — — —	superfluous*
boring	— — — — — — —	interesting
unexciting	— — — — — — —	exciting
appealing	— — — — — — —	unappealing**
mundane	— — — — — — —	fascinating
essential	— — — — — — —	nonessential*
undesirable	— — — — — — —	desirable
wanted	— — — — — — —	unwanted*
not needed	— — — — — — —	needed

---

*Indicates item is reversed scored. Items on the left are scored (1) low involvement to (7) high involvement on the right. Totaling the 20 items gives a score from a low of 20 to a high of 140.

Methodology: Surveying takes place during the event. The researcher approaches people attending the event and asks if they would participate in marketing research and complete a survey.

A second surveying technique is to mail the survey to the attendees and ask them to complete it and send it back. This requires gathering a mailing list with names and addresses of people who attended the event.

Source: Lascu, D. N., Giese, T. D., Toolan, C., Guehring, B., Mercer, J. (1995). Sport involvement: A relevant individual difference factor in spectator sports. *Sport Marketing Quarterly*, *4*(4), 41–46.

Topic of Study: Consumer behavior, purchase intention, the Internet

Purpose in Sport Marketing: The purpose of this research is to study consumer behavior. More specifically, the purpose of this study was to examine consumer confidence about Internet purchases and purchase intention of sport product on the Internet. The sport company might use this information to design and use the Internet as a distribution channel.

Instrument: Survey

Survey 6: Consumer Behavior, Purchase Intent, The Internet

Survey Instrument

1. In the next 12 months, do you think you are likely to buy XXXXXX over the Web?

Definitely will buy   1   2   3   4   5   Definitely will not buy

2. Overall, the thought of buying XXXXXXX over the Web causes me to be concerned with experiencing some kind of loss if I went ahead with the purchase.

Strongly Disagree   1   2   3   4   5   Strongly Agree

3. All things considered, I think I would be making a mistake if I bought XXXXXXX over the Web.

Strongly Disagree   1   2   3   4   5   Strongly Agree

4. When all is said and done, I really feel that the purchase of XXXXXXX over the Web poses problems for me that I just don't need.

Strongly Disagree   1   2   3   4   5   Strongly Agree

5. The thought of buying XXXXXXX over the Web causes me concern because some friends would think I was just being showy.

Strongly Disagree   1   2   3   4   5   Strongly Agree

6. Purchasing XXXXXXX over the Web would cause me to be thought of as foolish by some people whose opinion I value.

Strongly Disagree   1   2   3   4   5   Strongly Agree

7. Purchasing XXXXXXX over the Web will adversely affect others' opinion of me.

Strongly Disagree   1   2   3   4   5   Strongly Agree

8. The demands on my schedule are such that purchasing XXXXXXX over the Web would create even more time pressures on me that I don't need.

Strongly Disagree   1   2   3   4   5   Strongly Agree

9. Purchasing XXXXXXX over the Web could lead to an inefficient use of my time.

Strongly Disagree   1   2   3   4   5   Strongly Agree

10. Purchasing XXXXXXX over the Web will take too much time or be a waste of time.

Strongly Disagree   1   2   3   4   5   Strongly Agree

11. Purchasing XXXXXXX over the Web would be a bad way to spend my money.

Strongly Disagree   1   2   3   4   5   Strongly Agree

12. If I bought XXXXXXX over the Web, I would be concerned that the financial investment I would make would not be wise.

Strongly Disagree   1   2   3   4   5   Strongly Agree

13. If I bought XXXXXXX over the Web, I would be concerned that I really would not get my money's worth from the tickets.

Strongly Disagree   1   2   3   4   5   Strongly Agree

14. Purchasing XXXXXXX over the Web would not provide value for the money I spent.

Strongly Disagree   1   2   3   4   5   Strongly Agree

15. As I consider the purchase of XXXXXXX over the Web, I worry about whether they will perform as well as they are supposed to.

Strongly Disagree   1   2   3   4   5   Strongly Agree

16. If I were to purchase XXXXXXX over the Web, I would be concerned that they would not provide the level of benefits that I would be expecting.

Strongly Disagree   1   2   3   4   5   Strongly Agree

17. One concern I have about purchasing XXXXXXX over the Web is that eye-strain could result due from looking at the computer.

Strongly Disagree   1   2   3   4   5   Strongly Agree

18. I am concerned that using the Web may lead to uncomfortable physical side effects such as bad sleeping, backaches, and the like.

Strongly Disagree   1   2   3   4   5   Strongly Agree

19. I am concerned about the potential physical risks associated with purchasing XXXXXXX over the Web.

Strongly Disagree   1   2   3   4   5   Strongly Agree

20. Considering the possible problems associated with an online XXXXXXX vendor's performance, a lot of risk would be involved with purchasing them over the Web.

Strongly Disagree   1   2   3   4   5   Strongly Agree

21. I am confident about the ability of an online XXXXXXX vendor to perform as expected.

Strongly Disagree   1   2   3   4   5   Strongly Agree

22. If you purchase XXXXXXX over the Web, your credit card details are likely to be stolen.

Strongly Disagree   1   2   3   4   5   Strongly Agree

23. I am concerned that if I purchase XXXXXXX over the Web, the vendor will not keep my personal information private.

Strongly Disagree   1   2   3   4   5   Strongly Agree

24. The thought of purchasing XXXXXXX over the Web makes me feel psychologically uncomfortable.

Strongly Disagree   1   2   3   4   5   Strongly Agree

25. The thought of purchasing XXXXXXX over the Web gives me a feeling of unwanted anxiety.

Strongly Disagree   1   2   3   4   5   Strongly Agree

26. The thought of purchasing XXXXXXX over the Web causes me to experience unnecessary tension.

Strongly Disagree   1   2   3   4   5   Strongly Agree

27. To me, the World Wide Web is:

important	1	2	3	4	5	unimportant
of no concern to me	1	2	3	4	5	of concern to me
means a lot to me	1	2	3	4	5	means nothing
matters to me	1	2	3	4	5	doesn't matter
boring	1	2	3	4	5	interesting
unexciting	1	2	3	4	5	exciting
appealing	1	2	3	4	5	unappealing
fun	1	2	3	4	5	not fun
says nothing about me	1	2	3	4	5	says something about me
tells me about a person	1	2	3	4	5	shows nothing about a person

28. In general, I would be one of the last people to buy something over the Web.

Strongly Disagree   1   2   3   4   5   Strongly Agree

29. If I heard that a product I wanted to buy was available over the Web, I would be interested enough to buy it in this manner.

Strongly Disagree   1   2   3   4   5   Strongly Agree

30. Compared to most people, I purchase few, if any, items over the Web.

Strongly Disagree   1   2   3   4   5   Strongly Agree

31. In general, I would be among the last in my circle of friends to buy something over the Web.

Strongly Disagree   1   2   3   4   5   Strongly Agree

32. I would buy something over the Web even if I had not heard of the online vendor before.

Strongly Disagree   1   2   3   4   5   Strongly Agree

33. I like to buy things over the Web before other people do.

Strongly Disagree   1   2   3   4   5   Strongly Agree

34. In selecting from the many XXXXXXX vendors operating on via the Web, would you say that:

I would not care at all   1   2   3   4   5   I would care a great deal
as to which one I use   as to which one I use

35. Do you think that the various XXXXXXX vendors operating on via the Web are all very alike or very different?

They are all alike   1   2   3   4   5   They are all different

36. How important would it be to you to make the right choice of Web-based XXXXXXX vendor?

Not at all important   1   2   3   4   5   Extremely important

37. In making your choice of Web-based XXXXXXX vendor, how concerned would you be about the outcome of your choice?

Not at all concerned   1   2   3   4   5   Very much concerned

38. What is your age? _____

39. What is your gender?   ❏ Male?   ❏ Female

Methodology: Surveying takes place during the event. The researcher approaches people attending the event and asks if they would participate in marketing research and complete a survey.

A second surveying technique is to mail the survey to the attendees and ask them to complete it and send it back. This requires gathering a mailing list with names and addresses of people who attended the event.

Source: Pope, N., Brown, M., & Forrest, E. (1999). Risk, innovativeness, gender, and involvement factors affecting the intention to purchase sprot product online. *Sport Marketing Quarterly, 8*(2), 25–34.

Topic of Study: Consumer behavior, factors influencing attendance

Purpose in Sport Marketing: The purpose of this research is to study consumer behavior. More specifically, the purpose of this is to examine the many factors that influence the consumer's decision to attend a sports event. This information is useful in making decisions concerning several aspects surrounding the event over which the marketer has control, such as, parking fees, ticket prices, seating assignments, cleanliness of the facility, and friendliness of the staff. There are other factors that the marketer has limited or no control, such as, parking, weather, competing events or entertainment, and quality or outcome of the event.

Instrument: Survey

Part I—Demographics

Survey 7: Fan Attendance Survey

Directions: The following information is being requested for statistical purposes only. Please answer the following questions by placing a mark or circle on the appropriate box.

1. What is your gender?   ❏ Male?   ❏ Female

2. What is your age?
   ❏ 13–18   ❏ 19–24   ❏ 25–29   ❏ 30–34   ❏ 35–39   ❏ 40–44
   ❏ 45–49   ❏ 50–54   ❏ 55–59   ❏60–64   ❏65–69   ❏70+

3. What is your marital/household status?
   ❏ Single   ❏ Married/Partner   ❏ Divorced   ❏ Widowed   ❏ Others

4. What is your highest education level?
   ❏ Elementary   ❏ Junior High   ❏ High School
   ❏ Undergraduate   ❏ Graduate

5. How many children are in your household? (18 yr. old and under)

6. What is your annual household income?
   ❏ Less than $19,999   ❏ $20,000–$29,999   ❏ $30,000–$39,999
   ❏ $40,000–$49,999   ❏ $50,000–$59,999   ❏ $60,000–$69,999
   ❏ $70,000–$79,999   ❏ $80,000–$89,999   ❏ $90,000–$99,999
   ❏ $100,000–$109,000 ❏ $110,000–$119,000 ❏ $120,000+

7. What is your ethnicity?
   ❏ African American   ❏ Caucasian   ❏ Asian
   ❏ Hispanic   ❏ Others:

8. What is your occupation category?
   ❏ Blue collar   ❏ Clerk   ❏ Education
   ❏ Housewife/husband   ❏ Management   ❏ Military
   ❏ Professional   ❏ Sales   ❏ Student
   ❏ Technical   ❏ Others: ❏ Your title:

9. How many games do you attend each year? _____ games

10. Are you a season ticket holder?   ❏ Yes   ❏ No

11. What kind of transportation do you use when you come to the stadium?
    ❏ Driving a car   ❏ Bus   ❏ Taxi
    ❏ Motorcycle   ❏ Subway   ❏ Walk
    ❏ Others:
    _____

12. How many miles did you travel to get to the game?
    ❏ 0–10   ❏ 11–24   ❏ 25–49   ❏ 50–74   ❏ 75–100   ❏ 110+

Part II: Factors

Directions: Please circle the number that best reflects your perspective opinion.
   ❏ Factor   ❏ Influence Rating

How do the following factors influence your attendance at home games?

1 = Not at all
2 = Very little
3 = Somewhat
4 = Very much
5 = Extremely

1. The price of a ticket 1 2 3 4 5

2. The price of season ticket 1 2 3 4 5

3. The price of concessions 1 2 3 4 5

4. TV/Radio coverage of the home game in local area 1 2 3 4 5

5. TV coverage of another sport event at time 1 2 3 4 5
   of your home game

6. Other sporting events in the area 1 2 3 4 5

7. Other activities taking place nearby 1 2 3 4 5

8. Other professional franchises in your area 1 2 3 4 5

9. Record (won-loss) of home team 1 2 3 4 5

10. Record (won-loss) of visitor team 1 2 3 4 5

11. Number of star players on home team 1 2 3 4 5

12. Number of star players on visitor team 1 2 3 4 5

13. Offensive performance of the home team 1 2 3 4 5

14. Defensive performance of the home team 1 2 3 4 5

15. Offensive performance of the visitor team 1 2 3 4 5

16. Defensive performance of the visitor team 1 2 3 4 5

17. Closeness of competition 1 2 3 4 5

18. Games with rival teams 1 2 3 4 5

19. A chance to see a record-breaking performance 1 2 3 4 5
    by a team or athlete

20. Special promotion (hat day, poster day, etc.) 1 2 3 4 5

21. Home team's place in the division standings 1 2 3 4 5

22. Home team's place in the league standings 1 2 3 4 5

23. Home team's involvement in race for a playoff spot 1 2 3 4 5

24. Media advertising 1 2 3 4 5
    (TV, radio, newspaper, Internet, etc.)

25. Day games during the weekdays 1 2 3 4 5

26. Night games during the weekdays 1 2 3 4 5

27. Weekend day games 1 2 3 4 5

28. Weekend night games 1 2 3 4 5

29. Weather conditions 1 2 3 4 5

30. Cleanliness of the facility 1 2 3 4 5

31. Easy and/or multiple access to your facility 1   2   3   4   5
    (via subway, highway, transit, etc.)

32. Availability of parking at or near facility. 1   2   3   4   5

33. Size of the facility (seating capacity). 1   2   3   4   5

34. Crowd behavior at the game 1   2   3   4   5

35. New stadium or arena 1   2   3   4   5

36. Number of years the team has been in the area 1   2   3   4   5

37. The variety of concessions available 1   2   3   4   5

38. Violence in the game 1   2   3   4   5

39. The design and color of uniform 1   2   3   4   5

Methodology: The people to be studied include any group of potential consumers. The sport business might determine to target any group of consumers in order to assess general attitudes toward purchasing their product via the Internet.

Sources: (1) Lu, D. (2000). Factors affecting attendance in professional baseball: A comparison of Taiwan and USA. Paper presented at the Florida Association for Health, Physical Education, Recreation, & Dance annual conference, October, 2000. Paper available from the author, Florida State University. (2) Zhang, J. J., Pease, D. G., Hui, S. C., & Michaud, T. J. (1995). Variables affecting spectator decision to attend NBA games. Sport Marketing Quarterly, 4(4), 29–39.

Index

sport business industry, 2–3, 38, 73. *See also* sport business industry, factors influencing
  definition of, 4, 5
  industry segmentation, 190–194
  product examples, 3, 4–5
  size of, 5–10
    monetary size/value of, 7–8
sport business industry, factors influencing, 11
  commercialization and marketing of sports, 25–29
    growth of corporate sponsorship, 28–29
    growth of licensing and merchandising, 29
    increase in endorsements, 29
    increase in marketing orientation for sports, 27
    promotion and marketing, 28
    sport as entertainment, 25–26, 32
    and understanding of consumers, 27–27
  diverse market segments, 14–17
  education, 35–38
  media, 30–35
    benefits of mass media exposure, 31–32
    increase in radio and television coverage, 32–33
    increase in sport magazines, 33–34
    and the Internet, 34–35
  people, 12–13
    human interest in sports/recreation, 13–14
  professional service businesses for sports, 29–30
    growth of, 30
  sporting goods, 22–23
    diverse market for, 22–23
    influence of technology on, 23
  sports activities, 17
    growth of professional-level sports, 21
    growth of traditional sports, 20–21
    increase of new sports, 17, 20
    increase in sports tourism, 21–22
  sports facilities and sports medicine, 23–25
    increase in number of facilities, 24
    movement from single-purpose to multipurpose facilities, 24–25
    sports medicine and training centers, 25
sport business management, 4
sport management, 3–4
  as an academic discipline, 36–37
  academic journals of, 36
Sport Management Association of Australia and New Zealand (SMAANZ), 36

Sport Management Program Review Council of NAPSE-NASSM, 35
sport marketing, 25–29, 69–70, 91. *See also* 4 Cs; marketing mix strategies (the 4Ps); sport marketing research; sport marketing segmenting, targeting, and positioning
  academic journals of, 72
  "cause" marketing, 28
  definition of, 70–72
    as a business activity, 71–72
  and different consumer groups, 75–76
  foundation of, 74
  fundamentals and theory of, 72–76
  management model of, 76–77
  marketing research and analysis, 78
  specialized areas of study in, 74
  and a sport company's mission, 77
Sport Marketing Association (SMA), 97
sport marketing research, 93–95, 116
  academic journals of, 97, 104
  designing market research, 107–109
    analyzing data, 115–116
    conducting the study, 115
    defining objectives, 107
    determining research design, 112
    determining type of information needed, 108–109
    determining use of gathered information, 116
    locating existing data, 107–108
  evaluation and monitoring of marketing actions, 101
  and the marketing concept, 93
  methods of, 112–114
    focus groups, 113
    mail surveys, 113
    observation, 114
    online research, 113–114
    purchase behaviors, 114
    scientific research, 114
    survey research, 112–113
    telephone surveys, 113
    test marketing, 114
  process of, 95–97,104–105
  purposes of, 97–101
    defining marketing opportunities, 98–101
    linkage between consumers and the sport company, 97–98

United States Sports Academy, 47, 309
University of California at Los Angeles (UCLA), 313
University of Michigan, 315
University of Northern Colorado, 165
University of Oregon, 168
University of Pittsburgh, 319
University of Tennessee, 266
University of Texas, 265
U.S. Agency for International Development, 51
U.S. Customs, 42
U.S. Information Agency (USIA), 50
Utah Jazz, 322

V

VALS (Values and Lifestyles program), 141
value-in-kind (VIK), 256
Valvano, Jim, 309
Veeck, Bill, Jr., 265
Veltri, F., 298, 300
Vietnam, 50
Votaw, Ty, 298

W

Wade, Tom, 303
Wild Adventures Water Sports Park, 220–221
Williams, Serena, 298
Williams, Venus, 193, 298, 323–324
Winick, M., 170
Women's Basketball Hall of Fame, 85
Women's Basketball Online, 39
Women's National Basketball Association (WNBA), 39, 127–128
   marketing of, 103–104, 140
Women's Professional Basketball League (WBL), 39
Women's United Soccer Association (WUSA), 211–212
Women's World Cup, 15, 149, 211
Woods, Tiger, 263, 305
   endorsement earnings of, 297
World Cup, 61, 303, 314. *See also* Women's World Cup
World Tennis Association (WTA), 323–324
World Trade Organization (WTO), 52

X

X Games, 15–16, 20, 32, 288, 294

Y

Yao Ming, 64, 65, 296

Yeh, K. T., 41
Yiannakis, A., 74
York, T., 170
Yudkin, M., 286

Z

Zmelik, Robert, 296

About the Authors

Brenda G. Pitts, EdD

Dr. Pitts is currently professor in sport marketing in the graduate sport administration program at Georgia State University in Atlanta, Georgia, after having spent six years at Florida State University and 12 years at the University of Louisville. Dr. Pitts is author/coauthor of several sport marketing textbooks and numerous publications and presentations, primarily in sport marketing and published in several scholarly journals such as the *Journal of Sport Management, Sport Marketing Quarterly, Journal of Vacation Marketing, Sport Management and Other Related Topics Journal,* and the *International Journal of Sport Management.* She has consulted in sport marketing for several sport businesses, has reviewed materials in sport management, and spoken at numerous conferences. Her international stops have included such countries as Japan, Sweden, South Africa, Hong Kong, Singapore, Malaysia, France, Australia, Germany, Hungary, England, The Netherlands, Scotland, Cyprus, Belgium, and France. In recognition of her scholarly achievements, Dr. Pitts was the recipient of the Dr. Garth Paton Distinguished Service Award in 2004, Dr. Earle F. Zeigler Scholar Award in 2000, one of the first Research Fellows of the North American Society for Sport Management in 2001, and a nominee for the Sport Management Council's 2007 award. Some of Dr. Pitts' service accomplishments have included: member of the committee that wrote the Sport Management Curriculum Standards (first published in 1993), served on the first Sport Management Program Review Council, Program Chair of two NASSM conferences (1990 and 2004), and was Council Member, President-Elect, President, and Past-President of NASSM, 1990–1995. Dr. Pitts is a founding member of the Sport Marketing Association and was the Vice-President for Academic Affairs for the first three years of the new Sport Marketing Association, managing the conference program and editing the three conference papers books. In addition, she was an Editorial Board Member (1991–1998) and later Co-Editor-in-Chief of The Sport Management Library (1998–00), a project that has produced more than 20 textbooks in sport management.

David K. Stotlar, EdD

Dr. David K. Stotlar teaches on the University of Northern Colorado faculty in the areas of sport marketing, sponsorship, and event management. He has had more than 60 articles published in professional journals and has written several textbooks and book chapters in sport management and marketing. He has made numerous presentations at international and national professional conferences. On several occasions, he has served as a consultant in sport management to various sport professionals; and in the area of sport marketing and sponsorship, to multinational corporations and international sport managers. Dr. Stotlar was selected by the United States Olympic Committee as a delegate to the International Olympic Academy in Greece and the World University Games Forum in Italy and served as a venue media center supervisor for the 2002 Olympic Games. He has conducted international seminars in sport management and marketing for the Hong Kong Olympic Committee, the National Sports Council of Malaysia, Mauritius National Sports Council, the National Sports Council of Zimbabwe, the Singapore Sports Council, the Chinese Taipei University Sport Federation, the Bahrain Sport Institute, the government of Saudi Arabia, the South African National Sports Congress, and the Association of Sport Sciences in South Africa. Dr. Stotlar's contribution to the profession includes an appointment as Coordinator of the Sport Management Program Review Council (NASPE/NASSM) from 1999–2001. He previously served as Chair of the Council on Facilities and Equipment of the American Alliance for Health, Physical Education, Recreation and Dance and as a Board Member and later as President of the North American Society for Sport Management. Dr. Stotlar was a member of the initial group of professionals inducted as NASSM Research Fellows. He is also a founding member of the Sport Marketing Association.